/ **T4-ABM-239**

RISK CENTRIC THREAT MODELING

RISK CENTRIC THREAT MODELING

Process for Attack Simulation and Threat Analysis

TONY UCEDAVÉLEZ AND MARCO M. MORANA

Copyright © 2015 by John Wiley & Sons, Inc. All rights reserved

Published by John Wiley & Sons, Inc., Hoboken, New Jersey
Published simultaneously in Canada

No part of this publication may be reproduced, stored in a retrieval system, or transmitted in any form or by any means, electronic, mechanical, photocopying, recording, scanning, or otherwise, except as permitted under Section 107 or 108 of the 1976 United States Copyright Act, without either the prior written permission of the Publisher, or authorization through payment of the appropriate per-copy fee to the Copyright Clearance Center, Inc., 222 Rosewood Drive, Danvers, MA 01923, (978) 750-8400, fax (978) 750-4470, or on the web at www.copyright.com. Requests to the Publisher for permission should be addressed to the Permissions Department, John Wiley & Sons, Inc., 111 River Street, Hoboken, NJ 07030, (201) 748-6011, fax (201) 748-6008, or online at http://www.wiley.com/go/permissions.

Limit of Liability/Disclaimer of Warranty: While the publisher and author have used their best efforts in preparing this book, they make no representations or warranties with respect to the accuracy or completeness of the contents of this book and specifically disclaim any implied warranties of merchantability or fitness for a particular purpose. No warranty may be created or extended by sales representatives or written sales materials. The advice and strategies contained herein may not be suitable for your situation. You should consult with a professional where appropriate. Neither the publisher nor author shall be liable for any loss of profit or any other commercial damages, including but not limited to special, incidental, consequential, or other damages.

For general information on our other products and services or for technical support, please contact our Customer Care Department within the United States at (800) 762-2974, outside the United States at (317) 572-3993 or fax (317) 572-4002.

Wiley also publishes its books in a variety of electronic formats. Some content that appears in print may not be available in electronic formats. For more information about Wiley products, visit our web site at www.wiley.com.

Library of Congress Cataloging-in-Publication Data:

Tony UcedaVélez
Risk Centric Threat Modeling : process for attack simulation and threat analysis / Tony UcedaVélez, Marco M. Morana.
    pages cm
 Summary: "This book describes how to apply application threat modeling as an advanced preventive form of security"– Provided by publisher.
 Includes bibliographical references and index.
 ISBN 978-0-470-50096-5 (hardback)
1. Data protection. 2. Computer security. 3. Management information systems–Security measures. 4. Computer networks–Security measures. 5. Risk assessment. I. UcedaVélez, Tony, 1976- II. Title.
 HF5548.37.M67 2015
 658.4′7011–dc23

2015000692

Cover Image: Courtesy of Fromold Books, http://www.fromoldbooks.org/
Typeset in 10pt/12pt TimesLTStd by SPi Global, Chennai, India

10 9 8 7 6 5 4 3 2 1

1 2015

To Suzanne, my patient and loving wife, who supported me throughout the five years of writing and research; thank you for your patience and endless support. –Marco

To Heidi, Simon, Serina, Sofia, Samson. For all the soccer balls I missed to kick in the backyard, the tea times I failed to sit in, and the date nights I couldn't make due to fulfilling this project, this is for you. Deo gratias. Deus lux Mea. –Tony

Special thanks to Sarah Varnell and Caitlyn Patterson (VerSprite) for all of their review, edits, and writing guidance.

CONTENTS

Foreword	ix
Preface	xv
List of Figures	xvii
List of Tables	xxiii

1 Threat Modeling Overview 1

Definitions, 1
Origins and Use, 3
Summary, 8
Rationale and Evolution of Security Analysis, 9
Summary, 19
Building A Better Risk Model, 19
Summary, 31
Threat Anatomy, 33
Summary, 48
Crowdsourcing Risk Analytics, 48

2 Objectives and Benefits of Threat Modeling 63

Defining a Risk Mitigation Strategy, 63
Improving Application Security, 82
Building Security in the Software Development Life Cycle, 92

Identifying Application Vulnerabilities and Design Flaws, 104
Analyzing Application Security Risks, 118

3 Existing Threat Modeling Approaches   137

Security, Software, Risk-Based Variants, 137

4 Threat Modeling Within the SDLC   195

Building Security in SDLC with Threat Modeling, 195
Integrating Threat Modeling Within The Different Types of SDLCs, 205

5 Threat Modeling and Risk Management   235

Data Breach Incidents and Lessons for Risk Management, 235
Threats and Risk Analysis, 259
Risk-Based Threat Modeling, 282
Threat Modeling in Information Security and Risk
    Management Processes, 289
Threat Modeling Within Security Incident Response Processes, 306

6 Intro to PASTA   317

Risk-Centric Threat Modeling, 317

7 Diving Deeper into PASTA   343

Exploring the Seven Stages and Embedded Threat Modeling Activities, 343
Chapter Summary, 478

8 PASTA Use Case   479

PASTA Use Case Example Walk-Through, 479

Glossary   633
References   653
Index   657

FOREWORD

The cover page of this book includes a drawing from George Kruger Gray's "The Siege of the Castle." The picture depicts castles under siege and illustrates the challenges to protect against the different attacks used in the Middle Ages such as siege equipment; mobile armored shelters, ladders, and wheeled ramps, by attackers trying to scale the walls built to protect the castles. This picture is a stark reminder of the challenges that cyber-security faces to defend from cyber-attacks of the modern era. In the Middle Ages, attackers stormed the castle from different positions, bypassing the defensive walls, and breaking into the main entry castle doors. In the modern era, attackers strike from the different data interfaces that are available, breaking into the applications user and data interfaces, attacking the firewalls, and application access controls. This picture is also a reminder that defenses such as castle walls, fortified gateways, towers, turrets, arrow loops, drawbridges, and moats become obsolete with the emergence of new threats. In the case of castle defenses, this was the increased presence of gunpowder weapons, such as cannons, in the fourteenth century. In the case of cyber-defenses, the emergence of sophisticated cyber-crime tools that can successfully bypass security defenses, such as anti-viruses, firewalls, and user authentication; require that we be vigilant, monitoring, and improving our defenses before they are rendered obsolete.

Today, businesses that conduct operations online (which is almost a requirement in order to remain consumer friendly) are targeted by motivated threat actors seeking to steal customer's personal and private data, and to obtain business's intellectual property for a competitive advantage. Small-medium businesses (SMB) have gone out of business as their bank accounts have been drained. Businesses that accept credit cards online or at Point of Sale (POS) machines, are the target of fraudsters and organized cyber-criminals. Bank customers who are accustomed to checking their account balance and making payments and money transfers using online banking are the target of fraudsters armed with banking Trojans/malware. Once customers, personal and identifiable information is compromised, customers are notified by the bank of the breach, customer accounts are suspended, and the security incident has to be reported to the data privacy officer(s) and released to public in accordance to the data breach notification law enforced in the specific country. For most consumer customers, banks will take liability for the fraud being committed and repay their customers for losses, while commercial customers might face lawsuits from their clients when they refuse to pay for their losses. When business are found negligent of not applying the standard security controls and found noncompliant with information security standards, they are also impacted with additional fines and audits. Often businesses suffer large data breaches despite being compliant with technology security standards and conducting regular audits by qualified security auditors. This fact also challenges the assumption that adopting traditional security measures, processes, and technology, and compliance checks are enough to protect businesses from cyber-attacks. The assumption that security measures are "good enough" is often backed by evidence of successfully testing networks, systems, and application software for vulnerabilities, which is a factor in reducing the opportunity for an attacker to exploit them in targeted attacks.

Today, the risk mitigation effectiveness of the traditional approach of compliance driven security is challenged by the emergence of new cyber-threats and the fact that these threats have increased in sophistication and damage potential, which have rendered several security measures used today as obsolete. The adoption of sophisticated attack tools also referred to as cyber-crime toolkits for cyber-criminals and fraudsters as well as increased sophistication in the type of attack techniques, procedures, and tactics used are among the causes of an increased number of security breaches and the resulting increased economic losses felt by businesses. These cyber-crime tools are often freely available for attackers to download over the Internet and ready to be used for specific attacks against targets, such as Distributed Denial of Service (DDoS). Attacks tools can be purchased in the black market or rented for a fee such as in the case of malware and botnets. This increased availability of high-tech cyber-crime tools at very low cost severely increases the risks that businesses face when protecting customers data and company intellectual property from these attacks.

Due to this increased level of risk caused by emerging cyber-threats, businesses today cannot base their security on compliance and evidence of assurance followed by traditional information security standards and processes. Chances are that several business today that have audited for information security compliance with ISO 27001, PCI-DSS and have traditional security measures in place can still be targeted by cyber-attacks and experience losses of confidential data and fraud. Public and private organizations whose services and business depend on the web to generate a significant part of their revenues cannot look at compliance alone for security, but also need to consider a risk management approach that is based upon threat analysis, attack modeling, and simulations. This multifaceted risk management approach will reveal the level of resilience to targeted attacks and aid in determining the necessary countermeasures for reducing the risks to a manageable level. In addition, the analysis of threat actors, the modeling of attacks, and the execution of threat driven tests cannot be restricted to security practitioners but needs the collaboration of the application stakeholders that include information security officers, application architects, software developers, application architects, security testers, and business owners. Engineering systems and software that are resilient enough to withstand the impact of cyber-attacks is necessary, and requires organizations and businesses to adopt new processes such as risk-based threat modeling.

Many of the cyber-attacks occurring against web applications today are facilitated by exploitation of design flaws and security bugs in the applications, such vulnerabilities that are introduced because of coding errors in the software components. For this reason, a focus on identifying design flaws using threat modeling is critical and this is best done during the software engineering life cycles. Threat modeling is an activity that can be executed during the early stages of the Software Development Life Cycle (SDLC) to identify and remediate design flaws prior to coding and prior to security testing. The adoption of threat modeling in the SDLC is risk effective in building attack resilient software as well as cost effective, since it allows for identifying design issues as early as possible and provides time to make changes to the design before the application product is built. Today, there is a need to adopt a risk-based threat modeling process to engineer business critical web applications and software. For example, consider software that is used for credit card processing, software that is used in critical industrial systems, such as SCADA, and runs oil, gas, water, and electric utilities; manufacturing controls; traffic controls; and mission critical systems for the military. In the financial sector, this software is used to handle online banking, make payments, and trade stocks and bonds. A little bit closer to our everyday experience as consumers, consider software used for mobile payments and for online purchases, which processes and stores credit card information and other personal data.

The main question for security practitioners and risk managers today is how businesses can design and implement applications and products that are engineered to withstand cyber-attacks and yet be cost effective to build. This is the call for security practitioners to look at engineering software from the perspective of a risk manager, to understand the threats and types of attacks and be able to identify solutions that are cost effective, yet still able to mitigate the impact of attacks. There is also a call for "cyber-threat application security and software awareness" since businesses and organizations still focus on protecting the network infrastructure and the perimeter, and overlook how web and mobile applications are built and how they securely store and process sensitive customer and corporate data. Today it seems that there is disconnect among the information security practitioners and risk managers between the escalation of emerging cyber-threats and the effectiveness of the countermeasures implemented. This disconnect can be bridged by the adoption of new approaches, such as risk-based threat modeling. For threats that specifically target applications and enterprise software, it is important to build countermeasures into products during the software development life cycle, rather than bolt on security at the end. In order to understand how these attacks can be prevented and detected, the identification of countermeasures to mitigate threats needs to be driven by threat analysis and modeling of the attacks. For awareness sake, when making the case of software security to executive management, you can make parallels between the software industry and the car industry. "If applications today were built as resilient to cyber security attacks as cars are built resilient to car accidents, we would have software that is built with security controls equivalent to that of the car air bag. The car still needs to be repaired, but the consumer, the data, is protected."

Traditionally, threat modeling as methodology has been advocated by software security consultants to model threats to software and to identify design flaws that could be remediated during the SDLC. Examples of these thereat modeling methodologies include Microsoft Threat Modeling that is based on categorizing threats as STRIDE (Spoofing, Tampering, Repudiation, Information Disclosure, Denial of Service, and Elevation of Privileges). Software developers can use MS STRIDE methodology to design software with countermeasures for these threats such as data and channel encryption, digital signatures/hashes, mutual authentication, authentication, and authorization. This is certainly a good start, but it is not enough to design applications that can withstand sophisticated threats, such as one used today against business-critical software and web applications, the designs must be implemented. Consider the example of a threat that exploits the business logic of an application, such as a financial application that uses credit card data to validate the identity of a customer to conduct a specific financial transaction. An attacker can abuse this functionality to enumerate which credit card numbers previously stolen are valid so that they can be used for online purchases or counterfeit credit cards. This type of threat exploits abuse of functionality and logic flaws, and can be analyzed for specific threat actors and specific attacks using methods such as "use and abuse cases." This type of threat can also create a set of attack vectors and attack-driven test cases that are based upon this dynamic type of analysis, not a static assumption of threats. Another important reason for a risk-based threat modeling is the modeling of attacks to derive a set of tests that can be used to emulate the attack, and identify the presence of vulnerabilities and design flaws that need to be remediated. This modeling of attack starts by considering the product surface that is the available point of attacks for a threat actor such as the data interfaces and data channels. An attacker will seek to compromise the application by identifying the path of least resistance, exploring different channels that lead to the data assets, such as online, mobile, B2B channels, and in the cloud where data is either stored or processed.

A threat model can be used to emulate a real attack and test critical application functionality and software. To be realistic, the threat model needs to imitate the threat actors, tools, and attack techniques used, in order to derive a set of test cases that can be used by security testers to test the application resilience. This book advocates the use of risk based threat modeling, which is the analysis of threats and modeling of attacks in the context of information security and management of application and software as business assets. The main drive for the adoption of risk centered threat modeling is that using threat analysis and attack modeling allows risk managers to focus on the emerging threats to determine which countermeasures are most effective in mitigating these threats. Such a risk-based threat modeling process "bakes in" all the essential ingredients of compliance; threat analysis, business impact analysis, software security, and risk management; and can be proven in the field by application security practitioners and risk managers.

Though there is not a silver bullet or a single solution for the complexities of software development, the authors offer a new application threat-modeling methodology, the "Process for Attack Simulation and Threat Analysis" (PASTA), which is documented in this book. PASTA is a risk-centered threat-modeling process that focuses on understanding first and foremost the business context and inherent risk profile of the application that needs to be secured. Secondly, PASTA factors threats and attacks and risk managers in designing web and mobile applications that are resilient to the emerging cyber-threats. As application security is a journey and not a destination, I also hope that the risk-based threat modeling methodology documented in this book will be useful as one of the ways to mitigate risks of the numerous emerging threats targeting your web applications and software.

Hon. Howard A. Schmidt

PREFACE

"The Senate determined to bring eight legions into the field, which had never been done at Rome before, each legion consisting of five thousand men besides allies. ... Most of their wars are decided by one consul and two legions, with their quota of allies; and they rarely employ all four at one time and on one service. But on this occasion, so great was the alarm and terror of what would happen, they resolved to bring not only four but eight legions into the field."

Polybius, The Histories of Polybius

Battle of Cannae in 216 BC [1] when Hannibal employed defense in depth in order to encircle and destroy 10 Roman Legions all at once, resulting in the largest single slaughter of Roman troops in the history of the republic. Edward Luttwak used the term to describe his theory of the defensive strategy employed by the Late Roman army in the third and fourth centuries AD.

This book introduces the Process for Attack Simulation and Threat Analysis (PASTA) threat modeling methodology, an asset, or risk-centric approach. Its purpose is to provide a framework for risk mitigation based upon viable threat patterns against various types of threats. This book was written to usher in a new approach on threat analysis and risk mitigation. Both the methodology and the book have been inspired by more than 50 years of collective IT and Information Security experience where lackluster risk management measures and predictable security testing has yielded bloated and ineffective responses to instill organic security controls. The PASTA methodology is for both IT and Security professionals alike who recognize that there is no such thing as a "risk-free" utopia. The methodology appeals to IT, Security, Compliance, and Risk leaders who want to mitigate the residual risks that matter and understand the causal threat factors that make them relevant in the first place.

This book intends to illustrate how the impact, attributed to threat scenarios, has never been properly addressed. It shares the status quo problem of risk today and how risk management today is simply the shuffling of best guesses and control gaps that do not speak to the heart of the risk equation. While there are many threat modeling methodologies, PASTA presents a step-by-step, risk-centric threat modeling approach that is centered around understanding business impact, focused on threat research, and concerned about countermeasures that truly demonstrate risk reduction. PASTA is an iterative, maturing process that can be measured and aligned to several different frameworks and existing best practices. Its design centers on the understanding that threat motives and targeted attacks are truly unpredictable and require a more sophisticated method for identifying their possible target assets. PASTA is supported by a logical consideration around attack patterns, and considers the multiple ways in which threat successes can be achieved across a myriad of targeted exploits. With this broad understanding, PASTA aims to provide a linear approach to attack simulation while considering impact levels attributed to compromised data, infrastructure, and even reputation.

From CISOs to Security Engineers, this book provides a wrapper to enterprise security processes that work together under the framework of PASTA. We hope you may consider a risk-centric approach to threat modeling as your next evolution to targeted threat analysis and response.

REFERENCE

1. Polybius, Friedric Otto Hultsch (1889). The Histories of Polybius, Vol. 1, Macmillan and Company.

LIST OF FIGURES

1.1	Relating Environmental Factors to Attacks	11
1.2	Developing Metrics in Threat Modeling	25
1.3	Development Factors Affecting Scalability	25
1.4	Cyber Crime Motives	34
1.5	Simple Data Flow Diagram supporting Threat Model	35
1.6	More Evolved Data Flow Diagram supporting Threat Model	36
1.7	STRIDE Threat Classification Visual Example	39
1.8	Incorporating Vulnerabilities within the Threat Model	40
1.9	Vulnerability Mapping	42
1.10	Sample Attack Tree	48
1.11	Deriving Risk via the Application Threat Model	60
2.1	Example of Use Case Diagram 1	85
2.2	Manual and Automated Vulnerability Assessments	106
2.3	Example of Data Flow Diagram	110
2.4	Root Causes versus Symptoms	115
3.1	Essential Process Areas for Threat Modeling	139
3.2	Security Areas for Greater Unity via Threat Modeling	141
3.3	Process Overview of Vulnerability Assessment Integration to Threat Modeling	147
3.4	Building Security Process in System/Network Administration from Threat Modeling	152
3.5	Security Centric DFD for Distributed Attacks	159

3.6	Components Represented by DREAD Risk Model	168
3.7	Stages of PASTA Threat Modeling Methodology	173
3.8	Cone of Fire Encompassing Multiple Targets	176
3.9	Relationship among Assets, Use Cases, Actors in Application Decomposition	181
3.10	Interrelated Asset Variables within an Application Environment	182
3.11	Factors Influencing Attacks	183
4.1	Threat Tree	203
4.2	Use and Misuse Case of User Log-on	208
4.3	Sketched Architectural Diagram	210
4.4	Data Flow Diagram	212
4.5	Mapping Threats Vulnerabilities and Countermeasures	213
4.6	RUP SDLC	218
4.7	Integrating Security in the Agile SDLC	220
4.8	Integrating Security in the Agile Sprints	222
4.9	Integration of Threat Modeling in MS SDL	224
4.10	SDL Phases	227
4.11	Generic Online Banking Application Threat Model	232
5.1	HPY Stock Price at the Time of the Data Breach Disclosure (January 20, 2009 datalossdb.org)	243
5.2	Characterization of Risk by considering Threats, Vulnerabilities, and Assets	262
5.3	Five (5) Level Risk Calculation Heat Map	266
5.4	Threat-Vulnerability-Asset Risk Calculation Heat Map	268
5.5	Overall Threat-Vulnerability Domain	279
5.6	PASTA Threat Modeling Phases and Activities	285
5.7	Risk Calculation and Management Heat Map	293
5.8	NIST Risk Assessment mapping to Application Threat Modeling	299
5.9	Dissecting Cyber-Threats	302
5.10	Phases of Security Incident Handling Process (NIST via Coordinated Response)	309
6.1	Impacting Factors Across PASTA: A Checklist for Success	320
6.2	Threat Modeling Team Selection	323
6.3	Business Cross Section of a Threat Modeling Team	324
6.4	IT Operations Cross Section of a Threat Modeling Team	325
6.5	Security Operations Cross Section of a Threat Modeling Team	327
6.6	GRC Cross Section of a Threat Modeling Team	329
6.7	Givens Before PASTA Walk-Through	337
6.8	PASTA RACI Model	341

LIST OF FIGURES

7.1	Deriving Use Cases from Business Objectives	348
7.2	Converging Security, Compliance, and Privacy Requirements in Stage I	350
7.3	Hierarchy of Objectives Addressed by PASTA	354
7.4	Relating Compliance to Business Impact	359
7.5	Business and InfoSec Balance in Stage I	363
7.6	PASTA Roles for Stage I	364
7.7	PASTA Risk-Centric Threat Modeling – Stage I – (DO) Definition of the Objectives	367
7.8	Software/Data Enumeration Containers	370
7.9	Stage III Application Containers	379
7.10	PASTA Risk-Centric Threat Modeling – Stage II – (DTS) Definition of the Technical Scope	392
7.11	Enumeration of Use Cases, Services, Stored Procedures, Batch Scripts, and Actors	393
7.12	Use Case to Application Component Mapping	395
7.13	Common Syntax of Symbols for DFDS	400
7.14	Data Flow Authentication Example	401
7.15	Data Flow for Data Exchange Across Two Entities	401
7.16	DFD Example Using Physical Boundaries for Organizing Components	403
7.17	Whiteboard DFD of User Self-Enrollment	404
7.18	DFD Health-Care Example Using Container Approach	405
7.19	DFD Using Architectural Considerations for Component Grouping	406
7.20	Spectrum of Trust for Defining Trust Boundaries Across Architecture	409
7.21	Decomposing Mobile Web App Example	412
7.22	API from Stores Local Transaction Server with the Following Metadata	413
7.23	PASTA Risk-Centric Threat Modeling – Stage III – (ADA) Application Decomposition and Analysis	417
7.24	Areas to Consider around Threat Evaluation	421
7.25	Sample Threat Possibilities per Industry	423
7.26	Mapping of Threat Agents to Asset Targets	436
7.27	PASTA Risk-Centric Threat Modeling – Stage – IV (TA) Threat Analysis	440
7.28	Missing Architectural Countermeasures among Application Components	449
7.29	Abuse Cases & Vulnerability Branch to Attack Tree Added	450
7.30	Logical Flow Considering Threats to Assets to Vulnerabilities	454
7.31	Targeted Application Testing in Web Applications	455

7.32	PASTA Risk-Centric Threat Modeling– Stage V – (WVA) Weakness and Vulnerability Analysis	458
7.33	Linearly Thinking about Attack Patterns	460
7.34	Snapshot of Related Control from CAPEC ID in Library	463
7.35	Completed Attack Tree	465
7.36	MITRE CAPEC Library Snapshot – CAPEC 117	466
7.37	Vulnerability Portion of Attack Tree	469
7.38	Attack Pattern Portion of Attack Tree	469
7.39	PASTA Risk-Centric Threat Modeling – Stage VI – (AMS) Attack Modeling and Simulation	470
7.40	Visualization of Attack and Countermeasures	472
7.41	Data Flow Diagram With Architectural Risk Analysis of Vulnerabilities and Controls	473
7.42	Completed Attack Tree w/Countermeasures	474
7.43	PASTA Risk-Centric Threat Modeling – Stage VII – (RAM) Risk Analysis and Management	477
8.1	PASTA Threat Modeling: Stages and Activities	481
8.2	Entering Business Functional Requirements/Use Cases Using the ThreatModeler™ Threat Modeling Tool	491
8.3	ThreatModeler™ Tool Wizard Capturing the Level of Risk for the Project HackMe Bank	497
8.4	HackMe Bank Users	509
8.5	Representation of a Bank Account Query Transaction Through the Different Tiers of an Online Banking Application	510
8.6	Internal Services Deployed with the Application Architectural Components	512
8.7	ThreatModeler™ Association of Widgets with Client Components	512
8.8	Architecture of Online Banking Application	514
8.9	Component-Based Functional Use Cases of Online Web Application	519
8.10	Data Flow Diagram for Online Banking Application	521
8.11	Functional Component Trust Boundaries Using ThreatModeler™	523
8.12	Campaign of DDoS Attacks Against Banking Sites Announced by AQCF Threat Agent Group	532
8.13	Ontology of (STIX) Structured Language for Cyber Threat Intelligence Information (Courtesy of MITRE Corp)	537
8.14	Example of Kill-Chain (Courtesy of MITRE corp)	541
8.15	Web Incident Hacking Database Attack Library	542
8.16	ThreatModeler™ Tool Threat Library	543
8.17	Threat Model Using STRIDE per Element	546
8.18	Threat Risk Factors	549

# LIST OF FIGURES

8.19	Threat Dashboard with Threat Risk and Status	549
8.20	OSVDB Open Source Vulnerability Database source http://www.osvdb.org	555
8.21	Architectural Risk Analysis Component of ThreatModeler™	560
8.22	Architectural Risk Analysis of Authorization Controls	560
8.23	Threat Tree (Source OWASP)	562
8.24	Mapping of Threats with Vulnerabilities of Different Application IT Assets	563
8.25	Number of Attack Observed in 6 Months by Imperva 2013 WAAR	565
8.26	Test Cases to Validate Vulnerabilities at Component Functional Level ThreatModeler™	568
8.27	Sequence of Events Followed in Banking Trojan Attacks	576
8.28	Anatomy of Account Takeover and Fraudulent Wire Transfer	577
8.29	Attack Vectors Used in Banking Trojan Malware, Source OWASP Anti-Malware Knowledge Base	578
8.30	CVEs Exploited by Drive-By-Download Attacks	593
8.31	CAPEC Attack Pattern for HTTP DoS	595
8.32	Engineering for Attacks Source MITRE	598
8.33	WHID Attack Library in ThreatModeler™	599
8.34	Banking Malware Attack Tree	605
8.35	Use and Abuse Cases for MFA Controls	608
8.36	Threat-Level Security Test Cases	613
8.37	Threat and Risk Dashboard	623
8.38	Risk Calculation Heat Map	624
8.39	ThreatModeler™ Threat-Risk Management Dashboard	625
8.40	ThreatModeler™ Threats to Functional Components and Security Controls That Mitigate These Threats	626
8.41	High Level View of Threats-Attacks-Vulnerabilities-Countermeasures of Online Banking Application	627

LIST OF TABLES

1.1	Correlating Environmental Factors to Attack Motives – SAMPLE	12
1.2	Correlating Motives to Application Threat Vectors	16
1.3	Recommended Frequency for Environmental Threat Factor Analysis	17
1.4	Key Reasons App_Sec Fails Today	20
1.5	Threat Modeling Benefits for Various Roles	27
1.6	Threat Model Stack	35
1.7	Taxonomy of Attack Terms	46
1.8	Tools for Testing	54
1.9	Elements of Risk – Generic Listing of Key Risk Components	58
2.1	Application Security Roles, Responsibilities, and Benefits	69
2.2	Example of Threats and the Technical and Business Impacts	74
2.3	Criteria for Threat Modeling Scope	92
2.4	Criteria for Application Threat Modeling Updates	93
2.5	Mapping of Threats to Vulnerabilities	132
3.1	Example of Mapping Threat Modeling Efforts to Security Processes	143
3.2	Security Experience Meets Threat Modeling	148
3.3	Factors Affecting Time Requirements for Threat Modeling	155
3.4	DFD Symbols (Microsoft ACE Team) (59)	156
3.5	Traditional Network-Based Denial of Service Attacks	163
3.6	STRIDE Threat Categorization Table (60)	164
3.7	Example of STRIDE Classification Model	166
3.8	Threat Rating Table Example	169

3.9	Sample Risk Rating Exercise Using DREAD	169
3.10	DREAD Risk Rating Applied to Sample Threat	170
3.11	Security Objectives in support of Business Objectives	175
3.12	Application Decomposition for Mobile J2ME App	180
3.13	MITRE's Security Content	189
5.1	Example of Assignment of Risks Of A Threat Event based upon probability of the event and impact on the asset	265
6.1	Enterprise Process Mapping to PASTA Threat Modeling Methodology	334
6.2	Artifacts for Making PASTA	338
7.1	Relating Business Objectives to Security Requirements	346
7.2	Enumeration of Business Requirements to Understood Use Cases	349
7.3	Governance Artifacts Relevant to Stage I of PASTA	352
7.4	Considerations for Factoring Business Impact	357
7.5	Possible Inherent Risk Issues by Application Type	361
7.6	Simple CRUD Mapping Across a Product Application	373
7.7	Software Enumeration from Automated Tools	375
7.8	Free Hardening Guidelines/Tools for Inherent Risk Mitigation or Blind Threat Modeling (Stage II – PASTA)	381
7.9	Sample Identification of Use Cases for Health-Care Application	394
7.10	Hypothetical Functional Requirements/Objectives for Marketing Application	397
7.11	Deriving Use Cases from Functional Requirements	399
7.12	Sample Threat Considerations for Various Applications	422
7.13	VERIS Framework of IR Metrics	433
7.14	Threat Analysis of a Mobile Based Loan Application Serving Higher Ed	438
7.15	Threat Analysis for Bluetooth Enabled Medical Device	438
7.16	Threat Analysis Artifact against a Single Asset/ Use Case	443
7.17	Labeling Relevant Threat Modeling Variables during Targeted Assessment Efforts	456
7.18	Attack Considerations for POS at Restaurants	461
7.19	Residual Risk Analysis	476
8.1	Sensitive Data Analysis and Business Requirements of Online Banking Application	492
8.2	Online Banking Application Risk Profile	500
8.3	Online Banking Application Components S/W Technology Stack	508
8.4	Online Banking Web Application: Data Interfaces	509
8.5	Security Function Transactional Analysis	525

LIST OF TABLES xxv

8.6	Overall Cyber-Threat Scenarios Affecting Financial IT Systems and Applications	534
8.7	Structured Threat Information eXpression (STIX) Architecture vs 3.0	538
8.8	Example of Description of Browser Exploit Threat Using STIX	540
8.9	STRIDE Threat List	546
8.10	Application Security Frame	547
8.11	Secure Architecture Design Guidelines	559
8.12	Mapping of OWASP-WASC and CWE Source CriticalWatch: OWASP to WASC to CWE Mapping, Correlating Different Industry Taxonomy	565
8.13	Malware Banking Trojan Kill-Chain and Security Measures	588
8.14	Attack Vectors Used By Banking Malware	593
8.15	DDoS Attack Vectors Extracted from the Analysis of DDoS Attacks Against Web Applications	594
8.16	CAPEC SQL Injection Attack Sequence 1. Determine User-Controllable Input Susceptible to Injection	596
8.17	CAPEC SQL Injection Attack Sequence 1. 2. Experiment and try to exploit SQL Injection Vulnerability	596
8.18	CWEs Exploited in SQL Injection Attacks (CAPEC SQL Injection)	597
8.19	CAPEC-66 Security Requirements For Mitigation of Risk of SQL Injection Attacks	597
8.20	Attack Surface of Online Banking Application	601
8.21	Malware-Based-Attack-Driven Security Test Cases	610
8.22	DDoS Attack Driven Security Test Cases	612
8.23	Security Measures Proposed for Mitigate the Risks of Malware Banking and DDoS Threats	628

1

THREAT MODELING OVERVIEW

DEFINITIONS

[Application] Threat Modeling – *a **strategic process** aimed at considering possible **attack** scenarios and **vulnerabilities** within a proposed or existing **application environment** for the purpose of clearly identifying **risk** and **impact** levels.*

Definitions for any type of terminology are necessary evils. While seemingly elementary and potentially annoying, they provide a common ground from which to build. Providing a well-constructed definition also level-sets threat modeling's intended design as a process-oriented control for application security, versus interpretations that mutate its intent and true capability.

In this book, the expression "threat modeling" is reserved for software development and application security efforts. Within the topical boundaries of application security, the aforementioned definition provides some fundamental terms that should resonate with anyone who understands the very nature of security risk management and has implemented the threat modeling machine.

A closer examination of the definition provided reveals greater insights into the essential components that are threat modeling. The first emphasized term, *strategic*, describes a quality of threat modeling reflected in its ability to anticipate threats via

---

Risk Centric Threat Modeling: Process for Attack Simulation and Threat Analysis, First Edition.
Tony UcedaVélez and Marco M. Morana.
© 2015 John Wiley & Sons, Inc. Published 2015 by John Wiley & Sons, Inc.

calculated and simulated attack patterns. Each major function within the threat modeling process requires a great deal of consideration and anticipation of multiple risk factors influenced by threat, vulnerability, and impact levels.

Process is one of threat modeling's key, distinguishing qualities. A chain-like reaction of tactical events is conducted across multiple domains (business objectives, system/database administration, vulnerability management, etc.) where additional review, input, and contribution is provided by other stakeholders within the process – all in relation to a protected application environment. To date, the lack of process within information security efforts has accounted for several shortcomings in mitigating security risks introduced by deficiencies in application security, and in many cases acted as causal factors to those noted deficiencies. Although there are isolated victories in traditional security efforts, a growing sentiment is that the war against software exploitation is being lost. Threat modeling is intended to greatly revitalize the effort in securing data via a collaborative, strategic process.

The next term, *attack*, reflects a major science to threat modeling – the discipline of researching how attack patterns can potentially exploit software vulnerabilities and/or poorly designed countermeasures. The hierarchy of an attack becomes dissected via threat modeling techniques, exposing faults in application design and/or software development, as well as other practical yet key areas, such as unveiling plausible motives for which an attacker initially sought to launch their assault.

Vulnerabilities is a term used far more prevalently within other information security efforts. In the scope of threat modeling, however, its use extends the manner in which software vulnerabilities are understood. Vulnerabilities at the platform and software levels are aggregated and correlated to possible attack scenarios. As a result, this term is an essential component to its definition, as we will see in later chapters.

The *application environment* expression serves as the object of the threat modeling process. Other traditional security procedures simply address a single aspect of an entire application environment, thereby negating a more holistic approach to application security. This is not to state that these more isolated procedures are not important, but rather that the sum of their individual benefits is encompassed in the process of threat modeling and applied to the entire application environment.

The term *risk* serves as the object of key interest to threat modeling. Threat modeling, as a supportive role in fulfilling business objectives, seeks to identify risks associated with the cumulative effects of an ever-evolving threat environment, compounded by software/network vulnerabilities, and fueled by attack motives or interest in business information – all managed and/or driven by an application environment. Threat modeling provides greater precision in conveying risk through providing a clear path on how a business application environment could be compromised and the probability of the actual risk. In essence, risk becomes the common glue that unifies security and business professionals in a collaborative effort to protect the enterprise.

Within the threat modeling definition, *impact* is the ability to answer the question "How bad is it?" Unless security professionals consider all possible threat scenarios in order to generate a prioritized, risk-based analysis, they cannot provide an effective and credible answer. As answers morph into speculations and continue downhill, security professionals are again unable to convey an adequate and plausible answer to this question. Threat modeling divides a threat into multiple attacks, making it easier to see how each attack scenario unfolds. For each scenario, impact of any adverse aftermath can be ascertained with greater accuracy, thereby reestablishing the credibility of the security analysis. The ability to understand impact is central to reporting a threat. Devoid of this capability, identifying and communicating threats merely becomes an exercise built around hype and fear factor.

ORIGINS AND USE

> *It is only one who is thoroughly acquainted with the evils of war that can thoroughly understand the profitable way of carrying it on.*
>
> Sun Tzu, Art of War

Despite its trite and oversensationalized use in numerous other security publications, Sun Tzu's quotation is still very relevant to application threat modeling, particularly in its goal to imagine attack scenarios from possible adversaries. Although we are focusing on threat modeling as it applies to software development and application security efforts, we must also consider the origins of threat modeling and other ways it is applied. This chapter provides a comparative look as to how threat modeling, in its original form, has been applied in hostile environments that encompass both physical and logical attacks, most notably in tactical military operations. Though looking at threat modeling in a context outside of application security may seem irrelevant, it is important to understand a historical use. Threat modeling's past uses are not only useful to learn and remember, but also provide an appreciation as to how strategic analysis becomes a fundamental part of the process.

Topicality of Military Threat Modeling

By understanding the historical usage of threat modeling, security professionals at large can evolve a mindset built around strategy rather than segregated and disorganized knee-jerk responses. Thus far, the outcomes of reactive methods have fallen short of adequately addressing a growing number of threats to application environments worldwide. The gap between the complexities of attack patterns and advancements in countermeasures continues to widen. Lending from military origins, threat modeling develops the discipline behind threat analysis. For decades, the US military has leveraged threat modeling to obtain improved insight as to how an enemy could adversely affect US interests or military forces. This analysis encompasses the examination of an enemy's motives, capabilities, and likely attack scenarios as part of an overall objective of defending against as many viable attack scenarios as possible. Similarly, application threat modeling extends the capabilities and resources of security professionals. Lending from this process, professionals can dissect and understand attacks, correlating them across multiple application vulnerabilities. Security professionals who learn from the military's application of threat modeling will be able to introduce innovation where it has been significantly lacking – intelligence correlation. Specifically related to the ability to correlate exploits and vulnerabilities and ultimately map these factors to possible misuse cases prove to be a key value-add to threat modeling.

Profiting from Threat Modeling in War

In Sun Tzu's quotation, the phrase "*profitable way of carrying it on*" noticeably stands out. While profit is not usually associated with war, here it refers to the gain or reward received from understanding the *evils* of war. The gains are the avoided risks that could have introduced mission critical impact levels. In essence, most military strategists adhere to the philosophy of profiting from the realities of war via improved preparedness. A military's application of threat modeling is able to provide this capability in part through the use of threat modeling techniques. Threat modeling allows the *evils of war* to be better recognized using thought-out simulations. Although not all possible scenarios can be considered and modeled, the military seeks to play out the most probable attack scenarios. Ultimately, threat modeling is not able to eliminate the possibility of attack, but instead increases the state of readiness for which a military unit can effectively respond to a threat.

Threat Modeling @ DoD

Several divisions within the US Department of Defense have effectively applied threat modeling techniques to identify war's collateral risks such as casualties, illnesses, and adverse economic and environmental effects. The US Army and NASA have used Ballistic Missile Threat Modeling for more than 50 years. By applying intelligence gathered from foreign missile systems, the United States fortified their overall missile defense system. Over the years, the DoD used threat modeling to build a stronger missile defense program by identifying threats (with underlying attacks) that were able to permeate US defenses. Deriving impact levels and correlating them back to the threat model quantified the level of risk associated with branches of the attack tree models. Impact levels are critical and complicated pieces of information that require thorough understanding to effectively apply the appropriate level of countermeasure to the identified threat. Overcompensating controls can deplete resources in other areas where threats are potentially more probable and damaging. As a result, reliable threat models of foreign missile systems are periodically studied to determine likely threat scenarios in an ever-evolving global arms race.

Ballistic Missile Parallel

Similar to application threat modeling, ballistic threat modeling revolves around the necessity for good intelligence. In broad terms, intelligence refers to pieces of information that can be used to reveal strategy, strengths, and weaknesses of a force's military capabilities and assets. Within the framework of various application threat models, intelligence takes the form of a vast knowledge of attack patterns (via a growing and up-to-date attack library) as well as access to a well-managed and continuously updated vulnerability database. Information surrounding application vulnerabilities and attack patterns provide two key areas of intelligence for building a strong application threat model. Each varying source of intelligence is correlated to other sources by using a tree model where a root threat is supported by multiple branches of attacks and corresponding, perceived vulnerabilities that facilitate the introduction for an attack. A threat may encompass various branches of attacks (as part of a studied attack tree), each with a vulnerability for which the attack's probability of success is elevated. It is evident, therefore, that an extensive supply of intelligence (understood attack patterns and vulnerabilities) needs to be present to provide for realistic threat simulations. Limited insight into existing or evolving attack patterns or, conversely, the understanding of vulnerabilities in infrastructure, can greatly diminish the worthiness of a threat model. Related to the military example of ballistic threat analysis, the military has sought the assistance of internal and external experts to best understand both current and projected missile threats. Intelligence is key. The establishment of and interaction with intelligence communities greatly assists in itemizing what existing and future missile threats are likely. In turn, missile defense teams leverage the gathered intelligence to refine their internal missile defense capabilities. Comparatively speaking, these efforts are synonymous to the attack/exploit research in today's application security. Acquired intelligence is correlated to one or many vulnerabilities or defects by software systems that could be labeled as targets.

A Continuous Process

The military applies threat modeling as an ongoing process aimed at assessing both internal capabilities and external threats. Continuous evaluation has many advantages over one-time or interval evaluations: namely, it allows for more accurate data via increased frequency in which data is obtained, reviewed, and reported. The unique characteristic of the military's threat modeling process is that data research, review, and reporting are incorporated into many job duties, particularly in defense areas where threats are more probable. Nearly all personnel are required to report threat data, regardless of job function. For example, status reports are deliverables within the US Army that reveal the condition of a designated group, combat unit, or military installation. These efforts take place daily and provide up-to-date synopsis of capability. These reports (or assessments) provide a current status on physical and/or logical infrastructures capabilities, integral to offensive or defensive strategies. This aspect of integration is quite interesting when correlated with existing security efforts at most global organizations. The majority of companies have opted for a different approach by filtering out information security procedures from daily business processes and assigning accountability to segregated security groups. As a result, security groups are predestined to assume an adversarial role when interfacing with business groups. Security professionals are faced with numerous Chinese walls from business and technology groups who serve as the audience to their assessment efforts, thereby limiting the critical first research step to initiating an effective assessment. The schism between managing and evaluating capability inhibits the overall ability to effectively develop a continuous process for accurate assessments.

Looking Within

Internal assessments within military operations take many forms. Readiness reports, for example, reveal in-house technical and physical abilities for offensive, defensive, and/or supportive efforts. The Army leverages readiness reports to measure the capabilities of its troops and to provide flexibility for those who access this data. Military personnel at multiple levels use an infrastructure to input their respective readiness reports, reveal changes in capability, or report problems. Multiple layers of military personnel can review the information gathering using various computer-based systems that centralize threat intelligence. Moreover, the continuous assessment process cultivates strong countermeasures against security breaches, constantly evaluating data on internal capabilities. US Army officials use any readiness gaps found for clear direction on what countermeasures are needed to address adverse changes or declines in readiness levels.

As previously mentioned, the US Army has taken the time and investment to develop an internal system that manages data associated with internal assessment efforts. The Defense Readiness Reporting System (DRRS) catalogs personnel, logistics, and equipment readiness from a centralized location. The DRRS (along with other systems) gives the US Army close to real-time assessment capabilities, maintaining various reports that are frequently updated with new information. This information repository assists in addressing changes in process and/or resources that may adversely affect defensive and offensive tactics. Overall, these ongoing internal reviews of resource and/or process level changes will undoubtedly reduce the viability of possible threat scenarios against the US Army and its military installations.

Private or publicly owned companies would do well to imitate a similar process for which continued assessments reveal up-to-date platform, control, and process changes. Organizations where software development is central to client-facing product or services would benefit most from a program that periodically makes gap analyses of ongoing technical and security assessments. Such a program would expose process or technical deficiencies more quickly, hastening the rate at which countermeasures are applied to discovered vulnerabilities. Devoid of such a program, the status quo manner of conducting assessments on infrequent timetables will needlessly elongate the remediation time on existing vulnerabilities. Queued vulnerabilities, compounded by potential internal threats, may produce highly viable threat scenarios if outside interest groups can be certain that vulnerable targets are not scheduled for remediation within their attack time frame.

Thus far, we have addressed the introspective look within an organization and seen how the military assesses their resources and capabilities to provide a readiness measurement. An inward regard of capabilities at most organizations (albeit outside the context of threat modeling) may encompass points related to awareness programs, governance, and audit programs. Internal compliance to one or more baselines is already common practice. The frequency that such assessments are made, however, is not to the level necessary for a solid foundation of up-to-date information sources. Next, we will look at how the military looks outward to its adversaries to understand their capabilities, vulnerabilities, and potential interests – all key variables within the context of threat modeling.

Art of Espionage

Surveying internal readiness is parallel to the necessity of gathering information about an enemy's intent and capabilities. Reconnaissance exercises within the military follow several degrees of complexity and sensitivity to time, risk, and available resources, among other factors. Threat models must account for various critical factors such as an enemy's attack motive, capabilities, vulnerabilities or flaws, and amount of information. The complexity of threat modeling lies in expedient analysis and process development. In ballistic threat modeling, for example, the process must allow intelligence gathering to feed missile defense designers in a sufficient time frame so they can defend against future threat scenarios. A race condition emerges between two intervals. One-time interval relates to when information from reconnaissance efforts is evaluated and used to guide designs efforts in a missile defense system. The second interval is the time associated with a rapidly maturing threat scenario, accompanied by underlying attack sequences. Adding to the complexity, sometimes reconnaissance efforts do not yield credible information. Misinformation can derail a threat model. Following an incorrect set of attack scenarios also misleads defense efforts from designing an effective countermeasure. While the stakes are not as high as those in ballistic threat modeling, the ability to obtain highly reliable, recent data will better equip threat models to convey probable threats and impacts with greater accuracy. In turn, the ensuing security requirements serve as guidance for the development of countermeasures that reduce risk scenarios revealed by the threat model.

Reconnaissance is multifaceted. Espionage requires covert operations behind opposing lines, often requiring the ability to perpetrate enemy actors or personnel. Finding good, reliable information often takes extreme conditions and efforts. Within the military, reconnaissance carries its share of risk: jeopardizing mission objectives, involved resources, and even compromising sensitive information. In application threat modeling, reliable information is also vital, although the risks are much less extensive. External information sources may include application/platform vulnerabilities, as well as a thorough attack library containing current and past exploits that could be used in the form of an attack. An attack library would encompass the exploit or series of exploits that are necessary for the attack to be successful. These information sources drive the robust application threat model, similar to how missile defense designers rely on good intelligence for developing a successful ballistic threat model. Both models depict realistic threat scenarios that a defense system should be prepared to defend. The effort becomes even more daunting for missile defense designers who base much of their design efforts on a baseline threat models that have been affected by intelligence reports. Obtaining good information is easier said than done when fueling application threat modeling efforts and similar to ballistic threat models, are highly dependent on solid information. Similar to the problems that missile defense designers face in adjusting missile defense programs to an evolving threat model, software architects and developers will also have to consider flexibility in their products so they can respond to changing threat scenarios presented via application threat modeling. This makes threat modeling a "living" or ever-changing process that requires updating. An already constructed threat model is rigid in form but assumes greater flexibility by the inputs it receives in terms of threat intelligence. Ultimately, countermeasures designed to incorporate a "living" threat model will have to either evolve in capabilities or give way to newly developed countermeasures that extend beyond a countermeasures current state of defense measures.

Designing Countermeasures

Beyond good intelligence, ballistic threat models have employed good design. According to the Aerospace Corporation, some of the best threat models developed combine both good intelligence of foreign ballistic systems and *superior* knowledge of defense designs. Designing effective countermeasures in software applications is one of the key differentiators of application threat modeling over other traditional security efforts (which may only address a portion of the overall threat and associated risk). Designing good countermeasures in ballistic defense systems involves not only addressing perceived threats via good information and attack assumptions, but also foreseeing how the same threat may evolve or assume a different form. At times, attack patterns may revert to historical, classic attacks that are perceived to be ineffective. This perception provides a false sense of security and a way for attackers to revert to more classic attack patterns. In 2007, a decade old boot-sector virus, named Stoned.Angelina, infected many Vista machines being sold at retail stores. The machines were equipped with A/V solutions; however, the signature sets that were loaded onto the machines did not include defense for the classic virus because it was not perceived to be a threat. This simple example demonstrates that countermeasure design must be (1) ongoing, (2) based upon both historical and new data, and (3) flexible to encompass changes in design. The same type of flexibility is required by defense system designers who must understand what factors periodically change relative to the original threat. To ensure a good defense system, designers must address static and dynamic criteria of the threat that are likely to change (behavior of missile, projectile path, etc.) and those that are not (i.e. – size of missile). Similarly, in application threat modeling, there are threat elements that are more consistent in nature as well as those that are more variable. Application threat modeling users will have to diligently ensure that changes in a threat model, previously used to create adequate application-level countermeasures, are regularly updated so both the model and the countermeasures used are commensurate to the threat.

SUMMARY

Unfortunately, the threat modeling within the Software Development Life Cycle (SDLC) has not reached a maturity level comparable to that of the military. However, agencies within the US Department of Defense have had a lot more time to refine their process and have a few more resources at their disposal. This vast difference in maturity levels of applying threat modeling across two distinct environments allows software development teams and security professionals to leverage the many lessons learned by the military and see how their procedures for intelligence gathering, threat assumptions, and design can be achieved as part of an integrated process. The chances that a banking institution, utility company, or even software provider will incur the costs of managing one too many standalone processes that support threat modeling efforts is far fetched; however, the roles and responsibilities that each subprocess follows may be easily executed by members of existing resources. This will indeed be yet another difficult, process-related challenge that companies will have to face when adopting threat modeling as part of their strategic security initiatives.

Perhaps the most difficult challenge for today's security groups is the need to change the status quo perception that security equates to compliance. This viewpoint quickly negates more strategic approaches for application security. It particularly undermines threat modeling as a possible enabler to a strategic security assurance program. Ironically, a type of mutiny takes place within organizations as security professionals attempt to convince information owners that achieving compliance is not the same as achieving security. Within the military, conflicting or competing objectives would never provide meaningful threat modeling results if the process was challenged or stunted from fulfilling its full potential for analyzing threats.

RATIONALE AND EVOLUTION OF SECURITY ANALYSIS

> *"Other than a nuclear device or some other type of destructive weapon, the threat to our infrastructure, the threat to our intelligence, the threat to our computer network is the most critical threat we face ..."*
>
> FBI Director, 2009

Cyber warfare ... zero-day ... botnets. These terms depict the insurmountable challenges facing information security professionals today. The FBI's quotation reveals a growing rationale for bolstering technology, innovation, and collaboration in the area of information security. This quotation for many should simply be a trite expression of the obvious – a dire need to secure information borders within the public and private sectors. The intent behind this chapter is not to overplay the same incentives, business cases, or moral justifications behind information security efforts. This chapter will bolster the rationale of evolving application security to a new paradigm that extends beyond the mentality of equating security to compliance, rather than be content with entrusting the reigns of security to the latest prominent security vendor, regardless of magic quadrant ratings. The intent is not to minimize these efforts, but to learn from them – building upon their use to a new echelon of applying strategic thought to information security.

Although freethinking groups exist across various security disciplines throughout the world, this sort of progressive thinking erodes within the walls of many companies where more practical, stale security philosophies are driven by the concept of best practices. There is nothing best about "best practices." Such catch phrases have misled organizations into a false sense of security by encouraging them to only strive for a basic maturity level of security controls and processes. There is no question behind the intent of *best security practices*, as well as the many frameworks, policies, standards that are omnipresent within our industry. The responsibility truly lies with executive leadership and the follow-through that needs to take place beyond a primer application of best security practices. The shortcomings in adopting new forms of security strategy may be attributed to the perception of additional cost factors in technology, resources, or services. Most security leaders, perhaps due to higher level influences, are reluctant to break a good thing. The colloquialism "*if it ain't broke, why fix it*" is pervasive across security management, especially when having to justify new budget numbers. As senior executives continue to only live in the now, their adversaries are quickly looking ahead at the future of their attacks. Given all of the aforementioned information, the rationale for introducing threat modeling is to evolve security processes to a higher level of strategy, efficiency, and foresight, as well as being conducive to improved fiscal responsibility. Could application threat modeling point to a new utopia between security and business enterprise? Not exactly, but it is definitely a good start.

Environmental Threat Factors

Both opportunities and motives are key elements of threats and attack plans. Both are affected by environmental factors within the global ecosystem of politics, business news, and events. The opportunities for exploitation and/or well-defined attack motives can be greatly influenced by these environmental conditions and ultimately alter the following characteristics of an attack:

1. Intensity of a planned attack.
2. Sophistication of an attack.
3. Probability for successful exploit.
4. Ability to distort/eliminate forensic evidence.

In this section, we will examine motives and opportunities in relation to environmental factors. By understanding their roles in originating threats and attack plans, we can apply a stronger preventive and strategic program via threat modeling.

Product of the Environment

Even before these attack motifs become produced, environmental factors provide the trace of accelerant to ignite motives into fully operational attacks. The term *environment* is not to be confused by the application domain or application environment, which is limited by the functions of its authorized and unauthorized user base.

RATIONALE AND EVOLUTION OF SECURITY ANALYSIS 11

Instead, the term *environment* describes the social, political, economic, belief-based, and/or financial factors that serve as key drivers upon which software adversaries act. Revenge, spite, corporate espionage, and fraud are motives fueled by environmental conditions such as war, layoffs, recessions, financial distress, social injustices, and much more. This is just a short list of environmental examples for which hypothetical attack plans can evolve into mature attack plans. Coupled with opportunity, a motivated attack becomes even more precarious as environmental factors increase the probability of an attack. Environmental factors tremendously facilitate attack windows of opportunity similar to how they inspire attacks. Events in the social, political, environmental, or economic climate can provide a ripe occasion for conducting attacks. Changes in the environment oftentimes reduce barriers or obstacles that naturally or artificially exist to mitigate threat scenarios. The following diagram provides a cause and effect flow of events stemming from environmental factors and resulting in attack patterns.

Figure 1.1 provides a visual representation of how environmental factors serve as additional intelligence when identifying probable attack scenarios during application threat modeling. The environmental condition of an economic recession creates multiple motives for attacking a financial application, per se, where the attackers may fulfill their multiple objectives. In this minor example, these objectives reflect a growing need for either financial self-preservation or gaining auxiliary income to offset financial shortfalls. Each of these motives becomes associated with possible attack scenarios against an application environment, along with the targeted asset(s).

Threat models in application security traditionally address threats and underlying attack patterns, along with their intended targets (as well as other variables that will be covered extensively throughout this book). None of these other variables within the threat model preface the phase in which threat assessments and attack analysis

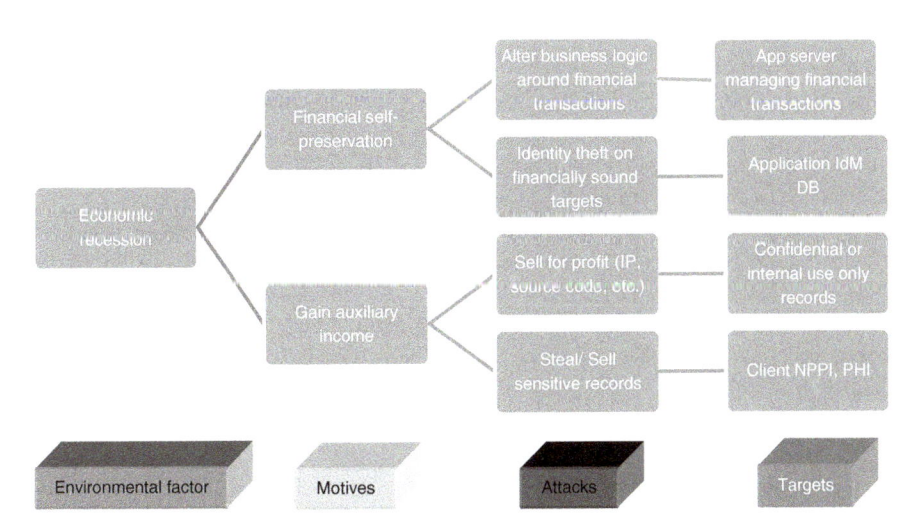

Figure 1.1 Relating Environmental Factors to Attacks

TABLE 1.1 Correlating Environmental Factors to Attack Motives – SAMPLE

Industry	Environment Factor	Possible Motive
Government	Increase antigovernment chatter	Upholding political or personal beliefs
Utility (nuclear)	War	Retaliation
Financial	Downtime economy	Financial gain
Software company	Increased turnover	Revenge, spite

occurs. Threat modeling exercises should include environmental factors as variables. Incorporating these factors may be simply anecdotal to any given threat model or may serve as key evidence in substantiating threat claims. In either case, environmental factors, motives, and opportunities are elements that undoubtedly affect threat characteristics and greatly influence the ability to better forecast the timing and probability of attack scenarios.

Forecasting attack scenarios is accomplished by first having a thorough understanding of environmental factors that may encourage certain types of motives. Table 1.1 lists examples across multiple industry segments and relates them to possible attack motives.

Qualifying environmental factors, as a precursor to threat modeling exercises, bolsters the strategic forethought associated with threat assessment efforts on application-based attacks. In the following section, we examine how motives, combined with ripe environmental factors, can compound attack probability levels and even exacerbate the sophistication level of an attack against an application.

Judging by Motives

Behind every threat is a motive, even if the motive is simple curiosity. Application-based attacks differ no less. Before a scan is run, payload is altered, or business logic is abused, the attack design must have an objective. Even seemingly benign attack probes or reconnaissance efforts against an application environment carry their own set of motives, quite possibly ulterior motives. From random injection attacks fueled by curiosity and bragging rights to elaborate plans to circumvent layers of security protocols, motives propel threat scenarios to attack plans. Most importantly, they begin by serving as an initial probe against any defense mechanisms that can foil attack plans or complicate goals for repudiation. Motives should be analyzed within the application threat model because they had better identify probable attack scenarios plotted against an organization's application environments. Additionally, identified motives can assist in forecasting the attack's sophistication level.

Assuming that all attack scenarios are driven by financial gains is flawed. Although these gains do represent the primary motives behind most attacks, universally presuming all attacks are financially motivated could mislead those responsible for defending

RATIONALE AND EVOLUTION OF SECURITY ANALYSIS 13

against them. Understanding attack motives provides clarity to possible targets, attack vectors, and, consequently, related countermeasures to defend against attacks. For example, a politically charged attack against a government site could involve attacks related to site defacement and Denial of Service (DoS) instead of those attempting to compromise data sources. Another example is that of a disgruntled employee at a financial firm who, given the right opportunity, may focus on high-impact business applications. In instances where motives are driven by revenge or spite from a company employee or former employee, high-impact targets are susceptible to attacks that affect data integrity, business continuity, and confidentiality.

An added layer of complexity to understanding motives is attacks solely devised to distract or deceive by simply serving as a diversion tactic. These types of attacks are exceptionally difficult to decipher since they may be launched from disparate networks, making event correlation difficult to accomplish. In these cases, the intent is for one or more attacks to lure resources and attention away from intended targets. These types of attacks are generally highly motivated and prefaced with a significant amount of planning. For this level of sophistication, counterintelligence efforts are invaluable in order to isolate possible sources. Counter-intelligence provides a preventive approach to understanding the greatest threat to an application environment. Tactics such as threat profiling are used to profile attack sources, entities involved, motives, capabilities, and access to resources.

Unfortunately, most organizations do not have their own counterintelligence groups to uniquely identify and qualify threat agents, particularly in the area of application security. Such an effort would require an enormous amount of time, effort, and money – all of which most organizations have sparingly. Some companies may obtain such intelligence via threat monitoring service providers, who aggregate growing lists of threats and attack exploits and deliver them via data feeds, or threat feeds. Threat feeds help build robust and up-to-date attack libraries that can be leveraged during threat modeling. However, companies employing threat feeds should be wary of overly depending on such feeds as the sole pieces of information for determining probable threat scenarios. Threats observed over public networks, honey pot farms, or in-the-cloud service providers only reveal a breakdown of threats to public infrastructures and do not precisely assess what may affect a specific organization. Although some threat feeds reflect data obtained from deployed network or host-based sensors across relevant industries, such data should not be taken as gospel for threat analysis. There may be other motives for unique and targeted attacks. As a general rule of thumb, a single source of information should not drive preventive application security measures, but simply serve as an added form of intelligence in building improved application countermeasures.

In an industry driven by benchmarks and outside influences, a balance must exist within security groups to leverage external research data and internal self-assessment exercises. Skimming the top attack scenarios from a threat feed and adopting it as the main source of information from which to build countermeasures follows a misguided mindset: whatever is good enough for the security masses is good enough for my security strategy. Such a myopic form of threat assessment places a greater emphasis on external sources for threat intelligence (as a basis for forecasting threat scenarios) over a company's own ability to assess analyzed threat scenarios, including unique characteristics of a company's physical and logical infrastructure. Adhering to the "Top 10" approach can easily give an organization a false sense of security based on the belief that relevant threat scenarios have been adequately addressed. An organization might learn a harsh lesson if lower ranked threat scenarios, not detailed within a received threat information feed, proved to be the most likely threat scenario to them. In light of the fact that all company resources and efforts may have been placed on top-level threat scenarios, countermeasures in other areas of the physical, or network infrastructure where the likely attack took place may have been overlooked.

The point to be made is *not* that these threat intelligence subscriptions are ineffective – on the contrary, they are extremely capable of identifying prevalent threats that have been observed and reported by a multitude of sources. This form of intelligence is highly useful when applied in the uniqueness and context of an organization's application environment. They are also precious resources in curtailing the time and effort to prepare for blanketed attack infrastructures, namely botnets, which may exhibit an array of threats identified by a threat aggregation service. However, beyond using such threat feeds, which may only encompass high-level or "Top 25" threats (depending on subscription), companies must consider other threat agents that make up their respective threat landscape. This may very well be some threats not provided by the threat aggregator service provider. In general, security information sources and tools should always be used after having established a strong understanding of the application environment and most importantly, the data with which it interfaces. Application walk-throughs, along with data flow diagramming, greatly develops this level of understanding for the threat modeler. These exercises can also attract a broader audience, fostering collaboration among developers, architects, business analysts, system administrators, security analysts, and QA team members. As each team becomes better acquainted with an application environment in review, vulnerable points can be collaboratively identified. Since the SDLC process should already encompass these individuals, all having varying insight into an evaluated application environment, application walk-throughs and data flow diagramming can quickly achieve the following objectives:

- Improve understanding of an application across multiple levels
    - Platform Level
        - Interrelated software dependencies
        - Local/Domain level privileges
        - Required ports and services
        - Hardening system requirements
    - Application Level
        - Use cases
        - Business Logic
        - Application privileges
    - Network Level

RATIONALE AND EVOLUTION OF SECURITY ANALYSIS

- Network-based security (ACLs, network device security policies)
- Scalability and bandwidth concerns
- Redundancy
- WAN/LAN based data requests
- Use of PKI
- Whitelisting/Blacklisting requirements
- Identify misuse cases that exploit poor business logic or code in software application
  - Login process
  - Registration process
  - Data requests (example: reports)
  - Application alerts (e-mail, SMS, etc.)
- Identify possible attack motives to data application data sources
  - ID Theft
  - Revenge
  - Financial motivation
  - Intellectual Property Theft
- Correlate attack motives to possible threat vectors in order to depict an initial threat landscape
  - Table 1.2 reveals how threat scenarios line up with motives and a subset of attack vectors.

Table 1.2 is an example of a well-designed matrix of how possible motives against an organization can be uniquely defined through simple assessment efforts. These assessment efforts may already exist either internally or through an external group. Surveying a diverse pool of technology and business users will help determine what potential threats are perceived by the organization's members and help identify those unique, targeted attacks. Table 1.2 reveals how threats encompass motives, target assets, and possible attack vectors to be used against an application environment. The table is meant to serve as a template for future use by threat modelers and risk analysts in beginning to correlate environmental factors to the vectors in which an attack would ultimately be introduced.

Attack environments will undoubtedly vary among one another and will be driven largely by unique factors, related socioeconomic conditions, and other personal ideals. Combined with strong motives, the makings of targeted attack plans began to unfold in the minds of the attackers. Many argue that the focal point should simply be the actual application attacks that target an application, such as session hijacking or elevation of privilege type exploits. The problem with this approach is that two essential questions remain unanswered: (1) who are they? and (2) what do they want? Understanding environmental factors and motives fueling attacks allows security groups to create multiple attack profiles. This leads to answers on the most likely profile types to conduct an attack with the greatest impact. Such a profile will also

TABLE 1.2 Correlating Motives to Application Threat Vectors

Threat	Target	Motives	Attack Vector
			Web Server(s) / Mail Server(s) / Intranet Sys / Authentication Trust Model / App Server / Portable Media / Wireless APs / External DNS / Network dev./app / Offshore Dev. / Social Eng. / Call Center (domestic) / Phy. Intrusion / Emp. Insider / LAN Based / IVR/VRU / API's / VPN

The following table represents simply a subset of possible threats and relevant targets, driven by motives over well-defined and understood attack vectors.

Threat	Target	Motives
Corporate espionage	Source code	Imitate a competitive application
		Inject objectionable code
	Business plans	Gain insight into service roadmap
	Emerging technologies	Replicate patented solutions
	Business processes	Business disruption
		Product/service imitation
	Confidential business records	Identify weak points
		Establish leverage
		Create competitive adv.
	Network schematics	Understand weaknesses in application architecture
Identity theft	Personal identifiable information	Facilitate repudiation
	Financial records	Financial leverage,
DoS, DDoS	High-impact/visibility business systems	Competitive reasons
		Politically charged
	WAN/LAN	Fueled by beliefs
	DNS ext./int.	Retaliation
Elevation of privileges	Access control mechanisms	Data access

16

reveal attackers' interests in specific application environments. Validated by log/incident data analysis over a sustained period of time, companies could prepare and refine threat profiles as a mitigating step against targeted attacks. This approach largely benefits the targeted attacks, which are often the most damaging and costly.

A final key difference between analyzing environmental factors and simply responding to top application-based threats is a stronger understanding of intent obtained via the former. Understanding the basis of an attack allows an application threat modeler to emulate the mind of the attacker.

Practical Application

Environmental factors provide improved calculations on attack probabilities as well as the prognosis on severity levels of observed attacks, either before, during, or after they have taken place. Admittedly, these efforts do require a significant amount of time. Across most industries, time and resources continue to deprive security groups from adopting techniques to assess environmental factors. As a realistic approach to executing these recommendations, organizations can adopt one of the following frequencies for analyzing environmental and motivational factors.

Table 1.3 aims to provide some degree of regularity in reviewing new and evolving environmental conditions. Constantly changing conditions heightens the probability for attack scenarios and their associated impact levels. The frequencies and scopes are driven largely by the overall historical and future sense of cyber-attacks against an organization's many application environments. The data obtained from each review should only be valid for a maximum of one year given the onset of new and developing environmental factors, both internal and external, that may trigger or accelerate threat scenarios against application systems and related data environments.

TABLE 1.3 Recommended Frequency for Environmental Threat Factor Analysis

Frequency	Scope	Details
Yearly	All business units	A comprehensive assessment determines the unique environmental factors and motives that adversely affect all business units.
Bi-annually	Alternating top 7 business units	If number of business units is less than 7, then a repetitive cycle of existing business units can be performed.
Quarterly	Alternating top 3 high-impact business units	Review top 3 high-impact lines of business, followed by a new 3 lines of business for each sequential quarter.
Monthly	Single high-impact business unit	Alternate across the organization, addressing one high business impact unit per month. If less than 12, repeat with the highest impact business units beginning the new cycle.

Sources of information during these periodic assessments will also vary greatly and be spurred by available resources. Internal personnel will ultimately be required to conduct analysis of internal factors to the organization. These may include the following types of evaluations:

- *HR Meetings:* Interviews with HR to identify cases where previously reported personnel cases provide a level of indication that certain employees may wish to act against the organization or its objectives. Obtaining information on disgruntled employees, for example, may provide early threat detection capabilities for certain types of information and operational threats.
- *Personnel Surveys:* Any HR surveys that seek to identify personnel viewpoints on the organization. This will help define enterprise- or department-level issues that could become organizational and/or environmental factors to consider for insider-based attacks.
- *Threat Feeds:* Threat feeds from external sources in which data reflects recent and aggregated attacks against similar companies, companies within the same industry sector, and companies of similar cultural and organizational makeup.
- *Third-Party Assessments:* External assessments performed by third parties help identify environmental factors and possible insider attack motives that would not have been discovered via internal assessments or employee surveys. Existing service providers may provide such assessments if their core competency includes those services.
- *Ingress Traffic Analysis:* Comprehensive review of ingress traffic across multiple entry points and correlated by geographic source, date/time, protocol, and separated by authorized IP sources (authorized third-party vendors) and unknown/unrecognized sources. Existing software may already detect and log network anomalies.
- *Access Audits:* Sensitive applications with logs set to record successful and failed logins. Correlate successful logins to time of day and frequency and perform the same correlation for failed events. Unify both data sets to cross-check for failed and successful logins on certain days/times. Anomaly detection would also be useful if it is inherent to the application or to a security product that interfaces with authentication application events.
  - *User Entitlement Reviews:* A subset to this is to review the current entitlements of users on a periodic basis. This may take place monthly, quarterly, or yearly. This exercise alone does not point to environmental or motivational factors; however, they may provide clues to unauthorized operations in user provisioning, which may point to future security circumvention.
- *Socioeconomic Analysis:* A review of external environment factors outside of the organization will ultimately affect employees in order that they behave either more or less rational with respect to their job functions and the due care that they would need to have with application environments used within their job functions. Economic distress, fears for personal security, personal beliefs fueled

by current events may all play a part in triggering some degree of action that can adversely affect an application environment.

All of these practical exercises are simply a subset of what can and should be analyzed as a part of a periodic assessment. Studying such environmental factors that may ignite attacks against application environments, either internal to the organization or against other application environments foreign to the company, is a vital part of any assessment. Unique factors to each organization will ultimately help create a customized assessment plan for ongoing evaluations.

SUMMARY

Attacks against applications are influenced by environmental factors and driven by motives. Socioeconomic conditions may provide a ripe time for attacks against application environments to yield either greater results or improved probabilities for success. Assessing these factors in conjunction with technical threat analysis within any given threat model provides greater readiness levels on behalf of the defending application owners.

BUILDING A BETTER RISK MODEL

> *"More people are killed every year by pigs than by sharks, which shows you how good we are at evaluating risk."*
>
> *Bruce Schneier*

Identifying risk should always be the key objective to application threat modeling. Threat identification and attack mitigation via countermeasures are important, but of greater importance is the ability to identify and mitigate business risk stemming from threats to application environments. Despite the many advances in security technology, understanding how existing and emerging security controls mitigates true risk is elusive.

The Inherent Problem

The problem with measuring risk today is that it is clouded by fear. Perception and subsequent reaction to perceived threats draws misguided conclusions for many attempting to mitigate risk. Information drives perception, and in application security, the manner in which information is handled determines whether or not appropriate risk mitigation efforts are properly executed. Fear has crippled many organizations into becoming less effective in dealing with application security. Organizations are paralyzed in HIGH-risk remediation queues and compliance gaps. Instead of adopting a strategic approach for application risk mitigation, reactive

TABLE 1.4 Key Reasons App_Sec Fails Today

1. Discrepancy between perceived and actual threats
2. Gap between current threats and existing preventive measures
3. Misconception of attack exploits against software
4. Greater use of detective/reactive app_sec controls versus preventive security controls
5. Inability to apply security controls as designed and/or as intended
6. Nonsecurity professionals involved in software development efforts or other key areas have limited security knowledge
7. One-dimensional approach to app_sec
8. Inability to factor in insider-based attacks
9. Misguidance attributed to FUD factors
10. Applying general security principles to a specific app_sec problem

---

responses drive one-dimensional security plans centered on those same HIGH-risk areas or compliance shortcomings. At the helm of this misguided approach is senior management, continuously seeking the best silver bullet at the lowest price. Over the years, fear has obscured reason and ingenuity within the realm of application security. Although great strides have been made in app_sec[1] related tools and technologies, their introduction and use within the context of reducing application risk has been nominal. The key reasons are mentioned in Table 1.4.

Table 1.4 is not meant to be a comprehensive listing of variables that lead to certain failures in application security, but instead a synopsis of commonly observed factors that inhibit a more strategic approach to app_sec. All of these factors, in varying degrees, affect the accurate depiction of application risk, which in turn limits that ability to derive any degree of business impact from identified application risk factors.

The rationale for threat modeling is to achieve a level of risk mitigation via a preventive, strategic approach to app_sec. This is a clear breakaway from the status quo mentality, where ingenuity is replaced with popular security trends, regardless of the unique nature of their industry, business, observed attack patterns, and environmental factors. In the next couple of chapters, we will take a look at how security strategy can evolve beyond a *keeping up with the Joneses* mentality. In the upcoming sections, we will explore the rationale or business case for threat modeling, which primarily revolves around the following paybacks:

- Better Form of Preventive Control
- Improved Application Design
- Effective Remediation Management

Business Case for Threat Modeling

Among all the rhetoric surrounding maturity modeling, six sigma–inspired projects, and ISO-driven benchmarks, one would think that implementing a framework for

---

[1] Application security.

improved application design and reduction in application risks and remediation time frames would be quickly adopted by members of the business community. However, the reality is that the majority of business groups are more concerned with the implementation of functional requirements versus security requirements. Traditionally, security requirements featured in the country that originated and mastered the fast-food concept, rate of service is paramount, especially for software development. The race to market with new products and features is always a high business priority. One of the numerous risks of such a speedy application development tempo is introducing multiple viable application exploits, which can jeopardize customer or business information. Unfortunately, these risks are generally lumped into an acceptable risk category. For many businesses, mitigating legal, financial, and/or regulatory risks take place via alternative countermeasures, such as improved contractual language or insurance policies that protect against financial fraud, loss of intellectual property, or unauthorized data disclosures.

Recognizing that process efficiency does not sell like cost savings, and realizing that compliance FUD has lost its luster in validating security investment, particularly when trying to lobby for executive sponsorship, it is important to highlight the various cost saving opportunities that can realistically be achieved through the adherence of a threat modeling program.

The following is a list of key benefits in developing and sustaining threat modeling efforts within an enterprise.

1. *Business Applications as Attack Vectors:* Software applications are low-hanging fruit for cybercriminals since software vendors do not have the same level of maturity in testing and patching as platform vendors for various operating systems. The differences in disclosed application vulnerabilities versus those at the application level are worlds apart. Microsoft's MSDN site has an excellent blog revealing numbers from their annual Security Intelligence Report (December 2012), showing that only 12.8% of vulnerability targets disclosed were operating systems. For this reason, businesses need to focus more on addressing threats to business applications, particularly early on in the SDLC. Today's reactive efforts to thwart security-based attacks equates to a rowboat trying to catch up with a motor boat. Strategic forethought has been needed for a number of years now; however, the paradigm for application security has focused on processes and controls on the heels of discovering that a major breach has occurred, or that a critical vulnerability requires immediate remediation. As sophisticated malware artists exploit the power of this knee jerk reaction, more advanced attacks can encompass diversion tactics in order to spread out the presence and effective use of any mitigating processes and controls. Application threat modeling introduces strategic forward thinking for probable attack patterns and vectors for a given enterprise, allowing organizations to mitigate possible threat scenarios based on current and good threat intelligence – another key component to the overall threat modeling process.

2. *Reduced Remediation Time and Efforts:* Anything that equates to more time in business also equates to additional cost. Remediation, traditionally taking place

in a postimplementation sense, has resulted in a workflow that, for most organizations, is truly insurmountable and costly. Since the threat modeling process addresses the most probable attacks and vulnerabilities that affect an application, remediation of weak or missing software countermeasures is addressed early in the development process. Most organizations have reached a level of remediation backlog almost matched by the number of security exceptions filed by business unit managers who oppose remediation efforts on their own information assets. Adding more chaos to this broken process are the current methods for tracking and managing remediation tasks, which continue to operate without any major changes to a highly ineffective and inefficient process. The amount of time and money consumed supporting a process that yields little to no risk reduction is immeasurable. Remediation and exception management – two out of control GRC efforts today – are both costly and ineffective in their production of security controls and risk reducing efforts. Nearly all information security and enterprise risk managers can truly identify with this problem today and welcome a new era of greater risk management efficiency. Application threat modeling lends to an improved risk model by injecting itself into a process that prefaces actual development efforts, thereby addressing security concerns up front in the SDLC. When platform vulnerabilities and software/service components are built and hardened to the specifications of the supported business application, remediation tasks are greatly curtailed and risk levels are reduced. In either case, time and money are saved through the proper use and application of a threat model to identify attacks, vulnerabilities, and key information assets of the greatest business impact. As with any security control or process, nothing completely eradicates risk. However, much of what is mitigated up front via application threat modeling will ultimately provide hundreds of hours in savings within the realm of exception/remediation management as well as change control requests that formalize any and all remediation tasks.

3. *Collaborative Approach:* Security risk assessments have historically taken an adversarial approach to both finding and addressing security risks in application environments. Threat modeling workflows foster more of a collaborative approach since they include all constituents that are normally a part of the remediation process. Via threat modeling, these key members are able to truly appreciate how existing application flaws translate to vulnerabilities that can be exploded by defined attack patterns. As a result, teams work together and learn much more about application security compared to simply being told to remediate unclear issues. This is currently the sentiment felt by most IT professionals (in development or system administration). Traditional IT professionals truly wish to understand the viability of how vulnerabilities foster exploitable attacks. The limited direction and guidance for corrective actions on hosts systems and software applications, however, leave most feeling that they are expected to automatically understand and quickly correct obvious security holes. Part of this problem is attributed to the poor guidance provided by security professionals to both information owners and asset custodians. Along with this intrinsic flaw is the antagonistic rapport between security professionals and those actually

delegated to address remediation efforts. Application threat modeling revolutionizes this approach by tackling two key fundamental flaws: (1) the timing in which vulnerabilities or configuration gaps are communicated and (2) the manner in which they are communicated. Namely, under the threat model approach, security professionals, and IT professionals work together to identify, validate, and rectify vulnerabilities and configuration flaws that introduce risk scenarios depicted by plausible attack patterns, as shown by the model. Needless to say, the unison approach in application threat modeling is refreshing and far more strategic than the current divisive ways that security flaws are identified and queued for remediation.

4. *Building Security In:* Contrary to security requirements previously established and socialized by separate and adverse groups (in either security governance or security architecture), security requirements now become an innate part of software development. Coupled with developers who would much rather know what to build in first than fixing bugs postproduction, building security in is a philosophy inherent in any secure software development life cycle (or secure development life cycle) – a highly recommended foundation for application threat modeling. Threat modeling could thrive in the absence of an S-SDLC/SDL process; however, it would be activated during the pseudo definition and/or design phases in which an application is being contrived. The presence of S-SDLC/SDL-IT efforts does award application threat modeling the proper context to operate within, versus a more ad hoc development culture, which would not properly assign responsibilities in various processes depicted by a threat model. For example, who is responsible for creating the proper attack library to be used within the threat model? Who will perform the various data flow diagramming exercises and what application boundaries will they encompass? Who will enumerate the actors, assets, and data sources that are applicable in the threat model? The answers to these questions are more streamlined within various phases of an S-SDLC/SDL-IT, or accomplished more haphazardly within an ad hoc development methodology. In either case, application threat modeling introduces attack considerations during a time in which functional requirements are being designed and outlined. Threat models help to determine attack vectors, inherent vulnerabilities (attributed to employed software or platform technologies), as well as an understanding of high-impact application areas that need to be protected. Incorporating this knowledge incorporates the premise of building security in and furthers the rationale for employing application threat modeling for key business applications.

The aforementioned points simply touch on a comprehensive list of points for a business rationale for threat modeling. More targeted benefits, appropriate to various security functions (operations, emergency response, risk, etc.), can easily be derived from these four points as well as others not mentioned. In the following section, we will expand on and correlate multiple business and security use cases. We will expand upon application threat modeling's ability to influence improved application design – yet another rationale for which enterprises should further consider adopting application threat modeling.

Improved Application Design

Application design has been more of a conceptual idea versus an actual work effort funded by most IT organizations. This may explain the poor state of application security that we find ourselves in, or at the very least serve as one of its contributing factors. Even when implemented, application design considerations always seem to be one sided or built primarily around software features, diluting other variables that should influence the overall application design, including key business, IT, and *security* objectives for the application. In recent years, security groups have slowly been allowed to provide input to application design, but the effort is still scarce, spotted, and inconsistent at best. With the fruition of S-SDLCs (*Secure Software Development Lifecycles*) and Microsoft's SDL-IT (Security Development Lifecycle) Methodology, a stronger security voice will hopefully continue to grow over time and build a rationale within corporate IT boardrooms.

If a business rationale for application threat modeling is going to take flight, metrics have to be incorporated into any given threat model. Although metrics can be a key ingredient in building a business rationale for application threat modeling, the criteria in which metrics are understood and utilized within the vernacular of IT and business groups needs to be properly defined. For example, we can migrate over many traditional security risk variables that include single loss expectancy (or annualized loss expectancy), attack probability percentages, business impact levels, asset value, cost of countermeasure, and more. As expected, these variables will ultimately vary in importance and use across various organizations given their preferred set of metric values that are consistently monitored, either formally or informally. Overall, metrics for application threat modeling need to encompass the following requirements (as shown in Figure 1.2).

More guidance on metrics and threat modeling will be provided in Chapter 8. For now, simply consider metrics as a valuable by-product from application threat modeling. Improved application design will provide the consistency across any application environment in order to repetitively extract metrics. The following sections reveal qualities in software applications that are fine-tuned via the procedures applied from application threat modeling. Just some of the application-related traits that act as beneficiaries from the structure and analytical rigor of application threat modeling include factors related to application scalability, support of application components, and information/application security. Each of these three areas encompasses several factors within traditional IT objectives as well as goals in information security, further illustrated in the following sections.

Scalability One key aspect of improved application design is the ability of the application environment to accommodate changes, such as future business needs, infrastructure, and security requirements. As all of these factors may require code modifications, the impact (whether good or bad) to scalability is ever present.

BUILDING A BETTER RISK MODEL

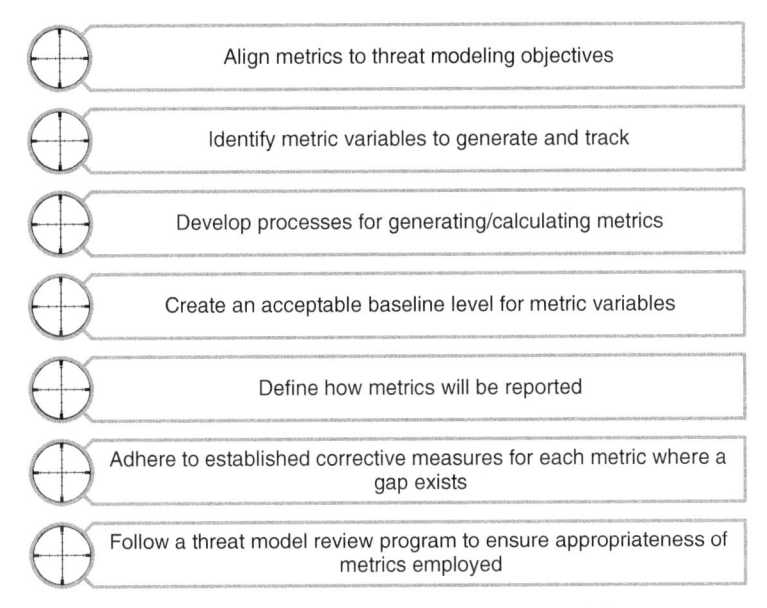

- Align metrics to threat modeling objectives
- Identify metric variables to generate and track
- Develop processes for generating/calculating metrics
- Create an acceptable baseline level for metric variables
- Define how metrics will be reported
- Adhere to established corrective measures for each metric where a gap exists
- Follow a threat model review program to ensure appropriateness of metrics employed

Figure 1.2 Developing Metrics in Threat Modeling

The ability for application architecture to be open and adaptable demonstrates a strong business case for application threat modeling beyond its security benefits. The thought that application threat modeling could provide direct benefits to application scalability may seem far fetched, but not if one unravels the layers that comprise software scalability. Microsoft's online Visual Studio Developer Center does an excellent job of depicting the key factors that impact software scalability. Figure 1.3 provides a graphical representation of these influential variables to software scalability.

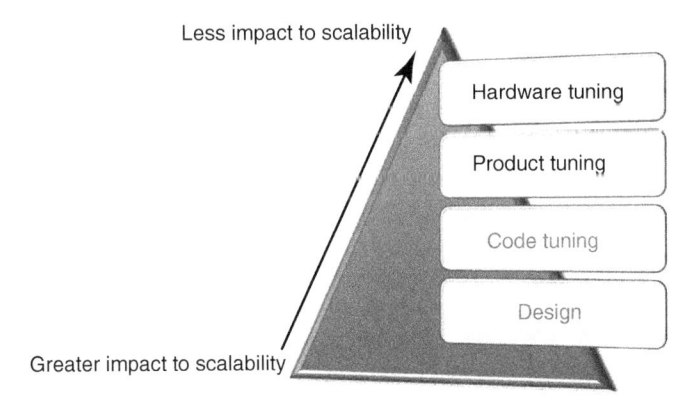

Figure 1.3 Development Factors Affecting Scalability

Design and code tuning efforts pose the greatest threats to the scalability of a software application. Taking this and today's security remediation efforts into account, modifications to code bases (code tuning) or application reengineering (redesign) efforts to incorporate new security countermeasures, such as input validation or error handling functionality, may unknowingly undermine any level of scalability that a given application may have had prior to such changes. A major reason is poor regression testing that encompasses all possible use cases that were initially tested during the first major roll out of a software build. Security changes implemented after the fact may ultimately resolve security gaps found by traditional security scans or assessments, but their objectives are simple and isolated. The reality is that security code modifications today are *quick and dirty* even when conducted through a formal change control process. Change control in most organizations has become so ritualistic that many of the considerations for how changes can affect a software environment are settled in a conference room instead of via a formal model. An application threat model provides the medium. It begins by addressing or readdressing the business objectives of the application and filters its way down to specific use cases, possibly impacted by the newly introduced security countermeasure or control. Additionally, it focuses on permission sets that may have been awarded inadvertently through design changes or code tuning. Since application threat modeling essentially *walks through* software application components (assets, communication channels, data repositories, and permission sets), a smaller degree of risk exists for when changes need to take place, thereby sparing possible setbacks in software scalability. Threat modeling essentially provides a higher degree of rigor in the analysis needed to determine adverse impacts to code tuning or software design changes. Threat modeling's differentiator is its systematic approach for breaking up the application security analysis into a hierarchy of key components, beginning with business objectives and ending with proper countermeasures for security gaps. In between is analysis to data sources based upon business impact or criticality levels, communication mediums, permission sets, plausible attacks, and clearly defined APIs. As a result, any considerations for design modifications and code tuning can take part within the boundaries of a threat model to ensure that previously defined functionality and objectives for application scalability are preserved and retested.

A more obvious relationship exists among the two worlds of scalability and security: nonscalable software can introduce future and serious vulnerabilities to software applications. Let us take the following scenario of a growing and profitable online retailer whose business focuses on ergonomic furniture. After years of perfecting their online store to reflect their vast inventory of ergonomic office furniture, primarily focused on the commercial sector, they are getting many inquiries from the federal government on their service line. In an effort accommodate this change quickly, project managers push new application requirements to development. Developers will in turn churn out new code to accommodate the desired changes on the retail portal. At this juncture, an effective application model is critical, particularly when ensuring that security controls are present. An application threat model therefore provides a framework where not only security countermeasures can be developed, but also processes related to continuity of service and scalability can be preserved by

BUILDING A BETTER RISK MODEL

the manner in which modifications are validated against application intradependencies. As a result, a heightened level of application design adds further rationale for employing the use of application threat modeling. Most importantly, security strategists will be able to recommend (with greater ease) what, when, and where security countermeasures should be incorporated.

Support Supporting software, such as any other IT-related process, must be properly aligned to a business objective. Such a lofty, idealistic goal may seem impractical if all support efforts will be validated against a broadly defined business or IT objective. Ensuring that support efforts on software applications are in alignment to these objectives, however, will ensure that not all supportive product efforts deviate from principal features of an application. If a process for supporting code modifications or application design changes does not revert to an initial blueprint of business objectives, the supporting code modifications can mutate into fractured and disjointed support efforts. Essentially, the faulty action that may result is scope creeping in supporting software. Good and even excellent ideas can easily take a quick turn to spawn unintended features or functionality. An application threat model will not catch such deviant actions until functions or features are reviewed from within the threat model and found to be discordant with defined business objectives as defined for the application.

What does support mean in this context of application development? Key members at the focal point of *supporting* software, examples of their related work efforts, and the benefits reaped from application threat modeling (ATM) are summarized in Table 1.5.

The proliferation of modular development efforts today makes supporting any application-related modifications nearly impossible without a proper framework. Application threat modeling is not aimed to be a replacement for proper application architecture and product management. However, since its process is embedded within the review of software features and functions, it provides an ongoing check

TABLE 1.5 Threat Modeling Benefits for Various Roles

Support Role	Responsibilities	Benefits From TM
Developer	Make changes to source code based on new or revised functional and security requirements	See related impacts from support-related changes to the application threat model
QA engineer	Validate new code through test cases	Understand the severity of application components and adhere to security test cases
Support personnel	Address questions related to the application's features and functions	Have a holistic reference to the application, from a security context as well as a feature/function point of view

for new features that may stray from intended objectives. Added functionality is a security risk because it typically introduces new interfaces, which may or may not include a new set of privileges for data access, among other types of application use cases. Improperly managed software modification (either from code tuning efforts or application redesign) can introduce tangents in functionality, which in turn introduces new doorways for attack vectors (i.e. – new forms, data interfaces). Essentially, supporting new code requires newfound oversight for secure coding practices, security architecture, and secure interfaces. Application threat modeling – an absolutely necessary security framework for addressing application risk on all of these levels – fosters improved application support by providing a context for new features and changes to abide by defined business and IT objectives. Unsanctioned features give way to process deviations in support operations, which are only as effective as the scope of features in which they are trained or introduced to support. New features or changes to an application, if not properly corralled back to operational project managers, will ultimately slip through the competency of support personnel who find such foreign features difficult to support. Moreover, application threat modeling, as a qualitative security process that is in line with validating newly developed or altered code, is positioned to identify anomalies in functionality and features, and then communicate outliers in application changes to support. This will preserve consistency and knowledge base in supporting the application.

With multiple parallel development efforts taking place, it is easy for code ownership to get lost amidst a sea of domestic and even offshore developers. However, improved application design can result from application threat modeling via its organized assembly line approach addressing multiple functional components as part of the application security analysis. Given most fractured development efforts, application threat modeling pieces together the various platform, database, network, and software-related components, which are all relevant support vehicles for change at some time in the future, thereby providing an excellent understanding of the application's design. In doing so, applications can be better supported in the future from various perspectives, including QA efforts, support operations, IT audit, project management, and software development. Application threat modeling provides an architectural view to support personnel in understanding how various application components (Web Services, Databases, Web Servers, Applets, etc.) interact among other application areas. This inherent holistic approach allows greater introspection to support the application by both developers and support personnel as threat models provide both high level and intimate details on an application's functionality. Lastly, support personnel at any level will be able to refer to deliverables or artifacts from an application threat modeling exercise as a key point of reference for understanding the following critical aspects of an application environment:

- Criticality of the software application
- Functional requirements as they relate to defined business objectives
- Security countermeasures incorporated into the application
- Type of data managed by the application

Although many will inevitably argue that it is not the place for application threat modeling to provide any level of blueprint for an application, the process does provide an updated overview for an application's various components, *particularly from a security context*. It cannot be emphasized enough that application threat modeling *is not* being taken out of context when it is depicted as a benefit to support operations for software applications. Ultimately, application threat modeling still preserves its security-focused objectives via improved application design by enhancing support efforts in software application:

- Elevates support teams' knowledge of security provisions, as identified by the application threat model:
  - Features related to access control
  - Controls related to confidentiality, integrity, and availability
  - Countermeasures that ward off spoofing, tampering of data, repudiation, information disclosure, DoS, and elevation of privileges
  - Superfluous features or functions that extend beyond objectives as defined within the application threat model
- Fosters a healthy validation of what features and functionality are actually to be developed. Also helps to limit out of scope software features that impact the following:
  - Stray from business objectives
  - Deviate from core competencies of the software application or environment
  - Introduce security risks via the expanded scope
  - Augments the scope of knowledge and expertise that is potentially required to support the application

Security Application Threat Modeling yields improved application design, driven by security efforts via strategic, streamlined, application hardening efforts, ideally all within the context of a secure software development process. Application threat modeling provides an architectural advantage over more traditional security assessments on software applications through the use of data flow diagramming techniques and application walk-throughs. It also embellishes traditional IT architecture by incorporating functional requirements for service delivery, continuity, and scalability; all obtained by threat modeling's collaborative workflow that fuses security analysis with traditional IT architecture and software development.

The key security contrast between application threat modeling and more traditional application assessments (achieved via automated scans or qualitative assessments) is that identified risk issues are derived from attack possibilities that are unique to the application environment and not solely to the discovered vulnerability. Motivational factors for launching specific types of attacks are conceptualized in a library in order to provide the most likely description of an attack landscape for an application. In essence, application security today does not truly map out specific attack scenarios for given vulnerabilities or series of vulnerabilities associated for an assessed application. As a result, an incomplete portrayal of risk is presented to information owners for remediation. Unfortunately, the owners do not understand the nature and likelihood of possible attack scenarios to their particular application and what likely attack vectors would be launched to introduce these risks. Supported by vast attack libraries, threat modeling provides a process for multiple security threats to be addressed, each encompassing a set of possible attack patterns, and corresponding vulnerabilities. Security professionals can walk-through an attack that specifically relates to an application use case, represented within the threat model, which is invaluable to the process. Threat modeling goes further by addressing weaknesses in business logic that should be reconsidered and IT components that may also introduce additional attack vectors (at the platform level or via third-party software). These security-weak areas are discovered prior to a production release or production build. Ideally, these efforts should take place within the early stages of an SDLC, thereby allowing remediation of vulnerabilities to be addressed prior to production.

Effective Remediation Management

The English saying of "an ounce of prevention is worth a pound of cure" is very appropriate when applied to remediation management in security risk management. Since application threat modeling is best applied within the early stages of the SDLC, it naturally adheres to this preventive philosophy and truly enhances remediation efforts by reducing the amount of time required for remediating software vulnerabilities as well as by correcting security gaps prior to introducing the application to end users. The following is a brief list of key factors that reveal how application threat modeling triggers effective remediation management.

1. Defines security requirements to be baked into the application
2. Incorporates security requirements into application design
3. Fosters the development of security countermeasures as features
4. Allows the development of security test cases

The aforementioned factors are far more difficult to achieve after an application has been developed, for reasons previously mentioned within this chapter. Besides limitations in time and availability, the process of reactive remediation efforts forces development teams to remediate production software (in a test environment) that may be n versions behind the current set of software. As a result, developers may not be too inclined to address software vulnerabilities in older versions versus alpha or beta releases that are currently being developed.

Adding further complexity to late remediation is the decentralized manner in which many developers write code – each focusing on a specific aspect or module of the application environment. This may force the necessity of an application architect or technical project manager who can oversee remediation efforts across all vulnerable areas. Since application development generally encompasses the involvement of multiple developers or even development teams, understanding an application and its environment may prove challenging, time consuming, and ultimately ineffective. Doing so at this junction may not include other key members who affect the integrity of the environment, such as system administrators, network engineers, or members from IT architecture who may have valuable insight and knowledge on how an application was built, behavior and reasons for any applicable data interfaces, technical/security exceptions made, and more. The likelihood that all (or even some) of these members will have time to address security vulnerabilities, particularly within a relatively similar time frame, is near negligible. Even if achieved, the window of time is small for both their initial feedback and corrective actions (programmatic or configuration related).

The need for evolving beyond current remediation management efforts in security is timely, given the increased need to reduce application security risks. Regardless of application environment (web, mobile, client-server and/or fat-client), threat modeling has its use and benefits, as we will later see in future practical applications of various methodologies and tools. Most methodologies can be applied parallel to maturing SDLC or SDL-IT processes. The key challenge is whether there is a formal SDLC process that repeatable application threat modeling efforts could become embedded within. Statistically speaking, most organizations do not adhere to any form of SDLC methodology or, if implemented, they are in an early stage of adoption. A formal SDLC process is a prerequisite for implementing application threat modeling as a repeatable security process; however, a fully functional QA process may also anchor and support a developing threat modeling program as well.

In some instances, an SDLC process is not uniformly adhered to across all business units involved with developing business applications. As a result, disparate security levels may exist across implemented application environments that share data. Applications disassociated with the application threat modeling program may introduce APIs that actually serve as ripe attack vectors. Internal application domains often use trusted authorities across application environments, thereby exacerbating the disparate security posture between the two application domains. This is important to consider when and if minimal gains in improved application design are witnessed, subsequent to the implementation and use of application threat models.

SUMMARY

As reflected in this chapter, there are several factors that account for the business rationale for threat modeling. These factors are both process and technical in nature and extend beyond the benefits of traditional application risk assessments and vulnerability assessments today. Although traditional risk assessments and vulnerability assessments provide ways to identify risk issues, they do not ultimately translate into new security requirements for the existing or even subsequent application development efforts. Conversely, threat modeling is able to address what security requirements must be present across multiple levels of the application environment as well as identify new attack vectors and potential exploits during the testing and validation efforts within the threat modeling process. All of these efforts take place prior to code migration into higher application environments, thereby reducing remediation efforts and risk exposure levels. Additional factors for its implementation relate to the following:

1. *Outline of Application Use Cases:* Use case scenarios have never truly been tracked or managed from the inception of an application's life cycle. As a result, the overall intent of use for an application may encompass functional aspects that were never meant to be pervasive over the life of the application. Use cases help define exploitable misuse cases, most notably through the rise of attacks based upon the misuse or abuse of application business logic. Threat modeling brings to light the need to address misuse case scenarios from within the testing stages of the SDLC or SDL-IT process as well as the necessity to disable features that should no longer be made available to the intended and unintended user base. Threat modeling brings greater focus on both use case and misuse case scenarios within an application.
2. *Discovering Application Security Land Mines:* Application walk-throughs are virtual simulations of an application's functionality and greatly assist discovering errors in business logic or vulnerabilities in the code. Walk-throughs are intended to be very thorough and aimed at identifying how object or resource calls can be compromised at various points of the application. This simulation allows a well-defined attack tree to develop and serve as a baseline of attacks for future threat modeling exercises.
3. *Comprehensive Data Security via Data Flow Diagrams (DFDs):* DFDs are nothing new to software development, but they do provide a fresh perspective to mapping out design and coding flaws within software applications. Essentially, DFDs provide a visual on how data moves between functional points within an application environment. These exercises provide insight into what actions against data are happening at various points and if additional controls for protecting the integrity and confidentiality of the data should be applied. Similar to application walk-throughs in the sense that they are thorough and comprehensive to the various features of a software application, DFDs are different in that they focus more on the data object being called than the functionality and parameters of the caller resource.

Most notably, the reduction of software vulnerabilities reduces remediation time and efforts. Less time translates into less cost. In order for threat modeling's business rationale to evolve from the theoretical to the practical in this area, key metric values must be collected and trended over time. These metrics should include residual risk levels, loss expectancy ratios, number of vulnerabilities for beta versus production versions, remediation time, and so on. These values will help provide choice metrics that can be used to sustain the business value of such threat modeling efforts. Application threat modeling embellishes much of what has been lacking in application design by fostering a greater intimacy with application requirements across business, IT, security levels, and beyond.

THREAT ANATOMY

> "A little while ago, the Pentagon demonstrated in an exercise that it was possible – even easy, actually – to hack into the power grids of the 12 largest American cities, and to hack into the 911 emergency system, and shut all of those off with a click of a button. Now, that isn't somebody getting shot, and you don't see the blood coming out of the body, and the body collapsing on the ground. But I can assure you, tens of thousands of people would have died."
>
> *PBS Interview with former iDefense CEO, James Adams*

Earlier in this book, we discussed attack motives in order to answer the question of why attacks occur. The range of answers to the why question are vast, but with a strong degree of overlap among various key factors. Before we delve into the answers on how attacks are planned and launched in cyber warfare, let us quickly revisit the list of drivers that propel white hats to black hats, hobbyists to criminals, and script kiddies to wanted cyber felons.

No matter how much we have advanced technologically, the elements of war and attack are still age-old intrinsic human sentiments rooted in hatred, greed, envy, or simple idle curiosity. This chapter aims to dissect the elements of cyber threats and attacks for the purpose of selecting the proper countermeasures.

One motive not represented in Figure 1.4 is the motive geared toward creating a diversion for a simultaneous or delayed threat or attack. These become more sophisticated and may or may not encompass a clear motive. More sophisticated diversion attacks seek to create a false motive for which opposing resources can take time, money, and effort to investigate, while core threats and attack plans continue to evolve. Now we build upon this notion to dissect the elements of attacks within an application context and related threat model.

In this chapter, we will dissect cyber-related attack patterns. We begin by understanding the progression of attacks with the encompassing threat and how understanding cyber threats can help a security professional to identify probable attack plans. Building upon the brief recap on attack motives, an understanding of threats to an application threat model is the next sequential step to see what attacks comprise an overall threat. It is important to understand the hierarchy of terminology used thus far, particularly *motives, threats,* and *attacks,* as they each represent both a unique and interrelated component to the application threat model. In software applications, a *threat* is very much like *risk* in that it will never be zero or nonexistent. There always is a degree of *risk* primarily due to the fact that *threats* are always present within or around an application. With enough *motive, threats* serve as mobilizing agents to conduct *attacks* against software environments. Table 1.6 provides a threat stack that emphasizes the hierarchy and interrelationship between these factors.

Motives, software/platform vulnerabilities, and risk levels stand independently; however, threats are comprised of viable attack patterns. Devoid of any probable attack, a threat becomes near negligible and is only retained as a theoretical or possible threat scenario. Table 1.6 reflects the interrelationship between attacks and threats and the dependency in which they coexist. No threat equates to no possible forms of

Corporate espionage/intellectual property theft
- Obtain competitive advantage
- Thwart new product/service developments by opposition (competition?)
- Copy new developments in order to be first to market

Terrorism/Counterterrorism
- Affect energy supplies access to basic daily necessities (clean water, electricity, etc.)
- Create fear and internal backlash in targeted civilian population
- Eliminate livelihood of enemy civilian life

Curiosity/Bragging rights
- Intellectual challenges/professional notoriety
- Thrill of the chase
- Hacking High/addiction

Religious/Cultural/Moral beliefs
- Freedom of expression in opposition to a central religious institution or group of people
- Impersonating religious organizations to tarnish image of target religious group
- Demonstration against social law, moral authorities, or lack thereof

Organized crime
- Financing illegal drug, contraband, and criminal activities
- Facilitate the ability to repudiate criminal activity

Figure 1.4 Cyber Crime Motives

34

THREAT ANATOMY

TABLE 1.6 Threat Model Stack

Threat Model Stack
−Motive
+Threat(s)
−Attack(s)
• Probabilities
• Vulnerabilities
• Assets
+Risk

attack. The absence of an attack or series of attacks reduces a threat to only conceivable or theoretical threat levels. Although reflected by any application threat model, it is important to note that a given threat model is evolving or only valuable for a defined period of time as the sophistication and plausibility of application-based attacks will ultimately evolve over time, as will the other components of the threat model stack.

The Threat Wrapper

Threats' complexities lie in bundling varying degrees or attack types, vulnerabilities, and impact levels, and there is variation among application types. For this reason, we will explore a handful of threats and varying types of application environments, and dissect the encompassing attacks that could accompany them. First, let us look at a very simple threat model that expresses a highly generic flow of input/output from a user base, between two trust boundaries, to a target information source.

Unrelated to any methodology, and assuming illicit data access is the primary motive, the foremost question should be: How can an attacker complete their objective? Now that the threat of data compromise is assumed, the focus becomes where and how the threat will be carried out. Revisiting our data flow in Figure 1.5, we have to identify how data sources can be leaked via the boundaries of the application environment. In this case, the trust boundaries are neatly drawn between the client or

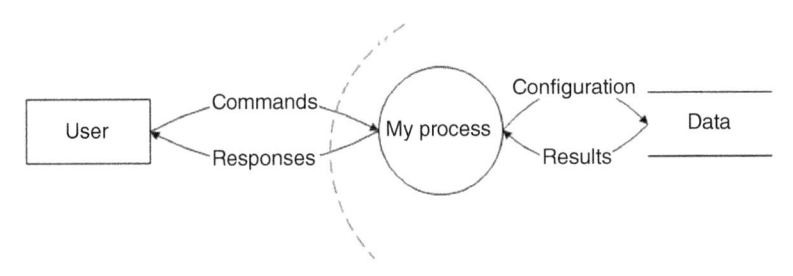

Figure 1.5 Simple Data Flow Diagram supporting Threat Model

user environment and the application environment. At this point, although we have not defined the business or IT objectives that should provide governance, we are proceeding to understand how the imminent threat should be addressed. Incorporating these objectives ultimately allows us to understand the appropriate countermeasures that equate to a formula reflecting the probability of each attack identified, the business impact if successful, and costs associated with implementing security control measures. In this case, we assume that all threats will be mitigated to the best of our ability.

Upon understanding the objectives of our threat model as well as all plausible motives for the identified threat, we need to evaluate the threat landscape. The threat landscape is comprised of target areas (client, server, middleware, or proxy), communication channels (wireless, Ethernet), layer seven[2] protocols (SMTP, SNMP, HTTP), physical security considerations (easily accessible server closets), and services probed to be present across the application environment. With these variables in mind, the previous threat model can now be updated with an overlay of a hypothetical threat landscape. Items represented in red reflect potential malicious misuse of the application environment.

Referencing the aforementioned figure, we see how a slightly more evolved threat model can manifest the components of possible threat scenarios against a generic application. In reality, the threat model may reflect any number of motives, as discussed earlier in this book, and those motives might shed some light into the types of attacks that are most likely to achieve a given motive. In Figure 1.6, we begin to understand some of the components enveloped within a threat. Motives trigger actions on behalf of malicious individuals or irresponsible employees to create some degree of threat. These threats may be geared toward target assets or information sources, as part of their objective and will ultimately rely on intel to discover software vulnerabilities or misconfigurations to exploit via attacks. As the threat traverses across public, semipublic, private, and restricted application zones, other variables related to threat begin to take form such as probability of successful exploitation, business impact of compromised business data, presence, or void of security countermeasures, and much more.

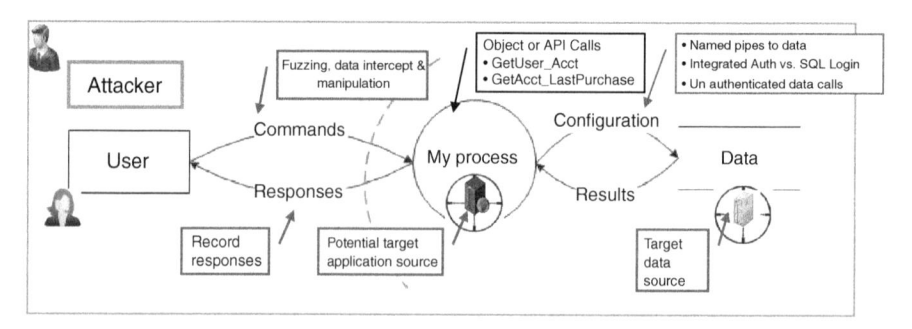

Figure 1.6 More Evolved Data Flow Diagram supporting Threat Model

[2]Related to the OSI model.

Understanding threats begins with understanding the attacker and the available information and expertise they may have to conduct their targeted attacks. Most times, an attacker's identity or the profile of an assumed attacker cannot be derived until after the attack has happened. The timing in which this information is obtained does not undermine its value; it can be used to create an attacker profile for future events, particularly if their actions are recorded in the application server log, network logs, or at the platform host level. Most private or commercial organizations do not have an attacker profile database; however, government or military IT operations may find this worthwhile in order to predict attack patterns based on commonalities in attack patterns. Banks and financial institutions may also find this essential.

Beyond this type of attacker profiling, threat classification provides the most common form of analytical and preventive defense that any organization can begin as a formal security operations effort. Threat classes are preventive in the sense that they help classify types of threats from any security control that provides both alerting and logging of actions taken against a system. Threat classes help to create "bins" for organizing attack data into decipherable forms of attack. Injection attacks, elevation of privilege attempts, and DoS attacks all become organized into appropriate classes for analysis and reporting. Coupled with external threat feeds, any organization has the ability to prioritize concretely their security controls for the *short term*. An emphasis on short term is made here because attack patterns and exploits that are en vogue may be blasted across target sites few months to several years. Overall, the idea is to have both a process and technology that can aggregate and classify threats appropriately.

From the threat classification efforts, an association map can be made by correlating attack scenarios and vulnerable application components. Additionally, both the possible exploit and vulnerability can be mapped back to the application within the threat model to obtain business impact values and risk levels. At this level, even before taking a deep dive into the practical logistics of the attack, such as attack vector, exploit, or associated vulnerabilities, obtain a high-level picture of risk and business impact, which may help formulate preliminary risk strategies. After all, the end goal associated with any threat model should be to mitigate risk.

Brief Intro to Threat Classification Models

Some threat classification models include STRIDE and DREAD – two Microsoft-originated threat classification models focused on identifying business impact and risk, in varying degrees. Additionally, the Web Application Security Consortium (WASC[3]) periodically revises its threat classification, which is a great technical reference for grouping various types of threats by their technical nature in lieu of any business impact or risk model. The WASC's listing is more of a technical briefing of the latest web application-related threats, and less of a threat classification model. A model could easily be built, however, from the classes defined within this periodic reference, as can one be built from the Open Web

[3] http://www.webappsec.org/.

Application Security Project (OWASP[4]), which also releases a top ten list of threats aimed at web applications. The OWASP top ten listing is updated every few years and reflects the most prevalent threats to web applications and is an excellent start for a technical-based threat class model.

Several threat models may also be built with the help of product-based security solutions from both open source and commercial grade products today. Many network- and host-based solutions have threat intelligence modules or feeds. Security operations centers then analyze and aggregate the provided data to understand what threats are traversing various types of networks and interfaces over a defined period of time. A security incident and event monitoring solution within an organization, or a managed service program where companies send logs of alerts and events to a security cloud for threat analysis can provide this information. More autonomous organizations can operate in a self-contained manner by leveraging threat feeds from large security organizations that leverage deployed security products and monitor networks from around the world. This gives these vendors great visibility into active threats as well as provides trending data for such recorded events.

In the end, threat classes are useful for categorizing vulnerabilities and attacks identified by the threat model. Figure 1.7 provides a visual synopsis of how threat classes can organize a laundry list of attacks and vulnerabilities. This simplified figure depicts how threat classes cannot only encompass elements of the threat, such as attacks and vulnerabilities, but also the countermeasures or controls that mitigate their associated risks.

Vulnerabilities – The Never-Ending Race

Dissecting any given threat reveals a number of vulnerabilities that serve as windows of opportunity. Without them, acting as a threat agent proves to be a lot more difficult and less rewarding given the decreased likelihood for success. Hackers and cybercriminals value their time as much as anyone else does, and if no clear vulnerabilities in process or technical controls are present, it is very likely that they will threaten other information doorways.

The evolution of vulnerabilities has migrated in overwhelming numbers from platforms to applications, making vulnerability management exponentially more difficult to track and manage simply due to the sheer number of applications that are present across enterprises. As a result, threat modeling is a bit more complex, needing a more extensive and up-to-date vulnerability listing.

As part of an application's threat model, an inventory of up-to-date vulnerabilities is key. Vulnerabilities can be linked to asset and architectural elements in the threat model through the inventory. These elements include both software and hardware assets and their related software or firmware that can be misused by released exploits. Considerations for zero-day exploits should also be made within the model, but they are more difficult to predict. Automated and continuous vulnerability scans should provide a good amount of vulnerability information quickly for aggregation,

---

[4] http://www.owasp.org.

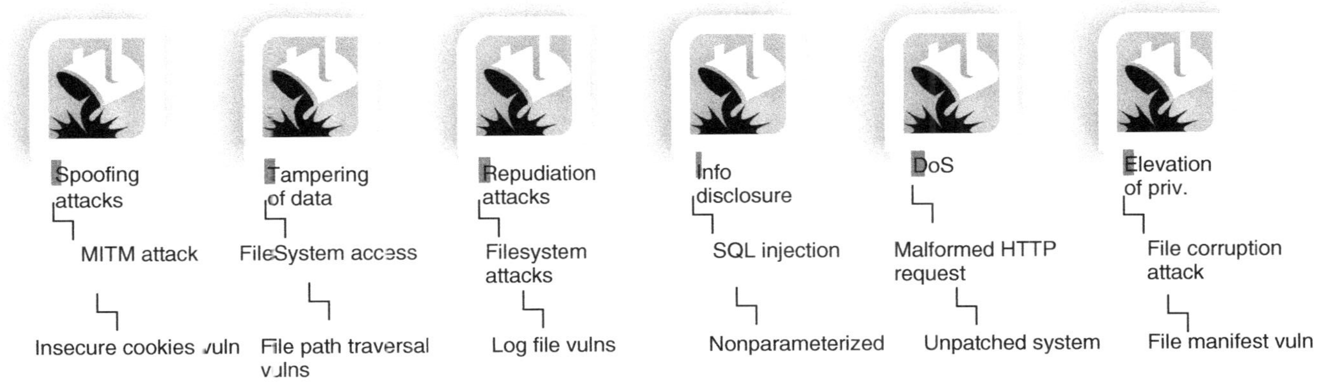

Figure 1.7 STRIDE Threat Classification Visual Example

- Spoofing attacks
  - MITM attack
  - Insecure cookies vuln
- Tampering of data
  - FileSystem access
  - File path traversal vulns
- Repudiation attacks
  - Filesystem attacks
  - Log file vulns
- Info disclosure
  - SQL injection
  - Nonparameterized
- DoS
  - Malformed HTTP request
  - Unpatched system
- Elevation of priv.
  - File corruption attack
  - File manifest vuln

39

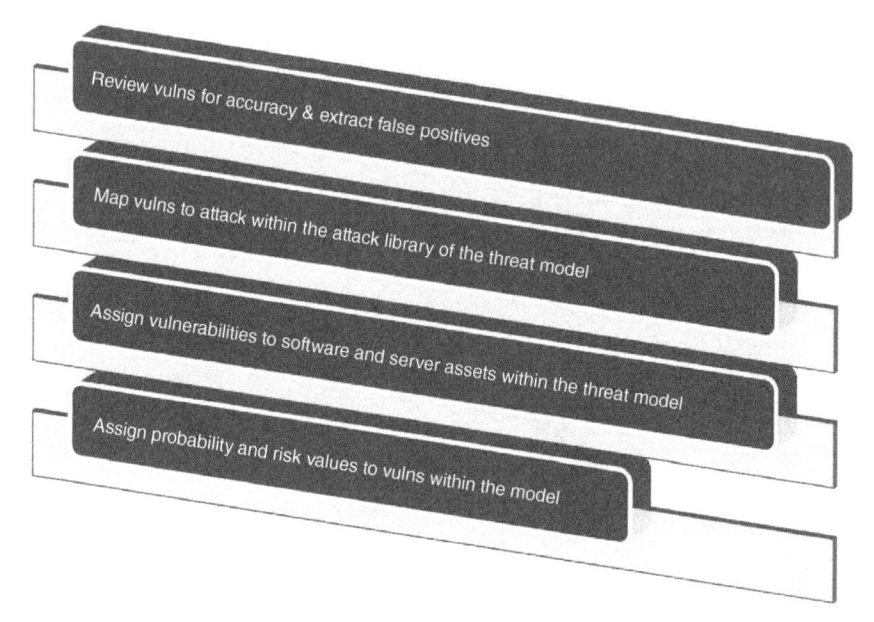

Figure 1.8 Incorporating Vulnerabilities within the Threat Model

- Review vulns for accuracy & extract false positives
- Map vulns to attack within the attack library of the threat model
- Assign vulnerabilities to software and server assets within the threat model
- Assign probability and risk values to vulns within the model

analysis, and use within the threat model. The following suggested workflow reveals the necessary steps needed to leverage vulnerability data within an application threat model (Figure 1.8).

The aforementioned diagram assumes the following as part of incorporating vulnerability details into the application threat model:

- A proper application scope has been defined, limiting the threat modeling analysis to logical boundaries of the application environment.
- Sufficient insight into vulnerabilities can be obtained on a periodic and regular basis to evolve the threat model's risk landscape for the application.
- The expertise to identify false positives within a vulnerability assessment is available as a repeatable process.

Apart from product-based security solutions that specialize in vulnerability scanning, multiple external data sources help any security operations group to build a "living" vulnerability database that can be used and correlated to an asset inventory of both platforms and software. SecurityFocus™ provides a vulnerability listing that encompasses multiple vulnerabilities for both open and closed platforms and software types. The National Institute of Standards (NIST) also provides a National Vulnerability Database (NVD) that includes a free listing of up-to-date vulnerabilities across multiple platforms. NIST's site lists all vulnerabilities by their Common Vulnerability and Exposures (CVE) reference, which is a useful data identifier that allows for some interoperability among security products and solutions. The Federal Government encompasses CVE as one of its criteria for the Security Content Automation Protocol (SCAP). More references to SCAP are included later in the book; however, this notion of common security language is key for application threat models and any security solution, particularly as these standards evolve and become more widely adopted within security products. Their intent is aimed at receiving security data from multiple sources in order to have a complete and accurate vulnerability and attack library.

As part of the threat components, multiple vulnerabilities may be relevant, which require countermeasures and risk mitigation. The following tree focuses on a hypothetical spoofing threat to a utility company's use of a Smart Card to gain access to the sensitive, central operation center. Although this example embellishes aspects of physical security, its simplicity helps to define the various components of a threat revealed thus far, namely, a definite threat, series of attacks, and software vulnerability. Ultimately, this hypothetical example aims to dissect a particular threat to the level of isolating related vulnerabilities that should be encompassed within the threat model.

> *GIVEN:* Employees use the MiFARE Classic Smart Card to gain access to various control rooms where power distribution is controlled and managed. The data that it stores and transmits to physical receivers is related to authorized personnel.
> *THREAT OBJECTIVE:* Gain illegitimate access to one of these control rooms by leveraging a legitimate key code from a Smart Card.
> *ATTACK VECTOR:* Wireless transmission of Smart Card over the air broadcasts.
> *VULNERABILITY:* The card uses a weak cryptographic scheme for encrypting data over the air (OTA). As a result, data-transmitted OTA can be intercepted and cracked.
> *ATTACK:* An off-the-shelf reader can be used to query or probe the card for its information.

In a more prevalent attack scenario (e.g. web application, web service), a vast range of vulnerabilities and attacks should be itemized in order to map out all possible attack scenarios and corresponding vulnerabilities that would be used. Similar to how attack libraries should be built, a relevant listing of applicable security vulnerabilities should be tracked through their existences within the application that serves as the object of the threat model. This process is not easy to instantiate; however, it is foundational for any threat model to work properly since possible vulnerabilities will reveal the likelihood of various attack scenarios for an application. Given the exhaustive list of vulnerabilities, an underlying process to support technical reviews is foundational to employing a threat model. This does not mean that threat modeling forces the need for additional or available resources; it all depends on the number of threat modeling efforts that are conducted across an enterprise or business unit. As previously mentioned, vulnerabilities are typically discovered automatically via an internal security operations group or managed service that provides vulnerability scans against application environments. From this preexisting and nearly parallel process, vulnerabilities found can be mapped to assets within the threat model as well as attacks within their respective libraries. The following figure reflects a short sample of how this process should unfold.

In the single vulnerability mapping that is accomplished in Figure 1.9, we see a single vulnerability that is mapped to both a subset of attacks (within a larger attack library) and the assets (either hardware or software), which the vulnerability affects. Ultimately, as the vulnerability is understood to be a material weakness for the application and ultimately the data it controls, risk mitigation efforts should proceed via code-related modifications or application redesigns.

Making logical groups is essential for the application threat model to efficiently use the vulnerability findings from preexisting and preventive security operations. This figure portrays a micro level version of the comprehensive level mapping that should take place among vulnerabilities and target assets. A more macro-level portrayal would encompass a large mapping tree that reveals a list of relevant security vulnerabilities to possible attacks, thereafter a map to affected software and hardware assets.

Threat class has been purposely left out of this and other examples thus far so that we may focus on mapping *known* security vulnerabilities to possible exploitable target end points and attack patterns. Predefined threat classification models such as STRIDE, DREAD, or Trike (an open-source threat modeling methodology) would successfully encompass vulnerability data presented from a preventive standpoint, meaning that discovered vulnerabilities are mapped to possible attack scenarios and

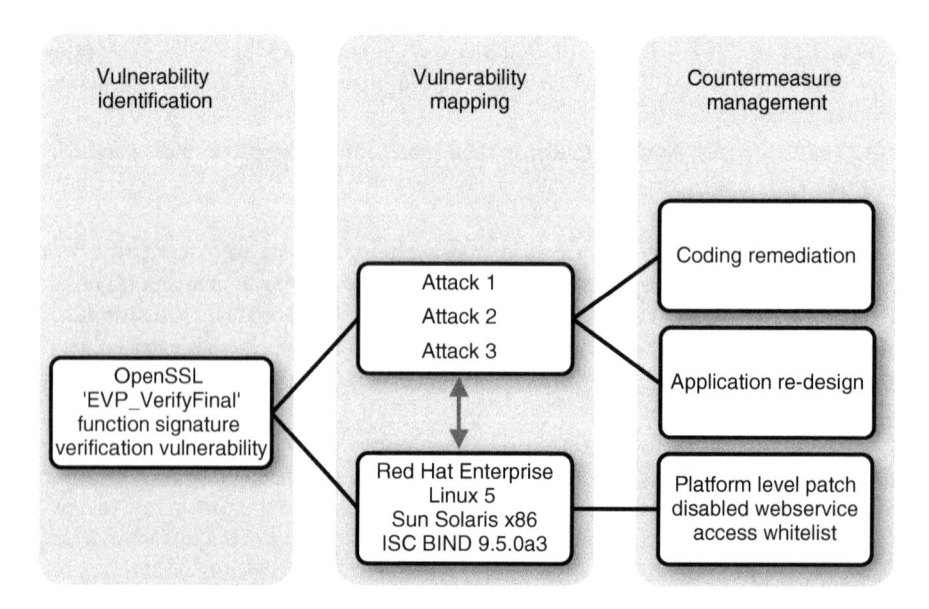

Figure 1.9 Vulnerability Mapping

then appropriately categorized. However, threat classes would be best derived less from preventive security processes, such as vulnerability management, but more from detective security measures, such as via security incident and event monitoring systems or threat feeds. Both reveal possible weaknesses for an attack within the threat model; however, detective security controls and processes reflect recent attack data that has taken place historically across the dark Internet abyss within the networks of internal application trust boundaries. This information *does not* replace but supplements the mapped information, linked back to possible attacks or exploits and affected technology assets. The notable difference is that a more precise threat categorization model could be developed for an organization versus one that may only have some relevant threat categories.

Attacks

Attacks are difficult to predict and understand uniquely. This takes us back to the motive discussion – something rarely addressed in information security and honestly not a traditional component to most threat models, although it does have a parent component to identify attack motives at the root node of an attack tree. At some point, however, a list of likely motives has to be maintained and correlated to information types to imitate the use of attack libraries within an application threat mode. Some governments are investing in such efforts to thwart possible attacks before they happen, recognizing that their adversaries are in the planning stages and waiting for an opportunity or particular data. Overall, it is a science of foreseeing the inevitable and the utmost damaging. *Counter-hacking units* have been developed in Great Britain to detect and counteract threats from Russia and China as well as many other countries (1–56). Part of what a counter-hacking unit does is study predictive patterns against government targets and private businesses with highly sensitive intellectual property. Great Britain's MI5 (Military Intelligence Group, Section 5), as well as the Singapore Intelligence Agency, have established counter-hacking units that are responsible for such efforts.

Profiling attackers helps to derive plausible attack vectors that could be sought to achieve such motives. In some cases though, the true motives behind an attack are not easy to decipher. In January 2010, Google Inc. (GOOG) reported that they were the victims of an elaborate attack against their infrastructure and that intellectual property was stolen. Within the same vein of communication, it was openly revealed that these attacks originated from within China, potentially organized by the Chinese government. The investigation grew when 33 other companies said that they were affected by the attacks and that information may have been compromised since the summer of 2009. One of those companies, Adobe Systems Inc. (ADBE), announced in early January 2010 that they also detected attacks from China against their infrastructure but declared that no information was compromised. As more and more details surrounding the attack surfaced, many security researchers involved with the actual forensic analysis released details on the attack vectors. Forensic experts and security researchers actually traced the attacks back to two key hosts that served as the command and control centers. Exploits related to PDF attachments and IE flaws were cited as part of the attack vector (57).

Initially, a human rights inquisition was said to be the central motive for this and other attacks that encompassed comparable attack vectors, vulnerabilities, and exploits. However, parallel to the theory that these attacks were fueled by a persecution of human rights activists, the notion that communist China had more capitalistic intent, specifically profiting from IP (intellectual property) theft, clouded the true motive and intent behind the Google attacks. In deciphering the true motive (the basis for these attacks), the following questions should preface a threat model in order to gain a focus on target data, applications, and related infrastructures in the future.

- Are the attacks interrelated?
- Is IP theft the true object of these attacks?
- Were these attacks aimed at probing intrusion detection, response capabilities, and protocols, along with any formal communication afterwards?
- Are these attacks diversion attacks – secondary targets used to occupy time and resources in order to conduct even more sophisticated attacks on primary targets?
- Is the true target for these attacks aimed at US corporations (Google, Adobe, etc.), government, or even citizens?

All of these questions revolve around motive and allow a threat modeler to focus on the possible end goals for the attacker, namely the type of data being sought. Naturally, many may wonder why we even worry about motive since the possibilities are endless. There is a difference, however, between likely motives and possible motives. Within a threat model, identifying the likely motives may ultimately draw focus to a key piece of an application or application environment that is the central target. Attacks alone will not provide such clarity to the possible target source, particularly with more sophisticated layered attacks. Attacks are the means to an end and motives are the keys to understand the desired end.

The motives in the Google–China case are most likely both IP and human rights related. Given that these attacks have targeted many US companies and government agencies since 2005, China may be desperately seeking to supersede advanced and existing software and hardware technologies by building upon IP theft and leveraging it to offer new, "original" alternatives to its billion-plus population and the global market. Business Daily Handelsblatt in Germany writes:

> Behind Google's threat to cease business activities in China, one motive stands out: The company, whose business is that of collecting and storing highly sensitive data, must protect itself from being spied upon by a country which seeks to play a major role in shaping the next generation of Internet standards. Beijing is following a strategy meant to prove that an authoritarian regime can survive in the Internet age. But the Chinese are lacking expertise, which is why they are seeking access to protected source codes.
>
> (58)

Perhaps IP theft is the focal target of these attacks and they were disguised as persecuting human rights activists. After all, the negative rap that China has had on human rights violations has something that multinational companies and world governments have come to apparently accept via their tepid and inconsistent reactions. Due to China's continued prolific success and sustainable economic utopia, doing business with MNCs only to target their IP, is an image that would quickly dissuade many from speaking to Chinese government and businesses. Regardless, the previously mentioned attack motives still remain likely motives and help to identify target assets for their past, present, and future attacks. Considering motives at the inception of a threat model will help shape countermeasures and controls across data sources and related infrastructure. These targets serve as the assets, a formal terminology in a threat model that will be discussed later. For now, these assets require software developers and application architects to respectively code and design countermeasures within the application environment to safeguard these target assets. These actions reflect security disciplines related to data and process classification techniques, where data sources and business processes are identified, mapped, and classified for their business impact level to devise controls commensurate to their worth.

Identifying Attacks

Attacks carry out threats, while threats are driven by motives. Digressing into application-based attacks within a threat model will encompass a greater deal of structure and formality. Although understanding motives within a threat model is not commonplace, it has prefaced the introduction of attacks (within the threat model) to introduce a comprehensive visual of how threats become actionable via motives and access to attack resources and opportunities. Application attacks build upon motives in the sense that hypothetical attack scenarios and applied exploits are correlated to the targets of these motives. Stringing all of these elements together will ultimately improve the overall readiness of the security professional who must create a threat model for an application environment. Motives undoubtedly influence the complexity in attacks that are launched against an application. Some attacks encompass known security exploits that target vulnerable applications, while others are fueled by zero-day use cases. Layered attacks are even more complex, as they use all of the aforementioned, coupled with other characteristics that make forensics challenging (attack source(s), timing, and collaborative actions).

Understanding attacks within the context of application threat modeling requires common terminology that security professionals note so that they do not confuse the vernacular associated with the use and execution of application threat model. The following table provides a short yet important list of terms leveraged by the threat model, specifically attack-related components.

As shown in the list of terms to describe application attacks, the term *attack* has been dissected into many components that capture its characteristics. This level of analysis is essential to understand the behavior of each attack cataloged by the application threat model. Many of the previously listed terms may be synonymous to other terms referenced by threat modeling methodologies, tools, or frameworks. Attacks within a threat model are adverse actions taken against an application or its environment for the sole purpose of sustaining or realizing a given threat.

Once all possible application threats are clearly understood, an attack tree encompasses all of an attack's characteristics, as depicted in Table 1.7. Building an attack tree involves creating a vast and comprehensive library of attacks or exploits that correlate to an equally vast and comprehensive list of vulnerabilities. The complexity of managing an attack library extends beyond its initial conception into its ongoing management and upkeep. The importance of an up-to-date attack library runs parallel to a well-maintained vulnerability management database. A broad attack and vulnerability library should ultimately allow an application threat model to address probable threat scenarios and underlying attacks and vulnerabilities. This laborious effort can be eased under the right environments, particularly within larger organizations. Security Operation Centers (SOCs), for example, may already be aggregating threat feeds and identifying repeated exploit attempts from outside and inside the company network. Additionally, such groups often administer vulnerability scans across the enterprise, which provide an inventory of discovered network, host, and even application-level vulnerabilities. From these large information sources, associations can begin among discovered vulnerabilities and attack libraries. The actual

TABLE 1.7 Taxonomy of Attack Terms

Term	Definition
Attack tree	A model that encompasses multiple attacks that may or may not be related to one another but that all support a given motive. Oftentimes interchangeable with *threat tree*.
Attack vector	A channel or path that encompasses an exploitable application vulnerability. Seen as the multiple hierarchical nodes that also encompass entry points in an application environment or system, which may facilitate an exploit execution or malware attack. Also known as an *attack path*.
Attack surface	Refers to the area in which an attack has the opportunity to introduce itself.
Attack library	A catalog of possible attacks that could be launched against an application environment. Used by security professionals to identify the likelihood and impact of attacks as well as possible countermeasures for such attacks.
Vulnerability	Preexisting weakness in an application component that allows the successful execution of an attack.
Attack (Exploits)	Malicious payload executed against a known or unknown vulnerability. Follows a many to one relationship.
Target (asset)	The focal point for a threat and the object of attacks or exploits.
Threat landscape	The logical surface area in which an attack or threat can be conducted. The threat landscape does not need to be continuous, meaning that threat components can be a part of different environments and not physically or logically connected.

repository of attacks will build the attack or threat tree for the application threat model. The tree itself encompasses a multitude of branches and nodes (or leaves) that describe associated vulnerabilities, attack vectors, and targets (assets).

Unlike traditional preventive security models that mitigate attacks by incorporating *best practice* guidelines, application threat modeling depicts probable threat scenarios along with their associated attacks. Given the proliferation of targeted attacks, threat modeling is an essential ally in thwarting their possibility of success. Even when addressing nontargeted attacks, the threat model lends strategic readiness via its attack library, which can correlate exploitative attacks to target assets and vulnerable hosts or networked systems. As a result, possible attacks or exploits need to be "tagged" and inventoried for research and applicability to software use cases, platforms, and networking services.

The following figure provides a visual representation of a simple attack tree. As demonstrated in Figure 1.9, a well-defined threat encompasses multiple attack branches or nodes, which in turn encompass targets (or assets) and their associated vulnerabilities. The term "assets" should not be misconstrued and solely relate to workstations or servers. Attack targets can also be related to network appliances, network devices such as Firewalls, Intrusion Prevention Systems (IPS), network or application proxies, content filtering devices, web servers, databases, and more. *Assets* are any exploitable hardware or software target for an attack or a necessary component to persist with a layered attack. The attack tree is used to visually represent the logistical manner in which single and layered attacks can be conducted against these targets. Apart from dissecting attack patterns and mapping them to assets and vulnerabilities, attack trees offer a conceptual understanding as to where countermeasures should exist and where they should be applied within the context of the threat. These countermeasures lessen the overall business impact as well as the associated risk or impact levels introduced by the threat. Such attack models are best developed at the inception of the application development process.

As shown in Figure 1.10, not all attack vectors introduce exploitable technical vulnerabilities. Some of the attacks take advantage of process-related weaknesses that are very difficult to mitigate, therefore making them more attractive to attackers. For example, a vishing attack is a technical threat introduced via an e-mail that lists a phone number for the target user to call. The exploit is deceitful messaging and the vulnerability is a trusting reader. For this scenario, there are few countermeasures that would prevent a user from having to defend against this ploy. Mail scanning technologies are not yet sophisticated enough to counteract vishing attacks, which contain no URL or images with hyperlinks. The e-mail simply includes a phone number and a misleading message, which may state that the company would never ask its members to click on links for their own security or divulge sensitive e-mail via e-mail or a website. With this disguise, recipients of vishing attacks would unknowingly call into a malicious VRU or IVR and provide sensitive data through those channels. Some of the other vulnerabilities associated with technical-based attacks involve software or platform vulnerabilities, as may be shown with any vulnerable e-mail attachment that can introduce or carry the exploit. In the chapters to follow, we will cover attacks in detail and show a sample of attack-vulnerability mappings via data flow diagramming.

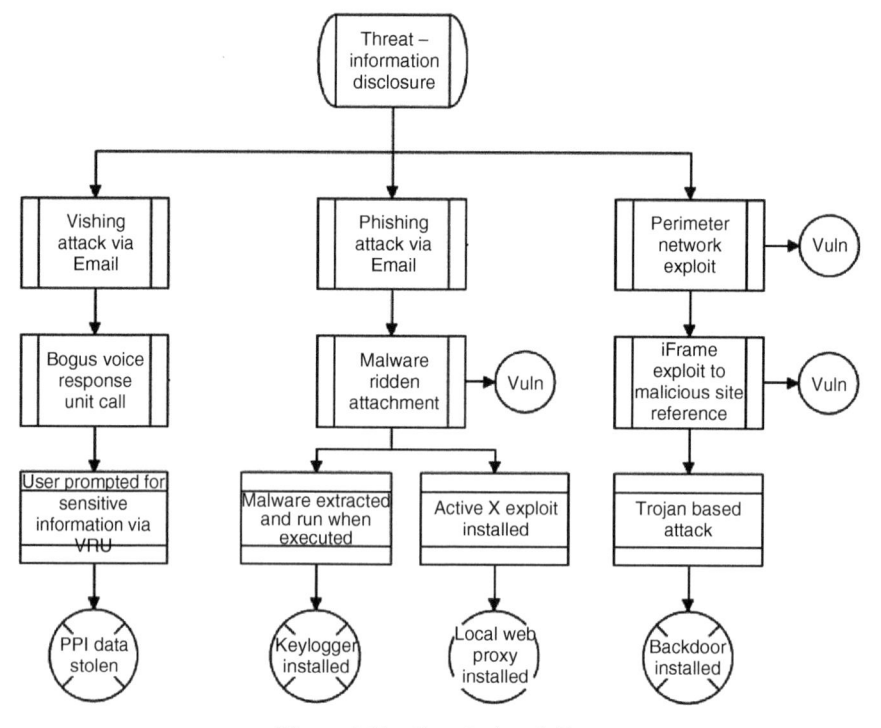

Figure 1.10 Sample Attack Tree

SUMMARY

Stepping through a threat requires a great amount of analysis and perception as a security threat modeler. Threats are driven by motives and are comprised of several dynamic pieces of content (exploits, vulnerabilities) that each require a light to heavy degree of research. These dynamic components force the threat model to be updated periodically to make sure libraries of attack exploits and vulnerabilities are up-to-date. It should be more and more apparent that application threat models can be effectively integrated into multiple IT and IS processes, such as security operations, IT change control, and SDLCs. As changes to an application environment are introduced, and as new threats or incidents are observed from centralized security logging, the threat model can evolve into an integrated security assessment model for key applications.

CROWDSOURCING RISK ANALYTICS

> *"It is not a question of how well each process works, the question is how well they all work together."*
>
> Lloyd Dobens

> "*The evil that is in the world almost always comes of ignorance, and good intentions may do as much harm as malevolence if they lack understanding.*"
>
> Albert Camus

Collaboration does not seem to be a word that effectively describes processes that support information security efforts today. In fact, many security and nonsecurity professionals will agree that a lot of effort is wasted on security initiatives today. The security industry as a business continues to leverage fear, uncertainty, and doubt, particularly those whose intentions are profit-driven rather than altruistic goals of personal data security or even national security. Gloom and doom type marketing efforts continue to push product-based solutions, particularly in the United States where the idea of simply injecting secure process into any business operation is devastating, forcing many to gravitate to the "quick and dirty" fix. The infamous "silver bullet" continues its path in the security market, even as its benefactors argue against the premise in open forums, yet celebrate it behind closed doors. Many will argue that security solutions have in fact given way to improved security process. Although this may be true to some degree, the improvements have been primarily within security operations, compliance, and internal audit. Today, those same processes are stunted with inefficiencies and generally embellish an adversarial role toward the rest of the enterprise that inhibits collaborative work.

Isolated security groups, with their respective isolated security toys, have created multiple forms of tunnel vision – each group only seeing the value of their processes, objectives, and related technologies. Often overlooked is the ability and opportunity for integration and building a more comprehensive value-added security solution to the larger picture. Threat modeling provides the opportunity to reshape all of these inefficiencies. From a process standpoint, many groups benefit from threat modeling efforts as they receive valuable insight into risk factors associated with any application environment. Process-wise, threat modeling fosters a high degree of collaboration across the following groups:

- Developers
- QA Engineers
- Governance Leaders
- Project Managers
- Business Analysts
- System Administrators
- Security Operations
- Network Engineers
- Risk Management
- Security/IT Architects

In this chapter, we will discuss how each member benefits from the application threat modeling process and understand how the generated workflow creates a repeatable process that security professionals can leverage.

The Developer, the Architect, the SysAdmin, and the Network Engineer

Developer, architect, system administrator, and network engineer are traditional technology roles that provide integral support to application environments. The holistic picture of how the application, network, and platform all interact will ultimately be driven from the application designer or the architect. From a functional standpoint, developers bring life to the application, in all of its forms and functions. Upon having a successful software build, both the network engineer and the system administrator focus on addressing network and platform level configuration efforts to secure the application environment and the various protocols that the application will support from both a user and administrative perspective. As a result, their inclusion in application threat modeling is essential in order to contribute to the overall security posture of the application ecosystem.

Wired for developing feature-rich components, developers are focused on feature-rich applications that reflect both their creativity and the list of business requirements for the application system. Security measures that counteract any adversity aimed at infiltrating or misusing their application are absent from their development approach. Today, software development takes on a new shape and form as many of the most popular coding frameworks have prepackaged modules that address common software traits such as concatenation, mathematical formulas, and even authentication. Undoubtedly, software development today is less of a disciplined art form than prior years. Much of this is attributed to the advancement of development frameworks, which have evolved greatly to facilitate application development. As a result, a floodgate of subpar developers have flocked to developing mobile, server-side, client-side, and web apps, with little experience. The demand for software developers in the United States has been overwhelming, introducing challenges for security brought on by the shortage of qualified coders. The shortage of experienced developers has allowed looser restrictions on what is expected of software developers. This has forced many companies to look overseas for more experienced coders or domestically for average coders. As a result, the requirement for improving proper coding disciplines, particularly in security, has taken a lower priority. Given the rate at which application development needs are being sought and the rate at which software builds need to take place in order to match demands in the marketplace, a retrofitting action to build security is far-fetched. Additionally, training alone does not provide any incentive for developers to code securely since that is not what they were hired to do nor are they paid to do this. Furthermore, it is not always the developer's fault; there are system, database administrators, as well as software implementors that all share the same sentiment that security is an auxiliary component to their primary focus in building a technical solution. This perception requires a recalibration of various variables that exist in the mindset of developers that include (but are not limited to) viability of attack, impact of vulnerabilities, significance to the business.

Beyond training, security assessments have attempted to bridge the misunderstanding of some of these variables to the developers, but with very limited success. Traditional assessments against application environments take an adversarial approach when interacting with development teams – they highlight any flaws that could *possibly* be exploited. Application threat modeling provides a process in which security professionals can address developers in a more collaborative manner to address likely attack vectors and vulnerabilities within their software applications. Developers are traditionally very responsive to these types of efforts, provided the security professional conducting the threat modeling exercise has the ability to transcend between security concepts, software development frameworks, and languages in use. To date, most experienced developers are well aware that their applications are under attack; however, they lack the understanding of how they are attacked and what type of measures they can take to limit the probability and risk that these attacks succeed.

A developer's undeclared adversary is the hacker. An experienced hacker has a solid IT background that encompasses software development, thereby allowing him/her to be intimately familiar with native methods, functions, and library objects that may be used to mitigate application threats. Unfortunately, most developers do not have such a well-rounded background and the ability to think like both a developer and a hacker, thereby creating an uneven playing field in the realm of application security. Developers are not able to think with a destructive mindset against their own application. They are focused on building up the features of their application. In this builder-like mentality, the developer does not spend time thinking of the destructive ways that their application could be compromised through various nefarious forms of attack. The purpose of threat modeling is to provide an ongoing process that allows them to understand the destructive vision of an attack against a software application by dissecting their own creation to find the weak areas or vulnerabilities. If nothing else, threat modeling allows developers to think destructively about their own application. The methodology employed by most threat models provides developers the opportunity to see their own application in the eyes of a likely attacker. It also allows them to think like an attacker while reverting to the mentality of a developer who now has a better understanding of possible attack patterns and what vulnerabilities may exist within their code structure.

Last, the threat modeling process allows the formal introduction of security requirements at the inception of the SLDC life cycle. Building security into the various stages of any SDLC process reflects a new movement in secure software development practices to design and develop security controls from the early stages of the SDLC process. The Building Security In Maturity Model (BSIMM) is a security framework that allows development groups to measure what security measures they currently have in place versus those that are recommended. The Software Assurance Maturity Model is another framework that development teams may leverage to continuously measure the security and effectiveness of their developed applications.

If developers are the artistic minds behind any given application, the system administrators serve as guardians of their creation. The security requirements that were alluded to earlier help form the necessary guidance in which system administrators should maintain the various platforms that encompass application components. There is nothing new with security requirements. Their traditional and dependable downfall today has been attributed to the lack of process of socializing the information and requiring their use by IT management. Again, human error and inefficiency is to blame for well-intentioned security requirements not becoming implemented as a realistic practice. This is most readily observed in larger enterprises where security leaders author standards, typically from industry renowned sources such as NIST, CICS, or the platform manufacturer. From there, the socializing of these standards to IT groups, who most likely were never a part of the drafting process, begins to fail miserably as yet another adversarial approach from security attempts to dictate how IT should do their job in the name of security and compliance. The message that threat modeling fosters is one of collaboration among IT and IS professionals to mitigate risk factors. People usually want to assist or help if they have a better understanding of what their threats are as a company and as a group of system custodians (or system administrators) charged with maintaining and safeguarding IT assets. Since they do not currently have a glimpse into whom or what their adversaries might be, system administrators today are less cooperative in light of the compliance and FUD (Fear, Uncertainty, and Doubt) communication that they receive from their IS counterparts. Threat modeling's ability to depict potential attackers, their profiles and motives, likely attack surfaces, and vectors allows for a wealth of information to help system administrators understand the underlying reasons to adopt any suggestive platform guidelines or formal platform standards that need to be leveraged when creating, cloning, or configuring platform components for the application environments.

QA Engineers

Quality assurance efforts test functionality using test scripts and manual methods. QA engineers or analysts have a pivotal role in identifying bugs within their test cases. They test newly developed features and functions from the development team and are theoretically awarded the ability to accept or reject new builds depending on the outcome of their test cases. This workflow generally does not receive the recognition and power that it deserves, mostly because of the rate at which software development efforts take place and the push to migrate code to production. Most software companies accept a level of imperfection when rolling out code to production; however, the level and frequency in which flaws are introduced to a software product may affect the reputation of a software company in the long term.

Organizations where QA efforts maintain a well-established process, supported by product and project management, are ideal for incorporating application threat modeling. Given the time and effort that threat modeling imposes against a release cycle, adoption from these management groups is key to convey the value and necessity of incorporating threat modeling in the SDLC process. Client requirements and service delivery goals may influence the manner in which threat modeling is ultimately adopted. There is no question that some internal *selling* is needed to foster faith in application threat modeling and its long-term value to creating better software. This may be accomplished by identifying factors that benefit project and product managers in the end. These factors will be revealed in detail in the next section.

Threat modeling within the QA software process should not simply be added as an additional task to a QA engineer who is performing functional testing. In order to accomplish threat modeling within the same vein of QA process, a dedicated and experienced security engineer should be included. An ideal security tester will possess the following background and skill sets:

- Understanding of application design
- Understanding of multiple development frameworks
- Wide breadth of use and understanding of security testing solutions
- Solid understanding of network protocols leveraged by the application environment
- Ability to create abuse or misuse cases from all identified use cases within an application
- Ability to develop and maintain a vulnerability database and understand how inventoried vulnerabilities can be applied against various network and system level resources
- Ability to develop and maintain an attack library that addresses key threats to any identified vulnerabilities within any tested application environment
- Solid understanding of database related protocols, authentication models, and objects
- Some development experience so he/she can review available source code for possible exploits in logic or information processing
- Ability to conduct application walk-throughs to create data flow diagrams that represent the attack tree, which encompasses related vectors, vulnerabilities, and attack exploits
- Understanding of business impact and risk as it relates to viable attacks that are represented by the threat model
- Strong communication skills geared toward developers, product and project managers, and senior management. Ability to understand and relay risk-related business concerns as well as probable attack scenarios that can be depicted via threat model and data flow diagramming exercises and exploit attempts
- Experienced in risk management frameworks and their application to business environments

Knowledge and hands-on use of various security solutions is a great compliment to a solid foundation of security experience. A *brief* list of such tools is provided in Table 1.8. This list is not meant to represent the best of breed within security testing, but to simply provide an inventory of solutions that will catalyze the overall testing process.

This arsenal of tools tests for application insecurities from which a wealth of information will be obtained and subsequently used within any given threat model. The information resulting from any automated scans must undergo a validation process to extract any false positive findings that may misrepresent the security posture of

TABLE 1.8 Tools for Testing

Tool	Use
Discovery/vulnerability scanner(s)	Nessus (Tenable Security)
	SAINT (Saint Corp)
	NeXpose (Rapid 7)
	Qualys Scanner (Qualys)
	Nikto
	OpenVAS (openvas.org)
	Retina
	NMap
Web application testing	WebInspect (HP)
	Acunetix
	AppScan (IBM)
	Wikto
	Wapiti
	Burp Suite Pro
	Paros
	WebScarab
Penetration testing/fuzzers	Core Impact
	Armitage (www.commonexploits.com)
	MetaSploit
Social engineering/phishing	SpoofCard/Phone Gangster
	Social Engineering Toolkit (SET)
	LittleSis.org
	Maltego Radium
	reconNG
Static analysis	Fortify 360
	Ounce Labs (IBM)
	FxCop (MS Visual Studio plug-in)
	Parasoft
	Veracode (Binary Analysis)
	O2 Project (OWASP)
	Brakeman (Source Code Review – Ruby)
	Yasca (Open-Source Code Analyzer

the application in question within the application threat model. False positives are detrimental to the application threat modeling process since they consume time and resources chasing unsubstantiated threats. Qualifying false positives may take some time and encompasses validation against platform, network, and/or application components. Exploiting vulnerabilities within a QA environment will best qualify attacks and vulnerabilities into legitimate threats, with the ultimate objective of understanding relevant risk factors for an application environment.

Security testing, as with more traditional forms of functional or regression testing in QA, adheres to a very pragmatic approach for finding possible security flaws. As a result, it is not the most opportune juncture to require risk analysis from a professional who is focused on exercising a suite of security test scripts. This is where the necessity to have a dedicated security professional (embedded within the QA process) is warranted since most QA professionals will have limited to no exposure to applying risk-based approach to their functional testing. This risk-based approach to security testing will foster interoperability of results among the QA and Enterprise Risk Management groups. Security testing today is nothing new for mature organizations that incorporate multiple security processes within the operations group; however, applying a risk-based approach to vulnerable findings is scarcely applied. More information on how application threat modeling leverages risk management workflows is forthcoming in the next few sections as in other portions of this book.

Security Operations

There may not be consistent security processes universally represented by a security operations group or center; however, they typically oversee the following efforts:

- Vulnerability management and penetration testing
- Incident response and security event monitoring
- Security log review and auditing
- Threat aggregation and analysis

Security operations often perform the aforementioned list of functions that fuel excellent intelligence to security professionals who are building the various components of the threat model. Specifically, information from this group provides greater accuracy in deriving probability coefficients for identified attack vectors. Alerts from managed network and application intrusion solutions provide an excellent level of information in understanding the following:

- Trend analysis of attacks over a given period of time
- Origin of malicious traffic (IP space, networks, geographic regions, etc.)
- Frequency and intervals of malicious traffic patterns
- Correlation of observed traffic patterns
- Threat feeds from subscribed threat or alert feeds
- Breakout of malicious traffic across certain criteria:
  - Internal versus external
  - Resemblance of targeted versus broad range of attack
  - Distribution of network protocols for observed attacks

Inclusion of security operation groups in the threat modeling process builds upon efforts during the QA or security testing phase of a given software application. Security testing can take place at a time interval that best suits that sponsoring organization; however, it is best incorporated into QA simply because its testing process is very much akin to the functional security testing conducted during traditional functional test cases within the SDLC.

The efforts from security testing should be comingled with the aforementioned information from security operations to refine estimates on probability coefficients that accompany various attack variables (discussed further later). This information can be correlated to attacks identified from the threat modeling attack library to legitimize further the attack scenario against the assessed application environment. Observed network patterns that resemble variants of exploit traffic are invaluable to the threat model as it helps to refine risk scenarios that are derived from the application threat model.

Observed malicious traffic tells one-half of the story, as it relates to possible threats to a company's application environment. The threats that have yet to be observed are equally important within the application environment. This information can be obtained from threat feeds, typically sent to security operation analysts for tracking and is especially useful if obtained for the company's industry sector. Threat information related to DoS attempts and exploits may be prevalent to companies in the energy sector, while injection-based threats may be more highly reported for those in the online retail business. Threat feeds provide the same level of benefit (to a slightly lesser degree) as the security incidents observed from a security operations center.

Correlation – The Final Frontier?

It goes without saying that information correlated and/or aggregated from security operations will have to have some degree of topicality to the assessed application environment within the threat model. For example, an HR SAS solution that is assessed within the threat model would not benefit from a broader scope of network or application areas to accounting if there is no application programming interface (API) among the two disparate systems. If such is the case, logical networks, assets, and applications that tie the two disparate application environments should be inclusive of the application threat model, but not anything further. This is done to ensure the proper scope of the threat modeling exercise. A larger scope may undermine the time and efficiency of the threat modeling process. The following is a graphical representation of properly defining scope among two unique application environments that are bounded by an API.

Enrique Salas, CEO from Symantec stated in his 2009 keynote RSA speech that one of the differentiating factors of managing security risk is how massive amounts of security information stemming from intrusion detection/prevention systems (IDS/IPS), firewalls, host intrusion prevention software (HIPS) agents, antivirus clients, host-based firewalls, network content filters, data loss prevention technology, web application firewalls, vulnerability scanners, spam filters, threat feed subscriptions, web application scanners, and more are all correlated to maximize the security risk insight across an enterprise. Companies that employ a part of the aforementioned network and host-based technologies can have a plethora of threat intelligence, regardless of whether the information is administered and managed internally, via a cloud-based service provider, or as a managed security service

(MSS) – the information exists and should be to help fuel threat scenarios simulated by the application threat model. Many of these solutions provide a historical view of threats to a given environment that is monitored by these and other security technologies.

(Security) Risk Management

Weeding out false positives within an application runs parallel to the need to understand risk and impact levels from qualified threats. Leveraging the security testing that should take place, preferably within the QA process; a level of unmitigated security risk issues will undoubtedly be present and can easily be manifested to security risk management groups within the process of application threat modeling. Unmitigated risks are those related to clearly marked attack vectors that present viable threats against existing vulnerabilities, which have negligible countermeasures to limit either the introduction of the attack into the environment or the exploitability of the vulnerability. Understanding risk entails a comprehensive understanding of multiple factors, all of which become better understood through a formal risk management process. Since most threat models provide a greater level of application risk by illustrating mappings among attack exploits and vulnerabilities, coupled with business impact values and probability values based upon informed research on attack complexities, ease of access, sophistication level, and so on, variables are largely missed by more traditional risk management efforts in enterprise security.

This section focuses on how introducing a basic liaise among security risk management and application threat modeling leverages the common objective of identifying and managing risk. Application threat models substantiate risk models: they provide greater credibility by simulating threat scenarios and thereafter establishing a full etymology of attack branches, related vulnerabilities, and associated countermeasures where residual risk can be addressed through risk management practices.

Within the realm of traditional risk management efforts, the following security elements are the bare essentials for any generic risk management framework (Table 1.9).

Regardless of the employed risk framework or risk model within an enterprise, threat modeling provides greater precision in some of the aforementioned risk components. Some globally renowned risk frameworks and standards include OCTAVE (Carnegie Mellon), NIST Risk Management Framework (800-53, 800-60, 800-37), the revised AS/NZS 4360 standard, which is now the ISO 31000:2009 Risk Management Standard, COSO ERM, and the new RiskIT integrated risk management framework from ISACA which encompasses many key elements from these more widely recognized frameworks and standards. Although well-known throughout the globe, many of these frameworks lack the technical specificity to provide actionable implementation of effective countermeasures or controls during a remediation phase of the risk management process. Additionally, many of these risk management frameworks or standards do not foster the ability to extract precise technical information to further diagnose application-level risks. Those who argue that this granular level of risk does not convey business risk do not apply a threat modeling perspective, which

TABLE 1.9 Elements of Risk – Generic Listing of Key Risk Components

Security Risk Components

1. Scope of affected Hardware and Software assets
2. Business impact analysis (consequence) related to scope of assets
3. Identified and confirmed vulnerabilities
4. Enumeration of possible attack patterns and supporting rationale
5. Threat model denoting probability or likelihood of exploitation
6. List of physical and logical countermeasures
7. Identification of residual risk
8. Implementing countermeasures and controls
9. Informing and Training
10. Monitoring

begins the process by identifying the scope of business or information assets encompassed by a threat model and later defines what elements of the asset, if not its entirety, are affected by the depicted attack branches. The scope definition also encompasses the business objectives that are supported by the assets or targets in the threat model, thereby allowing business risk analysis to be derived via the threat modeling process.

Beyond some of the more globally recognized risk management frameworks or standards are comparable risk frameworks/standards that have been developed by private and/or public organizations, including Microsoft, Google, Verizon Business, OWASP (Open Web Application Security Project) and more. Although these publications are not as widely adopted and practiced, they are based on the fundamentals of some of the previously mentioned industry standards for risk management, with emphasis on certain types of technology environments. They also incorporate a greater level of technical detail, which incorporates more meaningful content for articulating risk-remediation activities to system/data custodians across a given enterprise. We will take a closer look at existing models, frameworks, and risk management guidelines in further sections of this book, to further correlate existing risk models to the risk analysis capabilities provided by an application threat model.

An application threat model conveys application risk values that can be incorporated into a greater risk model managed by enterprise risk management professionals. The by-product of threat simulations, achieved by application threat modeling, allows a more sophisticated value of application risk. This sophistication is attributed to the application walk-through and attack simulation that gives way to well-defined attack scenarios, which are likely and associated with validated vulnerabilities. Once a well-defined attack tree contains a full set of layered branches (reflecting assets, associated vulnerabilities, attack exploits, and attack vectors), many of these branches then need to be assigned probability and impact values.

Probability and impact variables will ultimately help derive risk levels for the assessed application. The compounded net effect of vulnerabilities to attacks (or threats), along with associated impact or consequence values, probability estimates for successful exploitation, and net of existing countermeasures provides a far more accurate representation of risk compared to more general security risk equations that equate risk to simply a product of vulnerability and threat. Some traditional risk models do incorporate impact (or consequence) as well as probability, but none can truly represent probability variables in the risk equation since there are so many assumptions built on these probability levels. These assumptions have to be made under more generic risk models since the attack is not simulated. Under a threat model, the attacks are simulated in a controlled environment and a greater degree of accuracy can be made as to ease of exploitation and access to attack vectors as compared to a purely theoretic risk analysis exercise.

With an improved risk analysis, obtained by the application threat model, remediation takes on a greater level of importance since the overall risk analysis clearly shows a linear representation of cause and effect of not having existing countermeasures for a given set of assets or subject targets in the application threat model. For nonmanaged risk (meaning nonaccepted or nontransferable risk findings), countermeasures can be developed with greater direction. Ultimately, the dominant objective of any risk model or framework is enabled by the application threat to the application threat model – deriving risk to identify what countermeasures need to be developed, if any at all. This is the light at the end of the tunnel for risk management professionals since it focuses on completing the life cycle of risk management for discovered risk issues. Remediation efforts via countermeasures in process or control fulfill risk mitigation efforts, greatly aiding enterprise risk management professionals in fulfilling their group goals and objectives.

Elements of risk bolstered by an application threat model are depicted in Figure 1.11. Most traditional risk assessment efforts within a risk management practice are inherently qualitative, making it difficult to get complete adoption by some of the target audience of its deliverables. Via an application threat model, the following formula can be applied to substantiate risk designations, via its inclusion of impact values and greater precision in probability estimates, both influenced by the actual threat modeling exercise, whether they adhere to a quantitative translation of qualitative risk or simply a traditional heat map of risk levels.

Elements of quantitative risk analysis are concentrated around probability and business impact values, which encompass projected values for financial loss. Probability values in threat modeling encompass any statistical reference that supports ease of exploitation as well as successful exploitation attempts realized during the application threat modeling security testing process. The ability to exploit an identified vulnerability within the testing phase of the threat modeling process greatly substantiates probability estimates as compared to more theoretical values encompassed in traditional risk assessment methodologies.

A traditional risk formula generally encompasses the following variables for *risk*:

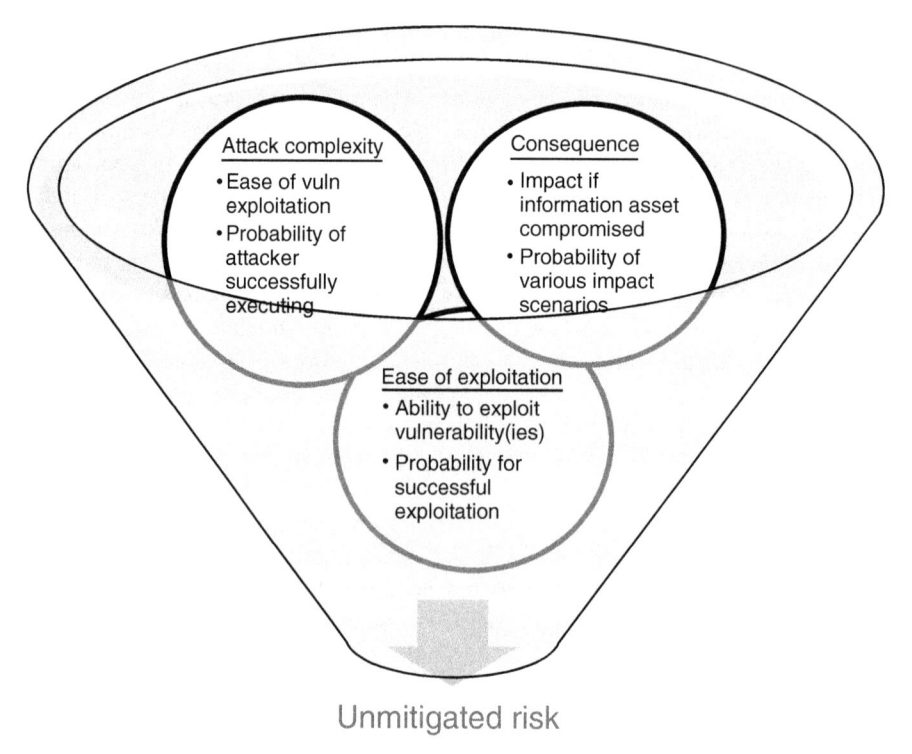

Figure 1.11 Deriving Risk via the Application Threat Model

- *Impact* (or *consequence*)
- *Threat* (or *attack*)
- *Vulnerability*

There are a multitude of risk models used today, both quantitative and qualitative, that incorporate the aforementioned risk variables. Undoubtedly, it would take the remainder of this book to argue each risk model's worth. It would take even longer to demonstrate how an indisputable or universal risk model may exist that properly addresses information security risks across all industry sectors and infrastructure types. Among the various risk models and methodologies, only one universal truth should exist relative to application risk: risk is relative. This is the reason that application threat modeling is essential for feeding an overall risk model to improve its risk analysis capability.

Application threat modeling can feed and bolster the risks maintained and calculated in more traditional risk models due to its ability to supersede traditional risk methodologies in four very important areas. They are as follows:

- Identifying uniquely identifiable threat scenarios
- Incorporating business objectives

- Improving on probability calculations
- Performing attack exploits to simulate real life risk scenarios

Application threat modeling, as a process, allows unique risk factors to be evaluated. It focuses on identifying technical application risks that are programmatic, platform, and network related, while aggregating this information to its relevant impact to the business that the application supports. Application threat modeling's objective centers on the uniqueness of various risk factors: unique threats, unique attack vectors, unique assets, and unique information sources, targeted by nonunique vulnerabilities and nonunique attack exploits. The context of *unique* reflects the fact that distinct application technologies are not, in aggregate with one another, found across other application environments owned by other corporate entities within the same industry segment or business type. A retail site that sells automotive parts will indeed have vast similarities with other retail sites that offer comparable products and services; however, the application architecture, associated platforms and software technologies, development frameworks, and application designs will be largely unique. Most importantly, the application use cases, gateways over which an attacker can interrogate an application (viewed by attackers as attack vectors) will be unique among distinct sites and business entities. Application threat modeling provides a process for understanding these unique variables through the use of the attack tree, where attack simulations encompass all relevant risk variables, including vulnerabilities, attacks (exploits), impact levels, and application countermeasures.

Regardless of whether a risk model is qualitative or quantitative, risk ultimately embellishes unique threats, vulnerabilities, and business impact scenarios that are often organization specific. Two competing banks may offer identical online banking sites, but the initial and ongoing efforts behind those B2C sites will encompass unique development teams, software and platform technologies, and architectural design for interoperability within and outside the overall application environment. IT and IS governance within the two disparate companies may also differ, thereby potentially affecting the security posture of an application, mostly as a result of having clearly defined application, network, and platform configuration standards. More traditional risk models exclude business-related objectives and features when identifying risk scenarios for an application environment. Application threat modeling, conversely, begins with the inclusion of defined business objectives. Risk analysis begins by identifying any underlying use case, feature, or functionality that does not support business objectives for the application's continued support and use. The distinguishing characteristic of risk within an application threat model is that the model for understanding risk is centered on the nature of unique information and technology assets (or targets) for an organization as well as its countermeasures and process-driven controls. The end result is a more precise risk model for deriving information security risks for software.

Probability values in calculating risk are another improvement via the application threat modeling process. As stated earlier, *probability* is a value that is often incorporated into more traditional risk formulas, albeit with less precision than application threat models. Via a threat model's attack tree, and the opportunity to simulate attacks in a white hat (or ethical hacking) scenario, greater accuracy in estimating probability is sustained. Within the threat model, attack tree branches allow visualization of a threat over a series of sequential attacks, thereby allowing probability values to be assigned to those attack branches. The probability value is still an estimate; however, its integrity is improved upon the opportunity to exercise an identified attack in a controlled environment. Not all attacks can be realized in a practice scenario within the threat modeling process. This does not reduce the value that threat modeling brings in improving probability values for an overall risk calculation. The attack trees within the model still provide a visual flow in which known attack exploits can be exercised over discovered application vulnerabilities. Each branch or layer of the attack tree will allow unique probability assignments for those attacks to be realized against discovered vulnerabilities and their exploits. Ideally, the traditional *probability* variable should be used as multiple coefficient values that reflect the likelihood for the following to take place:

- Likelihood that the vulnerability or set of vulnerabilities become successfully exploited.
- Possibility that the attack vector becomes accessible for exploitation and the attacker has necessary time and resources to conduct the exploit.
- Likelihood of various impact scenarios to become fully realized.

This coefficient use of probability $_{(p1), (p2)}$ is best illustrated by the following altered risk formula.

$$\text{Residual Risk} = \frac{\text{Vuln}_{(p1)} \times \text{Attack}_{(p2)} \times \text{Impact}}{\text{Countermeasures}}$$

Overall, enterprise risk management programs will greatly benefit from an application threat modeling process. More details related to application threat modeling's relevance to widely used risk models will be elaborated in greater detail in subsequent chapters.

2

OBJECTIVES AND BENEFITS OF THREAT MODELING

DEFINING A RISK MITIGATION STRATEGY

> "There are known unknowns; that is to say there are things that we now know we don't know.
>
> But there are also unknown unknowns – there are things we do not know, we don't know."
>
> United States Secretary of Defense Donald Rumsfeld

In today's digital economy, businesses provide valuable information and services to their customers online. The value of this information might vary depending on different factors such as the sensitivity of the information content such an intellectual property and confidential data. Since sensitive data flows through online channels and between the customer web and mobile clients and the web applications that are managed by the businesses, it is suitable target by value driven threat actors. Examples include cyber-criminals seeking to steal confidential data from bank customers for committing various crimes such as identify theft, stealing money from bank accounts, account take over, money laundering, credit/debit card counterfeiting, and online fraud. Fraudsters have an arsenal of cybercrime tools at their disposal for targeting online bank applications and bank customers. Online banking money movement transactions such as transferring money between bank accounts, for example, are targeted by fraudsters using banking malware. Personal customer details are targeted for identity theft and to impersonate the real customers in online banking transactions. Credit card data is targeted for online fraud such as for card-non-present transactions

---

Risk Centric Threat Modeling: Process for Attack Simulation and Threat Analysis, First Edition.
Tony UcedaVélez and Marco M. Morana.
© 2015 John Wiley & Sons, Inc. Published 2015 by John Wiley & Sons, Inc.

and debit card data is targeted for counterfeit debit cards and to withdraw money from the victim's bank accounts.

The Importance of Threat Analysis and Risk Management

To protect customer personal data and business sensitive data from cyber-criminals and fraudsters, businesses typically enforce information security processes in compliance with information security standards and risk management processes to manage the cyberthreat risks. The initial step toward enforcing information security policies is typically to create an inventory of assets that need to be protected with an assignment of the level of risk. This level of risk depends on the sensitivity levels of the of information assets. Once the data sensitivity is classified according to the confidentiality levels (e.g. public, internal, confidential, and restricted), it is possible to enforce the necessary levels of protection for the sensitive and confidential data. For example, a certain business might decide that all customer sensitive information should be protected with encryption when is transferred outside the business such as when is processed online by customer's use of web applications. For banks and for what concern online banking transactions that allow making purchases and money transfers, there is a risk of these being targeted for compromise by fraudsters, therefore banks will implement additional levels of security such as multifactor authentication as well as additional types of data validations. The risk associated with these money movement transactions might vary depending on the money amount that can be transacted online and have associated different level of security control and transactional risk. For example, a payment limit of small money amounts for online purchases can be considered low risk per each user-transaction while a transfer of money from one person bank account to another person bank account might be considered high risk. Once the risk associated with the value of the data and the value of the business transaction is being assessed, the next step consists of determining if the level of security controls that are put in place is sufficient. Typically, the higher the value of the asset, the higher is the level of risk and the stronger is the level of protection required.

In the case of sensitive data, the determination of risk level depends on different factors such as the type of threats targeting specific data attributes such as confidentiality, integrity, and availability of the data. The level of risk of the data also depends on the presence of vulnerabilities on the security controls such as encryption, authentication, and authorization that are put in place to protect the data and the access to this data from unauthorized malicious threat actors. Such vulnerabilities might be the ones that are exploited by threat actors to compromise the data and the business functions. Since vulnerabilities represent a "condition" for an exploit and a threat represent a "possibility" to cause an impact on the data and functional assets it is important to determine the level of risk of the threat by association of factors such as threats, vulnerabilities, and assets. By analyzing and associating these factors, a risk manager can determine the overall level of risk. Threats can be analyzed based upon information of the type of threat agent, his or her capabilities, and motives. This is the "who" factor for threat analysis. The other aspect is to analyze the "how," that is, the

DEFINING A RISK MITIGATION STRATEGY 65

type of attacks that are used including the types of attack techniques, tools, tactics, and procedures. The final aspect of threat analysis is the "what," that is, what type of assets and vulnerabilities are targeted.

Once assets, threats, attacks, and vulnerabilities have been analyzed, the next step consists of determining the level of impact of the threats being analyzed on the company assets and to determine the level of risk. Besides impact, such level of risk depends on factors of probability of the threat to be realized. The determination of the level of risk based upon the factors of likelihood and impact is the main goal of risk analysis. Once risks have been analyzed, the next step consists of deciding how to manage this risk to keep it at a level that is considered acceptable by the business/organization. At this stage, risk decisions are made on how to handle the risk to make it acceptable by the business, examples include apply countermeasures, to reduce the risk likelihood and impact, transferring the risk to another party, avoiding the risk by either not exposing the asset to the threat or not implementing the application feature that will increase exposure and do nothing, that is, to accept the risk based on the realization of compensating controls and measures.

Threat Intelligence

Knowing which threats might target the business's digital assets and how a compromise of these assets might affect the business is essential for determining the level of risk that the organization/business might face. Threat knowledge can be gathered through threat intelligence sources. Threat intelligence sources can provide businesses information on the types of threats targeting the business and the tools, techniques, and procedures used by the threat actors to compromise the organization's assets. Example of these threat intelligence sources might be public open sources, also referred as OSINT Open Source Intelligence, as well as nonpublic sources such as Information Sharing Assurance Center (ISACS). Oftentimes, the threat intelligence information might come from internal organizational sources such as reported instances of internal security incidents from Security Incident Report Teams (SIRTs), security events from monitoring-alert tools and last but not least fraud instances.

Threat intelligence is critical for the determination of the possible risk levels and also for the implementation of an effective risk strategy. By looking at threat intelligence, risk managers can proactively determine the level of alert and focus on monitoring specific events to trigger measures and actions and be prepared to respond to possible security incidents.

To proactively mitigate application threats, businesses can gather intelligence on threat agents and analyze threat events to determine whether the business is under the target of possible attacks. Threat intelligence helps business to build a threat intelligence knowledge base and derive threat libraries to analyze how threats can affect the application before the application is being attacked. After the threat and the threat agents are analyzed in detail, the next step consists of understanding the type of attacks and attack techniques that might be used by the threat agents and the vulnerabilities that are potentially targeted by these threats so that these can be prioritized for remediation. Often the answer to whether a digital asset is the target of a threat agent is strictly dependent on the type of assets and the value they represent to a threat agent when stolen and used for malicious and fraudulent purposes. For example, if an application stores confidential data such as personally identifiable information of a customer, it might be the target of data identity thieves who would use this information to impersonate a victim (a threat usually referred to as identify theft). If the application stores bank and/or credit card records of its customers, it might be the target of fraudsters who could profit from using this type of data to make counterfeit credit cards and execute fraudulent payments online. If the application stores proprietary software, algorithms, and trading secrets, it might be the target of either country- or business-sponsored threat agents that seek to gain competitive and/or strategic advantage.

Risk Management Strategies

A risk management strategy of the company can be proactive or reactive depending on the culture and appetite for risk. An example of reactive risk management strategy consists of focusing on the security problem as it occurs and devote resources to manage the risk when the business is impacted such as in the occurrence of a security incident such as a data breach. When a security incident such as a data breach occurs, the company will often follow a security incident response procedure. After the security incident has been escalated for investigation and response, the next step consists of determining its severity and take measures to contain the business impact and the damage. Examples of measures that organizations can take to limit business impact and the damage include suspending the compromised credit cards, blocking transactions, and issuing new user credentials such as passwords. Once the damage of a security incident such as a data breach incident has been contained, the next step is to conduct a "postmortem analysis" to determine the possible causes of the incident and take measures to prevent similar incidents in the future. Actions that can be taken by businesses in response to security incidents include fixing the root cause of the incident such as fixing vulnerabilities and apply new countermeasures to reduce the impact to the business if similar security incidents will occur in the future. A proactive risk management strategy consists of adopting preventive risk mitigation measures, investment on risk management tools, people and process that reduce the likelihood of security incidents such as data compromise and impact in the future. Often proactive risk management decisions are taken because the organization has suffered a security incident that caused an impact to the business such as a massive breach of confidential data.

The initials assessment of risks such as the analysis of the probability for threats to occur and their impact levels are one of the objectives of risk analysis. One possible factor for determining the probability of a threat to occur is the availability of vulnerabilities that allow the realization of such threat, the complexity and reproducibility of the attack, the skills required by the threat agent to conduct the attack, and the costs of tools and resources to conduct the attack.

Examples of factors that might influence the threat impact are the exposure to threats by the presence of vulnerabilities in application and software, the value of the asset (data classified as sensitive), the volume of such data, and the type of access controls necessary to get these data. For example, a threat can be facilitated by different factors, such as the availability of tools to the attacker and the knowledge required for using them. Often the tools used by the attackers are the same of the tools used by security testers to test a given asset for vulnerability such as an application vulnerability scanner. For example, consider a tool that is used by a tester to scan a given web application for identifying an instance of a common vulnerability such as cross-site scripting. Once the web application is found vulnerable to such vulnerability, it is flagged as issue in a report and this issue is remediated in compliance with the business information security policy. If the organization does not fix such vulnerability before the product/feature is deployed in production environments and released to customers, an attacker can use a similar vulnerability scanning tool to discover the vulnerability and then seek to exploit it for his advantage such as for compromising the web application and gather unauthorized access to sensitive customer data as well as web application functionality that is only available to authenticated and authorized users.

The secure testing of the applications and software, such as by conducting an ethical hacking and source code analysis are important risk mitigation activities and should be considered part of the application risk management process.

The Importance of Focus on the Emerging Threats

Identifying and fixing vulnerabilities before these can be exploited by possible attackers should be one of the sound security principles that businesses and organizations need to follow. Nevertheless, in today's threat landscape that is characterized by threat actors seeks not just to exploit known vulnerabilities but also nonpublicly disclosed vulnerabilities such as zero-days and design flaws that have been undetected by vulnerability assessment processes, the standard security testing to identify and fix common vulnerabilities is not enough.

Besides zero-days and design flaws, the other factor to consider by the businesses is the emergence of sophisticated and targeted threats relying on cybercrime ware tools. These are the tools that can be acquired by threat actors and are designed and configured to attack specific targets, for example, online banking with malware. Once the malware is configured to attack a specific target, it is delivered on the targeted client machine through phishing and social engineering as well as drive by download. Once the malware is installed on the target machine, it will be under the control of the attacker and will seek to compromise the customer sensitive data and the business transactions such as money transfers. Today cybercrime tools for attacking bank customers can be acquired and rented from cyber-criminals whose main activity consists of designing cybercrime tools for later selling or renting for profit.

Since cybercrime tools are developed in the economic underground with a sizable on tools and people that is reinvested from the proceeds of sales of these tools to the fraudsters and cyber-criminals who use them, there has been recently an increase of sophistication of the features of these tools such as use of malware clients and command and control servers that use bot agents and web proxy for controlling the traffic of stolen data.

The sophistication of these cybercrime tools today is of big concerns for certain industry sectors such as banks and clients that are targeted but also other business sectors that deal with sensitive and intellectual propriety data. The increased sophistication of the cybercrime tools also goes hand in hand with the challenge for business to react proactively to these threats and deploy controls that mitigate the risk. Because of this lagging behind the threats, today's cyber-ware tools such as malware and botnets can bypass most of application and network security controls deployed by the business such as firewalls, intrusion detection systems and multifactor authentication. The effectiveness of cybercrime ware tools today is as such that the cybercrime tool herders offer a money-back guarantee in case the fraudster is not satisfied because missed the fraudulent proceeds from the use of this tools against the victims.

Threat Resilience and Application Security

Because of the increase sophistication of cyber threats such as malware, hacking, data breaches, online fraud, identity theft, money theft, exploits of zero-days, and denial of service attacks and others, there is a need today to engineer web applications and software that are designed, implemented, and tested to be resilient to these types of cyberthreat. For this to occur, it is important that the different application stakeholders in the organization such as the software development teams that include application architects and software developers collaborate with application security architects and penetration testers and provide the risk information such as reports about application threats, vulnerabilities, and countermeasures that risk and information security managers can use to make informed risk decisions and apply the risk mitigation strategy that is best suited based upon the risk management process of the organization. Fostering this collaboration among different users involved in securing web application assets requires the adoption of a risk management process that is beneficial to each of the user roles and responsibilities involved. Table 2.1 provides an example of application security stakeholders, their role and responsibilities, and the benefits such as the value added to application security/risk management that this role can play for the organization/business.

Threat Analysis

After the value of the assets has been analyzed, the main factors for the analysis of risks are to focus on the analysis of the threats and the attacks. At high level, the goal of threat analysis is to analyze the "who" that is the threat agent, the "what" that are the targets that reattacked such as the data assets and vulnerabilities and the "how" that is how the threats are realized in attacks and specifically the types of attack tools, attacking techniques, tactics, and procedures used by the threat agents.

Essential for the threat analysis is the knowledge of threats. For most organizations, businesses, and governments, the acquisition of threat knowledge relies on sources of threat such as threat intelligence. Threat intelligence means different things

DEFINING A RISK MITIGATION STRATEGY

TABLE 2.1 Application Security Roles, Responsibilities, and Benefits

Application Security Stakeholder	User Role and Responsibility	Benefits
Application architects, software developers	Design and implement (e.g. coding) new applications as well as change the design and coding of an existing application	Adherence to the application security standards and secure coding requirements
Application security architects and pen testers	Conduct secure architecture risk analysis and threat modeling assessments	Identify application vulnerabilities, determine technical risks, and recommend fixes or countermeasures.
Risk and information security managers	Manage risks to the business in compliance with governance and risk management processes	Make decisions on fixing vulnerabilities based upon risk and business criteria

to different types of organizations. For example, for government organizations, threat intelligence can be a matter that concerns intelligence agencies, national security, and the military. For businesses, such as private companies, threat intelligence gathering can be considered a service to which the company subscribes to learn about potential threat agents targeting their business assets. The threat intelligence information that is captured can help the business determine to whether these threats can target the company's business assets and how they can be attacked. This type of threat intelligence information if properly disseminated to information security and risk management can be used for proactively manage the security of applications and the risk of threat agents targeting specific application assets before these threats are realized in attacks. Threat intelligence could come from different sources and can be gathered by different entities and disseminated through different channels.

Today there are several private threat intelligence services that provide this type of threat intelligence gathering for companies. This type of service varies from threat reports from public sources, such as publicly reported data breaches for similar businesses and organizations, to classified information, such as information gathered through secret services and law enforcement sources. From the risk awareness perspective, threat intelligence shifts the perception of risk, helps reduce the appetite for risk, and drives the risk mitigation strategy to take necessary preventive security measures to manage risks.

Analyzing the potential threat scenarios that target the digital assets is critical for the risk mitigation strategy, and particularly both "known" and "unknown" threats. A threat is considered known when it has already occurred either directly or indirectly (e.g. to a similar business and application), and it has been possible to analyze what the threat agents are, the attack tools and methodologies used, the type of vulnerabilities exploited, and the impacts to the company assets. For example, an online banking application that allows customers to conduct financial transactions online might become the target for fraud and data compromise by banking malware threat agents. The analysis of the attacks used by the threat agents might include information about the type of the banking malware used as well as the type of actions taken to drop the malware on the targeted machine such as by using social engineering tactics including phishing campaigns and infecting vulnerable websites for drive-by-download infections. Once the malware is installed and has compromised the target, it will attack the assets such as the user credentials using a key logger and then attack the authenticated online session using a man-in-the-middle attack. With the control of the user session, the threat agent will gather customer's credit card and bank accounts and conduct fraudulent transactions, such as transferring money from the victim's account to an account under the attacker's control. The knowledge of this attack scenario is critical to determine the type of preventive security measures that need to be implemented to mitigate the risk, for example, antimalware software, device fingerprinting, multifactor authentication, and detective measures such as fraud detection and event monitoring.

The unknown threats are not yet fully documented and analyzed but are hypothetically possible. These types of threats are also referred as "emerging" threats. These are threats for which not enough information is gathered to determine the "who," the "what," and the "how." Examples of emerging threats include threats that do not have a history of associated events such as security incidents that can be used for learning about the threat actors, the targets and the tools, techniques, and tactics used. The drive of such emerging threats can be business or political events as well as new opportunities presented to the attackers such as the availability of new tools for conduct exploits, the availability of new channels such as social media, mobile channels, and the emergence of new technology that represents an opportunity to attack such as cloud computing, virtualized environments, mobile devices and so on.

From risk management perspective, it is important to be able to learn about emerging threats as well as known threats, identify the type of assets and vulnerabilities that are targeted, and how these are targeted, that is, the type of attacks and attack techniques used to determine the type of countermeasures that are effective in mitigating the risks.

The analysis of the different threats and attacks potentially affecting an application helps determine the likelihood of a threat scenario for the given application. Specifically, this determines how different threats can be realized by a threat agent using different attack techniques. In the case of malware attacking the application, for example, the threat agent might seek first to compromise the application interfaces with the user (e.g. the browser) and subsequently attack either the transmission media (e.g. the online channel) or the servers where the data is stored (e.g. database). Once the attack scenario has been analyzed and it has been determined that the application is at risk, the next step of the risk mitigation strategy is to determine if similar digital assets and businesses are also exposed and can be affected by either the same or similar type of attacks. To conduct this type of analysis, it is important to look more in

DEFINING A RISK MITIGATION STRATEGY 71

depth at the application architecture and specifically how the application processes the data and the type of layered controls available to secure the data.

Analyzing risk at the architectural level to determine how a threat can affect an application is one of the main steps of architectural risks analysis. The risk to an application asset is determined by the chances (likelihood) of a threat agent to be capable (skillful and resourceful) of exploiting vulnerabilities of the application and of causing an impact (fraud, theft) to an asset.

Analyzing the Attacks

The relevance of a threat for the application asset depends on the likelihood of the threat to occur and the potential negative impact. After it is found that a certain threat can be relevant to the asset, the next step is to determine the impact that this might pose to the assets. Since threats are realized through attacks, analyzing the different attack scenarios allows an analyst to describe the various ways threat agents can attack the application, analyze the attack vectors, and determine how these can exploit vulnerabilities to cause an impact to the application assets.

To analyze these attack scenarios from the perspective of risk mitigation, it is important to consider both the attacker and defender perspectives. From the defender perspective, the classification of data drives the scope for specific security requirements to protect the data. For example, any data that can be used to uniquely identify a customer, such as the customer demographic information that includes his name, address, and date of birth, is considered confidential by the data owners and it is mandatory that the confidentiality, integrity, and availability of such data are protected from unauthorized access and compromise. This is usually documented in the company information security policy as a security requirement and is validated by putting the application in the scope of security processes such as application security reviews and vulnerability assessments.

From the defensive perspective, the scope of which assets need to be protected depends on the intrinsic value of the asset and is different for different types of organizations. In the case of a financial organization, for example, data assets whose business transactions such as payments and money movements are usually considered confidential and business sensitive information and need to be protected from unauthorized access and compromise.

A company that produces Customer Off the Shelf (COTS) software most likely will consider this software as proprietary and in some cases a trading secret whose intellectual property needs to be protected. When the software is considered intellectual property, the main threats against it might include spying, reverse engineering, copying, and cloning. A company whose application allows customers to register and subscribe to news and receive alerts on new products and services can be considered low risk since the information that is handled and stored is mostly nonconfidential and nonproprietary.

As the data are classified according to their intrinsic value, the web application's inherent risk depends on the data classification that the application uses for business. The higher is the value of the data that is stored and handled by the application, the higher is the risk for the application. Moreover, other factors need to be considered as well, such as the volume of confidential and sensitive data that is stored and handled as well as the type of service and transactions that are dependent on such data.

From the threat agent perspective, the higher is the gain resulting from the compromise of the target, the higher is the interest on pursuing the target attempting different attacks and vulnerability exploits. In a targeted attack, a threat agent will target specific exploits of vulnerabilities that allow him to reach his goal. Since vulnerability exploits are a cost for the attacker, the more common and easy is the vulnerability to exploit, the lower the cost is for the attacker and the higher are his chances to succeed in the attack.

From the risk management and application security perspective, the approach is much different than the threat agent attacker perspective: a defender ought to fix all possible vulnerabilities that can be exploited by an attacker. That means any potential weakness in any of the security controls of the application. For the defender perspective, it is therefore necessary to protect the application data from attack vectors targeting all the user entry points and analyze any malicious data that can be entered from these entry points to gain unauthorized access to the application. A threat analyst has to continuously shift from the attack perspective to the defensive perspective to identify which data flows can be attacked assuming that these entry points are in the control of an attacker. From the defensive perspective, the threat analyst ought to assume that these entry points and data flows are compromised and identify any potential vulnerability that can be exploited by an attacker.

From the defender perspective, protecting the application data means being able to protect the application confidentiality, integrity, and availability. From an application design perspective, this means building preventive controls in the application such as encryption, digital signatures, authentication and authorization, session management, input validation, secure fail over, and safe exception handling. Detective controls might consist of logging and monitoring security events as well as feeding the application parameters in secure incident and event monitoring controls.

This type of threat analysis often requires the analyst to think like a threat agent that is trying to break into the application defenses and exploiting any possible design flaws and vulnerabilities of the application. If the main goal of the attacker is getting the customer's confidential data, for example, he or she might exploit flaws in authorization, such as escalating privileges, breaking into the application through weak authentication, impersonating or reusing a session through weak session management, injecting commands into the application through weak input validation such as SQL injection to gain unauthorized access to the application data and functions. Other possible vulnerability exploits for this threat agent include the exploitation of poor or nonexistent cryptographic controls, malicious file execution vulnerabilities, injection flaws, remote file inclusion-upload vulnerabilities, weak user authentication, and lack of transaction authentication, and flaws in authorization and session management controls.

An important factor for analyzing attacks is that attacks can be either opportunistic or persistent. Opportunistic attacks take advantage of the application vulnerabilities already present in the application and exploit the ones that allow the threat agent to affect the asset sought. Persistent attacks take advantage of the unlimited time for trying different attack vectors to break into the application and affect the assets. By persistently trying to attack an application with different attack vectors and techniques, eventually the threat agent will succeed in finding a new vulnerability that can be exploited to conduct the attack. Vulnerabilities that are identified for the first time and for which there is no remediation (e.g. patch) available are considered by security researchers zero-day vulnerabilities. When these are found, they represent a high risk for the application because there is no known mitigation being implemented, tested, and deployed, therefore, exposing the application to the potential attacks. For these zero-day vulnerabilities, it is also not entirely known which threat agents will use them since these were never exploited before.

Analyzing Vulnerabilities and Impacts

One of the standard definitions of risk is that a risk is realized by a threat agent seeking to exploit vulnerabilities with an attack to cause an impact to the targeted asset such as data and functionality. Within this definition of risk, a vulnerability represent a condition of realize the impact. When vulnerabilities are identified and fixed, the risk is mitigated. In the case of web applications and software, the identification of vulnerabilities is the main goal of vulnerability assessments such as pen testing and source code analysis. Analyzing the exposure of vulnerabilities to potential threats such as by using threat modeling is also essential to determine the risk severity of the vulnerabilities in presence of threats. For example, the threat model can provide the information to assess if vulnerabilities' exposure to a threat agent is either external or internal. If the exposure to the threat agent is external, this might represent a higher risk to the asset rather than when the exposure is only internal.

For penetration testers, using a risk scoring method to assign the severity of the risks of vulnerabilities such as CVSS allows to determine the risk level of the vulnerability. This can be done by considering factors such as exposure of the vulnerability and the confidentiality, integrity and availability of the data that is exposed by the vulnerability as well as other factors that depend on the threat environment and exposure of the vulnerability to the threat agents. For example, a high-risk level can be given to an SQL injection vulnerability that might be exploitable pre-authentication to access a database that stores authentication credentials where a low-risk severity level will be given to a vulnerability such as XSS that is only exploitable by injecting scripts via internal files, and therefore exposed only to internal threat agents.

Besides the exposure of vulnerabilities to a threat agent, an important factor to consider is determining the impact of vulnerabilities to the assets. The impact against an asset might be factored in terms of impact to the security properties of an asset such as the confidentiality, integrity, and availability of the asset in case it is compromised. A data asset that represents value to the business, such as customers' sensitive data like bank and credit card accounts and PII, might cause a monetary impact to the business if this data is compromised. In general, impacts to the assets can be both tangible and nontangible: examples of tangible impacts include monetary losses because of data loss and/or fraud, unlawful noncompliance, legal fees, and fines. Examples of nontangible impacts to the business are reputation loss, impact to the brand and franchise, loss of trust in the company business, and any type of negative information such as news of the data breach that will impact the shareholders' trust in the business.

In application risk analysis, quantifying risks by factoring the loss or compromise of an asset is the next step after the technical risks have been assessed. That is, determining the risk of the assets' confidentiality, integrity, and availability being exposed by potential threats. For example, this is how a risk manager determines the possible impact to the business caused by a threat agent targeting the application by exploiting a system weakness and/or vulnerability. From the technical risk perspective, exploiting a technical vulnerability might cause system failure, the loss or compromise of the asset, and fraudulent use of the asset (fraudulent financial transaction). From the business impact perspective, exploiting the vulnerability might cause a monetary loss due to system failure, regulatory fines, and lawsuits because of data breaches, direct and indirect costs for recovering from data breach incidents, and monetary losses due to fraudulent transactions.

Table 2.2 shows some examples associating threats to applications with the technical impact (e.g. system failure, data compromise, vulnerability exploits) and with business impacts (e.g. monetary losses and liabilities).

From the perspective of analyzing the threats targeting a web application, we should analyze first the context that is the threat landscape that includes specific threats to web applications as targets to understand how these threats could

TABLE 2.2 Example of Threats and the Technical and Business Impacts

Threat	Technical Impact	Business Impact
Malware infected PC taking over online banking credentials	Loss of users' authentication data allowing fraudsters to take over the account (impersonation)	Money loss due to fraudulent transactions by impersonating the logged user to move money to fraudulent accounts through third-party accounts (money mules)
External threat agent exploiting application's SQL injection vulnerabilities	Unauthorized access to users' data including confidential and PII, trading secrets, and intellectual property	Liabilities for loss of users' PII, lawsuits for unlawful noncompliance, security incident recovery costs, and revenue loss
Denial of service attack against the application	Unavailability of web server due to exploit of application and network vulnerabilities and lack of redundancies to cope with traffic overloads	Revenue loss due to loss and/or disruption of service denying customer access to services and goods. Lawsuits from customers and businesses and recovery costs

DEFINING A RISK MITIGATION STRATEGY 75

compromise the application assets. Application level threats at a minimum should include threats to both the application data and the application functions. One main subject to consider in this type of analysis is the application assets and how they are managed by the application. If the data stored by the application includes customer confidential data, for example, it is a potential target. When customer confidential data is stolen, it could be used to impersonate the customer in a fraudulent transaction.

Since the risk strategy seeks to minimize the residual risk to an acceptable level for the business, mapping attacks to vulnerabilities is a critical step in application threat modeling since it allows a risk manager to determine whether the exposure of the vulnerability to an attack can lead to an exploit and increased risk.

Protecting the confidentiality, integrity, and availability of data assets is usually addressed as a security requirement and depends on the classification of the data. Regarding the determination of impact on data assets, an important factor to consider is the classification of the data. Information disclosure of customer's PII or business sensitive information (e.g. bank accounts, credit card accounts) to unauthorized users, for example, is more critical than exposure of data that is not deemed confidential and is just classified as internal. The localization of the application assets in the physical and logical architecture of the application whose classification is either sensitive or confidential is critical to determine the exposure of these assets to potential attacks and is one of the objectives of the architectural risk analysis.

Architectural risk analysis is a critical assessment for determining whether the application's security controls mitigate impacts, such as using encryption to protect data confidentiality in storage and in transit between the end user and the application. Part of the architectural risk analysis is also to determine the data entry points to the application. The entry points' risk can be ranked by considering the type of exposure it provides to the threat agent (e.g. internal, external) as well as the likelihood and potential impact to the data asset value (e.g. public, internal, confidential, and restricted) whose data the entry point leads to.

An important factor of the risk mitigation strategy is whether one of the measures recommended addresses process gaps, such as when failing to apply information security requirements leads to a potential risk to the business. For example, failing to protect confidential data can be considered as either a gap in the documentation of a security requirement or in the application of the security requirement. Similar examples include unenforced authentication and the need to know (e.g. minimum privileges for the users).

The enforcement and validation of these information security requirements are critical not only to mitigate threats and attacks but also to mitigate unlawful noncompliance and audit risks. When security measures to mitigate such attacks are not implemented as required by information security policies and standards, the business faces a noncompliance risk.

For example, the countermeasure designs need to mitigate potential attacks to satisfy at minimum, the security requirements in compliance with the organization's information security standards and policies. For this reason, the risks posed by design flaws identified by application threat modeling need to consider noncompliance risks as well as business and technical risks.

To consider all possible impacts of exploitable vulnerabilities, we need to consider design flaws identified through threat modeling, security bugs identified through secure code reviews, and insecure configuration issues that can be identified with application penetration tests. Some of the design flaws that lead to attack exposure can only be identified by looking in depth at the application design that includes detailed examples of session management vulnerabilities. Session management vulnerabilities, for example, might include uncoordinated single logout between applications that share the same session when the user logs in. When the user logs out of one of the services used by the application, some sessions are left open for the user so that they can be still reused. Such vulnerabilities have a HIGH impact to the business since they might allow a session to be replayed so an attacker can gain access to the application. However, the severity of such vulnerabilities is MEDIUM in the presence of short-lived sessions and idle time outs.

Some application vulnerabilities that application threat modeling can identify include identifying weak authentication controls such as weak authentication. The attack agent targeting weak authentication might be a malicious user who installed malware to capture data in transit between the victim's browser and the application. Without compensating controls such as a channel to protect the confidentiality of the authentication data in transit, SSL, for example, the vulnerability in the authentication being used by the site might expose authentication credentials to an attacker. From the technical risk perspective, this could be a risk that can be classified as HIGH considering both likelihood of the exploit (e.g. BASE64 credentials can be decoded in transit such as in the case of HTTP basic authentication) and exposure (the application is external facing to the Internet). The business impact of this exploit can be rated HIGH since the exploit of the authentication weakness might allow unauthorized access to the application and the application data, which might include confidential data and PII. The impact for noncompliance audit risk is also HIGH because the disclosure of confidential PII data is usually a violation of the organization's information security policies. Other potential negative impacts from exploiting this vulnerability include reputational damage because of the requirement enforced by local data breach notification laws to publicly disclose a data breach of confidential PII, as well as potential fines and liabilities from regulators.

Estimating Risks and Impacts An information risk assessment consists of estimating the risk caused by a threat seeking to compromise the confidentiality, integrity, and availability of the data in the presence of vulnerabilities. The estimation of the level of risk is usually done using qualitative and quantitative risk calculation methods. Qualitative risk analysis factors the likelihood of the exploit of vulnerabilities and the impact of the confidentiality integrity and availability of the asset. For a given threat, the higher is the sensitivity of the data and the higher is the exposure to the data caused by a vulnerability, the higher is the information security risk. It quantitative risk analysis, the risk is quantified in terms of monetary losses that the business might incur in case of either a loss of the asset (e.g. data) or loss of business service that process that asset (e.g. business transaction with the data). To determine the business impact caused by the loss and compromise of an asset, is it important to first estimate the value of the asset and calculate the likelihood of such asset being compromised due to the exposure of the asset to a vulnerability by a given threat agent.

Determining the value of assets depends mostly on the value given by the business in the context of the service that application provides using that asset. An application that generates revenue for the company by selling goods online, for example, might suffer a revenue loss when that application service is not available to the customer because of a denial of service attack or other type of application vulnerability exploit.

Different types of threats expose different types of information, such as PII or intellectual property, and that information loss may cause negative business impact. For example, when a threat agent exploits a technical vulnerability, such as a design flaw, coding bug, or misconfiguration, it causes a negative impact to the application assets.

It is important to make a distinction between information security and business impact: An information security risk is the risk that affects the security properties of the data such as the confidentiality, integrity, and availability of the data. A business impact is the economic impact caused by either the loss or the compromise of the value of the data asset.

Sometimes the difference between information security risks and business impact is subtle: information security risks are not per se associated with business impact until asset values and negative impacts to the business due to the loss or damage of the asset are also considered.

From the technical risk perspective, mitigating information security risks is a risk management decision, while from the business risk perspective, mitigating the risk of a business impact is a business decision. The essential steps of a risk mitigation strategy need to consider both information security and business risk factors, which can be done by following a two-step process:

1. Perform the technical risk analysis that focuses on the determination of technical vulnerabilities and the analysis of their impact on the assets. Categorizing the vulnerability or technical risk framework is critical to determine the impact from a technical risk perspective. Since a technical risk is in essence a weakness in a security control, it can simply be described as weakness in protecting the confidentiality, integrity, and availability of the data. Such weakness can be identified as vulnerabilities in application controls, such as authentication, authorization, encryption, session management, data validation, error and exception handling, and auditing and logging.
2. Correlate the technical vulnerability with the asset value to determine in monetary impact such as the cost to the business when the data compromised or lost.

For an application risk mitigation strategy to be useful to the business, it is important to monetize the loss that may result from an exploited vulnerability. A risk assessment typically includes the evaluation of information security risks and the technical risks posed by exploit of vulnerabilities and the business impacts. By factoring both information security and business impact (e.g. monetary impact caused by the loss of data), risk managers can make informed risk decisions on how to best manage the information security risks and business impacts. For example, the business can choose either to accept the risks since they are of low or no business impact, or to fix the vulnerability and implement a countermeasure for the threat to reduce the potential impact to a level that is acceptable to the business.

The exposure of an asset to information security risks is also a factor of the severity of the vulnerability found in a security control whose function is to protect the asset. The severity of the vulnerability as well as the impact on the asset confidentiality, integrity, and availability can be used to determine the overall risk of the vulnerability.

A known vulnerability, such as failing to encrypt a password in transit, can be ranked HIGH because of both likelihood to exploit (the password is passed in clear text and can be eavesdropped with a web proxy), as well as impact (hijacking a password can lead to application access). From the business risk analysis perspective, the risk of disclosing customer confidential PII (such as a data loss incident) is generally considered a HIGH risk, both in terms of unlawful noncompliance and negative impact to the business due to the public release of the data loss incident.

The assigned risk levels to the severity of the vulnerability can be used by information security managers to prioritize the remediation effort. From the technical risk mitigation perspective, vulnerabilities can be prioritized for remediation based on their risk level (e.g. HIGH, MEDIUM, and LOW). High-risk vulnerabilities are prioritized for mitigation over MEDIUM and LOW risk vulnerabilities since these represent a higher probability of being exploited by a threat agent, which might lead to the higher impact to the asset. From the business risk mitigation perspective, the vulnerabilities whose exploits lead to the compromise of the more business valuable assets are the ones that should be prioritized first. When a risk mitigation measure is applied to the current efforts of protecting the asset, the risk that is left over is referred as residual risk. One of the main objectives of risk mitigation strategy is to reduce this residual risk to a level that is acceptable to the business. Determining whether the risk posed by vulnerabilities is acceptable will consider risk mitigation factors such as enforcement of security requirements, security by design and by configuration, and system and infrastructure security measures.

A risk assessment can be actionable for managing business impacts caused by threats by determining how security measures need to be designed, implemented, and configured to reduce the exposure of the assets to vulnerability exploits sought by that threat. Since security measures can be applied to mitigate the risk and vulnerabilities should be remediated to reduce exposure to threats, determining which vulnerabilities need to be fixed ultimately depends on their potential impact to the business caused by a threat potential exploiting them. In essence, a risk mitigation strategy that considers both technical and business impacts need to factor the risk caused by vulnerabilities and the business impacts caused on the assets.

From the perspective of managing risk by implementing technical controls, it is important first to understand the application technical functionality and discussing it with the business owners. The main objective of this business discovery stage is to capture essential information about the business functionality of the application and the basic business functions. Some of the application functions might be common across different applications, such as user credential registration, user authentication, and query data. Other application functions might be business specific, such as ordering a product or service, paying online bills, wiring money to a beneficiary account, trading stocks, or betting for on an online auction.

Once the business context is understood, the next step is to understand the technical context of the application. This might require gathering information about the application design (architecture documents) and the various components of the technical architecture, such as the client-browser, web and application servers, databases, and backend mainframes, including the protected assets that store data such as customer sensitive, bank, and credit card information.

Once the data assets of the application are identified and depicted in the application architecture, to the risk analyst will analyze each application's business function and how the application security controls (authentication, authorization, encryption etc.) provide the necessary security features to protect the data assets, specifically the confidentiality, integrity, and availability of the data.

To determine the business impact, it is important to consider the business context in which the application operates. This can be determined just by looking at high level application assets and the application functionality that the application provides based upon these assets.

The final stage consists of determining the business impacts to the business caused by threat agents targeting the assets. For this type of risk analysis, it is important to have a risk framework of threats, vulnerabilities and controls and to follow a methodology to evaluate the impact to the application assets of various potential threats targeting the application. This can be done by following a risk-based threat modeling methodology step by step including the execution of a predetermined set of activities with expected outcomes such as artifacts.

From the perspective of managing application security risks, there are several types of risk frameworks that can be used for analyzing risks and threats to applications, some of which will be covered in this book, simply for comparative purposes. This book also includes a new risk-based threat modeling methodology whose details are initially introduced in Chapter 6. In this chapter, we will cover more breadth rather than depth what the important areas that a threat analyst needs to cover for a preliminary risk analysis of an application using threat modeling techniques. In order to conduct a thorough analysis of the threats affecting an application, it is important to commit to specific goals and follow a set of predefined activities step by step.

This type of risk assessment is in essence the assessment of the risk posed by application technical issues. The main scope of this technical risk assessment is to analyze how these design flaws and gaps might cause a security impact to the data assets, such as causing a compromise of the confidentiality, integrity, and availability of the data asset. Nevertheless, to determine the technical risks, it is important to qualify the likelihood and impact of the vulnerability. This type of technical risk analysis needs to consider other factors besides likelihood and impact, such as the exposure to potential threat agents and attack vectors to these assets. It is therefore critical to consider different threat scenarios and determine the different types of attack vectors that threat agents can use against the assets and components of the application architecture and determine the impact when the application vulnerabilities are exploited. Essentially, technical risk analysis consists of assessing the risks posed by threats to the assets and attack vectors seeking to exploit vulnerabilities of the application. The application vulnerabilities that are in the scope of the threat analysis, that is, the analysis of the exposure to threats to assets and attack vectors, can be discovered by other application vulnerability assessments, such as secure design review, secure code reviews, and ethical hacking/pen testing.

In any case, it is important to consider a threat model as a dynamic risk assessment that needs to be revisited over time to consider new threats to the application. As any other risk assessment methodology, threat modeling cannot be considered a one-time application security process but rather an iterative process to keep updates the threat model with new threats targeting the application as well as with the new exposure of these threats due to changes introduced to the application.

An event that should trigger a revisit of an application threat model is the emergence of new threats potentially directed toward the same class of web application and/or software products used by the company. The objective of updating the threat model in this case is to consider if these new threats need to be mitigated by adopting new countermeasures. In today's application threat landscape, for example, web applications and application software might become the target of new attacks and new threat agents seeking to attack the application and the business that runs it for different reasons, such as monetary and financial gain, political gain, spying-intelligence, or terrorism. By updating the threat model with these emerging threats, it is possible to identify the adequacy of the security measures in place and plan for the implementation of new preventive and detective measures as needed to mitigate the risk.

Applying Security Measures

To determine the security controls that need to be designed and implemented to mitigate the risks, it is necessary to consider the potential vulnerabilities that can be exploited by the threat agent and the potential impacts of these on the assets for each specific threat agent and attack vector. Once the main threats, threat agents, attacks, and vulnerabilities are identified, the next step is to determine the risk to the assets in terms of likelihood and impact. By using an application risk framework, it is possible to systematically consider different types of threats and attack scenarios and to analyze the likelihood of the application assets to be impacted as well as the business impact. Only by understanding how the different threats might cause a technical and business impact, it is possible to determine which security controls in the application can effectively mitigate the risks to the business posed by these threats. A technical impact can be described in terms of impact to the security controls, such as compromised authentication, authorization, and encryption controls. A business impact can be described in terms of tangible and intangible losses to the business.

Identifying technical and business risks in a given application is a critical piece of information for deciding which countermeasures should be implemented to mitigate these risks. For example, the type of risk information that might help risk managers make informed risk decisions includes the type of threats targeting the application, the control gaps and vulnerabilities, and the countermeasures to mitigate such gaps and vulnerabilities.

Once the application risks have been analyzed and the necessary security measures have been identified, the next step is to communicate to the application development teams how these security measures need to be designed and implemented. The security measures to mitigate technical risks of the application are included in the technical risk assessment that is done after threats are analyzed, application vulnerabilities identified, and technical impact to the assets have been determined, such as the impact to confidentiality, availability, and integrity of the data assets.

When technical risks posed by vulnerability exploits have been identified in a threat model, the next step is to factor threats in the determination of the risk/severity of these vulnerabilities. Since threats, attacks, and vulnerabilities are correlated in a threat model, it is possible to determine risk severity by looking at their exposure to the attacks visualized in the attack tree. Since an attack tree provides the information about the step-by-step attack scenarios, it is possible to determine the exposure of the assets to these attacks and factor the exposure in determining the risk probability. Determining the factors of risk to assign a severity level to the vulnerability, such as probability and impact, allows the business to decide which vulnerabilities should be prioritized for risk mitigation and determine the risk strategy: higher risk vulnerabilities remediated before medium risk vulnerabilities and medium risk vulnerabilities before low-risk ones.

For a risk mitigation strategy to be consistent, it has to be the first and foremost based upon the objective evaluation of risks. Objective evaluation means that risks are identified and managed as a result of following a standard process rather than best practices and improvised ad hoc processes. The results' consistency depends on following standard process, tools, and technology used and training and awareness. Among these basic elements, probably the most important factor is the training and the experience of the personnel involved in executing the risk strategy.

Specifically in analyzing threats to the application, the threat analyst's experience in identifying threats and vulnerabilities is one of the most critical factors and should not be overlooked. Since threat modeling is not an assessment that can be automated by using threat modeling tools alone and is very dependent on human knowledge, the training of the threat/risk analyst who conducts the threat/risk analysis is the most critical factor contributing to the overall quality of a threat model. Even if using risk/threat modeling tools can help in the execution of the assessment, these are certainly not necessary for a good quality threat/risk model of the application. Ultimately a threat analyst with several years of experience in application security and technical risk assessment is probably the most important asset in conducting this type of analysis. Nevertheless, what is really important for a successful application risk strategy is providing actionable tactical results that can be used by the development teams to implement the necessary countermeasures and reduce the impact to the business to acceptable levels.

IMPROVING APPLICATION SECURITY

> "When solving problems, dig at the roots instead of just hacking the leaves"
> Anthony J. D' Angelo

We previously explored how business can more effectively manage the risk caused by cyberthreat agents by gathering threat intelligence on the threat actors and targets and by analyzing the type of attacks used against the targets including the type of vulnerabilities that could be exploited. The rationale of this analysis of threats and attacks is to identify countermeasures that are effective in reducing the impact to the application assets. Moving forward, we look at best practices and risk management strategies that organizations can business and follow to improve application security.

Documenting Application Security Requirements

A good place to start for improving application security is security requirements. Some of these security requirements can be derived by understanding the potential threats that might affect the application. For example, modeling how a threat agent can abuse an application by assuming that the application's use cases can be abused to cause harm to the application and the data, helps derive a set of security risk mitigation requirements.

The model of threats affecting the application and the various components of the application architecture also helps determine application assets' risk exposure to potential attack vectors. Security issues identified by architecture risk analysis and vulnerabilities identified with secure code reviews and penetration tests also help to improve the security of applications and software throughout the SDLC. By adding threat modeling activities during secure architecture reviews, secure code reviews, and penetration testing, it is possible to determine the likelihood and impact, both technical and business, of potential threats exploiting these vulnerabilities and determine the necessary measures to mitigate the risks.

Applications that are built for the first time or existing applications that are undergoing changes for introducing new features planned for future releases of the application and software represent an opportunity to improve security by applying new security requirements to either the application as a whole or just the changes that are introduced.

Parallel to documenting business requirements (also covered in functional requirement specifications), deriving security requirements leads to improved security by building it into the new functionality. Oftentimes, this effort is limited to documenting security requirements for protecting access to the application assets from unauthorized users, grating users the entitlements to read, create, and modify the application's data, protect the confidential and authentication data in storage and transit, validate the application inputs and outputs, manage the user session securely, and audit and log security events as well as requirements for the secure configuration and operation of the application. Threat modeling can help improve security during this stage by deriving security requirements for security controls as risk mitigation features. For example, threat modeling determines the strength of the authentication required to mitigate potential threats against assets when the value and the risks for these assets are high. More specifically, when the analysis includes the possibility of different attack vectors attacking the authentication control with brute force attacks, credentials enumeration, data injection, session hijacking by exploiting potential vulnerabilities such as not locking the account login, credentials harvesting through login error messages, SQL injection, session fixation helps derive and document a set of technical security requirements that are more control specific and help in the design of a more secure application and software.

Security requirements that are derived using a threat model and validated with security tests also provide the business a certain level of assurance that the application's security has been tested to mitigate the risks from known threats and attacks. If, for example, security requirements are derived using use and misuse cases, validating these security requirements provides a reasonable assurance to the business that the mitigation of the risks posed by these threats has been considered.

The drivers deriving application security requirements include applicable compliance risks with privacy laws, regulations, and standards. Typically, compliance with security requirements can be assessed using checklists that qualify which security controls should be in scope and when and how they should be implemented. In the case of financial applications, for example, the design of multifactor authentication needs to comply with the FFIEC guidance for implementing multifactor authentication for authenticating high-risk transactions.

In the case of a design flaw such as authentication that is too weak to comply with a regulatory requirement, application threat modeling can point architects to a set of recommendations to fix the design flaw, including the type of recommended countermeasures. Such countermeasures might include previously analyzed and approved multifactor authentication (MFA) controls, such as knowledge-based authentication, risk-based authentication, one-time passwords, soft and hardware tokens, challenge/response questions/answers, biometrics.

At the architectural level, secure architecture requirements can be derived from the documented application security standards and guidelines. These standards and guidelines provide development teams direction on how to design and implement secure application and software by covering all the critical aspects of secure application design, such as protecting the authentication data in transit and storage, session management, error logging and auditing, role base access controls, and configuration management.

An application threat model performed specifically as a secure architecture risk analysis also needs to validate the design's compliance with the security requirements set by the secure architecture guidelines. This validation can be done in a variety of ways that include the analysis of the architecture design diagrams and data flows as well as a threats and vulnerability assessment using checklists.

The depth and breadth required for the secure architecture analysis might vary depending on the overall objectives. A security requirement can be as generic as validating that simple requirements, such as external facing web applications that handle customer PII, are compliant with the privacy requirements stated in the privacy questionnaire.

A more in-depth security requirement to validate might require reviewing the design to validate that customer PII is masked when displayed in each documented user interface and is protected in storage, transit, and all data flow between the users and the application.

Application Security "By Design"

When an application security expert reviews the application design, one of the important aspects to consider is whether there are risks in the design of the application architecture, such as security design flaws, and to determine whether any assets (e.g. data) are exposed to these design flaws. When a design flaw that exposes the application asset to a certain risk and attack vector is identified, the security expert can determine the likelihood and the impact to the business and proactively mitigate this risk before the application software is implemented and the application/product is rolled out in production. Besides proactively mitigating risks, fixing application vulnerabilities during design and ahead of coding produces a return of investment to the business since it is much cheaper to fix these during design change when the application has already been implemented and tested. In summary, when security activities such as security requirement derivation, architectural risk analysis, secure code reviews, and penetration testes are integral part of the SDLC, we have the opportunity to also integrate threat modeling and analyze the likelihood and impact of potential security issues identified by these security activities.

Applications and software that are already developed and released into production environments can also be improved from the application security perspective. Application threat modeling helps improve the security of existing applications by putting them in scope of a risk assessment review to validate the application security against a set of security measures that are necessary to mitigate the risks posed by new threats targeting the application assets. When performing the assessment for the first time, this type of application threat model constitutes a baseline and can be leveraged to analyze new threats and vulnerabilities. These vulnerabilities can be introduced by design changes to the application and software during the product life cycle. Such an application threat model baseline can be stored in a repository and used throughout the product life cycle. The baseline threat model of the application can be updated as needed, such as when either the application is being changed or when the application risks need to be reassessed to consider emerging threats.

In terms of standard design documentation, threat modeling can also use standard modeling artifacts such as use cases, architecture diagrams, and sequence diagrams. As in the case of software development teams that follow formal design

IMPROVING APPLICATION SECURITY 85

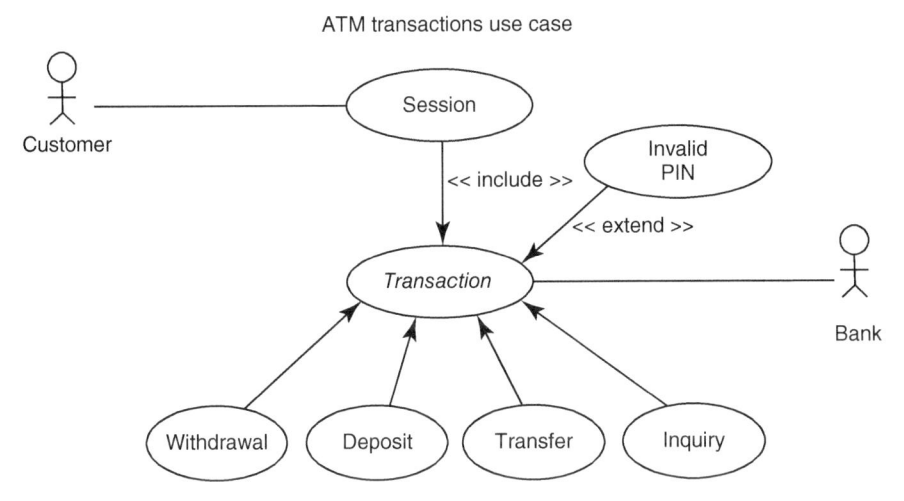

Figure 2.1 Example of Use Case Diagram 1

methodologies such as Unified Modeling Language (UML) artifacts such as use cases can be used to depict at high level how customers interact with the application functions of an application. An example of such use case diagram for ATM transactions is shown in Figure 2.1.

Other examples of design artifacts that can be leveraged for threat modeling include sequence diagrams that show how data flows sequentially through the different elements of the application architecture, architectural design diagrams that show the different tiers of the architecture and the components and servers, as well as network-physical architecture diagrams. When these design artifacts are documented by following a template, they can be very useful for the security design reviews and threat modeling since they capture essential information to identify potential security issues, such as design flaws or missing security requirements.

One important value of threat modeling conducted during the architectural risk analysis is that potential vulnerabilities, such as design flaws, can be correlated with vulnerabilities found with other assessments in later phases of the SDLC such as coding, verification, and testing. One example of this correlation consists of identifying whether design flaws found earlier in the SDLC with threat modeling result in reduced security flaws found later (e.g. during coding) with manual secure code review. This type of vulnerability data correlation helps to identify and address root causes earlier in the SDLC with improved process efficiency and security defect management cost reduction.

When applying threat modeling to architectural risk analysis, it is important to adopt a methodology that is used consistently across the organization so that threat modeling assessments can be compared across applications that are designed and implemented by development units. Oftentimes though, application threat modeling is conducted as an informal assessment, especially in the unfortunate cases when the application architecture is not documented and the security analyst SME can only assess the potential risks and impacts to the application by capturing them on a white board during an application development team meeting. This might be a useful exercise and effective in recommending improvements to the security of the applications and software in scope, but the effectiveness might be limited to the knowledge of the application brought to the table during the meeting as well as the experience of the application security SME in conducting this type of analysis.

When a formal threat modeling methodology is followed, the assessment can be conducted consistently by following the methodology step by step. Typically, the first step is to gather the necessary documentation to conduct the analysis. Once the initial design documentation of the application is gathered, it is possible to estimate the time necessary to conduct the assessment and plan the application threat modeling activities. For example, this is the time that is required for the review of the documentation such as business requirements, the review and the analysis of the design documents, architecture diagrams, use cases, sequence diagrams, and so on. Depending on how big the application is, this requires days or weeks to read the documents and set up meetings with the application stakeholders necessary to gather information and understand the application functionality and architecture more in depth.

As good approach toward the goal of improving the security of existing applications is to proceed gradually and plan a gradual, phased, and controlled adoption of application threat modeling among the different application development teams. Adopting a formalized, standard application threat modeling process might occur over several months or even years in large software development organizations. Companies that follow a standardized threat modeling process across the different teams within the organization are more likely to produce consistent and reliable results than companies that do not.

For increasing the changes of adoption of application threat modeling within an organization, it is important to leverage existing software engineering processes, such as security architecture design reviews. During these reviews, the security architect will review the architecture design documents and analyze the physical and logical architecture diagrams to identify the main components of the architecture, such as web and application servers and databases and to identify the data assets and the interactions with the data flows. Once the various assets and components of the application architecture have been identified, the next step is to enumerate possible threats to each component to determine how they can be affected. This step in the application threat modeling is often referred as architecture decomposition and involves decomposing the architecture into basic architectural elements such as assets, data flows and components (web server, application server, and database server), and considering how a predetermined list of threats such as STRIDE might affect these architectural elements. The outcome of this architecture security review might lead to identifying either errors or gaps in the design of security controls that are required to protect the application asset from potential threats. A change in design to address the security concerns has a substantial impact on the security of the application. For example, after reviewing the architecture of an existing application, the analyst finds that the communication channel between the application server and database storing authentication data is not encrypted to protect the data from information disclosure and spoofing. Additionally, there is no mutual authentication that prevents repudiation of the connection request to the database from an untrusted client. The information sent is also not digitally signed to prevent tampering outside the transmission channel. The security architect might request to roll out these changes to the application prior to the next release to mitigate these risks.

A more comprehensive application threat modeling process might also include a preliminary risk analysis of the application, the threat agents, the threat libraries used to identify likelihood and impacts to the assets, attack tree analysis of the different channels and assets that can be attacked, correlation of threats to existing vulnerabilities identified in the application, determination of technical and business risk, determination of security measures and prioritization of these based on a risk strategy whose objective is to maximize protection by minimizing cost to the business.

For a threat modeling process to be executed consistently, a standard application threat modeling methodology needs, at a minimum, to define the steps, the required inputs, and the expected outputs (e.g. artifacts) that need to be produced during each step. This will include, for example, architecture design documents that describe at a high level the physical and logical architecture and the design of the security controls. Conducting such a comprehensive application threat model can be very time-consuming and resource-intensive, especially when it is performed on new applications for the first time. On the other hand, the bulk of the effort is only required for the first threat model since it will be used as a baseline and just requires updating when new changes to the application are introduced, such as when integrating the application with new application components or services, as well as when changing the existing application data and components. Nevertheless, adopting a comprehensive application threat modeling assessment can be considered the ultimate goal for an organization and an application security investment that will lead to savings in vulnerability defect management efforts.

From the defender perspective, protecting the application assets is usually not just the task of one measure and one control but a set of measures and controls applied at the different layers of the application architecture. Applying security design principles such as defense in depth, security by simplicity of the mechanism, security as the security of the weakest link and security as security by default configuration, for example, is among the best practices that most application security practitioners can follow. The same security design principles can be applied to assess the security of the architecture during the secure architecture design reviews and threat modeling, considering a set of possible threats to each layer of the application architecture and assuming that when one layer is compromised, another layer would need to mitigate the risks and the potential impacts. In analogy to a defense in-depth evaluation of security controls, for example, a threat analyst needs to evaluate the potential exposure to threats by adopting an attack in-depth approach to identify how attacks can be mitigated at the different layers of the application architecture and to determine how application layered controls can work together to provide the best defense in depth for the application assets.

From the perspective of an attacker, trying to gain access to the application data, for example, if an attack vector causes one security control to fail, such as by exploiting a vulnerability of the client browser, the risk to the data asset protected by the application can still be mitigated by another control at the server layer, such as requiring the user to authenticate outside with out of band authentication. This type of threat analysis considers different threats to the different security controls and measures adopted by the application to protect the data assets.

Information Security Reviews

From the information security team's perspective, making sure that the company data assets are protected is one of the main information security requirements. For applications, software, and data assets, information security policies can be validated by asserting the security of the design against these requirements. Examples of such security by design assertions include validating the presence of security controls using a checklist and testing the application for vulnerabilities that need to be remediated to satisfy the information security requirements.

A security issue identified using the checklist requires further validation and can be assessed further during a meeting of the security analyst, application architect, and product teams. When the issue is identified, it can be addressed by adding a missing security requirement and/or a design change. When this type of validation of security requirements is applied to the application architecture reviews, it is meant to validate a negative requirement because of not having a security measure to comply with the organization's information security policy. If the checkmarks confirm that the security measure is in place, no further action is required. This type of assessment, even if useful as initial information gathering about the security of the application is not as useful as to take actions to mitigate risks when such risks are identified as a negative answer in the security checklist.

The scope of the checklist might include validating specific information security requirements, such as authentication and authorization access controls, password policies, user entitlements, protection of sensitive data, and auditing and logging. Such validation of security requirements unfortunately does not always translate to actionable security for the application. For example, validating the security of an application by conducting an interview with the application stakeholders might identify a gap but might not determine the level or risk when this gap is exposed to a specific threat.

With an information security assessment of the design of an application, the issue is identified as violation of information security policy and the fix consists of implementing a security control according to the specific requirements for security controls to protect the confidentiality, integrity, and availability of the data as these are documented in the information security requirements. The limitation of this type of assessments is that the findings of secure design review do not translate into actionable recommendation for mitigating the risk of the exploit of the security control gap by a specific threat. In an application threat modeling assessment, fixing a design issue in the application design comprise more specifically implementing a countermeasure that goes beyond fixing the vulnerability that exposing the asset. Since security issues in a threat model are typically identified by analyzing threats, trust boundaries, and data flow diagrams and are typically actionable by development teams that have an understanding of the architecture design of the application.

When security issues are identified using a threat model that considers the impact of threats and vulnerabilities to application assets, it would take the assessment of the application against information security requirements a step further. Beyond the basic compliance requirements and audit risks, a threat model covers the risks posed by threats targeting the application assets. By scoping the application design for application threat-model review, information security team could analyze the exposure of the application to threats and determine the countermeasures that mitigate the exposure to these threats.

From the risk management perspective, the strategic objective of threat modeling is to minimize risks and the associated business impacts. One of the risk management benefits of application threat modeling is helping information security professionals to manage vulnerability risks by prioritizing the remediation of these vulnerabilities according to their severity. Information security requirements can be set to manage the risk of vulnerabilities found with threat modeling during design ahead of releasing the application into the production environment. An example of information security requirement for critical vulnerabilities is that all security critical design flaws identified with threat modeling would require a design change before allowing the project to move to the implementation-coding phase and a security test to validate that such design flaws are fixed before releasing the application into production.

After completing a threat model, information security teams can look at the security flaws identified during threat modeling and, using architecture design reviews, validate that the application's design changed to remediate the security design flaws such as through the introduction of new countermeasures. During the validation phase, the effectiveness of such countermeasures to protect the application from threats and attack vectors identified during threat modeling is tested by specific security test cases. When the countermeasures successfully pass the security tests, the business can be assured that the countermeasures work as expected to mitigate threats and attacks identified during the threat modeling exercise.

Vulnerability Management

Threat models are very helpful in assessing the risk and exposure of vulnerabilities to the application assets. Another important application security improvement consist of the fact that security issues identified and fixed prior to the implementation and pen tests could reduce the number of vulnerabilities that need to be fixed at later stage of the SDLC such as during the validation phase of the SDLC. This will result in cost savings for the defect management costs associated with vulnerability management. From the defect management costs perspective, for example, using application threat modeling to identify security issues during design is more cost-effective than identifying and fixing them during coding or validation-test SDLC phases. Security issues that have roots in design can be fixed during design and reduce the overall security defect management costs. According to a study from IBM System Sciences Institute, the cost of fixing a design flaw during design is 7 times cheaper than fixing with coding and 100 times cheaper than fixing it during production with a new application patch. According to the same study, threat modeling is also the application security assessment activity that provides the highest Return of Security Investment (ROSI) in application security.

Typically, vulnerabilities with high severity risks take precedence for remediation compared to medium risk while low risk vulnerabilities can be remediated last. After the vulnerabilities have been prioritized for remediation based on their severity, the next step in risk mitigation is to determine the cost for fixing them. This depends on the type of vulnerability and the type of corrective action plan that needs to be implemented. The cost of fixing the vulnerability might differ depending on whether such vulnerability requires a design, code, or configuration change. In essence, the cost depends on the root cause of the vulnerability. For example, some vulnerability fixes might require a change in configuration of the application. These changes are cheaper to implement and roll out than changing the source code and/or redesigning the application.

By classifying each type of vulnerability by its origin and cause, it is possible to determine the necessary fixes. The origin of vulnerabilities is the type of information that tells us that phase of the SDLC life cycle; the security issue is most likely being introduced.

For example, a cross-site scripting (XSS) vulnerability most likely originates during the coding phase and is mostly caused by either not implementing output encoding or coding insecurely and missing the implementation of that requirement. *This type of information is actionable for managing vulnerability risks because it can be used by software developers to fix vulnerabilities in source code during the implementation phase.* An example of actionable information that leads developers toward remediating an XSS vulnerability includes encoding the outputs so that malicious JavaScript will not be executed on the browser.

In the case of SQL injection vulnerabilities, for example, the actionable recommendation for development teams consists of fixing the vulnerability with a source code change and construct SQL queries using prepared statements instead of concatenated strings. The classification of the vulnerability type helps development teams to develop the vulnerability fix. For example, vulnerabilities that are categorized by the type of security control that is affected (e.g. authentication, authorization, data protection, session management, data validation, auditing and logging, error and exception handling) direct the software development team to fix the security control in the application that is impacted by the vulnerability.

For organizations whose software is either developed internally by engineering teams or externally by vendors and only integrated and tested internally, applying threat modeling to the overall application as well as the components that are either integrated or developed by third parties/vendors provides several risk mitigation benefits. Firstly, for applications developed internally, applying threat modeling allows organizations to identify any potential design flaws and remediate them during the SDLC without introducing any risk in the production environment. Secondly, for vulnerabilities either found on external third-party components or exposed to external services and delivery channels, a threat model can provide an assessment of the technical risks during design and require the third party to address these risks before integration with the application. This is, for example, the case of an online banking application that relies on both in-house and third-party financial transaction processing systems and that can be accessed via different service delivery channels such as web, IVRs, and mobile. Because of the interconnected nature of such applications and systems, a threat to one of these application interfaces or channels can exploit vulnerabilities in any of these integrated and interconnected systems and services.

In the case of enterprise software where several complex systems and services are integrated, it is very important to define the scope of the application threat modeling to make sure that all critical components are covered. In the case of an e-commerce application, an online retailer might integrate the functionality to the online catalog-warehouse, shopping cart, and shipping applications. A complete application threat model would need to cover not only threats inherent to the application, but also threats to external components and services that the e-commerce application depends on, such as the credit card, payment services, and shipping services.

Application Risk Assessments

From the risk mitigation perspective, application threat modeling helps reassess the application against new threats and risks. As threats evolve, the exposure to these threats needs to be reassessed. For doing so, it is necessary to revisit the application threat model whenever application risks need to be reassessed or whenever new changes are introduced in the application that might pose new risks. From the business perspective, the main concern is first to understand the potential business impacts, and second, to determine if potential business impacts justify spending to introduce a change in the application to implement a countermeasure. A threat model of the application can help the business make such informed risk decisions to mitigate the risks and, for example, to decide that when the risk exposure is low, the risk can be accepted and that when risk level is high, the vulnerability needs to be fixed to mitigate the risk.

From risk mitigation perspective, a sound risk management practice is to update the application threat model every six months and each time the application design changes. One main reason for updating the threat model is that application design changes might expose the application assets to new threats. By updating the threat model, it will be possible to determine if application changes expose the application assets to new potential risks that require designing and implementing new countermeasures. Independent of changing the application, if the threat landscape for the application has changed and new threat agents and/or attacks need to be considered because they were used to exploit similar applications, for example, the existing threat model might need to be revisited.

From the security governance perspective, it is therefore important to consider updating the threat model with a frequency that depends on the initial risk profile of the application. The specific frequency that the application threat model needs to be updated depends on different risk factors such as risk associated with the classification

TABLE 2.3 Criteria for Threat Modeling Scope

Scope for Application Threat Modeling
Internet facing applications
Business critical function/services (online banking, brokerage-trading)
High-risk transactions (e.g. money transfers)
Access and handling of confidential data
Access and handling of authentication data
Access and handling of business sensitive data (e.g. credit card accounts, bank accounts)
Access and handling of PII
User administration functions

of the asset that needs to be protected by the application and the criticality of the services provided by the application. An example of criteria to decide whether an application should be in scope for Application Threat Modeling is shown in Table 2.3.

By using the criteria for threat modeling scope shown in Table 2.3, applications that are Internet facing and rated mission critical might be required to have their threat model be revisited semiannually. The same process might also require a review of the security of the application whenever a certain type of application change is introduced, such as a change to the classification of the assets and a change of security controls that protect the data.

Examples of application changes that might require an update of the application threat model include any application changes that might impact the overall security of the application, such as any changes to the application architecture and components, changes to the data and the information classification, and changes to security controls that protect the confidentiality, integrity and availability of the data. An example of criteria that can be adopted to determine if application changes should be put in scope for application threat modeling is included in Table 2.4.

Besides time-based and application changes criteria, another event that should be a reason to reevaluate application threat modeling is to reevaluate the application's exposure to new threats following a proactive risk mitigation approach, or reactively in case a security incident causes a data breach or fraud whose causes are still unknown.

BUILDING SECURITY IN THE SOFTWARE DEVELOPMENT LIFE CYCLE

> *"The most critical applications are generally developed internally. Thus, companies should focus on training their developers in secure programming and establishing a secure development process."*
>
> Gary McGraw, Chief Technology Officer, Cigital on PCI reference in Compliance Means getting your App Together, Darkreading security

TABLE 2.4 Criteria for Application Threat Modeling Updates

Scope of Changes that Warrants an Application Threat Modeling Update
Application design to introduce new functionality, processes
Application components, libraries
User interfaces
Data
Data classification
Network appliances, hosts, servers, backend data bases
Network configuration, topology
Integration with third-party components
Design of authentication
Design of role-based access controls
Design of encryption to protect data in transit and/or storage
Introduction of new data filtering, ingress and egress
Communication channels and data flows
Session management controls
Error and exception handling
Auditing and logging

A larger percentage of software used by businesses and organizations today is internally developed in support of business critical functions and processes. In the financial industry, for example, most of the online banking applications, including online trading applications, are developed by internal teams. Typically, internally developed software is subjected to several types of testing before release, such as integration testing and quality assurance testing. The internal software development has also to adhere to the coding standards and the various software engineering activities that are part of the SDLC used by the software development teams within the company. Internally developed applications are also required to be secure and prevent exposing vulnerabilities to potential threats, especially when operating in environments at risk such as the public Internet. For applications whose functionality is exposed through the public Internet, this requirement consists of testing the application for potential vulnerabilities before it is deployed into production. This type of vulnerability test consists of a web application penetration test performed during the validation phase of the SDLC. Typically, when new vulnerabilities that expose the application data and/or business transactions to high risks are identified, they need to be remediated prior to releasing the application into production. Securing applications by testing for vulnerabilities after releasing the application in production is not very efficient for several reasons: the engineering teams need to put off engineering resources to fix vulnerabilities late in the life cycle, eventually impacting the deadlines for the production release of the application. Another reason is cost. It is very expensive to fix vulnerabilities later in the SDLC since sometimes design and coding changes have to be reintroduced to fix the vulnerability and require redesign, recoding, and reintegrating and rebuilding the application so it can be retested to validate that the vulnerability has been remediated. A more efficient way to secure software and applications is to identify and fix security issues earlier in the SDLC such as during requirements, design, and coding. This can be done by adding information security review activities to software engineering activities such as security requirement reviews, secure architecture reviews, and secure code reviews. Another important aspect to consider is securing software by default to engineer secure software by requirements, design, and coding, a process also referred as software security engineering.

Rationale for Integrating Threat Modeling into the SDLC

There are several good reasons to integrate threat modeling activities within the SDLC. Threat models help information security reviews of software projects and assess the risks posed by vulnerabilities identified during the various type security activities that are built into the SDLC such as design reviews, secure coding, and penetration tests. A threat model help risk managers to assess application security risks by correlating the analysis of threats to the vulnerabilities identified in various assessments and these vulnerabilities to application data and functional assets. A risk analysis that factors threats, vulnerabilities, and assets can also factor likelihoods and impacts to determine the risk level and to apply security measures to reduce this level of risk. A threat model of the application also helps software engineers to derive security requirements such as by adopting use and abuse case analysis as part of the formal application design. As secure by design activity, threat modeling helps identify potential design flaws in the architecture that might expose the assets to potential threats and to document requirements in the architecture design documents. A threat model can also be used to derive secure coding standards such as by considering the threats and the vulnerabilities in the source code that these threats might exploit.

For the information security organization to adopt threat modeling in the SDLC, there must be a strong rational since both development teams and business sponsors will be impacted by execution of threat modeling and it is important to communicate the value to all the application stakeholders.

For any security initiative to be successful within an organization, it is important to consider both strategic and tactical goals of threat modeling. One important strategic long-term goal is, for example, identifying and remediating vulnerabilities earlier in the SDLC and possibly reducing the number of vulnerabilities caused by weak security requirements and design flaws that can be identified using threat modeling during the secure architecture reviews. Other important strategic goals of introducing threat modeling during requirements and design phases of the SDLC are actionable recommendations for fixing these security issues, assurance that requirements for threat-risk mitigations are documented and validated during design reviews, and secure coding and tests are used to sign off the application prior to release. From business perspective, an important strategic goal is to introduce savings in defect management costs during validation and tests since there will be fewer expected vulnerabilities identified at this stage of the SDLC.

From tactical security perspective, integrating threat modeling as activity in the SDLC needs to consider where and how it should be integrated. This might depend on several factors, such as the type of SDLC the development team uses (e.g. Agile, Waterfall, RUP), in which phase of the SDLC threat modeling needs to be integrated, and how it should be integrated as part of other secure software engineering activities such as security requirement engineering, secure design reviews, and secure testing and validations. Another important aspect to consider is the integration of these security engineering activities within the project workflows to establish which software changes need to trigger revisiting or issuing a threat model, which technical and business documentations are required to conduct the threat modeling activity, and the expected outcome of the assessment (e.g. threat profile with threats, attacks and vulnerabilities, risk profile),

The main prerequisite for the integration of the threat modeling activity in the software development process is the alignment of software engineering and software security objectives, essentially this means taking into consideration both security and engineering team goals. For organizations that did not yet adopted a process to integrate security in the SDLC also referred as S-SDLC process, integrating threat modeling as part of information security reviews and secure software engineering activities implies a lot of work to do up front to make it happen.

Typically the integration of security within existing SDLC activities, such as documenting functional requirements, designing application architecture, coding, integrating components, and testing quality, requires following security requirements in the SDLC methodology and engineering and security teams cooperating to make it happen. Even before choosing a standard for the S-SDLC to implement, this being MS SDL, Cigital-Touchpoints, or OWASP-CLASP, it is important to assess how mature and capable the organization is in critical areas such as secure software engineering domains. This can be done by assessing the capabilities and maturity of the secure software engineering practices using a standard maturity-capability models yard-stick, such as Cigital-BSIMM or OWASP-SAMM (Software Assurance Maturity Model), that helps to compare these practices against other organizations in the same industry sectors.

Depending on the maturity and capability of the software development organization, the size of the software development organization, and the resources allocated in terms of hiring and training the security engineering workforce, software security process, technologies and tools, the implementation of an S-SDLC process and the integration of threat modeling with the S-SDLC activities might require years. In essence, this is a task that requires following a "Software in the SDLC Strategy" as well as planning and cooperation from security and engineering teams within the same organizations.

Assuming that a strategy for adding threat modeling as part of S-SDLC process, roll out threat modeling training, and develop and/or acquire threat modeling tools has been approved by budget decision makers (executive management) of both the information security and the engineering organizations, the next step is to plan a roadmap and execution for the strategy. The successful execution of an S-SDLC strategy depends on the business commitment to push it within the information security and the engineering teams. Typically, the main obstacle to overcome at the beginning are the common security requirement misconceptions, such as security engineering and security reviews can be thought of later in the SDLC, added security controls to mitigate risk impact, application performance and usability. Adding threat modeling during requirements and architecture design reviews requires extra time and delays approvals in the project workflows. Security teams and development teams must therefore work together toward a common goal while understanding each other's agenda and limitations. Since responsibility of the application's security usually lies not with engineering teams but with security teams, it is important to work together as team and share the effort in terms of resources, processes, training, and planning to make software security a viable proposition for the company.

To plan the adoption of threat modeling with the organization, it is important first to understand the organization's capabilities and maturity in secure application development processes; understanding which application security processes have been followed by the organization and how well they are followed. The big distinction is between organizations that have adopted a "security built in" approach toward software development versus the one that has not.

Software development organizations that have just started adopting application security as one of their programs will probably execute a "bolt on" security on process and apply security to the application after development, such as by testing it for security toward the end of the SDLC and making changes to fix security issues just before release into production. Software development organizations whose application security capabilities have matured over time probably already adopted a "security built in" process and strive to execute several application security activities in different phases of the SDLC, such as architecture risk analysis during design, source code analysis/secure code reviews during coding, and security testing during validation. The implications of integrating threat modeling in these cases really depend on which security engineering model, bolt on or built in, the software development organization uses.

Applications that are developed following a security bolt on model are usually designed and implemented without necessarily performing any preliminary risk analysis or threat model. If an information security policy is enforced with a requirement to test an application for vulnerabilities prior to release, the only concern for security is to make sure that the application security requirements for testing are satisfied by putting the application in scope for a vulnerability assessment. As vulnerabilities can be introduced during design as well as coding of the application, security strongly relies on the vulnerability assessments.

Adherence with Information Security Processes Applications' compliance against information security policy depends on different factors, such as how the information security policies are enforced by the different information security processes rolled out by the organization, the information security review processes and tools used, and the amount of human resources dedicated to these assessments. Organizations that review the security of the data assets, including application assets developed internally, might already follow standard application and information security review processes for compliance and governance. A security in the SDLC process can first leverage information security review processes that already align with the

SDLC workflow activities and add additional security activities to be performed when security teams are engaged to review and assess the security of applications and application changes. For example, organizations that already have rolled out information security reviews during the design phase of the project can leverage this checkpoint to integrate also with security design review assessments, such as architectural risk analysis and application threat modeling. A security checkpoint to test the application for vulnerabilities prior to release in production can have a checkpoint for assigning the risk of the available threat model/risk profile.

In essence, before we start considering adhering threat modeling to the SDLC, we must consider adhering information security review processes to the SDLC. One of the evaluation criteria is to determine how well information security review processes allow security teams to validate compliance of development projects with information security requirements. The assessment of the project scope against information security requirements can also be leveraged to add additional security requirements that are derived by a threat modeling activity such as use and misuse cases. For example, by considering the potential threats, risk likelihood, and impacts of these threats to the application assets due to changes and new features introduced to the application, it would be possible to validate if new security requirements need to be documented in the new project to mitigate these risks. Later on during the design phase, modeling threats to the application is a critical activity to determine if there is any risk of these threats being realized by exploiting design flaws in the application architecture. A model of potential threats, the vulnerabilities that these threats might exploit, and the security controls that mitigate their risks can be used to derive a set of security test cases, such as use and abuse test cases or a battery of attack library tests.

Security test cases that are derived can later be validated via security tests to assess the security of the application against possible threats to the application and application assets. For example, information security policies define the security requirements to protect the confidentiality, integrity, and availability of company data based on the type of data classification (e.g. confidential, PII, restricted, sensitive, internal). The security requirement to protect the assets that are dictated by the information security policy applies also to the application security, as these can be considered an asset since the application handles the data by storing it for a user's later consumption. Based on the data classification, for example, the decision whether to encrypt the data is not made based upon threat modeling assessments, but upon documenting security requirements based on the application threat modeling and use and misuse cases and enforcing them through security governance and application security assessments, such as security design reviews/architectural risk analysis, manual secure code reviews, static source code analysis, manual security tests, and vulnerability assessments.

For a start, to determine the threats to the application and the business, we need to include a step that characterizes the business context in which the application functions, the type of data stored by the application, and the type of processing the application applies to the data. If the application business requirements for the application are already documented, the next step is to derive the security requirements for the application. Application security requirements can be derived from the information security policies and the applicable technology standards depending on the type of the application and the environment in which the application is meant to operate. Deriving security requirements can only be done after capturing business and technical requirements for the application. The engineering team can follow to design and build an application with security controls that are effective in mitigating potential threats based on these security requirements. Using threat modeling to derive security requirements is often referred to as security requirement engineering by security practitioners.

Application security requirements can be documented in different forms: "positive" or "negative" requirements. Positive requirements highlight the expected outcome of the requirement as described in the expected functionality, the requirement could state that the user is required to be authenticated to the application; the authentication will validate the user's credentials, username, and password. As a positive outcome, it allows the user to log into the application and access the application functions. In essence, a positive security requirement describes how a security control is expected to provide a security function, such as authentication and authorization.

Negative security requirements describe how the security control should react to unintended use of the control, such as when a malicious user tries to abuse the control functionality. An example of a negative requirement for a security control is to include a description of how the control would need to function to mitigate a threat. For example, the authentication will lock an account after more than six failed attempts to log in to prevent a malicious user from using brute force on the authentication.

In any application, a use case describes at high level the application functionality from the user perspective and helps derive the application's functional requirements. A use case describes either visually or textually who are actors using the application (e.g. users or external systems), the user's goals (e.g. query data), and the steps required to achieve such goals (e.g. log into the application, input data, process query, retrieve data).

In simple terms, to create a use case, the user of the application is considered the actor and the application function is considered the interaction of the actor with the application. The result of the user's action is also described in the use case as the actor's goal.

Typically, applications that are designed by following formal design methodologies such as the UML include use cases as artifacts for deriving the application functional requirements. Application use cases also describe the application's functionality from the security perspective as these requirements prescribe the security controls of the application, such as user authentication, authorization, encryption, data filtering, user session management, and audit and logging.

A prerequisite of the application threat analysis is therefore being able to capture technical and business data about the application. At a minimum, the threat analyst needs to be able to look at the application documentation, such as business and functional requirement documents as well as design documents. Without the application functional requirements, use cases help describe the main functional characteristics of the application and to describe how the user interacts with the application and the application data. From the business perspective, it is important that a threat analysts first and foremost understands the business context in which the application operates, such as the data assets that the application ought to protect, the different user roles of the application, the type of user interfaces, the type of data that is stored and transmitted, the type of functions supported, and the type of data processes supported (e.g. query data, send data, use service). It is therefore important to understand the business context of the application specifically from the perspective of the application value as the application functionality is considered an asset for the business as well as for the consumer of the application.

Considering the application as well as the monetary value associated to that data as an asset is a critical factor for the threat analysis, specifically for determining the business impact to the organization in case the data asset is either compromised or lost.

Besides considering the data as an asset, it is also important to consider the application itself as an asset for the type of service and functionality that is provided to the customer by using the application. When considering the application functions as an asset, from the defender perspective, it is important to determine which application functions represent the higher risk of being targeted by an attacker. For example, in a financial type of application such as online banking, any movement of money can be considered a high-risk transaction that needs to be protected from an attacker with additional authentication such as multifactor authentication. In any given application, functions that require higher privileges than user privileges such as administrator privileges to create and delete users of an application can also be considered of higher risk than normal user functions.

Since an attacker will seek to compromise the application data by abusing the application functionality with different types of attack vectors, a threat analysis that simulates these types of attacks is extremely useful to determine whether the application business logic can be abused. This type of threat analysis consists of analyzing how the application can be abused by an attacker by deriving the use and abuse cases of the application.

The goal of an abuse case is to describe the possible application abuses, such as the various malicious actions that are undertaken by a threat actor to try to steal confidential data from an application.

An abuse case describes the application abuses visually or textually through a sequence of steps that a malicious actor will follow to reach his goals. Since this type of analysis is also referred as use and misuse cases, it is important to qualify the difference between misuse and abuse. A misuse case describes the misuse of the application controls by incorrect use of the application, such as by error or an act of user negligence. An abuse case is meant to describe the application abuse, for example, when a malicious actor abuses the application with malicious intent for stealing data, steal money, and/or disrupt a service. For the sake of the terminology used in this book, we will refer to either misuse case or abuse case interchangeably since the same type of methodology will be used.

A use and misuse case represents the first artifact of threat analysis and can be used to derive nonfunctional requirements. Nonfunctional requirements help engineering teams build applications that are more resilient to malicious attacks since they are designed to withstand abuse of normal functionality. In software requirement engineering, use and abuse cases describe the various steps that a threat agent will follow to reach his goals. These use and abuse cases are translated in negative requirements, such as "the application will prevent brute forcing attempts of the password by locking the user account after several failed attempts." These negative requirements can be later formulated into testable functional security requirements, such as "the user account will lock after more than six failed log in attempts."

Adherence to Software Engineering Process One critical value of modeling threats to application security is not only the capability to derive security requirements, but also to design applications whose security controls are "risk mitigation effective," meaning implemented by following the principle of security by design.

Following a security by design principle means that security controls are designed by a default engineering process that keeps in consideration the threats to these security controls and the risks posed to the assets that are secured by these controls. From the risk mitigation perspective, in order to assess whether these application security controls are effective to mitigate threats, it is important to conduct first and foremost a security design review of the application architecture and analyze the security of different components, such as clients and the servers located in the different tiers of the architecture including web servers, application servers, databases, and backend servers. This type of analysis is also referred by security practitioners (e.g. security consultants and risk managers) as architectural risk analysis and consists of discovering vulnerabilities in the application architecture that might represent a risk to the application and the business.

Integrating security standards during the requirement phase of the SDLC is, therefore, an important proactive risk mitigation step that security teams should take for newly developed applications and for changes to applications. The security requirements might consider the security aspects of different domains, such as the application functionality, compliance with legal, regulatory and privacy laws, security compliance, and last but not least mitigation of threats against the application assets. Deriving application security requirements based upon input from these domains is not an easy task since it requires expertise to understand all these different domains and the impacts on the application.

An initial check on whether security requirements are implemented into design can be done through a security design review of the application whose objective is to review the application architecture and validate that security requirements are captured and followed in the design. In essence, the main objective here is to identify the design flaws. Once these design flaws are identified, it is important to understand the risk exposure to the application and the application assets: this can be done by analyzing which threats affect the application asset and how they can exploit these design flaws to cause a business impact, such data compromise, function compromise, and monetary loss.

As software security matures and is practiced within an organization, it is more efficient to develop secure software by building security into the SDLC. This is usually accomplished by integrating different security assessment activities in each phase of the SDLC. In the case of secure coding, this means performing static source code analysis during coding. In threat modeling, this means not only performing architecture risk assessments during the design phase of the SDLC, but also using threat modeling to derive security requirements and use and abuse cases that can be later used to test the security of the application.

One of the main values of integrating threat modeling as part of the SDLC, besides improving process efficiency and reducing the costs of fixing vulnerabilities, is proactive risk mitigation. For example, as the threat scenarios evolve, the security requirements need to evolve too to control the risk posed by these evolving threats. Application software that is developed today can only be secure if it is being built based upon security requirements that are derived based on today's threat and attack scenarios as well as newly discovered vulnerabilities.

In essence, this means that the application security requirements need to be derived using a new threat model specifically derived for each application users, data, environment, and business functionality. By using application threat modeling to derive these security requirements, security teams can understand how the application can be attacked (by adopting the adversary perspective) and determine which assets may be targeted by the attackers to make sure that the security measures that are implemented can be effective in mitigating these attacks.

A threat modeling exercise conducted during the imitation phase of the SDLC, such as to derive the security requirements of an application, also represents a great opportunity for knowledge transfer from security teams to business teams. For example, when the results of the threat model are communicated to the business analysis in the form of security requirements, it can be an opportunity to discuss the potential risks that the application might be exposed to and to proactively mitigate risks instead of waiting for vulnerabilities to be identified when it is too late or very costly to be remediated.

The value of integrating threat modeling as part of the SDLC in terms of proactive risk mitigation can be one of the main selling points for adopting threat modeling within a given software development organization. Nevertheless, before any organizations starts to roll out threat modeling as part of the SDLC, they need to consider the potential impact to existing processes, people, and technologies and plan the amount of resources needed accordingly. Since it might not be feasible to apply threat modeling to each software product being either a web application or software service produced by the company because of the limited resources in place, it is worth it to apply a risk scope criteria to consider in scope for the assessment only the applications that are considered high risk for the organization and the customers. As the execution of the application threat modeling process matures within the organization, it might be allowed to extend to cover all applications and software products being developed. The ultimate goal is to execute threat modeling as a security assessment and security engineering activity that is consistently performed by different development and security teams within the organization using common threat modeling methodology, processes, and tools.

Adopting a Security in the SDLC Process

Integrating threat modeling with SDLC activities during requirements and design is a win-win for security, business, and engineering. To realize this, application, business, and development teams need to work closely together to create a culture of cooperation based upon knowledge transfer and understanding each other's constraints and perspectives. For development teams, security is often seen as a feature of the product whose requirements need to be met, often at the expense of usability in order to release the application in production. In essence, it is seen as a tax on the release of the application. A threat modeling exercise can add value to engineering teams only if it helps them to build software with less vulnerabilities, a minimum impact on project resources to fix these vulnerabilities, and without causing any delays on the production release.

In the case of engaging with consultants performing application threat modeling, initial considerations about the benefits of application threat modeling are very important and allow the sponsor of the application threat modeling initiative to get the most out of the engagement. In particular, it is important to capture these in the form of contractual requirements documenting these in the consulting agreements and Statements of Work (SOW) between the consulting company and the organization committing the application threat modeling engagement.

In the absence of a formal threat modeling process adopted by the organization, the reliance on the vendor's threat modeling process is often done on the case-by-case basis to satisfy a tactical need such as to perform a threat analysis of a highly critical application asset for the organization. This threat modeling exercise might have specific goals and requirements such as to determine the impacts of potential threats to the application architecture at a high level. The requirements for this threat modeling exercise might be documented "ad hoc" for the specific risk profile of the application in scope for the assessment. At high level, the main requirements for the scope and objectives of the threat model might be documented after a meeting between the application security team and the application development stakeholders. Since an "ad hoc" threat modeling exercise not yet follows a standard process, it usually not repeatable and is only as good as the knowledge and skills of the threat modeling analysts performing the assessment including the quality of existing technical design documentation and knowledge that is brought on by the application development teams (e.g. architects and software developers) during the design walk-throughs.

Such a threat modeling assessment can be very valuable to the organization since several critical security issues can be identified just based on the expertise of the application security SME and his capability to gather the necessary information to conduct the analysis. Even if conducted informally, such threat model exercise can be very useful prior to and during the design of the application architecture as a preliminary risk assessment. For example, when the architecture of the application is sketched at high level, it is possible translate the security requirements in the high level design of security controls to design the type of authentication required for users and for each server, the need of encryption of the data in transmission and storage, and other security controls including authorization, data validation, session management, error handling, and auditing and logging.

In summary, for providing value to an organization, an application threat model should at least fulfill a few minimum requirements:

> Clearly define the scope and the objectives.
> Provide general documentation of the threat modeling methodology and process including SDLC checkpoints, assessment scope, application changes event triggers, prerequisites, and deliverables.
> Provide a threat profile of the application that allows business to make informed decisions based on information about threats, threat agents, attacks, vulnerabilities, assets, impacts, countermeasures, and residual risks.
> Be actionable for fixing issues and vulnerabilities by identifying origins and root causes.
> Provide a technical and business risk assessment of impact on assets based on technical and business impacts.
> Provide a set of different options for security measures that can be selected by the business for fixing vulnerabilities based on risk prioritizing and measuring effectiveness to mitigate risks.

If application threat modeling is one of the application security assessments performed by security teams or SMEs within the organization, it is important to document the scope of the engagement and the specific requirements for engaging the security team with the threat modeling service.

The goals of application threat modeling will also vary greatly depending on the type of organization. Organizations that produce commercial off-the-shelf software (COTS), for example, might use threat modeling to minimize both security and privacy risks for the client using the software as well as to reduce the costs of fixing security defects. Several ISV (Independent Software Vendors) have adopted threat modeling as part of the SDLC and significantly reduced the number of security bulletins to address vulnerabilities in newly delivered software.

In the case of organizations producing their own software and integrating third-party software in support of business services to customers (non-COTS products and non-ISV companies), the main objective of threat modeling is to reduce application security risks to acceptable minimum levels for the business by protecting both the business and the customers. Examples include organizations that use and develop their own enterprise-wide software such as financial organizations, government organizations, health care, telecommunications, production, logistics, online retailers, and sales-marketing companies.

After a vulnerability assessment of the application is complete and vulnerabilities have been identified, the next step is to decide which ones need to be remediated. One possible approach is to rate these vulnerabilities according to the likelihood of being exploited and the potential impact on the application assets. Assigning likelihood and impact to a vulnerability allows a security expert to determine the risk severity and prioritize it for remediation based on a qualitative risk scale such as high, medium, and low.

The business perspective of security should be considered when new security features need to be implemented to mitigate vulnerabilities identified by an application security assessment. For the business team, security is not the usually the primary concern unless security impacts customer's usability of the application, the application's performance, and the ability to perform business functions and transactions. The main concerns, rather, include implementing new features and products that can generate revenue for the organization, time to market the new product/application/software, and commitment to the deadlines for the product release. From the business perspective, a change to the application due to a security requirement of the costs and time that needs to be spent fixing application vulnerabilities is a detriment to the business since it might delay time to market of the product, introduce security features at the expense of product usability, and incur additional costs for allocating resources to the design, development, and tests of security features and application changes to fix security issues.

Therefore, before an application threat modeling initiative is promoted to the organization, it is important to consider the business perspective and be prepared for push backs with sales pitches. One of the pitches for selling application threat modeling to the business, for example, is cost reduction by saving time and freeing up resources dedicated to fixing vulnerabilities identified with other assessments such as penetration tests. As a matter of fact, when security issues are identified and fixed during design, it requires less effort for the development teams to fix vulnerabilities during validation since a smaller number of vulnerabilities will be left to be fixed later during the validation phase, prior to delivering the application/product to customers. As the security assessments are moved toward the end of the SDLC such as by analyzing threats during the requirement phase to derive security requirements and by using threat models to identify security design flaws, it would be less costly for the business to build security into the application and products. By emphasizing the cost reductions in fixing vulnerabilities and the efficiencies that can be obtained by rolling out application threat modeling as a proactive application security assessment, it is easier for the promoters of application threat modeling to make their cases to the business stakeholders.

IDENTIFYING APPLICATION VULNERABILITIES AND DESIGN FLAWS

"Measure what is measurable, and make measurable what is not so."

Galileo Galilei

One important risk mitigation strategy for any software development organization is to identify and remediate potential vulnerabilities prior to releasing the application to the customers. Typically identifying potential vulnerabilities in software and applications involves the execution of both manual and automated security tests.

IDENTIFYING APPLICATION VULNERABILITIES AND DESIGN FLAWS

Automated security tests consist of running vulnerability scanners to scan the application as well as the source code. After security issues are identified with a scanning tool, they need to be validated manually to determine possible false positives. After security issues are validated, the next step is to assign a risk severity value to the vulnerability. A standard risk scoring method such as CVSS can be used for assigning a risk score. By assigning a risk severity to each of the identified vulnerabilities, it is possible to prioritize them for remediation and mitigate any potential risks of these vulnerabilities being exploited to attack the application and the application assets.

Effectiveness of Automated Security Testing

From the security team perspective, applications are considered secure and ready for release commercially in production when the security has been tested and vulnerabilities have been remediated. Nevertheless, when these security tests consist only of automated security tests, to the security team might have a false sense of security since other types of vulnerabilities might not be found yet with manual tests because of the limited vulnerability coverage of security tools.

The type of security issues that can be identified with automated testing, such as Static Application Security Tools (SAST) and Dynamic Application Security Tools (DAST), are called Low Hanging Fruits (LHF). The security testing using an SAST tool is considered static since it does not require for the application to run, but just to compile source code to conduct the taint analysis and data flow analysis. The security testing using a DAST tool can identify issues in the application and is dynamic since needs the application to execute in order to conduct the assessment.

An LHF type of vulnerability is a common macroscopic vulnerability and therefore within the reach of identification by an automated security tool. For example, a tool can test and identify a cross-site scripting type of vulnerability without any inside knowledge of how the application is designed and/or coded. Note that "not requiring particular knowledge of the application" to identify the issue does not mean the following:

> Some of the instances of the vulnerabilities are false negatives (not an issue) and require a security tester to validate them with his knowledge of the application.
> Several other instances of the same type of XSS vulnerabilities are missed by the tool, also referred as false positives (did not find that instance/issue).
> Several other instances of the same type of XSS vulnerabilities can only be found with a human-based and comprehensive testing, considering the combination of all possible attack vectors, some of which are not part of the tool arsenal, as an attacker will do in weeks of trial and error analysis.

Fixing the XSS vulnerabilities will just require following the general recommendations of the tool without understanding the application architecture and the security options available to mitigate the risk of the vulnerability (e.g. output encoding, input filtering at different layers of the architecture).

For these reasons, it is important to realize that security testing applications and software, by relying solely on automated security tools, are not guaranteed secure. Even with the state-of-the-art security tools available today, such as automated testing, static and dynamic security application testing tools, it is only possible to get instances of potential security issues. These security issues can only be considered vulnerabilities when they are manually validated. Manually validating issues reported by tools is aimed at identifying false positives. Security tools might also miss identifying and reporting issues, leaving the vulnerability in the application. These are called false negatives. The main reason for false negatives is security tool vulnerability coverage. The tool's vulnerability coverage consists of the ratio between the number of different types of vulnerabilities that can be identified by a tool and the overall possible type of vulnerabilities that can be identified in an application. Previous studies have shown that the vulnerability coverage of all security tools combined, static and dynamic, is less than 50%. Because of the limited vulnerability coverage of security tools, fixing all vulnerabilities identified with tools alone does not provide a guarantee of security. Therefore, considering an application and/or software secure because no issues are identified by a security tool is wrong. A more comprehensive test of security vulnerabilities in an application needs to augment automated static and dynamic testing with manual code reviews and manual pen testing. These security testing techniques are shown in Figure 2.2.

Manual penetration tests augment automated vulnerability scanning by identifying other instances of vulnerabilities in the application through conducting a more thorough vulnerability assessment of the application. These manual tests test for common vulnerabilities by following a security-testing guide such as the OWASP security-testing guide. Manual code reviews augment automated source code analysis through a manual review of the source code line by line for possible vulnerabilities.

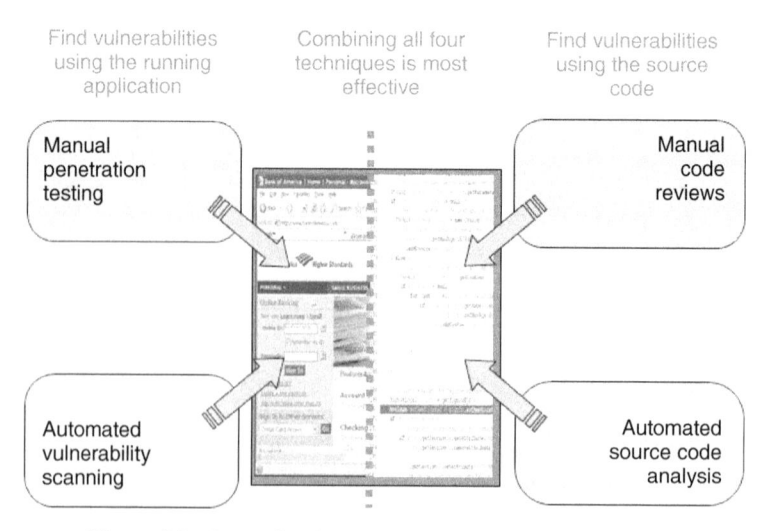

Figure 2.2 Manual and Automated Vulnerability Assessments

IDENTIFYING APPLICATION VULNERABILITIES AND DESIGN FLAWS

In essence, a vulnerability assessment, even when relying on automation/tools, requires human knowledge to assess the validity of the vulnerability findings. A comprehensive application security assessment needs to include manual and automated security testing as well to consider the exposure of these vulnerabilities to different types of attack vectors to determine probability and impact of these vulnerabilities.

Manual penetration testing and code reviews help identify a class of vulnerabilities that is usually not covered by security tools. These are omissions of security controls, flaws in design, and logical coding errors. Logical coding errors can be identified by a source code analyst with previous knowledge of the business logic of the application. Design flaws can be identified by a security architect armed with knowledge of the application security requirements.

Examples of design flaws that can be identified with manual source code reviews might include the following:

- Unencrypted passwords in storage such as when establishing a connection between application server and database.
- Unencrypted confidential data in storage and transit.
- Missing server side validation for potential malicious input.
- Unenforced authorization/role base access controls according to security policies and user access control matrix.
- Insecure exception handling in the source code.
- Not logging security events.
- Not implementing session logout and time outs.

To comprehensively test applications and software for these types of vulnerabilities, automated security tests must be augmented with manual tests, such as manual penetration testing, manual source code analysis, and manual security reviews of the application's design (architectural risk analysis and threat modeling).

Specifically, in the case of security design flaws, it is important to look at the possible causes in the design at the architectural application level so that they can be identified during design reviews. By looking at the possible causes of security design flaws, we can better understand where these design flaws might originate and what that type of vulnerability might represent for the application. Examples of security design flaws that are frequently identified during security design reviews include

- Not documenting a security requirement.
- Failing to design and/or implement a security control (e.g. authentication, authorization, encryption, auditing and logging).
- Leaving a gap in the design and/or implementation of a security control.
- Designing and/or implementing a security control that can be subverted and/or bypassed by a threat agent to conduct a business attack against the application.
- Not designing encryption to protect confidential data and exposing the data to information gathering threats.

- Authentication design flaws allowing a threat agent to either brute force or bypass authentication.
- Authorization design flaws allowing a threat agent to bypass authorizations (such as enforcing user entitlements based on client site parameters).
- Input validation flaws, such as relaying on client side data validations instead of server side validations, allowing a threat agent to bypass input validation to inject malicious data.
- Not logging security events, allowing threat agent attacks to be undetected and/or not conducting a forensic analysis of security incidents.

Since the chances of missing security requirements documentation leading to a security design flaw are very high, it is important to document security requirements as early as possible in the application/software development life cycle. By being prescriptive as to what the application/software is required to implement, it is possible to avoid several types of vulnerabilities. For example, not documenting security requirements, such as the requirement to implement authentication strength commensurate to risk of the transaction, can lead designing applications without MFA. Failing to document a requirement to encrypt authentication data, such as passwords in storage and in transit and restricting the use of hashes to standard hashing algorithms such as SHA-1 and SHA-256 and with salt, might lead to security design flaws that put all the application data assets at risk.

Not prescribing security requirements before coding might also lead to both design and coding flaws, such as not implementing a filter for malicious SQL injection commands before SQL queries are processed by the back end database and not requiring coders to use prepared SQL statements and store procedures to query data in the database.

Documenting the application security requirements is also important for software security assurance to assert these requirements with security assessments. By conducting a security design review against a set of security requirements, it is possible to identify any omissions in the design of security controls in compliance with the application security standards and information security policies.

Since security design flaws are usually not identified by automated tools, they require a subject matter expert/security architect to follow a methodology and to assess the application architecture by using an application security framework that considers both the potential threats to the application as well as the security controls that could mitigate these threats.

Identifying Security Design Flaws with Secure Design Reviews Security design flaws are in essence weaknesses and gaps in security controls that might originate from failure to document security requirements or in errors introduced during the architectural design of the application. The capability of a security team to identify all possible design flaws in an application depends on different factors, such as:

- Adoption of an architectural risk analysis/threat modeling methodology.

IDENTIFYING APPLICATION VULNERABILITIES AND DESIGN FLAWS

- Documented secure application standards.
- Documented design of the application to review.
- Secure code reviews of the application source code.
- Skill and experience of the security analysts.
- Cooperation of development teams to allow information gathering and sharing with the application security teams.

One of the prerequisites for security design reviews is gathering the technical documentation such as architecture design documents and technical and functional specifications of the application. This information gathering can also occur by conducting white board exercises with the lead application architects. To conduct the design reviews, it is necessary to refer to architecture design guidelines and standards, since these documents constitute the basis for validating the application security requirements.

The identification of potential security design flaws is facilitated by the understanding of the application logical and business context of the application more in depth. The business context can be understood by learning about the business objectives and requirements and the type of functionality that the application provides in support of the business objectives. Understanding the business and local context of the application is essential for determining potential business logic flaws that by might be exploited by a threat agent trying to attack the application. For example, assuming that the application executes online purchases by processing credit card data, it is important to understand the payment processing business logic and the controls including security controls such as authorizations and validation of payment data.

After a review of the business requirements, the threat modeling analysts focuses on the review of the technical and functional requirements and the design of the application architecture. One important aspect of understanding the application architecture is the decomposition of the architecture in its basic components such as user interfaces, servers, data assets, and data flows. This step is critical for threat modeling and secure architecture review process.

After the various components of the application architecture have been identified, the nest step of the threat modeling exercise is to determine the exposure of potential threats targeting these components. First and foremost, it is important to consider the potential threat scenarios. Depending on the type of application (e.g. intranet or Internet), the type of service provided to the application's user (e.g. money transfers, payments, filing tax forms, health records, trading secrets on products), and the classification of the data being accessed (e.g. public, confidential, restricted, top secret-classified), as well as other factors that constitute the risk profile of the application, it might be targeted by certain threat agents (e.g. fraudsters, malicious users, or corporate and country sponsored spies) and attacks (e.g. social engineering, phishing, PC infection with malware through drive by download, or exploiting application vulnerabilities and weaknesses in security controls).

To conduct a manual review of the data flows, it is important to document sequence diagrams and data flow diagrams that describe the various interactions of the users and application components with the data. Sequence diagrams, for example, show the data interactions between users and application components arranged in a time sequence. These diagrams are called sequential because data interactions with the various components are shown in time sequence. Sequence diagrams can be used to understand how the various data inputs and outputs are processed by application components and to determine the exposure of the data assets flowing among the different components of the application architecture.

Besides sequence diagrams, another graphical representation that can help a security architect understand how the data interacts with the components of the application architecture are Data Flow Diagrams (DFDs). DFDs help describe how the user's input is processed by the different processing components (e.g. web and application servers) of the application architecture. A simple DFD showing the flow of data credentials for both simple user and administrator and how these credentials are processed through the main components of the web application is shown in Figure 2.3.

In the DFD notation, each architectural component has a different graphical schematization:

- Input and output interfaces are schematized with squares.
- Application processes or functions with circles.
- Data storages with parallel lines.
- Trust boundaries with dashed lines.
- Input and output data flows across each of these components with arrows.

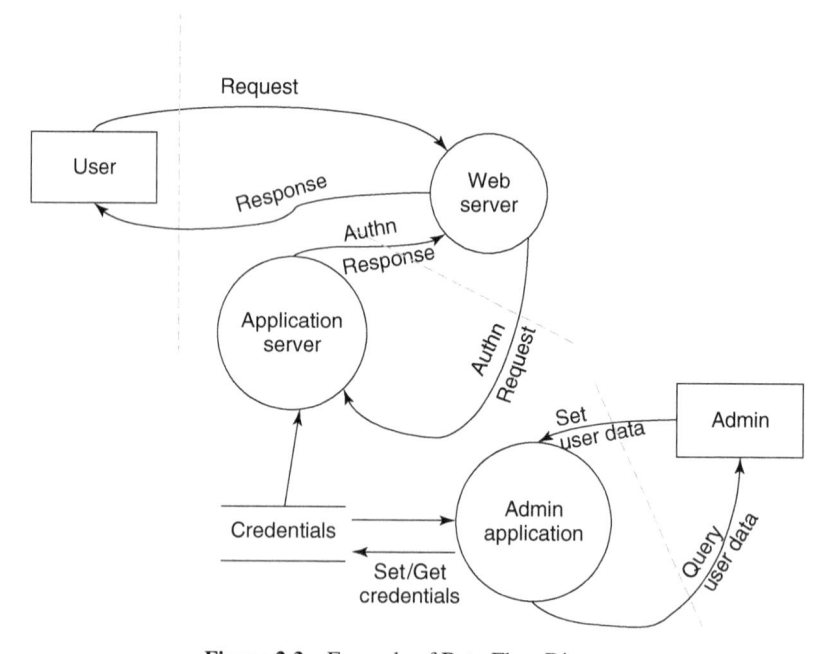

Figure 2.3 Example of Data Flow Diagram

IDENTIFYING APPLICATION VULNERABILITIES AND DESIGN FLAWS   111

At the architectural level, a threat analysis can be conducted by analyzing the exposure of potential vulnerabilities to different threats to the components of the application architecture identified in the data flows diagram.

The most important components to review for potential exposure of vulnerabilities to threats are the data assets, such as database storing confidential information and authentication data such as passwords. When these data assets are identified in a data flow diagram, it is possible to determine the data flows to query these data assets and how the data is potentially exposed while transmitted through the various components of the application architecture. When the potential exposure of an asset to a threat is identified, the next step is to analyze the risk of the vulnerability and the likelihood and the potential impact of that threat exploiting the vulnerability. The exposure of a threat by vulnerability might depend on the type of vulnerability, such as a security design flaw from a weak security control or not applying the security control all together.

Using Threat Libraries

An example of a threat library that can be used to identify the exposure to threats by potential vulnerabilities in application components is the STRIDE (Spoofing, Tampering, Repudiation, Information Disclosure, Denial of Service, and Elevation of Privilege) threat library. STRIDE can be used against the various components of a data flow diagram such as client, servers, backend mainframes, and databases, and the data flows in between to identify potential exposure to STRIDE type of threats. This type of analysis is also referred as STRIDE per element and is part of the Microsoft TM methodology.

A STRIDE per element analysis can help identify the likelihood of threats based upon the exposure of that component of certain vulnerabilities:

Spoofing the user ID to impersonate a legitimate user by exploiting a session hijacking vulnerability to pose as a legitimate user.

Tampering with a file during transmission to change its contents because of no digital signature.

Repudiation of sending a file from an untrusted connection because of not implementing mutual authentication among servers.

Information disclosure of the contents of the file because of unencryption.

Denial of service on a web server because of not limiting the size of the HTTP requests processed by the web server.

Elevation of privilege to access other user's data because of failing to enforce a role base access control on the server to restrict access to the data based upon user's session and user's role.

By taking the attacker perspective, it is possible to determine the potential exposure of the application components to potential threats due to design flaws in the application architecture. Determining these design flaws might be facilitated by using threat modeling as well as by the positive confirmation of the application architecture adhering to the security requirements and the application security standards.

From the threat modeling perspective, it is important to analyze how the data flows across the application components and validates the security controls at each component, starting from the various point of data entry through crossing boundaries to access the servers to reach the data assets. A trust boundary defines the boundary of trust that needs to be asserted as authentication and authorization checks for the data to move across a component, such as a web server, application server, or database server. By visualizing the different trust boundaries within an application, it is possible to determine whether basic security controls, such as user authentication and authorization, are enforced before the user is allowed to access the data under such a component's control. Another important aspect of the trust boundary is whether the connection among servers enforces nonrepudiation with mutual authentication (e.g. client to web before the data can flow across these tiers).

An important factor to consider for identifying design flaws is to characterize the goals of potential threat agents targeting the application assets. One possible goal might be to steal PII for identity theft. One possible threat scenario might include attacking the application to get the PII data by exploiting vulnerabilities in security controls to protect the confidentiality, integrity, and availability of such data. Therefore, a good place to start the threat analysis is to identify where PII data is stored, how it is accessed, and the security controls in place to protect the confidentiality, integrity, and availability.

Another approach to determine the vulnerability exposure to threats is to analyze at a design level how a vulnerability might be exploited at the different layers of the application architecture. Assuming, for example, that there is a known SQL injection vulnerability, we would like to determine how the risk of a threat exploiting this vulnerability can be mitigated by applying different security measures at the design level. These security measures might include for example:

- Input filtering in the web server using a Web Server API such as NSAPI or ISAPI.
- Input filtering in the application server using a servlet filter.
- SQL prepared statements for accessing the database, such as before serving the query to the database.

Because we can tie threats to vulnerabilities and vulnerabilities to the components of the application architecture, we can ultimately determine how to best apply defense in depth to mitigate the risk of the SQL injection vulnerability. For example, we could mitigate this risk by implementing countermeasure at all layers of the application architecture such as web server, application server, and data access components. The follow-up of this type of threat modeling/architectural risk analysis consists of documenting the design of input validation filter, such as NSAPI, to block SQL attack vectors as well as to enforce the secure coding requirement to use parameterized queries and/or store procedures for the application server components used to access the data assets. For complete assurance that security requirements for mitigating SQL injection vulnerabilities are followed, validate that SQL injection vulnerabilities previously identified and fixed with a design and code change can be closed by retesting the application. In essence, these security measures can be designed and security tested thanks to threat modeling during design reviews. The different types of options to mitigate the vulnerabilities both at design and source code level provides engineering teams with several risk mitigation options to choose from. These security measure options can be applied at the different tiers of the application architecture (e.g. web server, application server, or database) in adherence to the defense in depth security principle.

Remediating Vulnerabilities and Design Flaws

Once application security design flaws are identified, the next step is to properly report any issues by highlighting the risk and the corrective actions for fixing them. The corrective actions are usually referred to by security professionals as recommendations for fixing the vulnerabilities and are part of vulnerability assessment reports.

In the case of issues identified during security design reviews of the application architecture, these recommendations should be included as part of the threat modeling and architectural risk analysis reports. Possible recommendations might be documenting a missing security requirement, changing the design to meet a missing security requirement, or fixing a design flaw. The information of how a security issue should be remediated is usually part of the recommendation for each issue and included in the vulnerability assessment report along with the type of the vulnerability and the risk severity. For a finding to be considered actionable toward remediation by the development team, is it important that the recommendation is clear and detailed enough so it can be documented in the corrective action plan. The recommendation would also need to include what the most probable cause of the vulnerability can be:

- Missing security requirements.
- Design flaw (e.g. gap in design of a security control).
- Coding error (e.g. security bug).
- Misconfiguration (e.g. misconfiguration of security control).

Classifying the root cause of a security issue can fall in any of these categories and help the development team address it with a design, source code, or configuration change. Classification of vulnerability root causes is also critical for managing vulnerabilities identified across different assessments such as security requirements reviews, application threat modeling/secure architecture reviews, source code analysis/secure code reviews, and application penetration testing/ethical hacking. Examples of vulnerability root causes might include gaps in requirements, errors in source code, flaws in design, and application misconfigurations.

A security issues categorization that includes root cases allows security professionals to quickly decide where to fix the vulnerability, such as by changing/adding security requirements, redesigning the application, fixing the security bug in the source code, or changing the application configuration to adhere to secure configuration management procedures and guidelines.

The classification depends greatly on how the security issues are identified in the first place. In the case of security issues that are identified by testing the application inside out using testing tools such as automated source code analysis and manual code reviews, the causes of the vulnerabilities are typically either in the source code or the application binaries. The most probable causes of these vulnerabilities are insecure coding or insecure libraries that are integrated as part of the application builds. From a tactical perspective, fixing insecure coding would just require rewriting the code, removing the offending source code, and/or integrating with a nonvulnerable library. From a strategic perspective, the causes of insecure coding errors might be missing secure coding standards that developers can follow, not enforcing these standards, not providing adequate secure code training to software developers, not having dynamic application security testing tools, and not using secure components that are already validated for vulnerabilities.

In the case of security issues that are identified with outside-in type of testing, such as automatic dynamic security tests and manual penetration tests, there might be several origins, such as missing security requirements, design flaws, coding errors, integration and building with vulnerability libraries, or insecure application configurations and the servers where the application run before conducting these tests.

Therefore, when vulnerabilities are identified by testing the application from the outside in, it is not possible to determine "a priori" what the cause of the issue is since what is visible is the effect of the vulnerability and not the cause. To identify the cause of a vulnerability, we need to conduct a root cause analysis to correlate the non-visible causes of vulnerabilities within the application source code and/or design with their visible symptoms, the observable insecure behavior of the application. This type of analysis that identifies the non-visible causes of visible effects is generally referred as a root cause analysis and is exemplified in Figure 2.4.

To identify the root causes of vulnerabilities, it is important not to just stop at analyzing the symptoms but to look under the surface and understand what might cause them. To understand what the causes of vulnerabilities are, it is important to test the application both from outside out and inside in and to correlate the findings of the two types of assessments, a technique that is often referred to as gray box testing, a mix of black box and white box testing.

The black box testing goal is to test the application to identify vulnerabilities from the outside in by considering the application as a black box with no previous knowledge of how the application is designed and implemented. Examples of black box testing include manual penetration tests and using dynamic application security testing tools.

The white box testing goal is to test the application to identify vulnerabilities from the inside out by considering the application as a white box with knowledge of security requirements, design requirements, and source code. Examples of white box testing are source code analysis and using static application security testing tools.

Architectural risk analysis can also be considered a type of white box security testing for identifying potential design flaws (errors in the design of security controls)

IDENTIFYING APPLICATION VULNERABILITIES AND DESIGN FLAWS 115

Root cause analysis

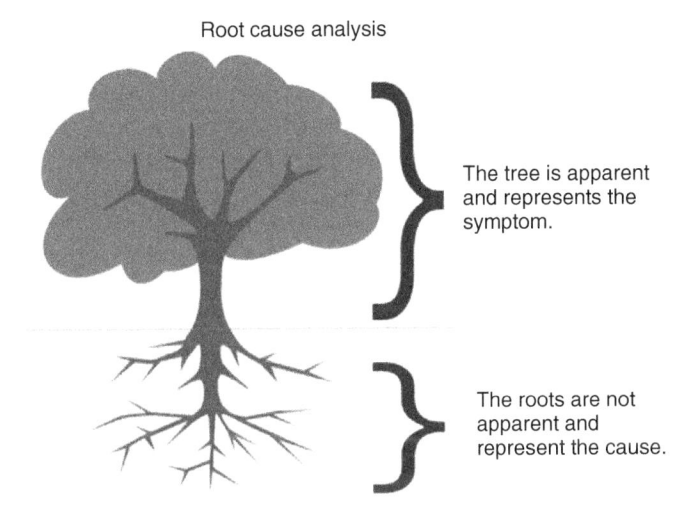

The tree is apparent and represents the symptom.

The roots are not apparent and represent the cause.

Figure 2.4 Root Causes versus Symptoms

and/or gaps (missing designs of security controls). Examples of the design flaws that can be identified include not implementing a security control, such as authentication, and storing sensitive information such as passwords in unencrypted form.

By combining the vulnerability assessments of architectural risk analysis, manual and automated source code analysis, and manual and automated dynamic testing, it is possible to cover different type of vulnerabilities and to correlate them to identify the causes of the vulnerabilities. For this reason, an overall application vulnerability report that aggregates the different types of vulnerabilities that are identified by other security assessment helps a risk manager determine the most effective risk mitigation measures to fix the root causes of vulnerabilities.

For example, security flaws identified with application threat modeling can be correlated to vulnerabilities found in secure code reviews and penetration tests to determine if these are the instances of the same root cause, such as a design flaw identified with threat modeling. A design flaw identified by threat modeling could be correlated to the same design flaws identified with a manual source code review. Reporting security issues by correlating them in one report helps risk managers focus on the corrective actions that address the root cause of the issue instead of the symptoms.

In general, to get the benefit of correlating vulnerabilities to identify the root causes, it is important to plan the threat modelling assessment ahead of manual secure code reviews. A threat model can be used to drive the secure code analysis toward the review of the source code of those components whose design flaws were previously identified in the threat model. The approach to use threat modeling for simplifying source code reviews is also referred as depth-first secure review instead of breadth-first for manual secure code reviews.

In general, the goal of vulnerability reporting is mitigation of the technical risks caused by vulnerabilities identified in the vulnerability assessments. The risk manager's main goal is to fix vulnerabilities depending on the level of risk based on the factors of likelihood and potential impacts to the application assets. Any vulnerabilities of high risk are typically prioritized for mitigation over vulnerabilities with medium and low risks. Once vulnerabilities are prioritized for risk mitigation, the development team must determine how to fix them and document the design and code changes in a corrective action plan. For this reason, it is critical that the recommendation included in the vulnerability assessment is clear and detailed enough to allow the development team to implement the fix. Vulnerabilities that are marked as fixed when it is reassessed through a retest that is no longer present. In the case of automated vulnerability scanning, vulnerabilities should be considered fixed when it is no longer reported by the tool as a finding. In the case of vulnerabilities that are identified with manual testing such as penetration testing, the validation consists of validating that the security test case is negative. For issues that are identified in the source code through either a manual or automated code review, the test consists of either reviewing the source code manually to validate that the offending source code is cleared, or by retesting it with the static code analysis tool.

In the case of security design flaws that are identified through threat modeling and architectural risk analysis, the report needs to clearly articulate the risks posed by the design flaw as well as the recommendation to mitigate the risk. Since the fix of a design flaw typically involves a change in the design, it has to be articulated in terms of architectural changes of the application that can be understood by the application architects. The recommendation can also refer to secure architecture guidelines and standards that can be followed to implement the fix.

Ideally, the organization's security architecture guidelines should include a set of security requirements derived from compliance and regulations as well as recommended technologies and frameworks for designing application security controls. A reference to these guidelines should be part of the recommendations as applicable to each case of design flaws being reported.

Similar to vulnerabilities identified by other type of application assessments, such as source code analysis and penetration testing, design flaws identified through the threat modeling exercise can be classified based on their risk severity. The qualitative risk ranking model used for assigning the risk severity to vulnerabilities identified by other assessments such as penetration testing and source code analysis can also be used for ranking risk of design flaws identified with the threat modeling/architectural risk analysis. One way to rank the severity of a threat-vulnerability is to use DREAD factors (damage potential, reproducibility, exposure, affected users, and discoverability). A qualitative risk ranking of HIGH, MEDIUM, or LOW based on the scoring method, such as CVSS, as well as calculating risk factors, such as likelihood and exposure, also allows risk managers to prioritize fixing these design flaws according to their risk.

An important factor to consider for determining the risk mitigation strategy is the business impact of the design flaw. Design flaws that pose an impact to the business, such as monetary losses when exploited by fraudsters, help build the rationale for risk mitigation to the business that ultimately has to allocate the budget to either implement the fix or to acquire the security technology, process, and tool to mitigate the risk. Reporting the business impact of the design flaw is therefore critical for empowering the business in making the informed risk mitigation decisions.

The recommendations issued in the threat modeling report need to consider the different levels of security knowledge and responsibility, including business, information and risk managers, and development teams. Ultimately, the real benefit of application threat modeling is that it empowers development, business, and security professionals to make informed decisions on how to manage application security risks throughout the software and application life cycles.

Another important factor to consider in vulnerability reporting is that the same application will be reassessed for vulnerabilities during its lifetime. This will include the vulnerability assessment in compliance with standard processes requiring security control effectiveness to be reassessed over certain time periods (e.g. every 6 or 12 months) or because of new application design and code changes.

As new types of assessments are rolled out for the organization, such as application threat modeling, it is important to be able to produce evidence to the business that threat modeling assessments are a factor of proactive risk mitigation and reduction of the overall risk to the business. One measure of proactive risk mitigation effectiveness is to correlate vulnerabilities that are identified earlier in the SDLC, such as during the design phase, due to adopting threat modeling as factor to a lower number of security defects identified later by other assessments such as source code analysis and penetration tests.

Another factor for proactive risk mitigation is classifying security issues by root causes, which is critical to correlate the vulnerabilities found by other assessment. A vulnerability classification that includes a categorization of the vulnerabilities by root causes, such as a design flaw in security controls including authentication, authorization, encryption, and session management for example, helps eliminate these issues before they are implemented and tested with source code analysis and penetration testing tools. The improved efficiency in managing the security issues attributed to threat modeling can also be shown in the vulnerability metrics when the number of vulnerabilities decreases over the lifetime of the different releases of the same application/software products. Typically, these positive trends in vulnerability and risk management are a factor of security activity, better training of the security team, and tools and technologies introduced to improve the security of the applications that are built and security tested.

The training provided to the security team and development workforce is probably one of the most critical factors in producing applications with less vulnerabilities to fix ahead of releasing the application in production. This is the case of applications that are designed and implemented by following security design principles and a security engineering process. Ultimately the threat modeling metrics, including the reports of the design flaws identified by threat modeling, need to take into account what is actionable to improve the security of the application both from the tactical risk perspective (e.g. fixing issues) as well as the strategic risk perspective (e.g. process improvements). From the tactical perspective, actionable security metrics include identifying the root causes of design flaws as well as pointed recommendations and resources on how these can be fixed and prevented in the future. From the strategic perspective, actionable security metrics include recommendations for process improvements, including security engineering and security training. As the author of the book Security Engineering and renowned University of Cambridge professor Dr. Ross Anderson pointed out, "the goal of a good security engineering process is the understanding of the potential threats to a system, and then applying an appropriate mix of protective measures both technological and organizational to control them."

From the tactical risk perspective, measuring the effectiveness of threat modeling might include producing successful trends that show that the organization is getting better at fixing issues. Remediation is now faster and cheaper than without using threat modeling. It is therefore important that the results of the threat modeling exercise provide enough information for the development teams to manage security defects more efficiently: a developer lead or an application architect would need to be able to take the results of the threat modeling and fix the design and/or coding to implement the fix for the security issue/vulnerability.

From the strategic risk perspective, measuring the effectiveness of threat modeling is possible when the organization has reached a certain degree of maturity so that a consistent security process, such as threat modeling, is being followed throughout the organization. Consistency in conducting the process is essential for producing consistent metrics so that design flaws are reported consistently by different security teams independently. This can be achieved when both security and application development teams follow the same methodology/process, take the required security training, and use the same technology and tools. The proactive risk mitigation improvements can be measured as positive trends in getting better at mitigating the application risks, being able to lower the overall risks to the business, and by providing visibility for the organization to become more efficient and effective in reducing the application security risks.

ANALYZING APPLICATION SECURITY RISKS

"Do not think of attack and defense as two separate things. An attack will be a defense and defense must be an attack."

Kazuzo Kudo

Analyzing Threats and Countermeasures

One of the main goals of information security is to protect the information assets such as company data from potential attacks. More specifically, this means protecting the data integrity, confidentiality, and availability.

From the business perspective, company data is considered an asset when data loss might have a negative legal and/or financial impact for the company. This valuable data includes PII, user credentials, and company secrets such as the company intellectual property. From the information security perspective, one of the main security requirements is to protect the confidentiality, integrity, and availability of data assets as well as of the functions that process such data. Protection of confidentiality, integrity, and availability typically requires implementing security controls such as encryption, digital signatures, and authentication and authorization. From the defensive perspective, these security controls include both preventive and detective defenses to protect the company assets, data, and application functions from potential attacks against these assets. Implementing these security controls is often driven by the enforcement of information security policies that define which data assets and functions need to be protected and the protection levels that are required.

The need to protect company assets is driven by other factors besides compliance with information security policies. Protection is also driven by enabling business with customers through establishing trust with the consumers of these assets, such as clients and customers and the service providers of these assets. This establishment of trust between consumers and providers of data assets and services depends on different factors such as evidence that security controls are implemented, evidence of security reviews and vulnerability assessments, and security certification/assurance from third parties that measures are in place to protect the data.

Examples of security measures include preventive and detective controls whose function is to either prevent or detect attacks against the application. Some defensive measures are user authentication and authorization to restrict access to the application assets to authenticated and authorized users, encryption to protect the confidentiality of these assets when they are stored and transmitted, as well as auditing and logging to identify "a posteriori" who gained access to the application assets. Enforcing security policies to protect the application assets is typically based on a defensive perspective of security, not an attacker perspective.

From the attacker perspective, application defenses might constitute a deterrent to prevent attacks against both the application and the application assets. A deterrent security measure costs too much for an attacker to break. For example, an attacker must have specific knowledge to exploit certain type of vulnerabilities. Another important aspect of this is the cost for an attacker to run an exploit. When the cost of breaking a security control becomes affordable for an attacker to exploit, then the security control only gives you a false sense of security. An example of this is cryptography. In 1998, it took the Electronic Frontier Foundation $250,000 to develop a machine to crack the DES encryption algorithm. Today a DES encryption can be broken by an affordable FPGA high-performance computer in a relatively short time (four or five days). DES is no longer considered a secure algorithm by US federal standards.

As the cost for acquiring tools to break into application security controls becomes cheaper, the deterrent effect of the security defenses becomes less important for an attacker. In some cases, the costs to conduct an attack compared to the possible rewards for an attacker, such as monetary gains of several million dollars, can justify the attacker's cost in cybercrime tools. A further justification might come by the reasonable low risks of being caught by law enforcement because these attacks can be conducted in complete anonymity using malware dropping services, attack proxies, and command and control centers hosted in different countries. In some cases, unmitigated vulnerabilities and design flaws in an application might represent an opportunity for an attacker to exploit security controls using relatively inexpensive tools. When this happens, the data breach might be undetected and the public disclosure of the vulnerability and data breach might represent a considerable reputational loss for the company.

Since the threat landscape has dramatically changed in the last 20 years, from exploiting vulnerabilities for fame and notoriety to targeted attacks for monetary gain such as fraud and identity theft, the challenge of who has responsibility to protect the application and the application asset has become much harder. The frequency and volume of data breaches occurring in the last five years represents a worrisome warning for companies today. The question is no longer IF but WHEN a data breach will occur.

Today, an application that is designed just to be compliant with information security policies cannot be considered secure enough to protect digital assets against motivated attackers. Just relying on application security because of compliance and audits only gives the defender a false sense of security. Securing data assets need to take into account both defensive and offensive perspectives of security, not just compliance and audits.

The defensive approach assumes that the application can defend against opportunistic and targeted attacks by focusing on preventive security controls and measures. Examples of defensive measures include following security standards and implementing security controls as required to protect the data and the application from unauthorized access, such as authentication and authorization, protection from malicious inputs by validating all inputs, protection from unauthorized access to sensitive data by encrypting data in storage and transit, and protection from exploits of session management vulnerabilities that can be used to hijack other user's sessions. Some defensive secure activities include designing applications by following secure architecture principles and adopting defensive coding following secure coding standards when developing source code for a given application/component.

The offensive approach assumes that the application can be targeted for opportunistic exploits of source code vulnerabilities, exploit of architectural design flaws, and functionality-business logic flaws. Targeted threats might use attack tools and techniques that are specifically crafted to exploit source code specific issues, specific business logic flaws for which the application is being designed and last but not least specific design flaws. Targeted attacks might also exploit common vulnerabilities but the attack vector might be specifically designed to exploit that common vulnerability type in an unique instance of source code error or design flaw.

From a defensive perspective, the fact that an application has been tested for common known vulnerabilities using generic attack vectors and the vulnerabilities are identified and fixed, is not a proof that the application security controls will not be bypassed and the data breached by an attacker. A simple example would be for an attacker to use social engineering and malware compromise on a host to steal the user's credentials to try and exploit the application business logic post-authentication. The offensive approach is the one that takes into consideration the fact that any layers of the application architecture, such as either the clients or any of the servers (e.g.

web server, application server, database servers, middleware, mainframes), can be compromised by using specific attack tools and attack techniques.

When considering the threat of targeted attacks, it is therefore important to consider all the factors of threat analysis that is the "who" the "what" and the "how" in essence who the threat agents are, what are the assets being targeted and how different attack vectors that can be used against a given application and its asset as a target.

By a general definition, a threat can be defined as a possible negative event whose occurrence might cause a negative impact to the application. The analysis of the potential threats targeting the application needs to take into consideration several characteristics of a threat, such as whether the threat is caused by an external or an internal agent, the type of threat agent (human and not), the likelihood of the threat to be realized (assuming possible points for attacking the application), and the degree of knowledge of attack techniques and tools required to conduct the attack.

For a threat analysis to be consistent and accurate, it is important to follow a threat analysis process step by step. Initially it is important to identify the possible threats and threat agents that could potentially target an application and the application assets. It is therefore important to identify the application's assets, such as the data that is stored and processed by the application as well as the application functions. Once the application assets and functions are identified, the next step is to determine their probability of being targeted. For example, an internal only application whose data is not confidential is less likely to be the target of an attack from an external threat agent seeking to steal confidential information. To conduct the threat analysis in objective manner, it is important to analyze the threat likelihood as well as the potential impact using a threat library. With a threat library, it is possible to enumerate all possible threats and the potential targeted asset types and choose the ones whose characteristics of threat agents and targeted assets match the assets (data and business functions) of the application. By matching the characteristics of the application asset to the potential threats affecting them, it is possible to put together a threat profile for the application.

If a web application is already operational, the theoretical threat profile can also be augmented by considering historical data of security incidents, such as security incidents that have targeted the application or applications that have a similar inherent risk profile (e.g. similar data, functions, and exposure to threats). One example of a data source that can be used for building the threat profile for the application includes the history of data breaches and fraud committed against the same or similar applications.

After building a threat profile for the application, the next step is to analyze the attacks. Attacks are different from threats. A threat represents a potential negative event whose risk be analyzed by considering the likelihood and impact to a certain target. At a high level, a threat describes a potential negative event in terms of threat agents and targeted assets. An attack is the action undertaken by the threat agent to realize a threat. An attack can be described in terms of attack techniques and tools and can be analyzed in terms of the different steps that a threat agent takes to cause a negative impact to an asset. For example, the threat can be described as a distributed denial of service against an Internet application from a threat agent classified as an activist group targeting similar applications in the past (online banking application). The attack involves using a compromised group of hosts to direct a high volume of network traffic and HTTP requests toward the website to exploit the servers processing resources and causing an impact on the availability of the website to customers.

Identifying how threats can be realized through the exploit of potential weaknesses in the application is one of the goals of an attack analysis. Vulnerabilities are considered valid independent of the threat and attack vector used to exploit them. The information provided by the threat analysis and the determination of the attacks is critical to determine how the vulnerabilities can be exploited, the assets that can be affected, and the potential impact on them. Vulnerabilities are not necessarily caused by flaws introduced during design, bugs during the coding of the application, misconfigurations of security controls, or missing a security test, but can be the cause of the lack of all these security controls and measures.

Identifying any gaps in the requirement of deploying certain security controls, such as missing authentication or input validation, represents a vulnerability for the asset that the security control is supposed to protect. A vulnerability such as security control gaps and/or control weaknesses represents an opportunity for conducting a certain attack. The type of attacks and attack techniques that exploit gaps and weaknesses in security controls have negative effects on the data assets and functions that these security controls are designed to protect.

The description of the attack includes the type of threat, the vulnerabilities that are exploited, and the asset impacted, and allows the qualification of the risk of the attack, such as the probability and the technical impact. In essence, attack analysis is a prerequisite for an assessment of the business risks faced by an application. For a security tester whose job is to identify vulnerabilities, exploiting the vulnerability is not required to assess the technical risk of the vulnerability. For a risk manager who needs to decide whether the vulnerability represents a risk to the business instead, qualifying how the application assets can be compromised by an attack such as an external or internal threat agent, the type of attack tools, and knowledge of attack techniques required to conduct the attacks is critical to make a decision on the overall risk of the vulnerability and decide what to do about it.

Some attack vectors that can be used for vulnerability exploits are used by security testers on applications. Often these attack vectors are embedded in security testing tools and are used to positively assert the exposure of the vulnerability by simulating the attack as a real attacker would do, but in a test environment and with test data to avoid any potential impact to either the application or the application assets. Identifying these vulnerabilities is limited to a black box analysis by using attack vectors and observing how the application reacts to them. A more comprehensive security test for vulnerabilities in an application also requires understanding the business logic of the application, how the application is designed, and the availability of source code to conduct a secure code review and identify potential security issues in the source code.

Often vulnerabilities originate prior to dynamic security testing. For example, vulnerabilities might be introduced as design errors and can be identified and fixed through reviewing the application architecture during the design phase prior to black box testing the application.

Other type of vulnerabilities might originate during the coding of the application as coding errors, or during integration with vulnerable libraries and components and during configuration. Vulnerabilities in the source code are not necessarily identified by applying attack vectors, but by examining applications for vulnerability conditions in the source code statically, without running the application. An example of static vulnerability identification techniques include static tainting, which is correlating a potential attack source to a place where the vulnerability can be exploited, referred to as the sink. The source of an attack in static tainting analysis does not qualify the type of threat agent that can be used for the attack, but the type of potential attack vectors that can be used. The threat agent can be internal or external and can be remotely controlled malicious software or a malicious user. Without specifically determining what the possible threat agents are and the attack vectors that these might use to the exploit the vulnerability identified in the source code, it is rather difficult to determine the risk of the vulnerability. This is where threat and attack analysis helps. By using a threat model that correlates the vulnerability with different threat agents and attack vectors, it is possible to determine the likelihood of the exploit and the technical risks of that vulnerability in terms of probability and asset impacted. Once the technical risk is calculated, the next step is to determine the business impact based on the asset value and make the final business decision of what to do about the risks. In case the risk is high and needs to be mitigated, the next step is to determine which and where security controls need to be applied. By using a threat model that includes a threat and attack analysis, it is possible to determine the type of threats and the different layers of the application architecture that can be attacked to exploit the vulnerability and negatively impact the asset. Through the threat and attack analysis, it is possible to determine which attack techniques the threat agents can use to cause a negative impact to the application assets and determine where and which security controls should be put in place to prevent and detect these attacks before any vulnerability is exploited.

Threat and attack analysis is a critical element of any threat modeling exercise and is essential to determine the risks and decide how to deal with the risks. Using information from the analysis and exercise, risk managers make informed risk decisions on whether to mitigate, transfer, or accept the risk. The effectiveness of such threat and attack analyses depends on the analyst's technical and business knowledge of the application and also on adopting a risk framework and a step-by-step process to conduct the analysis so that it can produce objective, consistent, and reliable results.

Analyzing Threat Agents and Threat Scenarios

The NIST special publication 800-30 Rev a, Risk Management Guide for Information Technology Systems, defines a threat as "the potential for a particular threat-source to successfully exercise a particular vulnerability." Characterizing threats is essential for analyzing risks. A threat, either human or nonhuman, is a condition of a possible adverse event that might negatively impact an asset. A threat can be characterized by different factors, such as the type of a threat, the threat source (e.g. the threat agents), and the targets (e.g. application assets).

An important factor in characterizing a threat is the cause of a threat. We will refer to the cause as the threat agent. Each threat has one or more threat agents. Identifying a threat agent is critical for qualifying risk. Risk is defined as "the probability of a threat agent to exploit a vulnerability to cause a negative impact."

A prerequisite to identify the possible threat agents targeting an application is adopting the threat agent taxonomy, which is the classification of possible threat agents. A comprehensive characterization of threat agents should include different types of sources for possible threats including human sources (people-based threats), nonhuman sources (e.g. malware), and mixed (e.g. a blend of human and nonhuman sources).

Examples of human-based threat agents targeting an information system might include the following:

- Political hacktivists.
- Cyber-criminals.
- Cyber terrorists.
- Disgruntled employees.
- Fraudsters.
- Cyber spies (Industrial and Government).
- Fraudsters.

This classification of human threat agents is important to understand the threat agent's motives, their ultimate goals, and the attack techniques and cybercrime tools that are used to attain such goals.

Examples of cybercrime tools that threat agents use to conduct attacks include:

- Malware software such as Trojans, Viruses, Worms.
- Key loggers.
- Spyware.
- Cyber weapons.
- Botnets (client and servers).
- Hijacked hosts and processes.

Nonhuman threat agents might include threats that are not initiated by humans, also referred as "acts of God," that can adversely affect an information system such as:

- a power-outage at a data center hosting an application caused by nonhuman event such as a storm, or
- the destruction of the computer and data resources whose application relies on caused by a fire, earthquake, or tornado.

Once the threat analyst has decided which threat agent classification then to use, the next step is to analyze the probability of these threat agents targeting an application and the potential gains derived from attacking the application.

From the threat agent perspective, an application could become a target when an attack provides a return on investment to the attacker, such as a financial, political, or strategic reward.

The first question that a threat analyst ought to consider is which type of threat agents might attack the application based on the functionality and data assets that the application stores and processes. It is therefore essential to capture the application business context: the type of application functions, the type of application functionality that is provided to the users, and the type of assets that are stored and processed in order to provide such functionality. After capturing the business context and having identified the application assets, the next step is to identify the possible threats agents targeting the application.

For example, a website that provides online services for a given organization, private or public, that is considered hostile by a certain group of hacktivists, could be targeted by attacks to disrupt or to take down the website hosting the application, such as denial of service attacks.

Another example is an Internet web application of a financial institution that provides financial services, such as online banking, whose data processed, includes customers' confidential information such as bank accounts and credit card data. Fraudsters might attack the application to take over the customers' accounts for fraudulent transactions, such as moving money from the bank into fraudulent accounts, as well as to gain unauthorized access to the customers' confidential information.

Identifying the threat agents is critical to the definition of a threat scenario that has the application as a potential target and includes the threat agents, their possible motives, and the likely targets that include both the application functions and the application assets. Different threat scenarios can be derived depending on the business context of the application. Some basic examples of threat scenarios are:

A business critical web application that provides online banking services for customers. Threat agents that have targeted this type of application in the past include script kiddies, hackers and crackers, fraudsters, carders, and organized cybercriminal gangs and groups. The type of attacks include exploiting application vulnerabilities to cause denial of service, defacing web pages, and compromising customers' confidential information for identity theft and fraud.

A site that provides services to citizens to renew a driver's license or pay car registration fees. Past attacks include actors that steal confidential PII for identify theft such as names, addresses, date of birth, and driving license numbers. Other attacks pursued by these threat agents in the past include exploiting application vulnerabilities to cause denial of service, defacing web pages, as well as compromising customer's confidential information for identity theft and fraud

A company website that provides R&D department users access to classified trading secrets and restricts access only to authorized employees. This type of application needs to consider insider and outsider threats for industrial espionage and unauthorized access to confidential and restricted information for financial and business gains.

An intranet workforce web application only accessible to company employees so they can access their salary statements and PII. This type of application needs to consider the risk posed by insider threats, such disgruntled and terminated employees abusing of their privileges to access some other employee's PII as well as damaging the company's reputation.

Deriving the application threat scenarios is a fundamental step for threat and attack analysis because it focuses on the characteristics of a specific threat landscape for the application based on the type of application, the assets, and the application functionality. Applications with similar functionalities and data assets stored and processed might have very similar threat scenarios and become the target of similar threat agents. By deriving a set of threat scenarios for each application, it is possible to focus on specific threats targeting the application, analyze the attacks, and prioritize the security measures to mitigate the risks. Since the threat agents' motivations, targets, attacks, and techniques evolve over time, it is important to keep the threat scenarios up to date by analyzing from different threat intelligence sources, new attack techniques being used, the types of vulnerabilities that are exploited, the reported security incidents, the types of functionalities that are exploited, and the types of data being breached.

Application Assets as the Threat Targets

After having captured the most likely threat scenarios for each application and keeping these threat scenarios up to date with threat intelligence information, the next step is to determine how the threat agents could attack the application and its components to realize their ultimate goals.

At the application architecture level, the focus of the threat analysis is to understand how different threats can target the several components that make the application architecture. In the case of a web application, the attacks that can be used to target the application assets might involve spoofing the confidential data in transit from the client to the server by exploiting flaws implementing a secure channel between the client and the server, tampering with the data to inject malware, hiding the source of the attack to prevent identification (e.g. by repudiating the source), or gaining unauthorized access to confidential information by exploiting weak authentication and so on.

In order to analyze the effects of threats consistently for each of the application components, Microsoft (MS) has derived a threat framework called STRIDE. The STRIDE threat framework is used in the MS threat modeling methodology to identify threats affecting each component of the application architecture. At the application level, identifying these threats points security professionals to security measures that need to be put in place to mitigate the risk posed by the threats. For example, since any data in transit can be attacked, security measures must be put in place to protect the application component from threats such as channel encryption to prevent spoofing, digital signatures to prevent data tampering, mutual authentication to prevent source repudiation, data encryption in transit to prevent disclosure, availability of the connection to prevent denial of service, and enforcement of role base access control while accessing the data to prevent elevation of privileges. By following the STRIDE methodology, a threat analyst can determine whether the application security controls are strong enough to protect the application components from these threats. If an absence of a security control is identified, a design flaw whose potential exploitation from an attack vector could negatively impact the application and the data.

A threat framework can also provide mapping between the threats, the vulnerabilities that can be exploited by these threats, and the security measures that can be adopted to mitigate the risk posed by these threats.

Analyzing how a threat can exploit one or more vulnerabilities to realize the threat agent goals consists of identifying the different type of attacks that can be used to realize these threats. A threat framework can include a predefined set of threats and attack libraries that can be used to specifically attack the several components of the application.

Threats of sniffing/network eavesdropping, for example, might be realized through man-in-the-middle attacks. MiTM attacks work by compromising the client through socially engineering the victim to accept a spoofed certificate that allows the attacker to capture any data traffic in transit between the client and the server. Threats of information disclosure affecting the data in storage and in transit might exploit weak authentication to access the data and weak encryption to protect the confidentiality of the data. Information disclosure threats might exploit input validation vulnerabilities by attacking the application with buffer overflows, cross-site scripting, SQL, LDAP and XML injection attacks, format string attacks, HTTP redirection, and response splitting attacks.

When conducting a threat analysis of the threats affecting different components of the application architecture, using a threat modeling tool that incorporates threat frameworks, such as STRIDE, and automates threats generation based on the information of the application components can be very useful. A threat modeling tool might include a visualization tool to capture the architecture logical diagrams depicting the different components of the application architecture such as user interfaces, data interfaces among components, and the different components such as web servers, application servers, databases, mainframes, and middleware components. Such visualization tools can be used to decompose the application into the different components and help identify the threats that affect each component. The characterization of the application architecture in components also helps identify the data flows, data interfaces, and trust boundaries that need to enforce authentication and authorization controls for the application users.

A threat modeling tool, such as the MS threat modeling tool, drives the threat assessment from the perspective of protecting each element of the application architecture from possible exploit of vulnerabilities that might result on a compromise of the data as an asset whose confidentiality, integrity, and availability need to be protected. By considering the threats, the vulnerabilities, and the impact to the data assets, the threat modeling tool facilitates the threat analysis by taking into consideration both the attacker and the defender perspectives.

Analysis of Attacks and Exploits of Vulnerabilities

An attack can be defined as the realization of the goals of a threat. An attack describes how a potential negative event is realized by describing how the source might use different types of attack tools and techniques that exploit previously known application vulnerabilities to cause a negative impact to the application assets that include both application functions and application data. An opportunistic attack might exploit common application weaknesses in the security controls, such as vulnerabilities in authentication and authorization, protection of confidential data, as well as gaps in detective controls such as auditing and logging and secure event monitoring.

A targeted attack will seek to identify first what defenses are in place by trying different attack techniques and by changing the attack vectors until the defenses can be bypassed. By comparison with opportunistic attacks, targeted attacks are more time-consuming for an attacker and require the attacker to adjust the attack to the defenses in place to try to bypass them and gain access to the application. Behind targeted attacks, there are typically motivated threat agents whose time and effort are justified by the financial gains and high return on investment of the time and resources spent attacking the application.

The extent to which a threat can be realized through an attack depends on different factors, such as the probability of success of the attack due to exploiting known vulnerabilities as well as the potential gains that might justify a threat agent acquiring knowledge of new attack techniques and investing in more powerful attack tools. It is important to look at these factors more in depth to analyze the possibility of an attack's success. Some factors that influence the success if conducting an attack are:

- Public information about the organization and press information that exposes it as potential target by motivated attackers.
- Public events that might facilitate the attacks such as company holidays or increased online shopping during holidays.
- Easiness of conducting the attack due to availability of attacking scripts and limited knowledge needed to run them.
- Knowledge and experience of the attacker/threat agents.
- Availability of information on how to conduct the attack (e.g. information shared among threat agents).
- Availability of tools for exploiting the application vulnerabilities.
- Availability of tools specifically designed to attack the application (e.g. banking malware).
- Reproducibility of the attack techniques to exploit a known vulnerability.
- Reliance on manual and automatic methods to conduct the attacks.
- Level of skills required to conduct the attack.
- Costs of tools and resources necessary for the attack, such as free attacking tools or tools that attackers can afford.
- Exposure of the application (e.g. attack surface) to the attacker.
- Exposure of the application vulnerabilities that can be either necessary or useful to conduct the attack.
- Public information about the application vulnerabilities and exploits.
- Not yet published vulnerabilities (e.g. zero-day).

ANALYZING APPLICATION SECURITY RISKS 129

- Public information about the application's inner workings such as source code, patents, technology stack and so on, which might facilitate discovering vulnerabilities and conducting the attack.

One methodology that helps analyze how a threat can be realized through different attacks is to use attack trees. An attack tree allow risk professionals to analyze different attacks by starting from the attacker's main goal and walking through the branches of the attack tree to determine the different ways the attacker's goal can be realized. Each branch of the attack tree represents possible opportunities for the attacks to be realized. Examples of these opportunities include the availability of vulnerabilities to be exploited, the availability of attacking tools, and knowledge of attack techniques that the attacker might have or need to acquire. In essence, each of the attack tree paths represents a possibility for an attacker to attack the target.

Once all attack paths are explored with an attack tree, it is also possible to determine which one among these attack paths an attacker would most likely pursue. The most likely attacks are the ones that have a high return on investment; the ones that minimize the cost in time and resources for the attacker goal while maximizing his gains. The top of the attack tree represents the attacker's main goal. By walking the attack tree from the root to the different nodes of the branches, it is possible to analyze all the different attack scenarios, explore the different attack paths, and validate the opportunities for an attacker to achieve his goals.

From the defensive perspective, understanding all possible avenues for an attacker to pursuit allows risk managers to identify the security measures that can be put in place to prevent these attacks. A very simple example is the condition of a vulnerability exploit necessary to pursue a certain attack path. Remediating that vulnerability will represent a lost opportunity for an attacker and will stop his attack at that node of the attack tree where the condition of the vulnerability is necessary to move further toward the attacker's goal.

The first step in analyzing an attack tree is to qualify what the possible goals of an attacker are. There are different types of attackers or threat agents, and each threat agent might have one or more goals to achieve by attacking the asset, application data, and application functions.

It is important to identify first and foremost which threat agents' goals would make them most likely to target the application. These agents pose the greatest risk to the application. If the goal of a threat agent is to commit fraud with credit card data, for example, one option for the threat agent is to attack either the credit card holder or a website that gives the credit card holder access to credit data information and transactions, such as requesting a credit card balance, linking the credit card to a bank account, and transferring money from that bank account to pay off the credit card.

Since attacking the credit card holder is much less expensive for an attacker than trying to attack the credit card web application, he will attack him first. An easy social engineering attacks directed toward a credit card holder is to use phishing e-mails with malicious links or malicious e-mail attachments that install malware on the credit card holder's PC to capture any website credentials with a key logger. Besides phishing, the attacker might try to use tools that exploit vulnerable web servers to install malicious software that infects site visitors through drive-by-download techniques and exploit of common browser vulnerabilities.

In case the selected attacks fail, the attacker might decide to attack the website directly by opportunistically exploiting common vulnerabilities such as XSS and SQL injection. If unsuccessful, the attacker might try a set of blended attacks that use phishing and drive by download to install Trojans that perform man in the browser attacks, or use more sophisticated attacking tools that allow him to capture the credit card data while in transit between the client browser and the application with man-in-the-middle attacks.

All these attack paths that could be pursued by an attacker can be documented in an attack tree to visualize how an attacker could pursue his goals based upon opportunities (e.g. vulnerabilities, exposure to data and functionality) and preconditions (e.g. attacker tools, knowledge and experience of vulnerabilities and exploits). To better analyze attack scenarios, using attack trees allows risk managers to explore the "what if" scenarios and understand how the attack can be realized. By assigning each node of the tree factors that qualify the likelihood (e.g. how easy and exposed is the vulnerability that can be exploited), it is also possible to estimate the attacks that are most probable or improbable to occur. By assigning a cost for the exploitation of the vulnerabilities, it is possible to estimate the attack scenarios that require the least resources. The combination of these criteria helps determine the attacks that are most probable and less expensive to exploit. The attacks that are most critical for likelihood and impact are the ones that need prioritized remediation.

Attack scenarios that are preventively analyzed using attack trees are also very useful for determining the best way to respond to a security incident by deciding which security measures are most effective to stop an attack. Attack tree analysis can provide useful information for incident response procedures during the preparation and identification phases. When attack scenarios are analyzed with an attack tree, it is possible to trace the possible conditions that might lead to an attack and devise the appropriate countermeasures to contain and mitigate the attack and similar incidents.

The attack tree analysis provides a methodology for a threat modeler to analyze graphically or textually the different possible means or ways to realize the attacker's man goal. Assuming that the attacker's main goal is bank account compromise, for example, the attacker could attack the user credentials to log into the application via social engineering/phishing attack or by trying to brute force the authentication. By using attack trees, it is possible to identify the main goals for the attacker and the means to deliver such attacks by exploiting different vulnerabilities.

An attack tree that visualizes many attack scenarios can help visualize these attacks. The attacker can try to exploit input validation vulnerabilities by attacking the communication channel between the user and the application, such as in the case of MiTM.

Data protection vulnerabilities, for example, can be exploited to get the user's credentials by sniffing them while in transit. The data flows between the user and the application help visualize the necessary controls to validate the data input at the entry points of the application tiers before being processed by the application components.

ANALYZING APPLICATION SECURITY RISKS 131

Vulnerabilities in authorization controls, for example, can be exploited by an attacker to elevate privileges through session hijacking. The threat model can visualize the several trust boundaries that can be bypassed or broken to gain access privileges to the application components and data assets.

For a threat model to be effective, all potential attack scenarios and attacker goals must be considered. Depending on the data and functional assets of the application, this will include any data assets, such as the customer's sensitive and confidential data, the user credentials, and the business functions-services offered to the customers through the application.

By identifying potential vulnerabilities in security controls and mapping these to the threat agents, attack vectors, and malware tools that can be used against the application, it is possible to determine the risk posed by the application vulnerabilities and prioritize them for remediation based on the risk that they pose. At this point of the threat analysis, a threat model can be used in conjunction with other vulnerability assessments, such as penetration testing and source code analysis, to assess the likelihood and business impact that exploiting these vulnerabilities might cause.

Identifying all possible threats and vulnerability scenarios can be a daunting task for a threat analyst, since in the real attack scenario an attacker might try a combination of several attacks that exploit all possible vulnerabilities in the application. From a defensive perspective, it is more important to focus on the most critical threats, such as the ones that are most likely to be realized and cause the most business impact.

In the case of attackers targeting a web application, for example, it is important to focus on characterizing the main threats and how these threats can be realized by the different attack vectors by exploiting vulnerabilities. An example of attacks and possible vulnerability exploits is provided in Table 2.5.

Mapping threat agents to attacks and attacks to vulnerabilities that these threat agents can exploit allows a threat analyst to get a better understanding of how potential threats to the application and the data can be realized through exploiting application vulnerabilities as well as weaknesses in security measures and controls at the high level.

Another factor to consider in attack analysis is identifying the attack surface. The attack surface represents the extent to which a target is exposed to potential attacks, such as through different entry points, either internal or external. An application that can be accessed through different interfaces, both web and mobile, has a larger attack surface than a web only access.

Entry points and access levels are also important factors to consider. The data entry points identified with a data flow diagram and document on the level of authentication and authorization required to access the data for different users is a very critical factor to determine the exposure of a given application to attacks. Entry points can also be qualified as high risk when they are exposed to external users whose access to the application is allowed from both visitors and customers from untrusted client browsers and desktops. Entry points are considered medium risk when they are only accessible to internal users whose client browsers and desktops can be trusted, since they are subjected to more restrictive security controls such as patching, event monitoring, intrusion detection, and prevention systems.

TABLE 2.5 Mapping of Threats to Vulnerabilities

Attack	Possible Vulnerability Exploits
Social engineering – phishing a user to deliver malware (*)	Luring users to select links to sites that are vulnerable to cross-site scripting, cross-frame scripting, cross-site request forgery, HTTP response splitting, and invalidated redirection flaws.
Attack application entry points to exploit application vulnerabilities	Weak encryption in storage and transit, weak authentication, weak enforcement of user authorization, forceful browsing, design flaws in business rule enforcement, authorization flaws, lack of input validation, access to data using insecure references to objects and resources, malware injection, exploiting lack of input validation, remote file inclusion, file upload vulnerabilities, lack of mutual authentication between client and server, unrestricted access to resources/systems, and lack of enforcement of minimum privileges and user roles to access data.
Attack the application session (account take over) to cause fraud and monetary loss	Client PC and browser vulnerabilities leading to malware compromise enabling online session and account take over. Additionally, exploiting site session management and authorization flaws and lack of adequate machine tagging information, logging, monitoring, and fraud detection to monitor, detect, and alert for occurring fraud.

(*) Note: social engineering a victim can be used to collect sensitive information directly from the user by redirecting the victim to a malicious link or indirectly by installing malware with key-logging capability.

Once all avenues of attacks against an application have been explored, it is important to determine the path of least resistance for an attacker. The attacker's path of least resistance is the one whose vulnerabilities are easier to exploit, or the attack paths that exploit gaps in security measures.

Any vulnerability or security control gap that is part of an attack path of least resistance needs to be prioritized for remediation since they represent the highest probability of exploit in an attack. By prioritizing vulnerabilities based on the likelihood of the exploit, risk managers can ultimately make better decisions on how to mitigate risks.

Analysis and Management of Application Risks

The risk exposure of the various data assets of an application depends on different factors, such as the availability of a user interface with data entry points that can be exploited, pre-authentication application functionality that can be attacked, unenforced data protection, and unprotected access to data. Any vulnerability in the application that allows an attacker to break into the application and gain unauthorized access to application assets represents an opportunity for exploit and could lead to a negative impact for the organization whose responsibility is to protect that data. It is important to look at each opportunity an attacker has to attack the application as a potential risk. The mitigation of the impact of this risk consists of removing the opportunity by protecting that application functionality and the data with a security control, removing the vulnerability, removing the functionality and the data, or making it difficult and expensive for an attacker to attack the application and the data by strengthening the security controls around it (e.g. adding MFA).

It is important to analyze the different layers of defense in an application and to analyze the different data interfaces and user interfaces and the possibility that these might be attacked by a threat agent. Assuming, for example, that an external threat agent's goal is to gather confidential data stored in an application database, he will consider different possible attacks. If the application is found to be vulnerable to SQL injection, the attacker would try to exploit this vulnerability first. If it does not appear that an application can be attacked pre-authentication with SQL injection vulnerabilities, the attacker will try to exploit other vulnerabilities, such as XSS to run scripts on the browser and steal user session cookies as well as run key loggers and proxies to entice the use to accept spoofed SSL certificates to spoof the channel with MiTM attacks.

The likelihood of the attack's success to exploit post-authentication vulnerabilities is usually much lower than pre-authentication. Nevertheless, there are other vulnerabilities that can exploited by attacking the client directly, such as browser vulnerabilities and social engineering attacks such as orchestrated phishing campaigns whose objective is to infect the client host and steal web application credentials to log into the application. Since multiple application layers can be attacked by a threat agent, data asset protection from potential impacts ought to employ multiple layers of protection according to "defense in depth" principles.

A threat modeling exercise that visualizes the different layers of the application architecture by decomposing it to architectural tiers that include front end interfaces, middle tier web servers, application servers, and backend tiers that include the data assets stored in databases and main frames, allows the threat modeler to validate if defense in depth principles are followed when designing the application architecture. After trust boundaries are identified and authentication and nonrepudiation controls are assessed at each tier of the application architecture, the next step in the threat analysis is to determine how the other components of the architecture, such as the data connectivity among servers and the processes themselves, are exposed to potential threats. The simplest way to look at threats impacting data flows and processes is to consider threats that impact data and process security attributes, such as the data confidentiality, integrity, and availability.

Once the likelihood and impact to the confidentiality, integrity, and availability of the data are evaluated, it is possible to qualify the risk as a factor of probability and impact. The evaluation depends on the technical risk model used to calculate the risk. One technical risk model that can be used to rank the technical risk of vulnerabilities is the industry standard MITRE CVSS model. This model makes it possible to rank the risks of vulnerabilities by assessing several intrinsic and nonintrinsic factors (e.g.

change of risk over time or environment factors); the basic factors of exploitability and impact.

According to CVSS, the intrinsic risk of vulnerability can be assessed for the following factors of exploitability:

- The vulnerability could be exploited remotely.
- Any pre-authentication condition required to attack.
- The complexity of the attack to exploit the vulnerability.

The following factors can be used to assess the impact of a given vulnerability:

- Exposure to confidential data.
- Possibility of damaging the data integrity.
- Possibility of impacting the data availability.

Analyzing the application architecture and exposure of the architectural components to potential threats can also be used to determine the CVSS factors of exploitability (likelihood) and impact and rate any vulnerability that is identified in a threat model. The information captured in a threat model, for example, can help determine whether vulnerabilities in an application are exposed to attack from a remote threat agent and if this threat agent has access to the vulnerabilities pre- or post-authentication.

The impact of the vulnerability can also be assessed by identifying any exposure of the confidentiality, integrity, and availability of the data due to presence of the vulnerability. For example, with a threat model that includes a data flow analysis, it is possible to analyze the flow of data from a threat agent attacking an external interface to the data storage component that can be impacted. If the data storage element stores confidential data, the vulnerability might have an impact on the data confidentiality and integrity.

By analyzing the data flow, it is also possible to determine if the vulnerability exposes the confidentiality and integrity of the data in transit. For example, assume that sensitive data can be transmitted between the user's browser and the web server. If the data is not protected with encryption during transmission, data confidentiality and integrity is exposed to spoofing, tampering, and information disclosure threats by a remote agent. Furthermore, if the connectivity between the web server and the application server is not authenticated and protected, attacks against authentication data might be exposed to repudiation threats post-authentication.

In case a vulnerability is found post-authentication, the probability of a threat agent exploiting it is diminished because the threat agent has to exploit weaknesses in the authentication first in order to gain access to the vulnerability and trying to exploit it. In the absence of a pre-authentication vulnerability, it is more difficult but not impossible for the threat agent to exploit it.

The easier attack for the threat agent at this point would be to try social engineering user to select a malicious link or malicious attachment in an e-mail whose end result would install malware on the client, such as a key logger to capture online credentials. Since the application users are among the weakest links in any security control, the threat agent would likely attack them first. This type of attack would also be facilitated by vulnerabilities that can be used to attack the client, such as XSS, XFS, and CSRF.

The least likely attack, but not as difficult, would be brute forcing the password to access a web application. In any case, the presence of another vulnerability that can be exploited pre-authentication would increase the probability of any post-authentication vulnerability. For example, a post-authentication SQL injection vulnerability can be rated as a MEDIUM risk when it is only exploitable post-authentication. However, in the presence of vulnerabilities that have collateral damage, such as weak authentication, the exploitability risk of a post-authentication vulnerability, such as SQL injection, should be increased from MEDIUM to HIGH. Examples of weak authentication vulnerabilities include using weak passwords policies (length of the password is too short or the format is nonalphanumeric), laws in the design of the authentication such as no rules to lock the user account for failed login attempts, too informative error messages when validating usernames and passwords, and usernames cached in memory and cookies or temporary files.

A threat model can also provide information to rate the complexity of an attack and help quantify the attack complexity risk factor. Typically, attack complexity analysis is best conducted using attack trees. Through attack tree analysis, it is possible to analyze the different avenues of attacks and exploits of vulnerabilities and also when an attack might be easy to exploit, such as when vulnerabilities are known and the type of tools and knowledge of the attack techniques are not difficult to obtain.

Using the CVSS model to determine the risk severity of the vulnerability, it is possible to assess the technical impact that vulnerabilities might cause to the confidentiality, integrity and availability of the data. The information provided by a threat model helps assess the factors of probability, such as exposure of the vulnerability to a threat agent, and impact: whether the vulnerability might be exploited to impact a data asset whose confidentiality, integrity, and availability need to be protected. Furthermore, when the technical risks due to vulnerabilities are qualified as HIGH, MEDIUM, and LOW risks, the next step is to associate the potential business impacts of such vulnerability exploits. A standard methodology to quantify the business risks is the quantitative risk analysis. This analysis calculates the value of the asset that can be lost in a single event, such as a security incident, whose cause is the exploit of a vulnerability factored by the frequency of this security incident measures on the yearly basis.

Based on an exploited vulnerability's economic impact to the organization, it is possible to make informed risk decisions, whether to accept the risk, mitigate the risk by applying a countermeasure, or transfer the risk to an external entity. Since the risk of the vulnerability exploit is monetized, it is possible to make decisions on whether to mitigate the risks by factoring the cost of the security measures and the potential economic impacts in case the vulnerability could be exploited. An investment in security measures, such as the remediation costs for fixing the vulnerability, is justifiable when the cost of the security measures is a fraction of the costs that the business will incur if the vulnerability were exploited. That cost is calculated based on quantitative risk analysis.

It is common sense, for example, not to spend on security measures per year to mitigate the vulnerability more than the possible economic loss that the vulnerability is estimated to produce in a given year. The challenge of this approach is not how much to spend, but to produce a reliable estimate of how much the organization should value an asset in case an incident causes the loss of the asset. The value of the asset needs to be estimated by considering both direct costs and indirect costs that are difficult to estimate. Direct costs associated with an asset either lost or compromised in a security incident vary. Typically, security incident direct costs include the cost for responding to and recovering from the security incident (incident response costs), the costs for fixing the vulnerability that caused the incident, and the costs for replacing the asset that is lost (account numbers). Indirect costs are associated with tangible expenses, such as legal costs in case third parties take legal actions because of the incident, regulatory fines and audit costs, loss of future revenues due to loss of existing customers, clients, and investors as they react to the incident, as well as intangible loss, such as company reputation. In case the security measures cost too much, the business could consider transferring the risk to a third party that is willing to provide service based on taking a liability of a potential loss as well as by signing cyber insurance with a legal entity willing to insure the organization for the potential losses.

3

EXISTING THREAT MODELING APPROACHES

SECURITY, SOFTWARE, RISK-BASED VARIANTS

"Knowing your own darkness is the best method for dealing with the darkness[es] of other people."

Carl Gustav Jung, Swiss Psychiatrist

As the subject around application threat modeling evolves in both theory and practice, the readers of this and any other related literature should judiciously apply the methodology and techniques that are appropriate to the time and resources of their respective enterprises. This chapter addresses three major methodologies in application threat modeling in order to provide objective insight across each one and denote the strengths and limitations of each. Among the present methodologies and those that may unfold in the future, there is not a wrong or a right methodology, but simply one which accomplishes varying objectives. Although none of these methodologies are flawed, the manner in which they could be selected can be flawed, particularly if the status quo approach to mainstream security is followed, which is simply a process riddled with imitation and the "best practice" speak. Candidly, the best practice of this and any other methodology is one that considers the unique variables that ultimately will be charged with deploying, sustaining, and adhering to such methods. As demonstrated in Chapter 1, application threat modeling involves time, talent, and resources of so many groups beyond those in information security. It is a process that naturally

---

Risk Centric Threat Modeling: Process for Attack Simulation and Threat Analysis, First Edition.
Tony UcedaVélez and Marco M. Morana.
© 2015 John Wiley & Sons, Inc. Published 2015 by John Wiley & Sons, Inc.

fosters collaboration, therefore, the methodology selection should strongly consider how collaboration can be supported and sustained via the right methodology, amidst common challenges that may be present in an organization, such as red tape, power struggles, bureaucratic red tape, and so on. Ultimately, the group or leader charged with formalizing application threat modeling should begin by determining what the overall business objectives are for implementing this new process.

There are numerous publications surrounding security and IT-related frameworks and methodologies that exist. Within those publications, there is generally little guidance as to how such methodologies and frameworks actually translate into successful launches within large organizations. As a result, this chapter is devoted to formulate the successful criteria that make threat modeling conducive to more effective forms of security risk management of an organization.

Right versus Appropriate Threat Modeling Methodology

Most professionals in any industry segment who have worked a substantial amount of years within a large enterprise, comprised of many diverse and complicated initiatives, will recognize that introducing a new process into an existing department or enterprise level process is risky business. Multiple factors can unravel the best of project plans, intentions, and corporate initiatives. As infamously coined by Bruce Schneider, security is indeed a process, and that process is ever changing, or at least it needs to be if it is to endure and mitigate the shifting landscape of threats against information sources.

As with any process, there is a starting point, and such a starting point is pivotal in supporting the various cornerstones of application threat modeling. Assuming executive sponsorship of application threat modeling within a given organization, there may be enormous pressure to achieve many of the theorized goals reflected in today's methodologies. As a result, organizations may elect to follow an application threat model based on where they see themselves versus what they realistically can achieve with their given resources. A maturity model would be appropriate in this situation to provide a form of measuring the adoption and use of an application threat model or methodology.

To distinguish between the *right* and *appropriate* methodology for an organization, an assessment of the following internal capabilities should be performed (Figure 3.1).

Properly assessing the aforementioned areas encompass a multitude of underlying processes, too numerous to mention and some more vast in number than others, depending on the size of the organization. Assessment efforts aimed at evaluating threat modeling as a possible new model for security software assurance will have to review the capacity in which these key areas are developed within their own domains of operation as well as the level of interoperability among them. A listing of these four IT and IS areas does not adequately provide the level of detail to fully understand how threat modeling is aimed to encapsulate processes within these areas to become fully optimized. The following sections will further describe each process and correlate to threat modeling efforts so that the *appropriate* methodology is selected for current

SECURITY, SOFTWARE, RISK-BASED VARIANTS

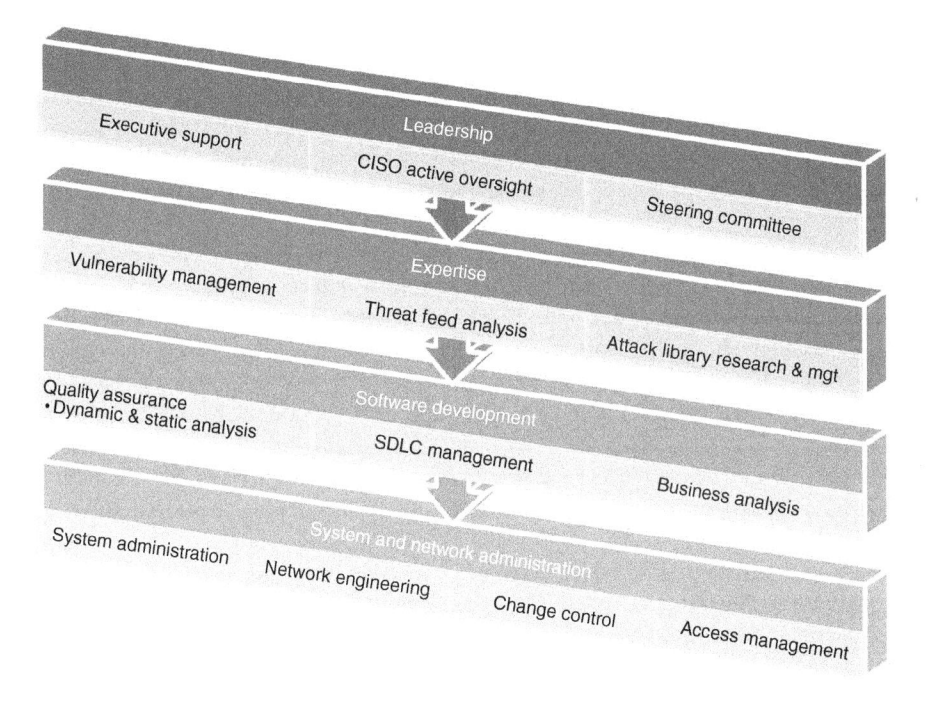

Figure 3.1 Essential Process Areas for Threat Modeling

[Figure shows layered process areas: Leadership (Executive support, CISO active oversight, Steering committee); Expertise (Vulnerability management, Threat feed analysis, Attack library research & mgt); Software development (Quality assurance, Dynamic & static analysis, SDLC management, Business analysis); System and network administration (System administration, Network engineering, Change control, Access management)]

use, while allowing sufficient flexibility for growth into the *right* methodology down the road.

Executive Sponsorship A common challenge in security for recent years has been the need to obtain executive support for security efforts. Executive sponsorship extends beyond formal communication from executive leaders at key public relation events or channels. Security messaging from executives should be consistent – which can translate to varying time intervals for many, but the recommended guidance is that key security messages from C-suite levels become reiterate quarterly at the very least, while underlying senior executives in security, technology, and risk management should provide more frequent and actionable security messaging. An example is a CIO's quarterly all-hands meeting where he/she may embed a persistent tone and message that stresses the company's need to be consistently vigilant in regard to data privacy issues due to recent legal battles that have crippled competitors in the same product and service space. Subsequent to this quarterly message to the entire company, senior level executives (non-C level) may address their department areas monthly in order to compartmentalize data privacy issues in a format that is more applicable to underlying management and staff. Such communication may reference administrative policies, guidelines, standards, compliance regulations, and other governance documents to sustain communication regarding data privacy issues. Senior executives may require the underlying management and team leaders provide evidence that these efforts are clearly understood via either training or auditable reports from control areas (i.e. data loss prevention technologies in e-mail, laptops, office suite products, file shares, etc.). In this top-down approach, we see how a pervasive security message can be achieved. Similarly, the longevity related to application threat modeling and possibly its ongoing use and adoption can be sustained if executive sponsorship can ignite and continually rekindle such efforts in the long term.

Leveraging the visible support of senior executives, the CISO has a prime opportunity to execute a less adversarial role in fulfilling his/her security management roles and functions. Without such support, the CISO would have a much more difficult, if not impossible, situation to socialize application threat modeling as a new and effective process for risk reduction and preemptive security remediation, regardless of case studies, metrics, and other tangible results that support its case. The greatest challenge would be in communicating with traditional IT groups who may continue to struggle with what may be regarded as doomsday application prognoses from their security counterparts, particularly when they may feel that risk issues are not clearly represented and greatly lack in any level of clear remediation guidance. This situation presents a significant challenge regardless of whether or not the CISO has obtained executive support. As a result, the CISO's oversight across all security efforts under his/her purview must be well developed and work well with the business and IT groups to properly socialize application threat modeling.

CISO Oversight Executive sponsorship is unfortunately a luxury across most corporate environments and therefore cannot always be depended on. With a dynamic array of shifting business priorities, *security* continues to be shuffled behind other business efforts. Given the many security efforts for which a security CISO must oversee, application threat modeling would greatly provide for cohesiveness across groups in order to sustain a common objective or mission. Depending on CISO's perspective, background, and departmental goals, application threat modeling may become either an effective abstraction layer for security operations or simply another security add-on that is conducted ineffectively. This will largely hinge upon their knowledge of application threat modeling and their degree of familiarity with varying methodologies.

Although an application threat modeling initiative can exist without the sanction of executive leadership (albeit very difficult), it is nearly impossible for application threat modeling to be effectively conducted without an active and supportive CISO. Given the breadth of involvement from multiple individuals, the required time and artifacts that are produced via threat modeling exercises such as data flow diagramming, security testing, attack simulations and more, at some point, these time requirements may come under question by security leadership and ultimately the CISO. Without a formal endorsement of the various sub-processes that support any application threat model methodology, the initiative is destined for failure. On the basis of this notion, either a *right* or *appropriate* methodology option would be eliminated, unless it is simply informal and partially implemented and followed by a subset of security or IT professionals.

SECURITY, SOFTWARE, RISK-BASED VARIANTS 141

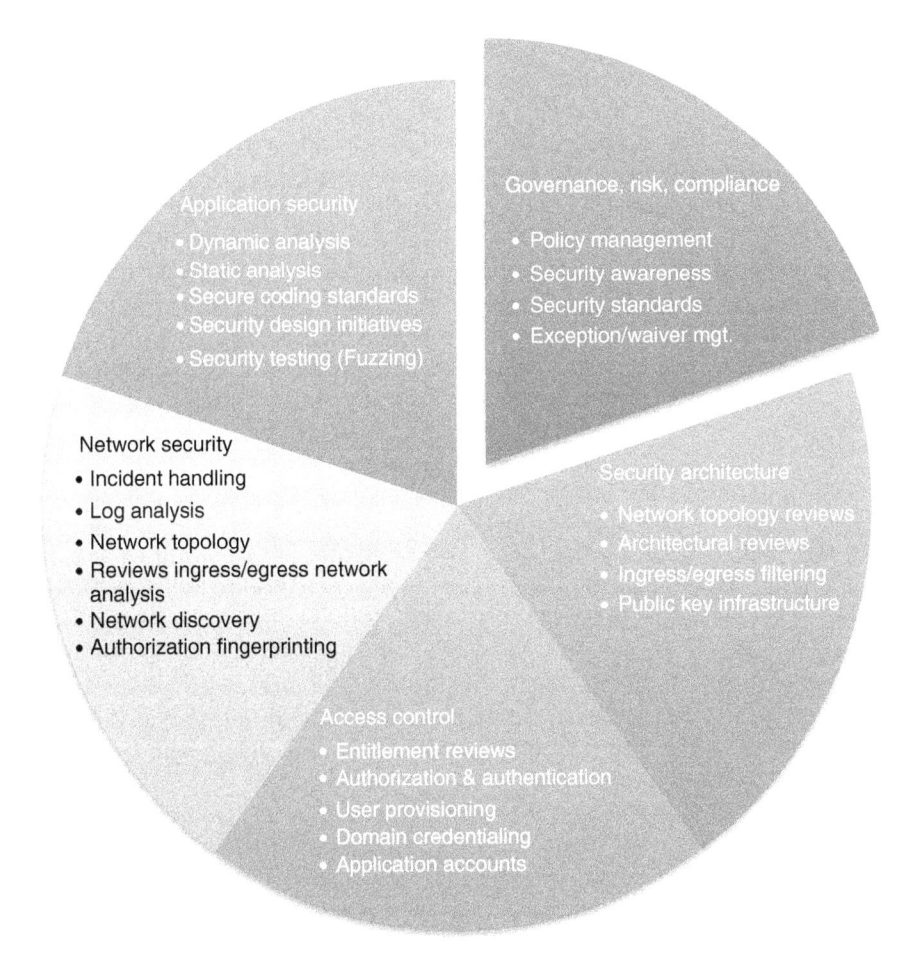

Application security
- Dynamic analysis
- Static analysis
- Secure coding standards
- Security design initiatives
- Security testing (Fuzzing)

Governance, risk, compliance
- Policy management
- Security awareness
- Security standards
- Exception/waiver mgt.

Network security
- Incident handling
- Log analysis
- Network topology
- Reviews ingress/egress network analysis
- Network discovery
- Authorization fingerprinting

Security architecture
- Network topology reviews
- Architectural reviews
- Ingress/egress filtering
- Public key infrastructure

Access control
- Entitlement reviews
- Authorization & authentication
- User provisioning
- Domain credentialing
- Application accounts

Figure 3.2 Security Areas for Greater Unity via Threat Modeling

To the image of the supportive CISO, we can effectively state that his/her active role and support will have a monumental difference on the success of this risk management process. Ideally, the CISO may integrate key security information into the application threat model, methodology, and multiple outputs. Application threat modeling provides the medium for collaboration among the following key areas depicted in Figure 3.2 that greatly affect application security. Under the right leadership, application threat modeling amalgamates the following areas, leveraging the many controls and deliverables that are produced by their respective efforts.

Assuming that a CISO's security leadership presides across some or many of the aforementioned areas, the following table provides a representation of how efforts carried out by these areas can both benefit and fuel the application threat modeling process.

Table 3.1 provides a glimpse of some of the functions that take place within each of the security processes and maps various stages of the application threat model. As shown in the table, the opportunity to leverage efforts across various security groups is possible when using an application threat model collaboratively. The challenge is having a centralized leader to endorse, support, and unify the many beneficial outputs that are created across the information security organization. These are some of the challenges that a CISO will ultimately face when looking to deploy application threat modeling effectively across the organization. Realistically, many of the underlying security groups may be opposed to the idea or doubtful of the intended benefits. As a result, enlightening the security group members on how threat, risk, and vulnerability information can be better applied across the enterprise can ultimately sway skeptics unless they are committed to the common security objective of protecting the enterprise.

These operational and administrative points related to security processes relate to methodology selection by how the enterprise's culture, leadership, and collaborative nature can sustain a desired threat modeling methodology. These factors should be considered heavily when selecting a methodology for implementation. In many ways, the selection of the methodology, in light of these factors, is synonymous with some of the criteria for selecting an SDLC methodology because time constraints, resource availability, and experience will all factor into the SDLC model that is selected.

An experienced CISO's leadership over security operations, access control, network security, risk management, and beyond will be a great asset in building and sustaining a repeatable process for application threat modeling within an organization's SDLC process and beyond. Selecting a threat modeling methodology by a seasoned CISO will allow him/her to opt for a methodology that is appropriate based on organizational/cultural challenges, resource restraints, and a collaborative environment *(appropriate methodology)*. Finally, the elected methodology should also allow for some flexibility in ascending to a vision of applied threat modeling for the future *(right methodology)*.

The Steering Committee Regardless of a stellar CISO, nothing is truly done alone, particularly when sustaining a process for which constant oversight and constituents need to be engaged. Threat modeling requires the expertise of many individuals, across varying domains for it to mature fully within an organization. Steering committees allow a balanced cross section of security and IT members to understand and develop a core set of threat modeling principles and objectives that are shared within an enterprise. These groups provide a simple yet vital role in socializing threat modeling tasks, goals, and objectives to their respective groups in security operations, risk management, compliance, and so on.

Members pertaining to a steering committee help to reiterate threat modeling use and benefits to the localized needs of their respective groups. Software development managers will provide credibility to the threat modeling process for his/her team of developers in the sense that they will be better informed on misuse case scenarios. Risk managers will speak to a team of assessors on how probability values in their risk formulas will be substantiated by attack simulations carried out by application threat

TABLE 3.1 Example of Mapping Threat Modeling Efforts to Security Processes

			Threat Modeling Processes				
	ID Business Objectives	ID Assets	ID Vulnerabilities	ID Attack Vectors	DFDs	Attack Simulation	Countermeasures
Access control	User roles and responsibilities	Include/exclude lists	ID process-related vulnerabilities to access control	ID weak process or control solutions	Rights of least privilege for data access (APIs), authentication, create-read-update-delete DB privs	Elevation of privileges in access	Platform/application access controls, centralized access control management
Security architecture	Continuity requirements (HA, QoS, etc.), data sensitivity	Application layers (security layers) for asset class, network segmentation for asset classes	Vulnerable infrastructure configuration/platforms	Ingress points, vulnerable network services	Ingress/egress points, insecure communication channels, request/response validation	Ingress/egress network points, network protocols leveraged (TCP, IP, SIP, ARP, etc.)	Layered security defenses, security hardening, platform standards

(continued)

TABLE 3.1 (*Continued*)

	Threat Modeling Processes						
	ID Business Objectives	ID Assets	ID Vulnerabilities	ID Attack Vectors	DFDs	Attack Simulation	Countermeasures
Application security	Business impact assessment on data and related systems, information asset classification, ID use cases	Scope of information assets, configuration	Internal/external vulnerability scans, application misconfiguration, static analysis	Application fuzzing, static analysis, ID misuse cases, business logic exploits	API calls, web services, XML-RPC (SOAP), SAML based requests	Dynamic analysis, penetration testing (application)	Data sanitization within application, validation checks (requests/responses), authentication checks
Network security	Network requirements, standards, guidelines	Hardening platform guides/standards, network discovery	Internal/external vulnerability scans (network)	Superfluous network ports and services, brute force, poorly configured network devices, IDS/IPS/FW Incident Analysis, Log Analysis	Network protocols supported, network authentication services	Penetration testing (network), social engineering attacks	Network authentication, PKI use, biometrics, multifactor authentication

| Governance, risk, compliance | Security policy, guidelines, standards | ID scope of assets that have been assessed in recent past to understand historically referenced risk levels | Risk assessment of process and control related application areas, compliance audits against control frameworks | Risk analysis or assessment results | Governance documents for preferred network topology and API channels | Risk issues that reveal proof of concept risk issues defined risk assessment efforts | Standards for both application and host configuration. |

modeling efforts. Security operations managers will also validate reasons security engineers or analysts should work to support a "live" threat model using information learned from security incidents tracked and trended against targeted networks or application assets. All of these scenarios help fuel a powerful and effective application threat model. The information maintained by security, compliance, and risk management groups all assume a strong level of expertise as resources fulfilling roles within these areas. In the end, the benefit of analysis that results from an application threat model is a direct representation of the information inputs that have been plugged into the model.

Expertise Threat modeling is an advanced form of risk management, applied toward various applications and related components that manage critical information sources. This form of risk management follows more advanced methodologies for information gathering (or discovery) as well as its analytical exercises. Given the many resources that help funnel information related to an application's vulnerabilities, effectiveness of existing countermeasures, and possible attack patterns, this places a great amount of dependency on this level of work and expertise. For example, when incorporating a list of discovered network/platform-related vulnerabilities, if these vulnerabilities have not been validated for accuracy and stripped of any false positive findings, it will ultimately affect the vulnerability nodes (or leaves) that stem from the attack tree, thereby having a cascading effect on how successful attack simulations are run and how the overall risk analysis is conducted. The result is an enormous amount of time wasted. For this reason, threat modeling requires a high level of expertise or the participation of subject matter experts (SMEs) within their respective security area to ensure the accuracy of the information that is relayed to the overall application threat modeler. For many enterprise organizations that have some of this expertise in-house, expertise challenges would not pose a problem. Smaller organizations where shared roles and responsibilities are common, would undoubtedly tell a different story as they struggle to develop a strong sense of expertise across more than one security area.

The expertise needed for application threat modeling itself will obviously not be found in someone who has had numerous years of applying application threat modeling across multiple application environments. The reason for this is the immaturity of the practice in today's security environments. The experienced threat modeler, similar to the hacker, will not obtain their skills via industry certifications, hours of CPE credits, or hours sitting in a classroom. Instead, the application threat modeler is one who can combine their hands-on experiences across multiple IT and information security domains. A practical list of *essential* and *supportive* areas across both IT and IS, as well as explanations, are as follows. The next page expands on the various security functions that are interrelated into the application threat modeling process.

These areas of experience serve as core fundamentals to fulfill various parts of today's application threat modeling methodologies. In reality, organizations have to grow the level of expertise across these areas over time to improve upon the effectiveness of application threat modeling efforts within an organization.

SECURITY, SOFTWARE, RISK-BASED VARIANTS

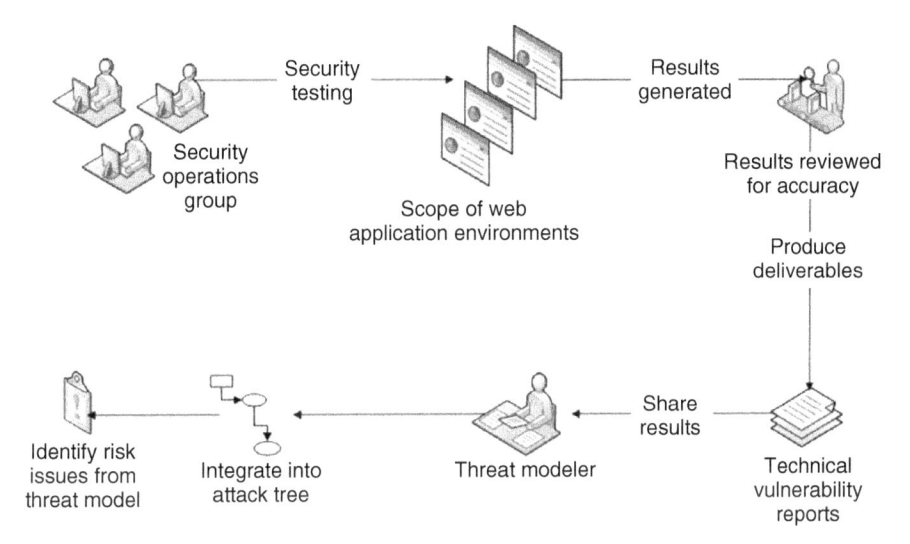

Figure 3.3 Process Overview of Vulnerability Assessment Integration to Threat Modeling

The areas depicted in Figure 3.2 and Table 3.2 reflect key security practices that generate important security information from which threat modeling analysis builds. This information can be managed internally or by a preferred security partner/vendor. If fulfilled externally, information management becomes a bit more challenging given its origin and the reduced level of control over the information. External threat feeds, for example, need to be effectively integrated throughout appropriate security silos within the organization. Figure 3.2 illustrates three distinct types of security processes that produce vulnerability and exploit information, which feeds the threat model attack tree. Figure 3.3 further illustrates how one of those processes, vulnerability management, can be successfully integrated into the application threat modeling process.

Practically speaking, the threat modeler in the aforementioned figure would have to validate, aggregate, and correlate related vulnerability information to nodes on the attack tree that list possible exploits to information assets or targets, as revealed by the threat model. This process leverages an existing workflow from vulnerability management and feeds the risk analysis by identifying the means in which an attack can be launched against an information target.

Incorporating vulnerability management into the threat modeling process further legitimizes and enhances the importance of this traditional operational security role within an enterprise as its information becomes an expected and much needed variable of the threat model, instead of vulnerability management simply feeding remediation tasks that typically either do not get completed or get deferred and then lost in exception management workflows. Via threat modeling, identified vulnerabilities get more attention as they are viable opportunities for vulnerabilities to be exploited against an application environment.

TABLE 3.2 Security Experience Meets Threat Modeling

IT/IS Area	SME Background/Experience
Software development	• You cannot speak about application software unless you have actually written code – theoretical concepts only go so far. It is hard to convey design or coding flaws to developers without understanding how to perform the remediation re-coding yourself. Nothing substitutes real world experience in working with different constructs, libraries, development frameworks, and compilers. • Without the experience of taking part in group think development efforts, it is difficult to understand how software development life cycles actually support application threat modeling. Real-world exposure to working within an SDLC methodology (or two) is invaluable.
System administration	• At least 50% of vulnerable applications stem from poorly configured software and system platforms. Hands-on system administration experience can greatly help articulate attack vectors through software or platform level configuration gaps.
Application security testing	• There is no substitute for real world hacking experience when trying to unleash a roster of different attacks based on both misuse cases and vulnerable software. The hands-on experience for application testing at both the dynamic and static level is key.
Vulnerability management	• A large part of application threat modeling requires having to marry vulnerabilities to possible attack scenarios. Vulnerability management experience is paramount in this effort to present exploits that can affect validated vulnerabilities across all layers of the ISO model. • Vulnerability management experience ties into formulating a "living" database of application vulnerabilities from which to correlate to attacks identified by the threat model attack tree.
Risk management	Threat modeling's core objective is risk mitigation. Risk management in information security bridges technical risk with business risk via its ability to depict how technical vulnerabilities and well defined attack patterns can affect clearly identified assets with a known business impact. Experience in this area is critical. • Risk management experience helps evaluate all the risk-related variables – probability levels, attacks, and vulnerabilities – that the threat modeler analyzes. Ultimately, risk values can be derived by this process.
Security operations	• The security engineer with security operations experience will be able to understand where and how to quickly identify security events that stem from firewall alerts, intrusion detection/prevention systems, host-based security agents, security appliances, proxy servers, and so on.

IT/IS Area	SME Background/Experience
	• Threat intelligence is one of many innovative sources of security information that security engineers need to analyze as part of application threat modeling simply because it allows the opportunity to develop an attack library that is up to date and reflects attack patterns that are researched and confirmed by security research groups. Threat feeds are now commonly sold as a service by many service providers and can be aggregated and analyzed and incorporated into a threat model.
• One of the most labor intensive efforts in application threat modeling is developing an up-to-date attack library that (a) provides a comprehensive and up-to-date listing of attack exploits and (b) reflects a library of attacks that correlate to information assets that are a part of the application threat model's scope. Given the ongoing vigilance that a security operations center or group has over historical and incremental threats, their experience for transferring this experience to application threat modeling is extremely beneficial.

Software Development Unless the majority of your revenue producing business software is 100% code-off-the-shelf (COTS), which would be frightening for many reasons, yet unlikely, then the following section and application threat modeling for that matter would be difficult to implement.

If application threat modeling were to follow the steps as yet another security process to lecture business units and IT groups on best practices or doomsday models in distributed application environments, there would be little worth in the rest of the content presented in this book. The fact is that application threat modeling, similar to its benefits to security operations, can bolster the effectiveness in which security is incorporated into software development practices. The hardest part of building security into an application solution is the fact that many nonsecurity professionals do not see the value or purpose of proposed functional requirements besides the fact that they comply with stated requirements from those same security professionals. Building on the last section, if the business can understand the viability of threats, the precision of what they are capable of doing, and the results that show their feasibility, there will be less misunderstanding of the value of application countermeasures. Like every functional application component, application countermeasures need development requirements as well. Leveraging the knowledge of the business analyst, who is traditionally positioned between understanding the business needs and the functional technical details of an application environment, this group can serve as a pivotal role in understanding and communicating the use of security requirements within an application environment. Referencing Figure 3.2, software development and business analysis are two of many facets that make up this broad area. Because one of the outputs from an application threat model's attack tree is the alignment of exploit leaves to vulnerability leaves to proposed countermeasure leaves, the practical development of security requirements can be incorporated into the business analysis process that often takes place in the design and definition phases of any traditional SDLC model such as Cascade (Waterfall) or Agile.

One example of the aforementioned is a banking application that is seeking a unique form of electronic signatures for account changes. A business-logic flaw, identified in a previously conducted manual vulnerability assessment, revealed that repudiation risks were still present due to weak or nonexisting transactional-based authentication. This specifically means that for major transactions that warrant additional validation and authorization from the authenticated user (e.g. large online transfer, name and address change, additional account members added), the authenticated user will need to provide authentication criteria to fulfill the transaction. Assuming that the vulnerability of not instituting any control is on the banking application, as well as other business and technical requirements that facilitate or complicate the use of transactional-based authentication, the business analyst can work with the threat modeler or security team to devise a suite of transactional authentication criteria that would mitigate the risks introduced by the discovered vulnerability. Such an example provides one of many instances in which application threat modeling can foster building security in through a process of bridging security risk to business impact to risk mitigation.

Once the business analyst team has developed a list of security requirements (in conjunction with the threat modeler or security group), these same requirements can be leveraged by the quality assurance (QA) team to test the effectiveness of the controls and their ability to mitigate risks identified by the threat model. The QA team can then reevaluate the application via testing similar to what was conducted by a security operations team (dynamic analysis, vulnerability assessment, manual fuzzing techniques) or provide a unique set of scripted testing criteria to test against a specific set of requirements defined by the business analyst team. Given the traditionally time-sensitive nature of QA testing efforts, it may be worthwhile to have their relevant tests be more targeted in nature to the security requirements that were set forth by the business analyst and threat modeler. Validation of previously discovered vulnerabilities can also be addressed at this time to ensure that developed functional enhancements adhere to security requirements and fully remediate previously discovered security holes. Leveraging the prior banking example, QA efforts may test the uniqueness of additional authentication values that may be used as part of a transactional-based security control, such as reauthenticating the existing session with a separate set of shared secrets that only the authenticated user and a unique security store or namespace may know.

Providing a repeatable framework to develop, implement, and test security countermeasures is not easy for any organization. Before security becomes a process, a software development process must already exist so countermeasures can be developed within the context of the definition, design, and development phases. A mature SDLC will also allow testing security requirements. Although the lack of a formal SDLC process does not necessarily mean that application threat modeling cannot be instituted within an organization, it does complicate its adoption and ongoing use simply because many of the traditional processes of requirements gathering and quality assurance testing may adhere to a dysfunctional process that is not fluid through the phases that span across conceptual design to implementation. Hence, application threat modeling should become interwoven within the process of the company's SDLC process. Later on, we will address how varying threat modeling methodologies synergize with SDLC variants in greater detail.

System and Network Administration Comparable to integrating security principles in software development via threat modeling, system and network administration are two critical efforts that can affect the security of the IT platform. System and network administration introduce the opportunity for *baking security in* by applying security countermeasures at the *inception* of an asset's deployment into the infrastructure life cycle as well as *during* its life cycle. As with software development, system and network administration has the opportunity to greatly improve its process and encompass security via application threat modeling's ability to distinctly identify configuration flaws that introduce possible exploit scenarios to an application environment affected by vulnerable network devices or systems. Exploited vulnerabilities depicted in the attack tree would yield the same preventive results as demonstrated for software development efforts during the SDLC. Ultimately, security requirements for network devices and platforms are developed so that network devices can be properly configured and positioned within the overall IT infrastructure. In some cases, changing how network or system assets are patched and updated can also improve via threat modeling efforts that identify possible threats early and introduce remediation early.

The example in Figure 3.4 (given subsequently) shows how threat modeling components, albeit incomplete and not encompassing privileges awarded to actors and other variables, can contribute in developing secure IT processes in network administration. The figure takes an actual Cisco vulnerability that exploits the http/https service that runs on the security device manager, which is susceptible to XSS attack.

Similar examples can be drawn from other threats against enterprise platforms or network infrastructure devices. The repeatable process of discovery and proof of concept exploitation (or ethical exploitation of vulnerabilities) will bolster either preventive governance activities, such as technology standards that ultimately are embellished in system images or network configurations, or improved IT processes such as patch management. For this reason, and in support of this chapter's objective, incorporating the role of system and network engineers into the application threat modeling process is essential for sustaining a threat modeling methodology that is pervasive across both security and IT processes, as system and network administrators address IT processes that impact security, such as patch management, configuration management, and access control. Application threat modeling supports the processes and technologies that enforce these controls by identifying vulnerable areas and probable threats that could exploit application systems without properly applying these traditional IT processes.

Figure 3.2 in the previous page revealed four key areas of traditional IT management that are essential in supporting threat modeling efforts. In summary, these four generalized areas are listed in the following sections with a brief description as

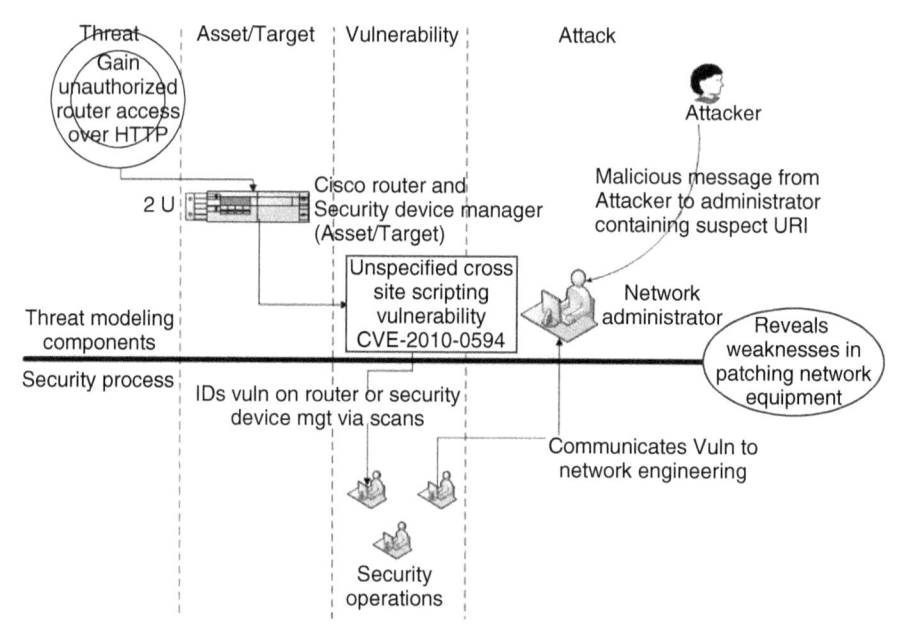

Figure 3.4 Building Security Process in System/Network Administration from Threat Modeling

to how they are prerequisites to successfully adopting, implementing, and using an application threat modeling methodology.

Access Control Actors are objects within any given model who interface with an application environment and who have varying access and privilege levels to application components. System administrators can properly assign rights to actors in order to sustain proper countermeasures against elevation of privileges, superfluous rights, or other attacks that leverage permission sets for a given user. Similarly, network engineers can govern access to network VLANs or enclaves to apply rights of least privilege to areas of the network that are commensurate to the responsibilities of the user.

Change Control Change can adversely affect security as well, particularly when not properly vetted through all checkpoints to ensure that security requirements are not compromised as a result. A successfully applied threat model against an application may be quickly thwarted with the slight mishap in change management. A network rule change could expand the attack surface for an application environment beyond the previously identified list of ingress network protocols that were allowed. Given change management's impact on network and system administration and engineering, it is important that changes be properly vetted against security requirements at the system or network administrator level. Since changes can affect the countermeasures for an application environment, along with the presence of unmitigated vulnerabilities, it is important that system and network administrators should be cognizant of changes to their respective environment and systems and transfer knowledge of those changes to the application threat modeling process.

Patch Management Despite the many evolutions in patch management, many organizations continue to experience major gaps in applying patches at both the platform and software level, thereby introducing numerous attack vectors that are difficult for the application threat model to catch. The reason is that an application threat model cannot address environmental outliers to attack vectors that are perceived to have the same patch levels across similar types of assets. This runs the risk of the application threat model excluding an attack or attack vector simply because it is assumed that there is equanimity across a certain type of asset (workstation, disk, which may be part of a cluster, or network devices that are legacy and manually updated individually).

Configuration Management Software and platform level configuration is essential in ensuring that software/OS settings are implemented consistently. Configuration management's impact to threat modeling is equal to that of patch management processes and technologies – requiring consistency so that security assumptions are sustained by the threat model. System and network administrators will have to have both the expertise and discipline to speak of any inconsistencies in process and technology that may exist, related to configuration management so that a proper threat model around a given application environment can encompass the proper level of accuracy in network-wide configuration management.

Time Commitments Those who hear of application threat modeling's numerous advantages counter with time and resource restraints as a key deterrent to adoption. Leveraging the point made earlier, a threat modeling methodology within an organization should follow realistic goals that match the level of resources, time, and expertise found within the organization. The most time-consuming portion of threat modeling is related to managing content: the content of threats and vulnerabilities into a "live" threat tree. Apart from this, the level of resources that have been depicted thus far across the organization would only need to be involved during two general phases of the threat modeling process: discovery and remediation. Since the threat model thrives on accurate and complete information around the application environment, discovery of technical and business process information involves those who can provide valuable information to the threat modeler for subsequent use. This describes the discovery phase of any given methodology, where use cases, actors, targets (assets), communication channels, APIs, data repositories, and more are tied to branches on the overall attack tree of the threat model. Second to discovery is the remediation phase of application threat modeling where governance activities or technical controls are introduced to mitigate any risks identified via the application threat model. Obviously, risk issues identified by the threat model will drive items to be remediated, therefore obligating time and resources for remediation. This will provide the best form for time projections on the remediation side, while most of the discovery efforts are assigned to a security professional who must spend hours performing the threat modeling efforts.

A unique application environment warrants a unique threat model. It may be tempting to reuse previous threat models where assets are shared across multiple application environments; however, this may affect the integrity of the threat model, which aims to understand data flow in the context of a unique application environment and unique business objective. Table 3.3 lists variables that influence the amount of time associated with an application threat model.

Table 3.3 provides some factors to consider when determining what internal resources have both the aptitude and availability to address threat modeling efforts against the technology makeup of a company's infrastructure. The first column of the table provides the main factors that should be considered when gauging the level of time commitment for application threat modeling.

Overall, there is no disguising the fact that application threat modeling is a time and resource investment that many would never contemplate given this realization. However, the time invested pales in comparison to the amount of ongoing inefficiency that exists today in addressing security as an after-thought to software development. Threat modeling is not the interoperability of multiple security solutions; therefore, it is not automated by software solutions or network appliances. It will require analysis and input from multiple SMEs across multiple phase of the application threat modeling process in order to contribute security countermeasures to identified vulnerabilities. A well-defined threat modeling methodology, as depicted in this chapter, ensures that the process of sustaining application threat modeling can be maintained without too much impact if resource constraints or turnover across threat modeling SMEs take place.

Threat Modeling Approaches The following sections address the various approaches to application threat modeling. Ultimately, the ideal approach is in line with the business's goals and objectives. To date, there are very few actual threat model methodologies. Instead, there are either frameworks or threat classification models that can be integrated or leveraged by a threat modeling methodology. Trike (v3) is one of the few that could be considered a threat modeling methodology, although it is self-labeled by its creators as a conceptual framework for application risk management and security auditing. Before a formal methodology is revealed for application threat modeling, we will address the existing threat classification models.

The approaches detailed within this chapter do not alter a general methodology for application threat modeling but simplify the manner in which threat modeling components (business objectives, actors, assets, information sources, use cases, communication channels, etc.) are depicted within the model. The next few sections compare two unique approaches to application threat modeling, each fulfilling unique objectives. The differing approaches that will be covered are *security* versus *risk* based-approaches to application security.

Prior to addressing approaches, a brief note should be made on the key illustrations leveraged in data flow diagrams (DFDs) so that subsequent illustrations can be made

SECURITY, SOFTWARE, RISK-BASED VARIANTS   155

TABLE 3.3 Factors Affecting Time Requirements for Threat Modeling

Factor	Description	Example
Number of use cases	The number of actions that an application can perform as a result of a client request, scheduled job, or API.	Actions that include buying items online, paying bills, exchanging content between entities, or managing accounts.
Popularity of technology	The notoriety of a platform or software technology will provide attackers with the ability to have a sophisticated level of understanding on how to better exploit the software or platform.	Any distributed servers, both open source and commercial related: SQL Server Database, Windows 2008 Server, LAMP Stack, IIS Web Server, OpenSSH, Adobe PDF, and Microsoft Outlook.
Availability of technology	The rarity of technology will affect probability levels of malicious users obtaining a copy of similar technologies to study its vulnerabilities for exploitation.	Legacy software or proprietary software.
Accessibility to technology	Cost of technology is not only a deterrent for legitimate, law-abiding companies but also for those organizations that subsidize cybercrimes.	IBM Mainframe, top secret software code base.
Level of expertise	Given that exploit scenarios move beyond the theoretical in application threat modeling, the appropriate level of expertise is needed to exploit vulnerabilities and take advantage of attack vectors. Depending on the level of expertise, a threat modeler or team of security professionals may have varying levels of time constraints in trying to exploit a given vulnerability. This is very common and would require the security expert to be well versed in multiple talents to exploit vulnerable systems.	Proprietary developed file systems, kernels, or software. Experience with rare software/platforms.

clearer within the book. A description of key illustrative icons for DFDs can also be found in the glossary.

The Assessment, Consulting, and Engineering (ACE) team at Microsoft has depicted the following illustration in their MSDN online publication, which provides a helpful understanding of symbols used in DFD exercises.

Table 3.4 provides some context to the DFD examples that will be discussed in this section. The threat modeling approaches themselves do not alter the nature of the DFDs as the purpose of the DFDs is to illustrate an application walk-through and

TABLE 3.4 DFD Symbols (Microsoft ACE Team) (59)

Item	Symbol
Data flow	One way arrow
Data source	Two parallel horizontal lines
Process	Circle
Multiprocess	Two concentric circles
Interactors	Rectangle
Trust boundary	Dotted line

denote use cases that can be used as misuse cases. A threat modeling approach is not intrinsic to the information represented by a DFD; however, the various steps of a threat modeling approach will undoubtedly reference DFDs in different ways to sustain distinctive motives.

Security Centric Approach to Application Threat Modeling

A security-centric approach to application threat modeling may also be referenced as an attacker-based or attacker-centric approach since the concern for threat modeling exercises is to catalog security holes for which an attacker can leverage against an application environment. This approach looks at threats to be launched against an application via the lens of an attacker toward security gaps for an application environment. The objective of this approach is to identify which threats can successfully be launched against a system given a number of identified misuse cases, vulnerabilities, accessible attack vectors, actors, communication channels, and more. The intent is to close security gaps in order to preserve the security of the application, thereby making the analysis binary in the sense that vulnerabilities are either identified or not identified so that countermeasure can be developed or aligned to vulnerabilities. Further, the analysis encompasses multiple levels of binary analysis, all with an underlying theme of security. Probabilistic threats may be determined to warrant countermeasures while less likely threats may be excluded from remediation efforts. Security-centric approaches to application threat modeling are focused on identifying motive, sources, and relative identity of the attacker or group associated with the attacker. The belief is that if the identity of an attacker is obtained, enough intelligence can be obtained to profile the attacker, his approach, level of perseverance, and resources. *Attacker identity* is not necessarily intended to narrow down an attack to a sole individual as that is becoming more and more difficult via the use of botnets and proxy-based attacks, which are the growing and preferred attack methods in recent years. Profiling the identity of the attacker may result in producing the following pieces of information:

- Organizations (ISPs, businesses, etc.) associated with attack branches of the attack tree in the application threat model.
- Metadata pulled from forensic evidence that may give clues to malware authors or groups.

- Techniques that give information as to the style or approach of a given attacker or entity. Attackers are now following a workflow so many actions or steps in their attack patterns may reflect the identity of the attacking entity.

The obvious challenge, related to ascertaining identity-related information for an attacker, is how organizations, who face resource and time deprivations, obtain a window of opportunity for producing this type of analysis. This is further compounded by the fact that most threat modeling efforts today do not properly leverage historical information that may include prior attacks or reconnaissance attempts by attackers. In support of a security-centric threat modeling approach, an analysis of internal, external, and host level traffic patterns is either not centralized, correlated, analyzed, or a combination of all of the above. Arguments may be made against such analyses by pointing out that these methodical steps warrant an enormous amount of time, energy, human, and financial resources. However, this investment solidifies the foundation of any application threat modeling approach since it accomplishes two goals: (1) it creates a process for centralizing and analyzing events for a workflow to threat modeling efforts and (2) it elevates the credibility of the application threat model by mapping historical traffic patterns to perceived future threats. Overall, a security-centric approach fueled by such information can effectively forecast more likely application threat scenarios in the future. Specific to web applications, the more security professionals actually understand both norms and anomalies in HTTP requests, network traffic, or misuse cases, the more information can be revealed of possible attack patterns depicted via the security-centric application threat model.

Applying a security-centric approach to a hypothetical attack from a disgruntled employee may be revealed by a series of actions against existing security controls or known vulnerabilities. The security-centric threat model would essentially be focused on the following questions:

1. What does the attacker want? (Target)
2. Why does the attacker want this? (Motive)
3. What can the attacker do with this information? (Impact)
4. How can the attacker gain this information? (Attack)

Bank Sys Admin – Security Centric Case Study The following illustrates a security-centric approach in a simple example of a disgruntled employee who recently left a business after nearly 15 years of service. New management and organizational changes forced the employee to become isolated and not valued as an integral part of the team of system administrators at a regional bank. The bank is moving away from a mid-range solution that the former employee administered for the past decade and is committed to new clustered banking solution on a farm of distributed servers. Ousted from his role and the company, the sys admin is knowledgeable of process-related deficiencies and security measures that will not be compatible with the new technology, namely, in implementing a comparable access control solution.

The former employee looks to exploit weak access control measures for APIs to the new distributed platform solution by (1) perpetrating a branch in order to request an application USERID and PASSWORD from the main branch's operations center (process vulnerability) and (2) leveraging the compromised account to make an elevated privileges attack on the application he knows does not properly validate application requests against roles and privileges.

These actions could be profiled by a security-centric threat model to walk through the application from the perspective of a former employee who may have intimate knowledge of application and/or process-related weaknesses.

The security-centric approach to threat modeling the aforementioned example is concerned with preventing the viability of such an attack from taking place. It does not take into account factors such as business impact, risk levels, or whether or not business objectives are compromised. Every organization needs to develop a threat model for insider attacks. A strategic way to apply a security-centric approach to threat modeling for insider threats is to develop models only for key business applications or applications that share common technology and process-related components so that the threat model can be transferred to other application environments.

Security Centric Threat Models for Complex Attacks Although this example is of a targeted attack, it is very simple and unsophisticated. Attacks that are more complicated are highly distributed in nature and camouflage true intentions, targets, and sources. They may even be deliberately spaced out over time to disguise further their overall objective. The following DFD of a botnet supported attack helps illustrate at what phase or level of a distributed attack a security-centric approach helps identify probable targets and sources. The illustration really only represents a minute part of the total possibilities that a botnet can bring to targeting a given application. Attacks launched by a botnet may simply be forms of additional reconnaissance in order to see if identified vulnerabilities are truly vulnerable by exploitation. Nonetheless, a security-centric approach can be applied in layers to derive how various phases of a botnet-based attack can be dissected into parts. For this, the STRIDE threat model from Microsoft provides a sophisticated threat categorization for such layered attacks and can allow the threat modeler to address attacks encompassed by these threats in layers. The following illustration represents a template view of complex botnet attack. A security threat model shows how attack vectors and observed traffic can be used to profile an attacker or attacking host, which is part of a distributed attack cloud.

Figure 3.5 can be used as a conceptual DFD template for addressing distributed attacks via a botnet cloud. Essentially, the value of the security-centric threat model addresses the *Analyze/Attack* phases of the threat as well as the *Review/Report* where successful exploits produce intelligence on where attacks may propagate or originate from (i.e. zombie hosts). The security-centric threat model shows how attacks can be mitigated from a security perspective, and, if they do become successful, how to prevent data leakage. The *Defines Scope* and *Tactical Approach* phases help fuel probabilistic values for likelihood of carrying out attacks depicted in a threat model's threat library. The shared resources of the botnet elevate likelihood levels for exploitation as the resources of the botnet may be collectively leveraged in order to execute an

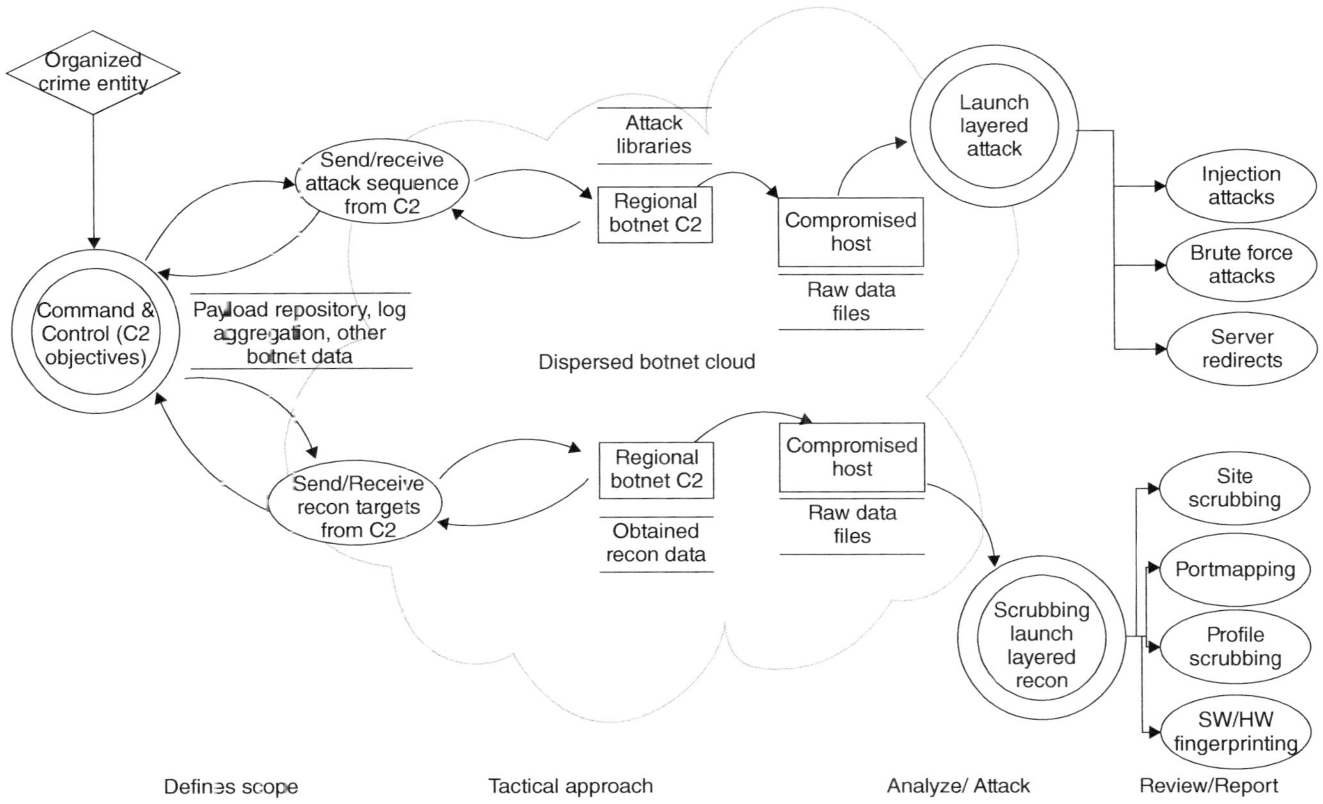

Figure 3.5 Security Centric DFD for Distributed Attacks

attack that was once believed improbable due to computation limits associated with one or two attacking hosts. The following section applies the STRIDE threat classification to demonstrate further the use of a security-centric approach to application threat modeling.

STRIDE – A Security Centric Approach to Application Threat Modeling

STRIDE is a threat classification model that facilitates a security-centric approach to application threat modeling. STRIDE is easy to use and understand for security professionals, developers, and so on. STRIDE is not an application threat modeling methodology since it does not define the process in which the threat model should be implemented, followed, and delivered. It does allow anyone to organize security threats against an application system by classifying them into the following six areas:

- *S*poofing: Attacks that mimic or impersonate another user account or application identity. This is not limited to identities assigned to end users or client users but also relates to any domain-related identities managed by an external data repository/store such as an Active Directory, LDAP, or ATOM server. This also may encompass any application level entities that are uniquely managed and stored by an application within a flat file system or a relational database management system, and that are not assigned to a unique individual, but mostly used to authenticate between application end points via APIs or other means. All of these areas relate to a primary form of authentication that may be a victim to a spoofing threat.

  Spoofing threats may also affect additional authentication measures that are traditionally used for two-factor or multifactor authentication. This encompasses digital certificates, additional layers of shared secrets authentication (encompasses challenge questions), biometric controls (something you have, know, are), out-of-band authentication channels (SMS, phone calls, etc.), authentication tokens (virtual, wireless, etc.), and any other secondary forms of authentication that may be intercepted, guessed, or brute forced in order to impersonate an identity at any level of the application environment.

  Motives for this threat classification include impersonating other users or identities to skew the audit trail of culpability, divert attention to impersonated users, and most importantly, gain illegitimate access to systems or application environments.

- *T*ampering: Altering application-related data, in transit, statically maintained in a repository or file system, or during data processing efforts by the application environment. Targets for these types of threats extend beyond client data and can encompass intellectual property, such as source code, classified designs of any project or product, formulas, or any form of proprietary information that provides competitive advantage to the data owner. Also in scope is data that relates to application or system configuration. Depending on how data is handled, the attack vector encompassed by this threat will ultimately introduce various types of exploits for intercepting the data in transit, manipulating the data while statically stored, or as part of a process or service that processes the data. Target examples for tampering static data sources include configuration files, data stored in databases, mainframes, mid-range file systems, and portable media. Target examples for data in transit encompass any wireless data transmission, Ethernet (LAN, VLAN), CDMA, TDMA, GSM, WiMax, Frame Relay, shared public infrastructures, as well as virtual networks.

Motives for data tampering-related attacks are driven ultimately by other threat classifications. Some may be spoofing-related efforts to impersonate other users via session hijacking, which alters session information on either client or server environments. Others may involve threats related to realizing repudiation goals aimed at avoiding culpability for crimes committed against an application environment.

- *R*epudiation: As briefly mentioned in the last section, the drivers for repudiation-based threats relate to avoiding detection and culpability of unauthorized events that took place against a system or application environment. There really is no logical instance as to when repudiation threats would not be present in conjunction with other types of threats since most attackers or nefarious groups will not like to deal with any investigation or prosecution. Therefore, the only instances where repudiation threats are unlikely are in the following cases:
  - Inexperienced attackers who do not consider repudiation tactics as part of their overall attack plan.
  - Layered attacks where acceptable collateral damage includes recognizing that certain members of a group may be compromised and prosecuted.
  - Attackers or organized groups who do not care if evidence is left behind for forensic analysis and possibly prosecution, most likely because the perceived or realized payout is worth substantially more than any response in the form of fines or imprisonment.
- *I*nformation Disclosure: As with threats related to repudiation, most attacks are focused on obtaining information illicitly, whether that includes cardholder information, patient heath information, intellectual property, bank records, user credentials, or any form of information valued by the attacker and the victim. If the victim does not also value this target information, the threat no longer becomes a threat, but merely an annoyance. Both parties must value the information for the attacks to be regarded as a perceived threat. The proposed victim organization or individual may feel that the target piece of information, if fully disclosed, does not realize a threat for anyone in the organization or its client/user base.

Motives for these types of attack are obvious and related to stealing information as leverage, collateral, or resale use.

- *D*enial of Service (DoS): DoS and/or Distributed Denial of Service (DDoS) attacks have one main purpose: to stop or severely impact the service delivery of one or more related application or network service. Theoretically, DoS attacks can take place at any level of the ISO or OSI Model, thereby introducing the reality of attacks to even the physical components of an application's infrastructure. Similar to other threat groups within STRIDE, DoS threats may be intertwined with other threats to given targets. DoS-based threats are difficult to defend, particularly if they are layered between the network and application, meaning that DoS attempts are made to flood network infrastructure equipment (and/or network services) and/or application level functions (logins, purchasing, report queries, etc.). In network-related DoS attacks, bandwidth consumption and/or overloading network devices to the point of preventing any additional ingress/egress network traffic to be properly handled and switched to the intended destination is the intended goal. Although these types of attacks have historically taken aim at public networks, malware coded to perform DoS attacks from within a LAN environment have taken place. Application DoS attacks seek more to affect the memory components of an application, particularly the stack and the heap, two distinct memory areas of the overall buffer. In these cases, elements of recursion or looping, as well as memory exhaustion can lead to DoS events.

Adding an extra layer of danger to these types of threats, DoS-based threats may sometimes encompass a degree of exploitability after a service or application component has been brought to its knees. This introduces other threat factors previously mentioned.

Motives for these types of threat classes include the following:

- Disrupting a site's function or uptime to prevent its services or information from being presented to its client base or
- Create a first layer of attack that results in exploitative opportunities for introducing malware, gaining authorized access, or conducting any other types of attacks that are within the context of other STRIDE threat categories.

DDoS-based attacks take advantage of more effective means to conduct distributed forms of DoS threats in that malicious traffic can originate from multiple locations, thereby incorporating repudiation threats as well as a more efficient means of load balancing an attack across multiple computing resources, not to mention the ability to easily bring down a system using a highly involved attack network of hosts makes defending DDoS attacks extremely difficult. Additional information on these types of threats and their related technical details are discussed in the subsequent chapters.

The following is a sample list of traditional DoS attack types that are generally geared toward networks. Physical and application level DoS attacks are discussed in the subsequent chapters. Most of the network-based attacks revealed subsequently are developed using malformed packets, amplified IP, TCP, or ICMP requests or simply recursive in nature and referencing the host IP of the target (Table 3.5).

The aforementioned table lists network-based DoS attacks, which are simply a subset of the totality of DoS attacks that can take place. More information

SECURITY, SOFTWARE, RISK-BASED VARIANTS 163

TABLE 3.5 Traditional Network-Based Denial of Service Attacks

Name	Description
ICMP flood	There are various types of ICMP flood-based attacks – all of which use an overwhelming amount of packets (whether ICMP, IP, or TCP) to overload the target system such that it becomes nonresponsive to legitimate network traffic.
P2P (Peer to Peer)	Not to be confused with attacks originating from a botnet, these network attacks are focused on traversing networks that support P2P protocols on numerous ports, but mostly on port 80. Attackers can leverage P2P hosts to wage attacks on other locations or points of interest.
Permanent denial of service	Long-term or permanent downtime is achieved via interruption to scarce network, hardware, or physical resources that sustain the uptime of a target asset or application.
Distributed attack	Occurs when multiple hosts take aim against a target network or host and leverage the totality of their hardware and software resources to overwhelm a target host or network.

related to these attacks as well as what countermeasures should be applied will be provided in the future chapters.

- *E*levation of Privileges – Most exploits do require some degree of privilege to work. Reduced privileges within an application environment at any level (client, application, or data) limit the possibilities for what an attacker can do. Not surprisingly, elevation of privileges is an attractive accompaniment to any type of attack as it helps introduce additional commands and malicious programs that target various portions of a given target environment. Successfully elevating account privileges for an application can take various forms, as a multitude of accounts are involved and serving as attractive points of interest for an attacker. Attackers will leverage reconnaissance efforts to get information on the platform, infrastructure, databases, and protocols the application environment uses. Elevation of privileges may also extend to the physical realm for those seeking to undermine biometric access controls for areas that require elevated privileges.

Classifying threats helps to show what security control is potentially vulnerable for exploitation. It provides an order of understanding to perceived attacks and it helps to organize remediation efforts. In security, we like to organize controls (or the lack thereof) into nice classification bins (Confidentiality-Integrity-Availability, or C.I.A., Administrative-Preventive-Detective-Reactive, etc.). These more renowned bins have no formal association to application threat modeling; however, they are represented to depict how security principles can be similarly organized during the application threat modeling process. STRIDE is an acronym that provides organization to application threats, which encompass attacks. Microsoft's ACE team is the authority

TABLE 3.6 STRIDE Threat Categorization Table (60)

Property	Threat	Definition	Example
Authentication	*S*poofing	Impersonating something or someone else.	Impersonation of notable company representative, trusted domain or trusted software, such as ntdll.dll
Integrity	*T*ampering	Modifying data or code	Modifying a DLL on disk or DVD, or a packet as it traverses the LAN.
Non-repudiation	*R*epudiation	Claiming to have not performed an action.	"I didn't send that e-mail," "I didn't modify that file," "I *certainly* didn't visit that web site, dear!"
Confidentiality	*I*nformation disclosure	Exposing information to someone not authorized to see it	Allowing someone to read the Windows source code; publishing a list of customers to a website.
Availability	*D*enial of service	Deny or degrade service to users	Crashing Windows or a website, sending a packet and absorbing seconds of CPU time, or routing packets into a black hole.
Authorization	*E*levation of privilege	Gain capabilities without proper authorization	Allowing a remote Internet user to run commands is the classic example, but going from a limited user to admin is also EoP.

on the STRIDE threat classification model. In order not to distort, reinvent, or misrepresent those threat classification values, Table 3.6 is a very useful table that Adam Shostack provides on Microsoft's blog on the Microsoft Security Development Life Cycle.

STRIDE is security centric in nature in that it focuses on security-related themes such as data tampering, spoofing-based attacks, elevation of privileges, denial of service, and integrity-based attacks. Attacks can be mapped to these threat categories to understand what security tenet is potentially violated. At a high level, the threat model that leverages STRIDE will map out misuse cases or attacks to targets, use cases, identified vulnerabilities, actors, connections, application or platform services, and data sources that are involved in defined attack vectors. Upon assigning possible attacks to threat categories, the threat modeler will understand the balance of threats as represented by STRIDE. The threat classification model also helps prioritize remediation efforts from the perspective of what type of threat is perceived to be most important for mitigation. Going back to the security-centric approach, the focus of applying countermeasures to identified attacks in an attack tree may be simply based on high probability values or high-risk designations from security sources (i.e. National Vulnerability Database (nvd.nist.gov), Common Vulnerability Scoring System (CVSS) values, or risk levels assigned to exploits by various global Computer Emergency Response Team (CERT) organizations). This furthers the objective of the security-centric threat model to address the most serious of security flaws for a given application environment.

As mentioned, the threat categories within STRIDE provide security professionals with the ability to segregate attacks into threat categories that matter most to the security group(s). Besides assigning attacks to assets and vulnerability leaves in the attack tree, STRIDE can help organize a threat modeler's threat library. Leveraging the default attack library from Microsoft's Threat Analysis and Modeling (TAM) tool (Version 2.1.2), the following illustrates how some of the attacks (A) managed by the tool can be classified by the STRIDE classification model. Furthermore, related vulnerabilities (V) can also be listed under each threat classification.

As shown in Table 3.7, the STRIDE classification model allows multiple attacks and vulnerabilities to be classified under one or more headings since it is possible that an attack or vulnerability can promote more than one type of threat.

Common Attack Pattern Enumeration and Classification (CAPEC) The Department of Homeland Security, as part of a special software assurance initiative with the National Cyber Security Division, has sponsored an initiative that would also help further the manner in which attacks can be enumerated and cataloged. The site, available via mitre.org, has an initial catalog of attacks along with a comprehensive schema and classification taxonomy. Release 1.5 of the catalog is currently available for download and is a great asset when populating a "living" attack library for an organization. The comprehensive catalog is broken out by catalog types or IDs, which encompass the following elements as part of the schema:

- Description of Attack
- Related Weaknesses
- CWE (Common Weakness Enumeration)
- Attack Prerequisites
- Resources Required
- Relationships (relates to mechanism of attack; maps to Web Application Security Consortium (WASC) Threat Classifications)

One of the more time-consuming efforts associated with application threat modeling is in building an effective attack library. For this reason, the CAPEC information that is available for download from MITRE is incredibly beneficial since it centralizes

TABLE 3.7 Example of STRIDE Classification Model

Spoofing	Tampering	Repudiation	Information Disclosure	DoS	Escalation of Privileges
Session hijacking (A)	Response splitting (A)	Repudiation attacks (A)	SQL injection (A)	Integer overflow/ underflow (A)	Forceful browsing (A)
Poor or predictable session IDs (V)	HTTP response not validated (V)	Anonymous access enabled (V)	Cryptanalysis attacks (A)	Ineffective performance considerations (V)	Poor authentication control (V)
Password brute force (A)	XML injection (A)	Poor RBAC model (V)	Use of weak keys (V)	Logic bombs (A)	Replay Attacks (A)
Weak passwords (V)	No schema validation (V)	No app-level logging (V)	Poor storage of secured key (V)	Poor program exits (V)	Poor validation of session requests (V)
Default/ shared passwords (V)	Dynamic XML generation from untrusted input (V)	Directory traversal to log files (A)	MITM, MITB (A)	Accepting arbitrary sized requests (V)	Lacking or inappropriate mutual authentication (V)
Session replay attacks (A)	SQL injection (A)	Improper security of log files (V)	Insecure communication channel (V)	Improper memory management (V)	SQL injection (A)
Poor session management (V)	Direct interaction to data repository (V)		No mutual authentication (V)	Buffer overflow (A)	Cross site scripting (A)

many current threats, is vetted by groups of security professionals, and is an evolving data feed that is free. Microsoft's TAM application also encompasses a small library that can help ignite a growing collection of attack patterns and can be consolidated with that data offered by the CAPEC catalogs to develop an effective attack library for threat modeling. Although the TAM is more closely associated with asset or risk-based approaches to threat modeling, the attack library is agnostic to approach and can be used to ignite an effective attack library for threat modeling efforts, regardless of employed approach.

Risk-Based Approach to Application Threat Modeling

An alternate approach to application threat modeling focuses on risk or asset-related themes that revolve around information loss or business impact of targeted assets. The analysis extends beyond identifying the motives and intentions of the attacker as well as discovering security gaps for an application environment. It also does not address such issues that relate to flawed or insecure coding/design practices, which would normally be addressed via software-centric approaches to application threat modeling. The focus of the risk- or asset-based approach to threat modeling is one that seeks to understand business impact of possible attack scenarios.

The following section introduces the DREAD model to calculate risk by its type. The purpose of the DREAD model is to illustrate the business risk area introduced by the viability of an attack. Attacks from a threat model can be organized by the following:

- *D*amage Potential: How extensive is the damage upon a vulnerability becoming successfully exploited? This assists in determining the overall impact of the attack against an identified vulnerability if successfully launched.
- *R*eproducibility: How easy is it for this type of attack to be reproduced? This helps identify whether the attack can be repeated.
- *E*xploitability: How easy is it for a known vulnerability to be exploited? This factor addresses the issue on the level of expertise or resources needed to exploit a discovered vulnerability.
- *A*ffected Users: Answers the question of forecasting the impact on a user base via their information assets or application environment that is leveraged by several users.
- *D*iscoverability: This helps identify how easily a vulnerability is detected for a given application environment. Such information helps identify how easily a vulnerability may be found for exploitation.

Like many other risk rating systems, DREAD encompasses the traditional HIGH, MEDIUM, LOW qualitative risk descriptors along with a quantitative risk value of 3, 2, 1, applied respectively. On the basis of the information that the threat modeler may have on both the vulnerability potentially being exploited and the expertise of the attacker(s), a similar analysis can be conducted to represent an attack branch off of the overall tree model. The following is depicted on Microsoft's Patterns and Practices MSDN section on .NET Framework Security. Although DREAD is another Microsoft-related by-product, its application can extend to non-Microsoft-related systems and applications as well. Related to an overall threat, DREAD allows the threat modeler to understand the following key variables in applying risk ratings to identified threats. Except the overall threat/threat description (which encompasses these variables), the main factors represented[1] by DREAD are as follows (Figure 3.6).

---

[1] Vulnerabilities are not uniquely identified by DREAD but implied in its association to attack techniques.

168 EXISTING THREAT MODELING APPROACHES

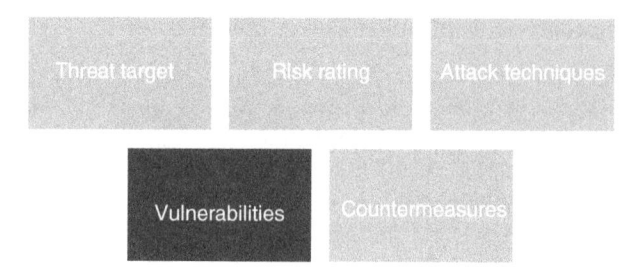

Figure 3.6 Components Represented by DREAD Risk Model

Vulnerabilities have been added to the original list as presented by Microsoft on their MSDN site on Threat Modeling (Chapter 3 of .NET Security) in order to clearly separate attack-related components to vulnerabilities in software, systems, or process. Vulnerabilities are meant to represent disclosed, undisclosed, and proof-of-concept exploits that may affect the asset or assets being evaluated under the threat model. The risk rating value is calculated using the qualitative-to-quantitative mapping of risk ratings as shown in Table 3.8.

The DREAD model encompasses a scoring system that affects that probability of occurrence for each of the five areas of the risk-based application threat model approach. Using the DREAD scoring system provides the risk rating value for a risk-based threat modeling approach. Here is a sample rating exercise depicted in table form from Chapter 3 of Microsoft's Pattern and Practices related to Threat Modeling (61).

Combining the risk rating values obtained for the overall threat with the other factors previously mentioned; the threat models could progress for each threat identified by the application. The following is a tabular representation of a very simple example of a threat model applied to a single use case of user authentication for a web application. The Microsoft provided table follows the same context of information depicted in Tables 3.8 and 3.9.

DREAD in essence provides a way for a quick risk analysis to be performed on threats within a threat model using five distinct categories that should have some degree in which the threat modeler views risk. Undoubtedly, some will argue that other risk factors are missing from DREAD to conduct a quick yet more complete risk analysis on threats. The DREAD rating category primarily addresses risks that lead to the attack but it does not encompass enough risk areas that result from a realized threat, with the exception of *Affected Users* and *Damage Potential.* Deniability of an attack (comparable to Repudiation in STRIDE, which is not a risk model for threats) may be worthwhile to consider as a risk factor for analysis. In attacks that are difficult to enforce accountability because they are conducted on an attack landscape that allows repudiation, proper accountability and consequences are limited. Accountability and consequence may affect the financial and business responsibility that the media, customers, and regulatory bodies all fault against the assumed security recklessness of an information or system owner (Table 3.10).

SECURITY, SOFTWARE, RISK-BASED VARIANTS

TABLE 3.8 Threat Rating Table Example

Rating	High (3)	Medium (2)	Low (1)
D Damage potential	The attacker can subvert the security system; get full trust authorization; run as administrator; upload content.	Leaking sensitive information	Leaking trivial information
R Reproducibility	The attack can be reproduced every time and does not require a timing window.	The attack can be reproduced, but only with a timing window and a particular race situation.	The attack is very difficult to reproduce, even with knowledge of the security hole.
E Exploitability	A novice programmer could make the attack in a short time.	A skilled programmer could make the attack, then repeat the steps.	The attack requires an extremely skilled person and in-depth knowledge every time to exploit.
A Affected users	All users, default configuration, key customers.	Some users, non-default configuration	Very small percentage of users, obscure feature; affects anonymous users
D Discoverability	Published information explains the attack. The vulnerability is found in the most commonly used feature and is very noticeable.	The vulnerability is in a seldom-used part of the product, and only a few users should come across it. It would take some thinking to see malicious use.	The bug is obscure, and it is unlikely that users will work out damage potential.

TABLE 3.9 Sample Risk Rating Exercise Using DREAD

Threat	D R E A D	Total	Rating
Attacker obtains authentication credentials by monitoring the network	3 3 2 2 2	12	High
SQL commands injected into application	3 3 3 3 2	14	High

Is DREAD Dead? Microsoft really has no formal obligation to sustain DREAD as a risk-rating model for threats, given that it has not invested too much in its ongoing development, marketing, and use across some of its threat modeling products that are free to the public, namely, TAM and the SDL Threat Modeling tool. Given its simplicity, it really does not matter if DREAD is supported by its original creators

TABLE 3.10 DREAD Risk Rating Applied to Sample Threat

Threat Description	Attacker Obtains Authentication Credentials By Monitoring the Network
Threat target	Web application user authentication process
Risk rating	High
Attack techniques	Use of network monitoring software
Countermeasures	Use SSL to provide encrypted channel

and supporters since the threat rating system fulfills a valuable role in simplifying risk ratings for attacks in a threat model. DREAD is not formally represented by any popular threat modeling tool, such as Microsoft's TAM or SDL Threat Modeling Tool; however, its application can be made out of band to these, and other threat modeling tools for the purposes of rating threat scenarios.

A Word about TAM and SDL Threat Modeling Tool The Threat Analysis and Modeling Tool by Microsoft is a free tool that is better equipped to address a risk-based or asset-centric approach to application threat modeling due to its inclusion and focus on threats against (1) defined business objectives and (2) identified information sources and assets. Given this focus, DREAD may be informally incorporated with TAM in order to derive risk rating for threat identified within the threat model. Its more sophisticated cousin, the SDL Threat Modeling Tool (another Microsoft creation), does encompass embedded risk elements; however, they stem from the fundamental design components of the application environment. The SDL Threat Modeling Tool applies STRIDE's threat categories to application components reflected in the application design. Along with those threat categorizations, the SDL Threat Modeling tools allow the business impact of those threats to be identified and captured within the tool. Additionally, those impacts are in turn associated with corresponding countermeasures or solutions (as it is labeled) within the threat modeling tool. The difference among the tools may not be very obvious, particularly if the user has little to no software development background. Both the SDL Threat Modeling tool and the TAM adequately fulfill the threat modeling objective; however, the key differences are in the inception of the process and the order in which the threat modeling variables are addressed.

At the inception of the process outlined by the SDL Threat Modeling tool, there is a slightly less focused regard of security vulnerabilities to use cases or assets. Instead, a greater view on software design, software development practices, software dependencies, and external factors (vendor environments, COTS risks, etc.) becomes a very noticeable theme when applying the model. The approach within the SDL Threat Modeling tools offers a very detailed understanding of the application environment through a very thorough process of application decomposition.

In short, STRIDE and DREAD, as two distinct forms for, respectively, categorizing and identifying threats and related risk factors, can be embellished in either TAM or the SDL Threat Modeling Tool by Microsoft. The approach to threat modeling varies on the slightly more valued paradigm – one that focuses more on security or one that focuses more on efficient and secure software. When given the option, most would choose both, which is the sensible approach. The issue is not to choose one, but rather, which is leading in greater importance for a specific point in time. Recognizing that both are important tenants to software development security, a security and/or software-centric approach to application threat modeling will ultimately yield similar results, but not via the same formula.

Trike Methodology and Tool Trike is another risk or asset-centric application threat modeling approach that actually comes with its own methodology, formally depicted in a paper as a band of security professionals (Eddington, Michael, Brenda Larcom, and Eleanor Saitta) who have shared this methodology and accompanying tool under the MIT license. The tool does a superior job in catering to a risk-based approach to application threat modeling and also encompasses many of the other phases or actions that are adhered to by other threat modeling tools, such as identifying assets within the application environment, actors that interface with or within the application environment, related privileges, and underlying communication channels. Currently, the Trike tool has only had one major release but there is a strong fan base looking forward to its second iteration. The analytical and risk-based approach depicted by the Trike methodology paper and tool has fueled worldwide interest from application threat modeling enthusiasts and security professionals. Trike will be covered in greater detail in subsequent chapters.

Methodology As previously stated, there is no widely accepted application threat model methodology. This is both good and bad, depending on whether or not the team executing threat modeling exercises understands the tasks associated with each phase of a standard threat modeling process or methodology. Prior to threat modeling becoming overly misrepresented or made to be something it is not, people conducting threat modeling exercises will be able to apply threat modeling concepts that fit the unique capabilities of their people and employed technology.

So what is the *standard* threat modeling methodology or process? This part of the chapter builds upon previously discussed approaches and terminology to outline the fundamental parts of the application threat modeling process that are relatively consistent and somewhat similar to other more traditional types of security assessment efforts, such as risk and vulnerability assessments, which both contain phases for scope definition, discovery, assessing, evaluating, and reporting. Similarly, application threat modeling needs to establish a proper boundary for an application environment to be analyzed through related threat modeling exercises, such as data flow diagramming, application decomposition, attack-vulnerability mapping, and so on. Threat modeling will also require a substantial amount of information to be collected and analyzed in order to make effective conclusions on threat scenarios for an application along with an overall risk analysis. Ultimately, there is some congruency at a very high level to more traditional assessment efforts and they will be apparent as we cover each phase of a standard application threat model process.

Thus far, we have addressed realistic expectations on resources and opportunities for threat modeling integration among both business and technology groups, particularly those involved with software development. Now that some realistic scenarios for threat modeling integration have been presented, we begin to focus our attention on understanding and applying a repeatable threat modeling process. Indifferent to approach (security centric, risk based, etc.), application threat modeling revolves around the stages depicted in the proposed threat modeling methodology, Process for Attack Simulation and Threat Analysis (PASTA) in Figure 3.7, which begins with a phase for understanding key business objectives to be supported by the application threat modeling process and completes with a risk mitigation phase that provides the opportunity to mitigate any business risk issues that have been identified and qualified as part of the threat modeling effort.

The aforementioned stages provide a fundamental framework for an iterative threat modeling methodology. This iterative process can be applied to an application that is preferably under development within the boundaries of a relatively mature or quickly maturing SDLC life cycle. Each of these seven phases are critical to the overall success of fulfilling the objectives of application threat modeling whether they are related to risk mitigation, threat identification, or improved application design and software behavior (essentially regardless of threat modeling approach). For each of the aforementioned phases of this *vanilla* methodology, we will examine the key reasons for which these phases provide supportive context to the other subsequent stages of the application threat modeling process.

Stage I – Define Objectives

This stage is central for fulfilling security, risk, and improved software security by the business boundaries that it creates. For example, a dentist who wishes to better manage patient schedules, cancellations, reminders, and insurance/bill processing may look toward an application as a facilitator of these goals, but these goals are driven by the needs of his/her business. Now that a generic mission is established for a technology solution, the boundaries in which that application should operate can be refined by the needs of the business. This is a critical point to the application threat modeling process because it is where application use cases are founded. Improper scope control for these functional requirements can ultimately affect the security of the application as well as the design and possible flaws that are inherent to almost any application. We have mentioned briefly before that grandiose scopes and unending functional requirements establish a very large scope for which security and software design measures should be instituted going forward. Superfluous functional features, lobbied by business leaders as must-haves, introduce additional use cases that may be abused if they are not properly secured. In many cases, these must-haves are functional features that sometimes do not receive the full adoption of the intended user base, thereby becoming a neglected functional feature over time and a ripe attack vector that does not receive a lot of attention for further feature or security enhancements. Last, excessive use cases may become unsupported by development over time due to various reasons (turnover, mismanaged development efforts, etc.) and may remain dormant compiled

SECURITY, SOFTWARE, RISK-BASED VARIANTS

1. Define objectives
- Identify business objectives
- Identify security & compliance requirements
- Technical | business impact analysis

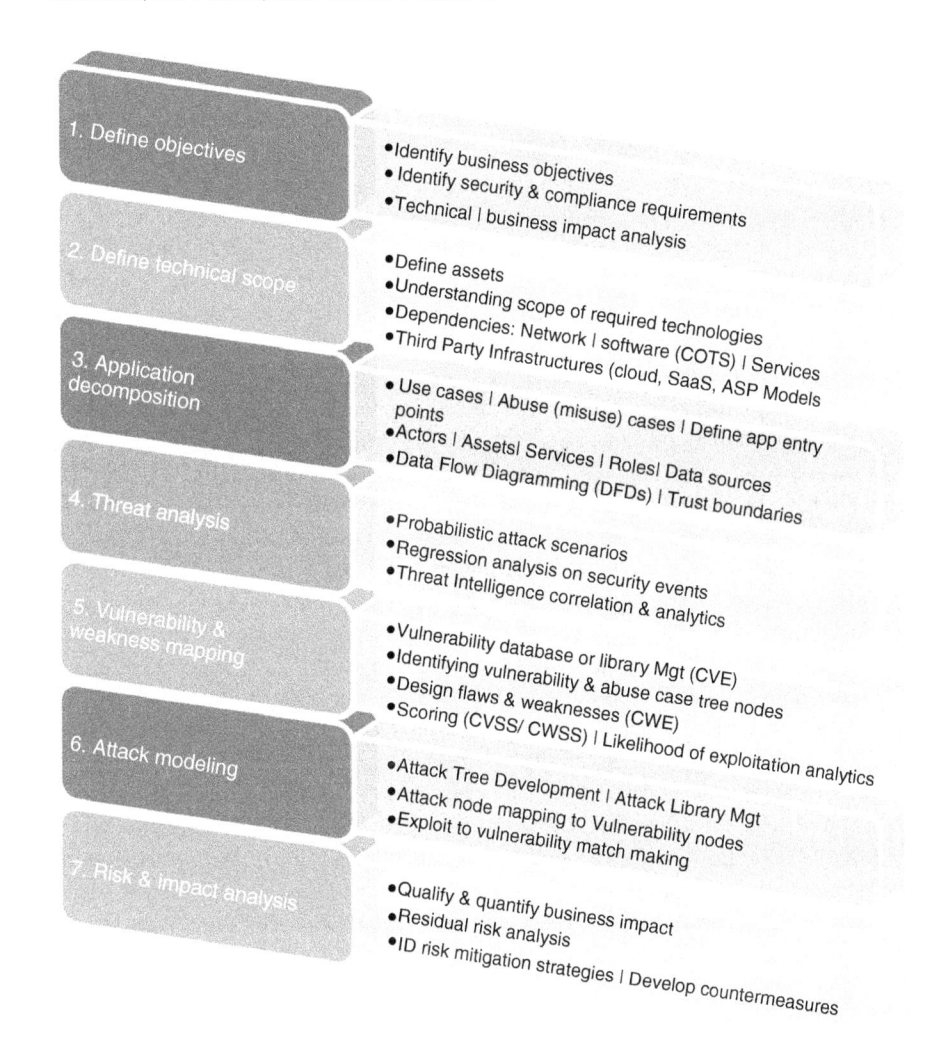

2. Define technical scope
- Define assets
- Understanding scope of required technologies
- Dependencies: Network | software (COTS) | Services
- Third Party Infrastructures (cloud, SaaS, ASP Models

3. Application decomposition
- Use cases | Abuse (misuse) cases | Define app entry points
- Actors | Assets| Services | Roles| Data sources
- Data Flow Diagramming (DFDs) | Trust boundaries

4. Threat analysis
- Probabilistic attack scenarios
- Regression analysis on security events
- Threat Intelligence correlation & analytics

5. Vulnerability & weakness mapping
- Vulnerability database or library Mgt (CVE)
- Identifying vulnerability & abuse case tree nodes
- Design flaws & weaknesses (CWE)
- Scoring (CVSS/ CWSS) | Likelihood of exploitation analytics

6. Attack modeling
- Attack Tree Development | Attack Library Mgt
- Attack node mapping to Vulnerability nodes
- Exploit to vulnerability match making

7. Risk & impact analysis
- Qualify & quantify business impact
- Residual risk analysis
- ID risk mitigation strategies | Develop countermeasures

Figure 3.7 Stages of PASTA Threat Modeling Methodology

code objects that also contribute to expanding the attack landscape for an application environment.

Even within the proper scope boundaries, functional use cases in support of business objectives can introduce insecurity and inefficiency simply because they overlap each other, if multiple functions allow the same result to be accomplished. Parallel functional use cases for different application roles in a reservation web application system may inadvertently foster competitive functionality among the two use cases. For example, having two different authentication stores where credentialing information is maintained and stored may be an idea that security conscious developers have for their multirole CRM application. The problem: over time, if this model is not supported, the other data store and related interfaces may become vulnerable to attack simply because of prolonged neglect. Another example is as simple as neglected hyperlinks under a poorly architected two-tier application environment where both are aimed to provide database calls for reporting. One hyperlink is continuously used as part of a control panel menu option, while the other is located in a submenu option that is only visible in a "Reports" page. If the GET requests seek to obtain the same exact data set from the database, development groups must ensure that any countermeasures or functional improvements that update factors such as authentication strings, privileges to database/file system objects, or access rights are properly enforced against the two small portions of the code base. This is an example where business objectives, matched with security objectives, can ensure that business requirements become fulfilled without introducing attack vectors that become exploited through procedural neglect in the SDLC process.

Upon solidifying a strong set of business objectives, ensure that this stage of the application threat modeling process incorporates the appropriate level of security objectives to sustain those business goals for the application. Security objectives at this phase of the application threat modeling process need to be detailed and precise, not only in their intent but also in both the process and technology level controls that will fulfill their effectiveness. Security objectives that are not properly defined can lose credibility and therefore never become enforced within the development phase if they are not socialized from the inception to all project stakeholders. Beyond the support that they provide for sustaining business objectives, security requirements should also never impede their fulfillment. Obviously, this goes hand in hand with defining acceptable business risk considerations so that security objectives can be cognizant of what those are. A supportive security objective is one that compliments the defined business objectives by either protecting the fulfillment of those objectives or introducing risk mitigation techniques against internal/external elements that could adversely affect those objectives. Table 3.11 provides a couple of examples where an individual business objective for a sample application is married with an exemplary security objective.

The requirements gathering phase of the SDLC will provide an opportune time for both business and security objectives and related requirements to be properly defined among stakeholders of an application. These requirements should be captured in the application threat model to ensure that the last phase of the threat modeling process properly addresses risks that affect the business objectives defined as part of stage I.

Stage II – Defining Technical Scope

Assuming that business objectives and functional requirements have been captured, along with security requirements safeguarding those same objectives, an understanding of the software design and underlying software and hardware assets that sustain the application architecture is now warranted in order to identify what the attack surface and threat landscape may be for the application threat model. The technical scope

TABLE 3.11 Security Objectives in support of Business Objectives

App Type	Business Objective	Security Objective	Notes
Student loan application	Automate student loan processing.	Ensure proper data security via web interface.	This 1:1 business to security relationship demonstrates how the security objective supports the defined business objective of processing loans online.
Content propagation service	Centralize and normalize content for consumer use in consumer electronic device (CED).	Ensure that proper data validation checks are present to preserve the integrity of new content.	Content management is key for entertainment content for CEDs. Ensuring the accuracy of the content so that it does not affect the integrity of the overall product upholds this business objective. Compromised or tainted content jeopardizes the adoption and use of the product.
Social network site	Provide multiple ways in which to engage the subscriber and encourage ongoing use in their daily professional and personal activities.	Provide appropriate level of data privacy controls and checks so that users can confidently use the site and not get a sense that their privacy is being jeopardized by social predators. Ensure proper authentication and authorization controls to fulfill this objective.	Data privacy is one of the determining factors for which a successful social networking site will continue to thrive. The key determinant, adoption, and use of the site will be susceptible to lower numbers if there is a sense that a user's information is not private, they may be targeted, or there is a negative association with the site to online social predators.

may change for a given application environment over the life of that application, particularly as it loses or gains functionality over time or undergoes a technology refresh. The goal of this phase is to identify the tangible resources that may be targeted to realize a given threat. It allows greater clarity in understanding what could make up a broad range of opportunities that an attacker may have against a target environment's assets. The value of these target assets may have direct or indirect consequence to the

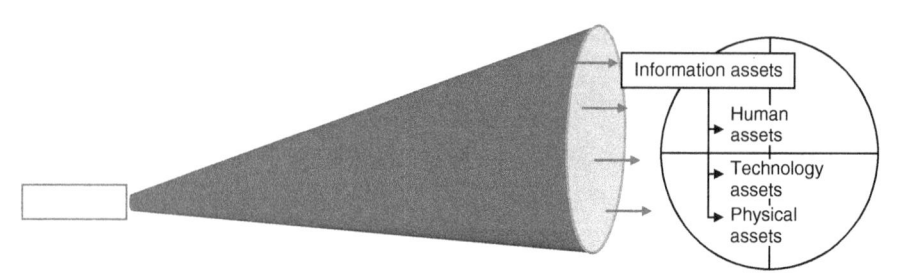

Figure 3.8 Cone of Fire Encompassing Multiple Targets

attacker's goal, as encapsulated by the overall threat and his/her motive as the driving force. Figure 3.8 can be considered a scope of attack or cone of fire as illustrated that would be addressed by activities in this stage of the threat modeling process.

The cone of fire represents the scope or range of attacks against accessible targets within the application environment. Without knowing the possible attack vectors of a would-be attacker, the threat modeler must understand what is being defended. This requires understanding the four W's of the application. Now that we know the business objectives behind the application and the functional requirements that support them, it is time to carve out those requirements into what tangible assets are involved. The who, what, when, and where of an application are defined in the following table and reveal aspects of an application environment providing a strong scope that the initial threat modeler should apply this stage of the methodology.

Four W's	Description
Who?	Who uses this application? Human users and application level user accounts apply here. How do human-based processes affect existing countermeasures or safeguards for the application environment? Who supports this application? Who is responsible for the security of this application?
What?	What is this application? Does it have a name? What was it intended to do? What is the extent of the information boundary/ownership defined by this application? What type of information does it manage? What is the demographic of the user base?
When?	How available is this application supposed to be? Are there peak usage times associated with this application? When do users or scheduled jobs interface with this application?
Where?	Where are the information assets and data kept? Where are the human resources charged with managing or maintaining this application environment? Where does the information that supports this application come from? Where does the code base for this application come from?

As you can see from the four W's, they represent questions at a high level about the application environment to ensure that a proper scope of assets, resources, infrastructure, third parties, and technology are brought into the picture to define the proper boundaries of this application.

The architectural review groups all of the relevant application components together in a holistic manner to begin developing a comprehensive view across the various layers of the application environment. Everything from the network, host platforms, third-party sites, system/network services, and application interfaces – all of these application components play a role within the application's ability to process, communicate, store information, and provide an interface to an end user or another application domain. An architectural overview does not walk through the application, but identifies the overall blueprint for how the application works. Since an application's threat model must encompass all possible attack vectors, an architectural review should overview and provide a quick, yet comprehensive list of the following:

- Network and communication protocols used among or within architectural layers (TCP, UDP, HTTP, SSL, IPSec, SMB, etc.).
- All data interfaces by the hosts represented within the application domain.
- Number and type of host platforms to be used within the application architecture. This may vary between production architecture reviews and those designed within lower environments, such as TEST and DEV.
- Network devices and services that are to be used in support of the application environment. This includes but is not limited to load balancers, routers, switches, firewalls, intrusion detection/prevention systems, web application firewalls, content filters, spam filters, network area storage, network access control, backup, virtual servers, AD, LDAP, ATOM, DNS, and DHCP services. There may be more related to network devices or services, so they may also be inventoried under the overall architecture stage.
- If a public key infrastructure needs to be put in place to support this application, the related assets need to be clearly understood as part of the overall application architecture.
- API with third party vendors via FTP, XML-RPC, SOAP requests, web services, or any other medium need to be properly depicted within the architectural representation of the diagram.
- Integrated software solutions that relate to Identity Management (IdM) solutions, application or network-based proxies, middleware, or any other COTS product that would be integral to the functionality and maintenance of the application environment. PKI infrastructures, LDAP, AD, and/or any other domain directory structure.

As with security objectives, the application architecture needs to support the defined business objectives of the application by not adding unnecessary network or asset components that complicate the overall service delivery of the application's design and overall architecture. Doing so may present attack vectors via these additional components.

Feeding stage II of this application threat modeling methodology is the design phase of the SDLC life cycle, which can provide many useful network schematics and application modeling artifacts that facilitate a proper architecture review of the assessed application. The threat modeler can leverage these diagrams to prematurely conceptualize attack vectors to the focal target points of the application environment. Greater amount of detail on this stage will be revealed in Chapter 7.

Stage III – Application Decomposition

In this stage of the threat modeling process, the application is broken down into individual components that can be uniquely targeted by an attacker. This exercise allows an attacker to dissect an application into parts to identify the best form of attack. Multiple attack scenarios can be devised as part of this effort in order to provide redundancy to an overall attack plan. Depending on the ultimate target, non-technology-related processes as well as physical security might also need to be examined to see how application-related attacks could be supported by attacks or diversions conducted in either the physical realm or the logical domain. Sometimes it is just easier to infiltrate a broken or weak process supported and managed by human capital than to go through layers of web application firewalls, HTTP proxies, firewalls, and intrusion protection systems.

Application decomposition encompasses many stages and requires professionals who carry the "jack of all trades" title fairly well. Decomposing an application environment may traverse network, application, and physical domains and into other areas that include processes, data, and/or mobile environments. Any interoperability of information infrastructure to the target application environment is key as part of this exercise. Application decomposition should also encompass auxiliary software that resides on platforms within the application environment which can serve as an attack vector to the information or target asset that is being sought. Simply said, it is very easy to decompose the application in a way that it is software centric, and thereby not taking into account other factors that could introduce a threat, such as platform operating systems, third-party software, or vulnerable ports and network services. They also may seek to exploit platform and network-related threats that are overlooked by a security conscience development team, given that is not their functional responsibility. For this reason, application decomposition within the context of application threat modeling needs to be comprehensive across employed technology components yet bound by the restrictions of the defined application environment in which information flow is managed and maintained. The *defined application environments* stem from the architecture review and objectives defined by the business earlier within the threat modeling methodology.

Application Decomposition High-Level Example – Mobile Phone App

In order to provide greater insight into this key stage of the threat model, we will take a mobile phone application as an example of the efforts that should take place within

SECURITY, SOFTWARE, RISK-BASED VARIANTS 179

application decomposition. The mobile java app, developed by a banking entity for its client base, is intended to allow end users to check their balance across multiple accounts (savings, checking, IRA, home/car loans, etc.), transfer funds across accounts, update account information, and manage online bill pay schedules. This example will be further exemplified in subsequent chapters with greater technical detail; however, we can still apply application decomposition at this level to demonstrate the approach and use of application decomposition.

For the sake of maintaining a topical and succinct example on application decomposition, our attention for now focuses on mobile client applications versus the entirety of what would normally be considered the mobile client-server environment. A more comprehensive threat model would encompass the mobile server environment as well as other infrastructure equipment that may help relay mobile phone communication. For now, this example on application decomposition focuses primarily on dissecting the mobile application client environment in order to understand what key components can be subverted by an attacker. Several misuse cases can be extracted just from the use cases developed for the mobile client environment as well as vulnerabilities related to the actual mobile platform. Each of the components listed in the following table may be exploited using an existing vulnerability against a software framework, plug-in, or even a developed use case for a given smartphone application. Table 3.12 enumerates possible application components that are present on Java ME-based smartphone running a banking application.

Through a simple exercise of understanding application components for a mobile application, the threat modeler is able to see what existing vulnerabilities would be most choice to carry out against a population of mobile phone users. Assuming that an attack plan encompasses a DoS attack against the proverbial mobile banking application, the threat modeler needs to prepare for this type of attach by breaking up the application environment into manageable components via application decomposition. In this way, the threat modeler can identify and correlate target assets, associated vulnerabilities, misuse cases, and trust boundaries to the identified application components that may serve as attack vectors. Exercises in application decomposition dissect the application environment in order to understand the fundamental technologies that support the application's use cases.

As discussed earlier, motive will play a large role in exploits to be used. Prevalent attacks against mobile computing platforms have encompassed DoS attacks, which have been traditionally motivated toward debilitating a victim's use of the phone or mobile phone application. From a hardware perspective, mobile phones typically use a chipset that supports a 16–32 Mb architecture, which introduces obvious limitations for complex or massive data computations across random access memory (RAM). With a smaller computing environment, limitations for multithreaded information processing, memory allocation, and load balancing APIs can prove challenging. Through an application decomposition exercise, we see that Java-based application environments (employing the Java Wireless Toolkit) leverage Connected, Limited Device Configuration (CLDC) v1.1 in order to contend with smaller resource pools for computing. We also discover through this dissection process

TABLE 3.12 Application Decomposition for Mobile J2ME App

Application Component	Use	Possible Exploit
Compiled client executable(s) (jar)	Used to run the application	Impersonated compiled app
Other installed java apps	Provides distinct uses but may be invoked by other apps depending on permissions set	Leveraging functionality of other apps in order to see if they may be leveraged in order to execute a misuse case or exploit
Connected limited device configuration (CLDC v1.1)	Java run time libraries and virtual machines (KVMs)	Exploiting vulnerabilities in libraries or overwhelming the performance of the application via saturated calls to VMs
File/directory objects (manifest files)	Use to manage both configuration and app-related data	Sensitive application data can be stored in these files and illicitly read by other apps or copied
Smartphone memory card	Physical auxiliary memory storage to phone RAM	Can be read by other apps anytime as persistently stored
Smartphone RAM	Temporary memory storage for apps and phone data	Shared by all phone functions and apps; no proper segregation of data
Mobile information device profile (MIDP)/midlets	API Specification for smartphones/apps that leverage MIDP/CLDC frameworks	Untrusted midlets could intercept API calls from other platform sources

that Java-based mobile applications also leverage MIDP v2.0 (Mobile Information Device Profile), a specification that encompasses APIs, tools, and other schematic components for smart phones and PDAs. Although these API and technology-related references have improved the sustainability of mobile applications, they port their own set of vulnerabilities based on their native functionality and built-in features.

Indifferent to the mobile computing application example, where a quick representation on how application components can be identified for subsequent use and analysis within the threat model, application decomposition's key objectives are to identify other threat modeling workings such as those previously mentioned and recapped in the list as follows:

1. Application Components – Services, Named Pipes, Software Libraries, and so on.

2. Actors – Human and nonhuman roles interacting with a given application environment.
3. Assets – Both hardware and software assets that interact with the application ecosystem.
4. Data Repositories – Relational databases, file systems, flat file data repositories, cached memory where data may be stored.
5. Trust Boundaries – Despite not being tangible objects, they become more clearly defined as part of the process of dividing up application components.

One important item not covered by this mobile application is the issue of user roles for a given application environment that is being "decomposed" in this phase of the threat modeling methodology. Most mobile apps have a single security context for a client mobile app environment. Client-server actions and requests may encompass a greater variety of user profiles for which different actions may warrant a different level of privileges. An online banking app for a mobile device, for example, may interface with a mobile banking web application using basic authentication. The security context of subsequent requests, however, may vary across inner layers of that part of the application environment. Use cases defined for the client mobile application may require a security context with read-only access to a given data repository. In other instances, the ability to change the data for a banking user (such as profile data or account notification settings) may require elevated privileges to the inner layers of the server-side application environment read. Overall, application decomposition not only encompasses listing application use cases and enumerating asset-related components for an application environment, but also mapping what actors (or users) and associated privileges are present for each asset and use case. A simplified visual on how this relationship would be represented is shown in Figure 3.9.

It is important to be constantly cognizant of what an asset is in its use within application threat modeling. An asset can be a physical server, which can encompass multiple other assets such as COTS or virtual servers – both of which may have integral roles within the scope of an application environment. For these assets identified via application decomposition, a subset listing of actors and use cases should be

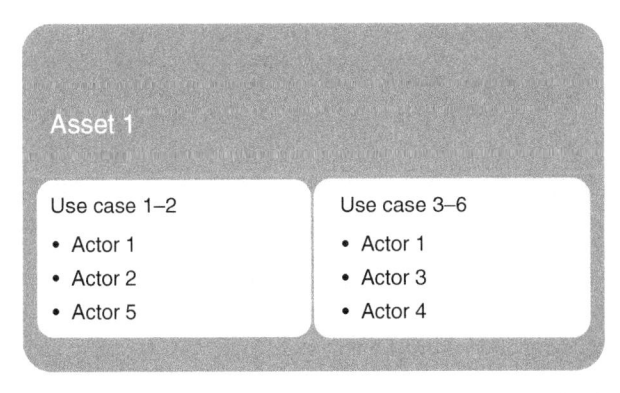

Figure 3.9 Relationship among Assets, Use Cases, Actors in Application Decomposition

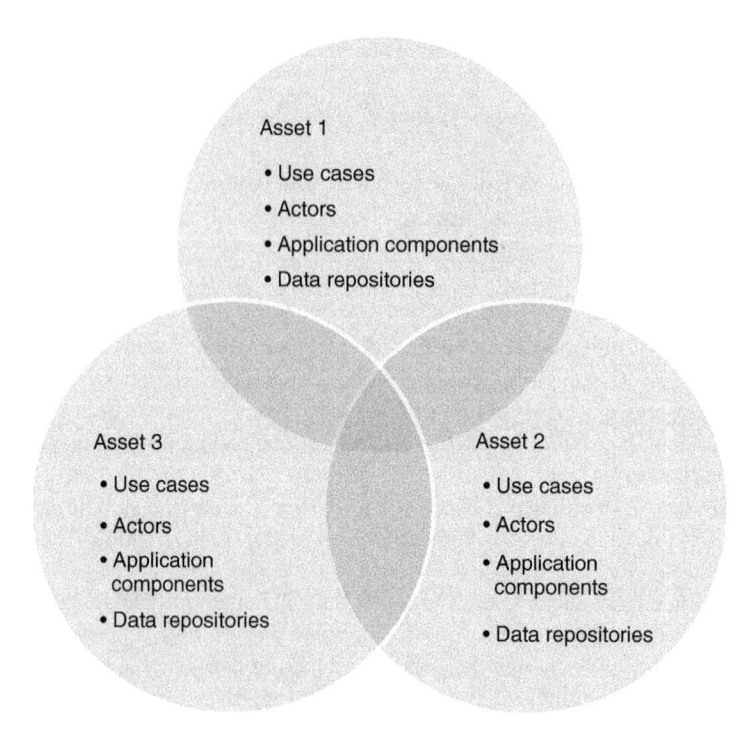

Figure 3.10 Interrelated Asset Variables within an Application Environment

identified. Excluding or overlooking a set of actors or use cases for any asset, belonging to an application environment makes for a less effective threat model since the missed area may encompass the threat that is most prevalent or likely to be utilized by an adversary. This is an example of the level of granularity and attention to detail necessary to effectively apply threat modeling.

As shown in Figure 3.9, a given asset as part of an application environment may encompass multiple use cases, which may in turn interact with multiple actors for those use cases. Although this figure portrays that use cases and actors are neatly wrapped under the boundaries of an asset, the actor's role or executed use case may extend to other assets within the application environment. This would best be represented in Figure 3.10.

Stage IV – Threat Analysis

By this stage, we now have a transparent application environment where use cases, underlying technologies, and supported network topologies are well understood. At this phase of the threat modeling methodology, the threat modeler now has the opportunity to envision why and how attacks to the application environment could be realized. Threat analysis within a threat modeling context begins with a series of questions that help to envision the motives behind attacking the application environment. A good list of self-examination questions is provided as follows and helps

Data as a driver (The nature of the data create motive)
- Social security info
- Driver's License, National ID Card, Passport Numbers
- Credit card number
- Financial/Banking account data
- Sensitive data around critical infrastructures
- User credentials
- Private health information

Emotional drivers
- Revenge/Spite
- Disgruntlement
- Anger towards nature of business
- Politically inspired
- Religious inspired
- Nationalism based

Botnet expansion
- Increase footprint of malware distribution
- Compromise other botnets

Business competition
- Intellectual property/source code
- Product designs
- Market strategy

Cyberwarfare/Military
- Military intelligence/secrets
- Building/Plant schematics
- Military research

Figure 3.11 Factors Influencing Attacks

provide a formal process of understanding motivational factors behind attacks against an application (Figure 3.11).

There are other driving forces not mentioned here that will serve as motivational drivers for launching attacks. Ultimately, threat monitoring groups can be tasked with identifying what these factors are or what they might be in the near term for a specific organization or department.

This exercise often poses the question: How is it possible to enumerate all positive motives from individuals on both the inside of the organization as well as those from the outside, not to mention possible attack vectors? The answer is that it is not possible since we recognize that our threat model reflects a finite level of hypothesizing on how an attack would take place. However, this threat analysis extends beyond simple, educated guessing as it leverages historical, logged events for the application environment. It also can embellish researched threats from external security companies that specialize in analyzing emerging threats across networks, web applications, middleware, databases, and other forms of technology and deliver this content via threat feeds. Both play an important part in forming a threat analysis against a particular application environment – one builds upon the known attacks and reconnaissance from inside and outside the traditional application boundaries, while threat feeds help draw correlations between similar application environments in order to derive similar attacks that may affect the application being assessed. Today, the latter takes place to some degree in a general sense that a perceived threat exists and is reported by many in the field of information security, thereby creating a false sense of threat that many follow simply because they do not have a threat model for their own organization's application environment. Hence, in a very general sense, security practitioners are accustomed to looking outwardly to identify what relevant threats risk mitigation efforts they should address. External information sources, such as threat feeds, security alerts, vulnerabilities listings, and top vulnerability and attack listings are all external sources of information that drive how many view potential viable threats. However, threat perception should not begin from a foreign or outside consensus on universal threats for various types of application environments (mobile, web, client-server, etc.). Instead, threat analysis should first examine the actual events that have taken place against an organization's internal and external networks. This does not mean that embellishing external threat information is nonstrategic or ineffective. The point to be made here is that it should not be the first step in conducting threat analysis for a given application environment. Entirely too much outward facing analysis has trumped the wealth of information that companies have within to identify and profile probable threat scenarios. This is most likely attributed to the ease of leveraging external threat analysis versus conducting correlative analysis of platform, application, and/or network logs. These information sources log many events that can help to understand better an attack or an attacker.

Those who have actually done correlative analysis across multiple logging sources know that this effort, although valuable, is difficult to sustain and manage. Even with advanced correlation engines and sophisticated filters, isolating alerts to diffuse the noise of the varied alerts into a decipherable security threat is not easy and requires a lot of patience, stamina, and an enormous amount of concentration. Security Incident and Event Monitoring (SIEM) products have definitely helped in this regard, particularly when they port a powerful correlation engine that facilitates or even automates filtering based on regular expressions or technical/business driven logic. Those who do not have such technical resources will be faced with a time-consuming challenge when performing a threat analysis based on internal log information and events. For those that do not even perform any level of centralized logging, this becomes an almost insurmountable dilemma. In these situations, a managed solution for infrastructure wide incident analysis makes sense so that the sophisticated level of threat analysis can take place with a provider that has invested the time, money, and expertise into a threat analysis as a service option.

Reverting to the traditional, non-outsourced model, threat analysis fundamentals actually begin without having to review one logged event or recorded incident. Prior to monitoring recorded events, a threat analyst must identify internal information sources or physical assets in some degree of detail and understanding for their intrinsic worth. Comprehending the value of information, above and beyond its worth and outside the context of what the organization may leverage its use is very important. Is it too close-minded to think that information fuels all attacks for your organization? Would reputation-based attacks be likely? Are attacks most likely to be fueled by insiders? Are our competitors simply out to ensure that your innovation becomes

SECURITY, SOFTWARE, RISK-BASED VARIANTS

stagnated and interrupted with a costly distraction? This core step in the threat analysis will help to accomplish two things: (1) provide a basis or motive for which attacks may take place and (2) augment the level of threat perception to a level that impacts the probability for which certain attacks may take place (in conjunction with proper incident and event analysis).

Simply knowing where your data resides can be sufficiently challenging for most companies. Understanding the value of data, both within and beyond the context of legitimate use will help pinpoint what areas of the application need the greatest layer(s) of countermeasures. It will also serve as a good primer prior to embarking on event and incident analysis efforts within this stage of threat analysis.

In summary, threat analysis and the underlying activities and exercises that support its cause foster threat perception – a key ingredient for catalyzing remediation, fostering "on the job" security awareness (since it is an integrated by-product of application threat modeling). The threat analysis embraces enumeration as a technique that attackers know all too well. From the perspective of the white hat during threat analysis, enumerating threats is based upon the following:

1. *Possible motives:* With an understanding of data locality, understood worth, and its overall use cases, a proposed threat landscape can be loosely defined.
2. *Observed "noise" on the wire/asset:* Will ultimately bridge threat perception with tangible historical evidence that is relevant to network, software, and host-based events.

Granted that enumerating threats can borderline becoming a perpetual exercise, thereby making subsequent attack enumeration for each threat to be infinite, the objective here is not 100% coverage, but instead targeted coverage to probable threat scenarios. It is worth reiterating that these threat scenarios are not qualitative, feel-good assessments that dilute risk representations. Instead, the threat analysis stage fosters a granular manner of understanding the threat and its underlying attack branches. Later in this book, we will go over some practical examples on how to build a proper threat analysis via gathering information from standalone IT assets or interrelated syslog information to a SIEM solution.

Stage V – Vulnerability Mapping

Up to this point, the threat modeling methodology has been able to define business objectives that should support the multitude of use cases for an application environment. This was followed by properly defining scope for the application environment, which allows the threat modeler to encompass the varied use cases and functionality associated with the application components. From that point, the methodology allows us to enumerate what those components are by enumerating the assets, services, and software that represent the inner gears of the application environment. In this section, we will build upon these aforementioned steps in the threat modeling methodology in order to identify the flaws in design or functionality to each component of the application environment.

Vulnerability mapping is a time and energy intensive stage within the methodology. The good news is that vulnerability mapping can largely be automated and leverage the existing workflow of vulnerability scanning efforts managed by a Security Operations Center (SOC) or individuals who are responsible for an enterprise's ongoing vulnerability scanning of application environments. While much efficiency is gained by leveraging output from such scanning efforts, threat modeling, as a beneficiary to the information stemming from vulnerability management, depends on reliable data where false positive rates should be significantly reduced as compared to standalone vulnerability scanning efforts that do not feed a threat modeling program. The reason for the elevated dependency on improved vulnerability detection is due to the proximity that vulnerability mapping has to the next phase of the methodology: building the attack tree. We will expand on this phase in the next section; however, reliable vulnerability data must be obtained here in order to shape the various attack branches of the attack tree. Each of these branches will identify probable and feasible attacks to which existing vulnerabilities exist within a dissecting application environment. False positives will distract the threat modeler and his/her audience from addressing viable threats and will ultimately affect the end goal of addressing risk scenarios that are not probable.

Mapping vulnerabilities to assets introduces several pragmatic challenges. Each individual asset, for which vulnerabilities are mapped to (within an assessed application environment), is ever changing. The types of users accessing said application component, version of software, auxiliary services or programs, number of users (actors), associated privileges, and type of platform each have their own set of vulnerabilities to which they can be paired. This mapping exercise can become extensive and difficult to balance since it may be tempting for most threat modelers to focus on types of vulnerabilities that they can relate to best within their environment (platform vs network).

Besides being cumbersome, mapping vulnerabilities to assets introduces other logistical challenges for those seeking to successfully implement one of the most difficult stages of the threat modeling process. As if vulnerability tracking was not difficult enough in a nonthreat modeling context, maintaining a repository of vulnerabilities and assets and creating ongoing relationships between the two are very time-consuming. To date, there is no solution that can facilitate mapping and managing these relationships in an ongoing manner, thereby creating the opportunity to fall behind quite easily in maintaining these assets to vulnerability associations. No stage in application threat modeling is more burdensome for this reason. Despite the high levels of time investment and expertise needed to manage these information relationships, the benefits of properly executing these assets to vulnerability mappings will help build a more accurate threat model since vulnerabilities affecting infrastructure assets will be attractive conduits for attacks, thereby enumerating areas where countermeasures and subsequent risk analysis should take place.

An optimized state of maturity level may never be achieved for the process of asset to vulnerability matching. However, if that level is close to being achieved, an advanced stage can and should ultimately be encompassed within the phase of mapping vulnerabilities to asset data. This phase involves pairing evolved exploit testing software of business logic vulnerabilities that are not easily detected by commercial or automated solutions. This process requires a greater level of expertise in the field of vulnerability management in order to properly identify and research vulnerabilities and thereafter develop proof of concept exploit testing against a subscribed set of platforms, network technology, or applications that would be vulnerable to these exploits. The need for this evolved form of testing and mapping is to supersede the lag in vulnerability detection and disclosure. Some companies are looking for ways to extend beyond the typical vulnerability management program that simply detects vulnerabilities that have been published for quite some time. Instead, some more advanced firms or security service companies are developing proof of concept exploits and testing them against an array of technology assets in order to discover new vulnerabilities based on simple reconnaissance efforts. It is in these types of services that many companies can truly emulate the attacker's workflow when targeting a system or network, thereby elevating the sophistication level of the attack model.

Stage VI – Building the Attack Tree

Assuming a proper mapping of current and active vulnerabilities to assets within a given application environment, identifying attack branches on the attack tree follows as the next step in the application threat model. Focusing on attack patterns for given assets requires a strong level of confidence in the vulnerability data as its integrity will assist in validating the feasibility of exploitation for some of the vulnerabilities that have been identified in the prior phase. Missing vulnerabilities or false positives will undoubtedly waste a lot of time and effort or reduce the readiness level with which a company can address probable attack vectors.

This phase of the threat modeling methodology will incorporate a pen tester at multiple levels, but mostly as it relates to exploiting some of the identified vulnerabilities. This stage's objective focuses on determining the feasibility of exploiting identified vulnerabilities that pertain to the application scope of assets. The success of this stage stems from the ability of the pen tester to prove that these identified vulnerabilities are indeed exploitable. This is critical and difficult given the time constraints in testing many of the identified vulnerabilities, even if limiting the testing to only critical or high level vulnerabilities. It is suggested that a diversified pool of automated pen testing tools compliment manual-based reviews and exploitative test scripts to balance automation and qualitative manual testing, given the challenges with managing time effectively during this phase.

As was the case with vulnerability-asset mappings (where associations were made among vulnerabilities and assets), attacks are also correlated to both variables in order to give way to more mature attack branches on the attack tree. Metaphorically speaking, the tree represents the threat with underlying attacks that sustain the realization of the threat. This best represents a security-centric approach to building an attack tree. Given the many to many relationships that assets may have with vulnerabilities and attack patterns, the fullness of the branch may evolve dramatically, thereby giving way to a mature attack tree as part of the threat model. An asset- or risk-based approach will represent the trunk of the tree to be the application environment from which assets support the overall application ecosystem. From these branches, nodes related to application use cases, misuse cases, vulnerabilities, attacks, actors, and privileges can be identified.

In an asset-centric-based threat model, the branch from the "trunk" or core of the application environment may represent the software or hardware asset, since the focus is to discover risks relatable to the asset level. A software-based approach to application threat modeling may take a more targeted approach and divert attention from network and platform-based vulnerabilities and attacks in order to focus on more software-related vulnerabilities that give way to attacks, such as insecure coding practices or design flaws in the application architecture. Although some regard of network- and platform-based analysis is incorporated, it is more focused on flaws at the application or software level. This makes more sense because the maturity level of system and network level security typically exceeds that of organically developed software, which is ever changing and therefore changing either positively or negatively in terms of overall security.

Overall, building a well-represented attack tree depends on a well-maintained library of vulnerabilities and attack patterns. It is quickly apparent that normalizing, organizing, and maintaining vulnerability and attack data are essential for building an effective attack tree for the vulnerability mapping and attack tree phases of the threat modeling methodology. From a risk management perspective, these phases are the essential ingredients to elevate current day security risk management efforts as they both provide the smoking gun to the risk analysis – something that has been sought and difficult to provide under traditional application assessment efforts. Until now, the threat modeling methodology leverages the expertise of so many different security silos, making it a more reputable model from which to build a risk analysis framework.

A Note About Security Content Automation   The MITRE organization, in its ongoing pursuit to seek support for its standardization of security information, has several data protocols and schemas, which many companies in the private and public sector can leverage. The shared content helps achieve a standardized format for security information, vulnerability/threat enumeration, and security reporting. In collaboration with the National Institute of Standards and Technology, MITRE has put forth various protocols related to application vulnerabilities, weaknesses, and attack patterns. These internationally recognized standards are already widely leveraged across the information security industry, particularly by security vendors and their associated products as part of a move toward a security content automation protocol (SCAP). There are a select few companies that are not security vendors and are now looking internally or externally to develop SCAP-related content that encompasses the many formats MITRE has made available to the security public at large.

Collectively as an industry, the drive has been to create greater standardization related to how security configuration and vulnerability data are normalized across security technologies and ingested across disparate data stores. NIST currently funds SCAP, which helps define the data and technology requirements that solutions should

TABLE 3.13 MITRE's Security Content

Name	Description	Threat Modeling Use
CVSS	(Common Vulnerability Scoring System) Used to determine the overall risk level to identified vulnerabilities in software applications	Can be used to fuel risk calculation across all threat modeling approaches (Software-, Asset-, Risk-based approaches)
CVE	(Common Vulnerability Enumeration) Provides an enumeration of vulnerability data for software/system platforms	Building a better vulnerability library to integrate while building an attack tree
CCE	(Common Configuration Enumeration) Reveals configuration gaps for various system platforms and software applications	Can be related to vulnerabilities or weaknesses in various application components. Attack tree integration potential
CAPEC	(Common Attack Pattern Enumeration Content) Identifies attack patterns that are associated with given platform systems and/or software applications	Leveraged in developing an attack library from which assets, vulnerabilities, use cases, and attack vectors can be mapped to
CWE	(Common Weakness Enumeration) Identifies a list of common flaws/weaknesses in software applications. Unlike CVE, weakness enumeration identifies software flaws that are not related to technical software weaknesses but instead to the lack of countermeasures against software attacks	In conjunction with CVE and CCE, weak application points help define nodes in the attack tree for which attack patterns can be viable exploits launched against an application

have in order to foster interoperability of security information. MITRE's effort contributes to fulfilling this new initiative taking shape across the security industry. Tying back into application threat modeling, many of these standard security protocols represent threat and vulnerability information that can represent attack and vulnerability libraries, respectively. A list of these data sources provided by MITRE and what they encompass are provided in Table 3.13.

Stage VII – Risk and Impact Analysis

The final stage of the highlighted threat modeling methodology ends with risk and impact analysis; two efforts that bridge the efforts made by security groups into the concerns and agendas of any organization's business leaders. This stage is not left with the "burden of proof" to derive risk and affect values for application environments. In fact, each of the previously recapped stages of the application threat modeling methodology aim to contribute and sustain proper risk and impact analysis in various degrees.

Risk and impact analysis within InfoSec needs a serious level of improvement and revitalization in order to restore its credibility. The underlying objective of this book focuses on outlining an option, application threat modeling, for restoring that tarnished image. Security risk management is faltering today, not because of a lack of guidelines or frameworks (which we can all agree that there are several), but rather from the lack of convincing and substantial evidence that accounts for gaps in security controls, whether automated by technology and/or sustained by processes. Sharing blame for this dysfunction, both professional and technical security professionals have a lot to learn and leverage from application threat modeling.

Many of InfoSec's critics cite that the technical and even nontechnical communities are unable to deliver a risk analysis using a business perspective. The blame here is equally shared by both the "suits" and the security "rock stars" that represent our myopic security world. Highly qualified and very technical security professionals (whether they are pen testers, source code reviewers, malware engineers, or beyond) are to blame for their lack of business relevance. These "rock stars" dominate their technical fields but are unable to bridge how their findings or analysis, no matter how sophisticated and advanced, equate to something that business leaders in operation, management, or even IT should be concerned with outside of the usual motivational drivers that include one of the following points:

- Everyone else is securing their data/environment in the same way.
- Compliance with <insert regulation> requires that you listen to the changes that I am talking about.
- All of your data and network will be compromised in x time frame if you do not comply with these remediation findings.

Although there is a hint of over simplification in the aforementioned standard repertoire of answers that technical security professionals provide to their business counterparts or managers, the fact remains that elements of business impact and risk are not effectively communicated within the deliverables or communications from security rock stars. Many management officials do not see the business relevance on how exploitable software or permeable networks translate to an imminent business risk outside of simply not meeting a regulatory requirement.

Conversely, the "suits" *generally* fail where the rock stars succeed. The key word here is generally, as there are several security professionals who, although fully certified with all the latest credentials, are still inept when it comes to business fundamentals. Nevertheless, many suits have come to understand the various components of a business well enough to understand the criticality of how application environments sustain organizational goals and objectives. They are more proficient with business operations at multiple levels of the organization and are therefore able to articulate the key concerns of what matters most to a company. This proves to be effective in conveying elements of risk and business impact to upper management. Unfortunately, suits have many known deficiencies in communicating with their technical counterparts, thereby weakening, or extending the remediation time period for open risk issues. Application threat modeling is not aimed to create a hybrid of a "rock star" and a "suit." It does, however, channel the positive strengths of each type so that they can effectively collaborate toward a common goal of identifying both risk and business impact. Examples that are more concrete will be revealed later on in this book.

Application threat modeling can be a game changer to the areas of security and technology risk management. This assumes an adoption of the risk-centric approach although some manifestation of risk is also possible with either the software or the security-centric approaches that have been previously discussed.

All of the various stages of the highlighted threat modeling methodology support the objective of identifying and managing risk and business impact. The first stage reveals the business objectives that provide qualitative baselines on qualifying risk. Impact against the fulfillment of these baselines would undoubtedly constitute a risk since these baselines represent business objectives. For example, an IVR or voice response unit (VRU) may have been implemented to reduce call-waiting times at a customer operations center. The business may look at this application development effort as a solution to historical problems related to long call-wait times, which ultimately contributed to their poor customer service issues.

Other criteria could not be used as a baseline to qualify risk in this first stage, but certainly, the impact of not achieving the defined business objectives in the first stage should easily denote that this should be a risk factor for the application environment. It is also important to consider other possible objectives that extend beyond the application environment as part of the risk analysis, but these remain secondary unless clearly defined and prioritized by the business. For example, having adverse impact to other, more critical application environments, where their respective business objectives supersede the value of those defined for the currently threat modeled application, should be considered. Additionally, nonapplication business objectives that represent more steadfast and ongoing objectives for the overall organization would naturally supersede the importance of all, more granular business objectives defined by the application environment.

Above and beyond creating a relevant point of reference for security risk analysis, phase one also allows for defining a proper scope for the risk analysis. This helps to preserve the integrity of the final deliverable as the analysis maintains itself topical to risks identified by the threat model and ultimately its impact to business operations. Phase two (scope definition) further fulfills this objective. Proper risk analysis should always fall within defined boundaries for the analysis. The scope of the threat model should encircle only the application components that are (1) core to the application, (2) essential in the fulfillment of the defined business objectives, and (3) within a set of trust boundaries that are under the control of the team conducting the threat model. Otherwise, a boundless scope dilutes the effectiveness of scrutinizing application level controls, embedded business logic, and varying forms of configuration across the application environment. A scope that is too large also complicates the understanding of other threat modeling variables such as actors, roles, and particularly vulnerabilities since any new piece of hardware or software introduced may exponentially exacerbate the threat modeling scope to an endless cat and mouse game. For this reason, the scope of the threat model must be well defined unless the threat perception necessitates that other related application components become part of the threat model. Many professionals will argue that even the smallest and most infrequent API could serve as the attack vector that can ultimately compromise an entire application, rooting both its platform and software. Although this is theoretically true, threat modeling's objective is to provide a thorough and likely attack simulation for a given application environment and not the dozens of adjacent application environments that it may interface with. Those application environments should instead have their own respective threat models with anecdotal reference to previously threat modeled applications. Essentially, there should be an assumption that these surrounding environments are in fact compromised and therefore warrant a layered set of countermeasures to protect the environment that is the object of the threat model.

Now that we have defined a scope for analysis, we need to carve out the areas of the environment that will be systematically reviewed. Application decomposition (stage III) further elevates the objective of risk and impact analysis via granularity. An application walk-through of compiled libraries, ACLs, system or application level processes/domains and more elevate the level of detail that the comparable, yet vastly different, risk assessment efforts do not currently offer. One of the problems with traditional risk assessments is the lack of precision in details, hence the reason many associate it with speculative analysis at best. Application decomposition seeks to clearly ID the actors, use cases, APIs, stored libraries, and data sources that are involved with the application. As a result, weaknesses or vulnerabilities in any of the dissected application components can be addressed with greater precision and in-depth analysis, as it relates to risk and business impact. This extends beyond simple patch management gap analysis, configuration flaw identification, or generic security function checklist efforts that are more generic and nonspecific to the context of the application environment. Application decomposition is particularly effective when separated application components are correlated to vulnerabilities and attack patterns. This essentially performs a logical walk-through of how application components, use cases, and vulnerabilities can become exploitable and ultimately translate to risk issues for the organization. Truthfully, this level of detail, in correlation with the security testing that threat modeling efforts require, will help to bolster remediation by proving the viability of these attacks to developers, system administrators, third party technology affiliates, and so on.

The fourth stage of the threat modeling methodology, threat analysis, also provides substance to the risk and impact analysis stage of the threat modeling process via slightly less pragmatic means than application or network testing. The threat analysis stage qualifies threats that may spawn attacks geared toward the application environment. Part of the research in this area encompasses a review of historical incidents against similar companies, infrastructures, application types, or information repositories. The threat analysis will involve research from within the protected environment (integrated logs, application events, etc.) as well as threat intelligence from managed service providers who may be able to provide some trending analysis on similar types of threats and the observed attack patterns that may have been logged.

Stages V (vulnerability mapping) and VI (attack modeling) of the application threat modeling methodology also provide the same value of granularity to identifying and analyzing information paramount to proper risk analysis. Specifically, the level of granularity that is most useful surrounds the details of an attack, versus simply addressing the finer points. As discovered vulnerabilities are paired with exploits, the attack feasibility factor becomes quite apparent for those contending to remediate the risks identified by the threat model. These precise pieces of vulnerability and attack information substantiate risk findings and help demonstrate how weaknesses in developed software can be successfully exploited. It extends beyond vulnerability assessment efforts alone, which leave the attack logistics as theoretical principles that engineers, system administrators, and/or developers are forced to accept and thereafter remediate without specifics on how these vulnerabilities come to introduce risks as revealed in a traditional security deliverable. Altogether, stages III, V, and VI do something that prior application assessment efforts failed to do – emulate the attacker's plan of attack into an actual attack, particularly layered attacks, which are what most real world attacks represent. Most automated pen testing and dynamic/static web application tests perform scripted attacks, which only imitate common attack sequences against an application environment, but do not represent a true-targeted attack. The plan of attack and supportive reasons for an attack are also rarely built into the pen testing methodology, making the exercise less of an attack simulation but more of a throwing the kitchen sink of standard exploits against an application environment exercise.

This is not to discredit pen testing as a useful form of identifying security holes, particularly since we recognize the huge disparity of how pen tests are conducted today. The reality, however, is that many pen tests are not executed with a black hat ability and perspective, meaning that the abilities of the pen tester do not truly represent the efforts of a real attack. Since this phase of the threat model provides the smoking gun as to how discovered and validated vulnerabilities can become exploited, there is heavy reliance on the testing phase being somewhat successful. The success of this phase helps to convey risk and impact of a vulnerable application environment via the exploitability of vulnerable software or networks. This technical risk information would then need to be correlated to its role in supporting the business, thereby allowing a proper business risk analysis, all stemming from the application and technical risks that have been found within this stage.

A great deal of dependency and complexity exists in the integration of pen testing efforts to the vulnerability mapping and attack tree build-out phases of the threat model. The key challenge relates to attempting to simulate a real world attack via pen testing efforts. The other challenge is in not encroaching on the autonomy of pen testing efforts that may be managed by internal security operations teams and/or third party service providers. Since most organizations are not fully mature in a threat modeling workflow, the disparity between pen testing efforts and true attack simulations are bearable growing pains, especially considering that this is mostly a training issue that can be more easily overcome than creating and repeating a threat modeling workflow.

This final stage of the threat modeling methodology is ultimately focused on risk and impact toward the application environment and most importantly toward the overall business. The steps that have preceded the risk and impact analysis all provide the risk analysis the ability to supersede other forms of risk analysis. At this point, there is a clearly defined list of possible threats as well as an attack tree that encompasses assets, associated vulnerabilities, attack branches, and any associated countermeasures already present within the environment. The viability of the defined attacks have also been well accounted for at this stage as vulnerability assessments, pen testing, dynamic analysis, and static analysis efforts may all or partially have been triggered by the prior stages in order to legitimize the probability for some of these attacks. The threat modeler can leverage the results of such security testing efforts from security operations to quantify probability ratios for succeeding on some of the defined attacks listed in the attack tree (stages VI and VII). For attack probabilities to be credible, it may not be necessary to have all defined vulnerabilities successfully exploited. Time restraints for creating the threat model will mostly constrain the amount of security testing that takes place to attacks that represent defined motives and use cases that are most likely to be exploited. This is actually no different from most security operation efforts within large organizations. For threat modeling to become an effective and sustainable process, it cannot drag on with testing and create a bottleneck for development efforts' goal of migrating new software builds to various customer or production environments.

To culminate to a point where a final risk analysis can be made for the application environment, the threat model must reveal the net level of exploitable vulnerabilities that introduce measurable risk and business impact. The net level of exploits equates to a residual level of exploitable vulnerabilities that are not mitigated by the present set of existing processes, network, and/or application countermeasures. From this, the business impact resulting from the effects of these net exploits will help to derive the business impact. It is at this point that the threat modeling process can ingest additional foreign pieces of information from other security efforts to calculate a set of cost variables, which will help to quantify business impact. Typically, impact is qualitatively portrayed, which forces business leaders to reconcile qualitative descriptors to something with greater quantitative meaning. For example, existing deliverables that reveal High-, Medium-, or Low-risk findings would conceivably be less valuable to more granular, previously captured, annual loss expectancy (ALE) values (e.g. $1.2 million as a result of a breach or successful attack) from a previously conducted risk assessment on the target application environment. In such a case, the risk report deliverable provides some level of basis for an impact value to leverage. Ultimately, if impact values can be leveraged from these types of existing security efforts, including business impact analysis (BIAs), then identifying application risk and deriving a meaningful business risk is plausible, all using a collaborative approach unlike any other security disciplines.

Chapter 7 explores in detail all the stages of this proposed application threat modeling methodology. Included in that chapter are real-world, practical security workflows that address some of the existing challenges that inhibit the adoption and applicability of each stage of the application threat model.

4

THREAT MODELING WITHIN THE SDLC

BUILDING SECURITY IN SDLC WITH THREAT MODELING

> "Proactively identifying risks is one of the main benefits of threat modeling. Rather than waiting for something bad to happen and waiting for the risk to be realized it means taking control of risks and making risk informed decisions in advance and initiate design changes ahead of a future deployment of the application. But a lot of businesses out there don't see the return on investment, they look at it as a liability, and until they can understand that proactive security actually returns, gives them a return on investment, it's still a hard sell for people."
>
> Kevin Mitnick

Application and software are complimentary; software is what applications are made of. Applications are engineered by following a Software Development Life Cycle (SDLC) process that encompasses different phases such as software functional requirements, software design, coding, building the software to an executable, integration with other software libraries, and building to create an executable, functional, quality testing.

Rationale for Building Security in the SDLC

Historically, security in software has been mostly considered as a requirement to be validated with functional testing that usually takes place during the last phase of the

---

Risk Centric Threat Modeling: Process for Attack Simulation and Threat Analysis, First Edition.
Tony UcedaVélez and Marco M. Morana.
© 2015 John Wiley & Sons, Inc. Published 2015 by John Wiley & Sons, Inc.

SDLC. Any security issues that would have been identified at that stage, such as common vulnerabilities, requires implementing a fix for the issue, testing and release of either a patch or a new release of the application. The main purpose of building security in the SDLC is to create software that adheres to security requirements, is checked for software vulnerabilities and built and tested for security. Another main reason of building secure software from the beginning of the SDLC is cost efficiency. Since creating secure software by bolting on a fix after testing is rather expensive and inefficient, software vendors started adopting a proactive approach by considering security from the creation of the software requirements, followed by secure design, secure coding, and secure testing. This process of secure software development is often referred by the software security professionals in different terms, such as secure software engineering process, secure by design, secure by development, and secure by deployment and building security in the software development life cycle. For the purpose of this chapter, we will refer to this as secure software engineering.

By following a secure software engineering process, it is possible to embed software security activities during the different phases of the software development life cycle such as during requirements documentation, architecture design, coding integration with other software libraries, and building the execution and testing. There are key secure software development activities that can be integrated within the software engineering process: during requirements, the derivation of software requirements, during design review, that the design conforms to security by design standards (such as secure architecture standards), during coding, following secure coding standards and validation, and after coding, that source code does not include vulnerabilities due to coding errors. During testing, the application is security tested to ensure that the application built does not have any common application vulnerabilities. If it does, they are fixed prior to release of the application software in production. Typically, all vulnerabilities are rated according to their technical risk and remediated accordingly.

Software that is built and released with very few vulnerabilities and with no high or medium risk vulnerabilities is considered more secure than the same software with a large number of vulnerabilities and several rated high and medium risk. The approach considered is defensive, meaning that there are fewer opportunities presented to a threat agent/attacker to exploit vulnerabilities and the organization has the least risk of these being exploited and is better because of the security. The extent to which vulnerabilities can be exploited in application software depends on different factors, such as the likelihood of an attacker finding the vulnerability and then exploiting it. This type of risk analysis takes into consideration the attacker's perspective. From the attacker's point of view, some of application vulnerabilities can be identified by running some security testing tools against the application. If these vulnerabilities have not been tested and fixed by the organization that developed the software before releasing it into production, the attacker can now easily identify and exploit them.

Besides common vulnerabilities that can be easily identified by automation tools, referred to as low hanging fruits, there are vulnerabilities that can only be identified through manual testing and in some cases, only by having access to the source code of the application. These vulnerabilities are difficult to identify without access to the application source code and without some experience with manual testing techniques.

From the defensive perspective, it is important to reduce the opportunities for an attacker to exploit application vulnerabilities, hence these need to be identified and fixed prior to releasing them into production. From the security engineering perspective, vulnerabilities need to be identified and the causes of them removed at the different phases of the SDLC. Vulnerabilities in given applications might be the cause of different factors and can be potentially introduced in any phase of the SDLC. For example, application vulnerabilities might be caused by a gap in the documentation of security requirements, an error introduced during design such as a security design flaw/deviation from security standards, a coding error such as a vulnerability created by specific source code, an error in testing such as not conducting a specific security test as well as misconfiguration of the security of the application before releasing into the production environment. From secure software engineering perspective, it is therefore important to look at all the possible avenues for introducing vulnerabilities during the different phases of the SDLC and to adopt security measures for preventing them.

The Importance of Embedding Threat Modeling During the SDLC

Identifying security issues in software prior to these issues being exposed into the production environment is an important factor for mitigating the possibility and the impact of a threat agent targeting these vulnerabilities. Once security issues are identified, the next step is to determine the severity of the vulnerability such as to determine the likelihood, impact, and whether these vulnerabilities need to be remediated and how. From the risk perspective, vulnerabilities might pose a risk to the application depending on the possibility that this vulnerability can be exploited by a threat agent and depending on the potential impact to the assets if these are exploited. It is important first and foremost to identify the potential threats against the application and the potential threat agents, the functions of the application, the assets that can be targeted by these threat agents, the type of attacks and attack vectors that can be used, the type of vulnerabilities that can be exploited by these attack vectors, and the security measures that might be put in place to mitigate the risk.

Identifying the potential threats targeting an application can start first with the analysis of the potential threat agents, their motives, and their targets, such as the data and the business functionality that the application is intended to provide.

In essence, this threat analysis consists of conducting a preliminary risk analysis of the application before the application is developed. This threat analysis can initially be based on the knowledge of a set of high-level requirements describing the business objectives, such as the type of data and functionality that is described as necessary to fulfill these business objectives. At this stage, it might possible to define at a high level what the potential threats are that might affect the data and the business functionality and to determine a set of security requirements to mitigate the risks posed by these threats.

In essence, this means embedding a threat modeling activity to analyze these threats in the early phases of the SDLC. The main goal of embedding this threat modeling is to identify potential risks as early as possible so that they can be managed by designing, implementing, and testing countermeasures throughout the SDLC.

By doing so, one immediate advantage is that is possible to make engineering decisions on how to manage technical risks. By putting applications in scope for application threat modeling as early as the requirement phase of the SDLC, risk managers can make informed risk decisions on how to mitigate these risks, such as requiring specific countermeasures to be designed and implemented, accepting the possible risks, not requiring additional countermeasures either because of existing controls or because the potential risk impact and likelihood is low, avoiding the risk by deciding not to design that functionality, and finally transferring the risk to a third party who will take ownership and liability of the risk.

The main advantages of embedding threat modeling in all the phases of the SDLC are:

1. *Risk management* that is to allow risk to be managed proactively from the early stages of the SDLC.
2. *Security requirements* that is to derive the security requirements to mitigate potential risks of vulnerability exploits and targeted attacks against application components.
3. *Secure design*, that is to be able to identify security design flaws, their exposure to threat agents and attacks, and prioritize fixing them by issuing new design documentation prior to the next phase of the SDLC.
4. *Security issue prioritization* that is to determine the risk exposure and impact of threats targeting issues identified during secure code reviews and prioritizing them for mitigation.
5. *Security testing* that is to derive security tests from use and abuse cases of the application for testing the effectiveness of security measures in mitigating threats and attacks targeting the application.
6. *Secure release of applications after development* that is to allow the business to make informed risk decisions prior to releasing the application based on the mitigation of high-risk vulnerabilities and assertion of testing of countermeasures that mitigate specific threats.
7. *Secure release of applications after an incident* that is by determining the potential root causes that have been the cause a security to fix them and identifying additional countermeasures that can be deployed. Root cause analysis and countermeasure analysis can be based on a threat model that correlates the known effect of the attack (e.g. data breaches, denial of services) with the analysis of the causes of the incidents.

The determination of potential risks of threats targeting the application as well as inherent risks of potential vulnerabilities that can be introduced during the application life cycle can be done as early as the preliminary phase of the inception of the application, once the application business functionality is defined at a high level. The scope of this activity is the determination of a preliminary risk profile for the application.

The Importance of Security Requirements

Once business and functional requirements are defined, it is possible to derive the security requirements and mitigate potential risks of threats targeting functionality by exploiting potential vulnerabilities as well as through targeting attacks. By using threat modeling techniques such as use and abuse/misuse cases, it is possible to derive security requirements for the application and software being implemented.

Derivation of security requirements during the requirement stage of the SDLC is critical for the overall risk mitigation and the return of investment in security. Often, the majority of security issues that are identified and tested in applications later in the SDLC are introduced because of not documenting security requirements and could therefore be prevented, producing savings since there will be fewer vulnerabilities to be fixed later in the SDLC with testing before release to production.

The documentation of security requirements is also an important risk prevention activity that can be conducted prior to design of the application. At a high level, a gap in design of a security control to protect the application data can be the result of a missing security requirement to design that control. When the gap is identified later during the security testing of the application, it might add additional costs for design, implementation, and testing and delay the overall production release.

Besides gaps in design of security controls, security design flaws can be introduced because of lack of following security technology standards for the design of security controls such as authentication, authorization, encryption, input validation, session management, and audit and logging. By focusing on a security review of the architecture of the application in light of potential threats targeting the architectural components, it possible to secure proof of the soundness of the existing application design and prescribe design changes as needed.

The integration of threat modeling as an activity for deriving security requirements largely depends on the type of SDLC that is followed. In the case of SDLC such as waterfall, where the phases are linear and sequential, threat modeling can start as early as the requirement definition phase, when the functional requirements of the application are defined based on initial business requests of the business sponsoring the project to develop the application.

After deriving the security requirements, the next stage is to document the application design, including the application architecture at a high level that includes the design of the main components of the application architecture, such as user interfaces, data interfaces, servers, and databases for example. The design should also include the requirements for the design of major security controls, such as authorization and encryption.

Design requirements can be derived based on the various security technology standards that should be followed when designing and implementing security technology and security controls. Some of the security requirements can be documented based on applicable security technology standards that need to be followed during the design of the application. Some security requirements can be derived by applying threat modeling, such as by analyzing each of the components of the application architecture to determine whether these components are protected by security controls from potential threats targeting them.

At the detail design level, security requirements for implementing security controls can be derived by abuse cases that describe the interaction of a threat agent such as an attacker and the security control. Abuse cases can be derived from a use case by considering the threat agent goals in the interaction with the security control; in essence, by considering the possible ways a potential threat agent could try to break into the application controls.

By deriving abuse cases during the early phases of the SDLC, such as prior to documenting the detail design of the application, it is possible to derive security requirements for the design security controls, which will make that control more resilient to potential threats targeting it. The concept of "resilience" might be associated because of how the control is able to withstand potential attacks against the application and the data that control is designed to protect.

Designing For Security and For Attack Resilience

After the application high-level design is approved also for its application security aspects, a more detailed level of security by design that document how a security control could be implemented might follow. Some of the design flaws can also be introduced at the detail design level, for example, in the case of designing user authentication for an application, the possible exposure of the authentication data in storage and transit and the use of nonstandard encryption algorithms to encrypt such data.

At the detail design level, security controls are designed using "use cases" describing the type of interaction between the user and the controls. In the case of authentication, for example, the functional design will describe in detail the user control validation by the authentication server and the functionality to lock the account to prevent brute forcing of the password by an attacker upon a certain number of unsuccessful attempts.

Security controls can be designed to be more resilient to targeted attacks by considering how such control is normally used and how it can be abused by a threat agent. The more resilient to attacks a security control is designed, implemented, and tested, the smaller the opportunity for an attacker to find an exploitable weakness. In essence, the main goal of application threat modeling at the detail design level is to build security controls that are "resilient" to potential attack vectors, such as breaking into the application and gaining unauthorized access to confidential data.

To determine whether a security control is resilient enough to withstand attacks, it is important to consider both possible vulnerabilities and probable attack vectors. In the case of authentication, for example, this means considering brute force attacks, aimed at breaking into the authentication by trying different attack vectors to guess passwords, enumerate valid credentials, spoof authentication credentials, exploit weaknesses in account lockouts, exploit weaknesses in protecting the authentication credentials in storage and transit, exploit weaknesses in managing authenticated sessions, as well as social engineering attacks against the application user.

By identifying potential threats and attack vectors that can be used against security controls, it is possible to proactively design countermeasures to protect them. At the architectural level, a threat modeling exercise can include the threat analysis of these threats and attack vectors as well as the analysis of the architectural components that can be attacked, such as user interfaces, databases, and server components such as web and application servers and the data flows between them.

The modeling of threats that can be used against the architectural components of an application is one of the essential steps within application threat modeling. A prerequisite for determining how threats and attacks affect the application architecture consists of first identifying the different architectural components and analyzing their exposure to attack vectors, both internal and external. By following a step-by-step application threat modeling methodology, it is possible to analyze the exposure of application components to different threats and determine the type of measures that can be deployed at different architecture levels to mitigate such threats.

The assessment of the secure architecture of an application also represents an opportunity to design applications that are compliant with the organization's information security requirements to protect confidential data in storage and in transit, validate input and filter it from malicious data, implement access controls such as authentication, authorization, and secure session management.

The discussion of the security requirements and the security architecture review are usually conducted by subject matter experts in application security in conjunction with the application architects. A security architecture review session might include whiteboard exercises, interactive sessions with the architects to understand the architecture of the application and how it is secured at the component level, such as the security end-to-end from the client interface to the servers and backend where the data is stored.

In order to conduct the secure architecture review of the application, it is important to rely on an accurate documentation of the application architecture, including the high-level physical and logical diagrams as well as documentation of the security controls that might include the design of user and application to application authentication, authorization, secure session management, data protection such as encryption, data validation such as input validation, audit and logging, and error and exception handling.

Secure Architecture Design Reviews

As secure design review methodology, application threat modeling can be considered as a further review of the application to identify potential design flaws that might be exploited by targeted attacks and abuse of security controls. A prerequisite to conducting such an analysis is to have a design that documents the main elements of the application architecture such as clients, servers, middleware, and databases, as well as the data interfaces to these components.

As part of the threat modeling exercise, it is important to analyze potential attacks targeting the application data through the data interfaces that are available to a potential threat agent. While doing so, it is important to analyze how the data is validated and sanitized from malicious inputs. Once the user is authenticated to access the data, it is also important to analyze which authorizations and permissions are given to the user and to validate how these are provisioned and managed.

While reviewing the security of the architecture of an application, it is important to take both the defender and attacker's perspectives. From the defensive standpoint, applying security measures to protect the data in storage and in transit might just need to follow a set of security requirements and validate that these are enforced in the design of the application. From the attacker's perspective, one ought to consider the different attack scenarios and use threat models and attack trees to analyze how the application defenses can be effective in mitigating the risks of attacks against the application.

Training and Awareness

While conducting application threat modeling with the application architects, it is also important to consider that this represents an opportunity to educate engineering teams about application security standards, application security architecture, application vulnerabilities, as well as application threats and countermeasures. In essence, application threat modeling helps to bridge the knowledge gap between information security and engineering teams.

Another important aspect of application threat modeling integrated as part of the SDLC is that it can be used to communicate technical risk to application development stakeholders so that they can make informed risk management decisions. A list of vulnerabilities identified in a threat model whose severity of risk has been determined, for example, can help to prioritize the mitigation effort toward the vulnerabilities that bear the higher risks values.

Threat Modeling and Software Security Assessments

A threat model can also be used in conjunction with other application security assessments, such as secure code reviews to determine whether the issues identified in the software components might be exposed to potential internal or external attack vectors. For example, an SQL injection vulnerability found with source code analysis can be considered critical because a threat model has determined that it can potentially be exploited by an external attack vector without authentication. A gap in input validation at a specific data interface whose SQL injection might exploit could also introduce a high risk when the data interface allows an attacker to upload a malicious file and compromise the data that is accessible through that interface. The visualization of that attack data flow is possible when a threat model of the application is available to determine the possible exposure of the vulnerability.

Attack Modeling and Security Testing

Besides secure code reviews and static source code analysis, other application security assessments can benefit from threat modeling. A penetration test to test the application for common vulnerabilities consists of running a suite of common attack vectors against the application to validate whether the application is vulnerable to common vulnerabilities that these attack vectors might exploit. Specifically, the attack vectors that are used in the penetration testing can also be derived with a threat model exercise to conduct a more in-depth security test of possible abuse of the application trying to exploit design flaws in the application that might not be visible to the tester without previous knowledge of the application threat model.

As part of the threat modeling exercise, the different type of attacks that can be pursued by an attacker to reach his goals can be analyzed using attack trees. By analyzing the attack goal and by exploring the different means and techniques to realize that goal, it is possible to identify the potential vulnerabilities that can be exploited in an attack as well as the security controls and measures that can be used to mitigate the likelihood and the impact.

An example of how attack tree techniques can be used to analyze the attacker goal and identify the possible vulnerabilities and countermeasures is shown in Figure 4.1.

A privilege escalation attack, for example, is an attack where the intent of the attacker is to raise his privileges to access data and functions that he is not allowed to access, such as privileged administration functions and sensitive data. Some possible ways for an attacker to raise his privileges are either designs flaws or misconfiguration of role base access controls and forceful browsing. Fixing these vulnerabilities is critical for the mitigation of the risk. Fixing the vulnerabilities can be done by either addressing to the root causes, the source of the vulnerability, or the symptoms. A forceful browsing vulnerability might depend on a configuration management change, such as the setting of access control policy rules or the set of permissions to the resources at the application layer, such as through an access control list. Implementing a security control, such as Role-Based Access Control

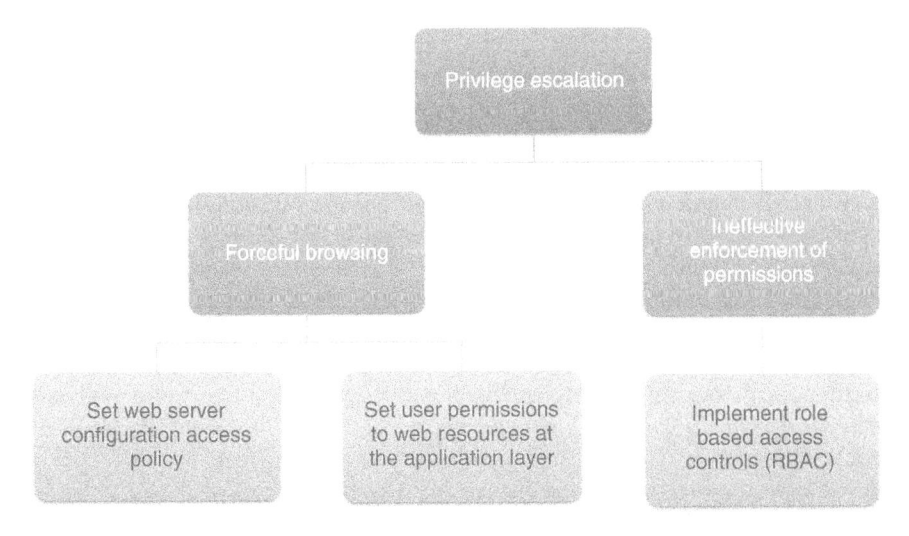

Figure 4.1 Threat Tree

(RBAC), can mitigate the risk that ineffectively enforced permissions will be exploited.

Through the attack tree analysis, it is possible to dissect attacks from the main goal of the threat agent down to the different avenues that the attacker can pursue to realize his goals. The execution of an attack depends on different factors such as the skill of the attacker, the tools at his disposal, and the knowledge of a vulnerability that can be exploited to pursue his goal. By assuming the attacker's perspective, it is possible to determine the likelihood and impact of various attacks and identify countermeasures to mitigate them. Mapping threats to vulnerabilities and countermeasures analyzed through an attack tree helps to identify which vulnerabilities should be mitigated. From the risk mitigation perspective, the decision to mitigate vulnerabilities depends on the vulnerability risk level determined by calculating the likelihood and the impact.

Threat Modeling and Software Risk Management

To proactively manage application security risks, using threat models in the SDLC can identify threats, attacks, and vulnerabilities throughout the different phases of the SDLC and make risk mitigation decisions. From the business impact perspective, mapping threats to vulnerabilities and mitigating them via security measures needs to also consider the impact on the organization's valuable assets that contain sensitive data or privileged application functions.

As a risk assessment methodology, threat modeling is concerned with modeling threats and their technical impacts due to the exploit of vulnerabilities. Mapping threats to vulnerabilities and vulnerabilities to assets and their values helps to determine the possible business impacts and whether the costs of the security measures to mitigate these vulnerabilities are worth the benefits of risk mitigation. By factoring the cost of countermeasures and the impact of exploits, such as in the case of the lack of security controls, the business can decide whether the cost of the countermeasure is less than potential business impact and the liability that the organization might incur by an attack exploiting such vulnerability.

Mapping threats to vulnerabilities and vulnerabilities to assets exposed by these can be analyzed using a risk framework for each of the business functions and application's data assets. The evaluation of the business impacts resulting from a threat attacking and compromising an asset such as data and/or functions helps to quantify the risk and monetize the costs to the organization. When the costs of compromising data and application functionality because of an attack are monetized, it is also possible to make informed decisions on how much money should be spent on countermeasures. Typically, an investment in countermeasures is justifiable when the cost of the countermeasure does not exceed the monetary loss caused by the possible threat attacking and compromising an asset. The higher the value of the asset, the more justifiable is the expense of investing in countermeasures to protect them. The analysis of quantifying the business impacts based on the value of the asset is also known in the technical literature as Business Impact Analysis (BIA).

The sooner a BIA can be performed on a given application, the better for proactively managing the application's risks. During the documentation of functional requirement phase, for example, it is possible to think through the "what if" scenarios that demonstrate how introducing new functionality and changing data can affect the overall risk to the application in case these data or functionality are compromised. The analysis of these "what if" threat scenarios and the analysis of what is at stake in case these threat scenarios are realized help determine if the risk is worth putting the new functionality and the data at stake, or rather, not implement that functionality and processing/storage of that data. If the business is willing to take the risk, it is important to justify that the risk can be controlled by a manageable level, such as by implementing countermeasures and the assurance that specific requirements are followed in the design, development, and testing of the application.

If it is not worth taking the risk because of the potential impacts to the organization, the business will consider implementing countermeasures to reduce the risk to a manageable level.

By conducting a threat modeling exercise to identify and analyze possible threats against the application, it is possible to determine the best course of action to mitigate these threats throughout the different phases of the SDLC and support important risk management decisions, such as how and when to mitigate application risks. By using the results of threat modeling throughout the SDLC, risk managers can advise the engineering team whether to redesign a component or to add new security measures before much effort is spent building the wrong solution.

INTEGRATING THREAT MODELING WITHIN THE DIFFERENT TYPES OF SDLCs

> "When to use iterative development? You should use iterative development only on projects that you want to succeed"
>
> *Martin Fowler, in UML Distilled*

Integrating Threat Modeling Into Waterfall SDLC

Software can be developed using different types of SDLCs. Traditionally, software can be developed using a linear process by following each of the phases sequentially, starting from the initial requirements phase, following through the design phase, the coding phase, and the final testing phase. Following the software development phases sequentially is also referred in the software engineering literature as waterfall SDLC.

Among the different types of SDLCs that an organization can follow for software development, the waterfall SDLC is the one that best suits the integration of security activities such as threat modeling.

During the requirement phase, for example, a threat model consists of identifying threats against the functional use cases of the application by considering a threat agent, such as an attacker trying to abuse the application functionality. At high level, when the use cases of the application are identified, it is possible to derive a set of abuse cases that map to each of the use cases with an abuse of functionality. The analysis of these abuse cases helps identify security requirements to mitigate the risk of application abuse.

During the design phase, threat modeling consists of identifying specific threats against the components of the application architecture, such as the user interfaces, the data processes, the data flows, and the data in storage. The goal of threat modeling during application design is to identify gaps in the design of security controls as well as design weaknesses.

During the coding phase, an existing application threat model can help determine the risk of security issues identified in the source code after either a manual source code analysis or an automatic source code static test for vulnerabilities.

During the testing phase, a previously executed threat model that helped to document security requirements with use and abuse cases can also be used to derive a suite of security tests that can be executed against the application to identify potential security issues. These tests' goal is to validate that any potential abuse of functionality of the application by certain threat agents and attack vectors is mitigated by the application countermeasures. In case these countermeasures are not sufficient to mitigate the threats and the realization of these threats through targeted attacks either toward specific assets or application functionality, countermeasures can be redesigned and reimplemented. By passing the final abuse test cases, the application can then be released into production.

This describes at high level the benefits of integrating threat modeling in the different phases of the SDLC. Let us walk-through more in-depth details of how this integration can be accomplished with some examples.

Assuming that the organization follows a waterfall SDLC, there will be at least four phases: requirements, design, coding, and testing.

Security Requirement Engineering

The requirements phase is the phase when security requirements are defined. During this phase, functional requirements are usually documented based on the documentation of business requirements. Security requirements for the application can be derived by considering different factors, such as compliance, privacy laws, and specific organization security policies. Security requirements can also be derived as a function of the potential threats targeting the application, specifically the data that is stored and processed by the application and the application's functionality. An example of threats against the data is threats to the confidentiality, integrity, and availability of the data. Examples of threats against the application functionality includes any abuse of the functionality with malicious intent such as for fraud, financial gain, or to damage the company's reputation. A possible way to identify threats against the application functionality is to analyze use and abuse cases. One or more abuse cases can map to each of the functional use cases of the application. For each of the abuse cases, security measures can be identified that mitigate the risk of the application abuse. These security measures can be part of the set of documented security requirements.

An example of a use-abuse case to elicit security requirements for secure authentication is included in Figure 4.2.

Use and abuse cases in graphical form depict the actions of the normal legitimate user in opposition to the abuses of these actions from malicious users. By analyzing the possible abuses of the user actions, we can derive a set of use cases to mitigate the risks of these abuse cases. In the case of a user action to perform a security function, such as authentication, the main abuse case that a threat agent/malicious user can attempt is to brute force user authentication, that is, to try to guess a username and password combination. To guess a valid username, the malicious user will try first to exploit an account, harvesting vulnerabilities to determine whether the error message can be used to distinguish between a valid username and an invalid username. Once a valid username has been harvested, the next step would be to guess valid passwords. First the malicious user will try to figure out the required format of the passwords and the minimum lengths. He will then try to attempt several passwords till the correct one is finally guessed and validated for logging in.

Once the main use and abuse cases have been analyzed for the application functionalities that might be potentially at risk such as user log-on, user access to confidential information, payments, money movement transactions, and so on, the next step consists of deriving functional requirements to designing security controls that are resilient to abuse of functionality for malicious purposes such as bypassing the functionality to gain access to unauthorized data and functionality. In the case of user log-on, for example, the security requirement for authentication that is derived from the analysis abuse of login for harvesting valid credentials consist on showing generic error messages to prevent a malicious user from harvesting the valid username from the error messages that are shown to the user. Designing authentication that require validation that passwords are constructed by enforcing information security policy requirements such as password minimum length and complexity. Locking the user account upon several unsuccessful attempts to log-on is also a measure that the authentication should implement to prevent brute forcing and can be derived by further analyzing the brute force abuse action against the password in the abuse case.

Deriving security requirements based on use and abuse cases is essential for the design of attack resilient security controls. These security requirements are characterized by making assumptions about potential threat actors targeting the application by assuming a "negative" condition and the potential risk that might further evolve from that condition. For this reason, these types of security requirements are seldom mentioned in the technical literature as either negative requirements or risk-based requirements. Risk-based security requirements are a subset of the security requirements that also include functional security requirements that describe how a security control should be designed to provide a security function such as authentication, authorization, encryption, and are also referred to as positive requirements. A subset of security requirements also include requirements for ensuring compliance with information security standards.

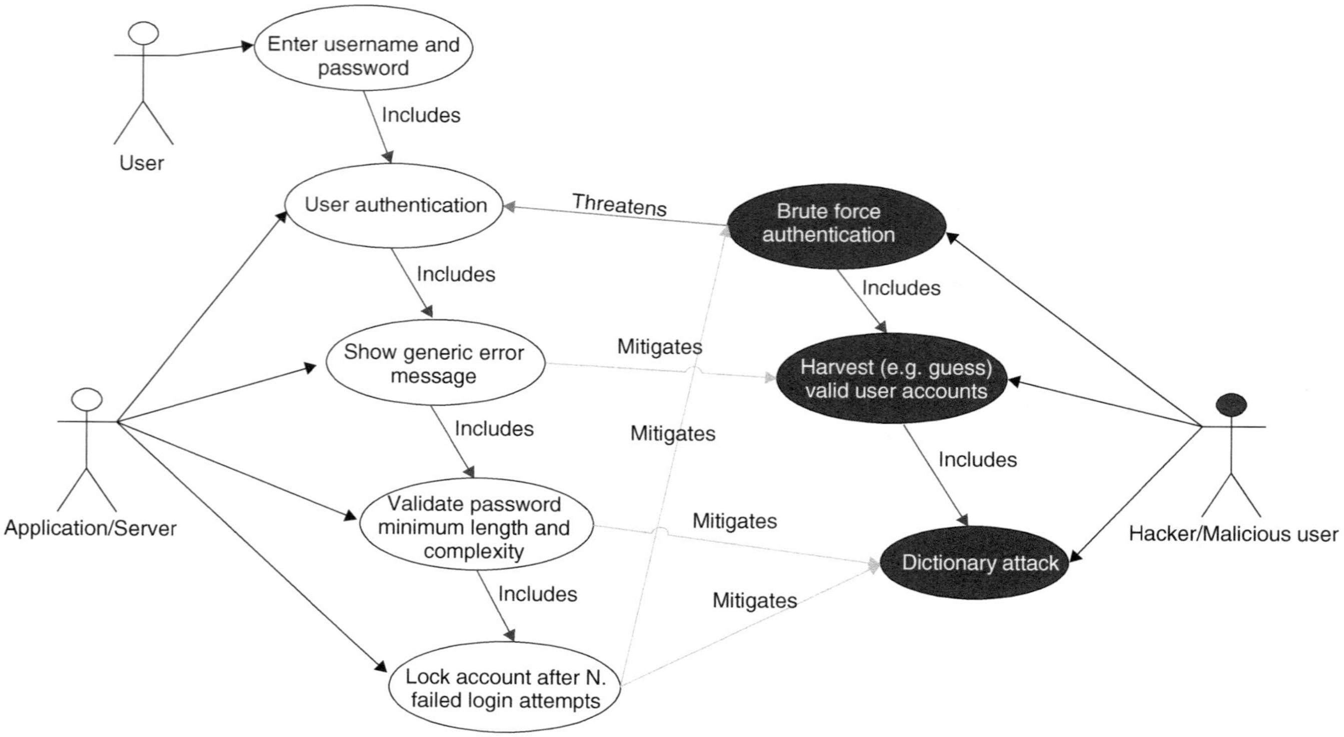

Figure 4.2 Use and Misuse Case of User Log-on

The security activity whose objective consists of deriving and documenting security requirements encompassing risk-based requirements, functional security requirements, and security compliance requirements is also known as security requirements engineering. Being thorough when deriving security requirements for an application to make sure that these requirements cover all aspects of application functionality, security functionality, and compliance threat mitigation is critical to the secure design of the application.

Secure Design Reviews

Several activities can be adopted during the design phase of the SDLC to improve an application's security. Examples of these activities include the application security review to validate that the design adhered to the security requirements, the architecture security review to identify any potential risks exposed by design flaws and gaps in the design of security controls, and threat modeling to identify potential threats targeting the application, the application components, and the countermeasures that protect them from the realization of these threats. Among the security activities that can be conducted during design, threat modeling is the only one that focuses on analyzing the potential threats targeting the application to determine if the security measures documented in the architectural design of the application mitigate the risks of these threats.

There are several benefits of performing threat modeling during the design phase of the SDLC architectural design review of an application, for example, risks can be mitigated proactively by documenting countermeasures for these threats in the design prior to these threats exploiting a vulnerability in the application. Typically, it is the responsibility of both risk managers and architects to make sure that the architecture of the application adheres to security requirements. An architecture security review of the application can be conducted with a walk-through of the documented design of the application that might also include whiteboard exercises to capture the essential elements of the architecture to identify the potential design flaws and how these could expose the application assets to these threats.

The effectiveness of secure architecture reviews of the application architecture depends on several factors, such as following a secure architecture review and threat modeling process for the review, documenting standards for the security of the architecture and availability of experienced subject matter experts in application security and threat modeling.

One prerequisite for the execution of secure architecture reviews and threat modeling exercises is the availability of documentation such as architecture design documents that include information of the logical and the physical architecture of the application, the layout of the infrastructure that supports the application, and the documented secure requirements that the design of the application needs to adhere to.

The objective of the secure architecture review is to validate that at high level the application design adheres to the security requirements; that the security controls such as authentication, authorization, and encryption are documented in the design to protect the confidentiality, integrity, and availability of the data as well as to protect access to the application functionality. If security issues in the design are identified during the secure architecture review, it is the engineering teams' and the application architect's responsibility to fix these design issues.

Threat Modeling

After the application design architecture design has been reviewed and approved to conform to security standards, the next step is to conduct a threat model. The scope of the threat model is to assess the architecture from an attacker's perspective to determine if the security controls in place are sufficient to reduce the potential impact of attacks targeting the application and the application data.

To conduct a threat model of the application architecture, it is essential first to identify the major components of the architecture, such as clients and servers, data assets, and data flows. A methodology for conducting this type of analysis is also known as data flow analysis. The scope of a data flow analysis is to decompose the architecture of the application into essential components and visualize them graphically by using a data flow diagram. Through the data flow diagram of the application architecture, it is possible for a threat analyst to analyze the interaction with the user of the application as well as with the data and validate the exposure to potential threats to each of these components.

An example of a data flow diagram is shown in Figure 4.3. It is sketched at a high level to show the end data flows in a typical web application. The decomposition of the application architecture includes web server, application server, and database server components, security controls such as encryption, authentication, authorization, input validation, session management, and exception handling and logging, the architecture boundaries that require a specific authentication and authorization in order to be crossed (e.g. the trust boundaries), and the different interfaces where the data is entered, either by the user (user interfaces), or by another component (data interface).

The overall purpose of these exercises is to conduct a preliminary secure architecture analysis to reveal the presence of security controls at the different elements of the

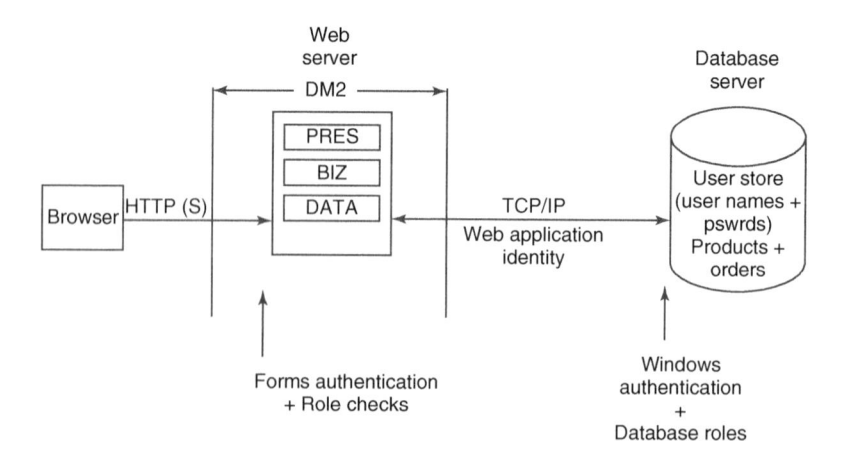

Figure 4.3 Sketched Architectural Diagram

application architecture to protect the data assets from threats against the confidentiality, integrity, and availability of the data assets and the application functionality.

For example, a database storing confidential data requires the confidential data to be protected by enforcing the access to only authorized and authenticated users. When such confidential data is sent to the user through the different internal and external lags of the application, it is exposed to threat agents seeking to capture this data while in transit. By sketching this in a data flow diagram, it is possible for a threat analyst to validate that a security control is in place to mitigate the possible threats. For example, to protect the data in transit, using SSL to protect the data traffic from the browser to the application server while the application server establishes a secure connection via JDBC/S to the data source keeps any sensitive data encrypted in storage on the DB. Usually after having captured the conceptual design on the whiteboard, the application architects go to the drawing board to produce a more detailed and formal design of the application. This might involve using a graphical tool such as VISIO to produce a more detailed view of the application such as in Figure 4.4.

At this stage of design, threat modeling helps identify weaknesses in the application, such as security flaws, that if exploited by a threat might affect the application functionality and the data assets.

In order to identify which threats might affect the application components, it is important to enumerate each of the possible threats systematically and identify which ones might or might not apply. For example, if the threat scenario were attacking the log-in of an online banking application, would the attacker brute force the password to break the authentication? A possible weak enforcement of strong passwords rules/policy by the application is therefore exposing this weakness to a potential threat. In another threat scenario, if a threat agent tried to bypass authorization enforcement to gain another user's privileges, would a gap in the enforcement of role base access control for restricting access to data and application functionality only to authorized users be a factor for the likelihood and impact of this threat?

For consistency, it is important to use a list of threats and enumerate each of the possible threats against the application's security weaknesses to determine if these can be a factor of risk.

A threat categorization such as STRIDE (Spoofing Tampering, Repudiation, Information Disclosure, Denial of Service, and Elevation of Privileges), for example, is useful for identifying countermeasures for each possible threat and for determining any lack of countermeasures that would expose the application to potential impacts from these threats.

Another technique to determine how a given threat agent could exploit different types of vulnerabilities to cause an impact is to use a threat tree as shown in Figure 4.5. Through a threat tree, it is possible to analyze whether the absence of a security control or the presence of vulnerability in a security control (depicted as the first level of branches from the root of the tree) might be a factor for a possible exploit of a threat agent (depicted as the root of the tree) and determine which countermeasure (depicted as the second layer branches from the root of the tree) should be in place to mitigate the risk of such threat (Figure 4.5).

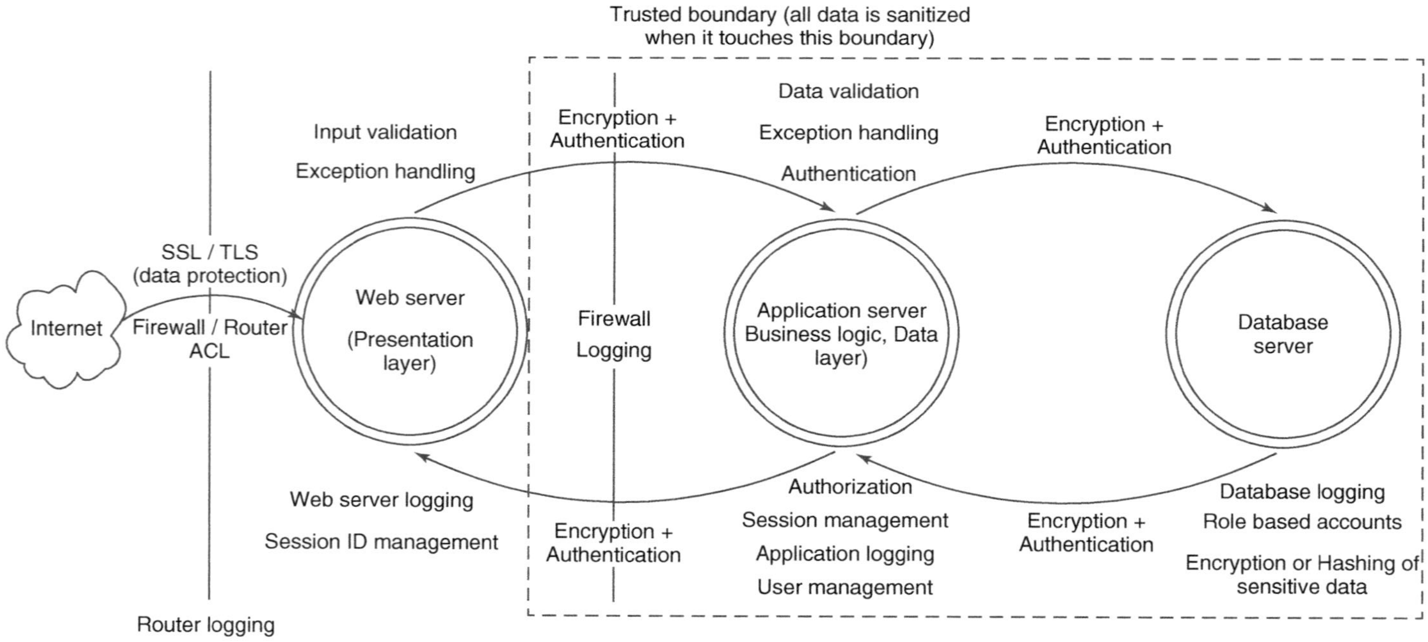

Figure 4.4 Data Flow Diagram

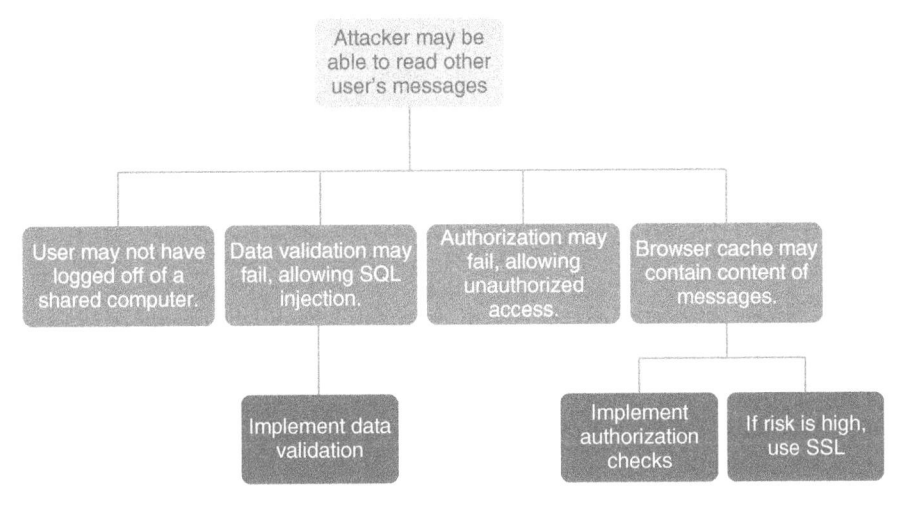

```
                    ┌─────────────────┐
                    │ Attacker may be │
                    │ able to read other│
                    │ user's messages │
                    └─────────────────┘
```

Figure 4.5 Mapping Threats Vulnerabilities and Countermeasures

The main objective of secure design reviews and threat modeling is the identification of any weaknesses in the security of the design of the application. Any design flaws that are identified during the design phase of the SDLC can be remediated prior to the coding of the software.

Threat Modeling and Secure Coding

From the software security assurance perspective, when the project reaches the coding phase of the SDLC, it is important to revisit the threat model that was previously created during the design phase to identify any architectural components affected by design flaws and exposed to potential threats. These architectural components ought to be considered high risk and therefore prioritized for an in-depth security code review during the coding phase. This approach of using a threat model to conduct secure code reviews on targeted components consists of a "depth first" approach instead of "breadth first" approach where all the software components of the application are treated equally independently from their risk.

The objective of source code reviews is to identify any security issues in the source code and fix them by introducing code changes prior to releasing the software for the final build and integration testing. Secure code reviews can be conducted either manually by experienced code reviewers following a secure code review process or with the help of tools, such as static source code analysis tools that can automatically scan the source code for security bugs.

Software developers typically have knowledge of programming languages and might follow secure coding standards as well as defensive coding principles when implementing source code for a given application. Once issues are identified in the source code, software developers can look at the threat model to understand the possible exposure of security bugs identified with the source code analysis to the threats that might exploit them.

Threat Modeling Driven Security Testing

Information security teams can use a threat model to derive the security requirements that need to be followed by software developers when developing the application source code. Whether source code adheres to these security requirements can be validated with security tests as soon as the software components are built and integrated with the overall application. These security tests can be conducted by quality assurance personnel, security auditors, and technical security testers (collectively referred to as security testers) based on a documented security testing plan. A security testing plan typically includes information on how to conduct a security test by describing the test set up, the several steps that need to be followed to conduct the test, and the expected outcome. Typically security testers are bound by time. On the basis of their experience, they rarely take a systematic approach to testing and instead focus on proving or disproving specific instances of vulnerabilities rather than identifying any systematic issues. This is where a threat model can help a security tester. A threat model can help security testers identify security issues and areas of concern in a focused manner, such as by prioritizing the security testing for the most critical components of the application and the ones where the exposure and the impact can be higher.

Security tests can also be prioritized based on risks such as the likelihood and impact to the application. Security test cases that have a risk of high impact can be prioritized for testing over the ones that have low probability and impact. It is therefore important to analyze the risks from the attacker's perspective as the risk depends on how likely it is for a threat agent to exploit a vulnerability to cause the impact to the application. It is, therefore, important to derive a set of test cases based on the attacker's perspective.

A useful technique for deriving these test cases from the attacker's perspective is to derive security test cases from use and abuse cases. The use and abuse case technique consists of deriving a sequence of possible events whose goal is to compromise the application functionality and the data. Since use and abuse cases are also used to derive security requirements for the design of security controls (e.g. authentication, authorization, encryption), the purpose of the security tests is to validate that these security controls reduce the likelihood and the impact. For example, based on a use and misuse case for authentication, it is possible to derive a security test case to validate that security controls such as account locking and password complexity are enforced to mitigate brute forcing of passwords and that is not possible to enumerate valid credentials based on the error messages.

Besides use and abuse cases, security test cases need to also include a series of security test cases for each of the potential attacks targeting the application. These potential attacks, the type of attack vectors/tools that can be used against the application as well as information on how these attacks can be conducted is critical to emulate the same in a security test case. Potential attacks against the application assets can be derived from the analysis of the attack scenario using the attack tree methodology. The attack scenario that is analyzed using the attack tree analysis can help derive a test case to simulate the attack against the application.

In order for security testing to be considered comprehensive, it is important to consider application specific security issues as well as common security issues. Examples of common security issues are the common vulnerabilities in web applications, such as the OWASP Top Ten. The effectiveness of security tests in identifying security issues depends on different factors, such as how detailed the security requirements are for the application, how comprehensive are the security test cases that are part of the security testing plan, the type of tools used for the tests, and the knowledge and experience of the security testers while conducting these tests.

Typically, security testers are given a security testing guide that documents the test cases and the step-by-step testing procedures that need to be followed to conduct the test and the expected outcomes. It is therefore important that such security test plan accounts for the most likely abuse cases and attack scenarios to validate the effectiveness of the security controls in protecting the application assets and detecting possible attacks. To document a comprehensive security test plan for the application of the possible attack scenarios and vulnerability exploits, it is important to capture the functionality of the application, including any business rules that could be exploited by an attacker.

Another important aspect to consider in the testing plan is testing the different layers of the application architecture. Security of an application has to be provided as security in depth mechanism by providing different layers of security controls. This type of information is usually documented in a threat model. A threat model provides the security tester with an end-to-end view from client to server of the different data interfaces and the type of security controls, such as user and application to application authentication, authorizations, input validations, and encryption for data in transit that exists at each of these interfaces. This end-to-end view of the security controls in an application also allows a security tester to determine the risk in case a security issue is identified by the negative result of a test case, the type of exposure of the asset due to the security issue.

Identifying possible security issues relative to the application environment will benefit most from documenting a comprehensive security test plan that includes both manual test cases and automated tools.

Once security issues are identified, it is important to substantiate the risk of these issues, that is, to consider the likelihood and impacts when these issues are exploited by specific threat agents. Substantiating threats through attacks will help to provide probability values that are not speculative, but based on testing efforts by the security tester or testing group.

Once attacks have been substantiated and probability levels defined, issues related to business impact are much more concrete and the risk analysis obtains a greater level of respect by the business audience members who are interested in threat forecasting efforts that have taken place as part of this stage. Once the risk of each of the test cases is determined, it is possible to prioritize these tests by the least difficult attack and the highest impact.

A security tests might include denial of service attacks toward preauthenticated URL/functions. In the case of an online web application, for example, this includes account registration process, queries for the location of a company store, as well as marketing surveys. By using the results of a threat model, a tester will prioritize testing these use cases for validating that denial of service defenses allow the application to function despite automation attacks try to exploit connection bandwidth and server resources to cause a denial of service.

A threat model helps security testers derive specific test cases for each specific threat, attack, and vulnerability. To successfully conduct this security testing, the main requirement is to validate that security controls are designed and implemented in the application to mitigate the risk of threats targeting the application, application data, and functions that process this data. A typical example would be to test that the implemented user authentication in the application locks the user after a certain number of failed attempts to prevent brute forced authentication. Another example might include security testing that the client host and the server mutually authenticate each other to prevent repudiation and Man-in-The-Middle (MiTM) attacks. Some of these requirements can be either implicitly derived by a threat model or more explicitly from compliance with information security policies. Protecting credit card holder's sensitive data, such as account numbers with encryption, can be driven by mitigation against information disclosure threat, driven by a threat model, but might be more explicitly required because of compliance with security technology standards such as PCI-DSS.

Among security requirements, risk driven security requirements can be derived from use and abuse cases: these risk driven requirements are also referred to as "negative requirements" since they are specifically documented to prove the application exposure to vulnerabilities, such as flaws in business logic, that allow the application to be abused to cause damage to the application and impact to the business. Use and misuse cases are also useful during the testing phase, such as for deriving the test cases and step-by-step procedures to validate that the application functionality cannot be abused since any potential flaws in business logic have been mitigated by secure design, coding, and configuration.

The objective of negative tests is to validate that an attacker cannot abuse the application functionality to damage the application and the data. This includes trying to bypass authentication to gain access to the application, bypassing authorization controls to perform unauthorized transactions, as well as other threat scenarios previously identified by the threat model. Since different threat scenarios are identified and investigated in the threat model with the purpose of identifying potential vulnerabilities, the tester could later validate that such threat scenarios cannot be realized.

Security tests need to validate that countermeasures are in place to protect against specific threats and attacks, such as data validation and encryption, and can then be tested at the relevant entry points by ensuring that the application filters attack vectors as well as that data assets are protected and data flows does not leave sensitive or personal information unprotected and vulnerable to potential attackers.

A security tester can look at the threat modeling artifacts such as the documented threat list, the associated vulnerability with each threat list, and the countermeasures visualized in a threat list to derive each of the test cases and include them in the test plan. A documented threat list identifies each threat from the perspective of the threat target, the target of the threat, the threat tree, and the identified vulnerability. A tester can look at the threat tree to identify the security failure modes and derive a test case to test that the countermeasures mitigate the realization of such threats by different attack vectors. Another important aspect of security testing related to threat modeling is to prioritize tests according to the risk rating given to each threat and prioritize the test cases by first testing the threat scenarios whose likelihood, exposure, ease, as well as impact are higher. Finally, a critical aspect of how threat modeling can drive security tests is to identify the same type of attack vectors that are used by the attackers and validate the resilience of the application against real attack scenarios.

Once the application has been security tested, the next phase of the SDLC is to deploy the application in the production environment. The deployment stage is the culmination of multiple exchanges between vulnerability assessments and security configuration management efforts.

The main objective is a secure configuration, installation, and operation of the application. The back and forth of this exchange, as part of any security risk management effort, aims to achieve an acceptable level of risk for the application and the information sources that it seeks to protect. Although the coding efforts may have accelerated to the deployment stage, threat modeling techniques are still applicable during the deployment/implementation stage. Security architects and build masters can apply threat modeling techniques in order to ensure the integrity of the deployment environment to the defined security specifications that relate to the configuration of hosts platforms, supportive services, and other environmental factors that may introduce vulnerabilities to the application environment. For this reason, security testers and build masters can apply attack simulations in the production environment to identified vulnerabilities at the platform and service levels. Misconfigurations account for a significant percentage of vulnerabilities for application environments. As a result, threat modeling techniques are very applicable in detailing attack vectors for the misconfiguration of these distributed assets.

Finally, after the application is deployed in the operational environment, it also has to maintain security during subsequent releases and before change management events. As consequences of these application changes, new threats have to be reassessed because of a design change in the system architecture, implementation of new component, integration with new library, and so on. By using the results of the threat model, it will be possible to identify and assess potential new security risks and make informed decisions whether to implement the change or determine new countermeasures to mitigate the new vulnerabilities that the application change would potentially introduce.

Integrating Threat Modeling Into Interactive SDLCs

An example of an interactive SDLC is the Rational Unified Process (RUP). RUP is an extensible software development process that in its standard form consists of four sequential phases (Inception, Elaboration, Construction, and Transition) and nine

Iterative development
Business value is delivered incrementally in
time-boxed cross-discipline iterations.

	Inception	Elaboration		Construction				Transition	
	I1	E1	E2	C1	C2	C3	C4	T1	T2
Business modeling									
Requirements									
Analysis & Design									
Implementation									
Test									
Deployment									

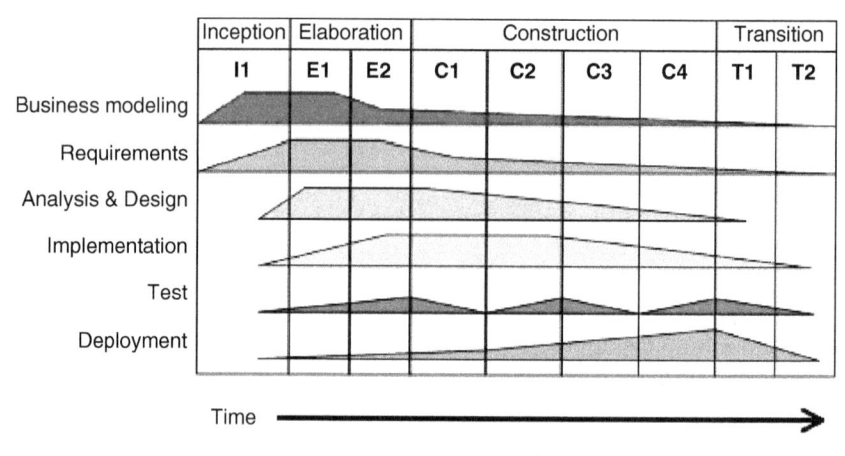

Time ⟶

Figure 4.6 RUP SDLC[1]

disciplines (Requirements, Analysis and Design, Implementation, Testing, Deployment, Configuration, and Change Management) that are used throughout the phases. Each phase has an objective and is considered accomplished upon reaching milestones (Life cycle Objectives, Life cycle Architecture, Initial Operational Capability, and Product Release). Milestones are similar to the quality gates found in a waterfall development process; however, RUP differs from a waterfall process in that each phase encompasses several iterations of a complete development cycle. From the security perspective, specific security objectives can be included in each phase of RUP. Reaching such objectives can be validated at each RUP milestone and used as a security checkpoint during the iterative development of the application (see Figure 4.6).

During the inception phase of RUP, the scope of the project is defined, including the estimate of project development costs, budgets, risks, and schedule. In order to meet the life cycle milestone objectives, stakeholders need to agree on the project scope and the schedule estimates, understanding the basic requirements for the project and any assessment of project risks. From the threat modeling perspective, time and cost for the threat modeling activity can also be estimated. In this phase, it is important that the security team is able to estimate the costs and to schedule the threat modeling engagement based on the scope of the project (e.g. size, complexity) as well as business and functional requirements.

During the elaboration phase of RUP, the architecture for the application is defined. In this phase, the bulk of the application requirements that need to be constructed are also elaborated. From the threat modeling perspective, abuse cases derived from use cases helps security teams to derive the security requirements. During the preliminary

[1] http://commons.wikimedia.org/wiki/File:Development-iterative.gif.

design of the application, a review of the design to validate the security requirements might also include validating security controls are elaborated and designed to mitigate the risk of specific threats. This type of analysis consists of conducting a threat model exercise. Such threat modeling exercise need to be revised and updated along with refining the design of the application architecture as well as identifying new threats at each iteration cycle.

The application software is developed during the construction phase of the RUP SDLC. During the application software coding, it is important that the source code is reviewed for security and that any vulnerability is identified with either manual or automated source code analysis tools. Secure code reviews can use the results of the threat model, such as the identification of security design flaws in the application architecture, to conduct an in-depth secure code review of the components that are more exposed to potential threats targeting them and are inherently more insecure because of the design flaws that were previously identified.

During the transition phase of the RUP SDLC, the application moves from the development environment to the production environment. From security perspective, the focus of this phase is to validate with security tests that the security controls of the application function as required and are acceptable for deployment as well as that the application does not include any known high-risk security issues that prevent release into the production environment. During this final phase, security tests can validate that risks of any security issues identified with the security tests are in scope for remediation prior to releasing the application into the production environment.

Applying Threat Modeling To the Agile SDLC

The Agile software development methodology is an evolutionary and iterative software development process. With the Agile SDLC, applications can be developed by refining the application requirements, design, implementation, and testing through different iterations of these phases until the final application is ready to be released into production.

In the Agile SDLC methodology, requirements, design, implementation, and tests are executed more than once at subsequent iterations of these phases, also referred to as "Sprints." In Agile software development methodology, the traditional SDLC phases of requirements, design, implementation, and testing do not produce final artifacts that are checked and validated upon completion of each phase before the project can proceed to the next phase, but are instead defined and refined with several iterations of these until the application is actually completed. The key objectives of the Agile methodology are to introduce flexibility, adaptability, and productivity into software development as well as collaboration between different teams. The flexibility of Agile methodology is due to its capability to adapt to changes such as new requirements and design since each iteration/sprint involves the full development cycle including the requirement analysis, design, coding, testing, and deployment of a working demo. Each iteration/sprint requires minimal planning and typically lasts from one to four weeks: this helps to minimize overall risk and lets the project adapt to changes quickly. Within Agile, the project stakeholders usually maintain and evolve a prioritized queue of business and technical functionality/requirements and produce and update design documentation as required. During each sprint, the development work is monitored and inspected frequently through daily "scrums" among project managers, product owners, and development teams. Incremental system tests at the end of each iteration/sprint validate that the new requirements added/refined during each sprint. The goal of the incremental system tests is to reduce the number of defects at the end of each iteration until the application can be released with a minimum number of defects.

Integrating threat modeling during Agile methodology represents several challenges:

1. *Incomplete scope assessment:* Since the design for the application is refined after each iteration/sprint, threat modeling can only review incomplete design artifacts produced after each sprint.
2. *Lack of security checkpoint enforcement:* Since the SDLC phases are not in sequence (e.g. start design and implementation before requirements are yet completed), threat modeling cannot enforce a security checkpoint to validate secure design before implementation.

Because of these constraints, integrating threat modeling in Agile is not as effective as secure architecture design reviews integrated as part of waterfall SDLC methodology to identify security flaws in design before starting implementation. Nevertheless, is possible to integrate threat modeling activities into Agile, such as during the definition of Agile security stories as shown in Figure 4.7.

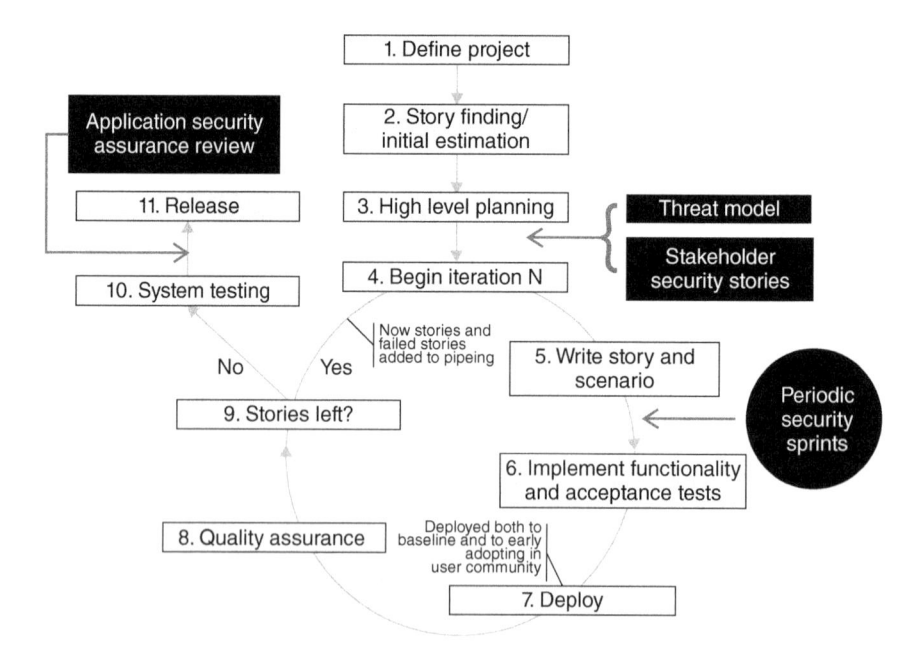

Figure 4.7 Integrating Security in the Agile SDLC

The Agile stories are in essence small, actionable statements describing a piece of business functionality such as "the authenticated users of the application can check their credit card balance through the application." The security SME working with the project stakeholder will look at each of these Agile stories and add security stories based on both general security requirements dictated by the security policies, information security standards, and the mitigation of potential threats affecting the use cases for the application to be built.

A threat modeling activity at the beginning of the initial story finding helps identify the threat scenario and derive security stories. An example of threat driven Agile story could be: "only authenticated users could access their account information" and "the account numbers displayed in the account balance will be masked to show only the last four digit of the account." Since an Agile story is in essence a finely grained use case that is describing piece of functionality, a security story describes an abuse case for the functionality and the security control to mitigate the abuse. When creating Agile stories, the developer teams usually take a business perspective, similarly, when creating Agile security stories, it is important to identify potential business impacts to derive the security story as well, for example, an Agile story such as "authenticated users of the application will be able to add payees and make payments." The security story will take into consideration that adding a payee and make a payment can be used for fraud, the security story derived from this abuse case could be: "only validated payees could be added" and "authenticated users will be challenged with secondary authentication before adding a payee." Another characteristic of the Agile stories is that they need to be testable, therefore they need to be expressed in terms of a user performing action and achieving results that can be validated with a test. Similarly, the expected results of the Agile security story need to define the security conditions for validation with security tests. Such conditions can be part of the acceptance criteria, also referred to as assurance. The validation of security stories can generally be part of the system integration tests (refer to the figure) as part of the final application security acceptance review before releasing the application in production.

The security stories introduced ahead of each sprint can drive the documentation of the security requirements as well as the secure design ahead of each sprint. A periodic security sprint is a security activity occurring during each sprint with the objective of validating the partial design being documented, coding artifacts being implemented, and the working prototype as it becomes available.

A typical Agile sprint, as shown in Figure 4.8, for example, includes a 2- to-4-week period with the objective of designing, developing build, and potentially shipping product increments. It is possible to integrate security reviews (shown as dashed arrows) as part of each sprint. During week 1, for example, development teams can start putting together an initial design and development from a set of high-level requirements that are derived from the use cases and the stories. During week 1, security can work with development teams to review the security requirements to include them as part of the design and the implementation of the working prototype.

During mid-week, security teams and SMEs can review the initial design to make sure it complies with the security requirements previously identified as part of the security stories. Finally, during the last week of the sprint, the security team

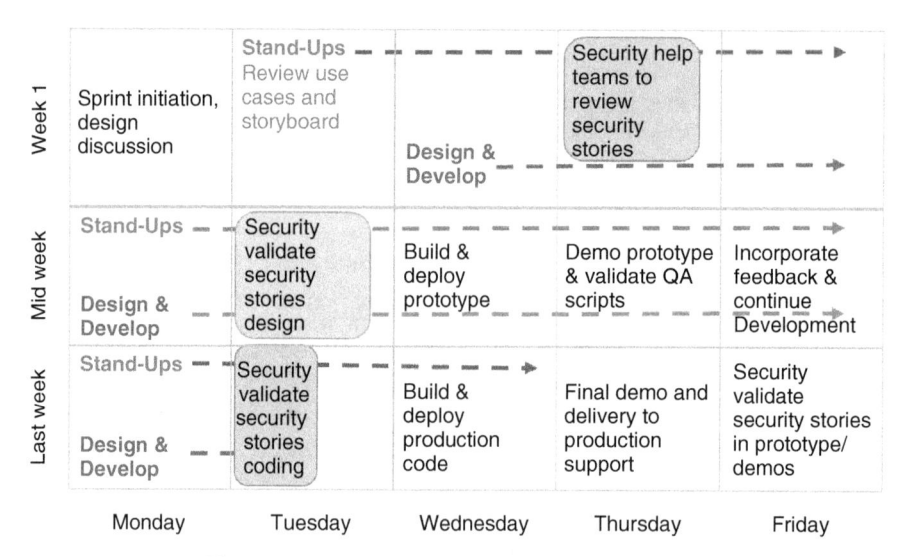

	Monday	Tuesday	Wednesday	Thursday	Friday
Week 1	Sprint initiation, design discussion	Stand-Ups — Review use cases and storyboard	Design & Develop	Security help teams to review security stories	
Mid week	Stand-Ups Design & Develop	Security validate security stories design	Build & deploy prototype	Demo prototype & validate QA scripts	Incorporate feedback & continue Development
Last week	Stand-Ups Design & Develop	Security validate security stories coding	Build & deploy production code	Final demo and delivery to production support	Security validate security stories in prototype/ demos

Figure 4.8 Integrating Security in the Agile Sprints

will validate that the implementation follows what previously identified security stories required by visually validating the security functionality of the working prototype/demo.

At the end of each security sprint, another opportunity to drive threat analysis in Agile is with an application security assurance review between system testing and the release phases.

Since Agile system tests are usually incremental, as new pieces of production ready working software are produced at the end of each sprint being integrated in the final application builds and tested according to the functional test plan. Similarly, a set of security tests integrated with the system tests, can validate that the software function as intended and is free of vulnerabilities, either intentionally or unintentionally designed or introduced as part of the software. Finally, an application security assurance review after each testing phase includes a review of all the security stories to make sure that they are being properly implemented and there are no vulnerabilities that can be exploited by known threats identified during the initial threat modeling.

Threat Modeling and Security Enhanced SDLCs (S-SDLC)

Security enhanced SDLCs are software development processes that already incorporate security activities to enhance the security of the application by design, development, and deployment. An example of Security enhanced SDLC is the Microsoft Software Development Life Cycle (MS SDLC). The MS SDL is a software development process developed by Microsoft with a specific objective goal to minimize security-related vulnerabilities in the design, code, and documentation and to detect and eliminate vulnerabilities as early as possible in the development life cycle.

Microsoft introduced threat modeling in 2002 as part the security by design best practice of the (SD3+C) process that included *Secure by Design, Secure by Default, Secure in Deployment,* and *Communications* (SD3+C). Among the security activities of the MS SDL, *"Threat modeling and mitigation"* is one of the *Secure by Design* guiding principles that include *Secure architecture, design, and structure, Elimination of Vulnerabilities and Improvements in Security*.

According to MS, the threat modeling and mitigation principle was to create threat models and include threat mitigation in all design and functional specifications for existing Microsoft applications. The (SD3+C) principles incorporated in each step of the software development process are shown in Figure 4.9.

The SDL Specification clearly defines which products and services produced by Microsoft should be in scope for the SDL. In the case of products, for example, this includes any software release that

1. is being used and deployed an organization/business;
2. regularly store PII or sensitive information;
3. regularly connects to the Internet or other networks;
4. automatically downloads updates;
5. accepts or processes data from an unauthenticated source; and
6. contains ActiveX or COM controls.

As part of the pre-SDL requirements, each technical member of a project team (developer, tester, program manager) is required to take training and security awareness courses on basic knowledge of secure design, threat modeling, secure coding, security testing, and privacy.

In the case of threat modeling, the basic concepts of designing, coding, and testing using a threat model are covered in the security training for software developers. A plan for when to conduct the threat modeling activity and the amount of resources to be allocated is included as part of the security requirements of the security plan created ahead of the design phase.

One of the security requirements that the MS SDL also mandates for any application software being developed at MS, is the security risk assessment (SRA) to identify functional aspects of the software that might require a deep security review. One of the assertions of the SRA is a decision whether the application software should be in scope for the threat modeling activities, as well as portions of the project that will require a threat model before project release. This might include, for example, all projects whose code is exposed to attacks via external interfaces or third party software, all features and new functionality being developed in new projects, updated versions of existing projects where new functionality if being added in the new releases.

For the applications whose threat model is in scope as an SDL activity, it is mandatory to threat model during the design phase to identify potential threats and vulnerabilities in the application components. Threat modeling is central to the risk assessment performed during the design phase to assess threat and vulnerabilities in

1. existing design or as result of the interaction with other software/applications;
2. code being created by third party;
3. legacy code;
4. high-risk privacy projects.

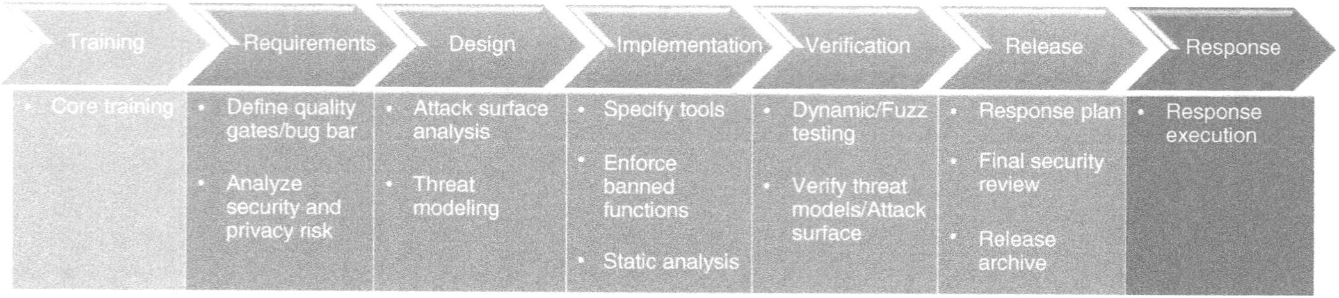

Figure 4.9 Integration of Threat Modeling in MS SDL

Among the security requirements for the design phase of the SDL is to "Ensure that all threat models meet minimal threat model quality requirements'; that is, all the required artifacts that are part of the threat modeling exercise are completed, such as data flow diagrams, assets, vulnerabilities, and mitigation. Another specific requirement for threat models is that they need a minimum review by at least one developer, one tester, and one program manager. As a best practice, a threat model should be reviewed any project stakeholder, such as developers and or architects who understand the software and can ensure that the threat model is as much as comprehensive as possible. A threat model also needs to be included as part of the project documentation and stored using the document control system tool used by the project management team. One of the prerequisites for the person responsible for conducting the threat model is to have completed the mandatory training on threat modeling.

From the perspective of change control request and approvals, a review of a threat model is required to identify whether the change will alter the existing threat mitigation and introduce new vulnerabilities. Any vulnerability identified in the threat model requires a work item to be assigned for remediation and the fix validated by the software assurance team.

During the validation phase, security testers ensure that the developed code meets all security requirements established in the previous phase. The validation phase includes all security and privacy testing as well as the software security assurance activities of the so called "security push" that includes threat modeling updates, secure code reviews, penetration testing, as well as documentation review. Security and privacy tests have the objective of validating that the software countermeasures mitigate any threats related to impact to confidentiality, integrity, and availability of the software, as well as the data protected by the software. The main objective of these tests is to "ensure that all security features and functionality that are designed to mitigate threats perform as expected."

During penetration testing, testers can use threat models to prioritize the tests on the areas of the software where the attacks are most likely to occur and have the highest impact.

Finally, the project is subjected to a final security review (FSR) before release. One of the milestones of the FSR is that threat models are completed. A security advisor (SME) reviews the threat models to ensure that all known threats and vulnerabilities are identified and mitigated.

In the adaptation of SDL for Agile, threat modeling is considered mandatory at every sprint since one of the requirements is to threat model all new features that are introduced at each sprint.

In particular, a threat modeling baseline is considered a one-time requirement that needs to be met before starting a new project with SDL-Agile. A threat model is referred by the SDL-Agile the "Cornerstone of the SDL"; the major SDL artifact that must be used as a baseline for a product. One of the requirements for SDL-Agile is that a threat model must be built as part of the sprint design and time boxes to include only the parts of the design that already exist or are already in development. The main focus of this preliminary threat model is to identify

1. any potential design security issues;
2. drive the attack surface analysis to the most at-risk components; and
3. drive the fuzz-testing process.

The goal of the threat modeling integrated with Agile is to update the threat model during each sprint as new features and functionality are added to the sprint. This should be reflected in an updated threat model that includes the new design being added. The SDL-Agile also identifies the minimum requirements for the threat modeling scope:

1. Anonymous and remote end points.
2. Anonymous or authenticated local end points into high-privileged processes.
3. Sensitive, confidential, or personally identifiable data held in data stores used in the application.

In order to keep the documentation overhead to a minimum, only new features introduced in the design at each sprint are threat modeled in the current sprint.

One variation of the MS SDL is the SDL for Line of Business (LOB). This MS SDL for LOBs defines the standards and best practices for security, new and existing critical enterprise such supply chain management, account-payroll, and human resources.

The goal of the SDL-LOB is to supplement the general SDLC (shown in Figure 4.10) with security activities and tasks that are more specific for LOB application.

In the SDL-LOB, asset-centric threat modeling and design reviews are the recommended tasks to be performed during the design phase. In particular, the SDL-LOB defines the level of oversight by an SME during the several phases based on a service level assessment questionnaire.

The application risk levels are determined as a function of the data classification, the presence of business critical function, and the exposure of the applications, such as when such applications are Internet facing.

According to the MS SDL for LOBs, a high-risk application is an application that is Internet facing and can handle both highly sensitive data and perform critical functions on the data. A medium risk is an application that is also Internet facing but handles no highly sensitive data and does not perform critical functions on this data. A low-risk application is an application that handles public data and functions that are noncritical.

According to the service levels performed by the application, there are different risk levels that can be assigned to the application (high/medium/low). Each service level has different level of service requirements. High-risk applications, for example, require compliance with threat modeling and design reviews, while a threat model is

Figure 4.10 SDL Phases

recommended for medium risk applications and to be performed as appropriate for low-risk applications. In the case of high-risk applications, it is the responsibility of the application teams to create/update the application threat model in consultation with security/privacy SMEs. The scope requirements for threat modeling are established ahead of the design phase based on the determination of the application risk type and the service level requirements.

In the MS SDL for LOBs, threat modeling is considered a critical security activity and is mandatory during the design of the application. The scope of the threat modeling activity is to assert the exposure of the application to threats and vulnerabilities due to the application environment and as result of the interaction of the application with other applications/systems.

A completed threat model is required during design along with the design review of a security SME. The completion of the threat model is responsibility of the application teams while the design review is responsibility of the security SME.

Application teams that have adopted the MS SDL have a choice of two threat modeling tools for conducting the threat modeling exercise: the Threat Analysis and Modeling Tool (TAM), an asset-focused tool designed for LOB applications, and the Threat Modeling SDL tool, a software-focused tool designed for rich client/server application development.

The goal of the TAM tool is to identify threats and vulnerabilities in security controls and design countermeasures for mitigating the risks and protecting the data assets. The TAM assumes that business objectives and data are clearly defined business assets. The focus of the SDL Threat Modeling Tool is rather to ensure security of the software's underlying code with no assumptions on the criticality of the data or of the business functions.

The SDL-LOB mandates some security requirements for conducting threat modeling during the SDL such as the following:

1. The threat modeling methodology needs to be consistent and repeatable so that objective results can be produced.
2. It should facilitate translating technical risk to business impact to determine the negative impact to the business due to realizing a threat and exploiting a vulnerability identified in the threat model.
3. It should provide management with enough information to make risk decisions using the results of the threat modeling exercise.
4. It should create awareness between application teams and security teams on the security dependencies and security assumptions that are made on each phase of the SDL.
5. It should be actionable: it should allow management to select countermeasures and prioritize them by risk.
6. It should be complete with the threat modeling artifacts, such as digital assets or data, business objectives, components, role information, use cases, data flow, call flows, generated threats, and mitigations.

7. It should be reviewed and approved by the security SME.
8. It should be part of the application portfolio and stored in a document control repository so that it can be later retrieved, consulted, and updated.

Using Threat Modeling in the SDLC as Hybrid Software Security Assessment

As security in the SDLC activity, threat modeling can be combined with other security assessments to improve the accuracy of the security issues that are identified in each of the assessments. For example, threat modeling used in conjunction with penetration testing can help reduce the number of false positives (issues identified that should not be considered issues or issues of high risk) and false negatives (issues that are either missed or are considered low risk). The use of two different application security analysis methodologies to improve the accuracy of the issues that are identified by each one separately is also known in application security as "hybrid security analysis."

An example of hybrid security analysis that is frequently used in software security is the one that combines dynamic security testing with static security testing. Hybrid security testing, for example, takes advantage of the different tools and testing techniques that are less or more suitable to identify certain types of vulnerabilities. Static analysis, for example, is better suited to identify vulnerabilities caused by security issues in the source code such as SQL injection vulnerabilities. Dynamic analysis is better suited to identify vulnerabilities caused by security issues in the application as a whole, such as issues in handling errors insecurely resulting in information leakages.

The main value of combining different security assessment/analysis hybrid assessment techniques is to reduce the number of issues whose risk is misclassified (issues considered high risk that should considered low risk) as well as to increase the security issue coverage (identify more issues). By correlating the vulnerability findings with the two assessments, it is possible to validate whether security issues that are identified in both assessments should be either false positives or false negatives and improve the overall accuracy of the assessments. A SQL injection vulnerability that is identified with both a dynamic and static analysis, for example, and whose insecure root cause belongs to the same instance and/or component of the application can be positively validated.

When the hybrid analysis is also automated to exclude false positives, it will reduce the overall costs since it will reduce the time dedicated to manually reviewing the findings. The correlation of static to dynamic assessments will also improve the remediation effort since it will highlight the root causes of the security issues and point the software developer assigned to fix the issue to the offending source code. An example of a false positive validation of a security issue is a vulnerability identified only with dynamic security testing that cannot be confirmed by a static security testing assessment and can be ruled out as a finding and considered a false positive.

An example of how combining different security assessments can improve the overall quality of the assessments is in the identification of the root causes of the issues. For example, the cause of the security issues can be attributed to either an error in the source code or a flaw in the design. Once the root cause of the issue is identified, it is also possible to determine whether the issue is exposed to a threat and might affect the application functionality, or to determine the level of risk. Typically, these types of security assessments require manual analysis and cannot be fully automated since they require a contextual understanding of the application business logic and functionality. Automated tests are no match for security analyst who has knowledge of the business logic and the application architecture being reviewed. Automated tools are agnostic of the application context and the business logic; what the application is used for, where it is being used, and by whom. This type of contextual information is essential in determining the business impact and quantifying the risks to the business of the security issues identified in the application. A secure code review, for example, might identify a cross site scripting vulnerability by looking at how a software component responds to a request and might point to an issue of invalidated URL parameter as well as lack of output encoding. By manually tracing the vulnerability from a manual review of the code, it is determined, that such component is not used to process user input, but rather to an internal processing function. A security test conducted manually can further validate that the level of access required to exploit the security issue is internal only. This information is essential to determine the exposure of the security issue and the risk. Since the XSS issue cannot be exercised by a user's input, it is not exploitable for phishing but only by an internal process that reads from input from configuration files that are only accessible by internal users of the application with administrative privileges.

By applying the knowledge of the application context and business logic, code reviewers and web penetration testers can assign a qualitative risk value to vulnerabilities when the root causes, exposure, likelihood to be exploited, and impact can be identified. For example, knowing whether the security issue can be exploited before or after user authentication is an important factor to consider when assigning risk to security issue. An SQL injection vulnerability found in web pages that can only be reached after authentication, for example, are considered lower risk than the same SQL injection issue found on publicly available web pages before authentication.

Knowing the vulnerability's root cause is an important factor to eradicate it and to decide how to mitigate it. An SQL injection vulnerability that is found with manual secure code reviews and is also exploitable with manual penetration testing can point the software engineer to the section of code that need to be fixed and to the attack vectors that can be used to exploit it. This therefore reduces the time required to fix and test the vulnerability. In cases where the root cause of the vulnerability is in the source code, such as in the case of SQL injection, but crafting the attack vector to exploit it is difficult without the knowledge of the source code, the risk of the vulnerability can also be revised accordingly to lower the risk.

To improve either manual-based or tool-based security hybrid analysis, considering the results of a threat model helps improve the accuracy of the assessment further when the security issues are analyzed by taking into account the security issue findings of static and dynamic security testing. One essential contribution of threat modeling is identifying the causes of security issues in the application design, such as in the application architecture. An example of a security issue that can be identified with a threat modeling assessment is a design flaw such as not designing a security control that compliance requires, such as the requirement to encrypt authentication data in storage and in transit. If such a design flaw is not identified and fixed prior to releasing the application into production, it may expose the application to risks and business impacts. If such a design flaw is identified with either a secure code review or a penetration test, it can be still remediated prior to releasing the application into production, but it would be much more expensive to fix than it would have been if the issue was identified with threat modeling during the design phase. Therefore, a good reason to perform threat modeling as early as possible in the SDLC is the return of investment in security and cost savings in security defect management.

A threat model conducted during the SDLC prior to other assessments, such as secure code reviews and penetration testing, can therefore identify issues including design flaws prior to being identified by other security assessments. A threat model can also be used to prioritize the scope of these assessments by scoping first for the source code analysis – the components of the architecture that have higher inherent risks due to higher number of security issues identified in them. This approach of using threat modeling data for prioritizing the scope of source code analysis is also known "depth" versus "breadth" first. Before starting a secure code review of the whole application, the focus is on the architectural components that have high-risk design flaws previously identified with a threat modeling exercise. This approach is the opposite of the "breadth first" approach that consists of scanning the whole source code of the application for possible vulnerabilities followed by manual source code reviews to validate the false positives as well as to identify additional security issues that cannot be identified with automated tools.

The prioritization of secure code reviews and penetration testing for the components of the application that have been previously identified as being more critical than others by a threat modeling exercise is also aligned with the overall risk management objective to prioritize the security issue remediation effort based on risk. The risk criticality of such components might be determined by different factors such as the type of the critical functions that such component provides, for example, the encryption of sensitive data and access controls for high-risk business transactions.

A value added by integrating threat modeling with source code analysis is that the analysis of the possible threats and attack scenarios including the data flows that can be targeted and the possible impact to the data assets and the functionality of the application. With a threat model, it is possible to visualize how the several components of the application can be attacked from the threat source of the attack to the final impacted data and functionality. The correlation of the attack threat source to the target of the attack is critical information for analyzing the countermeasures to mitigate the risk. A similar type of correlation between the source of the attack and the effect of the attack is done for the analysis of vulnerabilities in the source code where the "source" of the vulnerability that is the source code where the vulnerability originates and the "sink of the vulnerability" is the source code where the vulnerability ends and manifests itself by producing an impact. The difference between source code analysis and threat modeling in assessing the "sources" and the "sinks" of vulnerabilities and attacks is that in the case of threat modeling, the correlation between threat and vulnerability exploits relies on manually analyzing the architecture and the threats. In the

232 THREAT MODELING WITHIN THE SDLC

case of static source code analysis, this correlation between "sources" and "sinks" of vulnerabilities can be automated using a technique called taint analysis. Taint analysis is the technique that is used in static source code analysis tools to extract information about the relationships between functions, parameters, and calling paths to other functions and parameters.

Threat Modeling and Vulnerability Assessments

In a threat model, correlating the attack sources and the data and functions that are impacted by the attacks is done through manual analysis by considering the data flow diagrams, the architecture of the application, the type of environment, and the user cases. This data flow information is later used along with other information, such as attack trees, to identify vulnerabilities and countermeasures.

The data flow diagrams that are derived as one of the artifacts of the threat modeling exercise are also particularly useful for assigning the value of risk to the security issues identified with the secure code review and static source analysis of the application source code. Since a data flow diagram can visualize the exposure of a particular asset to the data, it can help determine the risk exposure in case that data asset is exposed to a threat by a particular vulnerability which affects that component.

For example, a cross-site scripting vulnerability identified by reviewing the source code of the application that runs on the application server can be considered LOW risk because a component such as a servlet filter in the application server *mitigates* the exposure of such vulnerability by input filtering and output encoding possible XSS attack vectors coming from external threat sources. An example of a threat model of possible XSS attack exploiting the XSS vulnerability and the asserted control in place is shown in Figure 4.11.

Identifying the access levels for the data entry points (shown in the DFD when the data flow crosses the trust boundary depicted in the dashed line) is also very

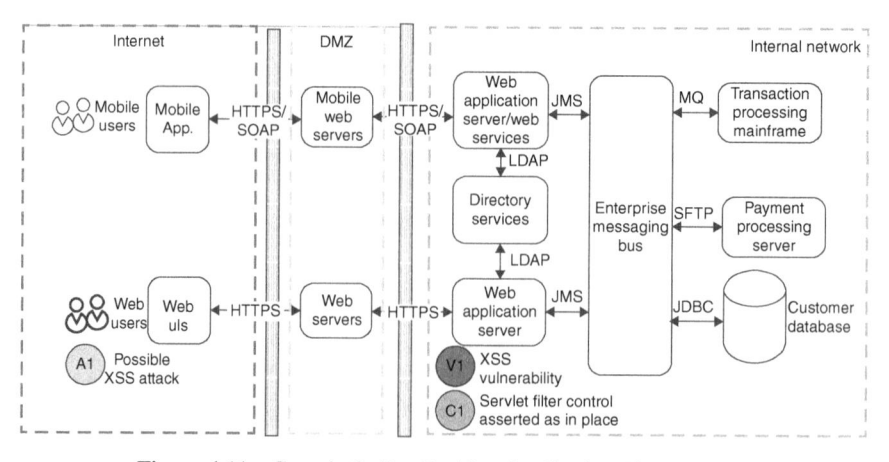

Figure 4.11 Generic Online Banking Application Threat Model

important for determining the level of authorization access required to exploit a vulnerability identified in the source code analysis. A source code vulnerability found in the application source code that can be accessed externally without authentication, for example, can be considered a higher risk issue than when the same source code vulnerability is found in the application source code whose functionality is restricted to authenticated users. By using a data flow diagram that is part of the threat model, it is possible to determine the severity of vulnerabilities in the source code.

Threat modeling is therefore a critical security assessment. It is important not just for the scope of the security review that includes the various components of the architecture in the context of the application business use and in the context of the possible abuse of threat agents, but also because it allows quantifying the risks of these issues by visualizing the likelihood and impact of security issues identified in other assessments, such as source code analysis and penetration testing, as well as correlating the causes of the security issues with the effects.

5

THREAT MODELING AND RISK MANAGEMENT

DATA BREACH INCIDENTS AND LESSONS FOR RISK MANAGEMENT

"Observe your enemies, for they first find out your faults."
From Antisthenes, Greek philosopher, quoted in Diogenes Laertius, *Lives and Opinions of Eminent Philosophers, vi. 12*

On August 5, 2009, Federal prosecutors in the United States charged Mr. Albert Gonzales with the largest credit card data theft and fraud ever occurred in the States, a combined credit card theft of 50 million credit cards and credit card numbers. According to the indictments proceedings, Albert Gonzales did not act alone, but as a member of a global cybercrime gang that included two hackers in Russia and a conspirator in the United States. During a period of more than 2 years, Albert Gonzales and his fellow cybercrime gang members attacked several corporate servers and Web applications and stole credit and debit card data by using attack techniques such as SQL injection, war driving, and installing network sniffers. To cover the tracks of these attacks, the members of the gang used different usernames, disabled programs that logged inbound and outbound traffic, and concealed the origination of the machines IP addresses by hiding them through proxies.

The main objective of these attacks was to steal credit and debit card data and economically profit from it. Specifically, the cyber gang profited from the resale of millions of stolen credit card and debit card numbers, cardholder personal information, magnetic strip/track data, and PINs on the black market and by counterfeiting

---

Risk Centric Threat Modeling: Process for Attack Simulation and Threat Analysis, First Edition.
Tony UcedaVélez and Marco M. Morana.
© 2015 John Wiley & Sons, Inc. Published 2015 by John Wiley & Sons, Inc.

debit cards to withdraw cash from ATMs. The money proceeds from the credit card fraud were money laundered by channeling funds through bank accounts in Eastern Europe.

Merchants, credit card processing companies, and credit card holders were all impacted by this data breach incident. Several million credit card holders had their credit card data stolen and funds withdrawn from their bank accounts using counterfeit debit cards. Heartland Payment Systems, the sixth largest payment credit card processor in the United States alone suffered a total loss of $12.6 million in fraudulent transactions. The volume of credit and debit data compromised totaled 50 million records. Besides Heartland Payment Systems, several merchants' Points of Sales (POSs) were attacked and large volumes of data were compromised. Hannaford Brothers, a large supermarket chain, reported 4.2 million credit card numbers and ATM card data stolen and T.J. Maxx, an American department store chain reported $45.6 million in credit card and debit cards being stolen.

Such a large data breach prompted the credit card processor Heartland Payment Systems to hire security experts to conduct a "postmortem" analysis to learn the root causes of these incidents and take additional security measures. The forensic investigation pointed to several causes, including the exploit of application layer vulnerabilities, such as SQL injection, and control gaps such as inadequately protecting transactions with credit and debit card data.

Audit and Compliance as a Factor for Risk Management

The postmortem analysis of the security incidents was done to identify the root causes of the security incidents and to determine which security measures worked and which did not. One of the security measures in question was compliance with industry security standards. Because of the mission critical Web applications and processes affected by the data breach and the fact that several of the businesses impacted were required to comply with security standards and were audited for compliance with these, one of the goals of the postmortem analysis was to determine if any unlawful noncompliance with information security policies, technology security standards, and regulations could be factored as the cause of the breach. Among the security technology standards that both credit card processors and merchants are required to comply with are the Payment Card Industry standards (PCI). Credit card brands such as VISA, MasterCard, and American Express mandate that credit card processors that process their branded credit cards and debit cards for payments comply with the PCI and Data Security Standard (DSS). Compliance with PCI-DSS is audited by certified PCI-DSS auditors called Qualified Security Assessors (QSA). The main goal of these PCI-DSS audits is to make sure that the various PCI-DSS security requirements are met before allowing merchants and banks to process credit card transactions. At the high level, PCI-DSS auditors validate that computer networks and systems have sufficient safeguards deployed to protect credit card payments from possible compromise of confidentiality, integrity, and availability of credit and debit card data. Examples of these safeguards include access control measures, secure networks, network vulnerability scans, and logging. Specifically with respect to the security of the Web applications and systems that process credit and debit card data, one of the requirements of PCI-DSS is that merchants and credit card processors develop and maintain the security of systems and Web applications, including assessing Web applications for vulnerabilities and correcting them and re-evaluating them after corrections. The Web application security assessments that can be adopted by credit card merchants and processors to satisfy PCI-DSS requirements might also include manual source code reviews, automated source code reviews, manual ethical hacking/penetration tests, and automated Web application vulnerability assessments/scans.

The various merchants and credit card payment processors that were impacted by the Gonzalez cybercrime gang credit and debit card data breach were all in scope for PCI-DSS and audited for compliance at different degrees to satisfy different security requirements. Nevertheless, despite the fact the both merchants and credit card processors were certified as compliant with PCI-DSS and audited by QSA, they were all impacted by the attacks and suffered direct losses of credit card data.

The security requirements that are validated as part of the PCI-DSS audit depend on the types of merchants and credit card processors and on their exposure to risk, such as the volume of credit card transactions. For example, PCI-DSS security requirements are different between merchants and credit card processors as well as between low and high transaction volume. Transaction volume in particular is used for determining the compliance levels: the higher the volume of the transactions, the stricter the level of PCI-DSS security requirements that need to be satisfied. Small businesses that process less than 20,000 online credit card transactions a year are considered level 4 merchants by PCI-DSS. Merchants that process more than 6 million transactions per year, such as T.J. Maxx and Hannaford Brothers, are considered level 1. To comply with PCI-DSS, level 1 merchants need to satisfy a more in-depth compliance audit assessment than level 4 merchants. A level 1 merchant, for example, is required to have an on-site security audit at least annually and a network scan at least quarterly while level 4 merchants do not require an on-site assessment except in some cases, such as when suffering a data breach. In this case, since level 1 merchants were involved, the strongest security requirements for PCI-DSS compliance were required and audited.

Since the companies involved in the data breach incidents were certified as compliant by PCI-DSS QSA, it is logical to question whether these audits were not thoughtfully executed and perhaps missed identifying the presence of vulnerabilities that were exploited during the breach, such as SQL injection. Typically, successfully passing a PCI-DSS audit implies that several of the PCI-DSS security requirements audited are satisfied by the presence of security controls, measures, and processes. This begs the question of whether PCI-DSS compliance could actually reduce the economic impact of a data loss.

One course of action after a security incident is to understand the root causes of the incident and to identify and mitigate any vulnerabilities to reduce the risk of further incidents. Another course of action after a security incident is to revoke the compliance certification and conduct further investigations to discover the possible causes of the security incident. PCI-DSS has strict requirements for protecting credit card, such as requiring business to either encrypt or mask credit card data numbers, not to store PINs even encrypted, and to identify and remediate web application vulnerabilities identified before they are released into production. When a PCI QSA identifies either gaps in security measures or vulnerabilities in systems and Web applications that process/store credit card data, evidence of corrective action plan to fix these vulnerabilities must be validated, along with proof that these vulnerabilities are tested as being fixed and the issues can be closed. Fixing Web application vulnerabilities is required for compliance with PCI. Failing to satisfy PCI requirements might result in fines and losing the required attestation and ability to continue conducting business with credit card brands. For example, a merchant that passed the audit for PCI-DSS can do business with the credit card issuer's organizations that are part of the PCI Security Standard Council that includes American Express, Discover Financial Services, JCB International, MasterCard Worldwide, and Visa Inc. A merchant that fails the audit of PCI-DSS compliance exposes itself to several unlawful compliance risks, such as fines, penalties, and higher costs for future PCI assessments. Ultimately, noncompliance with PCI-DSS leads to termination of the ability to process credit cards.

Since several of the PCI-DSS requirements are information security requirements for protecting cardholder information and transactions, successfully complying with PCI-DSS implies that these security requirements are followed and tested. The assertion that PCI-DSS security requirements are satisfied by a qualified auditor provide the credit card companies a level of assurance that credit and debit cardholder data and transactions are secure. This level of security assurance unfortunately is very limited to identifying low hanging fruits and does not require more thorough testing, for example, that systems are built with security controls resilient enough to protect credit and debit card data from emerging threats and attacks. A possible requirement for PCI-DSS would be to test that that Web applications and systems that handle credit and debit card data are resilient against an attack seeking to compromise credit and debit card data involving war-dialing, SQL injection, and network sniffers.

Lesson Number 1: Compliance Provides a Minimum Level of Security Assurance

It is often assumed that the organization compliant with information security standards and security policies increases the security posture of the organization and specifically provides assurance that the organization can operate in a condition of security and controlled risk. When a security incident occurs, trust is broken and questions are raised as to whether compliance with technology standards is strict enough to trust merchants and credit card processors to operate in an environment of high-risk exposure and emerging threats, such as cybercriminals seeking to compromise credit and debit card data for monetary gain.

According to NIST (National Institute of Standards and Technology) SP 800-33, "Assurance is grounds for confidence that an entity meets its security objective, it is a system characteristic enabling confidence that the system fulfills its intended purpose." In light of security incidents such as the 50 million credit and debit card breach and fraud perpetuated by the Albert Gonzalez cyber gang, the hard truth for merchants and credit card processors is that an attestation of compliance with PCI-DSS is merely assurance that the compliance security requirements are met and certified by a QSA. This level of assurance varies depending on different factors, such as the type of the organization (e.g. merchant or credit card processor) and the volume of transactions. In the case of Hannaford Brothers, a large supermarket chain that included 173 stores in four US states, QSA certified that the company was compliant with the PCI-DSS requirement of protecting credit card data in storage and in transit over public/open networks. At the time of the data loss incidents, the credit card processor Heartland Payment Systems was considered the sixth largest in the United States. QSA certified that Heartland Payment System compliant to the highest level of PCI-DSS requirements.

Unfortunately, it is known from public disclosure of data breaches that merchants and card processors were affected even if they were audited and certified as compliant with PCI-DSS. The lesson to be learned is that audited compliance with a security standard such as PCI-DSS by itself is not equivalent to applications and systems being protected from attacks seeking to compromise credit and debit card data.

There is often an assumption that compliance is a panacea of security and compliance is what businesses can rely upon to consider their systems and Web applications secure. This is a bad assumption that can put both businesses and consumers at risk since it drives a false sense of security. Compliance can be a factor for increased security of Web applications and systems, as it requires design of Web applications and systems that process credit card payments for merchants and credit card processors to satisfy a set of minimum-security requirements to protect credit card data. The extent to which the presence of these security measures is asserted by qualified auditors provides credit card companies a minimum level of assurance. Nevertheless, the compliance with security technology standards and information security policies does not necessarily provide assurance that systems, Web applications, and networks have been designed with security measures that adequately protect against threat agents seeking to steal credit card data.

The verification of these security requirements through an audit process, for example, provides a level of security assurance to the regulator that Web applications and systems in scope for compliance adhere to these security requirements. In the case of PCI-DSS, compliance with this standard by merchants and payment processors provides the companies that mandate the compliance a level of assurance that merchants and payment processors have implemented the required controls and processes to protect credit card holder data.

Lesson Number 2: Compliance Alone Is Not the Determining Factor in Risk Prevention of Security Incidents Caused by Emerging Cyber-Threats

According to the loss data publicly disclosed on March 17, 2008 related to the Gonzalez case, PCI-DSS compliant Hannaford Brothers was affected by a data breach involving 4.2 million credit card numbers.

PCI-DSS compliance credit card data processor Heartland Payment Systems was affected by a massive loss of credit card and debit card data on May 15, 2008. The total loss of credit card data amounted to 130 million credit card numbers. Subsequent to the data breach, Visa temporarily removed Heartland from its list of PCI-DSS compliant companies until countermeasures were implemented and it was re-certificated as compliant by QSA.

Other merchants that collected large volumes of credit card payment data were victims of the same attacks. T.J. Maxx, a retail chain of 2500 department stores in the United States and Europe reported a loss of 94 million credit card records including transaction details. T.J. Maxx was also in scope for compliance with PCI-DSS but, different from Heartland and Hannaford Brothers, it did not comply with PCI-DSS requirements and failed the audits.

Since both PCI-DSS compliant and noncompliant merchants along with credit card processors where affected by breaches of credit card and debit card data, both merchants and credit card processors need to reconsider the factors for compliance to make sure that this is not the only factor that is considered for managing cyber-threats targeting credit card data and transactions.

Some businesses, especially small and medium businesses that have limited budgets to spend on security, might consider unlawful noncompliance as a risk they are willing to take because of the costs of implementing security measures to comply with the provisions of the security standards.

Compliance with security processes and specifically compliance with vulnerability management processes is a critical factor for reducing risk. Nevertheless, mitigating any vulnerabilities identified by security tests, such as penetration testing or ethical hacking, will at best test web applications and systems for the most common web application and source code vulnerabilities. Security testing might be useful to identify common vulnerabilities, such as the OWASP Top Ten, but will only reduce the opportunity or the likelihood for an attacker/fraudster to exploit these common vulnerabilities. The enforcement of a security policy might require that security testing be done for web applications also in compliance with external regulations and technology standards such as PCI-DSS in the case these web applications process payments with credit cards. A successful audit for compliance with the industry-mandated standard would provide a minimum level of security assurance to the credit card issuing companies that common vulnerabilities have been identified and mitigated prior to processing credit card transactions. In case of compliance with PCI-DSS, for example, companies that look to satisfy the PCI-DSS requirement 11.3.2 need to perform vulnerability assessments for web applications. The scope of this vulnerability assessment is to identify "known" web application vulnerabilities.

When these vulnerabilities are identified and fixed (thanks to the enforcement of standards and policies), the likelihood of being opportunistically exploited is certainly reduced. Therefore, identifying and fixing Web application vulnerabilities that either process or store sensitive data and business critical transactions with these data, such as payments and money transfers, is a critical aspect for reducing the exposure to attacks seeking to exploit these vulnerabilities.

Nevertheless, just conducting a security test of common vulnerabilities is not enough to consider the web application secure. For example, the number of vulnerabilities that can be exploited by an attacker can greatly exceed the most common OWASP Top Ten vulnerabilities that are routinely tested. Assuming that a Web application is security tested for all known vulnerabilities, the scope of the test might miss hundreds if not thousands of other vulnerabilities that are not considered in the OWASP Top Ten. In addition, different types of vulnerabilities represent different risks for the organization. As not all these vulnerabilities have the same severity when exploited, most businesses prioritize the remediation of vulnerabilities that have the higher risks – those whose severity is either considered MEDIUM or HIGH risk.

It is important to notice that the scope of testing for vulnerabilities is not limited to web applications, but also includes servers, network infrastructure, and source code vulnerabilities as well as possible insecure configuration and deployment of web applications in the production environment. Furthermore, security testing a website for vulnerabilities, even a very comprehensive test that covers a wide scope of web application vulnerabilities, the underlying systems and networks might still not include zero-day type of vulnerabilities and business logic type of vulnerabilities. This is the case of vulnerabilities, such as zero-day, whose exploit does not have a remediation/fix yet and therefore might be exposed and exploited by an attacker. This is also the case of vulnerabilities that are often not tested because they require a specific manual security test case, such as logic vulnerabilities. They are often not identified due to the lack of threat modeling assessments, such as use and abuse cases to identify such logic vulnerability.

State-of-the-art vulnerability management executed by an organization typically makes sure that zero-day vulnerabilities are prioritized for mitigation and patched as soon as a patch is made available from the vendor, and that a threat modeling process is in place to analyze the design and identify business logic flaws that can be exploited by business logic attacks.

But even with a state-of-the-art vulnerability management process, there are other important aspects of risk management that are beyond managing the risk of vulnerabilities. One example is identifying control gaps and assessing the effectiveness of the security measures in place to protect the web application assets (e.g. data and functions) as well as to detect potential attacks targeting these assets.

Lesson Number 3: The Economic Impact of Security Incidents is Far Bigger Than the Impact of Unlawful Noncompliance

In the case of a breach of credit card data of a PCI compliant merchant, the fines are not levied by the PCI council but by the card associations (e.g. Visa, MasterCard) against the merchant bank, which will pass it to the merchants involved in the data breach security incident. The fines are typically a maximum of $500,000 per occurrence of an incident and the final amount includes fines that are dependent on the extent of data compromise such as the total number of card data stolen, the circumstances surrounding the incident, whether the track data was stolen or not and the timeliness of reporting the incident. If a company was validated as compliant by a QSA, the fine could be limited, but it all depends on when the data breach occurred since validation is one point of time. As an example, the incident costs for non-PCI compliant T.J. Maxx totaled $200 million, including fines and PCI required investigation costs. This did not include the additional costs for legal fees and lawsuits from banks and consumers.

One of the main lessons that merchants can learn after a security incident that results in data loss is that the fines are just a fraction of the overall costs/damages. In the case of Heartland Payments Systems, for example, most of tangible losses sustained after the breach consisted of the costs of re-issuing payment cards and the costs of fines and legal settlements. In May 2010, Heartland spent more than $95 million on legal fees and had to write off $35.6 million or 59 cents a share for the third quarter of 2009 to cover costs related to the data breach.

Possible sources for estimating the impacts of the security incidents involving losses of confidential and sensitive data for public trade companies are the quarterly reports. In the case of Heartland Payment Systems, the quarterly financial report released in Q1 2010, 2 years after the data breach incident reported that Heartland Payment Systems had accrued $139.4 million in breach-related expenses. A breakdown of the data breach costs incurred by Heartland consists of the following legal costs:

- $60 million for settlement with Visa related to the payment processor's data breach.
- $3.6 million for settlement with American Express.
- $12.6 million for MasterCard (levied against Heartland's sponsor banks).
- $19.4 million to settle claims related to the hacker intrusion.
- $4 million settlement toward a consumer class-action lawsuit to pay up to $175 to individuals for out-of-pocket expenses from telephone usage or postage costs tied to card cancellations and replacement or for any unreimbursed charges resulting from unauthorized use of their cards.

This data can be useful in conducting an estimate of the business impact costs that credit card processing companies and merchants might accrue because of a security incident. The costs of a data breach can be considered as an impact of the incident and used to estimate the risk by factoring together the probability of such data breach incident occurring.

These business impacts, when estimated, can represent the possible tangible costs for the business.

In order to comprehensively manage the risk of all possible business impacts that an organization might be exposed to in the case of a security incident, it is important to consider the economic impacts of several different types of security incident costs such as the following:

- *Incident response* activities for responding to the credit/debit data loss incidents and identifying, containing, and remediating the causes.

- *Data breach notifications* to the customer and clients whose credit/debit cards were compromised as result of the breach.
- *Data replacements* of compromised credit/debit cards.
- *Liability* for refunding customers of the money lost because of fraudulent transactions (e.g. above the max customer liability of $50).
- *Legal fees and court settlements for lawsuits* from credit card companies, customers, and businesses affected by credit/debit card losses and fraud.
- *New measures provisioning* for customers such as identity theft services for customers and clients including indirect costs for deploying new technologies and processes to protect credit/debit card processing in the future.

Besides tangible (e.g. monetary) costs incurred by the company affected by the data breach in order to deal with the impact of the data breach, there are also intangible (e.g. reputational) costs that are important to estimate. Examples of intangible costs are damages to the reputation of the company and the perceived company value by the customers and shareholders after a security incident is disclosed to public. One possible correlation of security incidents to the damage to company reputation is to look at the impact on the company shareholder value. For example, Heartland Payment System shareholders' given value to the company after the data breach was negatively affected and the stock dropped 57% – from $14 to $8 per share when the data breach was released to public in January 2009 (see Figure 5.1).

Even if the correlation between the release of security incident involving a data breach information to the public and the drop in stock value cannot be proven in

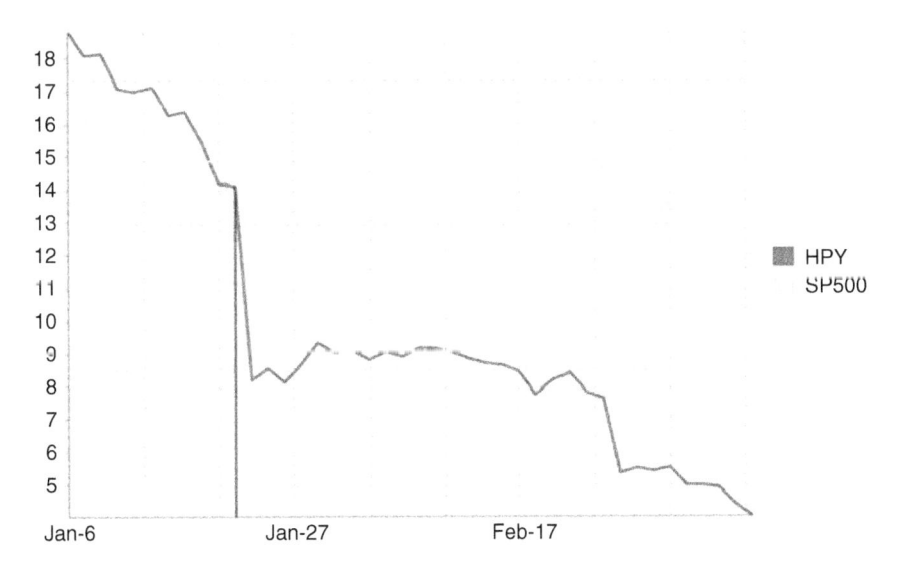

Figure 5.1 HPY Stock Price at the Time of the Data Breach Disclosure (January 20, 2009 datalossdb.org)

all cases of data breaches (this warrants more study), it can be used to estimate the impact on company reputational damage as one of the possible factors; others being an observed loss of revenue due to customer change of perception and trust of the company's business.

Lesson Number 4: Emerging Cyber-Threats Bring an Increased Level of Risk Exposure to Businesses

Another important aspect of proactively mitigating the risk of cyber-attacks leading to data compromises is assessing the organization's exposure to new cyber-threats. A methodology to assess this exposure consists of risk analysis to determine the probability that these threats might exploit control gaps and system vulnerabilities and cause a business impact. An important aspect of where the threat analysis can help assess risks is in helping derive a risk framework that includes a set of countermeasures proven effective in mitigating the risk of such threats. Such a risk framework can be used to identify gaps in security measures that are necessary to mitigate the risk of such threats. As threats constantly evolve and change, it is important that the organization's security measures, including information security policies, technologies, and tools, evolve as well to mitigate the risk of these emerging threats. The need of new countermeasures can be assessed by conducting a risk analysis based on a risk framework adapted and kept up to date regarding the emerging threats.

From risk management perspective, quantitative risk analysis provides a means for estimating the business impact of security incidents. The rough level estimates of the impacts of data loss incidents depend on the volume and value of the data assets that can possibly be lost. A comprehensive evaluation of the impacts of data loss incidents would need also to consider costs incurred for recovering the data and indirect costs, such as legal costs and fines from regulators/industry standards.

The larger costs that merchant and credit card processors might face after a security incident resulting in a large volume of credit card and debit data being compromised justifies an investment in additional security measures. These security measures are often above the minimum required to comply with security industry standards. The risk of impact to the business because of potential cyber-attacks targeting systems that handle a large volume of confidential data, for example, justifies focused security assessments above and beyond the ones required for compliance. These focused assessments focus on analyzing emerging threats and vulnerabilities in web applications and systems that could be exploited by these emerging threats.

The Importance of Focusing on Emerging Threats

For the sake of analyzing the risks posed by vulnerabilities that these attacks seek to exploit, it is important to consider the risks such vulnerabilities pose depending on the exposure to a specific threat. The other factors for determining the risks of data compromise incidents include estimating the easiness of conducting the exploit, such as reproducibility, discoverability of a vulnerability, and impact to the assets if the vulnerability is exploited. These are typically considered the main factors when calculating the risk of specific threats. An example of these factors is the DREAD risk ranking for threats that stands for damage, reproducibility, exploitability, affected users/assets, and discoverability to determine the risks that threats might pose.

Identifying the possible threat agents seeking to attack web applications and confidential data by exploiting vulnerabilities is essential to determine the likelihood and impact that such threat agents pose to web application/system. Some of these vulnerabilities might be identified during vulnerability scans, might be required by compliance with security standards and policies, and might reduce the risk of threats seeking to exploit such vulnerabilities, even if they do not fully eliminate the possibility of an exploit. Due to emerging threats, attacks, and vulnerabilities, some of which are not identified and or remediable yet, there are always new possibilities for an organization to become victim of data breach incidents even if due diligence and compliance were conducted and known vulnerabilities were tested and remediated. To cope with the emergence of these new threats, it is important that firms adopt threat and risk analysis as part of their risk mitigation strategy.

Emerging threats today target both the users and the web application. Attacks against users include social engineering with phishing e-mails, social media, and luring to click on links that apparently look legitimate but in reality point to a malicious website whose objective is to drop malware on the visitors of these websites. To protect their customers from malware threats, businesses need to adopt a threat and risk analysis process and determine the likelihood and impact that these threats might cause to the business.

In the case of threats seeking to compromise customers' confidential data, for example, it is important to analyze the different risk factors of these threats and analyze both the attackers and the type of attacks. This means performing a comprehensive analysis that identifies the possible threat targets, analyzing the type of attack tools and techniques used the type of network, system and web application vulnerabilities that these attacks exploit, and determining the potential impacts to the business in terms of economic losses, fraud, and legal costs. The vulnerabilities that are exploited in these types of attacks need to be analyzed by looking at the possible root causes to eradicate them. For vulnerabilities such as SQL injection, the exploit by a threat agent might lead to a negative effect such as loss, alteration, or deletion of data. The root cause of such SQL injection vulnerability might be a coding error. This coding error can be fixed prior to release of the web application in production, reducing the potential risk of exploiting this vulnerability.

In the Albert Gonzales case, one of the exploits reportedly used by the cyber gang is the SQL injection exploit. "The exploit of the SQL injection vulnerability provided a means for the attackers to compromise Heartland's internal network and sniff the credit card and debit card data traffic by installing network sniffer software." The sniffer software allowed the fraudsters to capture all data traffic among Heartland's processing systems, including financial transactions data and credit card data.

Since SQL injection vulnerabilities are typically identified as part of vulnerability assessments required in compliance with security policies and standards such as PCI-DSS, it is also important to reconsider the reasons businesses enact information security standards and how these standards are enforced. The purpose of technology security standards and information security policies needs to be prescriptive toward security requirements. An example is a set of application security requirements that are validated through governance and processes.

One of the main goals of a focused threat analysis is to help identify emerging threats and analyze the attacks used to compromise credit and debit card. Once threats are analyzed, it is possible to factor the risks and the business impacts and decide how to reduce the risk by applying effective security measures.

Identifying security measures that mitigate cyber-threat risks is one of the goals of risk management. It is important to provide risk managers with an analysis of threats and business impacts and a set of recommended security measures that can both protect and detect a cyber-attack seeking to compromise valued data assets such as credit card data.

Even if we cannot exclude that common vulnerabilities identified and remediated by a vulnerability assessment are a factor for improving security, we cannot be sure that other vulnerabilities can be exploited by an attacker, such as design flaws and vulnerabilities that are not tested with compliance-based vulnerability assessments. A focused analysis of the emerging threats possibly targeting web applications and systems is justified in addition to compliance depending on risk. For example, this is the case of systems and web applications that might expose large volumes of confidential data to cyber-threats. The main objective of conducting such a threat analysis is to determine the likelihood and the impact of security incidents caused by organized cybercriminals. Once these threat agents, types of attacks, types of vulnerabilities exploited, and technical and business risk are analyzed, it is possible to determine the type of security measures to protect against these threats.

This type of threat and risk analysis can also be used in conjunction with other security processes. These processes are typically part of the Chief Information Security Officer's (CISO) responsibilities and include security domains such as compliance, governance, and risk. Threat analysis is essential for managing risks and helping CISOs determine the exposure of their organization, managed web applications, and software to threats and make informed decisions on how to mitigate the risks. After these threats and risks have been analyzed, the next step is to apply countermeasures to reduce the impact of these threats and reduce the overall risk to the organization. The decision of which countermeasures to apply is considered part of risk management. In essence, this is the process of making decisions on how to mitigate the likelihood and impact of threats targeting the business and the business assets.

The inherent risk profile of each web application is different depending on specific asset values, such as data classification, the web application's business function criticality, and the potential business impact if the threat leads to a successful attack that compromises data and/or application functionality.

The inherent risk of an asset based on the type of attack that the asset can be targeted to help to determine the scope of the threat analysis as selection criteria to identify the assets that can be at risk of specific threats. Once the web applications at risk are identified, the next step is to determine which type of security controls are in place and which ones should be in place to reduce the risk to an acceptable level.

This type of analysis is also known in risk management as "control gap analysis" since it seeks to identify gaps in security controls, such as preventive and detective controls, as well as gaps in security measures that enable specific threats to be realized, leading to a security incident and a business impact. By implementing the security measures that mitigate the risks of specific threats, it is possible to reduce it to a residual risk that is acceptable to the business. The type of security controls and measures recommended to conduct the control gap analysis can be selected based on a group of security measures with different levels of effectiveness and costs in mitigating the specific threats. Typically, a web application requires more than one security measure and control to mitigate a specific threat since these measures work as defense in-depth, multilayered controls to mitigate the risk. For example, to mitigate the threat of malware compromise, the first layer of defense is provided by hardening the client/PC, running updated browsers and OS with minimum privileges, and antimalware and antivirus-spyware software installed. The next layer of defense, assuming that the malware has compromised the client PC and browser with key loggers or man-in-the browser, is to prevent attacks to the web application, the data, and the transactions. Security controls that can be used at the application layer are out-of-band authentication for logging and out-of-band transaction confirmation authentication of high-risk transactions, such as payments and money transfers.

Assuming that the preventive security measures are also compromised, the next layer of defense is to contain and limit the damage using measures that can detect an attack by triggering alerts based on specific web traffic parameters, either logged or fed in security event incident monitoring systems, as well as rules for detection of specific attack vectors implemented in web application firewalls and fraud detection systems. The threat analysis is, therefore, the driving factor in determining the bag of preventive and detective security measures that are required to mitigate the risk. The effectiveness of these security measures can be analyzed for each according to different criteria, such as effectiveness to protect/prevent or to detect/limit the impact as well as the 80/20 rule, which when applied as 20% of the overall recommended measures, mitigates 80% of the threats and attack vectors.

Compliance with security standards and security policies is an important driver for improving an organization's security posture and building systems and web applications that can better protect the data value assets from attacks seeking to compromise such data. The compliance with information security standards and policies also asserts that systems and web application vulnerabilities are identified and fixed in compliance with security testing processes.

Nevertheless, even when businesses have adopted security testing processes, such as vulnerability assessments in compliance with industry security standards (such as PCI-DSS), there is potentially still risk exposure to cyber-threats seeking to explore weaknesses that were not identified by compliance-based assessments. For the issues that have been identified and fixed thanks to a compliance-based vulnerability assessment, such a penetration test, there is always an element of risk posed by the severity rating of the vulnerability. When a violation of security standards is identified, such as a violation of information security policy, the business could still decide to accept the risk. This is when the risk is considered acceptable when reduced by the presence of existing controls.

The exposure to vulnerability risks is the least acceptable by the business when the severity of the vulnerability is considered critical. In essence, compliance with security policies might also help reduce the risk of security incidents and data compromises, but compliance alone is not necessarily enough of a reason to drive an organization to mitigate the risk of emerging threats targeting web applications.

Typically, compliance requirements have different levels that depend on different factors, such as the type of assets that need to be protected, the type of exposure, and the type of processes that use these data. Compliance with PCI DSS requires businesses to focus on sound risk management process to identify security issues and mitigate them depending on risk and exposure in compliance with the specific standard requirements. Unfortunately, apart from specific requirements for protecting the credit card data, such as masking, encryption, and testing common vulnerabilities, compliance does not specifically mandate threat analysis and threat modeling for emerging threats. This type of threat analysis might be used to derive security requirements to design web applications and systems that are resilient against emerging threats, such as DDOS and malware compromises.

It is therefore not surprising that security incidents leading to data compromise, such as the one caused by Albert Gonzales' cyber gang, also occurred to businesses that were audited and declared compliant with the security requirements mandated by specific industry security standards, such as PCI-DSS.

Compliance with industry security standards represents both a risk and an opportunity to improve security. There are several different reasons an organization would decide to comply with the standards. One possible reason is that this is a minimum requirement for operating as a business. For merchants and credit card processors, for example, compliance with PCI-DSS is justified by the need to operate with credit cards issued by the PCI-DSS council that include AMEX, Visa, and MasterCard. For the merchant and credit card processor required to comply with the PCI-DSS standard, the proof of compliance certifies their capability to operate with a stamp of approval verified by the QSA. Nevertheless, noncompliance represents an additional risk that needs to be managed. The likelihood of this risk might also depend on factors such as the likelihood to fail an audit and the impact of incurring fines and lawsuits. Nevertheless, from the perspective of reducing the impacts in case of an incident, such as additional fines and legal risks, compliance does not protect merchants from potential legal lawsuits and fines by the regulators in case of a security incident.

Unlawful noncompliance can also be a liability and bound to contractual agreements with a vendor, such as in the case of Service Level Agreements (SLA). Besides the legal impacts, noncompliance also impacts the organization's reputation and credibility. Since compliance with security standards certifies that the organization follows due diligence in maintaining a minimum level of security risks and can be trusted, the lack and loss of compliance with a security standard also diminishes trust that vendors have in the business. An example is the loss of trust of a bank in credit card payment processors when PCI certification is revoked following a security incident.

As with any type of risks, an organization manages noncompliance risk from the cost-benefit perspective. In some cases, the costs to comply with a certain regulation or standard do not justify the benefits. An organization could decide to transfer the risk to another entity, such as business partner, or operate in an environment that does not require such expensive regulation to conduct business. Some small merchants might deliberately choose to be unlawful and noncompliant with PCI when the cost of implementing the required security controls is higher than the costs of possible fines. This might explain why, for example, according to some data surveys, only 28% of small businesses (<1,000 employees) are compliant with PCI-DSS compared to 70% of large businesses (>75,000 employees).

Lesson Number 5: After a Security Incident, It is Important to Reevaluate the Effectiveness of Compliance-Based Security Measures

One of the lessons learned from Gonzales' cyber gang attacks on merchants and credit card processors is that security controls in addition to those required by compliance are necessary to protect credit card data transactions. Executive management shares this view when confronted with data breach evidence: to quote the CEO of Heartland Payment Systems, Robert Carr, "the fact that the security incident occurred despite Heartland's strong focus on data security and compliance with PCI has led me to the opinion that more must be done to increase the security of data transfers."

To identify what "more" than compliance should be done to reduce the risk of data breaches caused by emerging threats from cybercrime gangs, fraudsters, and cyber spies, it is important first and foremost to be able to analyze the threats, the type of attacking tools used, the type of vulnerabilities exploited, and the likelihood and impact of these occurring. One important aspect in this type of threat analysis is to consider the worst case scenarios, assume that defenses can be compromised, and that security controls can mitigate impacts by working at different layers as protective and detective controls. It is also important to learn from the organization's security incidents as well as from available threat intelligence reports how the attacks were conducted, how data was compromised, which vulnerabilities were exploited, and which security measures have been effective in stopping the data leak once implemented.

A "postmortem" analysis of the credit data breach that occurred at Heartland Payment Systems recommended several lessons to reduce the risk of similar data breaches in the future:

1. Share information about the threats among members of the banking and financial services industries and between the private sector industry and the public sector.
2. Adopt security measures such as end-to-end encryption to protect credit card data when it is shared among payment processing networks (data in transit) and when is stored in proprietary systems (data at rest).

3. Secure the system that processes, authorize, authenticate, and settle card transactions.

An important lesson to learn from these security incidents is whether the risks of these vulnerabilities and weaknesses enabled these attacks and whether they could be reduced by implementing security measures.

Besides the forensics analysis of data breach security incidents that occurred in the past, it is important to consider the potential for risk based on the exposure of new emerging threats and attacks. In addition to handling value-based data, such as credit card data, that can be used to commit fraud either by selling such data on the underground carding market networks or by withdrawing money from ATMs using the stolen data to counterfeit cards, merchants' web applications, systems, and credit card processing organizations storing and handling credit card data are primary targets for cyber gangs and fraudsters threat agents.

To determine the risk exposure for merchants, credit card processors, and consumers to value-driven threat agents, such as cyber gangs and fraudsters, it is necessary first to understand the threat agent's capabilities, motives, type of data sought, type of attacking tools and techniques used, and how these can cause an impact to the organization. Important sources of information for analyzing these threat agents are threat intelligence reports as well as any information available from internal sources, such as security incident reports. Threat intelligence can be used to build the organization's threat-attack-vulnerability knowledge base. The main objective of the threat analysis is to analyze the type of threat characteristics such as threat motives, capabilities, and targets and factor them into the risk evaluation – the probability that these threats might cause impacts to the businesses they are targeting.

The analysis of which security measures are effective in mitigating the risk of security incidents, such as data breaches, depends on a threat and risk analysis of the type of attacks used by threat agents that could be used against the assets to cause an impact.

The first step of the risk analysis for possible data breach incidents is to conduct a forensic analysis to identify the causes of the incident and determine whether the likelihood of data and functionality could be the target for similar cyber-attacks in the future. Often web applications have already been attacked by cyber gangs/fraudsters. The main question for risk managers is not how to prevent impacts "if" the organization is attacked, but "how" has the organization been attacked and what was effective in containing the impact and responding to the security incident. In both cases, it is important to analyze the type of threat agents and determine preventive and detective measures that can reduce the impact of security incidents to the organization. This is the scope of threat analysis, the discipline whose objectives are analyzing the possible threats, identifying the threat agents/actors motivations and capabilities, analyzing and identifying the targets of the possible attacks, as well as the different ways to conduct such attacks. For example, a fraudster can try to steal large amount of credit and debit card data by attacking with malware on specific targets, such as Point of Sale (POS) terminals at merchant stores and spoof communication channels with Man-in-the-Middle (MitM) attacks between POS and card processing servers, by exploiting vulnerabilities in these servers such as SQL injection to install remote access tools.

Initially, it is important to analyze the possible threat landscape, the type of attacks, and the likelihood and impact of these attacks. It is also important to understand the attacker's gain vs. risk perspective to identify the attacks that maximize the gains for an attacker by minimizing their effort, and which are most likely to succeed (the highest probability), because these can yield the greatest gain (e.g. installing malware to capture credentials) with the minimum effort (e.g. by opportunistically attacking vulnerable browsers with drive by download and by targeting the victims through social engineering).

Analyzing how malware and hacking attacks can be used to realize the attacker's goals is critical for determining which security measures are most effective in mitigating the risks of data compromise. For example, fraudsters seek to compromise the client's desktop PC first by attempting to exploit either vulnerabilities in the browser or the web application by directly targeting the victim with social engineering. The malware is typically downloaded when the victim either selects a link that points to a malicious site or an attachment with embedded malware. Once the victim opens the malicious link, the malware is silently installed on the victim's PC. This malware is specifically designed and configured to attack the victim's sensitive data, such as bank and credit card account data. Typically, this type of malware can be either purchased or leased as a cybercrime service for fee from a group of hackers and cyber gangs that profit from selling and renting cybercrime tools.

Since this type of malware is specifically designed to attack customers that bank online, it is also referred in the technical literature as banking Trojan malware. Once this malware is acquired, the next step is typically to plan the malware distribution campaign. This usually involves phishing and social engineering attacks to lure online banking customers into selecting links that might appear legitimate, such as a request to change online credentials and to enter personally identifiable information (PII) for further validation. Once the online banking customers select such malicious links, the malware will be installed on the victim's desktop. This malware will wait silently for the victim to log on to the online banking website to intercept the online credentials of the victim through a key logger, and with these credentials, will establish another web session. This web session will be used concurrently with the legitimate session to initiate money transfer transactions from the victim's bank account to another bank account under the control of the fraudster.

These attacks are usually effective in compromising the victim's confidential data and stealing money from the victim's bank accounts. Specifically, these attacks are designed to attack the weakest links of security such as the human element and the inadequacy of preventive and detective security controls in most web applications for certain type of attacks, such as MitM and Man-in-the-Browser (MitB). In order to proactively protect customers from these types of attacks, banks should consider a set of preventive and detective security measures at the different components of the web application that might be compromised during an attack, but also extend the protection to the user's browser and the desktop that represent the first layer of defense.

In order to decide which security measures should be deployed and where they should be deployed, it is important to analyze the sequence of the events used to realize an attack. Typically, the first step is to attack the user either through phishing or silently infecting the user's desktop browser indirectly through a drive by download attack. Once the user's PC is infected with malware, the second step is injecting HTML on the web pages that render the online banking web pages. This is an attack technique known as MitB. Since the malware installed on the victim's PC receives instructions from a command and control server, it will be instructed to inject a malicious frame directly into the victim's browser PC. Such a malicious frame/web page is designed to collect sensitive account and PII from the user and redirect it from the victim's browser to the command and control server. The malicious form would look authentic to the user since it will show during an authenticated online web session with the bank. Since the user will not be able to distinguish that this web page is under the control of the malware, it might lure the victim to enter data that is usually not collected by the web application, such as Social Security Numbers (SSNs), DOB, mother's maiden name, and any credit or debit card data including bank/credit card account numbers, PINs, and CVVs.

Since the user's host PC is compromised by the malware, the next step is to hook into the victim's operating system to control any data sent over the wire between the host and the web application. This is an attack technique that is known as MitM and is used by the attacker to sniff data in transit between the client and the server. Once the victim logs into the banking site, the bank Trojan included in the malware will intercept all the data traffic and any data entered by the user, including user credentials, such as passwords and answers to challenge questions used for Multifactor Authentication (MFA).

Another capability of this type of malware is to perform fraudulent transactions, such as transferring money from the victim's account to the fraudster's controlled account, also referred to as a money mule. The banking Trojan will exploit the user logged authenticated session to perform a wire transfer without the user noticing. This would be possible since the cybercrime tool is in complete control of the data traffic between the victim's browser, PC, and the online banking site; any credential or authentication factor input by the user into the site is captured by the fraudster to perform fraudulent transactions on behalf of the logged-in user.

These cyber-threats where malware is designed to target specific web applications such as financial websites, are also known as "Advanced Persistent Threats," or APTs. APTs are characterized by the use of cyber attacking tools specifically designed to attack certain web applications and websites and are therefore considered advanced in terms of attack sophistication with respect to simple scripts that seek to exploit common vulnerabilities in web applications. These types of attacks are also known to be persistent; that means persistently directed at certain targets, such as financial and government targets instead of opportunistically trying to exploit weaknesses in sites as these are identified. Examples of specific threats include attacks such as hacking and malware persistently directed toward online banking sites and the financial transactions performed through these sites using advanced cybercrime tools. Another type of malware typically used by persistent threat agents is Remote Access Tool (RAT).

RATs usually implement backdoors in systems to conduct an exfiltration of sensitive data from the organization, such as intellectual property and confidential customer information. A threat agent behind an APT might be a fraudster seeking valuable data for financial gain, but can also be a state/corporate sponsored threat agent seeking to spy on highly sought valued secrets.

In order to mitigate the risk of APTs, it is important to first analyze the threat and the attack vectors and then devise countermeasures that mitigate the risk by reducing the likelihood and the impact. A prerequisite for identifying countermeasures is to analyze the attack vectors. Assuming, for example, that a known cybercrime tool is used, it is possible to reverse engineer the tool to understand the functionality, attack vectors, and techniques used, and then design and deploy countermeasures that can be applied to the client as well as to different layers of the web application. This might include defenses against MitM attacks such as Out of Band (OOB) authentication, electronic signatures to digitally sign transactions to prevent tampering, and client side defenses, such as sandboxing and hardened browsers to protect the client desktop from key loggers.

Determining which security measures are most effective in mitigating the risk of specific threats, such as hacking and malware, needs to consider preventive and detective measures against targeted attacks. These targeted attacks are not only targeting the user's PC and web applications but also the human element with social engineering attacks.

One important aspect of managing risks is following a risk management strategy. To manage the risks of data breaches, for example, it is important to strategically look at all the security assessments of the information security program and at the effectiveness in reducing the overall risks for the organization.

Today, most businesses focus on identifying and mitigating vulnerabilities as required by compliance with industry standards and their organization's information security policies. The vulnerabilities exploited in an attack might expose the business's assets such as confidential data, PII, and intellectual property to attackers.

The process of identifying and mitigating vulnerabilities is known as vulnerability management. Traditionally, vulnerability management is a critical process for reducing risks to the organization since the main goal is to reduce the risk due to exposure of vulnerabilities to potential attacks that seek either opportunistically or intentionally to exploit vulnerabilities for financial gain. In essence, vulnerability management is a critical process for managing technical risks derived from either web application/system vulnerability or gap/weaknesses in a security control of such web application/system.

Indeed enforcing compliance with security standards and policies can be part of the engineering requirements of a new web application. For example, this might consist of deriving a set of security requirements that needs to be followed during the design phase of the Software Development Life Cycle (SDLC). Adherence of design to these security requirements can be asserted during the architecture design reviews and any security design flaws that are identified can be remediated prior to the implementation phase. As new threats emerge, it is important that the security requirements also change to adapt to these emerging threats by implementing specific countermeasures. For these reasons, the analysis of threats against data and functions might include formal methods such as use and abuse cases to elicit security requirements and attack trees to identify at a high level the possible attacks against the assets and to derive a set of security test cases to prove that the web application has been designed with security controls and functionality that is resilient enough to mitigate the impact of such attacks.

Ultimately, there is no one security measure that mitigates the risk, but a group of measures that include at least a few preventive and few detective security measures. The selection of which measures are worth deploying should consider other factors such as compliance with security standards, the cost of the countermeasure versus the effectiveness, and how it contributes to reducing the risk to a low residual risk.

Lesson Number 6: The Analysis of Threats and Attacks Help Businesses in Designing More Secure Systems/Web Applications.

Threat information can directly feed into risk analysis to determine the likelihood and impact of threats. When the threat and risk analysis is performed during the development of a web application, system, or software, such as during SDLC, it provides value from proactive risk mitigation.

For example, when the analysis of threats and countermeasures is conducted during the design ahead of the deployment to production, it can be used to prescribe a new set of security requirements that the web applications development teams, namely, architects and software developers, have to follow. During the architecture analysis, the risk assessment might include evaluating impact and likelihood of potential design flaws that have been identified during the security review of the web application architecture. These design flaws might expose the web application to threats seeking to compromise data and be remediated with a design change prior to the information security team approving the design. These design changes would also need to be security tested to make sure that they are implemented to mitigate the exposure of the data to the threats previously being analyzed.

The process described earlier is also known as architectural risk analysis. Risk analysis can also be integrated with other phases of the SDLC, such as during coding phase and testing to assess the risk posed by vulnerabilities that have been identified during these SDLC phases. Once the SDLC is completed, it would be important to update the overall risk metrics by reporting the issues identified to determine the residual risk of data compromises.

The residual risk is the amount of risk left after security issues have either been fixed or new countermeasures have been implemented. A residual risk might still be too high even after new countermeasures have been implemented to mitigate the new emerging threats. In such case, the risk of such threats needs to be managed. This is typically considered part of risk management and is the responsibility of the organization's web applications business owners.

An example of risk acceptance for the risk posed by an unmitigated vulnerability might need to consider all possible compensating risk measures. In the case of a high-risk issue identified in a web application such as SQL injection, the likelihood might be considered HIGH because the issue is exposed to the Internet preauthentication. The impact might also be considered HIGH because the vulnerability might expose the organization's sensitive data, such as customers' credit card data. Without compensating controls, the risk could be managed by considering (1) fixing the issue by deploying a new security measure that reduces the risk, (2) avoiding the risk (e.g. in the case of SQL injection, remove the account data query feature), and (3) transferring the risk liability to a third party by planning either a migration to a new web applications or to a new service (e.g. for query of client bank accounts) hosted outside the organization (e.g. cloud-based Software as a Service (SaaS)).

A threat analysis of today's threat agents might point to SQL injection as one of fraudsters' most sought vulnerabilities that can exploited for confidential data compromise in similar organizations (e.g. financial). This threat analysis was based on threat intelligence gathered from internal sources (e.g. application logs, fraud alerts, web applications firewall monitoring, and honeypots) as well as from open sources (e.g. threat reports, data loss incident reports). Some of today's incidents are reported to public because of data breach notification laws (e.g. SB 1386) enforced in some state jurisdictions in the United States. Information from the Information Sharing and Analysis Centers (ISAC) groups also share restricted information that similar web applications and organizations have been targeted with SQL injection attacks and put the entire business sector on alert.

Because of this threat analysis, one firm might decide that there is potential risk and conduct a focused assessment to identify all preauthenticated SQL injection vulnerabilities for web applications that match the business and risk profile of the web application being targeted by SQL injection attacks in a security incident that compromised data. The vulnerability assessment focuses on both known SQL injection attack vectors detected by automated scanning tools and manual testing for SQL injection attack vectors similar to the ones used by the fraudsters. The assessment identified that some web applications owned by the organization were indeed vulnerable to this type of SQL injection attack vectors.

There were three options to remediate the vulnerability as recommended by the risk analysis of the vulnerabilities identified. The options included either changes to the existing web application software or implementing additional countermeasures. One possible option might include fixing security issues in source code by reengineering all the data access components and using prepared statements, therefore eliminating the SQL injection vulnerability root causes. A second option required implementing a rule-set of filtering rules within the existing application servlet filter of the application to block as well as detect the new SQL injection attack vectors. A third option required adding filtering capabilities for emerging and existing SQL injection attack vectors by deploying Web Application Firewalls and also enabling alerts when SQL injection attack vectors were used against the web application. The risk assessment also included the effectiveness of these measures in mitigating the risk of SQL injection attack vectors, both as preventive and detective controls, and the total cost of the solution. Option 1 was considered 100% effective as a preventive measure, but was also the most costly to implement and test. It also did not provide detection measure/alert capability. Option 2 was considered partially effective as both a preventive and detective measure, but the least expensive to implement since required only a configuration change. Option 3 was considered as effective as option 2 but more expensive to deploy and maintain, even if less expensive than option 1. The risk analysis calculated the residual risks after each of these measures to be reduced to LOW risk.

On the basis of this type of information, business and risk management recommended option 2 as the most effective to mitigate the risk of this new SQL injection attack vectors and the least costly to implement. The business considered that option 2 was the best compromise between low cost and risk mitigation effectiveness (preventive and detective). Since option 2 just required a web application configuration change, it was also the fastest to deploy and test and most suitable to reduce the risk in the short term.

For the long term, the organization chose to implement option 1 (redesign the data access component libraries to code new prepared statements) directly at an internal cost or indirectly by a third party as part of a migration plan of a completely new and redesigned web application hosted and managed by a third-party organization. Nevertheless, after the business talked to risk management and legal, it was advised not to transfer this risk/liability to another entity/organization. So, option 1 was selected as long-term and a new project was budgeted to implement this feature in the next release of the web application.

Lesson Number 7: The Organization's Risk Management Strategy Needs to Evolve be to Ahead of Security Incidents Caused by Cyber-Threat Agents

One of the main lessons that businesses can incorporate in their risk management strategy for mitigating the risks of emerging threats is that it is important to identify a set of new security measures, such as people's security awareness and training, security processes, and security technologies that are adequate for reducing the risk of emerging threats for an organization.

Moreover, an effective risk mitigation strategy against cyber-threats needs to evolve from the traditional approach of managing security risks. Typically, the first step in risk management for businesses has been to identify the security domain that needs to be protected. This security domain ought to consider first the inherent risk profile of the assets to protect, such as the web application that processes confidential data, and then identify the type of exposure of the web application and the data assets.

For effective risk management, it is important to determine first what the inherent risks of the assets are that an organization is seeking to protect. These inherent risks are risks directly dependent on the value and volume of that asset independently of being at risk as the threat agents' target. Businesses such as credit card payment processors and merchants are subjected to higher risks than merchants of credit card compromise because of the higher volume of credit card transactions that they can process. An estimate of the impact that a breach at a card processing organization might cause depends on the maximum volumes of data being processed. Large credit card processing organizations might handle multimillion dollars' worth of credit card transactions every day. From the attacker's perspective, attacking a credit card processor represents a more desirable target than attacking a single merchant point of sale terminal. For a credit card payment processing company such as Heartland, the question is therefore which security measures, governance, and risk management processes could be adopted to mitigate the risk of credit card data breaches in the future beyond the ones that are required for compliance with industry security standards such as PCI-DSS.

Since compliance with today's industry security standards might be not enough to reduce the impact of tomorrow's emerging threats, it is necessary to revise these standards and add additional security requirements for mitigating the risks of new emerging threats. Businesses that were compliant with security standards one year ago are exposed to today's new threat agents, new attack techniques, and new vulnerabilities. It is, therefore, important to consider compliance with security standards as a catch up with emerging threats, not a proactive way to mitigate the risk of emerging threats. Businesses need to look ahead of compliance and use threat intelligence sources to determine which threats might target their businesses today.

It is also important not to get caught in the false sense of security that using a standard compliance security solution is enough to consider web applications, systems, and software secure. Compliance provides assurance, not the verification that web applications, systems, and software are attacker-proof. The main question is not whether web applications and systems have security controls that are complaint with industry security standards, but whether such controls are resilient enough to resist to today's attacks seeking to compromise data by preventing and detecting such attacks.

Since credit card data transactions are processed by systems and web applications, which are increasingly targeted by cyber gangs/fraudsters, it is important to put emphasis on security measures. Web application security's main goals for the organization's risk management is to make sure that systems and web applications are designed resiliently enough to protect against cyber-attacks and emerging threats specifically designed to compromise functionality and data.

An additional element that enhances the organization's capability of managing risks is to analyze the possible impact of specific threats, such as phishing attacks, malware and hacking attacks, MitM and MitB attacks, and denial of service and distributed denial-of-service attacks, and business logic attacks.

For specific threat sources, such as threat agents seeking to steal valued assets for monetary gain, the requirement for designing security features to protect web applications and systems from attacks seeking to compromise such data is a preliminary threat and risk analysis to determine the types of threat agents that might target the data, and the type of attack tools and techniques that could be used. This threat analysis is best conducted when each specific threat is analyzed separately. Threats targeting web applications for data compromise might include both human threat agents (fraudsters, hacktivists, script kiddies, cyber spies) and nonhuman threat agents (malware, scripts, botnets, remote access tools). A further classification of threat agents might include identifying the motives (financial, political), the goals (credit card data, confidential data, company secrets), and the capabilities (organized crime group, state sponsored hackers, etc.).

Once specific threats have been analyzed, the next step is to determine the risk that they pose data. Specifically, threat analysis is about considering the possibility of worst case scenarios that might lead to an attacker compromising data; in essence, analyzing "who can do what." After the threat analysis is attack modeling; analyzing how these threats can be realized in an attack to cause impact the data. The goal of risk analysis is to analyze the impact and the probability that the threat can cause an impact based on the presence of vulnerabilities. As part of the risk analysis, the risk is also calculated to determine the level of risk based on either qualitative or quantitative risk analysis.

One important aspect of the risk mitigation strategy is including threat analysis to determine the probability of threats targeting the web application. Since the web application functions in a specific environment, for example, for a web application in an Internet environment, the exposure of threat agents that seek to compromise valuable data can be determined by the environment in which the web application operates. In order to characterize the threat environment, it is important to gather threat data from threat sources, such as threat intelligence and reports on security incidents specific to the threats considered, such as data breach incidents. For example, threats that could cause data breach incidents or that have already caused data compromises can also be factored in the threat analysis to estimate the risks.

It is important that any security issues identified are reported, including the information about the type of threats that can be used to exploit them, the likelihood of such exploits, and the potential impact to the business. In order to make informed risk management decisions, businesses also need to know exactly which security measures are most cost-effective for reducing the impacts of potential data breach incidents. The ultimate goal for an organization is to reduce these risks to a manageable level. This is the level of risk that any given organization is comfortable to accept and is different for each organization, depending on the type of business/industry and the organization's risk culture.

The level of risk that businesses are willing to accept ought to be considered with the business goals. A risk that is deemed acceptable for given organization/business could be considered not acceptable by another. If the current security measures are deemed not enough to lower the level of risk to an acceptable level, the organization/business will implement a new set of security measures and controls to further control and reduce the level of risks.

In any case, it is important that these risks are properly considered and communicated to executive management and the business. It is important to be real with the business about the risks that cyber-threats represent to the business and quantify the possible impacts. Any justification for accepting these risks needs to be based on objective considerations and risk management metrics, including the assessment of risk and the compensating controls whose presence might reduce the impact and lower the level of risk that the organization might be exposed to and willing to take for future emerging threats.

THREATS AND RISK ANALYSIS

> "The time has come to invest resources into understanding and countering specific threats—a threat-centric approach will complement the existing preoccupation with vulnerability- and asset-centric security."
> *Anton Chuvakin, Research VP Gartner*

In the initial chapters of this book, we introduced some basic definitions for risk terminology including the definitions for risks, threats, attacks, assets, and vulnerabilities. These basic definitions are prerequisites to characterize application security risks. They are summarized as follows:

1. *Threat* – A potential negative event whose source might cause either a tangible or intangible negative impact to the business/organization and its operations, such as loss of revenue, monetary loss, legal lawsuits and fines, indictments.
2. *Vulnerability* – A weakness of the application/software and/or the environment in which the application/software operates that might expose the business' digital assets to attacks from threat agents when exploited.
3. *Asset* – A business resource that the business seeks to protect and considers of tangible and/or intangible value; examples include confidential data, applications, software, and functionality to process such data, hosts, servers, and network infrastructure.
4. *Risk* – The calculated probability of a threat agent causing an impact to an asset by exploiting a vulnerability.

Providing clarity on the risk terminology used is extremely important because there is often confusion on the meanings of threat, vulnerability, asset, and risk in the context of web applications and software. Agreeing on the definition for risk is the prerequisite for analyzing risks. The next step is to elaborate on the characteristics of each factor of risk and specifically on the attributes that can be used to assess threats, vulnerabilities, assets, and the impacts to these.

Before conducting the analysis of cyber-threats, it is important to select a set of attributes that can be used for characterize cyber-threats and specifically the threat actors(s). Examples of threat attributes are the following:

1. The threat sources such as the types of threat actors.
2. The threat actor groups and associated motives and tactics.
3. The threat event associated with a threat actor(s).
4. The threat actor(s) motives, goals, and their intentions.
5. The threat actor(s) targets such as the data assets and vulnerabilities being targeted.

6. The capabilities of threat actor(s) such as the knowledge of attack tools and attack techniques including knowledge of vulnerabilities and techniques of exploiting them.
7. The arsenal of various attack tools at the disposal of the threat actor(s).

For an in-depth threat analysis of cyber-threats, it is important first to adopt a taxonomy for cyber-threats and threat actors(s). To understand which threats are relevant, it is important to consider the history of these threats and analyze them in the risk context. For example, when considering the various cyber-threats targeting web applications, it important to consider the threat environment and the various types of threat agents that might target the application data assets. Examples of different types of cyber threats actors might include cyber gangs cyber gangs/fraudsters, script kiddies, political hacktivists, corporate and country-sponsored cyber spies. The characterization of cyber-threats can start from the "who" these threat agents are and then focus more in the details on the threat agents' motives that might include, for example, respectively, in the case of cyber gangs, stealing financial information such as credit card data by abusing web applications for fraud monetary gain; in the case of political hacktivists, attacking websites to denial service to customers, defacing it with defamatory information, and to expose confidential data of the political targets; in the case of cyber spies, stealing company secrets such as intellectual property documents and trade secrets.

To analyze cyber-threats, it is also important to look at the history of past security incidents and learn how these cyber-threats have evolved. In the past, threat agents sought to target hosts and systems and focused on creating vulnerability exploits mostly to fulfill their ego and gain notoriety. Web applications were not these threat agents' primary targets. These threat agents could be characterized primarily as script kiddies and secondly as techies mostly targeting vulnerable and insecure systems. Today's threat agents are driven by value, and they target web applications because web applications today allow users to remotely access value data assets and services. Any website that allows access confidential data, such as PII, tax information, or credit card data, is in essence a potential target because fraudsters can profit from stealing and reselling these data. Some business are more targeted than others, since the target is where the money is – financial websites that allow making payments, depositing checks, accessing bank accounts, or transferring money to other institutions.

Risk Analysis

Characterizing the exposure to threats by the organization assets, specifically Internet facing web applications that are exposed outside the internal network (accessible over the Internet), is the first step in risk analysis. Each business should have an inventory of web applications and classify them by the type of data and transactions they process and the type of transactions to determine the inherent risks. These risks need to factor the probability of these web applications already being the target of a threat, such as when the web application is either currently under attack or was targeted by specific threat agents in the past.

Understanding the capabilities of the threat agents, such as their resources, their supporting organization, the attack techniques and attacking tools used, the availability of these attacking tools (including the knowledge for using them), and the knowledge of vulnerabilities that can be exploited by these tools as well as manual techniques, is critical to determine the damage potential associated with a threat. This is an area where threat intelligence might help. For example, threat intelligence might help to analyze and determine the attack tools and techniques used against companies' web applications, including the type of vulnerabilities that are exploited.

The attack techniques that can be used by threat agents might vary depending on objectives and capabilities. This type of information can be gathered from threat intelligence and security incidents analysis. In most recent security incidents, for example, cyber gangs used phishing to install malware and capture user credentials through key loggers by gaining unauthorized access to confidential information. Another attack technique used by cyber gangs was sniffing the network by exploiting network weaknesses protecting data traffic and SQL injection. Hacktivists, for example, might use distributed denial-of-service attacks against government websites to gain public attention on their political agenda. Other type of attacks that can be used include phishing through social engineering to compromise specific user e-mails and expose their confidential and private communications to the public domain. Cyber spies might seek to target specific employees of a company known to have credentials for restricted internal websites whose access grants possession of company secrets. A cyber spies might use spear-phishing against specific corporate users' e-mails to install remote access tools and steal intellectual property.

Vulnerabilities represent conditions that are either necessary for conducting an attack or can facilitate an attack. An example of a vulnerability can be a gap in either security controls or measures. A security gap might be caused by lack of training and awareness of the company regarding phishing threats, a gap in applying a security measures protecting an asset, and most generally in a vulnerability of a network, system, or web application.

Assets represent the possible targets of threats. For example, the targets of an attack from a threat agent are valued assets, such as confidential data of either a user or a company/organization. In the case of cyber gangs, these value assets might be bank accounts, credit and debit card data, or anything that can be used for profit and economic gain. The assets that are targeted by hacktivists may be the organization's website with denial of service, stealing e-mails from public/political figures whose exposure to public domain might be of a political advantage. Cyber spies' targets can be certain company employees and systems at government organizations that are known to handle intellectual property, commercial/military secrets, and restricted information.

In general, the characterization of threats, vulnerabilities, and assets can be dissected and depicted as shown in Figure 5.2.

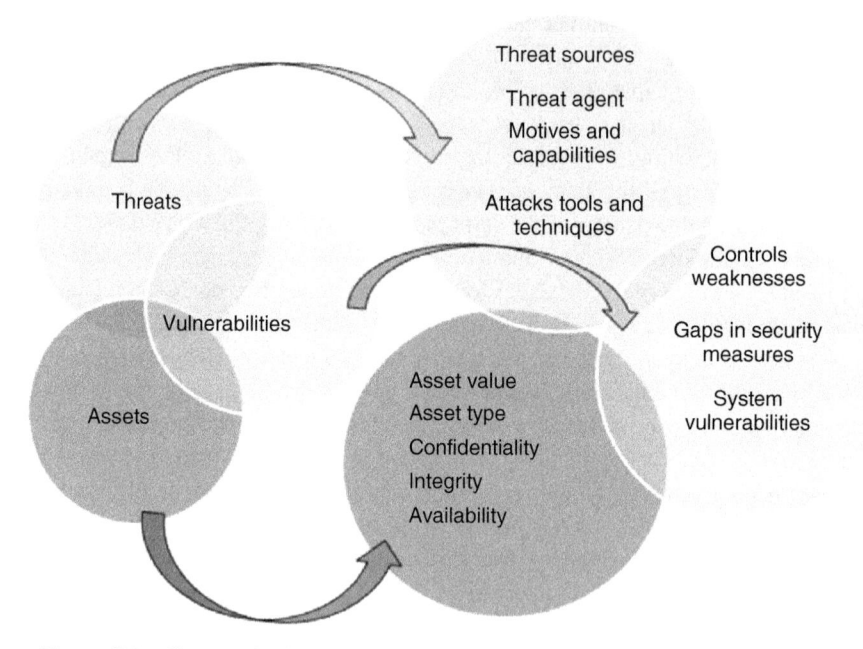

Figure 5.2 Characterization of Risk by considering Threats, Vulnerabilities, and Assets

Risk is identified at the intersection between threats, vulnerabilities, and assets. By characterizing the attributes for threats, vulnerabilities, and assets, it is possible to characterize the risk and analyze it in terms of probability and impact.

Analyzing the type of attacking tools and techniques used as well as the vulnerabilities, such as the security holes and vulnerabilities that might be exploited, also helps to determine which vulnerabilities need to be prioritized for mitigation as well as which security measures can be implemented to mitigate the risk.

The main goal of the threat analysis is to unveil how threats affect web applications and identify the probability that these web applications might be attacked in the future. This probability can be factored in the calculation of risk probability; the probability of a threat source to exploit vulnerabilities to cause an impact on assets. The probability for risk can also be characterized as the probability for a threat source/agent to target an asset based on the characteristics of a threat such as the motives, capabilities, and attacks, as well as of the assets, as a certain asset might be more valuable for the threat source/agent.

Probability can also be associated with the exposure of an asset by a vulnerability whose threat agent might seek to pursuit as target. When probability is characterized for threats, vulnerabilities, and assets, it is possible to determine the level of risks as probability level (high, medium, or low).

For example, a high-level risk can be associated with an asset whose inherent risk is HIGH, business value is HIGH, and whose threat probability is HIGH since it is likely the target for certain types of threat agents (e.g. credit card data for cyber gangs/fraudsters). The presence of HIGH-risk vulnerabilities (e.g. SQL injection) that can be exploited by the threat agent to conduct an attack against the targeted asset is also factored in the probability risk. The vulnerability risk can also factor the probability as the exposure of the vulnerability to the threat source and by the threat agent's capability of exploiting the vulnerability, such as the knowledge of attack techniques and the availability of attack tools.

Another factor that is assessed for determining the level of risk is the threat's potential impact if the threat agent is successful in his attack. This level of impact is an inherent characteristic of the asset. This impact can be factored as business impact by characterizing the value of the asset as well as technical security impact as this attack impacts the attributes of an asset such as confidentiality, integrity, and availability of an asset.

In this definition of risk characterized by threats, vulnerabilities, and assets, the assessment of the likelihood (probability) and impact are essential factors to calculate the level of risk. The risk likelihood is a statistical value that can be calculated based on the intrinsic values of the model used to calculate risks. The likelihood of a threat source to exercise vulnerabilities, for example, depends on the motives and capabilities of a threat source to a certain asset. For example, if a certain asset is considered valuable for an attacker, this can be factored into the threat motives and associated with certain threat sources. The likelihood of a threat depends on the type of threat source and the type of targeted asset. For this reason, is important to associate each threat with targeted assets. Other factors are inherently dependent on the threat agent characteristics, such as the attacker's abilities to conduct the attack including his knowledge of attack tools and attack techniques. Another element that influences the likelihood of a threat to be successfully attacked is the presence of vulnerabilities. Vulnerabilities are favorable conditions for the threat sources to realize their attack since they expose the assets to the threat sources. Vulnerabilities can inherently be associated to an asset such as the web application as a whole, a component of the application such as web servers, application servers, and databases. Since the presence of vulnerabilities determines the exposure of an asset to threat sources, it is important to determine whether such vulnerabilities are exposed to the threat agents to determine the severity of the vulnerability. For example, if the threat source is external to the web application, a vulnerability that can be exploited preauthentication is more likely to be exploited than a vulnerability postauthentication.

Another important factor to consider for determining the exposure of vulnerabilities is to determine whether security controls mitigate such vulnerabilities. The level of unmitigated vulnerabilities might depend on the absence/gap of security controls (fully exposed), as well as on a weakness in the security control that might partially expose an asset to the threat agents as well as the different characteristics of the assets such as confidentiality, integrity, and availability.

Threats can be mapped to the targeted assets and the vulnerabilities exposing such assets to determine the probability and the level of impact. The impact on the assets can be factored either as function of the value of the asset, usually determined by the business, or as a factor of the inherent intrinsic characteristics of the asset, such as confidentiality, integrity, and availability. These intrinsic characteristics of the assets are also dependent on the asset type and the asset's data classification.

In general, an asset can be a component of the web application, a function/transaction, or just the data. The asset value can be associated to the business criticality of the asset, such as in the case of a mission critical functionality and a business transaction of a certain value. The business criticality of an can be factored in terms of revenues that the application generates because of the business functions it supports, such as in the case of a company website that sells products and services to customers online. This type of criticality can be expressed in terms of business criticality of an asset and classified as high, medium, or low as well.

Another factor that can be used to assess impact is the inherent risk of the asset that is the value assigned to the data based on the data classification, for example, as public (low risk), internal (low risk), confidential (medium risk), PII (high risk), or top secret/restricted authentication data (very high risk). Understanding the threats that target assets and vulnerabilities and analyzing their characteristics help determine the risk as factor of likelihood and impact. This type of analysis is essential for calculating these risks and managing them as such and is a necessary step for deciding which measures need to be adopted to reduce the risk levels.

The level of risks can be calculated as function of the likelihood and impact of threat sources targeting certain vulnerability exploits. For determining the risk level, it is important to understand which type of risk assessments can be useful to determine these risk factors of likelihoods and impacts. For example, let us consider a certain type of asset classified by the business as high risk.

A web application that stores and processed a type of asset that is classified as high risk can also be classified as an high risk web application.

The next step is to conduct a threat analysis to identify the type of threat sources whose application assets might be the target. Identifying and characterizing these threat sources is the goal of threat intelligence. Through threat intelligence, it is possible to identify the type of threats seeking to compromise certain type of assets and characterize them by their motives and capabilities, attack tools and techniques used, and the type of vulnerabilities that these attacks seek to exploit. This type of information might be captured in a threat library and kept up to date with information of new and emerging threats and attacks.

Threat analysis can leverage the analysis of cyber-threats from threat intelligence sources and capture the information about these threats by building a threat library. The threat library needs to map these threats to the data and assets they target. This threat analysis will help to determine the likelihood of a certain threat targeting a certain data asset to determine the risk probability and impact. The more information is collected on these cyber-threats such as the type, motives, capabilities, and their history of attacks, the more accurate and actionable this threat analysis will be to determine the protection measures that need to be implemented in the web application and software.

TABLE 5.1 Example of Assignment of Risks Of A Threat Event based upon probability of the event and impact on the asset

Scale	Threat Probability	Impact to the Asset
Very low	Very unlikely to occur	Negligible impact on confidentiality, integrity, and availability
Low	May occur occasionally	Minor impact on confidentiality, integrity, and availability
Medium	Is as likely as not to occur	Notable impact on confidentiality, integrity, and availability
High	Is likely to occur	Substantial impact on the confidentiality, integrity, and availability
Very high/critical	Is almost certain to occur	Critical impact on asset confidentiality, integrity, and availability

Risk Calculations

The analysis of threats against web applications and software is a prerequisite for analyzing risks that that these threats pose to the business. Specifically, determining the probability that a threat might impact a web application can be factored based on the different characteristics of threats, such as the exposure of vulnerabilities and weaknesses in security controls that either "can be" or "are" already exploited by a threat.

The inclusion of threats in the definition of risk analysis is also part of the standard definition of risks such as NIST SP 800-53, which defines risk as "the determination of the probability of a threat agent/event causing an impact to the asset by exploiting vulnerability."

Intrinsic to determine risk is factoring likelihood and impact. This calculation can translate empirically into the formula to calculate risk that factors both the "Probability (P)" of a threat event occurring and the "Impact (I)" that threat event would have on an asset. A simplified formulation is:

$$Risk = P \times I$$

This empirical formula can be used to qualitatively determine the level of risks as a function of the levels of probability and impact. The main objective of qualitative risk analysis is to determine the levels of risks by assigning different levels to the factors of probability and impact. Different levels of probability of a threat and impact on an asset can be assigned by following escalation levels for threat probability and impact to the asset such as the one included herein (see Table 5.1).

Once the levels of threat probability and impact are assigned, the overall levels of risk that can be calculated using the risk assessment matrix/heat map such as the one in the example herein (see Figure 5.3).

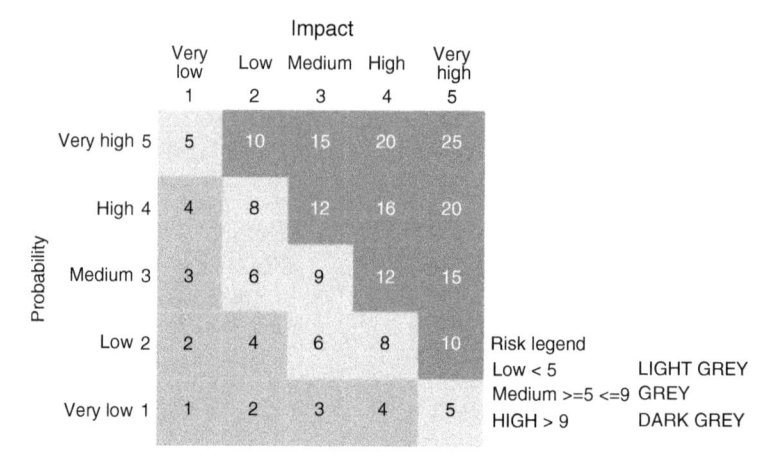

	Impact				
Probability	Very low 1	Low 2	Medium 3	High 4	Very high 5
Very high 5	5	10	15	20	25
High 4	4	8	12	16	20
Medium 3	3	6	9	12	15
Low 2	2	4	6	8	10
Very low 1	1	2	3	4	5

Risk legend
Low < 5   LIGHT GREY
Medium >=5 <=9   GREY
HIGH > 9   DARK GREY

Figure 5.3 Five (5) Level Risk Calculation Heat Map

By using this example, a level of threat can be assigned as the probability that a negative event, such as an attack against a web application, might occur. The threat analysis can help determine the threat probability.

By considering a threat such distributed denial of service (DDoS) against a certain organization's website located in a specific country, the type of threat agent motivation, capability, motives, and DDoS attack tools and techniques, the threat analysis indicated that the probability of either the same or similar threat targeting another organization-specific website to be very high.

Another factor that was considered for determining the threat probability is the correlation of the threat with the security events and logs detected, such as attempts to exploit network-based DDoS through attempts to flood routers, servers, and server applications layers and networking stack with junk traffic as well as exploit resource intensive preauthenticated URLs, such as document downloads and web forms as well as web application vulnerabilities that can facilitate DDoS attacks such as SQL injection.

One important factor to consider when determining threat probability is that the closer the threat agent is to the target, the higher the probability. When the target is detected under the discovery phase of the attack, such as during attempts to probe the defenses, the probability of suffering the impact of the attack is VERY HIGH.

The next step for the analysis of risks is to determine the impacts to the assets. For example, if a probable threat is realized and will cause an impact by exploiting weaknesses, such as vulnerabilities in the security controls that are designed to protect such asset, we must determine what the impact will be. Determining the level of impact of DDoS attacks can factor the lesson learned from the postmortem analysis of similar past attacks/security and factor the exposure by considering the effectiveness of the security measures in place as well as any weaknesses, such as web application vulnerabilities and how these affect the website, to determine the business impact that might be caused.

The analysis of impact needs to factor in both the analysis of the effectiveness of the security controls – referred to in risk management as "security control gap analysis," the presence of vulnerabilities and tools that exploit them, that can facilitate the exploit – and the impacts on the asset both from technical and business perspectives. At a high level without conducting a security control gap analysis and a vulnerability and business impact analysis, the determined level of impact is only a rough estimate.

One easy-to-use visual method to determine the level of risk is to use the risk heat maps. A heat map might consider the levels of risk based on five levels of probability and impact: for example, if the level of probability for a threat is considered VERY HIGH and the level of impact (such as the loss of availability of the asset due to the exploit of weakness in mitigating the risk of denial-of-service attack) is considered LOW, the overall risk is still HIGH.

The assumption of LOW impact is based on assurances that, for example, web application vulnerabilities that can be exploited by DDoS attacks have been tested and the risk mitigated, while anti-DDoS defensive measures at the network layer such as IP filtering, scrubbing Internet traffic, and other measures protect the website from DDoS attacks.

This high-level qualitative risk analysis can be useful to provide a rough estimate of the risk levels faced by web applications being targeted by specific threats by considering the effectiveness of the current security measures and mitigations of vulnerabilities. Since the probability of the threat impacting the web application is VERY HIGH, this high-level risk analysis can be useful for an organization to compare the different risks of web applications managed by an organization and to prioritize a more in-depth analysis of risks.

A more detailed analysis of risk would need to consider other factors to determine the levels of impact, such as the exposure of the web application to vulnerabilities, the ease of the exploits, and the value of the asset to qualify the level of impact when such vulnerabilities are exploited. Such analysis needs to factor web application weaknesses such as the "Vulnerability (V)" of a system/application that might allow the "Threat (T)" source to impact an asset depending on the "Asset Value (AV)."

A simplified formula for qualifying risk that considers the factor of impact on the asset and its value can be more explicitly calculated with the following risk formula:

$$Risk = T \times V \times AV$$

Since risk is associated with the probability of a threat occurring, we can also factor the "Threat Likelihood (TL)" and the probability of a vulnerability exposing an asset as "Vulnerability Exposure (VE)."

The overall formulation for risk is therefore

$$Risk = TL \times VE \times AV$$

Such an empirical formula for risk is useful for determining the risks of a threat, such as a threat agent, by factoring the opportunity of a threat agent to exploit either

Asset value	Likelihood of threat	Low			Medium			High		
	Ease of exploitation	Low	Medium	High	Low	Medium	High	Low	Medium	High
	Low	0	1	2	1	2	3	2	3	4
	Medium	1	2	3	2	3	4	3	4	5
	High	2	3	4	3	4	5	4	5	6
	Very high	3	4	5	4	5	6	5	6	7
	Critical	4	5	6	5	6	7	6	7	8

Low risk 0–2 | Medium risk 3–5 | High risk 6–8

Figure 5.4 Threat-Vulnerability-Asset Risk Calculation Heat Map

vulnerabilities or control weaknesses and compromise an asset to impact the confidentiality, integrity, and availability of the data. The value of the asset is the value that the organization gives to the asset if it was unavailable, lost, or compromised.

An example of qualitative risk calculation/heat map that uses these factors of risk to consider three qualitative levels and factors, threat likelihood, ease of exploitation and the asset values, is provided in Figure 5.4.

The value given to the asset might depend on different factors, such as the classification of the asset and the monetary value of that asset for the organization if such asset was unavailable, lost, or compromised.

To analyze which level to assign to the asset values, data can be assigned by an organization depending on the internal classification of the data as correlated to the value such as low (public), internal (medium), confidential/sensitive (high), PII (very high), and restricted/top secret (critical). The aggregated value of this data ought to be considered for determining the aggregated asset value of the data as well by factoring the number of registered customers using the web application whose data is classified as confidential or above.

To assert the value of the web application as an asset, some extra considerations are required, such as the loss of revenue generated through the website if the asset is either lost or compromised. The costs to an organization if a security breach occurred can also be factored, including recovery costs and impacts due to regulatory/disciplinary actions and legal lawsuits.

Other scale measures for asset values might consider the volume of aggregated classified data and the monetary values associated with it.

Another important factor is the business criticality of the application. For example, for a financial web-based application/site, the financial risk/impact can be associated with the monetary value of the financial transactions that are supported by the application. A financial impact can be considered LOW for a large financial organization when the loss of income is lower than $100,000, HIGH when above $1 million, and VERY HIGH when above $10 million. On the basis of these considerations, a web application that provides financial services for customers can be assigned an asset value level of VERY HIGH.

THREATS AND RISK ANALYSIS

Besides the asset value that helps to determine the business impact, there are other factors to consider for analyzing the risks. For example, in the specific case of DDoS threats, these factors are as follows:

- *Presence of Anti-DDoS Security Measures* that can be effective to mitigate DDoS threats and attacks (e.g. scrubbing of DDoS traffic, blocking and filtering rules for DDoS attacks, max network traffic capacity).
- *Presence of Vulnerabilities* that can be easily and opportunistically exploited for DDoS attacks at different layers of the OSI layer stack.
- *Availability of DDoS attacking tools* used by the attackers that can facilitate the attacks.
- *Knowledge of DDoS attack tools, techniques, and processes* by the attackers in order to conduct their attacks.

An organization might have assessed, for example, that the network and application layer defenses from DDoS attacks against the web application are basic and can be overcome using sophisticated attack tools, such as a botnet of DDoS attacking machines whose level of traffic that might be directed against the web application, is above the maximum bandwidth that can be absorbed by the web application. In such a case, a conservative assumption is to consider the ease of exploitation of anti-DDoS defenses as MEDIUM. By factoring the levels of threat probability risk as HIGH, the level of ease of exploit as HIGH, and the asset value as VERY HIGH, the DDoS risk for a web application asset is HIGH risk.

A qualitative risk assessment to determine the level of risk of a specific threat targeting a web application helps the business to prioritize the web application for mitigation of risk. This can be for emerging threats such as a specific DDoS threat against a website or a malware-compromised host threat against user's website credentials and others.

Prerequisites for this type of risk assessments are given as follows:

1. *Threat analysis* of specific threat agents under the scope of risk analysis including the identification of threat agents-sources type, capabilities, motivations, type of attacks/tools/techniques, targeted assets, and history of previous attacks, exploits, and impacts.
2. *Analysis of previous security incidents* such as SIRT reports correlated to the type of threat agent and targeted assets to determine the level of threat probability, the root analysis of root causes, and measures that eliminate them.
3. *Inventory of web application assets* with information to determine the level of asset value as a function of inherent risks, classification of the data, and the risk of transactions/functions.
4. *Vulnerability analysis* including reports of vulnerabilities for the web applications that were previously tested with pen tests and source code analysis and their status of remediation.

The objective of this type of risk assessment is to determine whether the specific threat represents a level of risk for specific web applications that have potential exposure to threat agents and represent a value for threat agents to be attacked or have been attacked in the past and have been impacted by security incidents and therefore might require a more in-depth risk analysis to determine the risk.

Residual Risk Calculations

According to ISO 27001, residual risk is "the risk remaining after risk treatment." NIST SP 800-33 defines the residual risk as "the remaining, potential risk after all IT security measures are applied. There is a residual risk associated with each threat." We can consider residual risk as the risk left after we have applied security controls that reduce the likelihood and impact of the risk posed by a specific threat agent.

We can refer to the notion of security measures as security controls. Intuitively, by applying security controls, it is possible to reduce likelihood of exploit and reduce the overall impact that threats and vulnerabilities have on the asset, in this case, web applications and data.

The reduction is a factor of how effective the control is in reducing the likelihood and impact of the inherent risk of a specific threat. The more effective the control in mitigating the risk of a threat is, the less residual risk caused by the threat is.

We define "Inherent Risk (IR)" as the risk of a web application in the presence of vulnerabilities and in the absence of any action to apply security measures to reduce such risk.

The IR, as previously calculated, is the risk that is assessed by considering the TL, "Ease of Exploitation (EE)" and the impact on the asset that is factored as AV:

$$IR = TL \times EE \times AV$$

The amount of "Risk Mitigation (RM)" of the inherent risk is directly proportional to the "Control Effectiveness (CE)":

$$RM = IR \times CE$$

The CE factors both the effectiveness of the control to reduce the likelihood and the impact on the asset value.

For example, assuming the security control is 40% effective (it works 40% of the time) and reduces the potential impact by 80%, the overall control effectiveness is 32% (40% × 80%). The amount of risk mitigation gained by applying this control is therefore 32%.

Since there is no one security control alone that mitigates the risk of one threat, it is important to consider the cumulative effectiveness of each single control. This is also a very useful criterion for a risk manager to determine if the controls that are planned to be applied are enough to reduce the risk to an acceptable level.

For example, let us consider that both preventive and detective security controls are applied and that among them some are more or less effective in mitigating the risk.

THREATS AND RISK ANALYSIS

In the case of a DDoS threat, for example, a preventive control that is always enabled and consists of application layer controls (web application firewall rules, fixing SQL injection vulnerabilities, etc.), network layer controls (IP whitelists and blacklists), and rate controls (blocking excessive HTTP client), requests can be considered 64% effective (works 80% of the time and mitigates 80% of the impact).

A detective control, such as monitoring the source of potential DDoS attacks such as SQL injection and issue alerts on suspicious spikes in the network traffic and rate of HTTP requests, is not effective in reducing the initial impact because it works as a reactive security control that buys the organization time to react with effective risk mitigation preventive measures by applying the principle of defense in depth.

The Residual Risk (RR) is the amount of Inherent Risk (IR) subtracted from the Risk Mitigation (RM). In simple terms, RR can be expressed by the following formula:

$$RR = IR - RM$$

By factoring the RM as function of the CE, the following formulas can be used:

$$RR = IR \times (1 - CE)$$

Assessing the residual risk is a critical step for managing web application risks after the inherent risks are analyzed.

For example, let us assume that the initial risks for a specific threat are analyzed and the level is found to be HIGH RISK. At this level of risk severity, the organization might require applying security controls to reduce the risk to a LOW residual risk. In order to determine how effective these security controls are in reducing the risk, the residual risk would need to be calculated. The usefulness of these residual risk calculations can be shown using these empirical calculations and making some assumption on the risk ranges. By assuming, for example, that the initial risk is considered HIGH (10 risk score) based on a risk analysis of risk and the control that is planned to be deployed is estimated to be 32% effective (works 40% of the time and mitigates the impact of 80% when it works) the residual risk can be calculated as follows:

$$RR = 10 \times (1 - 0.32) = 6.8 (\text{MEDIUM RISK})$$

As the risk is still medium, additional controls would need to be considered in order to reduce the residual risk to a level that is less than 5 and is considered LOW risk and acceptable for the organization.

For example, assume that the additional control is also 32% effective; the risk is finally reduced to LOW and deemed acceptable:

$$RR = 6.8 \times (1 - 0.32) = 4.62 (\text{LOW RISK})$$

When only one control can be applied, the control effectiveness should be at least 64%, such as 80% consequence effective in mitigating the impact and 80% likely (works 80% of the time).

If the residual risk is reduced to a level that is acceptable for the business, such as LOW or MEDIUM, then these security controls might be implemented. An important consideration at this point is to factor the costs of the security measures to determine if the cost to decrease the risk is less than the impact for the business; if it is not, then the management might decide to accept that risk.

One important value of the residual risk analysis is also to factor the cost of the security controls and compare them with the business impact if measures are not implemented. This is necessary because security controls, besides being risk mitigation acceptable, also need to be cost acceptable, therefore, it is important to determine if the controls are cost-effective as well as risk mitigation effective. For example, assuming that the potential economic impact caused by a DDoS attack against a website is $187,506 (year average impact according to 2011 Second Annual Cost of Cyber Crime Study Benchmark by Ponemon Institute), this can be considered the maximum limit that the organization is willing to spend on anti-DDoS measures for just one website. By considering this maximum limit, the measures that are most risk mitigation effective (at least 64% effective) and total cost of ownership most economical (<$187,506 per year) are the ones that can be selected to reduce the risk to acceptable levels.

Quantitative Risk Analysis

An important factor for risk management is the determination of the potential business impact resulting from the exploit of vulnerabilities by a certain threat agent. This business impact can be measured as monetary for determining the level of risk. An example is to use monetary loss threshold levels for assigning the different level of risk levels:

- Less than $100,000 million: LOW RISK.
- Between $100,000 and $1 million: MEDIUM RISK.
- More than $1 million: HIGH RISK.
- More than $10 million: VERY HIGH RISK.

By assigning threshold levels to business impacts, it is possible to determine the maximum amount that a business is willing to invest in security measures for managing such risks. For example, if the exploit of a HIGH-risk vulnerability, such as SQL injection, might compromise a database with PII of several million users, the costs for the organization might result in several millions of dollars.

Calculating risk as a monetary value of potential loss is critical for determining the business impacts that an organization might incur because of a specific threat exploiting a vulnerability. The standard calculation used by quantitative risk analysts considers both factors of probability and impact from economic loss. The factors that are considered for estimating the probability of the monetary loss caused by a security incident are the "Single Loss Expectancy (SLE)" and the "Annual Rate of

Occurrence (ARO)," or the annual frequency of the security incident to determine the Annual Loss Expectancy (ALE):

$$ALE = ARO \times SLO$$

The factors that can be used to estimate the impact are the "Asset Value (AV)" and the "Exposure Factor (EV)" to determine the "Single Loss Expectancy (SLE)":

$$SLE = AV \times EF$$

The accuracy of the SLE that a given business might incur because of a security incident depends on the estimated monetary value of the asset, such as loss of data because of an exploit of a vulnerability that exposed the asset. The reliability of these estimates depends on how good the source of the data is to conduct such estimates. It is, therefore, important to choose the data carefully. One possibility is to rely upon statistics from reliable sources or make conservative assumptions. For example, statistical data of PII loss incidents (identify thefts) reported and analyzed by the US Federal Trade Commission (FTC) in 2003 has determined that the SLE is $655 per person per incident and that 4.6% of the consumer population of the United States have been exposed.

On the basis of these data, the SLE for the loss of PII of a database with 1 million users is approximately $30 million. If we consider the frequency of a possible security incident as of one every 5 years, the ARO is 20% and the ALE is $6 million. On the basis of these calculations, an organization can put the threshold on the maximum amount that can be spent on mitigation measures to mitigate the risks of a particular asset, such as a company website that provides user access to a database of 1 million users' PII to be $6 million.

The quantification of the possible business impact incurred by an organization because of a security incident can also be used to determine whether a business should be considered liable for that cost in case of a security incident. The liability cost can be used by the business to determine whether the vulnerability should be mitigated at a cost or if it would be better to transfer the risk at a lower cost, such as by buying insurance with a cyber-security insurance company.

For example, assuming that a given organization would like to determine the company's "Liability (L)" for taking the risk of an exploit of vulnerability (such as SQL injection), the factors to consider are the probability of such exploit and the business impact:

$$L = P \times I$$

A rough estimate can be calculated using public sources for PII data breach incidents, such as Dataloss DB from the Open Source Foundation (OSF) and sources of threat intelligence such as the Web Hacking Incident Database (WHID) that correlates the hacking incident attacks to the types of vulnerabilities exploited. By assuming that websites are 9% of the reported breaches of confidential data (2013 Dataloss Db data), and SQL injection accounts for 65% of all attack methods (2013 Dataloss Db data), the probability of confidential data loss by SQL injection attacks is 5.8%. This probability is equivalent to the Threat Likelihood (TL).

The impact of SQL injection can be calculated by considering the EE, the EF, and the AV. Let us assume that the EE is MEDIUM or 50% (could be exploited using available tools and common techniques), the EF is 90% (high-risk preauthenticated vulnerability), the AV is $188 (average per capita cost according to 2013 Cost of data Breach Study from Ponemon Institute), and the data volume at risk is 1 million users' PII (SSN, Date of birth, names, and addresses), the overall impact is:

$$I = 0.50 \times 0.90 \times 188 \times 1 \times 10 \wedge 6 = \$84 \text{ million}$$

The liability for the business of a potential SQL injection attack compromising the PII of 1 million users by considering a probability of 5.8% is

$$L = 0.058 \times 84 \times 10 \wedge 6 = \$4.9 \text{ million}$$

The liability of the business for each of their customers is $4.90.

This monetary value of liability is the amount an organization can be considered liable for not protecting online customers' PII if the business suffered an SQL injection attack.

Similarly, in the case of a malware threat such as a banking Trojan, the threat likelihood, such as the probability of a personal computer becoming infected, is 0.2% for a person living in the United Kingdom. This is based on the fact that according to the company Trusteer in the United Kingdom, about 100,000 personal computers are infected by the banking Trojan Zeus and the overall population of Internet users in United Kingdom is 52 million (http://www.internetworldstats.com), of which 55% (Office of National Statistics, 2011) are using Internet banking, the likelihood for an online banking user's PC to be infected by banking malware is 0.34%.

The economic impact of banking malware needs to factor both the compromise of PII, including credit/debit card and bank account data, and losing money in a fraudulent wire transfer. Therefore, the potential monetary losses are much higher; one cybercrime incident alone might impact a business account holder in the amount of several million US dollars in fraudulent wire transactions.

Assuming one single commercial customer with a business account of $5 million, with an ease of exploitation as 90% (HIGH) due to ineffective countermeasures, the liability for one commercial customer with a bank account balance of $5 million is:

$$L = 0.0034 \times 0.90 \times 5 \times 10 \wedge 6 = \$15,300$$

Compared with the PII loss liability for an online banking consumer, the liability for a malware wire loss is several thousand times higher for a commercial bank account customer. If the bank cannot afford to take monetary losses for each of its asset-valued commercial customers, it should consider implementing security measures to mitigate the malware risks. One possible measure is to offer antimalware software that deploys strong out-of-band multifactor authentication and fraud detection for its commercial customers. Finally with these measures in place, the bank can also offer to insure the total amount of the customer's commercial deposit.

Risk Management Fundamentals

According to NIST SP 800-27rA, risk management is *"The ongoing process of assessing the risk to mission/business as part of a risk-based approach used to determine adequate security for a system by analyzing the threats and vulnerabilities and selecting appropriate, cost effective controls to achieve and maintain an acceptable level or risk."*

From the application security perspective, managing security risks is an ongoing process. Application security risks can be introduced through the life cycle of a web application, such as during development and operation. One critical aspect of risk management is to perform threat and risk analysis to determine the level of risk and identify security controls and measures to mitigate such risks. Identifying which security controls and measures can be applied needs to consider the effectiveness and costs to determine if the risks are lowered to an acceptable level in compliance with applicable policy regulations and laws.

The adequacy of the control to reduce the risk to a manageable level in compliance with the organization's risk management process is determined during the evaluation of residual risk. Specifically, an important step of the risk analysis is calculating the residual risks to determine if a certain security control is enough to reduce the risk to a level that is acceptable to both risk management and the business.

One aspect of application security risk management is managing application security risks by applying countermeasures. These countermeasures are identified using a security control gap analysis framework. The security measures and controls gaps that are identified by using these frameworks are derived by the analysis of which controls and measures have been proven effective in protecting the web application from targeted threats and attacks. A postmortem analysis of security incidents can also help to identify which application security measures have been proven effective in mitigating the risk.

After design, implementing new security controls to an application costs money. It is important to determine which security controls and security measures are most cost-effective. A risk management decision would also consider the cost of implementing new security measures besides the effectiveness and the potential liabilities in case these security measures failed. The organization's liability if a security control is breached and the cause of the security incident can be quantified based on quantitative risk analysis.

An organization can consider the liability costs as the maximum cost that the business is willing to spend on security measures to comply with policy, legal agreements with clients, regulations, and laws. The quantification of these liability costs for possible vulnerability exploits of web applications ought to consider the likelihood and impact of a security incident.

The final stage of the risk management process is when the report of the risk analysis is complete and the business needs to decide how to manage the web application security risks. During that time, different options can be considered to manage application security risks:

1. Mitigate or reduce the risk.
2. Accept the risk.
3. Avoid the risk.
4. Share or transfer the risk.

This decision on which option is the most suitable depends on the analysis of all the factors that were previously considered as part of the risk analysis. Often, the decision to how to manage risk is straightforward based on the organization's current risk management process.

For example, a given organization's risk management process might include the following guidelines when managing application security risks:

1. *Accept* risks whose assessed risk in absence of additional security measures is either VERY LOW or VERY LOW.
2. *Mitigate* or reduce risks whose level of risk, without additional security measures, is considered MEDIUM, HIGH, or VERY HIGH. To reduce the level of risks, determine which security measures and controls are both risk- and cost-effective to reduce the risk to acceptable LOW level, yet satisfy liability costs both for real risks (e.g. in case of an incident) and law-regulatory and noncompliance risks.
3. *Transfer* or share the risks to a third party through contractual agreements/cyber-insurance when the residual risks left after applying security measures are not cost- and risk-effective for the business but are still lower than the liability costs.
4. *Avoid* risks when they are not cost- and risk-effective to implement security measures to reduce the risks and when the liability for the business is still too high. One possible way to avoid risk is not to implement the application features that are considered high risk or process data that might be considered sensitive and represents too high a risk for the business in case it is either lost or compromised.

By following this risk management process, risk managers can manage risks consistently and proactively reduce it before incurring a security incident and a loss of either data or functionality. Asset management process is a prerequisite for risk management and might include an inventory of web application assets whose risk the organization/business is required to manage. Asset management can also be mandated for an organization in compliance with information security standards. Organizational information security policies that are derived for compliance with information security standards, such as ISO 17799 or ISO 27001 includes asset management as one of the requirements. This inventory would need to include the associated risk profiles for each web application to determine the level of inherent risk, including both information security risks and financial-franchise risks. An inventory of which web applications are at risk allows risk managers to identify which web applications are critical and prioritize them for threat analysis and risk assessment.

Another aspect of risk management is the ability to adapt the level of risks deemed acceptable based on the information from threat intelligence and monitored security events and alerts. When the levels of threat likelihood and impact are increasing, it is important that the organization responds by raising the bar on acceptable technical and business risks. A sound and proactive risk mitigation strategy is to plan the roll out of countermeasures for emerging threats before these countermeasures become requirements in policy and regulations. Since for most businesses today, the main question is not IF a web application will be attacked but WHEN will it be attacked, it is important to adopt a threat-aware risk management strategy.

Nevertheless, being proactive about mitigating security risks is not always possible. There will be situations when the organization ought to respond to security incidents and manage application security risks reactively. Examples of reactive risk management activities include security incident response, security incident investigation and forensics, fraud management, and vulnerability-patch management. Businesses that manage risks reactively spend most of their time responding to unplanned risk management events, security incident damage containments, and "stop the bleeding" activities. It is important to realize that reactive risk mitigation is not cost-effective. The cost of responding to security incidents and remediating web application vulnerabilities after they have been exploited in a security incident are much higher than investing in remediation of these vulnerabilities as they are identified while developing a web application, during secure design reviews, secure coding, and security testing.

Another important aspect to consider when managing application security risks is considering risks in the business contest, including both information security risks and business risks that is the economic impact to organization. Information security risks are often referred to as technical risks since their causes are technical defects of the security of the application, such as design flaws and vulnerabilities in security controls. When these technical risks are analyzed for impact, they are often measured based on the information security features, such as the impact on confidentiality, integrity, and availability of the data. The inherent risk of the data assets is typically based on the classification of the data. The level of technical risk caused by vulnerabilities can be determined by calculating the "severity" of the vulnerability using standard methods such as the Common Vulnerability Scoring System (CVSS). By using these vulnerability risk scoring methods, it is possible for an organization to consistently assign the risk to vulnerabilities that are identified and manage them according to their level of risk. For example, a vulnerability whose score is HIGH can be prioritized for mitigation over other vulnerabilities that are scored either MEDIUM or LOW.

CVSS scoring is a standard approach for scoring vulnerabilities and is commonly used by several web application security testing tools and for vulnerability risk management. However, to determine if the cost of fixing vulnerabilities is justified, it is important to consider the business impacts derived by the possible exploit as well as the potential regulatory and compliance impacts. From the business impact perspective, it is important to quantify the risk by considering the asset values and factor the likelihood of the asset being compromised and the business impact caused by the exploit of the vulnerability.

Fundamentals of Web Application Security Risk Analysis

When managing web application security risks, it is important to consider all the fundamental domains, such as the threats against the web application, the assets that are protected, the impacts that these threats might cause to assets that can be controlled by security controls, and reduce risk. The characterization of the web application security risk in these domains can be expanded to consider the threat, asset, impact, and control landscape. The risk for a specific web application security lies at the intersection of the characterization of the threat-asset-impact-control context of domains as depicted in Figure 5.5.

The characterization of web application security risk in these domains is critical for analyzing and managing the web application's risks. Specifically, the characterization of the threat landscape ought to include information about the types of attacks and the components of the web application that are attacked. This information is provided by the analysis of threats and attacks that are specifically targeting web applications. Threat intelligence provides critical information about emerging threats which includes collecting intelligence on threat agents, their motivations, capabilities, past and current activities, and the web application targets that also include client browsers, users, data, and functionality.

The next step of the threat analysis is to determine the type of assets that are targeted by the threats previously analyzed. At high level, this might include the customer's PII, confidential data, passwords, and other credentials to access the web application, including other factors used for authentication such as challenge questions and session tokens. This is where the threat landscape intersects with the asset landscape. To determine the threat likelihood, the probability of threat attacking, the threat landscape also needs to characterize the attack techniques, vectors, and vulnerability exploits and map them to the assets to identify whether the assets are exposed to these attacks and exploits. Examples of attacks against the web application that can be characterized in the threat landscape are social engineering, browser attacks such as man in the browser, drive by download and exploit of browser, host-based vulnerabilities, and exploits of web application vulnerabilities and business logic flaws.

The goal of attack modeling is to analyze the attacks of specific threats and includes formal methods, such as attack trees and attack libraries. Part of the vulnerability analysis is determining the vulnerabilities that can be exploited by these attacks to determine the likelihood of a threat affecting them. This is a where standard web application vulnerability assessment process can provide the necessary

THREATS AND RISK ANALYSIS 279

Impact landscape
Data losses
Online fraud
Card fraud
Denial of service
Defacing
Reputation loss
Client lawsuits
Unlawful non compliance

Controls landscape
Antimalware
Antiautomation
Virtual browsing
Strong authentication
Transaction verification
Maker/Checker process
Anomaly detection

Asset landscape
Customer data:
Credit/debit card data,
Bank account data
Confidential-PII data

RISK

Threat landscape
Attack customers:
Phishing emails
Malicious URLs
Virus infected documents
Social engineering

Application data:
Logging credentials
Challenge/Questions
passwords
Transaction data
Session tokens

Attack the browser:
Drive by download
Click jacking
HTML injection
Man in the browser

Attack the web application:
Vulnerability exploits
Business logic/flaws attacks
Session hijacking
Man in the middle

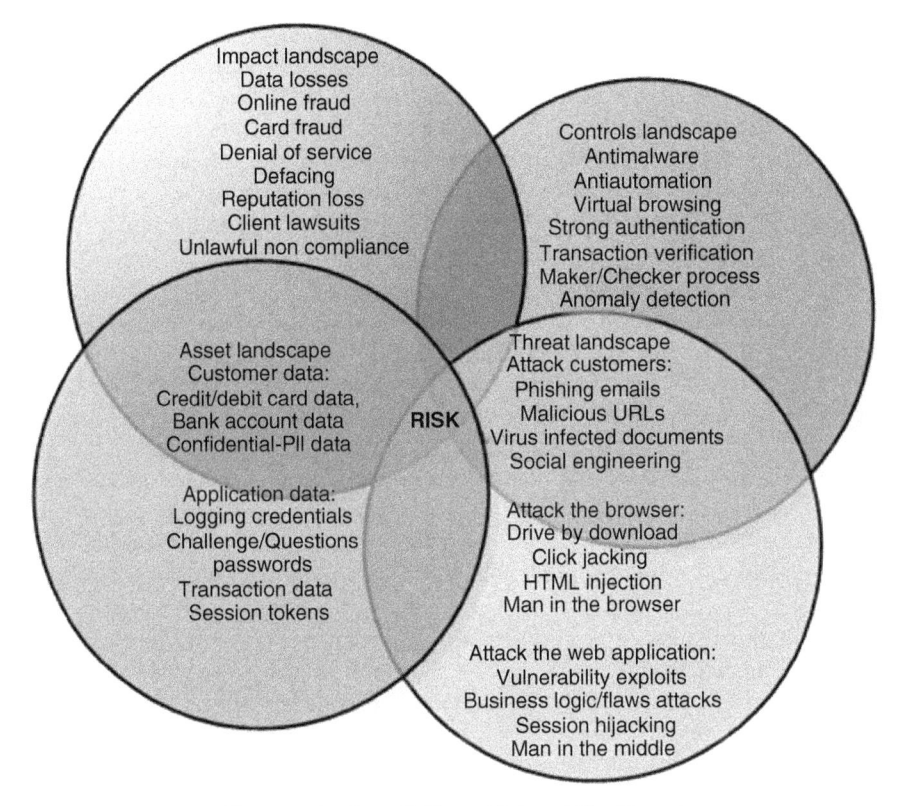

Figure 5.5 Overall Threat-Vulnerability Domain

data. Today, web application security is focused on assessing web application vulnerabilities mostly because of information security policies and regulatory compliance. Nevertheless, compliance vulnerability testing is often very limited in scope and coverage. Assuming that the documented and approved vulnerability assessment process is just relying on automation tools, for example, the potential coverage of threats, attacks, and vulnerabilities is limited to a very small percentage of all possible threats, attacks, and vulnerabilities that can be exploited by a threat agent; at best, no more than 40% of the overall known exploits of vulnerabilities. A larger coverage of vulnerability than automated pen testing includes manual security testing, source code analysis, secure code review, architecture/secure design review, and threat modeling. Architecture design reviews and threat modeling specifically are effective assessments for identifying security design flaws. A survey of vulnerability data shows, for example, that 70% of web application vulnerabilities are due to design flaws that can be identified using application threat modeling.

Once the threat and asset landscape have been characterized with information about threats, attacks, vulnerabilities, and targeted assets, it is possible to determine the likelihood of the various threat scenarios. The next step of the risk analysis is to determine the possible impacts to assets and analyze the risks.

The impact landscape can be analyzed by the type threats targeting the web application, such as losses of sensitive data of customers, denial of service, defacing, and for financial websites, wire transfer, and credit card fraud. From the perspective of quantifying the risk and business impact, being able to characterize the potential impacts for the business that a threat agent might generate by learning from previous incidents attacks is important. This is where the threat landscape domain intersects with the impact landscape domain by analyzing information from the impact landscape domain. From the threat impact perspective, for example, it is important to analyze how specific threat agents such as organized cybercrime might affect businesses by attacking web applications and the functionalities that these support. Today, threat agents attack not just the web applications but also the systems and applications that support their functionalities. Examples of systems that can be attacked are mobile channels, payment processing systems at POSs, and systems for processing financial transactions. The business impact of threats against web applications might account for losses of several million dollars in credit/debit card fraud and several hundred million dollars in fines, legal fees, and settlement costs. Assessing the levels of potential impact is critical to determine how much should be invested in security controls to reduce the risk and potential liabilities for businesses managing these web applications.

From the risk mitigation perspective, it is important to determine which controls can be implemented to mitigate the risks. It is therefore necessary to characterize the control landscape and determine which security controls are effective in mitigating the risks of these threats. This is where the threat landscape and the security control landscape intersect since security controls can be identified as those that are effective in controlling the risk. Besides fixing vulnerabilities and filling gaps in missing security controls, this includes applying additional security controls that are effective in reducing the risk to an acceptable level. For example, the risk posed by threats such man in the middle, man in the browser, session hijacking, and exploitation of web application vulnerabilities and design flaws can be mitigated by mutual authentication, antimalware client software, strong device fingerprinting, session management, focused security testing for specific vulnerabilities, secure architecture design reviews, and threat modeling to identify design flaws.

By walking through the different domains of threats, assets, impacts, and controls, it is possible to analyze and reduce the specific security risks. By walking through these domains and gathering, analyzing, and correlating information across these security domains, it is possible to characterize the risk.

One important aspect to take into consideration when performing this analysis is to determine which processes can provide the necessary information to characterize the threat, asset, impact, and control landscape of the web application. Some of the organization's traditional information security and risk management processes can be leveraged to provide the information required for the threat and risk analysis. Some information for the threat analysis might require adopting new activities, such as threat intelligence and threat modeling. Moreover, different businesses might have reached different levels of maturity and capacity in the analysis of threats and mitigation of web application security risks. One important aspect to cover in any type of interdisciplinary activity such as web application risk management is to foster collaboration among the different application stakeholders, including information security teams, application development teams, and risk management teams. Fostering collaboration among these teams is essential, since without collaboration and gathering necessary information for conducting the risk analysis from these stakeholders, it is very difficult to conduct the risk assessment.

Specifically, it is important to understand the organization's culture in relation to risk management from the information security compliance perspective and the maturity of the processes and tools used by the organization. It is important to understand especially how threats are analyzed, which processes are used to identify vulnerabilities, and how countermeasures are implemented. From the information security perspective, for example, it is important to understand the big picture: which regulations the business must comply with. The information security policies and standards and how the business adheres to these policies and standards is validated by information security and risk management processes. It is also important to adapt to the organization's software engineering process. It is important to seek opportunities to integrate threat modeling within the organization's risk management processes. These opportunities vary among businesses. Depending on the different levels of maturity reached in information security and risk management processes.

One critical aspect is to determine the level of awareness of application security risks among stakeholders. From the application security perspective, it is important to understand how critical web applications are for the business, how exposed are to cybercrime threats, and how exploiting vulnerabilities can potentially affect both the customers and the financial institutions serving them.

Sometimes there is very low awareness of cyber-threats and the impacts these might cause to the organization web application stakeholders might have different views and opinions on the impacts that threats might cause to web applications and have very little knowledge of threat- and risk-based web application assessments. The majority of web application stakeholders might consider traditional vulnerability assessments, such as pen testing, adequate, and information security and risk management processes sufficient to secure web applications in compliance with information security policies and standards. When there is little awareness among information security and risk management teams of the impacts that emerging threats have on web applications and the adequacy of current security measures and controls in mitigating these impacts, this is the case. In such case, it is important to spend time and resources in improving the organization's awareness of the impact of threats targeting web applications and on the inadequacy of current security controls and measures. The best way to raise awareness of cyberthreats is to refer to data such as security incidents and fraud either incurred directly or by similar businesses.

For some businesses, there is already awareness of the importance that threat, risk analysis, and information security managers have identified and a need to conduct more in-depth security assessments for web applications to identify potential risks, and risk managers are aware of the impacts of emerging threats to the organization and how these negatively impact web applications. Unfortunately, this level of awareness is not the same among different layers of management such as operational, senior, and executive. In this case, it is important to work with threat and risk awareness management teams, institute pilot threat modeling and risk analysis, and security control gap analysis and then present the results of these assessments to senior and executive management to improve awareness of the need for new risk mitigation measures and controls. Working with information security risk and fraud managers that could become champions within their departments for pushing new threat analysis and technical risks mitigation methodologies is critical to success.

The optimal case is when senior level information security managers and executive management, CISOs, COOs, and CSOs have a shared vision on the importance that application security has for the organization, and the focus is on making sure that web applications are protected from emerging threats and that potential risks are mitigated by adopting cost- and risk-effective security measures and controls. In this case, senior management can drive the adoption of new application security processes, such as application threat modeling from the top of the organization by pushing standardization, tools, training, and acquisition of human resources. At this level, organizations can push new application security initiatives, such as application threat modeling, across different lines of business by integrating it with information security and risk management processes.

RISK-BASED THREAT MODELING

> "You have to learn the rules of the game. And then you have to play better than anyone else."
>
> *Albert Einstein*

The Internet has become the primary digital media through which business serve their customers by allowing them to make business transactions such as purchasing goods and services online. While conducting these transactions, customers have an implicit trust in the company's websites. Banking customers, for example, trust the bank's website to open accounts, pay bills, apply for loans, book resources and services, transfer funds, trade stocks, view account information, download bank statements, and others. This trust is based on the assurance from the bank that the website is secure and protects the customer's privacy and confidentiality, bank accounts, and the various financial transactions that are enabled on these accounts. This trust is challenged when a security incident occurs, such as when the customer's bank account and credit card data are stolen and used for fraud, resulting in the customer losing both confidential data and money. Often when the trust between consumers and business is at stake and there is a possibility of losing the customer, businesses take action to make sure that the customers are compensated for their financial losses and offer new services, such as personal data privacy monitoring, for free.

Even if often businesses take the liability for the loss of online customers, it does not produce significant revenue loss. When the losses accumulate because of a massive amount of data compromise, it does produce a significant impact to the business both economically and legally. This is often the case when the security of a website

RISK-BASED THREAT MODELING

that was impacted and breached in the incident receives the attention of the business' senior and executive management and actions are taken to reestablish trust with both the consumers affected and the auditors whose business need to provide evidence of improved security.

When an organization is confronted with a security incident, the first reaction is usually to "stop the bleeding" and contain the damage. After the causes of the security incident are remediated, the main questions that need to be answered might include the following:

- *Who* is the threat agent that caused the security incident?
- *What* is the data that has been compromised and the impact to the organization?
- *When* the security incident took place?
- *Which* attack tools, techniques, and processes where used by the attackers?
- *How* the security incident occurred and if there was a security control gap or vulnerability that was exploited?

Seeking to answer these questions, Security Incident Response Teams (SIRT) typically work with the business and the application security, risk, and vulnerability management teams. Often this collaboration represents a challenge:

- *Business managers* do know which data and functional assets might be potentially at risk of compromise.
- *Application architects* do not know how well the application is being architected for security.
- *Software developers* do not know which vulnerabilities in source code can be potentially exploited by the attackers and the type of secure coding requirements that were followed during coding.
- *Security testers* do not know if the vulnerabilities exploited by the attackers were looked for and tested in previous security tests.
- *Information security managers* do not know which vulnerabilities exploited by the attackers were looked for and tested in previously execute security tests.
- *Risk managers* do not have information about the analysis of the risk posed by the threat agents that targeted the application, the vulnerabilities that were exploited, the assets compromised, and the business impact to determine the risk as well as information on the type of security measures that can be put in place to mitigate the risk including their cost and their efficacy.

One process that can help web application stakeholders from business, information security, and risk management to find answers to these questions is a risk-based threat modeling process. We define risk-based threat modeling as *"A risk-based process aimed at considering possible attack scenarios and vulnerabilities within a proposed or existing application environment for the purpose of clearly identifying risk and impact levels."*

The goal of risk-based threat modeling is analyzing threats, determining the type of attack used by the threat agents, analyzing the risks and quantifying the business impacts, and using this information to engineer attack-resilient web applications. Such risk-based threat modeling process can use formal analysis of threats and activities such as threat intelligence, attack modeling using attack trees and attack surface identification, identifying the assets at risk, such as the web application architectural components, the data and data flows between components, and functions that are at risk.

Risk-based threat modeling will also leverage existing security processes such as information security policies for deriving security requirements for the web application, vulnerability management, and reporting to map these vulnerabilities to the various web application assets that are targeted by the threats, security control gap analysis, architecture risk analysis, and risk management activities such as qualitative and quantitative risk analysis, technical and business impact analysis, residual risk analysis, and risk mitigation strategy.

Such a comprehensive risk-based threat modeling process can be executed through the development life cycle of a web application. It has been formalized and standardized by the authors of this book. We define this process as "Process for Attack Simulation and Threat Analysis" (PASTA). The details of this process will be covered in chapter VI PASTA. This chapter will focus on the genesis of threat modeling as risk-focused process that can integrate with information security and risk management process.

As a whole, the analysis of web application security risks can only be comprehensive if it considers at a minimum, the specific threats against web application assets, the attacks used, and the vulnerabilities exploited. In general, the scope for assessing web application security risks requires an in-depth analysis of the architecture, the software components, and the assets such as the confidential and sensitive data that is processed and stored.

In threat modeling, when the focus is the analysis of threats against software component the approach that is used is also known as "software security centric." When the focus is on the assets such as the confidential, the approach is known as "asset security centric." As a risk-based threat modeling process, PASTA is both software centric and asset centric in the context of web application security risks.

By following each stage of this risk-based threat modeling methodology, it is possible to conduct an in-depth and actionable technical threat and risk analysis of the web application. The end goal is to allow risk managers to make informed risk decisions on how and where to mitigate application security risks.

The approach that is followed in the assessment of risk is to render threats and attack visible to risk managers so that they can take informed risk decisions. Typically, application security is blinded to threats as security measures are applied in compliance with information security policies based on the inherent risk value of the assets and independently from the exposure to specific threat agents targeting the assets. Examples of processes that are blinded to threats are audit and compliance with information security standards and regulations. Compliance with information security policies is important and can be leveraged to enhance the risk profile for

RISK-BASED THREAT MODELING

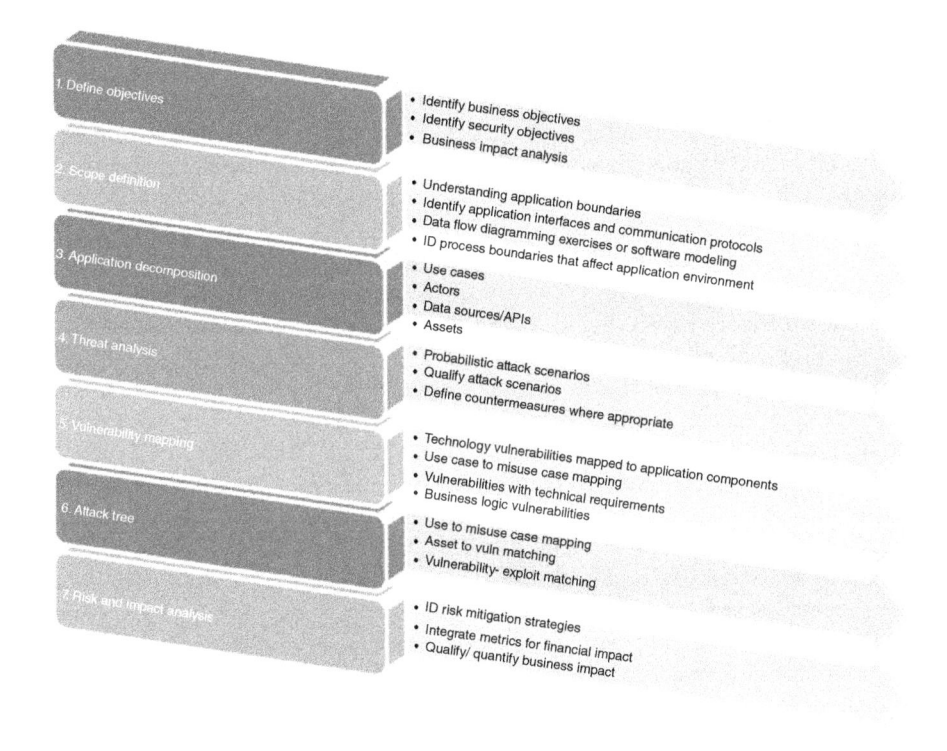

Figure 5.6 PASTA Threat Modeling Phases and Activities

1. Define objectives
   - Identify business objectives
   - Identify security objectives
   - Business impact analysis

2. Scope definition
   - Understanding application boundaries
   - Identify application interfaces and communication protocols
   - Data flow diagramming exercises or software modeling
   - ID process boundaries that affect application environment

3. Application decomposition
   - Use cases
   - Actors
   - Data sources/APIs
   - Assets

4. Threat analysis
   - Probabilistic attack scenarios
   - Qualify attack scenarios
   - Define countermeasures where appropriate

5. Vulnerability mapping
   - Technology vulnerabilities mapped to application components
   - Use case to misuse case mapping
   - Vulnerabilities with technical requirements
   - Business logic vulnerabilities

6. Attack tree
   - Use to misuse case mapping
   - Asset to vuln matching
   - Vulnerability-exploit matching

7. Risk and impact analysis
   - ID risk mitigation strategies
   - Integrate metrics for financial impact
   - Qualify/quantify business impact

the application in scope by considering possible threats targeting the application for unauthorized access to confidential and sensitive data and abuse of functionality for fraudulent transactions.

Documentation of security requirements is part of stage I of PASTA, "*define objectives.*" This is the stage whose goal is to capture the security requirements to protect the assets from specific threats in compliance with policies, standards, and security. Several threats can be analyzed: threat agents targeting web applications for personal information to commit identity thefts, compromise of financial transactions and abuse of data such as credit card data to commit fraud, exploit of web application vulnerabilities (e.g. SQL injection) and gaps in security measures and controls to compromise data, denial of service, and other type of attacks.

At the preliminary stage of PASTA, the objectives for the risk-based threat assessment are identified. In the general context of information security and risk, these objectives are set on high-level requirements for governing application security processes, managing web application risks, and complying with information security policies and regulations. For governance, PASTA includes governance objectives of the security of web applications, the establishment of a repository of web application security assets that can be managed throughout the SDLC, and the planning of application security awareness for the application stakeholders that manage web application security. Examples of risk assessment and management objectives for web applications include identifying the critical web applications and analyzing the inherent risks, analyzing the specific threats affecting these assets, and identifying the vulnerabilities and the security measures to needed reduce these risks to an acceptable level. Examples of compliance objectives include data privacy regulations, data breach notification laws, and security technology standards.

Once the objectives of the security risk-based threat assessment are identified, the next step is to identify the technical scope. The definition of the technical scope is the objective of stage II of PASTA. The technical scope for web application risk assessments includes identifying data assets that need to be protected, the potential exposure of sensitive data and functionality to the specific either external or internal threats. One important aspect of the technical risk analysis is to assess the risks of the architecture design and identify the data assets that should be in scope, since these are the ones targeted by the threat agents. Examples include architectural components with respect to the architectural tiers (presentation, application, and data) that store, transmit, and process data, data interfaces where data is input and transmitted between application architectural components, and data storage. Once the architecture design documents are assessed, it is possible to assess the compliance of the web application with information and security standards.

On the basis of the objectives of the risk-based threat assessment identified in stage I, specifically for concerns about protecting digital assets from specific threats, the definition of the technical scope of the assessment includes the web application and its components, including the digital assets that need to be protected. Once the technical and design documentation has been collected and a preliminary assessment of the security requirements is done to identify any noncompliance security issues, the next stage consists of understanding how the various digital assets are protected by security controls. This is done in stage III of PASTA: decompose the application. Application decomposition consists of identifying the web application components that protect the data assets and functionality targeted by threat agents. Decomposing the application into its basic architectural elements, such as users and services, trust boundaries, use cases, controls, interfaces, and data sources, allows identifying the security controls that protect data, functions, and transactions. Decomposing the application into its basic architectural components supports a granular analysis of security controls for both web application functions and transactions. The web application decomposition is necessary for conducting the web application threat analysis.

Stage IV of PASTA focuses on the analysis of threats. NIST defines threat analysis as "The examination of threat sources against vulnerabilities to determine threat to a particular system in a particular operational environment." Sources of threats are events that can be learned from the open source as well as from security incident reports. Emerging threats that are learned from the analysis of threat intelligence are used to build the specific threat library. When assessing the likelihood and impact of threats, the first step is to categorize and classify threats based on information reported from threat intelligence and web application relevant security incidents such as (SIRT), secure event monitoring events (SEMS) and Web Application Firewall

(WAF). Since this analysis is targeted toward specific threats to the web application assets, we can look at threats targeting these assets and functionalities used to access these assets. The main activities performed during the threat analysis are collecting threat intelligence information, categorizing this information based on the sources, motivations, goals, capabilities, past activities, events, and targets (e.g. web application, data, users, and functionality), mapping threats to the assets that were identified in stage III (application decomposition) to determine the threat probability, and mapping the threats to potential web application vulnerabilities exposing the assets to determine both likelihood and impact. Ultimately, the results of the threat analysis can be collected in a threat library and threat knowledgebase that can be used later on to assess the risks that these threats pose to the web application assets.

The threat analysis stage is a prerequisite to determine the risk severity of vulnerabilities identified in the web application by standard vulnerability processes such as pen testing, security testing, and source code analysis. This is stage V: "Vulnerability and Weakness Analysis." The objective of stage V is to analyze existing web application vulnerabilities and determine which ones have probability of being exploited by threat agents that seek to compromise specific web applications and data assets. At this stage, specific threats are correlated with vulnerabilities. This stage relies on the results of existing web application assessments, such as source code analysis and pen tests, that are performed in different phases of the SDLC.

During this stage, we also look at web application security issues, such as misconfiguration, that can be exploited by threat agents against specific assets (e.g. passwords, sensitive data, financial transactions), and any web application weaknesses, such as control gaps or lack of measures that might expose these assets to attacks. By determining which specific security control gaps and vulnerabilities can either be exploited or have already been exploited by threat agents (based on security incident information), we can focus on analyzing the risk and prioritizing these control gaps and vulnerabilities for risk mitigation. The prioritization also considers that based on the threat likelihood information, it is possible to determine the real risk of vulnerabilities as the true score not based on assumptions about the threat, but on the analysis of threats based on real data from threat intelligence and security incident reports.

Once we have analyzed the threats, determined the likelihood and impact on the web application assets, and determined which vulnerabilities and security control gaps can be exploited by these threats, we would like to know how these threats can be realized to understand the type of attack tools and techniques that the threat agents will be using to target these. To know this, we need to model the attacks used by the threat agents and determine how these exploit known vulnerabilities and security control gaps. Attack modeling implies that these attacks are real attacks against the web application. This is the goal of Stage VI of PASTA: "modeling of attacks and exploits to the web application assets." Attack modeling includes the analysis of the tools and techniques used by the attackers, such as Trojans that perform MitM and MitB attacks against the web application users and the security controls such as access controls (authentication and authorization) and data protection controls (encryption).

Attack modeling can use formal methods for analyzing the attacks that are most probable to an attacker, usually the ones that are easier to conduct and maximize their gain. One of the main outcomes of attack modeling is generating different models of the attacks that can be used in an attack library and then be used for specific security tests. These security tests augment the traditional security tests to test for security requirements and for common web application vulnerabilities, such as ethical penetration testing and static source code analysis. Attack modeling can also feed into an attack knowledgebase or attack library that can be used to conduct specific security testing, such as use and abuse cases of the web application. Ideally, only vulnerabilities that have not been tested before should be tested at this stage to determine if they can be exploited and need to be prioritized for remediation.

Once we have analyzed the threats, determined how and which vulnerabilities are exploited by the attackers through modeling the different type of attacks, we can analyze the risks and determine which security measures, such as security controls, vulnerability remediation, as well as processes such as additional security testing, security training/awareness, are recommended for reducing the risks. As these technical risks are analyzed, we also need to analyze the potential business impact to the value assets that are processed and stored by the web application.

From the business risk assessment perspective, this means mapping technical risk to business impact to derive the overall risk to the business. This is the overall goal of stage VII: Risk and Impact Analysis. Stage VII is centered on analyzing risk to the web application assets and identifying security measures to reduce impacts to the business. In this stage of the risk-based threat analysis process, we determine the level of risks using either qualitative or quantitative risk methods, recommend optional security controls/measures to prevent and detect data compromises, calculate the residual risks, we can provide different risk mitigation options to the business. These security controls/measures are both rated from cost- and risk-effectiveness in reducing the risk to the business to an acceptable level.

In summary, at the end of the risk-based threat modeling exercise, the various web application stakeholders that include business managers, web application architects, software developers, security testers, project and application managers, and information security and risk managers will benefit in different ways by the execution of risk-based threat modeling:

1. *Risk assessment:* Use the results of the threat analysis to determine which web applications and which specific data assets are at risk and incorporate application security requirements for mitigating these risks in compliance with information security policies and technology standards.
2. *Risk mitigation:* Incorporate the lessons from security incidents and threat intelligence into threat modeling tools, such as threat libraries and attack models that can be used to design and test resilient web applications.
3. *Awareness and training:* Develop application security training for web application/software developers and architects, focusing on specific design and coding of security controls and preventive and detective controls for mitigating specific vulnerabilities.

4. *Improved security testing:* Augment the traditional security testing for web application vulnerabilities with specific security tests to check the resilience of the web application as it either is or will be attacked.
5. *Improved vulnerability-risk management:* Prioritize the mitigation of web application security vulnerabilities based on the exposure of the web application to threats that have higher probability and business impact.
6. *Root cause exploit vulnerability analysis:* Use threat and attack models to analyze specific attacks and exploits for web application assets to determine the root causes and the viability of the exploits and recommend technical measures to reduce risks including specific security tests.
7. *Risk management:* Make informed risk management decisions to reduce risks of web application security risks by applying technical security controls/measures.

THREAT MODELING IN INFORMATION SECURITY AND RISK MANAGEMENT PROCESSES

> "Hackers are becoming more sophisticated in conjuring up new ways to hijack your system by exploiting technical vulnerabilities or human nature. Don't become the next victim of unscrupulous cyberspace intruders."
>
> *Kevin Mitnick*

Several organizations and businesses today enjoy the benefits of selling products and services to large population of customers through online web channels. These benefits do have costs: developing, deploying, and maintaining the web applications. These costs are justified because of the increased revenue generated from selling products and services online.

Among the web application development costs, it is also important to factor the costs for application security, such as ensuring that the web application complies with information security requirements. Often, having adopted a risk assessment process is also part of the requirements that organizations and businesses ought to comply with. Included in the compliance requirements of the ISO/IEC 27001 information security standards, for example, there is a requirement to demonstrate the adoption of a risk assessment methodology that considers the risks derived by violation of information security policies, as well as legal and regulatory requirements. This risk assessment methodology should include criteria for risk assessments, analysis, and treatment of risk. The treatment of risk should include criteria to determine which levels of risks are deemed acceptable by the organization/business.

Achieving compliance with information security standards such as ISO/IEC 27001 and obtaining an attestation/certification of compliance is a cost for the organization/business but also provides tangible benefits such as

- *Information security assurance:* Business clients and consumers can look at an information security standard certification for assurance that information security policies have been followed.

- *Vulnerability risk management:* The enforcement of process to identify and fix vulnerabilities provides evidence that risk posed by vulnerabilities is managed and the risk that these vulnerabilities pose to the confidentiality, integrity, and availability of the data whose security control is meant to protect to.
- *Trustworthiness:* Compliance with information security policies and standards and the audits of these by Quality Security Assessors (QSA) provides information security assurance to clients and customers that the security of the services being provided can be trusted.

Some businesses might look at evidence of ISO 27001 certification audited by qualified auditors as a factor for trust conducting business with a third party: in that case, certification ought to be considered a necessary business enabler. For merchants who accept online payments with credit cards, compliance with the technology security standard PCI-DSS is a requirement to conduct business with credit cards that are part of the PCI council, such as American Express, MasterCard, and Visa. PCI also requires performing periodic risk assessments. For PCI-DSS, the risk assessment process is designed to identify, analyze, and document risks. The assessment is the integral component of the risk management strategy and therefore should be used to manage threats and vulnerabilities and document control effectiveness.

Since the implementation of a risk assessment process is among the requirements for compliance with information security standards, the benefit of adopting such a process can be framed as satisfying audit requirements while enabling trust from consumers of online services and producers of these services. For these reasons, it is very likely that businesses that have achieved certification with security standards, such as 27001 and PCI-DSS have a risk assessment process in place. For these businesses, the main question is how well this risk assessment process is executed and how well it helps to assess the security risks that are managed by the organization/business. Specifically, as cyber-threats increase, seeking to attack web applications for stealing confidential data, denial of service, and fraud, it is important to know how well these risks have been assessed by the organization/business.

The unlawful noncompliance risks and cyber risk are equally important for an organization interested in assessing risks. To effectively manage of these risks, it is important to highlight their main peculiarities of compliance from risk perspectives:

- *Unlawful noncompliance risks:* These are the risks to which organizations and businesses are potentially exposed and impacted because of incurring fines from regulators, legal fees, and lawsuit costs when failing audits.
- *Cyber-threat risks:* These are the risks to which organizations and businesses are potentially exposed and impacted because of security incidents from loss of customer's confidential data, PII, intellectual property information, and fraudulent transactions.

Understanding of the difference between noncompliance risks and cyber-threat risks is essential to determine where the focus of an organization's risk assessment should be. For an organization whose online business has not been certified yet as compliant with information security, the main focus of managing risks should be on establishing a risk assessment process to manage information security risks.

For organizations and businesses that have achieved compliance with ISO 27001 and other information security and technology security standards, and either have not been impacted by a security incident yet or might be at risk of being impacted in the future, the focus of the information risk assessment also need to be focused on analyzing and managing the risk of cyber-threats targeting the organization/business.

For companies whose risk management process is required for compliance, it is important to understand the critical value of adopting a risk assessment process both as a certification requirement and as a business enabler. Assessing and managing cyber risks, on the other hand, is important for the business bottom line since economic impact caused by a security incident might also put companies out of business (worst case scenario). The negative consequences of a security incident might include the loss/compromise of data that the organization is required to protect, such as confidential data and customers' PII. The loss of such data confidentiality, integrity, and availability is a risk that organizations/businesses need to assess and manage. Protecting the organization's data assets such as PII is also covered by security requirements that are defined as part of information security standards. The potential risks of confidential data compromise is also a risk that organization/business ought to quantify and monetize since the monetary losses suffered during a breach of confidential data caused by a security incident are very high for an organization.

From the perspective of assessing and managing noncompliance risks, the probability that an audit could find an organization unlawful and noncompliant is a risk that could lead to fines and other penalties. From the perspective of assessing and managing the risks of cyber-threats, the risks are linked to a specific cyber-threat even occurring, such as a security incident that might impact the business with disruptions, denial of service, loss of revenue, loss of confidential data, reputation damage, and fraud.

If we consider both noncompliance events and threat events as general "adverse" events, we can use a general definition of risk to assess both noncompliance risks and cyber threat risks. For example, this is the definition of risk used by NIST SP-800-30: *"Risk is a function of likelihood of a given threat-source's exercising a particular potential vulnerability and the resulting impact of that adverse event on the organization."*

The determination of the application security risks that might produce negative impacts to the organization is dependent on the probability of a threat and the probability of exposure of that threat, such as an Internet facing website and a security measure/control or vulnerability that further exposes that website to that threat.

If we generalize a threat as the adversarial event that might have a negative impact, it is important to further specify the type of threat to determine the probability. One possible specification of threats can be a threat that impacts the confidentiality, integrity, and availability of sensitive/confidential data. Such a threat can be a threat agent, either internal or external to the organization, human, such as a malicious user/fraudster, or nonhuman, such as client malware. The probability of a threat agent attacking the web application might be factored as "threat likelihood" and can be determined by further analyzing the threat agent type, historical events associated with that threat agent, threat agent/group capabilities, and potential targets.

The probability of exposure to that threat can be called "vulnerability exposure." In the context of the web application, the exposure can be a gap in the implementation of a security control, such as user authentication, authorization rule/permission, encryption of sensitive data, or a web application vulnerability that when exploited can cause a negative impact to the business, such as compromise of application functionality and loss of the data confidentiality, integrity, and availability. Examples of web application vulnerabilities include the OWASP T10: injection flaws, broken authentication and session management, cross-site scripting, insecure direct object references, security misconfiguration, sensitive data exposure, missing function level access controls, cross-site request forgery, using vulnerable components/libraries, and invalidated redirects and forwards.

In the context of information security, a control gap might also include lack of general security measures, such as not enforcing processes such as documenting security requirements. Scoping the web application for vulnerability assessments and information security reviews prior to deploying the web application in the production environment is one example of a security requirement that should be enforced. In the context of risk management, a control gap might be an unenforced a control to manage risks, such as not enforcing information security policies as required by regulations and standards.

One critical factor for managing application security risks is determining which security controls and measures can reduce the likelihood of threats, vulnerability exposures, and negative impacts such as data breaches compromising the data CIA. The probability of a cyber-threat being realized can be determined by analyzing the threat agents and the type of attacks they use against possible targets. We can think of attacks in different ways than a threat agent/actor can to realize the objectives/goal of the threat. More specifically, the definition of attack that is most applicable to web applications as "computational resource" is NIST SP 800-28v2: *"The realization of some specific threat that impacts the confidentiality, integrity, accountability, or availability of a computational resource."*

One critical activity assessing risks is the threat analysis. A threat analysis allows the identification of the different types of threat agents and assessment of the likelihood of potential impact against specific targets. Attack modeling used to realize threats is part of an attack modeling activity. Attack modeling models attacks by analyzing different types of attack techniques, including vulnerability exploits. A generic threat to a web application can be realized by one or more attacks. For example, if the threat is to steal classified data, it can be realized by attacking a web application with an SQL injection attack, brute force authentication, session hijacking, as well as social engineering attacks. These attacks and vulnerability exploits can be modeled as real case attack scenarios to determine the presence of vulnerabilities that may facilitate the attack and increase the probability of being attacked in the future.

Once we have identified what the likelihood of a threat is and have factored the exposure of these threats for the assets that the organization seeks to protect, the next step of the risk assessment process is to determine the type and level of impact to these assets. The type and level of impact to a data asset can be an information security impact, such as an impact on the CIA of the sensitive/confidential data, or a monetary impact, such as the loss of the value of the data asset. Once we have determined the type of impact on the data, we can focus on assessing the risk levels of likelihood and impact using qualitative risk scoring methods. Once we have determined the value of the data asset in case it is lost or compromised, and the probability associated with a threat event causing the loss of that data, we can also quantify the risk using quantitative risk methods.

Note: Refer to qualitative and quantitative risk calculation formulas used in this chapter as a reference.

Now that we have analyzed the threats against a specific web application, modeled the attacks to determine the likelihood of these threats by identifying the exposure of vulnerabilities, and determined the impact on the assets, we have completed the risk analysis. The next step is to determine the level of risks so that these risks can be managed according to their severity/risk. Examples of risk management include accepting the risks, avoiding the risks, (not to accept the change that introduced the risk), transferring the risk to another party (by purchasing cyber-insurance), and remediating the risk by applying a security measure/control.

Determining which risk should be mitigated depends on the risk management strategy for example, an organization's risk management strategy might require mitigating only risks whose probability is MEDIUM–HIGH and impact is LOW–MEDIUM, accepting risks whose probability and impact are both LOW–MEDIUM, transferring risks whose probability and impact are both LOW–MEDIUM but impact is MEDIUM–HIGH, and avoiding risks whose probability and impact are both MEDIUM–HIGH. Such a risk mitigation strategy can be graphically represented in the risk management quadrants of Figure 5.7.

After the treatment of risk has been decided, the next step is to determine which security controls/measures are both cost-effective and risk mitigation effective in reducing such risks.

Businesses that seek to comply with the information security requirements of the ISO/IEC 27001 standard can choose several optional security controls for assessing

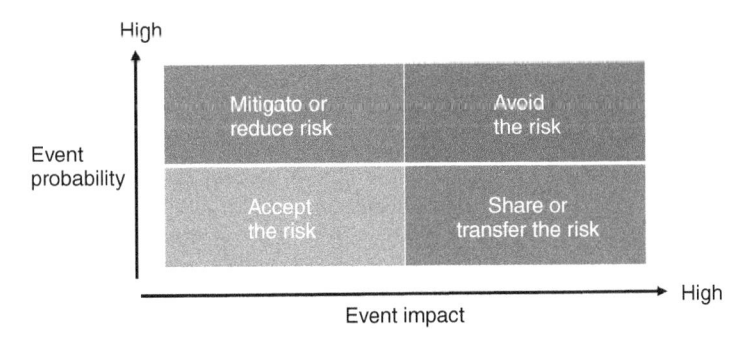

Figure 5.7 Risk Calculation and Management Heat Map

and treating risk. These are defined in the "Annex A – control objectives and Controls of 27001." For information security risks, different controls can be deployed. These controls depend on the type of impact to the assets, for example, if the impact is confidentiality, integrity, and availability, security controls such as encryption, digital signatures, and access controls can be implemented respectively to mitigate the specific impacts. Additional security measures can be implemented to further reduce the likelihood of a threat, such as reducing the exposure by making the web application only accessible from the internal company network or only from specific clients whose source static IP address is checked for allowing access. These types of security measures can significantly reduce the exposure for Internet threat agents. Security testing common web application vulnerabilities and the remediation of these also reduces their probability of being exploited by opportunistic attackers using hacking tools that are either free or widely available.

A criterion that can be used to determine which security controls should be implemented to reduce risks consists of determining the level of risk left after these security controls are implemented. This criterion consists of determining the residual risk. (*Note:* This chapter provides a methodology that can be used to calculate the residual risks). Typically, there is not just one security measure/control that reduces the initial security risks to both a qualitative and quantitative level that is considered acceptable. Organizations/business should consider implementing a set of security measures/controls, such as preventive and detective security controls, proactive and reactive controls, and multilayered controls that work together to reduce risk to acceptable levels for the organization/business.

Another factor for organizations/businesses to be considered to decide which security measures/controls are most suitable for reducing risks are the costs of the security measures and the risk mitigation/reduction benefits. Regarding the costs of security measures, it is important to consider all possible costs, not just the acquisition costs. A comprehensive estimate of the cost of security measures/controls includes the overall Cost of Ownership (TCO), such as the costs to acquire, deploy, and maintain the security measures/control. A comprehensive cost estimate of security measures/controls should consider the costs for designing, implementing, deploying, and maintaining such security measures/controls.

The assessment of the benefits of a security measure/control can factor the effectiveness in preventing the consequences of a threat and detecting it prior to the threat being realized in an attack and an exploit. Some security measures/controls are only effective if they are deployed together with other controls to provide the so-called "defense in depth." An example of security measures that work together as defense in depth are ones that provide detection and prevention at different layers of the web application architecture, starting from the outmost layer (the client outside the internal network) and ending at the innermost layer (the servers and backend services within the organization network). A good example of a set of security measures/controls that work together to provide defense in depth is anti-Distributed Denial of Service (anti-DDoS) attack security measures/controls. Anti-DDoS controls can be deployed in the cloud to scrub malicious traffic, within the organization network premises to prevent and detect DDoS traffic that reached the internal network, and measures to protect and detect DDoS attacks at the different layers of the OSI stack, such as the network layer (e.g. IP white list and black list filtering, ingress and egress filtering, velocity-rate controls) and at the application layer (e.g. load balancer/WAF, antiautomation defenses, server configuration hardening).

One important factor to consider is also how much an organization/business should budget for security measures/controls to mitigate the risk of a specific threat. For some organizations, the spending in security measures might be easily justified because they wish to comply with specific security requirements, such as ISO/IEC 27001. In that case, the budget for security measures/controls is allocated from the compliance budget. For organizations that are not strictly regulated by internal information security requirements, the budget for implementing security measures/controls can be a fraction of the budget allocated for IT spending and justified to provide information security assurance to both internal management and customers/clients. For the organizations that have had a security incident and have been economically impacted by fines from regulators, legal lawsuits from clients and customers, and possibly fraud, the budget of security measures/controls might be justified to prevent the impact of similar security incidents in the future. In that case, it is suitable to compare the costs of security measures/controls with the estimated costs due to the economic impact of a security incident caused by the absence of such security control/measure.

In summary, it is important to consider risk assessment and risk management as an important and essential process, not just for application security, but for any data asset the organization is responsible to protect. Organizations/business that have not yet implemented a risk assessment and management process should look first at establishing a web application security risk assessment framework and have a plan to treat web application security risks based on risk management rules. The risk-based threat modeling methodology outlined in this chapter provides an example of methodology with activities that can be performed in stages, either during the SDLC or after web application deployment, to assess and manage web application security risks efficiently and effectively.

Organizations and businesses that have already adopted a risk management process in compliance with ISO/IEC 27001, such as NIST SP 800 series, Factor Analysis of Information Risks (FAIR), or Operationally Critical Threat, Asset, and Vulnerability Evaluation (OCTAVE), can also leverage these risk frameworks to manage web application security risks and integrate risk assessment and management activities with PASTA. At a high level, information security risk assessment and management follow a similar process, but the focus might be slightly different between the different types of standard risk assessment processes: for example, FAIR is organizational risk-based, NIST is focused on security controls, while OCTAVE™ is operational risk.

In general, all standard risk assessment processes are based on a similar risk management framework for assessing risks. Web applications whose risks need to be assessed and managed can use the following risk framework ingredients:

1. *Asset management:* Identifying what the organization's web application assets are and who the web application management stakeholders are of these assets (e.g. business, application, project, development, testing, security, and risks).
2. *Inherent risk classification:* Assigning information security value based on the sensitivity of data handled and business risks based on the business value given to the web application asset if this asset is breached. This applies to each of the web applications that are managed by the business organization.
3. *Threat analysis:* Identifying the threats to the web application assets, including sensitive data stored and processed by the web application as well as functionalities that lead to a business impact if it is either loss or compromised.
4. *Vulnerability assessment:* Identifying the vulnerabilities that may be exploited by threats to the web application assets. This includes an analysis of how these web application assets might be compromised – how these threats can be realized in an attack.
5. *Impact analysis:* Identifying the impacts from both the information security perspective (e.g. loss of confidentiality, integrity, and availability) and from the business perspective (e.g. economic loss, revenue loss, reputation loss) if the assets, including sensitive data and functionality, are either lost or compromised.
6. *Risk analysis:* Assessing the level of risk based on the threat occurrence probability based on the exposure of the assets to vulnerabilities, the ease of the exploit/attack, and the level of impact if the asset is compromised.
7. *Risk management:* Determining security measures that can be implemented to manage risks and make informed risk management decisions whether accept the risks or set priorities for implementing security controls/measures to mitigate the risks.

The PASTA risk-based threat modeling methodology documented in this book also implements this general risk framework of activities, but is specifically focused on assessing and managing application security risks.

The main goal is to empower the organization/business web application stakeholders in effectively and efficiently assessing and managing application security risks by making informed decisions on where, how, and why to apply security measures and controls. In support of this decision making, it is important to rely on a risk management process that could scope the risk management objectives, identify the web application asset to protect, analyze threats, vulnerabilities, and model the vulnerability exploits and the attacks to determine the probability and impact to the assets and the business.

For businesses that seek to integrate the PASTA risk-based threat model with a generic risk assessment process, such as NIST Risk Assessment Methodology documented in the Special Publication (SP) 800-30, we provide herein an example on how this can be done.

Initially, it is important to highlight that there is no specific risk assessment and management process today that focuses on application security risks. The focus of

NIST SP 800-30 is assessing risks of information technology systems. If we generalize a web application as an information technology system the organization/business is responsible for managing, we can extend the scope of this guide to assessing web application risks as well. Nevertheless, we would also expand more on what traditional information security risk assessment processes can do, such as the assessment and management of risks to web applications beyond the inherent risks of the web application as an asset. These are, for example, the risk caused by threat agents targeting web application with malware for fraud, stealing PII, authentication credentials, and distributed denial of service.

By keeping these threats in mind, we can still look at which of the traditional standard risk assessment activities can be leveraged for a risk-based threat analysis of web applications.

First of all, it is important to look at the definition of risk used in the risk assessment methodology being used. The NIST SP-800-30 risk assessment methodology defines risk as "*a function of the likelihood of a given threat-sources to exercise a particular potential vulnerability and the resulting impact of that adverse event on the organization.*" The NIST risk assessment process consists of executing the following nine steps:

1. *System characterization:* The characterization of the system/web application boundaries, functions, data, and system/web application criticality and sensitivity.
2. *Threat identification:* The identification of threats and threat sources (human and nonhuman) that could exploit system/web application vulnerabilities.
3. *Vulnerability assessment:* The identification and assessment of vulnerabilities of the system/web application and procedure/process level that could be exploited by the threat-sources.
4. *Control analysis:* The analysis and identification of the controls (current and planned) that could eliminate or minimize the probability of a threat exercising a system/web application vulnerability.
5. *Likelihood determination:* The determination of the likelihood (HIGH, MEDIUM, LOW) that a vulnerability could be exploited by a threat-source.
6. *Impact analysis:* The analysis of impact level as a consequence of a vulnerability being exploited using qualitative scoring to assign HIGH, MEDIUM, or LOW levels.
7. *Risk determination:* The calculation of risk as a function of likelihood and impact for a particular threat/vulnerability. The likelihood includes factoring the probability of the threat and magnitude of the impact in the presence of planned or existing security measures/controls.
8. *Control recommendations:* The recommendations of security measures/controls (organizational, technical) that could mitigate or eliminate the identified risks.
9. *Risk reporting:* The risk assessment report that describes the threats and vulnerabilities, measures risk, and provides recommendations for control implementation.

After a risk assessment is completed, the second part of the risk management process consists of deciding how to treat the risks that have been assessed in compliance with the organization/business risk mitigation strategy. The NIST methodology includes common strategies to mitigate risks such as

1. *Risk acceptance:* To accept the risk using the existing control.
2. *Risk mitigation/reduction:* The prioritization, evaluation, and implementation of countermeasures/controls to mitigate the risks previously identified as part of the risk assessment and reduce it to a residual risk that is acceptable for the organization/business.
3. *Risk avoidance:* The elimination of the risk's cause by either removing an existing vulnerable component/process/feature or deciding not to implement it.
4. *Risk transference:* Transferring the risk to another organization/business by using other options to compensate for the loss, such as purchasing cyber-security insurance.

For businesses that have implemented an NIST-based risk assessment process and assess web application security risks by following the steps of this process, we can provide an example of how these steps can be leveraged for executing a risk-based threat modeling process such as PASTA. We can start, for example, by mapping PASTA to the nine steps of NIST SP 800-33 as shown in Figure 5.8.

The first step of the NIST risk assessment methodology is the characterization of the information technology (IT) system. As a whole asset, an IT system encompasses software, hardware, data, as well as the people who support and use that IT system. In order to characterize an IT system from a web application context/perspective, it is important to identify the parameters that can characterize the web application risk profile. PASTA provides guidance on characterizing a web application in the context of the risk assessment objectives in stage I (Define objectives), it defines the scope of the assessment in stage II (Define scope), and characterizes the specific data assets and functional assets of the web application in stage III (Application decomposition). Prior to characterizing the web application as a data and functional asset, it is important to define the risk assessment objectives in the context of information security requirements as mandated by compliance with information security policies, organizational governance processes, and risk management, including both risks that are inherent to the sensitivity of the data processed and managed by the web application, but also risks due to the specific operating environment and data exposure to threats specifically targeting the web application in that environment. Once these objectives are defined, it is then possible to define the scope of the assessment, including the technical scope based on any technical documentation available. Since threats can either opportunistically target web application vulnerabilities or specifically the data assets, such as confidential data, authentication data, and high-risk functionality, it is important to define the scope of the risk-based threat assessment around these specific data and functional assets and the threats that target them.

By following the PASTA methodology, the generic characterization of web application consists of defining the inherent risk profile. The risk profile of the

THREAT MODELING AND RISK MANAGEMENT 299

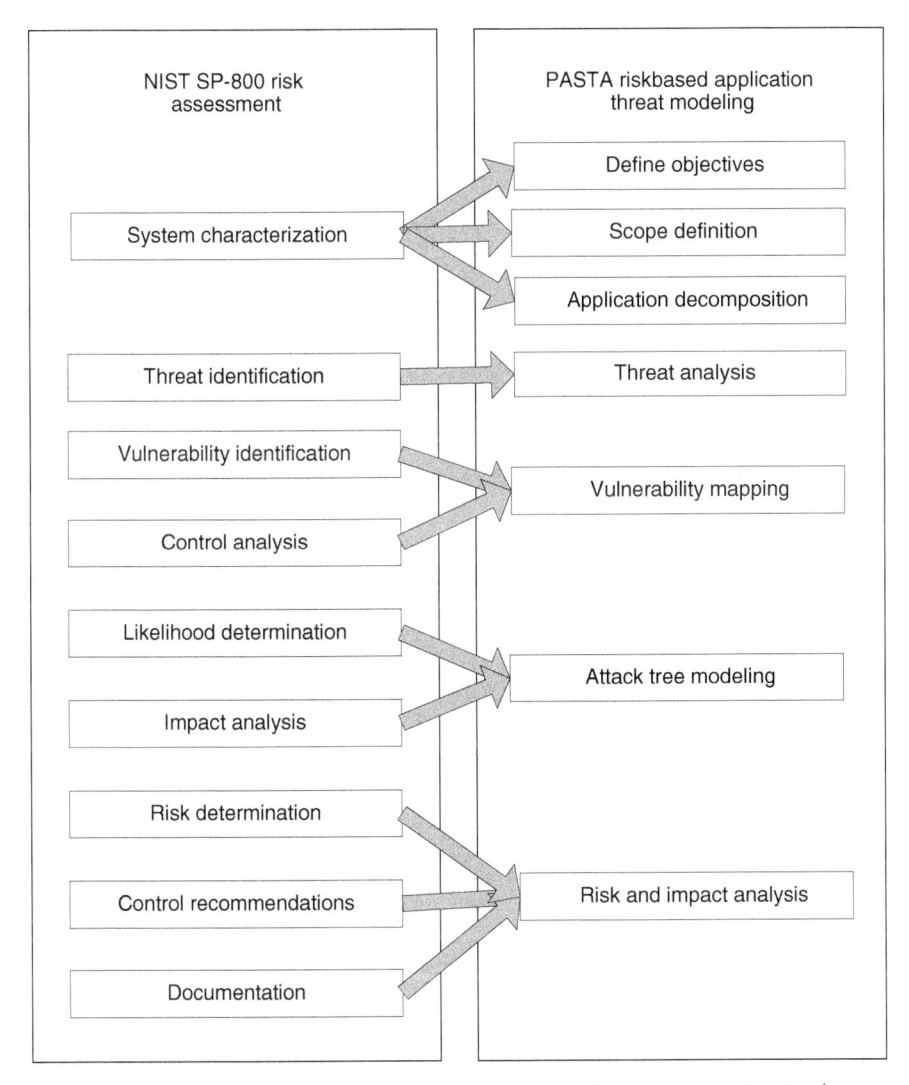

Figure 5.8 NIST Risk Assessment mapping to Application Threat Modeling[1]

web application in scope provides the initial information to assess and manage application risks in its operating environment. Such a web application risk profile might include the following information:

- *The type of operating environment* of the web application: Internet, intranet, extranet.

---
[1] NIST – National Institute of Standards and Technology.

- *The type of communication channels* (e.g. web, mobile, SMS, messaging, social media) that can be used to interact with the web application data components/services.
- *The type of data assets* used by the application according to the organization data classification policies (e.g. public, internal only, confidential, confidential/sensitive, PII, restricted/secret).
- *The information security risks* associated with the potential loss/compromise of the asset-valued data (e.g. confidential data).
- *The unlawful regulatory-compliance risks* potentially impacting the organization/business in the case of noncompliance.
- *The aggregated information security risks* as a volume of the confidential data stored by the web application (this is proportional to the number of registered users).
- *The risk dependencies* from third-party components and services used by the web application.
- *The type of risky business functions* performed by the web application that might be considered high risk, such as access to confidential data, financial transactions, administrative functions, and so on.
- *The business/economic value of the assets* such as web application and data as these are an asset and can be a business impact if these are either lost or compromised.

The Initial Risk Profile

The preliminary risk profile of the application is essential to determine the inherent risks due to the probability of the threat exposure and the possible impacts. These are possible impacts to the data (e.g. loss of CIA) as well as the value of the data (e.g. monetary loss). An initial risk profile allows a preliminary assessment of the application's risk independently of the likelihood of a threat as a factor of risk. This preliminary risk assessment specifically factors risks based on the classification of the data and the business functions as business risks. Other factors that can be assessed are the availability of risks if the service is lost and the risk to the company brand reputational loss.

The exposure to threats is an important factor to consider. For example, an application that is Internet facing is at higher risk of external threats than an application that is only intranet facing. The risk derived by storing confidential data, PII, and credit card account numbers can be considered information security risks. The risk of financial transactions that are made available to users through the web application, such as transferring money between bank accounts of different financial institutions, can be considered business/financial risk, as well as compliance/regulatory risk. This preliminary risk profile supports the identification of the inherent risk and the business criticality of the application.

In order to define the risk profile it is important to first define the technical scope based on the best available design documentation, such as architectural, logical, and physical network diagrams. In the absence of technical documentation, a possible way to capture the web application's technical scope is to create a rudimentary architecture diagram/sketch that captures the basic elements of the application architecture, which is the threat analyst's. It is important to realize that the absence of technical documentation that describes how security controls are designed and implemented, represents a risk that needs to be mitigated. A good security engineering practice to follow is to require updated architecture design documentation to be uploaded in a repository (e.g. SharePoint site, database) and accessible by the web application stakeholders including information security and risk teams.

Threat Analysis

Assuming that the architecture and the design of a web application is documented at a high level, the risks of the several components of the web application architecture can be further analyzed by identifying the specific data assets and architectural components that can be exposed to potential threats, such as the web application users and their roles (e.g. visitors, authenticated users, administrators), the web application use cases (e.g. query and modify data, business transactions), the web application trust boundaries (e.g. client, DMZ, internal network), the data interfaces, the type of servers (e.g. web servers, web application servers, web services), the communication protocols, and the data at rest (e.g. databases) and in transit (e.g. data flows) between the main tiers of the application architecture.

The next step of the NIST risk assessment methodology is to identify and analyze threats. For the web application in scope of the risk assessment, the risks to be assessed include specific threats against the web application data assets and business functionality. Independent of the inherent risk of the application, any authentication data that is stored and transmitted to the client for authentication needs to be protected with encryption. If the web application stores sensitive data assets such as confidential data, access to these data need to be protected by security controls such as authentication, authorization, encryption, session management, error and exception handling, and audit and logging.

This stage focuses on identifying potential threats targeting web applications either directly or indirectly both as human (human threat agent attacks) and as nonhuman (malware-automated threat agents attacked).

The purpose of threat analysis in the context of web applications is to identify specific threats and determine the likelihood of these threats targeting the web application. Examples of threats that can be considered are threat agents stealing customer's sensitive data, committing online fraud such as wiring money outside the bank, denial of service, and defacing the web pages for damage to the company's reputation. Analyzing these threats consists of characterizing the threat sources, capabilities, motivations, past activities, targeted assets, and attacks used. The information for analyzing cyber-threats can be gathered from sources of threat intelligence and more closely from analyzing the types of threat sources that were previously identified to be the origin of previous security incidents. This is depicted in Figure 5.9.

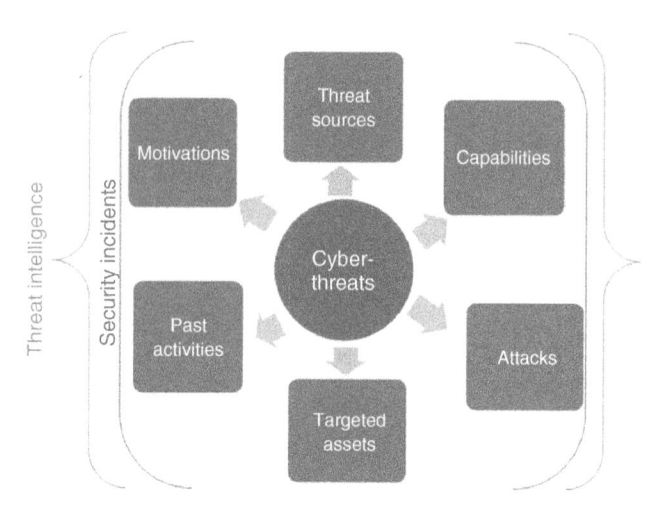

Figure 5.9 Dissecting Cyber-Threats

The analysis of cyberthreats can be used for the analysis of the risk of cyberthreats by factoring the threat likelihood, ease of exploits/attacks, and the vulnerability exposure caused by weaknesses in the web application security controls.

Sources of threat information from threat intelligence and security incidents, application logs, as well as Security Incident Event Monitoring (SIEM) systems and logs. Identifying threats includes characterizing the threat agents behind these threats, their motivations, capabilities, and attacks. Examples of threats affecting web applications include phishing/social engineering users, targeting confidential data stored for stealing identities and committing fraud, stealing user's credentials to gain unauthorized access, user's bank account takeover via malware hacking, and denying access to users by targeting it with DDoS.

Determining the probability of a threat targeting a web application includes analyzing previous security incidents that might be caused by these threats. If a security incident caused by a specific threat agent already occurred in the past, the threat likelihood of being attacked again by similar type of threats is very high.

Another factor to be considered when determining the threat likelihood is the exposure of a threat and requires an in-depth risk review of architecture, such as analyzing how a threat might affect each component of the application. Threats can be facilitated by the presence of vulnerabilities and control gaps exposing data assets to these threats. An important factor to consider is also that threat agents do not just target the web application directly by trying to exploit web application vulnerabilities, but they also target the user to steal online credentials by compromising the client/PC with key loggers and other malware.

The client browser can also be targeted by vulnerability exploits. A threat agent can attack the web application user through other channels, such as e-mail through a phishing attack vector that might contain a malicious link that either carries the malware as a payload or exploits a web application vulnerability such as XSS. Other successful attacks against the user's browser include MitB attacks to inject code directly into the browser outside the control of the web application to capture confidential data such as credit card data, PII, and authentication data such as PINs and challenge/response questions. Once the attacker is in control of the traffic between the client browser and the web application, he can also hijack the authenticated session and impersonate the user actions to commit fraudulent transactions. The outcome of this analysis is to determine the likelihood of a threat being realized and causing a negative impact to the web application by considering the most probable attack scenarios and attack vectors. The probability for a threat to be realized depends on other risk factors, such as the degree of risk mitigation and the ease of exploiting the vulnerabilities.

Vulnerability Analysis

Determining vulnerabilities that can be exploited by a threat leads to stage V of PASTA, vulnerability analysis. This stage maps to the NIST vulnerability identification step. The goal of this step is to identify web application vulnerabilities that can be exploited by the previously analyzed threats that had a high probability of attack and map these threats to vulnerabilities. If these vulnerabilities are identified in a web application by a security test, they might expose the web application to these threats. The vulnerabilities that are mapped to these threats are the ones that might increase the probability of realizing this threat. For example, if the goal of a threat is to compromise confidential data, finding web application vulnerabilities such as SQL injection will increase the probability of a specific threat exploiting this vulnerability.

Mapping web application vulnerabilities to threats previously analyzed during the threat analysis is done during stage V of PASTA, Vulnerability Analysis.

The vulnerability analysis maps to step 3, Vulnerability Assessment of NIST's risk assessment methodology. This step consists of identifying and assessing vulnerabilities that could be exploited by threat sources. It is not the purpose of this stage of PASTA to conduct web application vulnerability assessments, but rather to use the available vulnerability data from previous security tests such as penetration tests, source code reviews, and secure design reviews. During the stage V of PASTA, the previously identified vulnerabilities are mapped to threats to determine the asset exposure. For example, if vulnerability is identified during a pen test, it is possible to determine the exposure of this vulnerability to a specific threat and factor it with the likelihood of a threat to calculate the level of severity/risk of the vulnerability and prioritize it for risk mitigation. Specifically, this is the goal of step 5 of the NIST risk assessment, likelihood determination. Step 6 of the NIST Risk Assessment, Impact analysis, consists of impact analysis as a magnitude of qualitative impacts, such as either the loss or degradation of integrity, availability, and confidentiality of the asset that contains sensitive data and business functionality. Analyzing the impacts of a threat to the asset also needs to consider the probability of the threat occurring and the impact on the targeted assets as function of the vulnerability that exposes the asset to the threat and the attack viability of the attack as well as the asset value to determine the business impact.

Attack Modeling

For businesses that have adopted risk-based threat modeling, the determination of the likelihood and impact of an exploit can be analyzed only after modeling the attacks. In stage V of PASTA, vulnerability analysis, we map web application vulnerabilities to threats to determine the threat likelihood. The threat likelihood is the probability of a threat to target vulnerabilities and potentially damage them. The likelihood of a threat being capable of exploiting web application vulnerabilities to realize an impact can be analyzed by modeling the attacks. This is done in PASTA stage VI, Attack Modeling. Since an attack consists of realizing a threat to produce a negative impact (the goal of the attacker), modeling how this attack takes place is critical to determine if such attack leads to a successful exploit.

From a theoretical stand point, this can be done using formal methods such as attack trees and use and abuse cases to simulate how different types of vulnerabilities can be exploited by an attacker to reach his goals. For example, if the target of an attacker is the user's credentials to log on to a web application, the attacker might try different types of attacks, such as social engineering, dropping malware-key logger on the victim's PC when the victim visits a malicious website, exploiting web application vulnerabilities such as XSS to run a script key logger, exploiting an invalidated redirect to a malicious site to install malware-key logger, and attacking the web application database with SQL injection to run a query to get all the user's passwords stored in the database. These attacks that be modeled and simulated to determine the likelihood and impact of an exploit and factor these with the asset value to determine the risk. The attack scenarios that are analyzed through attack modeling can be included in an attack library and then used for security testing the web application to determine if these lead to possible exploits.

Risk Analysis and Management

Once we have analyzed the threat likelihood and mapped these threats to the presence of vulnerabilities and determined the likelihood and impacts caused by the exploit of these vulnerabilities, we can determine the risk level of a specific threat to the asset. By following the NIST risk assessment methodology, the risk determination occurs during step VII. The risk of a threat is calculated by multiplying likelihood with impact for a particular threat/vulnerability, including likelihood of the threat and magnitude of the impact of the threat in exercising the vulnerability in the presence of planned or existing controls. After calculating the risks on the assets for each threat and knowing how each asset is being impacted (e.g. loss of confidentiality, integrity and availability, monetary loss), it is possible to recommend the implementation of measures and controls to reduce the risks. In NIST risk assessment methodology, this is done during step VIII, Control recommendations. These are the recommendations of security measures/controls (organizational, technical) that could mitigate or eliminate the identified risks. Finally, during step IX of the NIST risk assessment methodology, it is possible to document the risk to produce a report that describes the threats and the vulnerabilities, the calculation of the risk levels, and the recommendations for implementing controls to reduce the risks.

The NIST steps VII–IX map to the final stage of PASTA, Risk Analysis & Management. The goal of this stage is to identify the levels of risks of each threat, the different security measures/controls to mitigate these risks, and to calculate the residual risk after these security measures/controls are applied. After assessing the residual risk, determining how the risk should be treated depends on the risk management strategy being followed. This organization's risk management strategy might also include NIST's recommended risk mitigation strategies, such as risk remediation, risk transference, risk acceptance, and risk avoidance. Qualitative risk analysis can be used to determine the level of initial risk before security measures/controls are applied and residual risk analysis can factor the effectiveness of different security measures/controls for reducing risk to acceptable levels.

Note: this chapter provides qualitative, quantitative, and residual risk calculation methods that can be used for these risk calculations.

Step VIII of the NIST risk assessment methodology, control recommendations, consists of identifying security controls that can mitigate the risk posed by the exposure of the data asset to vulnerabilities that were identified in the IT systems. To determine which type of security control should be recommended to mitigate the risks, it is important to look at the effectiveness of the control and the cost of acquiring, implementing, deploying, and maintaining the control. Determining which security measures/controls are effective in mitigating the risk is based on the previous analysis of the type of vulnerabilities and how these vulnerabilities are exploited in an attack to realize a specific threat (e.g. unauthorized access to sensitive data and functionality, denial of service). Threat analysis, vulnerability analysis, and attack analysis provide the necessary information to determine which security measures and controls are effective in mitigating the risk. These security measures/controls can map to vulnerabilities and control gaps and can be documented in a security control/measure framework to be used to assess web applications for the presence of potential gaps in the implementation of these measures/controls as well as in the presence of vulnerabilities affecting these controls. Besides the use of control risk frameworks to assess gaps, more specific countermeasures for each threat can be identified and recommended during the SDLC of the web application, such as secure architecture design reviews during design, source code review and static code analysis tests during coding, and security testing and penetration tests during the testing phase prior to release of the web application into the production environment.

During the final stage of PASTA, Risk Assessment, the overall risks posed by the threats that were previously analyzed are both qualified and quantified. Security measures/controls that are effective in reducing the risks to a low residual risk are identified and recommended during this stage. Analyzing threats, vulnerabilities, and impacts essential for the final assessment of risk and determining of security measures/controls that can reduce the risk. For example, the SQL injection vulnerability that is exposed to a publicly accessible interface and can be used to break the authentication and gain unauthorized access to the application is determined to be a high risk and is prioritized for risk mitigation. In determining which security measures/controls are effective in mitigating the risks, we ought to consider different options such as

1. deploying a filter API at the web server to filter incoming traffic to the site;
2. designing and implementing a servlet filter at the application server before processing the data;
3. changing the source code of the database access components to use prepared statements and/or store procedures.

The selection criteria of security controls/measures that mitigate the risks need to factor costs versus benefits, such as the cost of the security measure/control compared with the effectiveness of mitigating the risks. For example, among the optional measures to mitigate the risks of SQL injection, the prepared statements and store procedures are known by industry standards and application security best practices to be the one that is most effective in mitigating the risk of SQL injection because it will eliminate the root causes of the vulnerability but will not be more expensive to implement than the other optional security measures.

In summary, we have provided an example of how a risk-based threat modeling methodology such as PASTA can be integrated with an industry standard information technology system risk assessment process such as NIST to specifically assess and manage security risks of web applications.

THREAT MODELING WITHIN SECURITY INCIDENT RESPONSE PROCESSES

> "To competently perform rectifying security service, two critical incident response elements are necessary: information and organization"
>
> Robert E. Davis

The risk-based threat modeling methodology PASTA focuses on analyzing and modeling threats and attacks against web applications. This analysis leads to assessing risks, impacts, and the determination of security controls to mitigate these risks.

Businesses that have already adopted a risk assessment methodology to manage information security risks of information technology systems, such as NIST, can also integrate several risk assessment activities with PASTA to specifically focus on characterizing web applications as assets, identifying specific threats targeting web applications, assessing web application vulnerabilities, analyzing the effectiveness of security controls, determining the threat likelihood, and analyzing impact to qualify and quantify risks and recommendations of security measures and controls to reduce risk to a manageable and acceptable level. The benefit that PASTA provides to the standard NIST risk assessment is that it focuses on analyzing threats and modeling attacks to determine whether existing security measures and controls are effective in controlling the risk and the impact of threats. When these are found not to be effective based on the analysis of the attacks and the determination of impact, additional security measures are considered and recommended based on risk mitigation strategy considerations.

An important factor in risk mitigation decision making is determining the control effectiveness in protecting web applications when they are under attack. The effectiveness of these security controls can often be tested prior to the deployment of the web application into the production environment and possibly become the target of attacks from threat agents. Security testing allows businesses to be proactive in managing security risks. PASTA focuses on assessing the likelihood of threats, estimating negative impacts, and identifying and implementing security measures for proactively reducing the exposure of these threats before these risks materialize into security incidents.

Ideally, a consistently executed risk assessment process allows risk managers to identify and implement security controls that reduce the risk exposure to future threats and reduce probability and impact of security incidents in the future. Realistically, even with effective risk mitigation controls implemented, can still be considered targets worth attacking. If these attacks are detected the probability of information security incidents that the organization needs to be prepared for is increased.

Security Incident Response Preparedness

For several businesses today, security incident preparedness consists of implementing security incident response procedures so the organization is prepared by knowing exactly who and how security incidents should be handled in the event that they happen. First of all, it is important to agree on the definition of "security incident," as this will apply in the context of web applications. A standard definition of computer security incident according to NIST SP 800-61's "Computer Security Incident Handling Guide" is "violation or imminent threat of violation of computer security policies, acceptable use policies, or standard security practices."

For web applications, a security incident might fall in the same category, since, in essence, web applications are made of one of more computer resources. Examples of such computer resources include computer hosts, web servers, application servers, database servers, and backend systems (e.g. mainframes). Using the NIST definition for security incidents, some examples of security incidents affecting web applications might include the following:

1. *Detected unauthorized access to confidential data* (e.g. credit card data stored and managed by a web application).
2. *Detected infection or compromise of a computer host* such as by compromised by a threat agent such as malware.
3. *Observed crash of a web server* caused by unusual traffic of connection requests for that web server.

4. *Released public information of a vulnerability* affecting a specific website.
5. *Released vulnerable software* with a missing security patch.
6. *Announced breach of sensitive data* such as the action of a threat actor posting such data in a publicly accessible website.
7. *Unauthorized vulnerability scanning of a web application* allegedly originating from an external source/attacker to identify possible exploits and triggering an alert.

One important aspect of security incident response is to being able to analyze the security incident events from the perspective of the impact it might cause. Information security incidents affecting web applications might include the compromise of availability, integrity, and confidentiality of sensitive customer data. Analyzing the severity of a security incident is therefore critical in determining who and how the security incident should be handled and prioritized.

Traditionally, businesses that have adopted a standard security incident handling procedure have their security incidents handled by a specific team called the Security Incident Response Team (SIRT). SIRT are trained and prepared to handle security incidents in a timely and systematic fashion by following standard security incident handling guides. An example of this standard incident response guide is NIST SP 800-61-2 "Computer Incident Response Guide." This guide documents a four-step process to handle computer security incidents:

1. *Preparation*,
2. *Detection and analysis,*
3. *Eradication and recovery*, and
4. *Post incident activity.*

A graphical example of this four-step process and how it feeds data forward and backward is highlighted in Figure 5.10.

Security Incident Preparedness

The first step in handling security incidents is preparation. Preparedness is, in essence, the proactive part of security incident response. The preparation for handling security incidents includes following procedures to respond to incidents and knowing to whom to escalate the incidents when a response needs to be initiated. For example, notification-escalation procedures should be in place to know whom to contact and notify when the security incident is first identified. This might include key personnel within the organization, such as CISO, the Chief Information Officer (CIO), threat analysts, risk and fraud managers, web application technical managers, and legal. Outside the organization, the parties that could be involved and notified of a security incident might include law enforcement agencies (e.g. FBI, US Secret Service), public media, software vendors, internet service providers (ISP), members of Information Security Assurance Centers (ISACs), national Computer Emergency Readiness Teams (CERT), regulatory bodies (e.g. data privacy office), and so on.

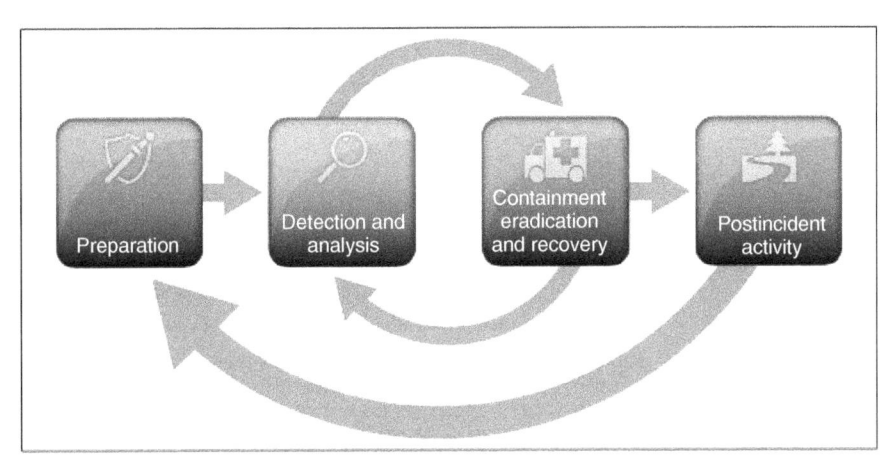

Figure 5.10 Phases of Security Incident Handling Process (NIST via Coordinated Response)[2]

Once the organization knows who to contact, the other important aspect of preparedness is to know which type of information could be shared by each of the people that are notified. Security incident information is obviously highly sensitive and should be handled according to the level of sensitivity required to protect the information confidentiality. In preparation for a security incident, a security team will prepare the contact list (e.g. phone numbers, e-mails) and conduct routine roll call to validate that it is up to date and accurate.

Another part of preparedness is also to make sure that the SIRT team is ready to engage with threat and risk analysts and receive the right information so that they can conduct further analysis of the threat sources and correlate them with the type of attacks and vulnerabilities that have been found exploited in the security incident. A threat analyst whose role is conducting threat analysis and risk-based threat modeling of web applications, such as using PASTA, is a critical resource for the SIRT in determining the security incident root causes, such as identifying how the compromised data assets have been exposed to potential vulnerability exploits and exposure of security control weaknesses and gaps.

Another important aspect of security incident response preparedness is to enable team access to the tools that are used to detect, monitor, acquire evidence, and respond to security incidents. These include security information event monitoring (SIEM), security incident monitoring and intrusion detection, tools for collecting forensic evidence for possible legal actions, and tools for tracking and reporting the incident, such as ticketing systems. Training the security incident response team to use these tools and execute the computer security incident handling procedures is also critical. Part of this training also includes conducting simulated security incident exercises routinely

---

[2]http://csrc.nist.gov/publications/nistpubs/800-61rev2/SP800-61rev2.pdf.

to assess the SIRT capabilities, measure effectiveness, and identify opportunities for improvements or greater efficiency.

Detection and Analysis

Assuming that a security incident team is prepared to execute the security incident handling procedures, the next step is to be able to detect and analyze security incidents when they happen. An important aspect of security incident response is to be able to proactively look for the signs of incoming threats before they are realized. Early detection of possible attacks can be done by monitoring threat intelligence sources, such as social media (e.g. Facebook, Twitter, and YouTube) for threat activities that might be correlated with future attacks. For example, the type of information that can be monitored includes recruiting activities by threat agents (e.g. hacktivists, cyber gang members, money mules) in preparation for an attack and requests to acquire/rent hacking tools (e.g. malware, botnets, weapon zed, Zero-day exploits, DDoS tools). Businesses whose websites are a potential target for cyber-threats should hire threat intelligence agencies to monitor social media as well as sites used by these threat agents (e.g. PasteBin) to monitor possible attack preparations and alert the interested parties. For DDoS threats, for example, some are publicly announced on YouTube and PasteBin, including who the targets are and when they will be attacked. When these threats are detected, it is important to raise attention toward these attack sources and be prepared to respond to incoming attacks.

Cyber-Threat Alert Levels

Other threat intelligence sources that can be consulted in preparation for future security incidents include cyber-threat advisories from law enforcement agencies, CERT, ISAC, and threat intelligence reports from private security companies. Specifically in the case of financial institutions, the Financial Sharing - Information Sharing and Analysis Centre (FS-ISAC) provides the group members with threat analysis (e.g. reports, advisories), information about new vulnerabilities, and security incidents. When incidents happen, the information shared also includes information about data breaches, impacts, and the possible causes. Members of FS-ISAC are allowed to both share and consume threat intelligence and information about security incidents. The information on threats, vulnerabilities, and incidents is given different data classification levels: "restricted" to only a specific group with the FS-ISAC members, "confidential" to all FS-ISAC members, "internal" to FS-ISAC members and partners (e.g. government agencies), and "public" that can be shared freely is subject to copyright rules. The information about security incidents, threats, and vulnerabilities is provided with a risk criticality level and, in the specific case of incidents with a level of severity, based on impact. FS-ISAC ratings for cyber-threats caused security incidents have five levels:

1. Informational
2. Minimal impact

3. Moderate impact
4. Significant impact
5. Major business disruption

FS-ISAC also rates the risk of cyber-threat attacks for the all financial industry sector as follows:

1. Low
2. Guarded (general risk)
3. Elevated (significant risk)
4. High
5. Severe.

The severity ratings given security incidents can help prioritize actions such as preparing defenses in case specific financial institutions are also targeted by these attacks. The financial sector's awareness to potential threats can also be prioritized for attention based on the severity of these attacks. Examples of these attacks include DDoS, spear-phishing, identity theft, and malware hacking.

Threat intelligence information can be distilled, analyzed to be included in threat libraries, and stored in the threat knowledge base for analyzing the threat likelihood as a factor of risk calculation. Specifically for businesses that have adopted PASTA, the threat intelligence gathered from the security incidents and attack sources can be used to update the threat and attack libraries that are used by threat modeling tools (e.g. ThreatModeler™) to conduct the threat modeling exercise.

When a specific threat that is monitored based on the specific threat severity and later on is also detected by a security information event management tool (e.g. SIEM) as an indication of possible attack against a web application, the correlation between threat and attack is much easier rather than looking at the attack without the knowledge of the threat source. When a security incident is also supported by threat intelligence, the response to the threat is also faster than when being detected just by looking at the log evidence without previous warnings.

Unfortunately for most organizations today, security incidents are detected only months after the initial compromise. On the basis of the information from the Verizon 2013 Data Breach Investigations Report, the majority of breach events (62%) were not discovered until months after the initial compromise. For this reason, it is important to put the effort on threat intelligence, attack detection, and threat to attack correlation.

Correlating information about threats such as threat intelligence, vulnerability assessments, and attacks from sources such as security information events (e.g. SIEM, WAF) can also help in the detection of security incidents. In the case of malware attacks such as account takeover, it is known that session hijacking is exploited by an attacker to impersonate a user and then transfer money from the bank account of the victim to the fraudster controlled account (money mule). A rule can be set to detect when multiple client sources (e.g. multiple IPs) are used to establish concurrent online web sessions as an indication of a possible malware banking Trojan attack. The attack detection rule is set by the knowledge gained from learning how online banking Trojans operate.

Specific rules for detecting attacks against a web application that attempts to exploit common vulnerabilities (e.g. XSS, SQL injection) can also be set in the Web Application Firewall (WAF). After the attack is detected and analyzed for correlation with other sources to verify, it can also be blocked and temporarily contained until a remedy (e.g. data filtering, code changes to use prepared SQL statements) of the vulnerability is deployed. Since the attack vectors used might change to try to bypass filtering rules, the information about new attack vectors that can be gained through threat source intelligence is also critical for maintaining a set of rules for the WAF that is updated for the most current attack vectors.

Similarly, in the case of DDoS attacks targeting web applications, specific rules can be set to detect attacks from specific DDoS rules such as Low Orbit Ion Cannon (LOIC). These rules can be set at the network layer (e.g. UDP, TCP/IP), in Intrusion Detection Systems (IDS), and at the application layer (e.g. HTTP) within a WAF.

By using PASTA risk-based threat modeling, threat analysts correlate the information about threats with the information about attacks and vulnerabilities targeted by these attacks, such as web application vulnerabilities. Threat analysis helps SIRT teams to "tune in" to security information event monitoring tools and detect specific types of attacks against web applications. Since SIEM tools correlate information from different logs, they might generate a lot of events. These events need to be accurately correlated to accurately determine (e.g. less false positives) whether the event detected might indicate a source of an attack.

Assessment of Security Incidents

Once the security event has been detected, the next step is to determine if a computer security incident case should be opened and a ticket issued. The organization's standard definition of what constitutes a security incident should be used to determine if the security information event that has been detected falls in scope of a security incident. According to NIST computer security incident response guideline SP 800-53r1, a security incident is "an occurrence that actually or potentially jeopardizes the confidentiality, integrity, or availability of an information system or the information the system processes, stores, or transmits, or that constitutes a violation or imminent threat of violation of security policies, security procedures, or acceptable use policies." On the basis of this definition, a detected unauthorized access to a web application, detected installation of malware to steal confidential data, such as network sniffers, posted stolen user credentials such as passwords, as well as attempts to exploit web application vulnerabilities with tools all fall into the category of possible computer security incidents.

The next step after a security incident is identified is to include information that characterizes the security incident. According to NIST security incident information might have one of more of the following:

1. *The status of the incident* (new, in progress, forwarded for investigation, resolved).
2. *A summary* of the incident.
3. *Indicators of compromises* related to the incident.
4. *Other incidents* related to this incident.
5. *Actions taken* by all incident handlers on this incident.
6. *Chain of custody*, if applicable.
7. *Impact assessments* related to the incident.
8. *Contact information* for other involved parties (e.g. system owners, system administrators).
9. *A list of evidence gathered* (e.g. alerts from IDS, SIEM, AV, File Integrity S/W, e-mails, system logs, application logs, network devices logs, e-mails).

An important piece of information that needs to be filed with the security incident event is the incident's severity level to determine how it should be prioritized for response. The severity of an occurred security incident can be assigned based on the degree of asserted or possible impacts. For example, the impact of the incident might be just "reputational," such as a security incident resulting in a defaced web page, or it might be "tangible," such as a data breach resulting in loss of confidential data and PII. The level of impact of data breach incidents can be calculated based on the following factors:

1. *The classification of data* being compromised (e.g. confidential, restricted, internal).
2. *The information security parameters affected* (e.g. confidentiality, integrity, and availability).
3. *The volume of data records* affected that are either lost or compromised.

According to NIST, the assignment of the severity levels for security incidents can also consider the extent of the incident's impact – whether it is both an information impact and a business-functional impact. Examples of information impacts include "privacy breach," impact on private information of customers that was accessed or exfiltrated, "proprietary breach," such as an impact on proprietary information that was accessed or exfiltrated, and "integrity loss," sensitive or proprietary information was changed or deleted. A business impact of "high" should be assigned when an organization can no longer provide critical business services to its customers, a level of "medium" applies to businesses that lost the ability to provide a critical online service to a subset of system users, and "low" when it can provide all critical online services to all users but lost full capacity.

Note: The level of information security and business impacts can also be assessed using the qualitative and quantitative risk analysis methods used in stage VII of PASTA and documented in this chapter.

Escalation Procedures

Once the security incident has been analyzed to determine the extent, type of impact (e.g. data breach and business/online service), and assigned a severity level, it is escalated for notification to the appropriate person/role within the organization as required by the security incident response process escalation procedures. Typically, the higher the severity of the security incident, the higher the role and responsibility of the person who needs to be notified. Once the security incident is filed, a meeting between the security incident stakeholders takes place (e.g. SIRT, CISO, CIO) to decide the course of action to handle the security incident. If additional evidence is collected it is also considered for evaluation.

Containment and Eradication

The next step of the security incident response process consists of taking actions for containing, eradicating, and recovering from the incident. For attacks against web application, examples of containing a security incident might include the following:

1. Disabling user accounts, changing passwords for online user accounts that were compromised.
2. Temporarily disabling/blocking access to URLs/functionality that is targeted by the attacker and compromised.
3. Fixing the vulnerability that was exploited.
4. Filtering the malicious HTTP traffic from a web server.
5. Blacklisting the source (e.g. IP address) of the attacks.
6. Disconnecting servers/databases whose data has been exfiltrated.
7. Taking the website offline until causes are investigated.

   The decision of how to contain a security incident depends on the analysis of the type and severity of the impact. The incident containment measures are temporary and ought to be carefully considered for the additional impacts that might generate, such as the unavailability of a web application functionality/service until root causes of the incident are identified.
   Containment helps the organization to limit further damage, "stop the bleeding," and buy time until the cause of the security incident is identified, eradicated, and fully remediated. During this phase, all the possible evidence of the security incident, such as SIEM events, web application logs, and system logs, are analyzed to determine the root cause of the incident. Often, collecting this information is required for possible legal law enforcement evidence and forensic analysis. In such case, the handling and preservation of evidence ought to follow specific rules and regulations established by law enforcement and rule of law. The type of information that ought to be collected also includes the source of the information (e.g. IP address, machine name), name of the individual collecting the evidence, date, time, and location.
   After an incident has been contained, the next step is to eradicate the incident by eliminating the root causes. These root causes need to be investigated based on

the analysis of the evidence (e.g. alerts and log events). Often, additional investigations and specific security tests are required to confirm the causes of the security incidents, such as determining the presence of vulnerabilities, analyzing of possible gaps in security controls, and application security misconfigurations. Examples of eradicating root causes include fixing the type of vulnerabilities that were exploited in the attack, eliminating the malware that caused the attack (e.g. computer Trojans, viruses), adding security controls/measures such as encryption, input filtering, stronger authentication, setting permissions, and applying changes to web application configuration policies.

Root Cause Analysis

One of the artifacts that can help when analyzing the security incident root causes is a threat model. A web application threat model whose data had been compromised because of a security incident helps determine the possible root causes of the security incident. Let us assume that the impact of the security incident is severe and the SIEM logs point to several potential causes of the incident, such as breach of confidential data. What is not known is what could have caused the incident, such as which type of vulnerability was exploited and whether the origin of the threat is internal or external. By knowing where the confidential data is stored, it is possible to use a threat modeling artifact, such as a data flow diagram, to identify the security controls (e.g. authentication, authorization) that could have been bypassed to access the data, and then assess and further investigate if these protections failed to either protect the data or failed to detect the access of such data by an unauthorized user/threat agent. Besides the data flow diagrams, the identification of the various use cases and of the type of user roles and permissions also helps to analyze which type of permissions and authentication levels were compromised in order to gain access to the confidential data. The transactional analysis of the web application also helps identify which web application functions allowed either querying or entering confidential data, such as user registrations and validations. Additional security measures and controls could be identified by analyzing the attack vectors that were used to attack the security controls and gain access to confidential data. Once the vulnerability root causes are identified, they can be prioritized for remediation. A postmortem analysis of the incident causes should also include an evaluation of the security measures that worked and the ones that did not work and issue recommendations for implementing additional controls and processes (e.g. threat modeling, security testing) to reduce the risk of similar security incidents occurring in the future. The postmortem security incident analysis can also provide valuable information to improve the current web application threat model. Examples include updating threat libraries with the new threats observed in the security incidents, updating the attack libraries with the attack vectors that were used, and updating the map of these threats to the vulnerabilities that were exploited.

The last step of the security incident response consists of analyzing how the incident response procedures were applied and identifying opportunities for improving the current procedures based on the lessons learned during the security incident handling.

6

INTRO TO PASTA

RISK-CENTRIC THREAT MODELING

"Risk comes from not knowing what you are doing."
Warren Buffet, Billionaire, Philanthropist, Investor

Understanding and exercising a broad scope of real-world attack patterns better depict the viability of threats. Combined with a risk-centric approach that centers on developing countermeasures commensurate to the value of the assets being protected, PASTA (Process for Attack Simulation and Threat Analysis) allows for a linear threat model to achieve both technical sophistication and accuracy and a marketable message around risk mitigation strategy. This can be achieved by realizing three key attributes as part of its methodology: topicality, substantiation, and probabilistic analysis. These attributes will be exemplified in the step-by-step coverage of the PASTA methodology in this chapter.

For any security process to be successful, it needs to be repeatable, measurable, yield results, and invite more stakeholders than those found in security and compliance. The risk-centric threat model detailed in this chapter provides a linear methodology to encompass all of these aforementioned characteristics. Its multistep process is combined with a multifaceted focus to various stakeholders. In lieu of IT, information security, and business groups maintaining disaccord over security deliverables, a risk-centric threat modeling approach unifies disparate goals over a linear workflow

---

Risk Centric Threat Modeling: Process for Attack Simulation and Threat Analysis, First Edition.
Tony UcedaVélez and Marco M. Morana.
© 2015 John Wiley & Sons, Inc. Published 2015 by John Wiley & Sons, Inc.

that is comprehensive yet simple to use. Aspects of this methodology have already been introduced; however, this chapter focuses further into each of the steps in PASTA so that readers can consider how each stage events' can be applied within their own environments. As previously mentioned, PASTA's approach is asset or risk centric; therefore, the following chapter will be focused solely on this approach and provide points for why this approach may be of best value over some of the software-centric threat modeling alternatives that exist.

Inherent Challenges to Threat Modeling

Some of the inherent challenges to threat modeling center around company culture, resources, maturity of process and control, and most importantly executive support. Lack of executive support truly nullifies even contemplating threat modeling for an organization. Beyond this, the other inherent challenges become more easily overcome, however, nonetheless a challenge. Next would have to be the company culture. If there is a lot of corporate politics that are centered on self-preservation or subscribing to the *blame-game*, this may thwart threat modeling before it ever gets into a beta phase. Tool dependency or the lack of any tools will also weaken any threat modeling methodology, although with far less impact as the lack of executive sponsorship. Conversely the lack of any tools for application testing will limit the sophistication of the application threat model.

Process maturity can be an inherent challenge as well since several inputs and outputs of the threat modeling methodology are dependent on somewhat established processes such as incident management, security governance, risk management, vulnerability management, system imaging, pen testing, project management source code reviews, asset management and more. Still not detrimental to overall threat modeling adoption and ongoing execution, immature processes can force the use of maturity models in order to track which threat modeling activities are initially performed and how they are refined over time. Those reading should not be discouraged to think that threat modeling adoption should only come at a time when all security and technology processes are running at a CMMI level 5. Most places are running in the low CMMI 3 levels and are quite able to adopt threat modeling initiatives while receiving benefiting from the various benefits that threat modeling provides outside of each stage's deliverables.

Again, threat modeling via PASTA is possible in nearly all scenarios except for when there is no executive sponsorship of its process and produced artifacts. The reason for this is that the deliverables produced by the PASTA approach are intended to be also socialized with senior executives.

Threat Modeling Methodologies: A Quick Comparative Look

A quick reminder that the application threat modeling that will be depicted in this chapter will revolve around a risk-centric approach. Nothing is actually lost in terms of steps, terminology, or even artifacts produced, it is just that PASTA prefaces many of the same activities around DFDs, building attack trees, threat enumeration, with some valuable context that makes that overall threat analysis to much more sophisticated than simply finding security weaknesses or application development inefficiencies, but discovering all of the aforementioned with the proper context and applying security commensurate to the subject application's importance to the organization. Security- or software-centric approaches to threat modeling cannot derive risk values *to the degree* that an asset- or risk-based methodology can deliver. Our desire to focus on a risk-based approach stems from the key principle that risk ultimately needs to be elevated back to the business; regardless of technical, security, or nonintrinsic business characteristics, risk needs to be effectively mapped, socialized, and accepted by information owners from the business unit that governs the application or system environment. Ultimately, technologists need to recognize that sponsorship of any software/system development life cycle or security program within an organization is in support of the business and its objectives. Software-centric or security-centric objectives that translate and elevate technical risk findings to only a developer, engineer, or manager will, in essence, not effectively communicate risk beyond that of a technical nature.

Before Starting Prior to diving into the application threat modeling methodology, we will address some planning prerequisites that have come from applying PASTA in large-size and mid-size enterprises. These prerequisites will help to organize the people, processes, technology, and third-party groups that carry an integral role in the PASTA framework.

As with any process function, readiness may be as just as important as execution. Figure 6.1 provides a brief but important checklist to review prior to adopting and executing the proposed PASTA threat modeling methodology. This checklist forces an organization to address key questions during each of the phases as they will greatly impact the success when considering adoption and use of threat modeling techniques as reflected by the PASTA methodology.

Sponsorship and Support

If you have been to a security conference of any type, from BlackHat to RSA, the message of obtaining executive sponsorship for security efforts is timeless. The message bears repeating: if you are going to launch an effective, repeatable threat modeling process within your organization of any size, you had better make sure that you have senior management's support and understanding. In order to make this less of a pain to sell, individuals will want to hone in on the following value points:

1. Threat modeling via PASTA allows greater cohesiveness among security groups in operations, governance, architecture, and development.
2. PASTA allows money and time savings by incorporating security governance at the inception of development efforts, thereby reducing compliance gaps, audit findings, and risk issues – all that warrant remediation management and exception or waiver management workflows.

Sponsorship and Support

Identify executives across swim lanes executive sponsorship	Know resource & time restraints from groups for better commitment	Establish close relationship w/ risk & business leaders for contextual use	Involve 3rd party service providers (Data Centers, Cloud Service Providers)

Maturity

Select a maturity model to track performance of threat modeling activities	List what enterprise/ department level processes will be leveraged	Identify technology that is leveraged for any threat model	Identify where weakest process areas are beforehand

Awareness and Communication

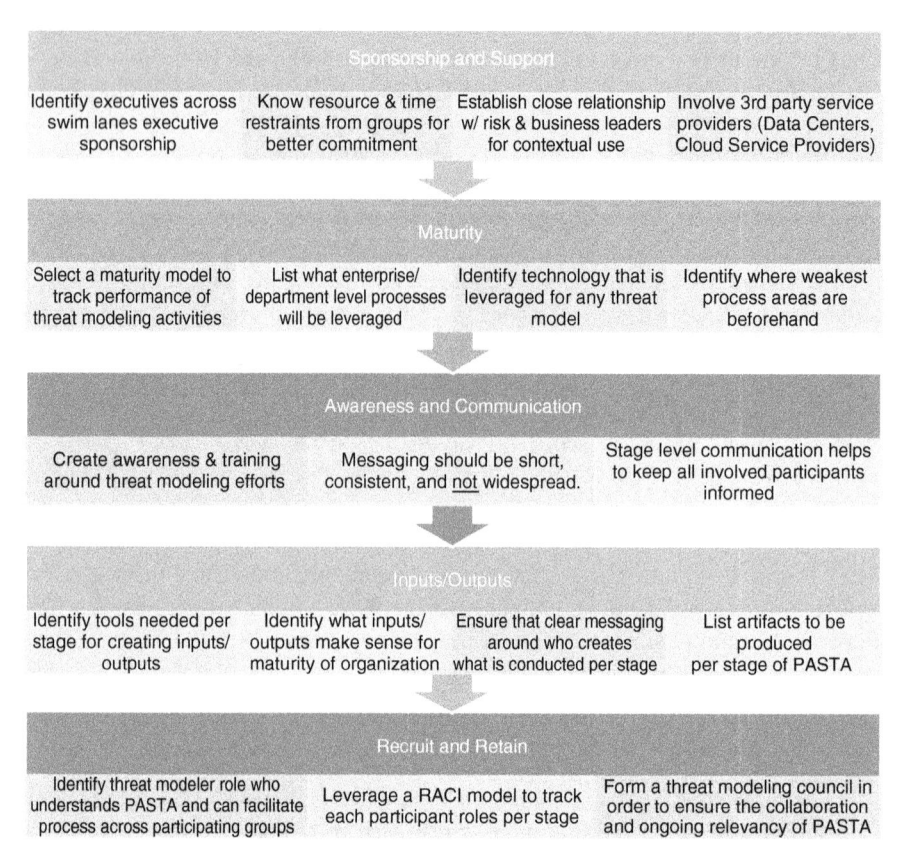

Create awareness & training around threat modeling efforts	Messaging should be short, consistent, and not widespread.	Stage level communication helps to keep all involved participants informed

Inputs/Outputs

Identify tools needed per stage for creating inputs/ outputs	Identify what inputs/ outputs make sense for maturity of organization	Ensure that clear messaging around who creates what is conducted per stage	List artifacts to be produced per stage of PASTA

Recruit and Retain

Identify threat modeler role who understands PASTA and can facilitate process across participating groups	Leverage a RACI model to track each participant roles per stage	Form a threat modeling council in order to ensure the collaboration and ongoing relevancy of PASTA

Figure 6.1 Impacting Factors Across PASTA: A Checklist for Success

3. Threat modeling with PASTA will foster greater understanding of likely attack sources. Current efforts may simply take prefabricated attack scripts from security solutions without truly understanding how those attacks are really addressing security weaknesses in their software or vendor software. If a company is serious about security and mitigating the advanced threats that continuously approach, a shift in approach and technique is warranted.
4. PASTA takes security principles to both business and IT groups as part of their normal workflow of the SDLC process, thereby introducing a type of security on-the-job training that serves as an effective awareness vehicle. Developers, QA, Network Engineers, and System Administrators are now better able to understand specifically how inaction in corrective security measures can introduce risks to the application and the data it manages.
5. PASTA makes things less adversarial in terms of addressing security risk mitigation. It is no longer an "us" versus "them" mentality. More collaborative, more warm, and fuzzy – overall, an HR love story in the making.

Culture, time, and availability of human resources and tools will obviously be a large determinant as to whether or not threat modeling of any flavor is adopted. Having consulted on the topic to a large and disparate population of companies and government entities, there is no common profile where threat modeling is well received. Large companies have different vantage points than smaller companies. Larger organizations will have the depth in resources to address some of the stages in PASTA that relate to objective building, security/technology governance, and risk analysis, while smaller organizations are less likely to be organized in those areas. They, however, will be more nimble in applying proper application decomposition exercises, threat analysis, and vulnerability/attack mapping than their larger Fortune 500 counterparts. In the end, as with any process, it will take time. During that time, sponsorship is the key as well as measuring the execution PASTA over time. Metrics will ultimately determine how effectively threat modeling serves the selected application environments as well as the overall enterprise.

Maturity

The maturity of processes and controls, leveraged by any threat modeling methodology (i.e. – Architecture, Software Development), will affect the success of PASTA. Immature processes should not negate the adoption of PASTA, but instead force the use of a maturity model in conjunction with the threat modeling methodology. In some cases, immature controls enable application threat modeling to become adopted easier since many of the processes could be developed in support of PASTA as the iterative methodology is carried out. This all depends on the level of resources available as well as the perception and executive support.

Awareness

No process or technology, aimed for the benefit of a wide audience, is successfully carried out or implemented in the shadows without proper communication. In too many instances, security artifacts become shelf-ware because they are developed and executed in a vacuum. For this reason, awareness efforts around threat modeling should take place before, during, and after the threat modeling process. The overall message should be directed to both participants and benefactors of the application threat modeling process. Some may scoff at this idea, but the reality is that the lack of communication in InfoSec has been the downfall of many security efforts. Most often, recipients of the communication around threat modeling efforts will appreciate their inclusion in this effort and be pleased to know that the objective revolves around preserving the business objectives for the application environment. Last, properly communicating application threat modeling procedures will ultimately lead to a greater understanding of what is expected regarding remediation patterns against the application environment.

In the spirit of launching effective awareness efforts around application threat modeling, simplicity and clarity of message is critical. There are many communication efforts that announce InfoSec efforts regularly. The announcement of a new Policy or Standard, changes to Access Control protocols, or implementation of new identity management software are a few examples that have benefited from centralized and formal communication. Application threat modeling, however, works best with quaint, short, clear messages delivered by the threat modeler. Regardless of approach, the message should be confined to those who will partake in the threat modeling exercises as well as those who will benefit from the varied artifacts and deliverables to be produced.

Clarity around threat modeling's taxonomy of terms or vernacular has been sabotaged by early adopters or security professionals that have distorted many of the definitions and usage. There is an enormous amount of misuse. Status quo security professionals who find themselves seeking to use the latest term or security colloquiums have often equated other security disciplines in security (i.e. - pen testing, static analysis, application risk assessments, etc.) to threat modeling. This exemplifies the need for greater awareness on what is meant by the term and associated terms and use of its vocabulary.

Communication around each PASTA stage needs to be met with clear timeliness and aligned to milestones for each stage of the PASTA threat modeling methodology. Embellishing simple project management principles for awareness efforts will help maintain a fluid communication plan absent of last-minute reminders supporting tasks. For example, last-minute communication of threat modeling efforts may obviously jeopardize the participation of much needed SMEs. With this in mind, timely communication of threat modeling efforts, across various stages of the methodology, will ensure everyone's knowledge on both the upcoming threat modeling process and remediation patterns that are manifested by one or more deliverables.

Inputs/Outputs of the PASTA Process

The ingredients for making great PASTA boil down to people, information sources, and artifacts to be created. They comprise the essential inputs/outputs for an effective threat modeling methodology. This section quickly addresses each, with even further detail to be provided within each phase of the PASTA methodology for threat modeling.

People as Inputs   People may be the most important input to consider when embarking on threat modeling efforts for your application environments. Do you have the right people in place? If not, can you leverage your security partners at various stages of the PASTA methodology in order to deliver where you may not be able to internally? These types of questions are important to answer prior to embarking on any application threat model methodology.

Behind any process is a leader or governing group. In this case, application threat modeling does require a figurehead more than a group, as a large number of figureheads can introduce dysfunction when creating a single threat model for an application environment. The threat modeler's primary function is to sustain a holistic oversight of the subject application environment in order to provide a threat model based on realistic and probable attack scenarios that could jeopardize the application environment in question. The threat modeler is well versed across multiple functional

RISK-CENTRIC THREAT MODELING 323

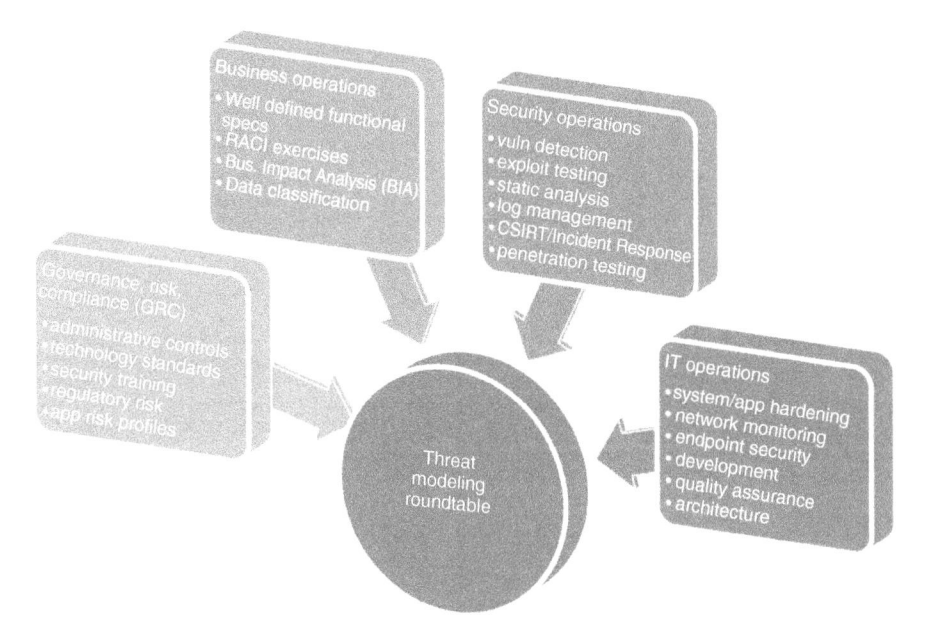

Figure 6.2 Threat Modeling Team Selection

areas in which the application environment operates (development language, system level, networking, client software, mobile technologies) or wherever the application environment extends. The threat modeler may add one or two other individuals to assist during the execution of the threat modeling process, particularly in areas where technical deficiencies may exist. Given that threat modeling encompasses the following organizational layers, it is preferred that the threat modeler seek representation from each one of the areas depicted in Figure 6.2 in order to establish a temporary committee around the threat modeling efforts.

Establishing an ambassador-like representation during the threat modeling process allows greater facilitation and funneling of ideas and feedback received during the threat modeling process. Initially, the participation of such ambassadors will entail a level of familiarity that would need to be established. Representatives from each of these groups will need to be trained mostly on the purpose and understand the ultimate goal of the threat modeling process, based on the overall approach to be used (asset based, software centric, or security centric). Representatives from each of these aforementioned areas will be used and leveraged at varying times of the threat modeling process but must be included on the threat model's development and maturity during the overall process.

The newly formed threat modeling team must be engaged with a strong sense of collaboration. It should be mentioned that the term "team" is used very loosely. It can mean a union of technology, security, and business professionals and does not necessarily have to be a formal process or event. This may seem to bear no mentioning in a security book, but the lack of tact in communication has been a sharp thorn to other security processes and for threat modeling to work, it must adhere to its

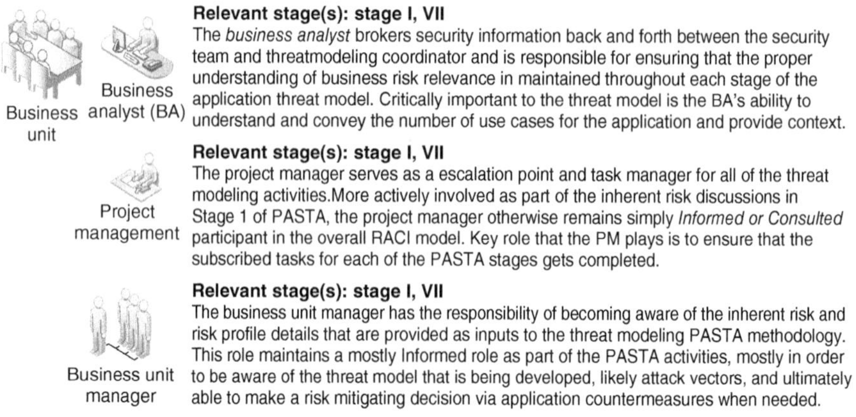

Relevant stage(s): stage I, VII

The *business analyst* brokers security information back and forth between the security team and threatmodeling coordinator and is responsible for ensuring that the proper understanding of business risk relevance in maintained throughout each stage of the application threat model. Critically important to the threat model is the BA's ability to understand and convey the number of use cases for the application and provide context.

Business analyst (BA) unit

Relevant stage(s): stage I, VII

The project manager serves as a escalation point and task manager for all of the threat modeling activities. More actively involved as part of the inherent risk discussions in Stage 1 of PASTA, the project manager otherwise remains simply *Informed or Consulted* participant in the overall RACI model. Key role that the PM plays is to ensure that the subscribed tasks for each of the PASTA stages gets completed.

Project management

Relevant stage(s): stage I, VII

The business unit manager has the responsibility of becoming aware of the inherent risk and risk profile details that are provided as inputs to the threat modeling PASTA methodology. This role maintains a mostly Informed role as part of the PASTA activities, mostly in order to be aware of the threat model that is being developed, likely attack vectors, and ultimately able to make a risk mitigating decision via application countermeasures when needed.

Business unit manager

Figure 6.3 Business Cross Section of a Threat Modeling Team

natural framework for collaboration to take place. Unified by identifying threats and mapping out probabilities and impact, the threat modeling team will ultimately seek risk mitigation for the defined application environment to preserve agreed upon business objectives. As part of this effort, a demographic breakdown of threat modeling participants is depicted in Figure 6.3 (see also Figures 6.4–6.6).

These prior illustrations are only a subset of the various possibilities for a heterogeneous representation of a threat modeling team. Other groups not represented may include key members of third-party diverse representation from each of the four groups. In some cases, an internal pen tester from the Security Ops group may be absent, in which case an alternative member from the group, say a web application security tester, may be brought in for depicting attack patterns under *Stage VI: Attack Tree Modeling*. Obviously, their strengths in identifying attack vectors and misuse cases will surround web-based environments or those that support http/https protocols. As a result, the threat modeler will have to compensate for shortcomings in identifying network-based or even host-based misuse cases or attack patterns. Overall, it is important for the threat modeler to identify where gaps in expertise may exist so that he/she can provide gap-fill level testing to those that would typically be covered by a pen tester. In this scenario, the threat modeler would have to arrange for vulnerability assessments, followed by penetration tests on discovered vulnerabilities for areas in which the web application security specialist would not cover with their level of testing. In doing so, those efforts, combined with the testing efforts performed by the web application security specialist, would reflect greater coverage across multiple levels of the ISO model.[1]

Ideally, the threat modeler will have access to security and IT professionals who have the greatest level of proficiency in niche areas encompassed by the stage of the application threat model (e.g. static analysis for PHP web applications, assessing middleware or web proxies). In the instances where these resources are not available

---

[1] ISO model encompasses the Physical, Data, Network, Transport, Session, Presentation, Application layer of network architecture.

Relevant stage(s): stage II, III, IV, VII

As a holistic overseer to a given application, the architect plays a pivotal role in application threat modeling by seeing how attack branches of the threat model unfold to reveal viable attack patterns, supportive vulnerabilities, target actors & affected application components. Having a 1,000 foot understanding of the application, the architect is able to see how and where countermeasures are weakest across an application's footprint. Based upon time, effort, and resources, the architect can work with network engineers, developers, and product managers to implement appropriate preventative, detective, and reactive countermeasures that affect access control, validation checks, network ingress/egress, authentication, audit trail, and encryption use.

Architect

Relevant stage(s): stage I, II, III, IV, VII

The developer is one of the key audience member in threat modeling. Across the seven stages, the developer will contribute in various ways. Developers will help to identify application related components, particularly those that are software based (Stage II). During Application Decomposition (Stage III), developers can map data flows among application components from the prior stage, Technology Scoping (Stage II). Where application developers have developed or contribute to existing application log engines, events within such logs can provide for contextual based threat intelligence (Stage IV). Last, developers will ultimately be responsible for application based countermeasures that reduce any level of residual risk identified by the threat model (Stage VII), so their role as an *Informed* player becomes important.

Developer

Relevant stage(s): stage II, III, IV, VII

The systems engineer will be savant to the system/ platform components that are relevant for the application threat model (Stage II). As such, they would also be well positioned to apply hardening techniques at the system level at this stage. The systems engineer would also be helpful in mapping any data flows that interact with the system or database server stack (Stage III), thereby contributing to the Application Decomposition discussion and DFD creation activities. Threat intel may also be needed from in-scope systems, therefore, they play a *Consulted* role under Threat Analysis (Stage IV). Last, countermeasures against the residual risk areas may come from system hardening techniques, therefore, Systems Engineers will be key during this stage.

Systems Enginee- OR SysAdmin

IT operations

Figure 6.4 IT Operations Cross Section of a Threat Modeling Team

325

Relevant stage(s): stage II, III, IV, VII

Network engineers can identify network assets, protocols, authentication controls, and overall network services that are being allowed across the system environment (Stage II). Within the Technology Scope stage, the network engineer can provide 'blind threat modeling' mitigation via the use of applying network governance standards that could harden the network related infrastructure supporting the application. Network engineers can also assist during the Application Decomposition (Stage III), especially as it relates to threat modeling for administrative use cases and defining network protocol use for APIs. Similarly, their knowledge of network log solutions, particularly those at an enterprise level make the network engineer an important Consulted or even Accountable role under Threat Analysis, (Stage IV). During this stage, the network engineer can help harvest relevant network logs from the scope of network components as well as from any Security Incident Event Monitoring (SEIM) solution. Last, network engineers may be involved under Stage VII in order to apply possible mitigation techniques at the network level.

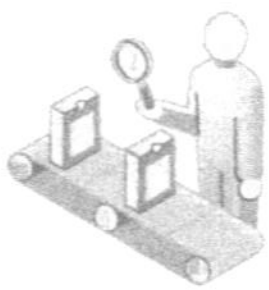

Relevant stage(s): stage I, II, V, VI

The QA tester will play an informed role across multiple stages since their testing requires a comprehensive understanding of the application environment. First, the use cases supported by the application (Stage I) as well as the employed application components (stage II) which may undergo functional testing. Across these two stages, the QA tester serves as an Informed party. Their role can become a bit more involved if their functional testing is also accompanied by security testing. If executing as a security testing entity, the QA Tester can validate the presence of software vulnerabilities and their exploitation levels (Stages V & VI).

Relevant stage(s): stage I, II, III, IV

Access Control groups are highly useful during Stages I and II by the fact that they can provide insight to application use cases that related to application support, remote administration, account provisioning/ de-provisioning. Also, under Stage II, Access Control technology components supporting access control functions for the application could be enumerated as part of a list of application countermeasures (e.g. – IdM, AD, ADFS, AD Proxy, LDAP, RADIUS, TACACS+). API calls to these components can be depicted during the Application Decomposition stage and members from these groups would only be suggested to maintain a *Consulted* role. A final piece of critical importance would be the access control violations across all access control logs (network, database, application, middleware, etc.) which would provide valuable threat intelligence in stage IV of the PASTA process.

Network Engineer

QA Tester

Support ops / access control

Figure 6.4 (*Continued*)

Relevant stage(s): stage IV, V

Security operation groups fulfill an array of different tasks across an enterprise. One of which is reviewing alerts, logs, and other types of technology related incidents. These functions serve a wealth of information related to threat intelligence. Sourcing this type of data during the Threat Analysis stage of the PASTA methodology can help map security events to threat patterns. Security engineers can substantiate or even dispel evidence surrounding threat scenarios depicted under the Threat Analysis stage. Separate to managing various logging events and alerts, security engineers execute multiple different scan types across an enterprise. Configuration scans, vulnerability scans, source code audits, network discovery scans are just a few types of key scans that lend to producing valuable information for a risk centric threat model. In general, scan results produced by this group provides insight to the nature of vulnerabilities or misconfigurations that affect the application scope of components. Security engineers can perform targeted scans against the scope of application components under the Vulnerability Analysis (Stage V) phase of the PASTA process. The various types of scans will identify initial flaws in the application's security model that can be mapped to the attack tree as a branch to a asset component The supporting attack tree illustrates how identified threats could be viable beginnings of legitimizing threat possibilities.

Relevant stage(s): stage VI

Building from targeted vulnerability scans from Stage V, a pen testing group will look to definitively prove the possibility for exploitation of identified flaws in coding, implementation, configuration, etc. Pen testers may actually be within the same Security Operations group, however, they are often times a third party that may routinely pen test a series of applications for a client organization. Inclusion of pen tests in the threat modeling processes seeks to qualify the viability of exploitation for discovered flaws from Stage V. If vulnerabilities become exploitable, both component weakness and the attack pattern(s) that were able to subjugate them now become relevant factors of residual risk calculations. Even if tested components do not become exploited during a pen test, the result doesn't necessarily mean that the that the overall exploitability of the component is negligible and/or the residual risk calculation is lessened. The use of pen testers as part of the threat modeling process provides an invaluable 'smoking gun' to both developers and architects who may not have understood the manner in which vulnerabilities translated into exploitable risks.

Figure 6.5 Security Operations Cross Section of a Threat Modeling Team

Relevant stage(s): stage IV
Incident response plays a key role in Stage IV: Threat Analysis as IR/CERT teams can provide historical context to historical attacks that correlate to the application environment based on variables such as business type, data type, data worth, accessibility (direct/indirect), user base, black market worth/use of data. Introduces attack profiling capabilities to threat model and supports probability values of risk formula in Stage VII: Risk and Impact Analysis.

Incident handler

Relevant stage(s): stage IV, V, VI
Managed Security Service vendors or other vendors charged with conducting periodic red team exercises (tactical social engineering, physical intrusion, covert ops exercises for illicit access and data compromise) may be incorporated in the threat analysis for a given application environment in order to identify weak physical/logical controls based upon prior assessments, knowledge of the environment, and comparable application environments that they have assessed.

Managed security provider

Figure 6.5 (*Continued*)

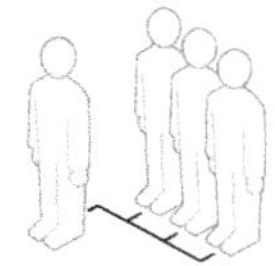

Governance, risk, compliance

Relevant stage(s): stage I, II, & VII

CSO and CISO roles are the figureheads to any security program, therefore, their influence across PASTA's threat modeling stages are always at an *Informed* level. Their roles are especially relevant however in potentially influencing what governance standards get promoted earlier in an SDLC process. Under the Define Business Objectives and Technology Scoping stages, the CSO/ CISO, and particularly the ISO have the ability to influence the adoption and use of technology standards as a form of blind threat modeling. In doing so, this allows the PASTA process to achieve yet another point of integration to legacy efforts in security governance. Similarly in Stage VII, these governance members carry an Informed role around residual risk issues that have been identified and presented back to a BU.

CISO/ CSO/ ISO

Relevant stage(s): stage I, II, & VII

Risk centric threat modeling doesn't forego compliance risks. Those risks are real and can be preemptively addressed by factoring in regulatory requirements around data security, encryption, etc. earlier within the SDLC process. Similar to the influence that Security Governance leaders (CISO, CSO, ISO) have on security adoption, compliance professionals have the ability to relay impactful regulatory restraints that could affect BU level goals for a product or application. Therefore, Stage I and II are equally relevant to these threat modeling participants. Equally, their Informed roles during Stage VII provide Compliance group members with the ability to maintain awareness on what residual risk levels can equate to regulatory compliance risks, when mapped back to their respective control frameworks.

Compliance

Relevant stage(s): stage I & VII

Risk assessors and managers are involved in stage I: Define Business Objectives, where they may incorporate relevant prior risk findings in order to factor in an application risk profile that should be addressed earlier in the SDLC process. This risk profile depicts inherent risk issues that affect the security of the application, thereby possibly affecting the obtainment of defined business objectives for the application. Also involved in stage VII: Risk and Impact Analysis, risk professionals will help to quantify the residual risk issues that extend beyond the technical risk issues identified across the various PASTA stages.

Risk assessors

Figure 6.6 GRC Cross Section of a Threat Modeling Team

for tasks deemed to be in their line of expertise, the threat modeler ultimately has to decide how those efforts are to be continued, if at all (e.g. by the threat modeler or another SME). Time delays as well as the criticality of fulfilling test cases in the areas associated with unavailable SMEs need to be considered against the fulfillment of the threat modeling objective.

Depth of experience and a comprehensive background in security operations and IT is reiterated by the aforementioned scenario where SMEs may not be always at hand. Since exploiting identified vulnerabilities is critical to the risk analysis in that it provides credibility to the probability coefficients within the risk equation, the threat modeler must elect how and when to proceed when a complete threat modeling team is not able to contribute, particularly in areas that improve the overall risk analysis. Devoid of this ability, the risk analysis under a risk-based approach to threat modeling is weakened, as is the risk message conveyed back to the business. Other scenarios where SMEs are absent from the threat modeling team or group may prove less damaging to risk analytics.

It should go without saying that there will be much smaller organizations that do not have the depth of resources that other larger organizations have to achieve these dynamic and synergistic teams. In such cases, the threat modeler must judiciously select and recruit a team that would work and not compromise the job functions of those individuals. The lack of resources across these operational areas should not dissuade the application threat modeling efforts from commencing. More information on how to apply application threat modeling for smaller organizations will be addressed at the end of this chapter.

In the previous figure (Cross Section of a Threat Modeling Team), organizational members (in the middle column) are either loosely or closely associated to defined groups (on the left). An example may be Information Security Officers (ISOs) that are part of GRC efforts on a day-to-day basis. These recruits to the threat modeling process provide additional expertise around specific subject areas at varying phases of the PASTA threat modeling methodology. Building upon this example, an ISO may provide invaluable information on the risk analysis of an application environment during the threat analysis or risk analysis phase. Given the ISO's interaction with the business unit sponsoring the application, he/she may have a strong knowledge of regulatory, customer, or vendor-based considerations that should be accounted for, whether they are technical or nontechnical. For example, vendor-based support that implies use of nonstandard technologies within the application domain may need to be articulated and addressed in the data flow diagramming efforts or application decomposition talks, where applicable. Conversely, in regard to the nontechnical realm, the ISO may raise relevant, regulatory issues around data privacy that limit the manner in which functional requirements are implemented during the design or requirements phases of the SDLC. This latter example is a slight departure from security-centric or software-centric approaches, however, inclusive to the goals of identifying various risk types in a risk-centric approach.

Regardless of the apparent dependency that the threat modeler has on the various SMEs that may be brought into the application threat modeling process, the threat modeler himself/herself must also be well informed of the topics brought forth by their SMEs so that they do not simply appear as a facilitator for a process that is self-guided by a series of SMEs. This reiterates the need for a well-rounded and experienced security professional to take charge of threat modeling efforts. Every organization is different so while in some places this could be a security professional, it other places it may be the architect, a PM, or even a developer who has some security background. Given that PASTA fosters more of a collaborative approach, the focus is less on this "threat modeler" role than the interoperability of all related members doing their part across each stage.

Ultimately, the members recruited to support various phases and areas of the PASTA threat modeling methodology only reinforce varying principles that support the type of approach that was selected. For example, under a software-centric approach, the role of the business analyst during the requirements phase of the SDLC will vary compared to that of a risk- or asset-centric approach to threat modeling. The software-centric approach will primarily call for the business analysts' depiction of functional requirements around the software. This provides a bare bones approach for sustaining code quality focused objectives that encase continuity, scalability, and efficiency. Separately, the security-centric approach seeks for the protection of these aforementioned objectives from security threats that include privilege escalation, information leakage, impersonation attacks, and so on.

The asset- or risk-centric approach may demand more from the business analyst in terms of conveying information that extends beyond the functional requirements for the application. The threat modeler may question the business analyst about operational uses of the existing or intended application in order to further refine the context understanding around business impact. This in turn enhances the overall risk analysis. This information would be sought in addition to their analysis of articulating functional requirements for the application. Another example (under the risk-centric approach) may be the threat modeler's interest in understanding the human use of the application environment once it is deployed into production. The user base (as a pool of application actors) is important for the threat modeler to identify in order to determine who may ultimately exert abuse cases in the threat model. For both human and nonhuman actors, this allows the threat modeler to qualify risks related to collusion, data theft, or malware proliferation, rogue API requests, privilege escalation, injection-based attacks and much more. This risk analysis extends beyond the exercises of the software- and security-centric approaches. This does not translate to PASTA being a more comprehensive threat modeling methodology but one that is focused with a different end goal – residual risk mitigation.

Tools

In terms of leveraging a tool that acts like a centerpiece to the threat modeling activities, there are several. Since Microsoft's approach to threat modeling are already encompassed within the PASTA threat modeling methodology, many of their tools serve as an excellent reference and documentation artifact for fulfilling PASTA's stages III–VI (inclusive). A good resource for conducting security-centric-based approaches to application threat modeling is the Threat Analysis and Modeling

(TAM) by Microsoft. Beta version 3.0 was released in the summer of 2009 and is a good supporting solution to capture many of the threat modeling variables such as actors, permissions (privileges), assets, vulnerabilities, and more. A software side-dish for software-centric threat modeling efforts is also provided by Microsoft and is geared toward both software developers and security professionals. The Microsoft SDL Threat Modeling tool focuses more on design flaws in the software development process and depicts these flaws in both security and nonsecurity contexts. For more information around threat modeling efforts sponsored by Microsoft, please visit their threat modeling blog at http://blogs.msdn.com/b/threatmodeling. Although distinct, much of the steps presented by these threat modeling approaches are already performed in PASTA's stages III–VI, inclusive. The key difference is that PASTA's focus is around threat mitigation to components that introduces material business risk. This is one key reason for which PASTA's threat modeling methodology encompasses more than just developers or architects since other roles can even provide greater contextual understanding of how functional specifications serve a business goal, not to mention on the impact sustained by identified technical risks. MyAppSecurity's Threat Modeler is building greater functionality to support the PASTA framework and is a free and intuitive threat modeling solution that can be used to simply capture many of the inputs for each stage.

Process and People

Multiple processes are impacted and leveraged as part of any threat modeling methodology. It should be stated that by "process" we are referring to security or IT processes that are occasionally found across various organizations. This includes (but is not limited to) IT, Support Operations, key third-party vendors, Legal, Executive Management, Human Resources, Facilities management and more. Some of these processes have been reflected in the aforementioned diagrams. Security Governance, Security Assurance, Security Operations are just a few major subsets of Information Security programs that are commonly found across various companies today. Most organizations do not have these groups uniquely staffed and equipped in the nonenterprise space. In most cases, security is fortunate enough to have a figurehead such as a CISO. Given this reality, it is foolhardy to expect that a unique group or individual be devoted to threat modeling efforts. Not only is this costly, it proceeds to follow in the same footsteps where isolated security groups reach nothing more than an adversarial relationship with internal colleagues in IT, Development, and the BU.

As shown in recent illustrations, several processes are leveraged by each stage of the PASTA methodology. Previously referenced groups and their corresponding processes are not generally foreign to most large enterprises, although they may be absent, developing, or maturing within smaller organizations. In those cases, companies will have to decide whether they can simply proceed with implementing PASTA while developing or further maturing those areas that require additional resources, refinement of process/deliverables, and solutions. Additionally, the threat analysis will also provide direction in terms of identifying which groups will be more important to leverage in both the short and long run. For example, a good sense that targeted attacks or even recon efforts have been taking place across business groups may automatically create a need to interact more with those groups. Signs of prior reconnaissance efforts around a guarded facility may warrant the need to include facilities management officials as part of the threat modeling activities for each stage.

A list of enterprise processes (focused primarily around security and technology) that heavily influence various stages of PASTA are referenced subsequently and correlated to each stage (see Table 6.1).

As shown in Table 6.1, a multitude of enterprise processes should be injected into the threat modeling process in order to sustain the integrity of the overall model. This will require various information inputs as well as generated outputs. Threat modeling using PASTA demonstrates the collaborative approach achieved across various enterprise resources. Although threat modeling is not something that every company may embark on, it should not be because of the lack of resources, since the threat modeling process should be measured and matured over time. Despite the fact that larger enterprises may have an advantage over smaller companies in terms of resources, smaller organizations are able to adopt and produce very powerful threat models simply via their quicker ability to mobilize people and decision making. During various consulting engagements, it has been very apparent which companies were threat modeling capable and which were not. In several instances, the smaller organizations performed application decomposition exercises, CRUD role and privilege assignments, identified attack sectors, and more. While they excelled in these areas, they had shortcomings in areas like governance, where larger organizations were a bit more mature. Smaller organizations may have the advantage of diving into stages III and IV (Application Decomposition and Threat Analysis, respectively) simply because the development teams are generally much smaller. Larger organizations may have tougher political hurdles to jump over within these stages as collaboration among development groups moves much slower due to the size of the application development group. Conversely, the governance groups of larger enterprise environments are generally more sophisticated in order to create a strong foundation of the PASTA steps that encompass stages I, II, and VII. This is largely because these larger groups have a more experienced and sophisticated process around Governance, Risk, and Compliance.

The purpose of Table 6.1 is to intersect and align various IT, Governance, and other enterprise-related areas with specific PASTA threat modeling methodology stages. The following section will perform a hypothetical walk-through of the various PASTA application threat modeling methodology stages in order to clearly define the steps and actions that should be taken, while simultaneously considering possible challenges and variants that a threat modeler or team may witness in their own respective environments. This next section will also provide detailed specifics on what deliverables need to be produced as artifacts or inputs to other phases across the PASTA methodology.

TABLE 6.1 Enterprise Process Mapping to PASTA Threat Modeling Methodology

Process	PASTA Stage Mapping	Reasoning
IT governance	Stage I (Define Objectives), Stage II (Technical Scope)	Business objectives need to understand what tech/security governance applies to supporting their business objectives. Additionally, maturity modeling can be applied as a way to allow each stage of the application modeling methodology to grow. BSIMM (Building Security-In Maturity Modeling), SAMM (Software Assurance Maturity Modeling), and OpenSAMM could be applied as part of this governance effort for stage.
Security governance	Stages I and II (Define Objectives and Technical Scope).	Same as aforementioned but in a security context of preserving the business objectives via confidentiality, integrity, and availability control measures.
Compliance	Stage I (Define Objectives). Neglecting regulatory issues may adversely impact the realization of business objectives, which have to be incorporated into the threat model's risk-based approach	Business needs to understand how regulatory factors may affect the functional design/requirements from business objectives.
Security awareness	All stages are affected by security awareness. Security lessons are informally introduced/ reiterated to threat modeling audience members	Each phase portrays lessons of security awareness, but acted out in a collaborative effort to secure the subject application environment.
Risk assessments (RA)	Stage I (Define Objectives), Stage II (Technical Scope), Stage VII (Risk and Impact Analysis)	RAs done on similar environments internally may create inherent risk profiles for the (a) overall suite of use cases for the app and (b) inherent risks associated with the types of technologies (software/hardware) to be used in fulfillment of business objectives and functional requirements. Risk assessments can also leverage completed threat models to bolster the subsequent risk analysis provided by future risk assessments of the same application environment.

Business impact assessments (BIAs)	Stage VII (Risk and Impact Analysis).	BIAs are enterprise deliverables produced in order to determine the financial and business impact of applications to the business. It helps to leverage this deliverable when creating a risk synopsis for the application environment.
Privacy impact analysis(es)	Stage I (Define Objectives)	Privacy impact assessments (PIAs) conducted against the application environment, prior models/version, or similar versions of the software architecture will ultimately help shape technical requirements and design countermeasures that should be in place to protect against threats related to data leakage.
Vulnerability assessments	Stage V (Vulnerability and Weakness Enumeration)	Vulnerabilities from common solutions can be paired with attack patterns as part of the attack tree build-out. False positives are excluded from the integrated analysis.
Static analysis	Stage V (Vulnerability and Weakness Enumeration)	Coding flaws and weaknesses in software design are detected as part of the subject application environment and labeled as nodes/branches of the attack tree that correlate to feasible attacks.
Dynamic application analysis	Stage V (Vulnerability and Weakness Enumeration)	Vulnerable responses from the application's interpreter are captured and aligned to branches on the attack tree as vulnerabilities that could be exploited as an attack.
Red team exercises/social engineering	Stage V (Vulnerability and Weakness Enumeration), Stage VI (Attack Modeling)	Supportive processes to the application environment could be compromised via social engineering techniques, thereby testing the "human factor" becomes just as important as defending the logical application/network testing.
Software/security architectural	Stage III (Application Decomposition), Stage V (Vulnerability and Weakness Enumeration)	Define application entry/exit points, identify application actors, software/hardware assets, information assets (configuration files, relational databases, flat files), data calls/responses (APIs), trust boundaries, system/software services, compiled libraries, utilized executables/binaries, data sources, technical (functional/security) requirements, and anything that sustains the application architecture, which may in turn be leveraged as an attack vector.

(*continued*)

335

TABLE 6.1 (Continued)

Process	PASTA Stage Mapping	Reasoning
Project management	All stages, however Stage I (Define Objectives) is key to defining strong project governance	Project management must encompass security objectives throughout the threat modeling methodology. One of the project objectives (for an asset-centric approach) is to identify residual risk for the application environment.
Incident management	Stage IV (Threat Analysis)	During the process of identifying possible threats, incident management may provide the threat modeling team with historical incident response events from aggregate infrastructure alerts or comparable environments in order to help define or substantiate a threat analysis.
Network/security operations	Stage IV (Threat Analysis)	Similar to Incident Management, NOCs/SOCs monitor various events across the network that could help substantiate the threat analysis.
Security partners/managed security	Stage IV (Threat Analysis, Stage V (Vulnerability and Weakness Enumeration), Stage VI (Attack Modeling)	Security vendors and managed security service providers can actually conduct various threat modeling methodology stages for organizations that have weak maturity levels with these stages. Security partners and managed security providers can manage attack-related libraries, vulnerabilities databases/findings, as well as help refine threat analysis with correlative analysis or monitored threats that are internally or externally managed by the environment.
Software development	Stage I (Define Objectives)	All stages of any given software development methodology have some degree of relationship to the PASTA threat modeling methodology. Specific to software development, stage I helps to ensure that development receives security requirements to adhere to when building out their application environment.
Quality assurance	Stage VI (Attack Modeling)	Security testing is delivered to the application using a robust attack library that can be applied against the newly released code build. Security tests are based on understood threats contained from the threat model.
System administration	Stage II (Technical Scope)	System administrators, or those who are charged with properly implementing a system build, will be able to leverage the technical security requirements revealed under stage II.

RISK-CENTRIC THREAT MODELING   337

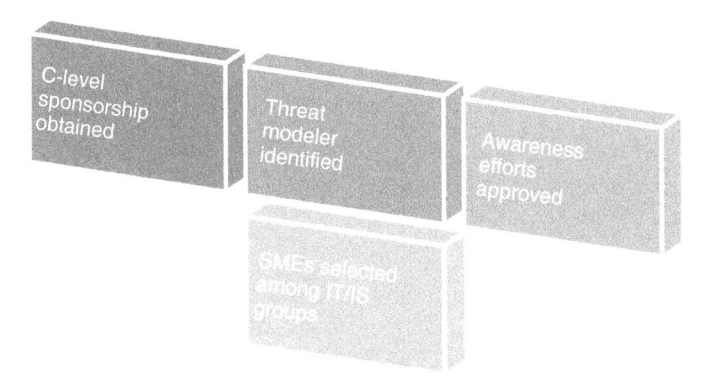

Figure 6.7   Givens Before PASTA Walk-Through

The following stages of the PASTA threat modeling methodology are depicted in the context of an application under development and governed by a Waterfall SDLC. The actions defined under each stage assume the following givens prior to formally commencing the methodology (Figure 6.7).

Expected Outputs from PASTA   Across all of the stages to be covered in the subsequent sections, there will be many deliverables or artifacts produced from each of the stages produced from the PASTA methodology. Many of these artifacts are produced by some of the processes and resources previously mentioned as inputs. More detail on each type of artifact produced will be covered within each detailed stage of the application threat model methodology. Some of these artifacts are summarized in Table 6.2.

In the past few sections, we have looked at what inputs/outputs (in the form of artifacts or information sources) are needed for each stage of the PASTA threat modeling methodology. We have also looked at the necessary foundation of people, processes, and governance that should be in place for successful threat modeling to be sustainable. Specific to the people involved with PASTA, the following RACI (Responsible–Accountable–Consulted–Information) model has been provided to identify a generic, yet common list of enterprise roles that can be leveraged and customized by any organization looking to adopt PASTA as a threat modeling methodology. The proposed RACI diagram is found on the next page and addressed under each of the detailed stages that follow (Figure 6.8).

As shown in the aforementioned RACI model, most of the participants across the PASTA process are assigned a "Consulted" or "Informed" role. This helps to visualize how PASTA leverages existing roles in InfoSec that may carry out these functions. SMBs would most likely have the greatest challenges of not having all of these internal FTEs; however, accommodations can be made in order to customize PASTA's RACI model to be more adaptive to a reduced security workforce at an organization with varying resource restraints. The legend for the roles is on the right.

TABLE 6.2 Artifacts for Making PASTA

Stage	Inputs	Outputs
Define objectives	• Business Impact Analysis • Business Risk Impact Analysis • Business Requirements • Functional Requirements	• Description of the application functionality • List of business objectives • Business Impact Analysis 　○ Compliance Reqs (PCI/FFIEC, etc.)
Define technical scope	• Platform Standards • Network Standards • Architectural Schematics/ Network Diagrams • Software Configuration Standards • Third-Party Security SLAs	• High level, end-to-end view of the application architecture • Protocol enumeration support by technical scope • Enumerated asset list, by criticality and technology dependency • List of all network devices/appliances
Application decomposition	• Architecture diagrams/design documents • Sequence diagrams • Use cases • Users, roles, and permissions associated with use cases • Logical diagrams of requests/responses within application scope	• Data Flow Diagrams (DFDs) of the application scope • Use and abuse cases ranked by criticality • User's access control matrix with roles, and permissions/trust levels on data and transactions • List of assets and APIs • Map of use cases to actors/assets

Threat analysis	• Generic list of threat agents and motives, internal Security incidents (**SIRT**) report
	• Fraud detection report
	• Secure incident event monitoring (**SIEM**) reports
	• Application and server logs (syslogs)
	• Threat intelligence reports, alerts and feeds
		• Report of the most likely attack scenario-landscape that includes:
		  ○ Documentation of threat agents and their targets
		  ○ Documentation of threat agents and likely attacks vectors used
		  ○ Documentation of observed security incidents-events that relate to likely threats and historical attacks
		  ○ Reference to threat intelligence reports for likely attack scenarios

Vulnerability/Weakness mapping	• Library of threat trees mapping generic attacks to vulnerabilities • Documented attack scenarios (from threat analysis, stage IV) • Vulnerability reports for assets queried from the centralized vulnerability repository • Standards for vulnerability enumeration (MITRE CWE, CVE) • Standards for vulnerability scoring (CVSS, CWSS)	• Map of existing vulnerabilities to the nodes of a threat tree • Enumeration of these vulnerabilities using CVE-CWE Scoring of these using CVSS-CWSS • A list of attack scenarios, the applicable threats, and the vulnerabilities that these threats can exploit
Attack modeling	• Application technical scope-boundaries • Data flow diagrams • List of entry points and trust levels	• Application *attack surface* representation • *Attack tree* mapping to vulnerabilities and exploits Pen tester's list of possible attack paths to exploit the vulnerabilities and defined attack vectors.

(continued)

339

TABLE 6.2 (*Continued*)

Stage	Inputs	Outputs
Risk and impact analysis	• List of communication channels • Attack libraries-patterns (e.g. MITRE CAPEC) • List of threats, attacks, and vulnerabilities to the application assets • Exploit Testing Results • Preliminary BIA of stage I • Application dependencies and technical boundaries identified at stage II • Granular application assets and components-data at risk identified at stage III • Threat Analysis Data provided at stage IV • Vulnerabilities mapping to threats and assets at stage V • Stage VI attacks simulated to cause exploits • Organization's information qualitative risk analysis models (e.g. NIST, OCTAVE, FAIR) and elements used (e.g. asset values) • Quantitative risk models • Mapping of attacks to countermeasures (e.g. OWASP TM) • Secure architecture guidelines and technical standards • Approved technical standards for countermeasures and technologies • Risk mitigation strategy guidelines (e.g. NIST)	• Detailed application *risk profile* that includes a description of the risks and the business impacts. • *Quantitative risk analysis* (e.g. ALE) for each vulnerability-exploit • *Qualitative risk analysis* for each vulnerability-exploit (e.g. likelihood × impact) • *Threat matrix* with threats, attacks, vulnerabilities, business impact, and the type countermeasure applied • Residual risk value to business after either (1) countermeasures are applied or (2) risks are compensated by current controls-measures • Risk mitigation strategies and cost-benefit analysis

APPLICATION THREAT MODELING ACTIVITIES per STAGE	MGT	PMO	BA	ARC	DEV	SYS	QA	SOC	VA	PT	RA	CMP	SA	TM
STAGE 1 - DEFINE BUSINESS OBJECTIVES	**R/A**	**A**	**R/A**	**I**	**I**	**I**	**I**	**I**	**I**	**I**	**A**	**A**	**I**	**A**
Define Business Requirements	A	I	R/A	I	I	I	I	I	I	I	I	I	I	A
Define Security/ Compliance Requirements	I	I	C	I	I	I	I	I	I	I	C	R/A	I	A
Define Business Impact	I	I	C	I	I	I	I	I	I	I	R/A	C	I	A
Define Risk Profile	I	I	R/A	I	I	I	I	I	I	I	I	I	I	A
STAGE 2 - TECHNICAL SCOPE	**I**	**A**	**C**	**A**	**R/A**	**R/A**	**C**	**I**	**C**	**C**	**C**	**I**	**C**	**A**
Enumerate Software Components	I	I	C	A	R/A	R/A	C	I	C	C	C	I	C	A
Identify Actors & Data Sinks/ Sources	I	I	C	C	R/A	C	C	I	C	C	C	I	C	A
Enumerate System-Level services	I	I	C	A	R/A	R/A	C	I	C	C	C	I	C	A
Enumerate 3rd Party infrastructures	I	I	C	A	R/A	R/A	C	I	C	C	C	I	C	A
Assert completeness of secure technical design	I	I	C	A	R/A	R/A	C	I	C	C	C	I	C	A
STAGE 3 - APPLICATION DECOMPOSITION	**I**	**I**	**I**	**A**	**A**	**A**	**I**	**I**	**I**	**I**	**I**	**I**	**C**	**R/A**
Enumerate all application use cases (ex: login, account update, delete users, etc.)	I	I	I	C	A	C	I	I	I	I	I	I	C	R/A
Perform Data Flow Diagram of Identified Components	I	I	I	A	C	C	I	I	I	I	I	I	C	R/A
Security functional analysis & the use of trust boundaries	I	I	I	C	A	A	I	I	I	I	I	I	C	A
STAGE 4 - THREAT ANALYSIS				**I**	**I**	**I**	**I**	**R/A**	**C**	**C**	**C**	**C**	**C**	**R/A**
Analyze the overall threat scenario				I	I	I	I	R/A	C	C	C	C	C	A
Gather Threat Intelligence from Internal Sources				I	I	I	I	R/A	C	C	C	C	C	A
Gather Threat Intelligence from External Sources				I	I	I	I	R/A	C	C	C	C	C	A
Update the threat libraries				I	I	I	I	C	C	C	C	I	C	R/A
Threat agents to asset mapping				I	I	I	I	R/A	C	C	C	C	C	A
Assign Probabilistic Values around Identified Threats				I	I	I	I	C	C	C	C	I	C	R/A

Figure 6.8 PASTA RACI Model

	VA	PT	RA	CO	DEV	SYS	QA	SOC	MGT	PMO	BA	ARC	SA	TM
STAGE 5 - VULNERABILITY ASSESSMENT														
Review/Correlate Existing Vulnerability Data					C				I	I	I	I	I	R/A
Identify Weak Design Patterns in the Architecture					C				R/A				I	A
Map threats to vulnerabilities					C				R/A				I	A
Provide Context Risk Analysis based upon Threat-Vulnerability									R/A	C			I	A
Conduct Targeted Vulnerability Testing									C	I			C	R/A
									C	C	C		C	A
STAGE 6 - ATTACK ENUMERATION														
Analyze the attack scenarios					C				I	R/A			I	R/A
Update the attack library/vectors and the control framework										R/A				A
Identify the attack surface and enumerate the attack vectors					C				C	R/A			I	R/A
Assess the probability and impact of each attack scenario										C			I	R/A
Derive a set of cases to test existing countermeasures										C			I	R/A
STAGE 7 - COUNTERMEASURE DEVELOPMENT / RESIDUAL RISK ANALYSIS	C	C	C		C			C	I			C	C	R/A
Calculate the risk of each threat		I	I									C	C	R/A
Identify the countermeasures.					C	C	C					C	C	R/A
Calculate the residual risks	C	C	C		C							C	C	R/A
Recommend strategy to manage risks	C	C	C		C							C	C	R/A

Roles Legend

MGT	Management	DEV	Development	VA	Vuln Assessment	SA	Security Assurance
PMO	Project Mgt	SYS	SysAdmin	PT	Pen Tester	TM	Threat Modeler
BA	Business Analyst	QA	Quality Assurance	RA	Risk Assessor		
ARC	Architecture	SOC	Security Operations	CO	Compliance Officer		

RACI Legend

R Responsible
A Accountable
C Consulted (2 way)
I Informed (1 way)

Figure 6.8 (*Continued*)

7

DIVING DEEPER INTO PASTA

EXPLORING THE SEVEN STAGES AND EMBEDDED THREAT MODELING ACTIVITIES

> "Knowing your own darkness is the best method for dealing with the darkness[es] of other people."
>
> *Carl Gustav Jung, Swiss Psychiatrist*

Knowledge is power. This is greatly exemplified in developing good and reliable software. At a basic level, poorly developed software compromises generally excludes an adequate SLDC process. As the SLDC process aims to ensure that requirements and design patterns are incorporate, PASTA aims to ensure that those are devoid of risk. Power comes from the knowledge of knowing what coding errors exist prior to a production release. Ignorance is not knowing what weaknesses and vulnerabilities are actually exploitable via abuse cases. As hindsight is always 20/20 in the world of insecure software, PASTA provides the ability to create security foresight.

The following section will now walk-through the PASTA process in the context of a newly forming application going through a generic, waterfall, SDLC methodology. For this example, we will assume a simplified version of Agile SDLC methodology. Regardless of the flavor of SDLC used, threat modeling applications should run parallel to such a process in order to integrate into the generic definition, design, development, and testing phases of software development. The following depiction

---

Risk Centric Threat Modeling: Process for Attack Simulation and Threat Analysis, First Edition.
Tony UcedaVélez and Marco M. Morana.
© 2015 John Wiley & Sons, Inc. Published 2015 by John Wiley & Sons, Inc.

of the various stages of PASTA is intended to highlight what efforts should take place in conjunction with a developing application. PASTA can also be applied in other circumstances that do not relate to full SDLC efforts; however, they are not covered at this time since much of the activities mapping to a full SDLC development effort can be applied and tailored as desired by a security organization.

The objective of this section is to provide a detailed walk-through of the PASTA process alongside software development activities, normally conducted via a standard SDLC process. As part of this walk-through, roles depicted under the aforementioned RACI diagram will be discussed along with the deliverables that serve as possible inputs/outputs of the activities for each stage of PASTA. This walk-through is not meant to be absolute in the number of activities that are conducted under each stage of PASTA, but provides a suite of core activities that should be performed in support of the listed objectives and goals for each of PASTA's seven steps. This walk-through is also intended to be simply an example to many possible examples in successfully applying PASTA as a threat modeling methodology.

Stage I of PASTA – Defining Objectives (DO)

Business objectives for a given application provide the key ingredients to ultimately define a functional system. Information technology and Information Security leaders are now tasked with understanding those objectives and correlating existing and new governance measures in order to support business objectives with both technology and security measures. This has been a recent message that is long overdue and bears reminding; after all, today's state of application security is the blatant absence of security requirements. A key factor is that security is not properly matched up to business requirements. Since security is looked upon as something that disables business applications versus something that protects and even enables them, as security professionals, we currently find ourselves in a very antagonistic state in the eyes of our business counterparts. For this very reason, it is important for any threat modeling methodology to lead off with well-defined business objectives that are supported with governance artifacts that (1) make sense, (2) are in line with the capabilities of the business and technology groups, and (3) address inherent risks related to both the regulatory landscape of the data being managed by the application environment as well as the inherent risks of the application architecture (mobile, ATM, traditional web, etc.).

Central to PASTA's application threat modeling process are understanding business, financial, and operational objectives that legitimize an application's existence. From a business perspective, discovering why an application was developed, who the intended users are, and how and why features were developed is very important. Essentially, all of these questions map to answers, or more specifically, requirements in any type of SDLC methodology. These requirements give way to use cases. It is these *use cases* that PASTA's stage I seeks to extract from business objectives. Being able to enumerate and inventory use cases has never been done in other security efforts and therefore inhibits the ongoing use of security evaluations. Beyond this culture shift in application assessment, the use cases found in stage I reveal detailed functionality that would not be captured in dynamic application analysis, source code reviews, risk assessments, application audits, or other types of application evaluations. Knowledge of application use cases enables security groups to bridge the schism that has traditionally separated productive collaboration between business and security professionals. Security professionals have long been categorized as being completely ignorant of business terminology and understanding. Through threat modeling, this notion can be disrupted and give way to productive and realistic discussions on how to apply security features to application functions and features.

From the knowledge of how use cases fulfill business objectives, security professionals are able to hone in on the business impact of adverse security threats affecting the functionality of the application and its underlying data. Understanding how an application fulfills business objectives will help in understanding how adverse threats affect not only the risk level around the application itself, but also the service level agreements, legal agreements, regulatory requirements, and more that are binding to the business. In summary, understanding business objectives behind applications provide the following value-added components to the PASTA threat modeling stage I:

- Knowledge of business drivers/motivators around the application and its core functionality.
- Understanding of the business impact around the application if objectives are not fulfilled or adversely affected by security threats or agents.
- Understanding of possible business liabilities if certain security considerations are not incorporated into the design and requirement building activities for the application. For example, applications operating in a highly regulated environment may have to retrofit compliance requirements if not properly considered within this stage, as it is a business objective to avert compliance requirements that may be costly postimplementation or development.

The inclusion of business objectives at the start of an asset- or risk-centric approach to threat modeling helps build relevant and meaningful context later when attacks, weaknesses, vulnerabilities, and exploits are addressed further in PASTA. Similar to how IT and IS governance begins with exercises to understand business objectives, PASTA initiates threat activities with these foundational concepts so that threats are more relatable and meaningful in stage VII.

The following is a brief and simple representation that helps capture how business objectives could be analyzed into certain prerequisites for factoring security into the process. Examples as to how defined objectives can pave the road to security governance, such as policies, standards, and guidelines, are as follows.

The right-hand side of Table 7.1 reveals examples of governance considerations that could support some of the business objectives that are reflected on the left side of the table.

TABLE 7.1 Relating Business Objectives to Security Requirements

Business Objectives	Security Requirements
High availability for app to process simultaneous requests	• DoS mitigation techniques, • High availability (HA) architecture
Ensuring client/customer confidentiality	• Input/output validation, • Strong authentication requirements • Client data segregation in database • Data encryption (in transit/at rest)
How reliance on data integrity (e.g. financial trading apps/content)	• Use of digital signatures with digital certificates • Proper logging and monitoring at system and DB level
Adherence to stringent privacy laws (per country)	• Proper authentication model • Secure role-based access control model for application access
Legal (e.g. client driven) and regulatory risks	• Translate security requirements to controls for mitigating regulatory and legal risks

Requirement Scope Creeps and Security

Beyond building a primer of procedural- and technology-based governance measures, defining business objectives in stage I provides other intrinsic benefits to the threat modeling process. It may be difficult to consider that business requirements can lead to security features or failures for many, but understanding this relationship requires the ability to have experienced objectives that give way to functional requirements that go horribly wrong. Consider poorly defined business objectives that beget functional requirements for the application environment. Many of those business objectives may be germane to support the business while some are loosely and/or poorly defined and, as a result, give way to poorly or loosely defined application functional requirements. Ultimately, as the application progresses over multiple builds in its life cycle, functional requirements that were defined based on business objectives that did not have clear relevance to the company's overall objectives may be susceptible to being neglected or even forgotten over time. Many on both the user and development sides have said, "Oh yes, I forgot this app could do that."

It is within the realm of those functional, orphaned use cases that dysfunction could arise via misuse cases of the application environment. For every functional aspect of the application, dysfunction can exist, particularly if that part of the application codebase is not well kept. Take, for example, an online B2C portal for sports jerseys. Many of the functionalities may be related to payment processing, account creation, cart management, or other functionalities that support selling sports jerseys online. However, a separate business objective of interfacing with newly formed partner sites (such as footwear) may have been introduced and ultimately neglected as that aspect of the business disintegrates over time. If APIs that were initially triggered from the online sports jersey store were poorly designed for security (such as anonymous web service requests to a web service namespace or end point), an ideal attack vector related to information leakage could be exploited after having been discovered on the B2C sports jersey web portal. It is for such cases that stage I allows parallel efforts challenge whether or not some of the business objectives defined by the SDLC are extraneous to the application's mission.

Stage I Activities

There are several activities to complete under stage I. Each activity within this stage is intended to correlate to activities that relate to *Defining Requirements* within a generic SDLC methodology.

From the perspective of stage I of the PASTA threat model, the activities that should take place here are aimed at the following:

1. Defining key business objectives to that application.
2. Understanding impact of application to business and thereby impact of functional features to business.
3. Developing a risk profile for the application.

Stage I: Activity 1 (S1:A1) Define Business Requirements

Now we will begin to look at the specific activities that make up stage I of the PASTA methodology. Cross references to the appendix RACI diagram will be helpful throughout this chapter in order to identify what roles are associated with each of the stage activities.

Much of the information relevant to completing S1:A1 already is addressed by some SDLC steps. Although distinctly different in their approach, Waterfall and Agile SDLC methodologies do gather business objectives and requirements that can fulfill this stage of the PASTA process. For the purpose of a risk-based application threat model, S1:A1 prescribes specific information gathering activities that need to be conducted in order to ensure that forward facing PASTA activities have a relevant anchor of context from which to build the overall risk analysis.

Figure 7.1 provides a representation on how obtaining business requirements becomes relevant in building a contextually sound threat model.

The arrow above reflects that use cases can originate in various phases of the SDLC process. For this reason, the process may need to be repeated if use cases are found to be different from earlier efforts as part of a repetitive requirement gathering process.

Rogue use cases may stem from poorly established SDLC practices where developers are left to decipher what requirements a product application should have with the resulting requirements devoid of any input or loopback from the business. Another way rogue use cases come about is via requirement gathering activities that are lost in translation and never become reconciled through repetitive development efforts.

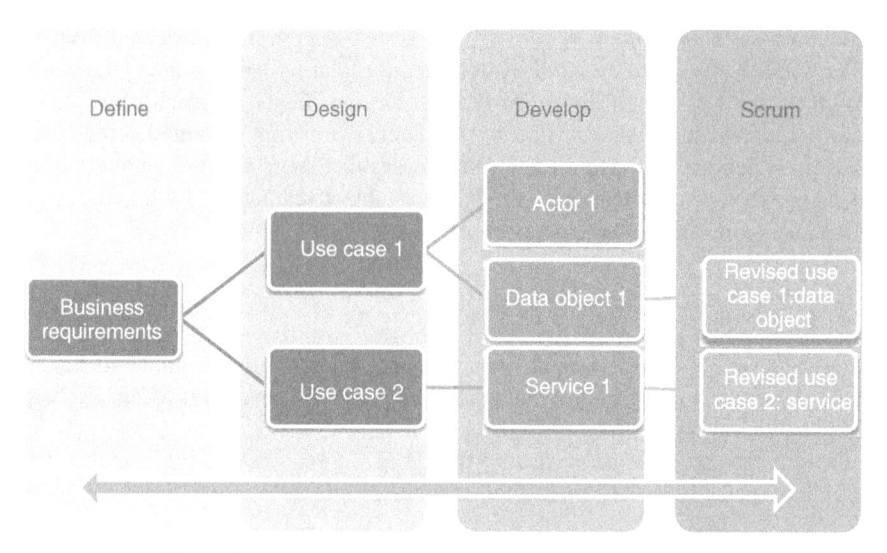

Figure 7.1 Deriving Use Cases from Business Objectives

If repetitive development steps do not catch possible rogue or orphaned use cases, activities in both stages I and IV will help make certain that there is a good mapping that supports identified business requirements. During these steps, requirements received by application development teams may be audited by those responsible for accomplishing threat modeling in order to reconcile whether the translated use cases truly fulfill some of the defined requirements for the application.

Where the information may not be captured or exist presently, a simple artifact can be used to capture the responses needed to complete this activity in S1:A1. The following is a sample artifact that could be used/developed.

In Table 7.2, the highlighted use case derived from the sample business objective does not tie into fulfilling the goal of the developed product application. This simple exercise does not necessarily mean that the use case will be excluded from development; however, it may be trimmed.

At the conclusion of this activity, the threat modeling team should have a strong understanding of what are the key functional requirements for the application. This may easily lend from the DEFINE stage of an SDLC. Furthermore, the end of this activity should provide for a good understanding as to what the key requirement(s) for the application is. In knowing this information, defining business impact in the next activity will be far easier to accomplish.

Stage I: Activity 2 (S1:A2) Define Security/Compliance Requirements

This stage is all about meeting business objectives. It is important to recognize that many businesses actually have both security and compliance as included areas in their overall objectives. The absence of security in their customer facing applications or products may spell trouble for many businesses. Similarly, ignoring or faltering on

TABLE 7.2 Enumeration of Business Requirements to Understood Use Cases

Business Requirement Example	Use Case Example
Become an industry leader in providing a paperless, mobile solution for collecting basic PHI	A mobile app on an iOS tablet is used to capture vital PHI by the physician (blood pressure, height, weight, age, temperature, etc.) upon check-in.
	Allow for PHI records to be sent via multiple protocols (RF, Bluetooth, e-mail, HTTPS, etc.) to avoid the need to print.
	Incorporate GPS location capabilities to allow doctors to inform patients about the location of a pharmacy near their home.
Grow a market presence in Western Europe where mobile tablet solutions are proliferating	Allow the user to select a default language from a wide range of languages found in Western Europe.
	Build in translation capabilities for the 15 most prevalent languages in Western Europe.

regulatory requirements for information security may introduce loss of accreditation or introduce fines – both of which would be vehemently avoided by most companies, particularly small to mid-size start-ups. Activity 3 of stage I provides the opportunity to address both regulatory compliance and security requirements for the application being developed. This provides an integration point for Governance and Compliance processes, artifacts, or deliverables that may have already been developed by the company. From a business point of view, this incorporation of security and compliance is mitigating potential business or reputational controls earlier in a product or software development process.

Working with compliance and privacy officers in this stage, this threat modeling activity can quickly derive what scope of both internal security requirements and external regulatory requirements is related to the application architecture model and most importantly, the data model. Resulting from an assessment of where compliance, privacy, and security overlaps, requirements that are key to implement during this stage are especially those where overlaps occur. Figure 7.2 attempts to portray this visually.

Maintaining topicality to the risk-centric approach of PASTA, this early adoption of security, compliance, and privacy requirements provides for both security and compliance risks to become mitigated earlier in the SDLC process. This allows for preemptive threat mitigation via hardening techniques against system, application, and/or even network components. Working alongside security governance groups, a review of IT and security standards can be applied to the application environment in order to provide a base layer of security. As previously mentioned, many external guidelines and security best practices from sources such as CISecurity.org

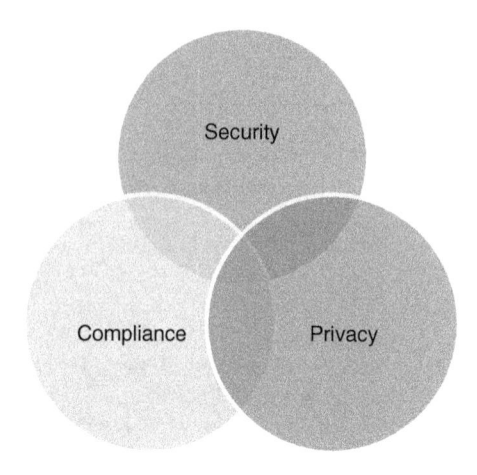

Figure 7.2 Converging Security, Compliance, and Privacy Requirements in Stage I

or OWASP.org can provide an ample external reference point if internal guides and security standards are nonexistent or lacking.

As an example, we can use a health-care product manufacturer. The product is an on-premises client-server solution that captures PHI data for new mothers and their newborns. From a security standpoint, let us assume that the health-care IT organization has internal security standards that are used to ensure that data is securely stored by flat file and relational databases. Internal security audit groups use these security standards as a benchmark for measurement when performing internal assessments. If the application is being threat modeled as part of an SDLC process, this security control would be presented as a requirement to be fulfilled. In doing so, the control has a greater certainty to be adopted and implemented in the DEFINE or DESIGN phase of the SDLC versus introduced, postimplementation.

Similarly, regulatory requirements from HIPAA/HITECH may potentially force the protection of PHI by a covered entity and in such a case, applying cryptographic controls[1] earlier in the process is far easier than having to consider impacts to data calls made by various actors or processes within the application.

Examples of controls that span across privacy, compliance, and security that may be referenced from internal security standards and/or guidelines are the following:

1. Standards for cryptographic controls.
2. Secure coding standards for mobile applications.
3. Network security standards (areas that govern network administration, allowed protocols and services, account hardening).
4. Password Complexity Standard (addresses use of password length, complexity, expiration, etc.).

---

[1] 45 CFR §§ 164.312(a)(2)(iv) and 164.312(e)(2)(ii).

5. Logging Standard (specifies what types of events are logged).
6. Authentication Standard (determines what acceptable authentication mechanisms need to be used).
7. Server Hardening Guide for [X] (includes requirements for hardening an Operating System based on security best practices and OEM recommendations).
8. Security Architecture Guide (outlines the secure architecture models for various types of applications – web, client-server, mobile, and cloud).
9. User Accounts Standard (defines how user accounts are to be governed by credential stores such as AD, LDAP, IdM solutions, etc.).
10. Data Security Standard (identified required controls that should be used to govern security for data at rest and data in transport).

Security Governance Artifacts for Stage I

In forging ahead with this part of stage I, it may be opportune to not assume that all readers understand what is meant by governance, standards, policies, guidelines, and other terms that may or may not be related to actual security governance. It first bears mentioning that there are both technology and security governances. Technology governance has predated security governance, and they traditionally have been managed apart from each other. This is somewhat dysfunctional since a separate group is responsible for configuring a system based on factors such as speed, efficiency, and reliability, among other factors that relate to performance of the application environment. In turn, security groups look to harden the same system environment, motivated primarily to "lock down" the same application environment so that it can reduce its threat landscape. For financial reasons and those related to improved security strategy, both governance groups should create hybrid documents in order to address the same audience and come away with agreed upon functional and security governance material that sustains both functional application requirements for the overlaying application as well as security requirements for CIA.

A suite of governance artifacts used within the early stages of the PASTA process are revealed in Table 7.3. They provide further evidence on how security and compliance requirements can be factored into the PASTA process early on.

Other terms such as guides, cheat sheets, recommendations, or lists may contain invaluable governance material. The aforementioned terms in Table 7.3 are commonly associated and recognized governance terminology that conveys security information for various audience members (end users, system/database administrators, network engineers, architects, etc.). Governance-like material may also stem from blog posts, instructional videos, whitepapers, books, or articles that basically convey what someone should do to a piece of technology, software, or code to improve its security state against any given number of attacks or threats. The act of security governance is not simply the production of standards and the like, but ingesting what sort of obligatory measures are going to be applied to the network, system platform, data repository, supportive network services, and software application so that attacks are less likely to succeed. This is why governance can be leveraged in stage I of the

TABLE 7.3 Governance Artifacts Relevant to Stage I of PASTA

Artifact	Definition
Plan	Details on how policies, procedures, and other governance documentation are to be enforced and made actionable by the audience for whom the plan is designed for. Common plans in governance include Business Continuity, Incident Response, and Disaster Recovery. Depending on the objectives of stage I of PASTA for a given application, these artifacts may or may not be used. They may also be relevant at different stages (e.g. – Incident Response plan may point to the high-level details on how threat feeds are consumed and used, thereby useful in knowing where threat intelligence sources may be found as part of stage IV – Threat Analysis).
Policy	Collection of policy statements that define required actions by personnel and contractors to ensure physical and information security, as well as data privacy. Truly relevant to PASTA's stage I if the policy supports a business objective. Also relevant to PASTA's stage II if the policy can serve as a process based or high-level technical control for which *blind threat modeling* or inherent threat mitigation techniques can be applied.
Policy statement	Succinct, yet clear statements around a specific area that people or processes need to adhered to, in support of company wide security measures. Provides high-level summations of policy goals that may pertain to stage I or II of the PASTA process.
Procedures	Steps or instructions to describe how to achieve the goals defined by a policy's set of policy statements. Provides the actual details on how procedures can serve as threat mitigation controls within stage II of the PASTA process. This allows for inherent risk to be mitigated within the early stages of any given SDLC process (primarily within the DEFINE or DESIGN stage of an SDLC process).
Standard	Requirements for systems or software in order to sustain functional and continuous technology within an application environment and organizational enterprise. This will be most applicable after stage II, since technical objectives/requirements will be defined. Given the technical nature of standards, these governance artifacts provide the most relevant controls to further reduce inherent risk and allow for architects and developers, along with system administrators to conduct blind threat modeling or inherent threat mitigation based on the technology scope or even the process scope (if a human process is an intricate component to the product application). This truly fosters the idea of Building Security-In by including such type of governance artifacts. Building in standards also has a beneficial by-product that exceptions or waivers to implementing controls are reduced by their inclusion and consideration to the system or application being threat modeled.

TABLE 7.3 (*Continued*)

Artifact	Definition
Guideline	Suggested or recommended technical/security measures that could be implemented based on industry expert recommendations on similar environments of application make and type. Given that guidelines have a more technical scope, they will be mostly leveraged during stage II of the PASTA process. Since they are not required (by their nature of being a guideline), these artifacts are irrelevant to stage I. Similar to Standards, they provide further risk reduction when applying against known inherent risk issues caused by identified architectural weaknesses, software vulnerabilities, or previously unmitigated attack vectors.

PASTA model; it provides an initial acknowledgement by the business and technology groups that they are going to develop this new application on the security foundation of hardened networks, architecture, software, and server environments.

The image that follows provides a simple visual representation depicting some of the interrelationships between security governance, technology governance, and ultimately the business objectives defined within this stage of the threat modeling process.

Reflecting on Figure 7.3, the governance materials, which, by definition, are aimed to support technology and security objectives, indirectly support the business objectives that represent the pinnacle of the objectives hierarchy shown. At this point, much of the governance introduced in stage I of the PASTA methodology is more precisely selected and applied and/or adhered to as the scope of technology assets are selected. Essentially, this means that in a heterogeneous ecology of systems, platforms, and software, generic governance material may be cited during stage I. If there is more homogeneity across employed web servers, application servers, proxies, and network devices used as part of the subject application environment, then stage II of the PASTA methodology will provide more specific governance material that conforms to the types of technology that are selected.

Stage I: Activity 3 (S1:A3) Define Business Impact

Deriving business impact for an application environment all centers on adverse events that prevent or limit the predefined business objective from being fulfilled fully or in a timely manner. One already existent source in larger enterprises is the use of a Business Impact Analysis or BIA. BIA exercises are common, especially in the financial industry sector, and allow business objective, self-assessment questions to be captured as well as other types of questions that establish impact criteria for the application as a whole, and in some cases for unique features or functions that the application supports. They can be time-consuming, but it all hinges on the amount

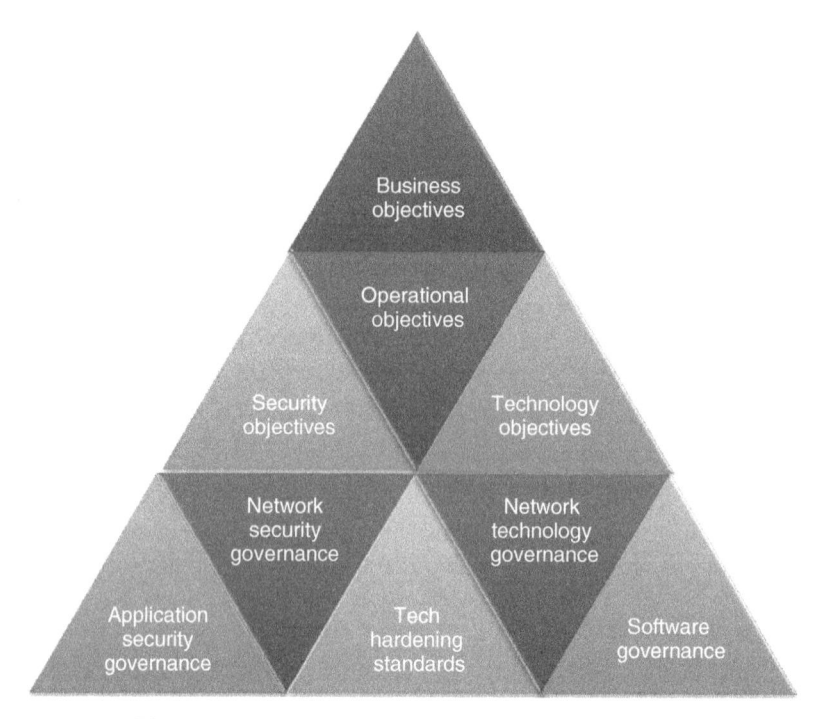

Figure 7.3 Hierarchy of Objectives Addressed by PASTA

of questions gathered as part of that process. For smaller organizations just embarking on threat modeling and not exposed to BIAs previously, a good recipe is simply to develop questions around CIA (Confidentiality, Integrity, and Availability) plus considerations for regulatory Compliance (the other "C"). For any organization, key questions that may be presented are listed as follows:

- Is the data used by the application classified, nonpublic, sensitive, or regulated data (e.g. ePHI (electronic patient health information), PII (personal identifiable information), PCI-DSS related (cardholder data)?.
- Is there a classification assigned to this data? (Internal classification assigned to data may elevate the consequences in the event the data is compromised.)
- What service level agreements (SLAs) to clients/customers are material in terms of loss of revenue, reimbursements, charge backs, and what use cases or data sources would serve as a trigger to these breaks in SLA?
- Can the application's function affect the health of one or more individuals (e.g. medical application in the Emergency Room, Bulk Energy System (BES) (in the Utility sector), direct or indirect operation of an automobile, civilian aircraft, or military device/vehicle)?
- What is the process for gaining access to the application?

- What compliance regulations are relevant based on the data managed by the application and relevant regulatory requirements?
- Does the application's function affect financial reporting for the organization or the integrity of any aspect of financial reporting vehicles?

Monetizing impact is extremely important in this activity and requires some financial analysis. Fortunately, financial numbers are very easy to be obtained from financial officials, particularly when attempting to explain the end goal quantifying business impact. Financial costs are needed in order to convey how an application risk can materialize to business costs, ideally at a unit level. The costs help to convey financial impact to business-minded roles and illustrate to them how technical risks can translate to business impact. Historical events that take place and have associated costs are best to exemplify costs. The following are a list of sample events from which financial costs can be extracted and analyzed.

- Security breaches.
- Litigation costs.
- Historical class action law suit averages.
- Credit monitoring fees.
- Postbreach audit costs.
- Newly required controls to be implemented.
- Loss of accreditation (HIPAA).
- Regulatory related fines (PCI-DSS).
- Opportunity costs associated with downtime.
- Intellectual property loss estimates (via valuation models).
- Direct costs related to downtime or deprecated functionality (annually = annual loss expectancy; per incident = single loss expectancy).

All of the impact considerations listed earlier can be unitized using a gross amount of potential revenue or estimated costs. For example, quarter revenues directly or indirectly related to the product application can be simplistically unitized by a time period (hour, day, month, etc.). In terms of costs, fees related to audit, litigation, and other types of postincident–related costs can be estimated and created into unit costs for different types of events. This will help to provide some degree of financial impact attributed to adverse events from the systems. This type of information and analysis will help to portray a risk picture that is ultimately conveyed in stage VII.

Most BIAs will be able to provide some level of financial context to impact, which is important for this activity. Leveraging the BIA is a powerful, yet underutilized process that generally fails in execution, mostly due to high levels of qualitative speculation with little to not substantiating evidence for financial loss numbers. The BIA process is extremely valuable for understanding risk as it represents the value of a given application to an operational area of a business. The by-product of the BIA process has not been adequately leveraged by other governance processes, such as risk assessments and business continuity planning efforts, particularly in mid-size and smaller organizations. Textbook BIAs are integrated in more mature governance efforts; however, even in those instances they factor very little into the overall risk evaluation. Related to the PASTA threat modeling methodology (particularly in the context of its use alongside SDLC efforts), BIAs provide a qualitative, baseline description of risk for the application environment. This is important as it may help divide the application environment into components and assets that require varying forms of countermeasures for risk mitigation – all based on the impact that could be sustained by a given attack.

Identifying impact in this stage's activity allows PASTA to have relevant context when addressing threats, vulnerabilities, and attacks against the application. This contextual understanding to threats, attack patterns, and vulnerabilities provides for a rational correlation to defined business objectives. The context for the following exercise will follow the development or rewrite of an entire application environment or substantial portion of said environment. Without yet addressing any aspect of the threat model or encompassed attack surface for the application environment, many of these governance-related aspects will still be able to provide the following value.

This book is not focused on teaching about BIAs; however, they are very important to substantiating a threat model's value under PASTA. Candidly, not having one does inhibit the risk analysis that PASTA attempts to emulate collectively across all seven stages; however, a rapid BIA analysis could be done in order to capture some of the main answers posed by some of the questions exemplified in the last page. The following is a quick example of such an approach in the context of a health-care scenario (Table 7.4).

Building quick questionnaires around simple yet comprehensive security themes (such as Confidentiality, Integrity, Availability, and Regulatory) can easily provide a rapid list of questions on what and how sensitive the business impact would be if threats to those areas were successfully launched. For example, how impacted would a business be if PII were compromised? The key to gathering these answers is to obtain some degree of precision around who, what, and especially by how much an impact would affect a business entity. The precision on the responses will help to ensure that general answers are not factored into the impact analysis, which will undermine the validity of the impact analysis.

It should also be considered that it may be a bit presumptuous to assume that any business impacted by PII leakage would be adversely affected. The reality is that impacts in such a case can greatly vary across industry, business size, country, and so on. Some would be impacted more if their services are focused on managing such data, compared to other business models where such a role is more secondary than principal. An example is whether a government agency in the social services sector experiences a PII breach versus that of an auto store that keeps basic personal data on its customers. The impact will be substantially different, even if the volume of data compromised is the same. Adding elements of government regulations as an overlay, as well as country, will greatly affect the compounded impact of regulatory involvement and fines.

TABLE 7.4 Considerations for Factoring Business Impact

Considerations	Samples
What is the business goal supported by the product app?	*Example:* Increase adoption and overall market utilization of a new product application for physicians who treat diabetic patients.
What is the goal of the app?	*Example:* Facilitate metrics, trending, and overall analysis around insulin shots given to diabetic patients.
What is the regulatory landscape that affects this product app? *(List all the apply)*	*Example:* HIPAA, HITECH (seek UCF guidance).
What is the most critical aspect of the application?	*Example:* Availability, Confidentiality, and Integrity of patient health information.
What is the criticality if the product app was not available over the course of x?	*Example:* The application does not have a critical uptime as insulin could still be distributed and quantities and patient data could be captured in the patient module of ACME Health.
What is the existing risk profile associated with the product app?	*Example:* Moderate Risk (4/15/2014).
What is the intended user base of the production application?	*Example:* Health-care practitioners, Loan officers, Tellers, Government employees, Legal, and so on.
Is the data used by the application classified, nonpublic, sensitive, or regulated data?	*Example:* ePHI (electronic patient health information), PII (personal identifiable information), PCI-DSS related (cardholder data)
Is there a classification assigned to this data?	*Example:* Internal classification assigned to data may elevate the consequences in the event the data is compromised
What service level agreements (SLAs) to clients/customers are in place related to the application?	*Example:* Loss of revenue due to SLA violations, reimbursements, and client charge backs.
Can the application's function affect the health of one or more individuals?	*Example:* Medical application in the Emergency Room, Bulk Energy System (BES) (in the Utility sector), direct or indirect operation of an automobile, civilian aircraft, or military device/vehicle, etc.)
What is the process for gaining access to the application?	*Example:* Self-enrollment application, access control workflow, and so on.
What compliance regulations are relevant based on the data managed by the application and relevant regulatory requirements?	*Example:* PCI-DSS, HIPAA, GLBA, NERC CIP, and so on.
Does the application's function affect financial reporting for the organization or the integrity of any aspect of financial reporting vehicles?	*Example:* SOX, FFIEC, NCUA, and so on.

Another thought is to classify impact into various groups, particularly if a bulk financial estimate around each one of those groups can be made. This can simplify the financial analysis so that impactful events are categorized into various financial classes. Organizing impact into various "classes may follow a CIA approach in order to have predefined costs associations for confidentiality, integrity, and availability. This breakdown does not have to follow simply a CIA approach, but any other approach that simply organizes impact scenarios into manageable groups of a similar type. In either case, the best starting point (devoid of a more formal or mature BIA process) is to simply ask questions that all tie to affecting a defined business objective for the application.

1. What are the key goals for the application (e.g. content propagation, provide robust B2C commerce site, employee enrollment, customer bill pay, Cloud-based file service manager, online CRM)?
2. How long can the application be down for?
    a. What would the impact be to existing customers? New potential customers?
3. What legal requirements is the application bound to in terms of service uptime?
4. What regulatory requirements affect the application in the wake of a breach or break in continuity?
5. What impact is felt by cost centers that support the business (e.g. accounting applications, A/R applications, ordering/shipping capabilities, phone lines)?
6. How does reputation factor into the ability for the company to sell its goods/services? Is customer trust a big factor for sustaining repeat business?

More advanced BIAs will have more poignant questions on technology and data use and will typically encompass third-party services, infrastructure, or solution providers that have an integral role in the application's maintenance. Additionally, impacts from various regulations at play should be considered, in order to define supplemental objectives that help to avoid audit risks or customer compliance mandates.

Regulatory Compliance and Business Impact

Faltering against regulatory requirements and mandates can provide their own level of business impact to an organization. Regulatory compliance gaps can negate the worth of an application if the application is found to have material weaknesses against a compliance regulation. This is why compliance is material to a risk-centric approach as it can affect the business objective of a product application. Remember that risk is only relevant if it undermines the objective of a product application. In some instances, even achieving the compliance requirements is not good enough to ward off business impact. In the last quarter of 2013, Target Stores revealed a massive breach that has introduced a massive backlash from both merchant banks, credit card companies, and the PCI Council. This does not include the hundreds of civil suits that have been filed against the company. All of this took place to a major retailer in the United States that was compliant with the Level 1 PCI-DSS security requirements. For this reason, it is important not to solely rely on simply a compliance driven objective for security, but one that looks at true security analysis, as revealed by a threat model. From a stage I perspective, requirements from security, compliance, and privacy can be adequately converged in order that the proper preventative, detective, and reactive controls can be put into place.

As mentioned in the prior list, threat modeling leaders will also have to consider how application use cases warrant change given any data, security, and/or privacy requirements stemming from compliance regulations. For this reason, the focus on data types are very important for stage I as they help see if the data usage is tied to prerequisites around data security across various compliance regulations. As part of this stage's activity, helpful white-boarding exercises among Compliance, Information Security Officers (ISOs), Business Analysts, and Security Engineers would help define what inherent system or application technology can be leveraged in order to build compliance into the product application. Figure 7.4 depicts a high-level triage representation of the relationship business objectives, application data types, and compliance requirements for a given application. Note how the ≈ symbol represents *resistors* or countermeasures to the risks introduced. The *resistors* in the following figure are supported by controls or countermeasures that may already exist in the environment and may be attributed to administrative, technical, or process-based mitigating controls. Labels on the outside of the arrows represent inherent risks while labels on the inside of the arrows represent mitigating controls (Figure 7.4).

For larger enterprises, sometimes impact is attributed to the lack of compliance to internal controls. Reverting to the first activity for stage I, the threat modeler may find that internal factors may trigger some level of impact that is either direct or indirect. For example, for publicly traded companies, adhering to internal controls around SOX becomes a key objective in ensuring integrity of financial numbers. As such, it provides an opportunity for such an impact to be noted as well as an opportunity to see if there are any internal governance standards that can help introduce controls around logging, authentication, validation of financial transactions, and separation of duties for the application being threat modeled. As part of the third activity in stage I, some

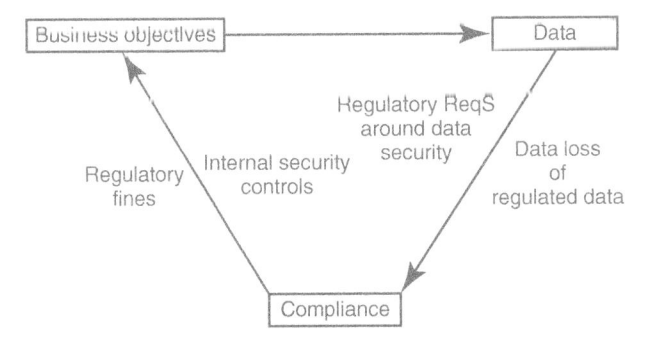

Figure 7.4 Relating Compliance to Business Impact

degree of built-in security considerations can be made at this point by factoring which security standards or guidelines should be introduced to the collective threat modeling process. Depending on the level of detail obtained about the application's business goals and objectives, certain governance material may be introduced in stage I of the PASTA methodology and ultimately considered for implementation as preemptive countermeasures in either stage I or II.

Stage I: Activity 3 (S1:A4) Define Risk Profile

The activity to perform within Stage I (Define Objectives) of PASTA is to identify or prepare a risk profile for the subject application. This exercise provides valuable insight to preexisting risk elements that have affected the application in the past or those applications with a similar technology footprint, deployment model, architecture, or overall use case. This preexisting risk is referred to as *inherent risk*. Different from the BIA, the risk profile seeks to comprehend what inherent risks affect the application from a vulnerability standpoint as well as what threats are inherent to the application being designed. Risk profiles can be derived from prior risk assessments from within a company's enterprise technology risk management group or a private outside professional service group. If an application is new, there may not be an existing or recent risk assessment. If such is the case, risk assessments that have been previously conducted and of similar type (based on technological use, data use, etc.) could be used to draw risk correlations to the application being threat modeled. This is done in order to establish an existing risk profile for the application across common areas.

Inherent Risk

If an application risk assessment has already been conducted, a threat modeling team can see what inherent risk issues carry forward into the PASTA threat model. Most technical risk assessments show open issues relating to newly discovered vulnerabilities from prior risk assessments. Accompanying the risk analysis is generally a remediation matrix that reveals relevant, top issues that represent the weaknesses for the application. Initially, it is important to first understand the technical risk issues for the application environment. Next, it is important to map these vulnerabilities to technical components across the threat model. Risk relevancy will be determined by whether technical risks can be mapped to application components such as assets, actors, data sources, use cases. If they can, they should help in forming a baseline risk level or risk profile for the application. The true risk analysis will arise from analyzing how business objectives and supporting application use cases have been adversely affected by the presence of these vulnerabilities and weaknesses.

Risk profiles provide a baseline of risk around the application and help provide a contextual understanding of some inherent threats to the design, underlying platforms, or even operating environment. As mentioned before, risk profiles can be derived from prior risk assessments. The most recent (last 12 months) risk assessments will provide the greatest level of relevancy around which inherited process,

TABLE 7.5 Possible Inherent Risk Issues by Application Type

Type	People	Process	Technology
Cloud application	Cloud service provider support receives no security training	Onboarding new tenants in multitenant environment receives no vetting	Multitenant cloud environment with only programmatic controls for logical segregation
Mobile application	Discovered that rogue threat agents are creating rogue instances of app in App Store	Nonprivate app store does not vet authenticity of applications or developers.	None-use of controls that help ensure authenticity of mobile application (e.g. hashing, digital certificates, web service authentication to unique application fingerprint)
Client server	Historical information leakage via internal threat agent	No restricted access to developers across lower environments (DEV, TEST, QA) and production environments (STAGE, PROD)	Liberal application access controls

technology, and even people components are considered relevant to the threat model. As most other threat modeling methodologies look at the technical, PASTA also considers nontechnical related process/people issues as well. In the end, building a better understanding of risk via threat modeling means identifying inherent risk issues that affect how application components are designed, developed, implemented, and administered. The following is a brief table reflecting examples of inherent risk across people, process, and technology (Table 7.5).

In many instances, application threat modeling solely focuses people to look at the application stack. Other methodologies may actually exclude the network or system stack. It is important to realize that threat agents and inherent weaknesses to process and human resources may circumvent the most fortified applications. These activities benefits quickly allow for an introspective look as to where other risk areas may warrant analysis and a mitigation strategy.

Prior risk assessments of an application that is being updated is the easiest scenario to depict under this activity. However, if there are no prior assessments that have been completed since the application is newly developed, prior risk assessments may still be used. Selecting prior risk assessments with similar attributes (use cases, deployment models, etc.), data sources, architecture, people components, and process components may allow for some level of similar risk *DNA* to be applied to the new application. For example, if two client-server applications (one is a legacy app while the other is newly developed) use the same authentication method that is homegrown and known to have prior risk issues, those details can be ported over to a new inherent risk profile for the newly developed application.

Context should drive the relevancy of risk to the application being threat modeled. Not all risk issues are relevant and in order to keep the threat model lean and topical, relevant risks need only be applied. Context will be driven by perspective as it is difficult to determine universally what and how risk associations from one environment to the next should be made. Overall, risk context should regard whether similar application components are being used and leveraged, particularly if using a similar framework, underlying system components, and data sources. Other components that may legitimize the need for inherited risk to be applied are around similar use cases, deployment models, hosting models, outsourced development groups, third-party software components, Open Source libraries, and network paths/protocols. Additionally, architectural similarities may warrant that risk issues become inherited from one application to the other. The following list provides some exemplary guidance on what components may warrant the need to port risk-related considerations from one application to the one being threat modeled under PASTA.

- Use of similar authentication models (e.g. OAuth, LDAP, Active Directory, Stored Credentials).
- Use of same system platform actors (e.g. host accounts used for API authentication).
- Use of similar architecture model (e.g. published web services interacting with mobile clients).
- Similar data stores/warehouses.
- Similar network communication protocols/services.
- Similar use of application and human actors.
- Similarities in system/platform types used in support of application environments.
- Similarities in use of application frameworks (e.g. Struts, Spring, Java Frameworks, .NET).
- Similarities in using third-party software (e.g. NHibernate, application proxies, Drupal, JAR files, OS extensions, Apache, memcache).

Participants of Stage I

Within stage I, the primary participants include project managers, business analysts, Information Security Officers (ISOs). These members provide primary "Responsible" and "Accountable" levels of support while other groups in IT (Developers, Architects, Engineers provide a secondary or tertiary level of support at the "Consulted" or "Informed" level. As shown in Figure 7.4, the BA (Business Analyst) role should have solid knowledge of what the goals and business objectives are for any given application. As such, they carry a *Responsible* or *Accountable* role. In this stage, they have

EXPLORING THE SEVEN STAGES AND EMBEDDED THREAT MODELING ACTIVITIES

Business objectives
WHAT: Functional features
WHO: Dev managers, project Managers, Business analysts, ISOs

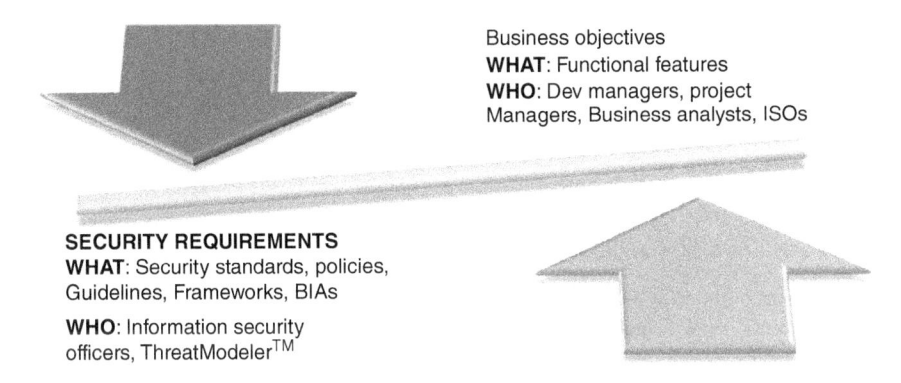

SECURITY REQUIREMENTS
WHAT: Security standards, policies, Guidelines, Frameworks, BIAs
WHO: Information security officers, ThreatModeler™

Figure 7.5 Business and InfoSec Balance in Stage I

the responsibility to share what the clear goals and requirements for the application are in order to ensure that scope creeping takes place and that proper understanding of business impact is documented and loosely associated with premature use cases or overall application functions. Given that the focus of stage I is to provide an overall objective to the application threat model in support of the SDLC process for a given application, these participants should focus on providing proper transparency around the business objectives and how the security objectives help fulfill them. This means that from the security perspective and in collaboration with the other roles in the RACI model (for this stage), the BA, PM, and ISO roles need to also receive input as to how security and/or compliance objectives could impair the fulfillment of those associated business objectives. Figure 7.5 helps to depict the type of communication and collaboration that should exist and over what topics.

Generally, the requirements phase of an SDLC process introduces the desire to pile on several functional features for a given application environment. The *WHAT* under the business objectives of the aforementioned see-saw diagram comprises varied application features that management feels too important and critical to exclude from the scope of the SDLC process. Conversely, the *WHAT* provided by the security side of the see-saw figure represents the countermeasures aimed at securing an application environment. Things such as security standards provide preemptive mitigation techniques that can be included based on the intended design pattern, platform solution, and even deployment model. The *WHO* listed under each side of the diagram includes key members that can provide appropriate business and security context in order to contribute to stage I activities under PASTA. Key roles during this stage include those who are responsible or accountable for defining business requirements for the business application as well as those who can articulate security requirements that would mitigate inherent risk issues and/or address regulatory requirements aimed at reducing compliance risk. These suggested roles, along with their associated definitions, are presented as follows.

For a full detailed breakdown of roles for this activity and all activities for this stage, please review the appendix area for the included Threat Modeling RACI diagram. While the aforementioned figure only depicts roles for which individuals will be either Responsible, Accountable, or Consulted as part of the relevant stage activities. All roles are best exemplified by the RACI at the end of the book.

Beyond roles, artifacts are needed to be consumed by various stage activities as well as produced by each stage activity. Under the following section, we will discuss what specific artifacts should be gathered as input as well as what expected outputs should be produced for this overall stage.

Integration and Collaborative Opportunities for PASTA

Every functional feature within an application can give way to dysfunctional use cases or abuse cases. Many feel that the conversations among security professionals and those on the business and IT side of the SDLC process come from two different camps of life: one from the glass half full, while the other coming from the glass half empty camp. Balance is the answer to balancing the marriage between software development teams and security groups. The collaborative and integrated approach to PASTA lends to provide a more balanced approach and purposively begins with the understanding of business objectives around the application as a way to educate security professionals a bit more on what exactly they are really protecting. Harmonizing the two camps will also come with collaborating across various activities where artifacts, organic to one group, are shared and discussed with another as an input to the PASTA stage's activity.

The previously referenced Figure 7.6 provides an image where each respective effort is applied in the right amount and with the appropriate resistance from the opposing force to achieve a proper balance of both functional features and security countermeasures. Such security countermeasures are applied against the residual risk that has not been accepted or transferred by the business unit sponsoring the

---

Management
- Members of this group represent product management officials, development managers, and business leaders who have a vested interest in the success of the subject application. Members of this group are sought for their business perspective, which helps validate the business objectives fulfilled by the product application that is being threat modeled. They also serve to validate the inherent risk profile that is achieved during this stage.

Project managers & Business analysts
- Project Managers and Business Analysts are both responsible for how business requirements are determined, shaped, and communicated. For this reason, they are responsible and accountable for the accuracy of representing the totality of these requirements during this stage. These members are intended to represent PMs and BA personnel from within an application team. Any role that is non-existent within the group can be substituted with the appropriate individual(s) that help define requirements for the application.

Compliance
- Compliance members are responsible for defining the regulatory blueprint that relates to the application. Regulatory requirements will most likely be addressed by security measures being factored in early in the SDLC, however, for greater assurance that both security and compliance is addressed early in the SDLC, the compliance members will be consulted in order to define a roster of relevant regulatory requirements that could affect business goals and objectives.

Information Security Officer (ISO)
- The ISO (Information Security Officer) serves as a bridge to collect business requirements and introduce security requirements to the conversation. They are responsible for conveying what internal security guidelines or standards may need to be followed as well as external security best practices that equate to pre-emptive, threat mitigation strategies.

Figure 7.6 PASTA Roles for Stage I

application environment. This effort represents the yin and the yang commonly depicted between business and InfoSec. Fortunately, this adversarial view is lightened via the PASTA methodology as it is very conducive to a greater level of transparency and understanding among each group's objectives. This is due to the fact that the PASTA stages force collaboration among disparate groups – all who support and the SDLC process in various ways.

Taking a historic look at IT, we can recall how the schism between technology and business was improved through introducing new roles such as the systems analyst and the business analyst – both roles that lobby between business and information technology groups, such as network engineering, system administration, and database administration. In InfoSec, the Information Security Officer (ISO) has similarly helped to provide this mediating role. The ISO plays an important role in the PASTA threat modeling methodology as they provide the bridge among security and IT groups. Over its iterative cycle, all participants in PASTA will grow more aware of activity objectives and appreciate both the business risk aspects as well as the technical risks considerations. In the beginning, however, ISOs play a pivotal role given their background in mediating across business units on topics related to business risk and technology risk. ISOs have also traditionally represented Governance, Risk, and Compliance (GRC) groups and are involved in producing many of the commonly used deliverables within that function such as Business Impact Assessments (BIAs), Risk Assessment reports, Vendor Risk Assessments, and standards documents. Being able to understand the objectives of both business and security will provide for greater unity and collaboration during the PASTA process.

A key benefit to PASTA's stage I is that it helps clear the negative image associated with ISOs and the artifacts produced by them or their GRC colleagues – namely Risk Assessments and Business Impact Analyses (BIAs and also Business Risk Impact Analysis. Instead, prior security deliverables are leveraged in stage I of the threat model in order to portray initial risk, security, or compliance issues that should be considered against the functional requirements for the application environment. In regard to the ISOs' roles and their inherent weaker abilities in more technical security issues, their inclusion in the threat modeling team helps to offset some of their more deficient areas. As a result, ISOs can continue to work with the business in order to gauge how the applications will embellish existing security knowledge as well as interpolate business risk more effectively compared to their more technical counterparts in security operations that are leveraged later on in the PASTA process.

Stage I Summary

So now that we have a good understanding of stage I (Define Objectives) of the PASTA methodology, we turn our attention to building from these efforts in order to apply them to the technical scope of the application environment in stage II (introduced and covered in the next section). To recap, stage I of the PASTA process allows business objectives to be understood and security-related generalizations to be made in order to drive obvious governance efforts that should be followed. Answers related to the following questions are some of the tangible takeaways from this stage that should be addressed.

- What is the scope of the threat model?
- What is the most critical objective supported by the application?
- What is the most critical objective supported by the threat model? (e.g. – identifying threats related to information leakage)
- What will this application do?
- What risk has traditionally affected this application in the past?
- Are there inherited risks based on deployment model, architecture, or third-party technologies that are assumed?
- How many inherent risk issues are associated with the application today?
- What data requirements does this application have?
- Who does the application serve? (internal, external clients, external consumers, government, etc.)
- Does this application have revenue generating/impacting considerations that should be noted/defined?
- What are the Service Level Agreements (SLAs) that would be associated with the application?
- What dependencies are created by the application to customers/consumers? (e.g. Cloud data backup service that is B2C, Utility/Energy related, Financial Reporting)
- What inherent risks are implicitly assumed by the service delivery associated with the application? (e.g. PII, Safe Harbor, Top Secret)
- What is the full scope of regulatory or compliance considerations that should be extracted as regulatory controls and considered for design considerations or building other types of functional requirements?

The aforementioned are the basic questions that any business should consider when brainstorming new ideas or enumerating features for a new software application. The answers to these questions help define the technology, people, and physical infrastructure that will be needed to help sustain the desired solution in the context of fulfilling the business objectives.

In conclusion of this phase, we take a look at the key steps and goals that should be achieved by stage I. They are as follows:

(a) Defining a list of key business objectives for the application.
(b) Defining security requirements (particularly around the data).
(c) Leveraging any existing Business Impact Analysis (BIAs) deliverables or have one launched.
(d) Determining the regulatory requirements associated with the application environment.

Figure 7.7 summarizes the steps for stage I of PASTA and reviews possible inputs and outputs associated with this phase of the threat modeling methodology.

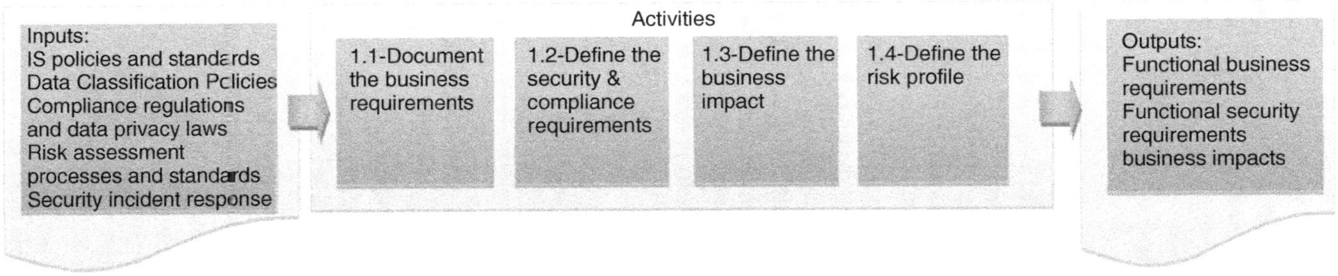

Inputs:
IS policies and standards
Data Classification Policies
Compliance regulations and data privacy laws
Risk assessment processes and standards
Security incident response

Activities

1.1-Document the business requirements

1.2-Define the security & compliance requirements

1.3-Define the business impact

1.4-Define the risk profile

Outputs:
Functional business requirements
Functional security requirements
business impacts

Figure 7.7 PASTA Risk-Centric Threat Modeling – Stage I – (DO) Definition of the Objectives

Stage II of PASTA – Defining the Technical Scope (DTS)

In a risk-centric approach to application threat modeling, the focus is on protecting high-risk assets. PASTA helps identify whether the risk of an asset's compromise is worth more or less than the time and effort to develop countermeasures. For this reason, the focus in stage II is to identify all of the assets in the application environment. The objective is ultimately to enumerate all types of hardware and software components that support the use cases of the application. Later in the process, the threat modeling team will help map relevant threats to the assets identified.

We recall that stage I of the PASTA methodology maps well into any *requirements definition phase* of a given SDLC process by listing any governance-related issues, along with inherent risk and business impact considerations. In this chapter, we build upon this foundation of defined business objectives, inherent risk, and associated impact to understand the application environment from a technical perspective. This collective understanding is very useful in order to define a technical scope for the application environment. Secondly, extend the use of *blind threat modeling* from stage I, we will have an opportunity to build a baseline of security controls aimed at reducing the attack surface for each asset component[2] contained within the scope of the threat model. Controls may traverse physical, logical, or network boundaries. As introduced in stage I, blind threat modeling seeks to reduce the scope of functionality for each component without reducing the overall functionality of its intended use within the application environment. Much of blind threat modeling is simply security hardening and functional deprecation in the absence of a defined threat pattern. In this stage, the technology scope can dictate what types of controls work best to divest needless functionality from software components and harden those services, accounts, ports, and overall component configuration. In summary, security hardening achieves preemptive risk mitigation, which in turn supports the preservation and fulfillment of business objectives associated with the overall application environment.

There are five key activities within Stage II of PASTA. They are as follows:

- S2:A1 Enumerate Software Components.
- S2:A2 Identify Actors & Data Sinks/Sources.
- S2:A3 Enumerate System-Level services.
- S2:A4 Enumerate third-party infrastructures.
- S2:A5 Assert completeness of secure technical design.

The activities of stage II provide a list of which the underlying technology stack will be comprised. This includes the platform/system, relevant databases, application servers, network servers, infrastructure equipment, biometric hardware, and any other

---

[2]Component is intended to refer to an asset or subasset within the threat model that could serve as the target to a direct or indirect attack.

IT asset that will be used to fulfill the objectives defined under stage I. Essentially, the activities across this stage defines the various components (assets or sub-assets) that will be later dissected by the application threat model. Any of these technologies could either serve as the immediate attack surface or target component within the threat model. The technology scope therefore helps form the environment in which a future attack tree will be representing, along with associated vulnerabilities, attacks, actors, and so on.

Stage II of PASTA (Technical Scope) attempts to answer the common problem or question, "I didn't know that we were running/using that technology in our app." Stage II is essentially a large enumeration project. It focuses on itemizing software and hardware assets in order to later define a lean and relevant attack surface whose components could be exploited by various possible threats. Activities in this stage should produce a roster of technological components that are inventoried. This in itself is incredibly useful and can be leveraged over time as the technology scope of the application changes. The roster of application components needs to extend beyond traditional realms (i.e. server, infrastructure appliance, end point). The list should span to include layered pieces of technologies that may be embedded. The simple rule is to identify anything that has a direct exposure to a caller or actor, whether it is from a human or a compiled library that only calls another component based on an event or interpreted result. Essentially, the asset breakdown should extend beyond hardware and include software-based technologies such as proxies, middleware, authentication servers, compiled libraries, open-source libraries, third-party APIs, browser-based plug-ins, and so on. Today's feature-rich UIs for example need to be dissected properly in order to ensure that all of the client and presentation layer technologies are properly enumerated.

Later on, these assets will serve as the main "trunk" to the attack tree to be developed in PASTA's stage VI. The tree will ultimately show underlying use cases, data components, and actors interact with each other. From each one of these nodes, further branches can be split out to show unique threats for each underlying node stemming from the initial asset component. Scoping is important for this exercise as too broad of a scope may confuse the subsequent steps. Too broad of a scope inhibits good analysis. For this reason, a tighter scope of assets is suggested in order that a simpler and more efficient threat model can be created.

Stage II: Activity I (S2:A1) Enumerate Software Components Achieving the objectives for this activity will come from the following exercises:

1. Interview Consulted or Accountable roles in the RACI as to what software and data sources reside in the application.
2. Review any existing data schemas to understand type of data managed by application.
3. Use tools to quickly enumerate software components, data repositories, file systems, and so on.

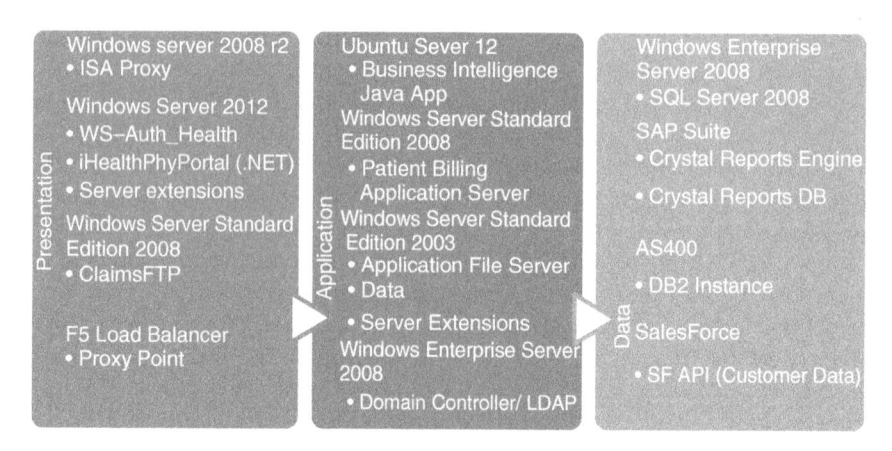

Presentation
- Windows server 2008 r2
  - ISA Proxy
- Windows Server 2012
  - WS–Auth_Health
  - iHealthPhyPortal (.NET)
  - Server extensions
- Windows Server Standard Edition 2008
  - ClaimsFTP
- F5 Load Balancer
  - Proxy Point

Application
- Ubuntu Sever 12
  - Business Intelligence Java App
- Windows Server Standard Edition 2008
  - Patient Billing Application Server
- Windows Server Standard Edition 2003
  - Application File Server
  - Data
- Server Extensions
- Windows Enterprise Server 2008
  - Domain Controller/ LDAP

Data
- Windows Enterprise Server 2008
  - SQL Server 2008
- SAP Suite
  - Crystal Reports Engine
  - Crystal Reports DB
- AS400
  - DB2 Instance
- SalesForce
  - SF API (Customer Data)

Figure 7.8 Software/Data Enumeration Containers

The easiest way to enumerate technology scope, particularly from software and data sources, is to establish "containers" for where the application software components reside across the overall architecture. For example, in a traditional three-tiered application environment consisting of Presentation, Application, and Data Layers, software technologies can be enumerated into these three containers. An example of how these three containers would look is presented in Figure 7.8.

The "containers" are ways to organize assets (both data and software) into groups. In the figure, the containers show four activities for which enumeration techniques are needed. Each "container" reflects a layer within the environment that has a clear difference in functionality across the application environment. If lists are used, a prefix to the type of application component also helps to organize the components by a type of value that reflects the server type, architectural layer, impact level, or other characteristic.

Building a technical scope begins with understanding how the data traverses the OSI model within the application scope. This analysis should be granular enough to understand how data is managed across the relevant network (within the application), encompasses file storage solutions (from file repositories to physical storage devices), as well as considerations for client software technology.

As part of this stage's activity, the following questions serve as sample questions around data use that can be used to ensure proper scoping within the threat model.

1. Where is the data originating from, what distinct actors or unique data calls are being made, and what sources are requesting the data? (Defining proper trust boundaries, API security implications.)
2. Where is the data ultimately being stored (short-term basis)? Considerations for caching, dynamically created flat files, and relational databases should be made.

3. How many types of networks/network segments will data traverse? (Network configuration and segmentation, data in transit security considerations.)
4. Are there any application servers that will provide any level of validation to the data and at what points? (Implies any distributed or middleware servers that may be in scope.)
5. Will the processes around my data provide use for nonrelational database considerations? (Data at rest considerations, file level encryption, file system-level security.)
6. Is there a long-term storage area for which the data will ultimately reside? (SAN implications, data classification, data retention implications.)
7. Will data be accessed remotely (outside of a company managed LAN)? (Implications for security access control models, authentication, authorization, network security.)
8. What software will interface with the data (web related, client related)? (Implies authorized use criteria, CRUD (create, read, update, delete exercises), data ownership/access models, whitelisted APIs, etc.)
9. In what format will my data traverse over the network (serialized data stream, file upload, xml data blob, etc.)? (Implies use of data in transit security measures, injectable data structures, overall security of data schemas.)
10. What network and application level services will help sustain my data or its user base across the application stack? (Implies dependencies to network services that affect the messaging and security of the data and use of any network standards to secure such services – DNS, DHCP, SNMP, FTP, Active Directory/LDAP, etc.)

These 10 questions provide a good starting point for understanding the context of an application via its data use. In knowing how system or application components are using data types and of inherent impact levels (per type), threat mitigation can be applied in a commensurate manner. Later in stage III (Application Decomposition), DFDs will help to produce the interaction of all system and application components to these data sources.

Providing a proper *technical scope* should begin with consideration of the data life cycle within the application environment and the technology that ultimately sustains and secures it. Purely looking at technical scope based on technology use versus data use will not make much sense via the PASTA threat modeling methodology because of its focus on risk. A large part of risk will stem from data value, information loss, and so on. During this stage of the PASTA methodology, considerations for data use will help define the technical infrastructure that will be used as part of the SDLC process. Later in stage III, a logical representation of data calls can be done via data flow diagrams (DFDs). DFDs help illustrate the interoperability of technology components across the application environment, including, but not limited to, application, database, and client software layers. Examples include how access control is used to control data access across various sources. Understanding data flow across schematics, blueprints, or architectural application designs will help to correlate the types of countermeasures that may need to be implemented should these measures be found to be either vulnerable or fostering ripe attack vectors.

Stage II: Activity II (S2:A2) Identify Actors and Data Sinks/Sources Achieving the objectives for this activity will come from the following exercises:

1. Identify what actors (human or application based) are serving as worker processes, requestors, callers potentially leveraging authentication criteria.
2. Run CRUD (Create, Read, Update, Delete) exercises against application actors to map associated permissions across the application layers.
3. Perform static analysis of configuration files, which may store username/passwords. This may reveal application level actors that are less well known.
4. Audit LDAP/AD servers that may provide integrated authentication techniques.
5. Sniff application traffic to other key asset components that may contain a pre-shared key, cert, authentication engine in order to see if authentication calls have been missed in enumeration efforts thus far.
6. Identify data repositories by identifying protocols common for data transfer among client and data repositories (SMB, MySQL, SQL Server, Postgres, DB2, FTP, SCP, XML-RPC, etc.)
7. Perform data discovery techniques in order to identify any data extracts/exports that may relate to application data sinks/sources.

Similar to the other activities around enumerating software, systems, and third-party software, this activity is focused on identifying smaller components that actually run or operate within the previously listed exercises. Within these two exercises, we will identify all database, system, and application actors that are making/receiving requests on each asset or across the application environment. There are tools to map actors associated with running system process IDs (PIDs) that help identify some of the inherent actors on a given system or third-party product. One example of doing this at the system/platform level for a physical or virtual Windows host is using SysInternals by Microsoft.

Mapping a user's activities to active PIDs on Windows is simple using Microsoft's Process Explorer.

1. To begin, download Process Explorer from http://technet.microsoft.com/en-us/sysinternals/bb896653.aspx.
2. Unzip process explorer into a directory where you keep utilities.
3. Next, run procexp.exe.
4. Process Explorer will present you with a list of all the processes running along with other information such as CPU usage, RAM consumption, PID, a description, and the software's manufacturer.

TABLE 7.6 Simple CRUD Mapping Across a Product Application

	Presentation Layer	Application Layer	Data Layer
Create	• ftp_user01 • dc1_super1	• soap_user01 • app_int01	• batch_usr1 • hostdb_user1
Read	• w3wp.exe • dc1_super1	• soap_user01 • app_int03	• batch_usr2 • hostdb_user1
Update	• Rrpc_app01 • dc1_super1	• soap_user01 • app_int02	• batch_usr1 • hostdb_user1
Delete	• N/A • dc1_super1	• soap_user01 • app_int01	• batch_usr3 • hostdb_user1

5. Select the Users drop down and you will be able to select which user's processes you wish to view.
6. If this data is needed externally, selecting Save from the File drop down will allow you to export the current user's process information as a CSV.

Design Time Exercise – CRUD Beyond using tool-based techniques to extrapolate the actors and services of the product application environment, application architects and members of the development team should be able to create an initial list of actors and required services that sustain the application use contained within the environment. Developers, for example, can perform CRUD exercises to determine what actors will be used to Create, Read, Update, or Delete data from the data repository, whether it be a backend database or a flat file system. An example of a simple CRUD exercise can be found in Table 7.6.

When searching for relevant data sources in application environments, these are best and easily identified via application schematic designs, which may explicitly identify a nice pair of database clusters that contain all data for the application, or better yet a single mainframe. In today's highly diverse word of data stores, understanding data flow and storage is a treasure hunt. In instances where schematic data flows do not exist, certain e-Discovery tools, along with other efforts, can help to build a DFD that makes sense. E-Discovery scans for certain known application file extensions (.xml, .csv, .txt, .dat, etc.) can all be used in order to regex the nonsystem related files of a file system to see where possible data sources/sinks exist in the application environment. Beyond e-discovery efforts, source code reviews can search for authentication strings that may authentication to data sources. This can further reveal what ftp, RDBMS systems, or file shares are being used to do data pushes/pulls across the data environment.

Stage II: Activity III (S2:A3) Enumerate System-Level Services Achieving the objectives for this activity will come from the following exercises:

1. Interview Consulted or Accountable roles in the RACI as to what platforms and system services are to support the application.
2. Review any existing network design documentation.
3. Run quick tools to enumerate platforms and ports/services used.

Platform enumeration seeks to discover what system types or operating systems are being used. This may also include middleware. Service enumeration is aimed at identifying what services are running on the system assets on which much of the application software will be running. Both of these exercises will require the use of some system commands and/or simple tools that facilitate identifying both services and actors in association with various use cases of the product application. A port scanner, for example, would be able to do both the platform identification and the service enumeration for a given scope. If, for example, my test product application runs on a 192.168.52.0/28 network, I can scan that and see what the scope of platforms and services are.

Note that system platforms encompass application servers and/or databases within each container. They also reveal possible third-party products or autonomous application environments (e.g. cloud services, SaaS services) that may support the overall application solution. Third-party products in general are difficult to include in the threat model since they are largely black boxes for which an underlying understanding of technology is absent. Third-party cloud environments are even more complex since the ability to scan or interface with any facet of the cloud infrastructure is not commonly permitted by the cloud or hosted operator. Vendor products and tools, although proprietary in nature, at least present the opportunity for security practitioners to scan and interface with the host in order to ascertain some level of security assurance. Both third-party services and appliances should be listed under the correct container for activities under this step.

There are scores of package management utilities available, including YAST, apt, and dpkg for Linux, and Windows Program Manager for Windows. While these tools do their jobs well, they are limited in their capabilities and if there is any diversity of operating systems on the network, then systems administrators will end up with a diversity of report types. To avoid this unnecessary use of time and resources, it is recommended that you use a security scanner such as Tenable's Nessus or Rapid7's NeXpose. These will produce formalized descriptions of installed packages in a heterogeneous network with much less time and effort than using the aforementioned options. They also provide functionality well beyond the scope of package management, including the ability to identify services open on a given platform as well as the ability to fingerprint the platform OS and any embedded OS that may be present. All of this information helps the threat modeling process by identifying a blueprint of assets with possible inherent vulnerabilities. Such data will be further leveraged in stages IV and V (Table 7.7).

TABLE 7.7 Software Enumeration from Automated Tools

Software	Count
Microsoft Office XP Professional with FrontPage [version 10.0.2627.01]	1
Microsoft Silverlight [version 2.0.40115.0]	1
Mozilla Firefox (2.0.0.2) [version 2.0.02 (en-US)]	1
Nessus [version 4.4.1.15078]	1
Symantec pcAnywhere [version 12.0.0]	1
Tenable LCE Client 2003 (×86) [version 3.6.2]	1
Adobe Reader 7.0 [version 7.0.0]	1
Mozilla Firefox (3.0) [version 3.0 (en-US)]	1
Microsoft Silverlight [version 3.0.40624.0]	1

Referring to the aforementioned figure, we see that the containers encompass software and system assets that operate within a presentation or DMZ layer of a fictitious architecture. The subsequent layers represent an application layer where business logic or some degree of validation may be applied to requests and responses for data exchanges that are both downstream and upstream. Lastly, a data layer represents where the greatest level of protection should be applied to the assets, given the presumed data centralization of key business and/or client data.

Missing from the example is a container for client-side technologies that are developed by the product/software development team. This includes the likes of JavaScript, Flash, and Silverlight technologies. These technologies should also be included in the threat modeling activities for stage II as they could be the target of threat mitigation in subsequent steps.

The collection of the data for technological asset enumeration can be contained in the Comprehensive Threat Modeling Workbook Tab labeled "S2-Define Tech Scope for App." With respect to technology enumeration, the worksheet will also allow technology components to be divided into various categories using the drop down features of each row. The objective is to create a comprehensive list of technology assets that can be reviewed for functional use cases, interoperability, and inherent security (or lack thereof) within the proposed product application design.

Stage II. Activity IV (S2:A4) Enumerate Third-Party Infrastructures Many application environments use various external networks. Some may be in the form of cloud-based services such as PaaS, SaaS, or IaaS while others will be along the lines of a more traditional third-party ASP or colocation model. Whatever the service, it is important to bring third-party infrastructures into the technical scope. Depending on the relationship and the legal terms around "right to audit," certain automated solutions could be used similar to the activities for a captive or self-hosted model. However, many third-party vendors do not like their environments to be scanned without proper permission, so it is important to ensure that any discovery scanning efforts against a multitenant or shared hosting environment is cleared beforehand. For this reason, realistic actions to perform under this activity include the following:

1. Interview third-party technology SMEs in order to identify what software, data, platforms, and system services are to support the application.
2. Review any existing network design documentation from the third-party.
3. Run quick tools to enumerate software used, data repositories (flat files, relational DB), fingerprint platforms, and ports/services used (may depend on legal agreements with the third party).

Generally speaking, technical points of contact are generally made available to nearly any customer of any size. Most account management teams themselves will have the information or know of the internal SME who can provide requested asset/component information pertaining to your hosted solution. For some of the larger hosting service providers (such as Windows Azure, Amazon AWS, Akamai, RackSpace, etc.), the hardest thing is simply trying to find the right point of contact with whom to correspond with. Although no hosting provider enjoys the inquisition-like experience of being asked questions related to their environment, the smartest hosting providers have actually organized technical information around the most common questions and answers, including a roster of what exposed services and APIs pertain to the services that are provided to most tenants. As most hosting providers are not keen on divulging their architecture and software components, even in the wake of audits from their most affluent clients, attempting to extract as much information from them via a light assessment process can go a long way. Second to that is the ability to interact with the hosted environment and derive what network, system, and application components are present within the hosted model.

The following is an example where a cross section of an application model may be using the Microsoft Azure Cloud solution. Azure Storage may provide a cloud-based repository for your application to leverage as part of an overall functionality. Within Azure Storage, there may be namespaces that your application is using or interfacing with. An example of some of the services found within the Azure Cloud product (Azure Storage) is listed as follows:

- *Microsoft.WindowsAzure.ServiceRuntime:* Classes in this namespace enable you to interact with the Windows Azure environment from code running within your role.
- *Microsoft.WindowsAzure.Diagnostics:* Classes in this namespace enable you to collect logs and diagnostic information from code running within your role.
- *Microsoft.WindowsAzure.Diagnostics.Management:* Classes in this namespace enable you to collect logs and diagnostic information remotely.

These classes may create new instances of objects that are used in the application that should perhaps be included as part of a software component hosted by a third-party vendor. Depicting the aforementioned components in an enumeration list will allow for subsequent application decomposition efforts to take place in stage III. Following similar exercises will help to enumerate other third-party technology components.

Stage II: Activity V (S2:A5) – Assert Completeness of Secure Technical Design
At the end of S2:A4, one will have the ability to organize the application components into groups that allow one to better map how defined use cases are supported by the underlying technologies and networks (in stage III). Classification of asset components also facilitates the strategy for inherent risk mitigation to take place, all depending on how the assets components are classified. Multiple classifications can take place to "tag" asset components in various ways such as architectural position (data layer, app layer, etc.), criticality level of server, criticality level of information, criticality level to business. All of these designations are not necessary to define immediately, but reaching a point where these characteristics are defined over time will provide for a much more streamlined form of identifying what asset components are worth performing some level of inherent risk mitigation during this activity.

This activity presents basic exercises aimed at organizing the identified application components and providing a level of security assurance that inherent risk mitigation strategies are applied to the identified components from this stage. It should be pointed out that this activity's efforts extend beyond enumeration and into applying some level of countermeasures that come from existing requirements for security. This activity provides for an analysis on how to classify the scope of technology components that will be threat modeled as well, therefore it looks to verify the thoroughness for which the scope has been created. Doing so affects so many other activities downstream, some of which we have already discussed, such as inherent threat mitigation. Others include correlating vulnerability research or threat intelligence to the components that have been identified. This is achieved by making application dissection both intuitive and comprehensive. *Containers* or dissection categories can be used to organize threat modeling *ingredients* or elements, which include actors, services, data, shared pipes, and so on across the breadth of the application solution. The criteria for a container can be anything (as previously mentioned-criticality, architectural role, etc.), but a good rule of thumb would be to use a criteria that is consistent. One of the easiest forms of criteria can be the architectural positioning of the application component. For example, the following seven containers reflect an architectural location of physical asset components in the overall technical scope of an application.

1. Client Software.
2. Client Platform.
3. Client Hardware.
4. Server Software.
5. Server Platform.
6. Server Hardware.
7. Network.

These seven areas are collectively broad enough to address most threat modeling targets and narrow enough to individually provide adequate threat modeling ingredient organization for the threat modeler. Items 4–7 (inclusive) can also be virtualized. You may have both traditionally hosted and cloud-based components that relate to software, platform, and hardware and this would not be redundant. The reason would be that the administrative service and process supporting such technology would be vastly different from a self-hosted physical asset versus a virtual hosted asset in a multitenant PaaS environment.

As the technology changes, the relevancy of these container groups may change or even disappear over a long period of time; however, even with the proliferation of virtual computing platforms, the hardware containers, for example, are still very much relevant given virtual host resource consumption levels of physical hardware components such as power, physical, and network interfaces – all of which can receive unique configurations that undermine secure implementation of the whole application. Overall, the platform security stack is often overlooked by other types of threat models; therefore it is important that stage III builds upon the successful enumeration of technology assets in stage II in order to define the interrelationships among all assets (both physical and virtual). Although we are engaging in application threat modeling, applications often times leverage the environment variables and configurations of its underlying platform or system host.

Containers formed under this activity help organize asset types and initiate how interrelationships are formed. A great example on how this activity can make for better application decomposition later in stage III is the area of embedded system security. Malware-laced hardware products, particularly in POS devices for retailers, health-care handheld devices with client software, and proprietary military equipment with an application stack embodied in a small ecology of asset types that have embedded kernels, users, roles, APIs, and more could easily be missed in other threat models. Depending on the Threat Analysis conducted in stage IV, these variables may actually become material to the overall threat model but should be considered and identified earlier. In other threat modeling methodologies, a threat analysis may legitimize this threat; however, there may not have been the necessary component enumeration and classification in order to identify which component to apply countermeasures to. PASTA provides this opportunity to prepare for such an organization to application components in this stage.

A representation of each of these seven containers for maintaining dissected application components is presented in the series of graphics as follows (see Figure 7.9).

Within this PASTA methodology walk-through, security analysis and countermeasures can be introduced across each stage in order to address and support business objectives related to the environment being threat modeled as well as mitigate risks identified by each phase of the methodology. Governance artifacts, however, are best consumed within stage II of the PASTA methodology. Within Stage II of the methodology, correlations are drawn to appropriate governance efforts in order to build security into preexisting SDLC efforts that are part of an established workflow. This allows traditional security shelf-ware, such as requirements, checklists, standards, and (in some cases) policies to become "actionable" and baked into the

EXPLORING THE SEVEN STAGES AND EMBEDDED THREAT MODELING ACTIVITIES 379

Client software
Description: End client software stack that handles input, application output, initial data integrity, authorization of APIs, client side storage, etc.

Considerations: Ajax, Silverlight, DHTML5, Javascript, Plugins, Fat client, mobile client software.

Client platform
Description: Client platform kernel level, file system, process availability, encryption capabilities, system logging, and more are addressed.

Considerations: Mobile iOS, Android, Proprietary Platform (ex: medical), or any client side platform where data is processing.

Client hardware
Description: Security of physical interfaces to server hardware, ease of hardware theft, hardware tampering, mobility of device.

Considerations: Mobile devices, tablets, ultrabooks, netbooks, notebooks, Mobile POS Devices, Mobile Medical Devices, Smartphones, etc.

Server software
Description: Server side application software(s) responsible for initial data receipt, processing, validation, and management.

Considerations: COTS software such as proxy servers, middleware, database abstraction layers, proprietary code aimed at applying business/data validation.

Server platform
Description: Server side application software(s) responsible for initial data receipt, processing, validation, and management.

Considerations: OS level considerations and security, filesystem level security, kernel hacking, elevated OS privileges, logging, filesystem/object level encryption and more.

Server hardware
Description: Security of physical interfaces, physical device security, hardware tampering, embedded system, security review of product manufacturer.

Considerations: Integrated server chassis, server blades, 1U/2U manufacturer devices, ease of replacements, failover and redundancy.

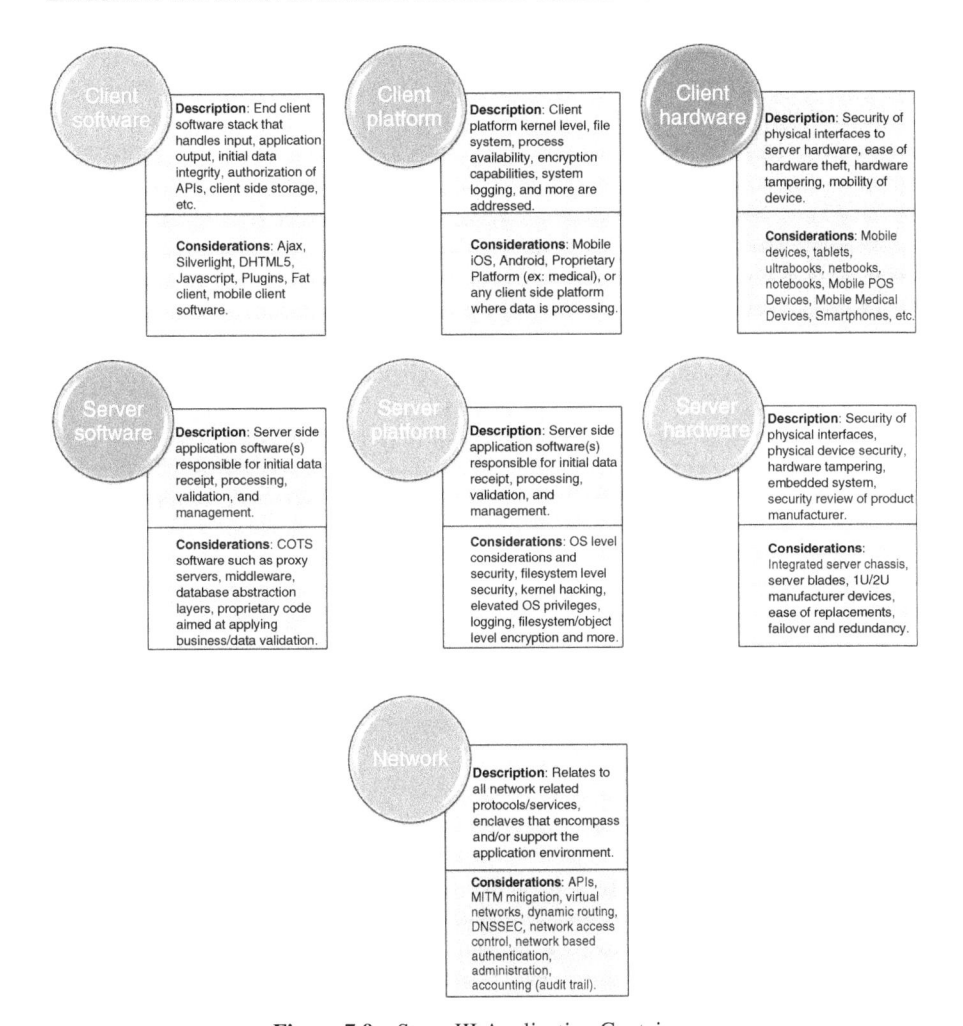

Network
Description: Relates to all network related protocols/services, enclaves that encompass and/or support the application environment.

Considerations: APIs, MITM mitigation, virtual networks, dynamic routing, DNSSEC, network access control, network based authentication, administration, accounting (audit trail).

Figure 7.9 Stage III Application Containers

development process or change control process for a given application environment. The translation of business to security objectives will ultimately create the opportunity for traditional security governance efforts to be injected into the application design – reiterating the idea that application threat modeling can finally integrate security efforts that have traditionally been excluded early on in the SDLC process.

Ultimately, upon reaching a clear understanding of the types of technology to be used under stage II (Technical Scope), a baseline of security considerations can be formed in order to create a baseline level of security configuration aimed at sustaining the technological, operational, and business objectives for a given application. Moreover, we see the potential to leverage technology and security governance in order to provide some degree of tangible evidence or examples of these governance by-products. The following table lists examples of governance documents and/or tools that may primarily be leveraged from the manufacturer of given technologies across the application environment. Most of the references given subsequently are denoted as external forms of standards for securing or hardening various technologies commonly found in application environments. A company's own internal technology standards would be the preferred starting point, presuming that they support the business objective via their given function. The following table is not meant to represent a comprehensive set of hardened security standards/tools, but are mostly used as examples to convey the point of applying various recommendations for hardened technology platforms. Most importantly, these references are completely free and are specific to a type of platform and are generally provided by the technology manufacturer, such as Microsoft, Oracle, Cisco, and so on (Table 7.8).

The point of the aforementioned table is not to provide a listing of security governance tools and documentations, which are bound to expire, but instead to demonstrate that a lot of resources for preemptive security hardening can take place during stage II as a technical scope of assets is defined for the application. Many of these resources can be found on the manufacturer's site of the OS or platform used. The key point to be made is that this layer of preemptive hardening provides a species of *blind threat modeling*, which simply acknowledges that a specific threat has not been defined, but as threats are inevitable, implementing an easy baseline of platform or system controls could add security to various layers, thereby supporting the age-old adage of defense-in-depth, which is still a reasonable and encouraged approach in general.

The previous table introduces countermeasures that address possible uses of technology within the application environment, all this without having entered into the formal threat analysis. This translates to something that can be termed *blind threat modeling* – considering and implementing base security controls prior to formally revealing defined threats and threat actors. The blind threat model is formed in recognition of data use cases for the application, protecting the fulfillment of defined business objectives, and preemptively addressing regulatory requirements that are naturally in scope. No other threat modeling methodology factors in this aspect of blind threat modeling and although this inclusion of controls and countermeasures may be criticized as nontopical to a defined threat, this process provides a primer of security controls supporting business objectives and fosters greater reliance to build security requirements early on in the SLDC. Many of the security standards that would be applied would naturally mitigate a large amount of system/network configuration and implementation flaws that would normally be present across system and software implementations (SSL Implementation, PKI roll outs, Authentication etc.). As a result, baking designated security controls into the application architecture preemptively elevates the level of risk mitigation and accomplishes a huge feat of truly building security-in.

In the event that limited technology governance material exists internally, external references to security checklists and/or hardening guidelines could be used as security governance for various assets (targets) in the PASTA threat model. For large company enterprises where technology and security governance is more prevalent, internal

TABLE 7.8 Free Hardening Guidelines/Tools for Inherent Risk Mitigation or Blind Threat Modeling (Stage II – PASTA)

Asset	Governance Reference/Tool	Reference
Windows asset (Win7, W2K8, and beyond)	Enhanced Mitigation Experience Toolkit (EMET) v3.0	http://www.microsoft.com/en-us/download/details.aspx?id=29851
ISA Proxy Server	Windows Hardening Guide for ISA Proxy 2006	http://technet.microsoft.com/en-us/library/bb794718.aspx
Windows IIS (Win7, W2K8, and beyond)	URLScan 3.0	http://technet.microsoft.com/en-us/library/dd450367(v=WS.10).aspx
Windows Servers or Computing Endpoints	Microsoft Baseline Security Analyzer (MBSA)	http://www.microsoft.com/en-us/download/details.aspx?id=7558
IIS Server (v6 & up)	IIS Lockdown Tool	http://support.microsoft.com/kb/235864
IIS 7 Web Server	Windows Server Hardening Guide (2308)	http://technet.microsoft.com/en-us/library/bb794718.aspx
Windows 2008 Enterprise	Podcast and Hardening Guide for W2K8	http://www.microsoft.com/events/podcasts/default.aspx?pageId=x344
Apache Web Server	Whitepaper on Hardening Apache Web Server	http://people.apache.org/~sctemme/ApconEU2008/Hardening%20Enterprise%20Apache.pptx
Oracle Database	Oracle Database Vault	http://www.oracle.com/us/products/database/options/database-vault/index.html
MySQL Database	Making MySQL Secure Against Attackers, Setting Up SSL Certificates for MySQL	http://dev.mysql.com/doc/refman/5.0/en/security-against-attack.html http://dev.mysql.com/doc/refman/5.6/en/secure-create-certs.html
Cisco iOS	Fortifying SNMP, General Management Plane Hardening	http://www.cisco.com/en/US/tech/tk648/tk361/technologies_tech_note09186a0080120f48.shtml#fortify http://www.cisco.com/en/US/tech/tk648/tk361/technologies_tech_note09186a0080120f48.shtml#configman

(*continued*)

TABLE 7.8 (Continued)

Asset	Governance Reference/Tool	Reference
W2K3 Server (Standard)	Windows Server 2003 Security Baseline (solution accelerator)	http://technet.microsoft.com/en-us/library/cc163140.aspx
MS SQL 2005 Server	Database Mirroring Best Practices and Performance Considerations (Availability)	http://technet.microsoft.com/en-us/library/cc917681.aspx
Sun Solaris 10 Application Server	Solaris Security Toolkit 4.2	http://www.sun.com/software/security/jass/
SuSe Enterprise Server Edition	SuSe Enterprise Security Tools and Documentation	The security tools that Novell has available ranging across an array of different topics that include everything from secure OS configuration to certificate implementation. http://www.novell.com/communities/coolsolutions/tools?filter0=securityandfilter1=All
Juniper Networks Firewall	Juniper Security Configuration for Switches	Provides reference to secure configuration guidance on the JUNOS Software. http://www.juniper.net/techpubs/software/junos-security/junos-security10.1/junos-security-swconfig-security/junos-security-swconfig-security.pdf
Windows 2010 SharePoint Server	Framework for deploying shared services across SharePoint farms	Reveals a best practice security model around the implementation of share service farms and hosts http://office.microsoft.com/en-us/windows-sharepoint-services-it/windows-sharepoint-services-security-model-HA001160771.aspx
Windows SharePoint Security Features	Security Features present within SharePoint servers	Windows SharePoint Services 3.0 around inherent security features http://office.microsoft.com/en-us/windows-sharepoint-services-help/about-security-features-of-windows-sharepoint-services-3-0-HA010021578.aspx
ESX Security	VMWare Infrastructure Hardening (v. 3.5)	http://www.vmware.com/files/pdf/vi35_security_hardening_wp.pdf

Ubuntu Server	Tools and guides around how to secure Ubuntu server instances	https://help.ubuntu.com/community/Security
Any client-side web technology	OWASP Anti-Samy	A collection of programmatic code snippets that allow for countermeasures to be factored into most web applications. https://www.owasp.org/index.php/Category:OWASP_AntiSamy_Project
Any web-related application code base	OWASP Cheat Sheet Series	A collection of cheat sheets that show examples of code snippets on how to best mitigate insecure coding errors in web applications and associated components. https://www.owasp.org/index.php/Cheat_Sheets
IIS Webserver	IIS 7.0 Benchmark	Prescriptive guidance for establishing a secure configuration posture for MS IIS 7.0 (source: Center for Internet Security (CIS)) Center for Internet Security
Apache Web Server 2.2.x (v3)	Guidance for securing Apache web servers on primarily RHEL platforms	Microsoft's Pattern and Practices site; Also referenced by NSA.gov
Microsoft Windows Server 2003 Security Standard	Hardening Guide release by Microsoft to secure the system level services and built-in applications	Defense Information Systems Agency (www.disa.mil)
Database Security Checklist and Guidance	Database security considerations from the US Department of Defense	Defense Information Systems Agency (www.disa.mil)
Microsoft ISA 2006 Proxy STIG Version 1, Release 2	Security technical implementation guideline for Microsoft ISA proxy	Defense Information Systems Agency (www.disa.mil)
z/OS RACF STIG, Version 6, Release 5	Guidelines for security mainframe environments' RBAC model via RACF	Defense Information Systems Agency (www.disa.mil)

Note that these URLs may change over time.

standards, guidelines, checklists, or other governance by-products can be leveraged. Additionally, there are several external references for which a secure baseline configuration at the application and system level can be introduced – all in support of the technical and security objectives, which are both areas that should ultimately support business objectives.

It should be mentioned that these external references should really only be used to inspire or sustain those organically developed by a governance group for an organization. If these and/or similar governance items are leveraged and applied against the application environment, the threat model must account for the controls or baseline countermeasures that are implemented as a result of adhering to these governing requirements or recommendations on security at the network, system, or application level. Given that we are attempting to lower the inherent risk profile of an application to an acceptable residual risk, we have to encompass the countermeasures that relate to the network or system environment, particularly if they have been hardened via the conformance to a body of governing security standards.

In the end, governance can stem from internal efforts as well as external sources driven by wider security-related groups. The benefit of these latter groups is a slightly more vast perspective, which may also be their detriment, particularly when in conjunction with Application Threat Modeling efforts. Nonetheless, the content is recyclable, usable, and provides a good baseline. The following is a varied list of external governance material that could be followed during this stage of the application threat modeling process in order to be assured that a solid security foundation is created at the foot of the application environment.

Participants Across Stage II Activities – Technical Scope

As will be reflected for each of the stages of the PASTA threat modeling methodology, the inception of the process hinges upon a clear understanding of the business purpose or focus for the threat modeled application. As we will see, the focus will shift slightly more to the security and technical aspect of the application environment analysis in order to deconstruct the functional into dysfunctional areas that can be analyzed for probable vulnerable and attack vectors. The nature of those involved will also slowly begin to exclude more of the business folk and encompass the likes of developers, security testers, pen testers, and web application specialists. For stage II (*Technical Scope*), the key people to be involved are application architects, system engineers, and developers. These three groups of individuals do not represent the entire participant base for this phase for every type of organization; however, they are central to addressing the security of the aforementioned components related to the network, application, system, and data handling within the developing threat model. Therefore, they carry a *Responsible* or *Accountable* role in the previously shown RACI diagram (Figure 6.8). The architects will conceivably have a strong domain over the interrelationships of application calls across the application/network environment. Therefore, their holistic view will allow them to perform application enumeration activities for this stage as well as consider blind threat modeling techniques to evaluate and potentially use tools and reasonable hardening measures. The network architect is also valuable here in order to understand the network infrastructure that is supportive of the environment and what underlying Layer 2/3 protocols are needed to support the application. For reasons similar to those of the system administrator/engineer, the threat modeler needs to understand the default network configuration and hardening that may exist as the underlying communication backbone of the application environment being threat modeled via PASTA – this includes the security configuration of network switches, routers, IPS/IDS devices, and more. The network professional may also contribute in the areas on how high availability network technology is leveraged for given application environments as well as other network-related services that may be used by the targeted application, such as DNS, LDAP, AD, PKI-related servers (Certificate Authorities), application/network proxies, IPSec services, and more. All of these considerations will affect the threat model by revealing countermeasures against attacks at the transport layer. As a joint effort, the architects and system engineers can provide an accurate assessment as to the total range of IT assets (both hardware and software) that would be needed and in scope for the application environment. Knowing what is in the application environment is currently a challenge for most security assessment efforts as several IT outliers find themselves outside the reach of traditional assessment efforts. Using a combination of technical discovery techniques by the threat modeler (or requested by the threat modeler to SecOps) along with Q&A efforts with architects and system administrators, a defined list of assets across an *n-tiered* environment is possible. The scope of effort for these individuals obviously encompasses the logistical boundaries of the application environment, but may extend to other areas where connectivity and access may exist, such as partner sites, cloud-based APIs, or lower computing environments.

Stage II also requires the role of the lead system administrator for the subject environment. As mentioned before, larger environments may have standardized their server side technology, virtualized on a given platform solution, or gone to their cloud for a hosted solution. The lead system administrator or system engineer is someone that above all else may have knowledge of the standard base image on a given server in any one of these environments. At this point, the threat modeler should work with the various individuals in order to derive what base security controls were configured into the disk image. This may range from a vanilla image from the manufacturer of the OS (Solaris, Windows Server 20xx, SuSe Enterprise Server, etc.) or application server software (Apache, Citrix XenServer, etc.) to a well hardened system based on technical and security requirements, as mandated by a technology or security governance entity within the organization. If no security requirements in the form of hardening guides or technological standards exist, then this is an opportune time to consider what security requirements should be in place. Such security standards derived from this process should be done agnostically of the specific use of any given server technology or platform within the threat model. The intent here is to not progress without some effort of security governance taking place during stage II of PASTA. At the very least, if no governance documentation exists, parallel governance efforts can begin here in order to understand at least what security controls could have been leveraged based on the high-level business and IT objectives understood for the application in stage I of PASTA.

Developers (as the last Responsible or Accountable group in this stage) know what types of software or hardware requirements will adequately support their application environments. In addition, they are quite particular about what types of application servers would function best for their data storage and API needs. Application servers such as databases, proxy servers, memcache servers, e-mail, and cloud-based applications such as Salesforce (CRM) or even Cloud-based services such as OAuth web services, Azure/Amazon AWS APIs, are all technology areas that provide additional information reference points (in terms of asset sources and overall expansion of the possible attack surface). These become relevant components or family of components (referring to Cloud technologies and services) that feed into asset enumeration activities performed within stage II.

Although the *Responsible* and *Accountable* groups are Architects, Developers, and System Administrators, *Consulted* roles are vast in this stage. This is to ensure that all technical assets, networks, and software are accounted for as part of relevant application components. Those consulted (refer to RACI diagram in Figure 6.8) are BAs, QA members, Security Operations (internal or external to organization), security risk management professionals, and those carrying the role of information security officers for various lines of business.

The involvement and activities completed by the aforementioned group of individuals introduces control maturity to PASTA, particularly realizing the case of technology security governance. Beyond nonexistent, a next level governance attempt that could be started from the PASTA process is to begin with general, server/technology agnostic governance documentations that point to base controls that could be applied regardless of asset use. For a supposed CMMI (Capability Maturity Model Integration) value of 1, this newly developed governance documentation may suggest more generic security controls at the system or application configuration level that can be leveraged, regardless of technology use. A common example is applying such generic guidance to web server assets of different use cases: Internet versus intranet presence. Specifically, protecting connection string information in both instances of a web server (assuming a relational backend database) is equally important. More lax configurations on certain server side controls will depend on the nature of the intranet application and its use cases; however, there may be greater leniency on the amount of network protocols that are open on a given host for an intranet server as compared to an internet server found in an external DMZ environment. This is simply one example where a given server type may need to have a security standard developed as a spinoff effort to the threat modeling process. The threat modeler will not be involved in this governance process, however. As it is outside of his/her scope, he/she may liaise the effort between IT and security governance.

Regardless of whether a new artifact of security governance is derived from this process, the key point to take away is involving the lead system engineer or system administrator who may contribute technical guidance as to the base level of controls that may be present across the proposed application architecture. The designated role of the threat modeler is to interface with chief architects, developers, or system administrators, who serve as custodians to the subject application environment, will help the threat modeler determine what topical, governance items can be leveraged. Similar to stage I of PASTA, this exercise under stage II allows the following to be achieved:

- An enumeration of baseline level security controls to mitigate attacks across the attack surface to be defined. The word "baseline" in this case is used in the context of what existing suite of technical controls are present at the OS level or application server level in order to enumerate a "default" set of countermeasures that may assist in attack mitigation or reduction.
- An understanding of technical dependencies among the application environment to platform, software, and network-related technologies.
- Cross reference to any existing technology standards/guidelines allows technology/security governance to become actionable as part of the threat modeling process.

Thus far, we have mentioned three groups of individuals that may be involved in defining the technology scope of PASTA's stage II: the developer, the architect, and system engineers/administrators. These three groups of individuals do not represent an exhaustive list of possible participants that are to be *Responsible/Accountable* within the Technical Scope stage of PASTA, but their inclusion is essential. Other members may be used who have a strong sense of technical understanding to the network, platform, or software components to be used within this stage of the application environment. Related to the SDLC process, it should be noted that this stage of PASTA can be tied to the Requirements Definition stage of a given SDLC process in order to see what underlying technology security requirements can be applied to the overall application environment, in support of the functional business requirements. In the following Stage, Application Decomposition, we will explore the interoperability of the system/platform, application, data, and technical components in order to map out things such as actors, assets (or targets), calls, requests/responses, and more. This stage of PASTA directly correlates with the design process of a given SDLC life cycle.

Contrasting Large and Small Enterprise use of PASTA's Stage II

Although large and small organizations may have similar business objectives for application environments of the same type (point of sale, inventory management, content distribution, etc.), the underlying technology governance implications that support these objectives will differ among the two during stage II. From a technology governance standpoint, larger corporations have an easier time applying a standardized list of inputs to a proposed solution. Large corporations tend to heavily standardize their use of technology. This includes standardization efforts across web servers, hardware, network infrastructure devices, and even third-party services. Due to their depth of financial resources, comparative to smaller companies, larger companies have the strength of both technology consolidation and standardization – which in turn provides a great value for achieving preventative administrative security controls in the form of standards, guidelines, and hardening techniques. This is not to imply that all large corporations standardize technology and services; however, they do possess more of an inherent capability to facilitate security governance. Greater access to employee resources within respective governance groups, financial resources, and overall purchasing power all lend to characteristics where larger organizations are better positioned when it comes to technology standardization, and overall technology governance. Conversely, smaller companies face inherent challenges that are nearly opposite to these same business traits. With limited access to financial resources, a smaller employee base to lead governance efforts, and limited funds for procuring technology, smaller firms indeed face an uphill battle to achieve a high level of threat modeling maturity in stage II of PASTA.

Procurement's Impact to PASTA's Stage II Activities

A word on procurement of hardware/software and how shopping for the most cost effective technologies may affect cost of administration as well as cost of securing these assets, particularly for SMBs. The greatest inhibitor for smaller firms in stage II of PASTA is money. Here is a great example of how other business functions can actually affect the adoption and growth of threat modeling in an organization, particularly among smaller firms. Smaller companies have less sensitivity to value calculations and philosophies such as total cost of ownership (TCO). As a result, their technology decision making is cost driven versus strategy driven. The focus of small or even mid-sized enterprises is more geared toward finding the most appropriate solution at the best possible price. This negates the ability to conform and develop technology standards, let alone security standards for technology governance. The reason is that as a greater level of technological diversity proves challenging to harden and securely configure. Note that the word *challenging* is used and not impossible. Securing heterogeneous pools of technology is very possible, but also very time-consuming. Faced with optimizing purchases versus strategizing how new technologies can be streamlined and supported more uniformly, smaller organizations allow a more heterogeneous pool of technology to take root within their organizations. Ubuntu servers running Apache, Windows desktop user environments, and a mix of infrastructure brands at the network level are common for both types of environments; however, when it comes to technology standardization, larger companies may defer to exclusively use one brand of technology over another in order to facilitate ease of administration.

Stage II provides opportunities for both small and large companies to consider a bare bones baseline of security across their procured and employed technology. Organizations that can streamline technology assets and third-party services to a select group of technology can allow security standards to be developed and maintained more easily. Maintaining standards is greatly undervalued from a security perspective. What has not been made apparent to most is that a linear relationship of implementation ease exists between IT (technology) governance and security governance. As a brief example, a yearly governance effort to revise policies or standards (typical for nearly all governance groups) is made increasingly difficult by technology variances across an organization over time.

Smaller organizations, such as start-ups, will lack in this area and will generally have neither the breadth of capital resources nor a standardized process for procuring and implementing technology. This thereby forces them to have a wider array of employed technology platforms that will extend their attack surface because of the more varied technology that will require unique security mitigations.

A standardized technology or service environment allows security governance to be more easily managed versus one where several different forms of technology are applied. Applying governance around disparate technologies, for the purpose of ensuring proper configuration, hardening, access control, logging, and so on, requires more time and effort than those environments that have been standardized.

This is why stage I of PASTA is to understand the objectives for a solution that is or has been developed in order to lead into stage II – defining the technical landscape of the solution. As objectives to a new or existing software application are defined/redefined, the threat modeler can at this stage begin to work out the inputs that would be needed in order to support such a solution and derive what inherent threats/countermeasures may be at stake. The opportunity for the threat modeler to illustrate how security governance becomes tied to these same inputs is even more important as it makes the notion of building security in more of a reality, as such base security controls are associated with the application environment based on revelations of data types, employed technology, and software solutions to be used within the overall ecology of the application environment.

Stages I and II activities brought forth opportunities for security governance to be instituted as a primer, particularly when applied in parallel to the SDLC process. Generally speaking, larger organizations are in a better position to sustain business objectives with well-defined governance standards simply due to their size and ability to have dedicated groups leading in those areas. Smaller organizations do not typically have the luxury of unique governance personnel who build a master library of strategic policies, standards, and guidelines for consumption. The harsh reality is that smaller organizations have more pressing matters to attend to, namely running and growing the company and putting out operational or business development fires that ignite along the way. This unfortunate disposition does not mean that smaller organizations are precluded from engaging in application threat modeling, but rather that their efforts in this area should be more creative, targeted, and staggered over time. For example, smaller firms can look to industry frameworks for quick-wins on existing governance standards from organizations such as OWASP in order to apply security principles to business objectives for a web-based application being proposed under stages I/II of PASTA. Larger firms can obviously apply the same approach, but they typically have enough resources to develop custom governance documents that can dictate the types of technology standards and processes to abide by. In their circumstances, material from places such as OWASP, PTES, CIS, ISC2, ISACA, Microsoft, Oracle, SANS, and more will help support or shape their tailored governance efforts applied during Stages I and II of PASTA.

It is possible for smaller enterprises apply specific governance material in stage II of the threat modeling process, since it is then that the business will understand the types of technology that will be utilized for the application environment being altered (via change control) or via new development efforts during the SDLC process. The smaller scope of security governance efforts is directly related to the amount of hardware and software supported by the application environment. With a smaller scope of technology to standardize (for potentially both IT and Security perspectives) specific hardening guides for the system environment can be applied with greater ease. This typically lends to an advantage for the smaller organization, although the lack of consistently applying technology governance often reveals inconsistencies over time, thereby reducing how effectively such companies mature under stage II of PASTA. Given their more complex and mixed technology, applying security governance during threat modeling is even more necessary for larger organizations, particularly in stage II. For larger enterprises, standardizing not only aligns well with applying security standardization and overall IT governance, it also ports other intrinsic benefits, such as cost reduction, improved TCO, better internal/external support from choice vendors, and others. This is because larger companies quickly realize that procuring the same technology lends to cost savings in administration and support, particularly when buying from a single vendor and potentially in bulk. Acquiring and using the same technology facilitate applying security standards and guide against these more uniform and dedicated forms of technology. Committing to a certain flavor of web server, network router, firewall, middleware, and code-off-the-shelf (COTS) solution provides the opportunity for governance and security to be enforced with reduced risk of changing the underlying technology. Over time, companies can quickly become "HP," "Windows," "Oracle," or "Unix" shops based on their standardized asset procurement and asset management practices. As an example, a large company that has a strategic partnership with Dell will build out their Web, Application, and Data environments based on the globally accepted technology standards for company web servers, application servers, or database servers. From there, associated security standards can be applied and "baked in" to the baseline configuration of the asset image.

Although there are obvious differences in terms of how small to large organizations address stage II of PASTA, the diverse extremes portrayed in both instances exemplify how IT governance and security governance can evolve into a synergistic effort where standardization is taking place. This shows how simplified IT and IS governance can coincide and be uniformly applied in a unified process. Standard builds of varying security levels can be built in conformance to industry inspired standards from NIST, ISO, CIS, MITRE, SANS, OWASP, DISA (military), and beyond. While the smaller firm may appear to have less of the advantage, they can actually grow from a smaller governance practice and develop a greater quality of governance through a reduced scope. Separately, larger firms have the ability to develop security assurance if their asset acquisition strategies are led by IT governance goals for standardizing technology types. Regardless, this phase allows PASTA's stage II to incorporate security governance as an inherent countermeasure to enumerated threats in subsequent stages of the PASTA model.

Stage II Summary

In conclusion of this phase, we take a look at the key steps and goals achieved by stage I: (1) understand underlying technology (network, software, system) and related dependencies associated with the application environment, (2) round up any applicable technology/security standards to be applied to technology assets used within the scope of the application environment, and (3) properly define an application scope for the threat model to focus on. Figure 7.10 summarizes this process for us and summarizes possible inputs and outputs associated with this phase of the PASTA threat modeling methodology.

Now that a business understanding of the application has been defined via stages I and II has built upon that information with the practical understanding of technological components, we look to analyze the application via exercises aimed at dissecting or decomposing the application. This phase builds upon Stages I and II by evaluating the dissection of each application component by how it supports business objectives defined in stage I, while leveraging basic controls via security governance in stage II. Stage III of PASTA, Application Decomposition, is truly a unique process that provides a collaborative setting where the threat modeler can facilitate discussion among development teams, security teams, IT/Security architects, and more on how the application is designed and ultimately built. This collaboration ties very well into design phases of any SDLC methodology and openly includes multiple SMEs over a tabletop exercise to understand the depth and breadth of how an application works. This unique component to PASTA fortifies this threat modeling methodology above others for the purposes of deriving risk. The analysis, however, must first begin with a thorough understanding of the application's intended design and use cases so that subsequent phases of attack enumeration, vulnerability analysis, and threat assessment are effective. The following section also explores data flow diagramming to a greater extent, as well as introduce the necessity of defining trust boundaries across a given application stack within the application environment. Additionally, the section will also focus on the heightened importance of security architecture and design to the PASTA application threat modeling methodology.

Stage III of PASTA – Application Decomposition & Analysis (ADA)

In relation to SDLC efforts, application decomposition can take place during the design phase. This is timely since by this point, requirements or use cases are generally more defined and can therefore be correlated to other areas, including but not limited to network routing, hardware, configuration (system/software), database tuning, and much more. This correlation and analysis provide an opportunity for security threats to be better understood and properly mitigated in the subsequent PASTA stages that follow. Since in the design phase, use cases become more clearly defined and connected to underlying technology, application decomposition helps to ensure greater familiarity with how use cases are (1) designed to behave and (2) related to other components of the threat model (use cases, actors, assets running stored procedures, services, etc.). With this organization of usage, the threat modeler can facilitate understanding how threats affect various parts of the subject application. Via the application decomposition stage, complex or confusing application architectures can be unraveled in a manner that allows all involved SMEs and threat modeling team members to truly understand how the application works and where it can be subjugated.

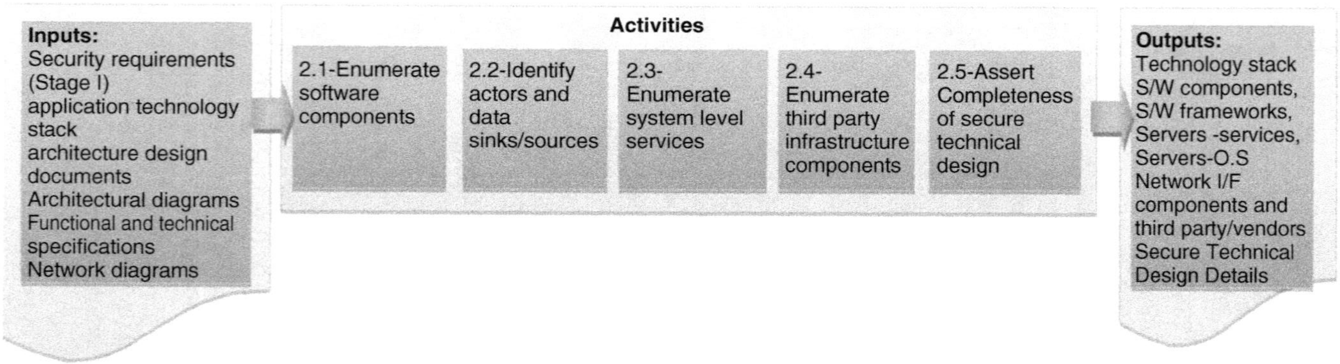

Inputs:
Security requirements (Stage I)
application technology stack
architecture design documents
Architectural diagrams
Functional and technical specifications
Network diagrams

Activities

2.1-Enumerate software components

2.2-Identify actors and data sinks/sources

2.3-Enumerate system level services

2.4-Enumerate third party infrastructure components

2.5-Assert Completeness of secure technical design

Outputs:
Technology stack
S/W components,
S/W frameworks,
Servers -services,
Servers-O.S
Network I/F components and third party/vendors
Secure Technical Design Details

Figure 7.10 PASTA Risk-Centric Threat Modeling – Stage II – (DTS) Definition of the Technical Scope

Stage III (Application Decomposition) of the PASTA methodology includes four key activities. They are as follows:

- S3:A1: Enumerate all application use cases (ex: login, account update, delete users, etc.).
- S3:A2: Perform DFD of Identified Components.
- S3:A3: Security Functional Analysis & the Use of Trust Boundaries.

In the following sections, we will review the details associated with each activity; however, first we will begin with a background on stage III threat modeling goals.

Stage III: Activity 1 (S3:A1) – Enumerate Application Use Cases   Use case enumeration is aimed at ensuring that all planned functionality is captured and revealed in the DFD. This benefits everyone involved (Architects, Developers, System Engineers, Business Analysts, etc.) by visualizing how the functional requirements are diagramed in a visual. The use cases should reveal the actors or processes that are part of the call/request. This provides the context for what use cases are most critical to protect and later, allows for vulnerabilities and attack patterns to be appropriately mapped to them. For this activity, begin to list the use cases for the application in the following manner (Figure 7.11).

As shown, use cases encapsulate other threat modeling components such as services, trust boundaries, actors, data sources, named pipes, and so on – all things that support application use cases. Use cases are developed from functional requirements, which largely reflect the understood objectives by the business for the application. As such, a use case enumeration exercise will help formulate a hierarchy of what actors, requests, responses, or data boundaries are used as part of each use case. This may have already been accomplished via the activities typically performed during the DEFINE phase of the SDLC process.

Use cases will have a one-to-many relationship with various components such as actors, data sources, named pipes, and so on. Since we have defined much of these under stage II, we simply now have to play matchmaker with the use cases identified in stage I with and application components identified under stage II. Application

Use Cases	Stored Procedures/Batch Jobs	Actors
• Register new patient • Update patient data • Add insurance information • New insurance claim • Update insurance claim • Delete insurance claim • Assign image to patient record	• [XML Data Blob Parser.py] • [ReportGen.sql] • [NormalizedEMR.sql] • [UpdateImageRecords.sql] • [PurgeRecordedFile.py] • [EncryptPHI.py]	• (L) [platform account1] • (L) [domain account] • (L) [DB Svr account] • (L) [DB Admin account] • (L) [DB User account] • (H) [Client User] • (L) [App WebSvc User account]

Figure 7.11   Enumeration of Use Cases, Services, Stored Procedures, Batch Scripts, and Actors

TABLE 7.9 Sample Identification of Use Cases for Health-Care Application

Use Case	Actor (Presentation Boundary)	Actor (Data Boundary)
Check-in patient	IIS worker process	(CREATE) MED001 domain user
Register patient	IIS worker process	(CREATE) MED001 domain user
Enter patient symptoms	IIS worker process	(CREATE) MED001 domain user
Validate patient symptom validation	IIS worker process	(READ) HealthUsr001 (SQL login)
Update patient record	IIS worker process	(CREATE) MED001 domain user
Pull patient medical history	IIS worker process	(READ) HealthUsr001 (SQL login)
Make imaging request	IIS worker process	(READ) HealthUsr001 (SQL login)

components should be identified within the architectural layer to which the use case is found. In some cases, the application component may be within a different architectural layer than that of the use case (e.g. – client request component sends coupon code to application web service). A simpler representation of the exercise that would accomplish this activity task is shown in Table 7.9.

White-boarding exercises can assist to "talk out loud" about how components support use cases across the overall architecture. Thereafter, it will be easier to map out their interoperability with one another within the DFD. Remember, that if the application is large, threat modeling the most attack prone layers may make the most sense, especially if time constraints are present and threat modeling is still in its infancy as a program within an organization.

The following is a brief example of how these associations can be tied to a root use case, as part of an application decomposition effort, which in this case applies to a fictitious stock trading application (Figure 7.12).

In order to better exemplify exercises associated with application decomposition, we will focus on building on the threat modeling stages and associated activities we have collected thus far. Using a hypothetical example of an online web application, the following example will extract and link the business objectives, associated technology, and use cases for a sample marketing application.

In this example, we will take an online software application that takes credit card purchases for a particular cardholder and performs a mash-up against current offers that retailers have for consumers. From a stage I perspective, an applicable business objective for this application may be:

Business Objective of Marketing Application *To leverage credit card transaction data with future advertisements of retailers in order to sell a mix of consumer spending information to interested retailers wishing to better penetrate geographic markets, cities, etc. Key supporting objectives are to ensure that the two types of data are current, well-managed, properly correlated, and protected.*

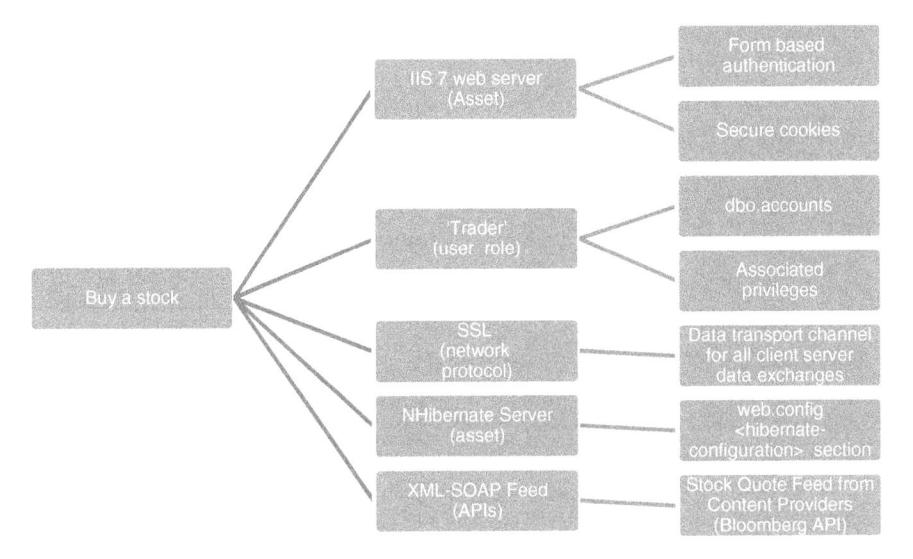

EXPLORING THE SEVEN STAGES AND EMBEDDED THREAT MODELING ACTIVITIES 395

Figure 7.12 Use Case to Application Component Mapping

Additional discovery efforts in this stage may also reveal that the subject application of the threat model will include a few published web services that support retailers' ability to interact with to backend data repositories. Some of these APIs will seek to obtain consumer buying trends for a particular geographic region (e.g. zip code, state) for a subset of cardholders. Other interfaces to the subject application may include content feeds from various coupon providers who offer small quantities of coupons or offer them in bulk. These could be correlated to cardholder accounts so that they may receive targeted offers for a particular retailer, product, or service.

In support of a subject application's intended focus, the threat model can continuously identify a myriad of application use cases, which we can dissect within stage III of PASTA. At this Stage, we presume that Stages I and II have been adequately been completed and documented for this fictitious marketing application. Stage III (Application Decomposition) will leverage the information from prior stages, so it is important not to lose sight of the business objectives defined in stage I or the technical scope defined in stage II when applying PASTA. With the understood business objectives from stage I, functional requirements that help ensure such an objective can be developed during the Planning and Design phases of a generic SLDC process. A sample of functional objectives from stage I may include:

1. Maintain a *customer profile* based on purchases made and other correlated demographic information (age, sex, location, etc.).
2. Securely *store and leverage customer profiles* in a normalized state that facilitates searches of customer profiles and transactions.

3. Maintain accurate customer contact information in order to *solicit new offers* based on prior buying history.
4. Provide a *marketing module* that allows marketing professionals to devise new campaigns or offers.
5. Provide a *financial module* aimed at defining offers, coupons, or promotional thresholds for given products in order to ensure some degree of margin.
6. Receive *batched data feeds* related to transactions made at stores, by various referential IDs, such as Store ID, zip code, and so on.

A tabular representation of the sample application is found on the following page and demonstrates how PASTA's first three stages build on one another in terms of dissecting the subject application. Objectives in the top header stem from stage I and give way to use cases in stage III, which support functional requirements that aim to fulfill those business objectives. Stage II provides that technical scope of what technology platforms the application will use. This will be increasingly relevant and important for other areas of stage III and looking ahead to stage IV – Threat Analysis.

This very concise table is not aimed to be a comprehensive list of all objectives, assets (both software/hardware), and use cases pertaining to the hypothetical application. However, it does provide a good example on how broken down components of the application can be organized.

In previous PASTA stages, outputs related to aforementioned business objectives, functional requirements, and technical scope help provide the proper context for application decomposition. It also provides the ability to gradually see what existing, inherent controls (physical, technical, and logical) are present. Each of the activities in the previously mentioned PASTA stages will help show how the application handles things such as secure design, data flow, inherited trust, inherent security controls, and user privileges around use cases.

Assuming a three-tiered, internal facing web application, the following can be depicted as a possible set of use cases for the application to be dissected against. The terms requirements and objectives have been used interchangeably later in order to denote some aspect for which application use cases can be built upon. Lending from the functional requirements or business objectives in the hypothetical application used thus far, a myriad of use cases could be identified and isolated within the application. A subset of possible use cases are supplied in Table 7.11. This sample set of application use cases, identified as part of define/design stages of the SDLC process (primarily) or the application threat model (secondarily). For the sake of brevity, use cases pertaining to only functional requirements "Customer Profiling" and "Customer Data Storage" were used from those depicted in Table 7.10.

Stage III: Activity II (S3:A2) – Perform Data Flow Diagram Exercise Stage III of PASTA (Application Decomposition) has the opportunity to ensure that each dissected area of the application supports the objectives defined in stage I and adequately run on the assets defined under stage II. In stage II, we inherit component names as well as descriptions around each component (e.g. type of client-side plug-in, versions around software components for web, application, and database servers).

TABLE 7.10 Hypothetical Functional Requirements/Objectives for Marketing Application

Functional Requirements/Objectives

	Customer profiling	Data analytics	Data harvesting and brokerage	Offer creation and management	Financial offer management	Batch processing
Stage I related (objectives defined)						
Stage II related (technical scope of software/hardware assets)	AppServer Profiling Engine (Apache/Tomcat/Java, Ubuntu Server 12; HP Integrity rx2800 i4 Servers (HA Pair))	DBServer (MySQL Cluster CGE, Ubuntu Server 12; HP Integrity rx2800 i4 Servers (HA Pair))	DBServer (MySQL Cluster CGE, Ubuntu Server 12)	CouponServer (Windows Server 2008, IIS, Enterprise SQL Server, .NET web services, FTP service; HP ProLiant DL320 G2)	Third-party service provider managing current offers via published web services; hardware supplied by third party	JobServer (Ubuntu Server 12 with Perl/Python scripts and cron jobs enabled; HP Intensity Superdome Server)
Stage III related (identified use cases from functional requirements)	Automatically capture store sales data related to purchases (name brand, price, time of day, store number, cc type, etc.)	Provide "canned" analytics around customer aggregate customer data	Allow data entry of Name, Address, Age, Sex, Zip, Marital Status, and Ethnicity (optional)	Allowance for entering new offers from retailers	API for COGS (cost of goods sold or costing data)	Nightly store uploads of store purchases

(*continued*)

TABLE 7.10 (Continued)

Functional Requirements/Objectives

Allow self-fulfillment for new online profiles to be created	Provide interface for user-driven dynamic queries around aggregate data	Allow interfacing with other marketing related apps to provide Name, Address, Age, Sex, Zip, Marital Status, and Ethnicity (optional)	Manage expiration of offers made automatically; allow revocation from offer administrators	Allow financial users to enter in unit costs for products sold	Batch processing of new financial thresholds
Cross reference in-store purchases with other marketing data servers containing "bulk" marketing information	Cross reference and validate with other marketing tools that maintain client data	Receive, process, integrate, and package demographic information from other marketing sources for authorized sale	Manage renewal capabilities of various campaigns	APIs to other financial tools and software in order to perform predictive financial analysis	Batch processing of new weekly offers

TABLE 7.11 Deriving Use Cases from Functional Requirements

Functional Requirement(s)	Use Cases	Description of Use Cases
Customer profiling	Capture store sales data	API stores local transaction servers with the following metadata: retailer, price, time of day, store number, cc type, and so on. and feeds this application's data repository w/the captured info.
	Self-fulfillment of new users	Form online-based enrollment, a web interface requesting e-mail info (such as username and password), mobile number, name and address, and credit card.
	X-marketing data lookup	Cross DB queries using "LIKE" statements in order to find counts of possible consumer matches to other marketing data sources.
Customer data storage	Canned reporting	Precanned operational reports. E.g.: <purchased item> by <zip code> and <gender>, <purchased item name> by <item type> with matching <store buyer profile data>, and so on.
	Dynamic reporting	Allows users to construct business queries to data repository in order to create their own types of marketing report.
	Cross reference foreign marketing sources	Sends SOAP requests to external marketing data web services in order to query if matches exist for existing customer profiles.

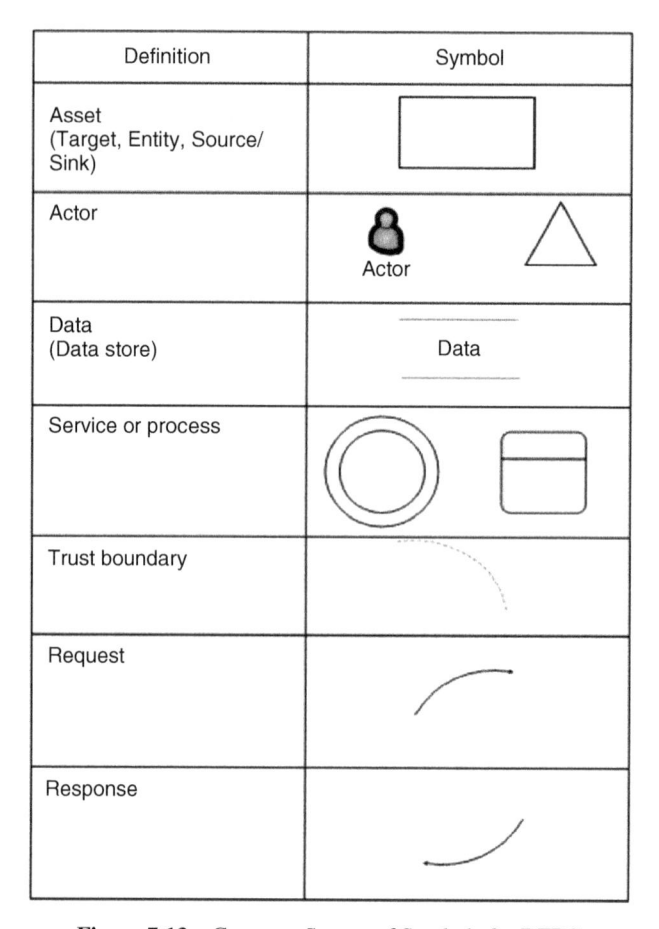

Definition	Symbol
Asset (Target, Entity, Source/Sink)	▭
Actor	Actor △
Data (Data store)	Data
Service or process	◎ ▢
Trust boundary	⌒
Request	⌒
Response	⌣

Figure 7.13 Common Syntax of Symbols for DFDS

Before we take to the whiteboard to pontificate on the application components within your application stack, two considerations should be made at this point. One is that a common set of DFD protocols and taxonomy of terms should be defined and understood for your organization. Although there is a common set of DFD icons and symbolic representations, it should be noted that DFDs should reflect the best use of terms and iconic figures that fit your organizational groups that are involved within stage III of PASTA. If a more generic and standardized set of representations is desired, then the following legend (Figure 7.13) should be considered, as they represent the common symbolic representations for components, processes, and requests/response within a DFD.

Labels in DFDs should contain descriptive information on what the call/request being made contains. It should provide sufficient information to denote the type of information being passed. Too much information can clutter the label and affect the legibility of the DFD. Add information that is material to understand the nature of

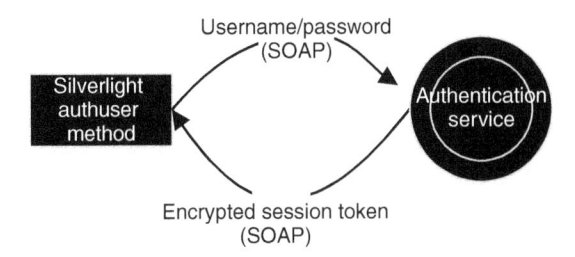

EXPLORING THE SEVEN STAGES AND EMBEDDED THREAT MODELING ACTIVITIES 401

Figure 7.14 Data Flow Authentication Example

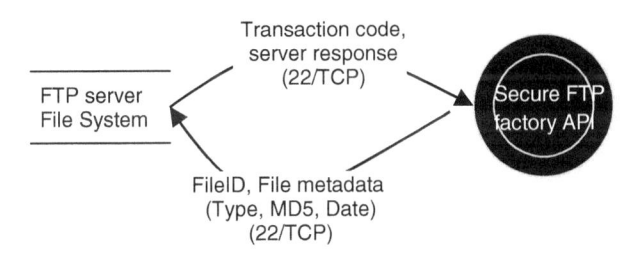

Figure 7.15 Data Flow for Data Exchange Across Two Entities

the call/request. The example (Figure 7.14) makes clear that the data flow revolves around web-based authentication. Developers can see what data is being sent/received as part of this request.

We see another example that includes the port/services used by application calls/requests. We see the target components (data sink of an ftp store) and the application server (source) that establishes a secure connection to send over files. Connection protocol and data descriptions of what is sent back is revealed (Figure 7.15).

In the following figure, the components from previously used health-care use cases have been mapped along with their application calls and responses. Although we will get into trust boundaries in detail shortly, note how trust boundaries are rendered as dotted rectangles around the components that are interfacing with a defined data store server. The trust boundaries represent distinct logical or physical boundaries between two distinct system applications, thereby using the physical characteristic as a basis for trust validation, previously covered in stage II of PASTA.

Note also that unique arrows were not drawn to the components under each system platform as it would have cluttered the DFD. However, the goals of reviewing the relevant actors as well as the use cases that trigger the flows among components are successfully depicted.

The point to be made in this section is that no two DFDs will look the same, particularly among organizations or even development groups. DFDs will vary in their appearance. The goal is to build a DFD that is understandable by *your* team and one that can be leveraged to denote where abuse cases may take place due to excessive trust awarded to application entities or insufficient amount of countermeasures.

As we look to yet another example of a DFD, it should be mentioned that the scope of components to DFD will be largely driven by time, topicality, and not creating an obnoxiously, complicated diagram. In this example, we will borrow from the previously mentioned Customer Profiling application mentioned earlier in Table 7.11 (S3:A1). As shown in Figure 7.16, the DFD is a targeted one; focused only on the self-enrollment feature of the application. Once again using the universal syntax of threat modeling icons, we see a whiteboard representation of how this DFD would look like (Figure 7.17).

All of the application components pertaining to this *use case* (not application) have been illustrated in the DFD along with the associated requests, responses, data, and main protocols utilized. Via the DFD see the application's use of Silverlight plug-ins, associated *.xap* files sent to the browser, it's interaction with a*n* MS Silverlight Web-Services instance and ultimately a data MS SQL store to where much of the user enrollment data would be kept. Although the aforementioned is a raw whiteboard drawing, the illustration is a key artifact for PASTA since it shows an activity that was largely worked upon by both security and development team members.

As one can see, all use cases *were not* depicted in the DFD and this is intentional. DFD exercises are best illustrated in manageable sizes. If all of the components for the application were to be illustrated, it may get too overwhelming to convey over one DFD. This in turn may discourage people to use DFDs in the first place or even application threat modeling. For this and other reasons related to simplicity of use, knowing what aspect of the application you need to DFD is important. Over time, the comprehensiveness of the exercises will be the sum of its parts (or other DFDs).

The online enrollment use case diagrammed also employs the most common syntax of DFD symbols. These symbols provide the most frequently used representation of application components and allow for some level of universality to be achieved for those who may have experienced DFDs before. It is important to point out that if the standard symbols prove to be nonintuitive for a collective group, it's perfectly fine to change what icons or symbols are used. Ultimately, since these diagrams are intended to be internal artifacts for those engaged in a secure SDLC implementation, determining what symbols to use should be based solely on what makes sense for your group. This is an example where best or common practices may not "best" for you and your team.

Using Containers to Organize DFDs   Reverting back to the manner in which components are grouped via containers in stage II, we can use a technology list to consider components at a physical layer in the DFD (MS SQL Server, IIS Server, Human Actor) as well as things from a logical sense in terms of what they do (e.g. handle web requests, process serialized xml streams). Architecturally, the DFD can also be divided by where each component exists in the scale of the overall application flow. More of this architectural-based criteria will be depicted when looking at the use of trust boundaries in DFDs. The previous example was simply meant to take a manageable portion of the application and portray how it interacts with other components. It is worth mentioning again that one of the main benefits of DFDs is that they allow for multiple groups (both in IT and in InfoSec) to understand application flow among

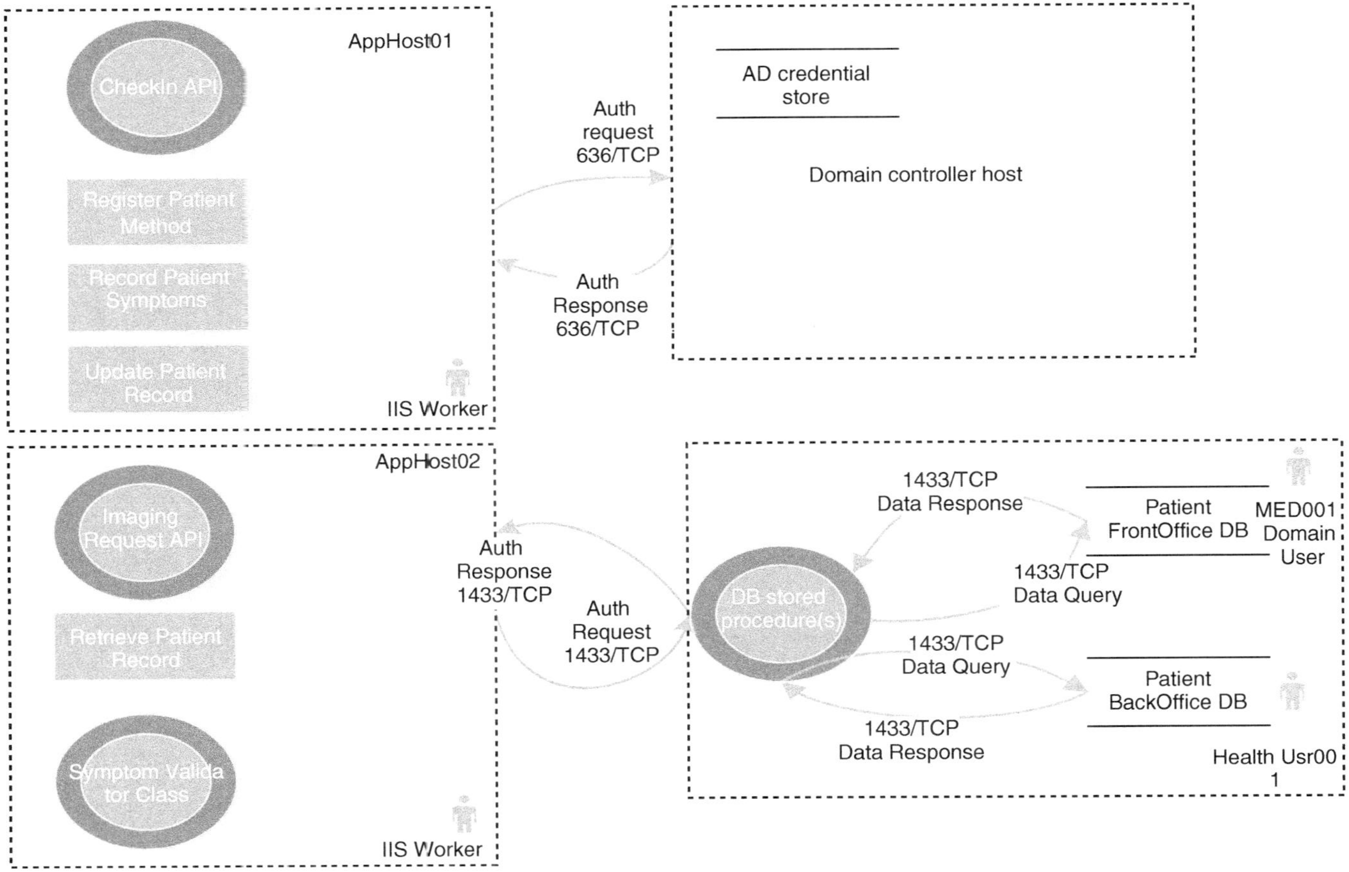

Figure 7.16 DFD Example Using Physical Boundaries for Organizing Components

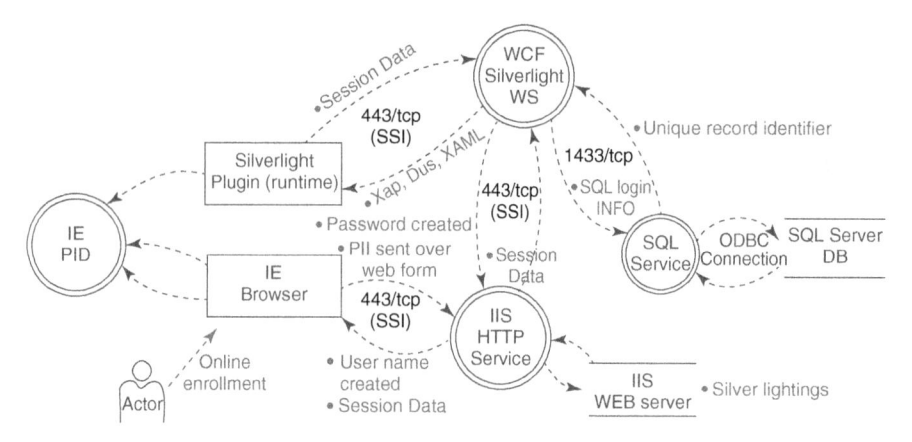

Figure 7.17 Whiteboard DFD of User Self-Enrollment

components that were not previously considered. It is in the awareness of how a subject application behaves that fosters security to naturally develop from earlier in the SDLC process.

Recalling our use of containers from S2:A5 (Classify & Map Application Components), we can begin to map out interactions of application components within a DFD that traverse logical, physical, or architectural boundaries. Leveraging the fictitious, health-care use cases from S3:A1 (Enumerate all Application Use Cases) (Table 7.11), we can map out the interactions among components via application methods, functions, calls, and APIs. The following is a separate type of DFD that uses slightly different symbolic representations but considers the relationship of logical application components to their physical hosts (Figure 7.18).

In application decomposition, the dissection process should address three areas for it to be thorough: architectural, physical, and logical. Although time may limit the depth of the decomposition process, future iterations of DFDs produced do have the opportunity to revisit how the application functions. Moreover, based on the criticality level of the components derived in S2:A4 (Assert Completeness of Secure Technical Design), the depth of dissection can vary for any iteration of a threat modeling activity for S3:A2 (Perform DFD of Identified Components). Over time, the criteria for building DFDs can vary, but as a basis it should consider components from the physical, architectural, and logical realm in order to be considered comprehensive.

The first criterion, architectural, focuses on what activities are taking place across an application environment and how threat modeling components are interacting with one another. These threat modeling components include actors (system/db/application), services, data sources, compiled binaries, batched/schedule programs, and hardware interfaces. Reverting back to our fictitious marketing application as an example, establishing trust boundaries across the application layers requires starting around the application architecture. This means that application calls and data flows from callers are mapped from data sources (databases), domain controllers, file servers, and so on to receiver sources. Actors associated with both caller and receiver

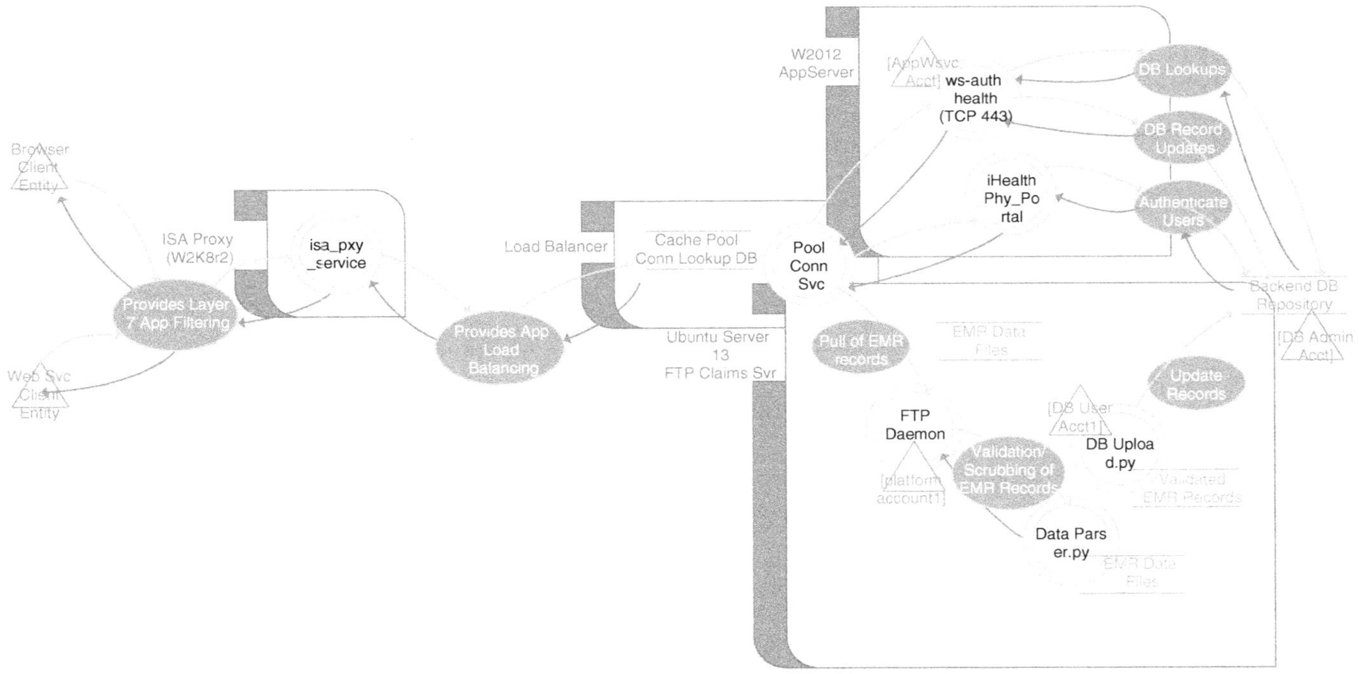

Figure 7.18 DFD Health-Care Example Using Container Approach

405

identities are also cataloged per call/data flow. Distinct callers, data sources, system environments (virtual/physical), software source, compiled binary source, and network segment (VLAN) would all contribute to the need for a trust boundary to be defined. In certain cases, trust boundaries should be even defined for when none of the aforementioned variables change, but this would be dependent on the risk profile for the application. A military-based application with top secret clearance may, for example, define more inner trust boundaries to increase security validation. Using security containers can greatly assist in this exercise as they define where many of these components reside within the threat model.

Grouping web servers within the DMZ, application servers in the application tier of the overall architecture, and lastly the database servers within the data layer, provides easy architectural wins for where trust boundaries can easily become defined. This is a basic depiction of using solely an architectural approach to define trust boundaries and does not include some of the other parameters that were recently discussed (such as data sources, batch/scheduled jobs, actors, etc.). This architectural approach also assumes threat modeling an environment that is traditionally located and managed under a single data center and not an application that relies on a distributed architecture model (e.g. multiple ASPs or Cloud service providers). We can touch upon this momentarily, but for now, we focus on a more traditional model in order to better understand the application S3:A2 (Data Flow Diagramming) efforts (Figure 7.19).

Stage III: Activity III (S3:A3) – Security Functional Analysis and the Use of Trust Boundaries Trust boundaries within DFDs introduce where new security countermeasures need to be developed. Both DFDs and embedded trust boundaries can be

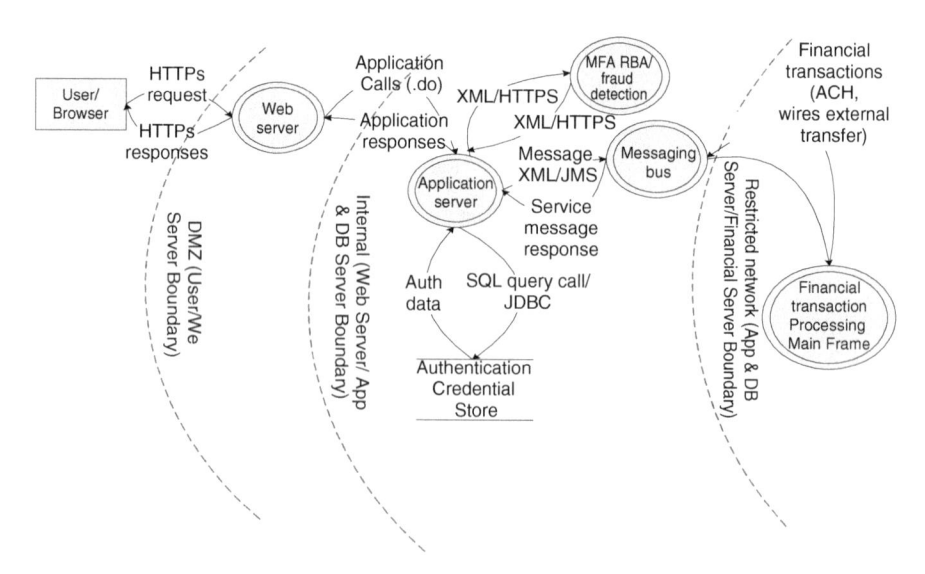

Figure 7.19 DFD Using Architectural Considerations for Component Grouping

best fulfilled as part of a Stand-Up SCRUM activity or in the Design phase of a Waterfall SDLC methodology. Note that trust boundaries are always represented using dotted lines between segregated application components. For this activity, use the architectural location of the assets identified in stage II to define unique trust boundaries between architectural layers and possibly among application components or assets. Although trust layers can be defined in multiple locations, the easiest will be using architectural layers. In doing so, you will be able to segregate the architecture into layers of trust where countermeasures can later be applied. Using the architectural approach, your DFD should have 2-3 trust boundaries defined among the presentation, application, and data layers. More can be used if needed. Generic rules of thumb for adding more trust boundaries include the following guidance:

- When and if data flows from one controlled network environment to another.
- Between sink/sources (external entities) and requesting process components.
- Among distinctly coded process components.
- Among data stores and process components that have a separate code base.
- When platform or system boundaries are crossed (Ubuntu Memcache server to IIS Web Server).
- Codebase changing between two systems where data flows exist.
- Groups responsible for software development/system engineering differ among assets in DFD.
- Actors among components/assets in DFD are different/have different privileges.
- Data request going to an external sink/source in DFD.
- Source (data source) to sink (data destination) of data flow is outside boundary of application.
- Data changes characteristics between two data flow endpoints.

Building off of prior activities conducted thus far, we can now effectively build a "trust model" into our DFDs given what we know of application components', such as use, physical location, architectural positioning, inherent risk, criticality to the overall application environment, and presumed range of actors using each component. From this information, members of the threat modeling team can collectively appreciate an illustration that defines trust boundaries among areas of the DFD. The goal of defining application trust boundaries is very important to PASTA's threat modeling methodology because it is the first time all involved RACI participants can see where and why distrust should be present within the application and from which container or container object threats may originate.

Examining the implied trust relationship among application components needs to be done methodically, particularly when the impact rating of the asset is determined to be HIGH. An example is a handheld device's biometric authentication control that interfaces with the client application software stack on the device. If the mobile device's security was solely dependent on the device's hardware security control measures, then any hardware-based circumvention or hardware-based exploit could undermine all of the mobile software security features. Applying this same example to Supervisory Control and Data Acquisition Systems (SCADA) in the Energy sector, one may have a more complex and impact-intensive threat model. An example here is the overlay of modern day graphical user interfaces (GUIs) to traditional administrative access and functions on an industrial control system (ICS) that traditionally may have only had console or serial cable access from a dedicated host and may now support TCP/HTTP protocols, which give life to a web UI for ease of access.

Leveraging how application components are organized under S2:A5 (Classify & Organize Components), containers can help facilitate where possible trust boundaries need to be established among actors, assets, technology assets, services, data, web services, APIs, and compiled binaries that interface with the SCADA environment. Defining trust will extend beyond how these components have been classified and will also consider how these components' authenticity, integrity, and authorization is validated or verified within the application model, based on their physical, logical, and/or architectural proximity and similarity to one another.

Architectural considerations to application decomposition presume that similar asset types have been grouped appropriately based on similar functionality. This essentially creates layers for a given application environment. These definable boundaries are aimed to separate distinct actions among processing entities for the application environment. A traditional three-tiered application environment may have two trust boundaries that separate the web layer from the app layer and the app layer from the data layer. As an example, web servers are not architecturally placed within the same trust boundary as client machines because these two distinct computing environments are managed by separate user groups and there should not be an assumption that they are being managed equally well and with equally judicious responsibility on security configuration. As a result, a trust boundary would naturally be placed between these two distinct architectural areas. A few application characteristics to help identify the location of where a trust boundary should be placed include the following:

- Unique entities are receiving unique data requests for processing.
- The Actors (or Callers) are unique among the sending and receiving processing agents.
- Technology or platforms vary greatly among the architectural layers of the threat model.
- Types of protocols across the application layers changes (e.g. web traffic only in one layer vs. XML-SOAP, SAML requests).

Architecturally speaking, it is a common approach that external facing assets should not receive any level of trust from inner layers hosting other application/data components. The reason is quite simply playing the role of devil's advocate or not hedging your bets against Murphy's Law.[3] Later under stage IV of PASTA, this level

---

[3] Anything that can go bad, often does.

Figure 7.20 Spectrum of Trust for Defining Trust Boundaries Across Architecture

of "paranoia" may be substantiated by internal logs and alerts or via external threat intelligence. More rationally, however, it is quite easy to understand that a semipublic network environment, such as a DMZ, may have already been compromised. As such, downstream communication to inner network layers should be questioned and validated. Architecturally focused approaches to placing trust boundaries within a DFD traverse a trust spectrum. A simplistic representation is reflected in Figure 7.20.

These architectural access levels help the threat modeler know that some form of countermeasures or controls will be needed in order to safely pass along requests from other assets/actors to target assets across other trust boundaries.

In general, trust boundaries are placed where boundaries of trust should be formed. These boundaries provide the foundation for considering various types of countermeasures around the calls made across the trusty boundary, both upstream and downstream to the application. The benefit of grouping assets based on trust levels is that it helps to develop or implement preventative, detective, and reactive countermeasures. From a preventative sense, trust boundaries help enforce proper access control measures among boundaries via the network, platform, and beyond. Trust boundaries also aid in detective means, providing audit-logging capabilities that can be fed to a Security Incident and Event Monitoring solution or central logging repository. Last, reactive measures can also be considered if the product application is okay in having automatic security responses be applied and potentially blocking certain access or network request automatically. This would equate to more active defense measures for example.

Beyond architectural-focused efforts in defining trust boundaries under stage III, additional trust boundaries may be warranted based on the other two criteria previously mentioned – physical and logical. Architectural considerations for trust boundaries provide a low maturity level for establishing trust boundaries since assets are grouped by a network VLAN or generic categorization of use (network services, web servers, application servers, database servers).

The easiest example of where physical considerations should denote that unique trust boundaries be defined are physical assets located in distinct networks, potentially that of a third-party service provider. It should be easier to understand the applicability of physical considerations in establishing unique trust boundaries since distinct networks, asset custodians, physical infrastructure may be noncongruent to those processes/control measures at a primary data center. It is likely, however, that a trust boundary had been previously defined with architectural considerations alone since a VPN connectivity, P2P connection, or API over SSL would reveal a separate network that would be architecturally apart from a presentation layer or application layer of an overall application solution.

More advanced threat models may extend beyond the architectural approach and leverage physical considerations for defining inner trust boundaries. In more sophisticated threat models where the impact or risk rating of the application scope is higher, physically separate servers will most likely warrant a trust boundary defined among other physical assets since the uniqueness of such an asset will encompass threat modeling variables that may be extraneous to those already enumerated (new actors, new services, new APIs, etc.). This requirement for a unique trust boundary will be affected by a few factors such as those listed in the following checklist:

- Is the asset currently found within a trust boundary defined by architectural criteria?
- Is the asset unique in its code base as compared to other assets within its same architectural realm?
- Is the asset host to a third-party application service/server?
- Does the asset physically host many virtual hosts, thereby building a unique application ecology within the physical realm of the asset?

The aforementioned list is good in considering additional "inner" trust boundaries that may need to be defined within a previously defined trust boundary, based on architectural considerations. Inner trust boundaries in general are found in more advanced threat models, since the interrelationship of applications and servers are more intricate and the data potentially more sensitive or critical. In most cases, it is highly unlikely that a trust boundary becomes defined solely based on physical criteria and not inclusive of architectural considerations. Even if a web server is found on the same physical host as a Java application server, virtual network/architectural segregation is possible, so architecturally, the segregation and trust boundary could be defined based on the need to achieve *architectural* separation. The greatest exception to this, of course, is if a physical host server encompasses several virtual guest machines. In relation to virtual assets within the threat model, they should be regarded as separate "physical" hosts and thereby potentially require trust boundary to be defined among them and other unrelated assets. The cloud-based scenario further complicates this and requires using the third criteria, logical considerations to further refine where new trust boundaries should be applied. Even within the ecosystem of virtual hosts, review of how virtual networking and virtual hosts are used and segregated should be evaluated for providing trust boundaries within such a virtualized environment.

Thus far, physical considerations to trust boundaries extend the basic architectural methods to decompose an application environment. Logical considerations increase the capabilities of application decomposition even further into more advanced techniques based on the logical flow of the data (APIs/feeds/scheduled jobs), the use cases for the application, data repositories, and identity/origins of the actors. This extra factor for possibly defining new trust boundaries should be applied similarly to other criteria, but primarily in considering the following:

- Are there new actors involved at the host or application level (upstream/downstream) that will be handling the data being sent/received?

- Is the code base for the receiving end point of an application programming interface different from that from which the data originated?
- Is the actor's identity and related security context as a user different between the source of a data exchange and its destination?
- Is exchange of commands or data extending across two distinct interpreter environments?
- Are the utilized use cases elevating or reducing the criticality/sensitivity of the information being exchanged?
- Is the application supportive of polymorphic data or one with an abstraction layer?

These aforementioned checkpoints help determine whether additional trust boundaries need to be depicted in a DFD exercise and extend the architectural and physical conditions for using trust boundaries. Logical considerations to defining trust boundaries are truly reserved for more complicated or advanced threat models where the importance of the application data or criticality of the services provided by the system is high. Similar to physical criteria for defining trust boundaries, logical considerations can be applied using a layered approach that incorporates all of the approaches mentioned. Overall, each approach should be considered and applied based on the context of both the application use cases as well as the inherent risk profile that pertains to the application.

Beyond introducing trust boundaries within an application, this stage III activity aims to create opportunities for other activities such as enumerating actors, unique data sources, services, kernels, interpreters, client technologies, or simply any place where alteration to data, schema objects, application commands, or source code could be altered. The dissection is typically achieved as part of a collaborative work effort among developers, system administration, network engineers, and architects. In some cases, one individual with in-depth knowledge of all these areas may possess the needed expertise to properly dissect the application; however, they will commonly rely on the collaboration and expertise of multiple SMEs for this type of stage II activity. The components dissected in this phase tie in the previous logical considerations around defining trust boundaries. Identified services, actors, and data sources all help to better define trust boundaries for the application in scope.

The DFDs presented thus far adhere to the common syntax of DFD symbols; however, if more high-level depictions are desired, DFDs such the following in Figure 7.21 can provide architects, business analysts, and project managers with a high level and very easy representation of where trust boundaries should be defined. The following figure represents an Android-based mobile application. It is not surprise that key components include a mobile client front-end communicating with a two-tiered, web application environment. In the diagram that follows, we see how the physical, architectural, and logical considerations that help define trust boundaries within the DFD.

Figure 7.21 shows various trust boundaries in shades of red with different labels; all depending on the types of trust boundary formed using the architectural, physical,

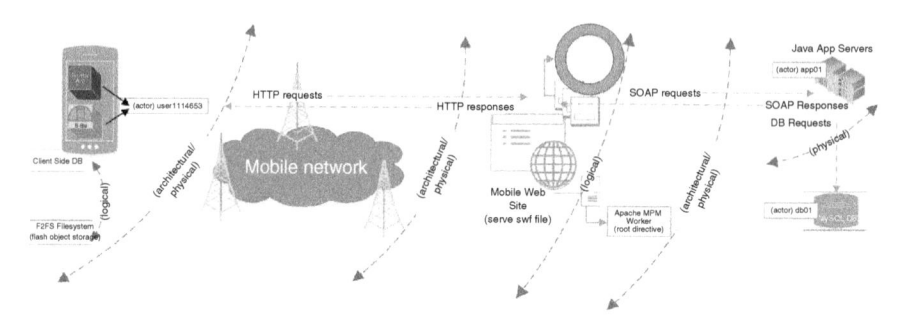

Figure 7.21 Decomposing Mobile Web App Example

and logical designations. This simple decomposition does not comprise all the possible actors, data sources, data flows, ad use cases that would be included in stage III of PASTA. However, the figure does reveal how application decomposition should begin at a high level. Depending on the inherent risk profile for the application, where greater governance of the software development actually takes place, greater focus may take place at the client side or the server side of the environment. Focusing on each of the embedded trust boundaries, further decomposition of application components can take place at the server level, application layer, network, and even client hardware device – in this scenario the mobile handset. The point to be made is that embedded flows are never too small or insignificant or too large not to be considered something to decompose the application into data sources, actors, requests/responses, processes, compiled objects, and more.

Do not Forget the Physical Interfaces You may determine that including nontechnical components in a threat model is nontopical, but we can guarantee you that the attackers will not. While decomposing the application in stage III of PASTA, it is also important to keep an open mind as a threat modeler on attack scenarios. Many security professionals and technologists will simply focus on areas they are most familiar with or ones that have been most discussed in the media. This is a disservice to any type of application decomposition exercise as it becomes biased to components that are "marketed" in security media and not based on relevancy to your product application. As an example, technology-focused mindsets may simply center on OSI layers two and up, while missing various physical elements that could directly or indirectly affect the security posture of the overall environment. For this reason, a balanced regard when dissecting the application environment is critical. If a physical exploit is possible and viable in a postimplemented scenario to a product or software application, countermeasures would need to be considered at the other layers of the OSI model as well.

A great example of this is in Figure 7.22. At first glance, the figure reveals an application's architecture with fairly secure transportation measures, employing both SSL and IPSec tunnels between satellite store locations and the corporate sales server where centralized daily receipts are processed and stored. A secure perception may even be sustained solely by an application risk assessment or even a software-centric threat modeling methodology. The PASTA methodology, however, will also

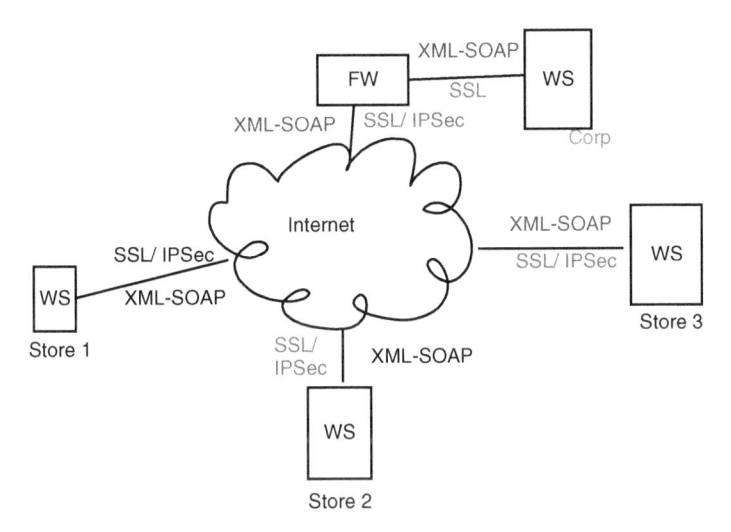

EXPLORING THE SEVEN STAGES AND EMBEDDED THREAT MODELING ACTIVITIES   413

Figure 7.22 API from Stores Local Transaction Server with the Following Metadata

consider physical or environmental factors that may affect the security of each individual store's web server or simply the introduction of rogue web service clients wishing to make unauthorized data interfaces with the corporate web service namespace. The physical scenarios for such authorized requests can range from a stolen or tampered-with web server at a store location to physically introducing a fake Certificate Authority (CA) or DNS server in the local environment. In either case, an altered host, or one that is successfully inserted into the local architecture of a POS environment, can introduce a perpetrating host containing unsigned or tainted compiled library files.

In Figure 7.22, we see the use case for batched or time driven XML SOAP feeds initiated by store web servers to their corporate operations web service end points using SSL communications run over a VPN tunnel. The data format is XML and the serialized data sent adheres to XML-SOAP calls under Microsoft's .NET Web Service Framework.

Under the depicted architecture, if such a physically compromised server had no authentication/integrity checks to application requests/responses, this can easily affect use cases related to authorizing or processing unauthorized credit card charge requests that could not be processed at the time of a transaction (which is not uncommon in a merchant retail environment). Even if authentication criteria are factored into the compiled libraries or binary files of each store's web server, reverse engineering such code in the scenario of a physically compromised host is not only possible, but also plausible. This is especially true if unsigned libraries or SAML requests are not employed per transaction where additional authentication checks related to identity of requestor are not validated.

Once again focusing on one of the use cases in a DFD allows us to more deeply explore areas where possible countermeasures may need to be developed. The aforementioned figure provides a backdrop to the subsequent security analysis that helps the threat modeler compartmentalize use cases reflected by the application architectural diagram.

Participants of Stage III – Application Decomposition

Understanding data flow is of utmost importance in stage III. As a result, who that work with data and know the data flow that it is designed to take across/within an application environment will be best positioned to speak to how trust boundaries should be defined and where appropriate countermeasures should be developed. The knowledge of the data environment and its role within the application are key in helping further define possible attack vectors and, most importantly, what types of countermeasures should be developed at various levels, whether it is at the data level or at the network/client level. Beyond the threat modeler facilitating the activities for this stage, those who play a *Responsible* or *Accountable* role in this stage are Developers, Architects, or System Engineers. Depending on the level of knowledge that BAs may have on proposed data flows, their roles may evolve from an *Informed* role to a *Consulted* role (based on Figure 6.8). All of the other defined roles will be working with BAs and PMs already in order to gather the high-level specifications around data usage so they will remain instrumental in executing many of the activities for this stage.

Stage III Deliverables

Practical inputs of this stage of the PASTA methodology could benefit from an array of different artifacts that the threat modeler could leverage as part of this stage. This list of artifacts as possible inputs is detailed in the following table. The lack of any of the following does not require these items to be produced, as much of them can be produced during the vulnerability analysis phase of the PASTA process.

Input	Description and Use
Configuration baselines	Provides a roster of configuration settings at the platform level as well as for any major software installation currently present on an asset within the threat model.
Software enumeration	Provides a roster of possible security countermeasures or pivot points of attack from a software perspective.
Network service listing	Provides a roster of possible network entry points that may be vulnerable for exploitation.

Input	Description and Use
Hardware (asset) enumeration	Encompasses a list of assets (e.g.: web, database, fileserver, software, network devices, VoIP equipment) for the application environment based on the proposed architecture to be used.
Identifying actors (role listing)	Considers the role of users (within an RBAC model) at various phases of the application and how they could either sustain or unfold security measures across the scope of the application environment within the threat model.
Manual processing	Considers human roles or physical controls that may be involved with manual processes the application environment depends on. This may include biometric measures, SmartCard technologies, call back authentication techniques, transcription services, data entry, courier services (tapes), physical records archiving, physical tape handling/processing, and so on.
Third-party roles	Role of third parties and similar listings of the aforementioned related to any infrastructure that will help either support or fulfill services on behalf of the application environment within the threat model.
Personnel considerations	Operations folk across technical, support operations that may be targets of social engineering ploys or those who have carte blanch, unaudited, or unmonitored access to key assets in the application environment.
Captured network flows	Beyond common network services such as DNS (53), SNMP (161), NTP (123), many architects do not have a strong handle on the amount of network services leveraged by the scope of application servers under a threat model. As a result, captured net flows for a brief period of time (month) offer invaluable data to get a glimpse of common network traffic that support valid use cases.

Stage III Summary

It is very easy to lead into the next stage of PASTA (Threat Analysis) without reviewing all the possible inherent flaws or strengths that a DFD has to uncover under the Application Decomposition stage. It is very tempting to follow the security rabbit hole by leaping into tangents where countermeasures or risk analysis can naturally take place. Instead, the threat modeler should ensure proper breadth of coverage in understanding the technology leveraged within the boundaries of the application environment and what likely threats should take precedence in their analysis. This is where PASTA diverges from other application threat models, as it attempts to focus on the most viable threats both inherent to the technology footprint of the environment as well as the industry segment and the data managed by the application environment.

The key takeaway for this stage's activities is that Application Decomposition is a stage in PASTA where comprehensive coverage should be applied to enumerate underlying platforms, technologies, software (and related versions), COTS (Code Off The Shelf), network services/equipment, physical security, and the overall process that governs all of the aforementioned for the scope of the application environment. Under application decomposition and the use of trust boundaries, PASTA provides considerations on where abuse cases may give way to data-focused attacks, platform continuity, authentication bypass, data integrity violations, and so much more. All of these types of considerations become more precisely defined, particularly during the threat analysis phase (stage IV) of the PASTA methodology.

Many of the activities in this stage leverage the use of a produced DFD. DFDs provide an illustration of how application components (from stage II) relate to one another. This is achieved through both analysis and some simple white-boarding efforts. The dissection or decomposition of the application truly is simply taking the enumerated components and mapping out their requests/responses with one another. In computer science, application decomposition or *factoring* provides a good form of dissecting a complex problem into more digestible components. Revealing application components and their calls to other components within the application boundary provides a visual depiction of use cases in the DFD.

Traditional assessments do not have activities that improve the level of understanding around how application components interact with one another. For most security assessments, knowledge of use cases, actors, or trust boundaries is part of a black box. For this reason, PASTA's application decomposition (or stage III) is a valuable stage to this risk-based threat modeling methodology. The stage III security analysis scrutinizes and focuses on network components, application services, on-demand events or triggers, RBAC models, batch processes, and more.

Already in stage III, as we decompose our applications, threat modelers must be cognizant of what inherent threats could be a factor. However, the benefit of how stage III is carried out is that its primary focus is enumeration exercises across physical and logical entities in order to simply determine what actors and use cases are supported by the application. A summary of key activities that should be performed in stage III is recapped as follows:

- S3:A1: Enumerate All Application Use Cases (e.g. login, account update, delete users).
- S3:A2: Perform DFD of Identified Components.
- S3:A3: Security Functional Analysis & the Use of Trust Boundaries.

In the next section, we will take a look at stage IV – Threat Analysis – which will now bridge the knowledge of what we know of the application to that of what we perceive as a threat agent to its understood business objectives and identified use cases. The following is a visual summary of stage III (ADA) (Figure 7.23).

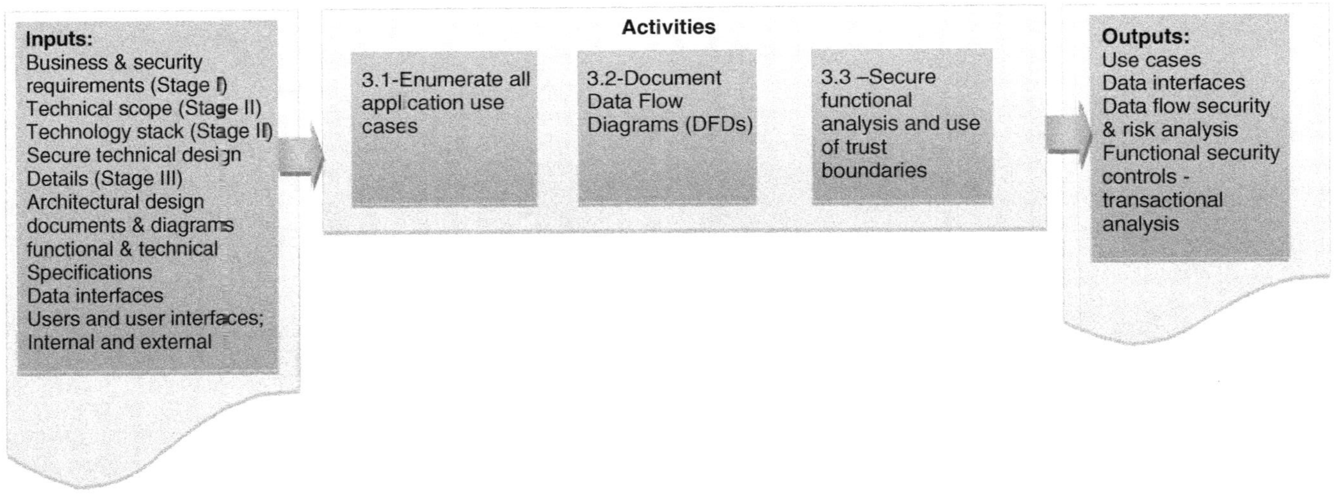

Inputs:
Business & security requirements (Stage I)
Technical scope (Stage II)
Technology stack (Stage II)
Secure technical design Details (Stage III)
Architectural design documents & diagrams functional & technical Specifications
Data interfaces
Users and user interfaces; internal and external

Activities

3.1-Enumerate all application use cases

3.2-Document Data Flow Diagrams (DFDs)

3.3 –Secure functional analysis and use of trust boundaries

Outputs:
Use cases
Data interfaces
Data flow security & risk analysis
Functional security controls - transactional analysis

Figure 7.23 PASTA Risk-Centric Threat Modeling – Stage III – (ADA) Application Decomposition and Analysis

Stage IV – Threat Analysis (TA)

Reexamining Threats Before we dive into threats, let us understand just how relative that word ("threat") really can be. As one may expect, there is no universality of threat to all industries, companies, or applications. Just like criminal groups and attackers do not have the same level of appreciation for information or technology assets across industries, companies, or applications. This being said, let us focus on the three major threat targets to which threat modeling can help protect: Data, Infrastructure, and Human Life. Directly or indirectly, these are the ultimate targets worth defending. For level-setting purposes, we examine all three below:

Data: Private or sensitive information pertaining to end users; also includes system information for which access or elevated assets to various parts of the application infrastructure could be obtained. In essence, data can be summarized into PHI or PII. If the product app does work with sensitive data, then there may be a clear threat. Therefore, a value should describe the level of threat to the data based on its attractiveness for both internal and external attack agents. We use a rating of high, moderate, or low for the assumed threat that the data naturally invokes given its usefulness in the black market or in other illicit venues where PII can be sold for pennies on the dollar.

Infrastructure: Beyond the attractiveness of data is the attractiveness of a robust infrastructure. Attackers who have knowledge of the power and sophistication of an infrastructure would truly enjoy being able to leverage the collective computing power in order to launch other types of attacks. This is a well-developed threat that in certain instances may be heightened if the computing environment gets worldwide attention. Likewise, less robust computing environments have traditionally received less intrigue from attackers, although recently in 2014, mobile-based Android attacks have surged seeking to leverage a small amount of computing power but in a collective network of compromised mobile devices. In the end, as the distributed nature of attacks continues to evolve, we are going to see a possible target-value shift from powerful distributed servers that are plentiful in the physical and virtual space to smaller computing assets, bound by a common malware agent able to perform essential malicious computing functions, consistently well over time.

Human: Wearable medical devices have been around for longer than most people think. Coupled with embedded software, wireless technologies, and a thin software footprint, human life is now well within the realm of exploitation and has been for nearly a decade. Before it may have been a lobby-con joke to think that JavaScript can hack humans, but now they really can. A recent example came in 2013/2014 when researchers announced that apps compiled against the Android 4.1 Jelly Bean API can exploit a bug in JavaScript. (Small tangent: both the Android 4.1 Jelly Bean API and the Google Glass itself would be listed as components to the threat model in stage II). The resulting exploit would allow hackers to obtain a live view from users of the Google Glass. All depending on the human – their role, position in society, wealth, status, and relevancy to a large plan can make human targets quite prevalent, particularly in the military when more integrated and wearable technology becomes introduced.

The point of identifying these threat areas is to have these considerations visible when fulfilling activities in stage IV. What could be intended threats around application X? Is it really the data? Is it something greater? Could other aspects of the application environment be really the focus (e.g. – human life, introducing service downtime, etc.)? These are key questions to consider as we fulfill the activities in this stage. In general, *threat*, much like *risk*, is going to be relative; relative to your data and your infrastructure. A practical guidance will be to continue monitoring emerging threats in a highly evolving Information Technology landscape in order to correlate what architectural, programmatic, asset, industry, or information related threats are relevant to the product application being threat modeled.

Stage Objectives The objective of this stage is to identify the relevancy of threats to the application being threat modeled and/or its underlying components. Thus far, in this risk-based approach to threat modeling, we have only really looked at a few variables in the risk formula, such as inherent risk and business impact. The viability of threats will be regarded in this chapter, thereby beginning our analysis of the right side of the traditional risk equation.[4] As all possible threat examples cannot be covered, the key takeaway from this chapter will be on how to identify good threat intelligence and apply them in estimating probabilistic threat instances that are credible for defensive measures to take place.

Threat feeds. Threat intelligence. Threat Data. Threat Landscape. Let us not forget Cyberthreat. There is a lot of threat talk out there and there is no security conference with a vendor hall in the world that will allow you to forget it. Beyond simply using it in security speak, it is important not to have the word lose value, particularly as it relates to threat modeling. In this portion of the threat modeling methodology, we focus on simplifying the term's use to two key areas: threat data and threat intelligence. Threat data is the data that is used to make effective threat analysis. Threat intelligence is the data that is collected and already analyzed, and largely served by service providers as a service feed for your operations center. In fulfillment of a risk-based threat modeling process, we are keen on having accurate and well founded threat data and threat intelligence. In doing so, we can drastically improve the threat modeling and overall risk analysis for threat mitigation.

Stage IV of PASTA begins to augment the level of risk analysis initiated in stage I, where risk profiling and business impact considerations were established. As part of the Threat Analysis, we will begin to substantiate various possible threat scenarios that are based on sound threat intelligence. This section will define how to interpret threat sources and apply them to existing or new software applications. Analyzing

---

[4]Risk = Threat × Vulnerability × Impact (Basic Risk Formula).

threat related data and tying it to application threat modeling is not done today – this is unique to PASTA. Even beyond threat modeling, threat aggregation is only taking place across major enterprises that have the time and resources to consume this data. Even in these circumstances, the received threat intelligence is generally consumed by a security operations team and if security measures are taken, they are localized to being primarily network driven in nature. Isolated from any level of threat knowledge are software development groups as well as system engineers who may be responsible for system/database administration. This is yet another demonstration that even with good threat intelligence, it means nothing unless properly consumed and applied within meaningful areas of the greater network architecture.

Stage IV's key objectives include the following:

- Review credible, diverse sources of threat data.
- Leverage internal sources of data, originating from security incidents, log/alert data.
- Enumerate likely threat agents who may be able to carry out supporting attack patterns for given threat.
- Identify the most likely threats to the application (should be less than 5).
- Determine a threat likelihood value for each threat that is developed.

The aforementioned objectives are intended to be fulfilled using the following stage IV activities listed. Each of these activities will be covered in the sections that follow:

- S4:A1 Analyze the Overall Threat Scenario
- S4:A2 Gather Threat Intelligence from Internal Sources
- S4:A3 Gather Threat Intelligence from External Sources.
- S4:A4 Update the Threat Libraries.
- S5:A5 Threat Agents to Asset Mapping.
- S4:A6 Assign Probabilistic Values around Identified Threats.

Stage IV:Activity I (S4:A1) – Analyze the Overall Threat Scenario The goal in this activity is to identify threat patterns that are most likely targeting similar application types with similar architecture, data use, deployment models, and other technology-related characteristics. Simply said, the goal for this activity is to list threats against the application. Some of the threats will be inherent to any type of deployment model. For example, adversarial goals for botnet propagation are indiscriminate to architecture, platform, hosted model, and other application environment characteristics. Some threat patterns will not apply based on the application type or even industry that it is in. Take for example inventory applications of automotive car parts. There is very little mass use for such information to be compromised or even be affected from an integrity or continuity point of view. As such, considerations for threat patterns may be lessened. Of course, there are always exceptions, especially

EXPLORING THE SEVEN STAGES AND EMBEDDED THREAT MODELING ACTIVITIES   421

if the information around a car part can be used as leverage as part of an overall threat. However, such a targeted attack would be addressed under this activity of stage IV – Threat Analysis.

Considerations for viable threat patterns are a lot simpler than it sounds. The world of InfoSec will have you believe that if you do not start by consuming their threat intelligence, you will not know how to protect your own environment. I think that may make more sense in highly distributed, noncentralized, and outsourced environments, but if you have a good hold of your product/application deployments, your team within your company will be best suited to say what threats are most likely to happen.

For this activity, internally assessing the perceived threats from members of the product team, application team, and senior management will undoubtedly provide the most realistic threat patterns that could possibly affect a product application. Ideals team members for this activity would be middle managers, product managers, IT managers, and senior business executives who are familiar with the application and its intended use and benefit. Conversations around threats to the application and company as a whole should be discussed. The reason for such a broad scope is that threat agents may not necessarily be looking at an application as a sole target but simply a means to a bigger target, particularly if the application itself is publicly accessible. For this reason, it is important to begin with threats that are germane to the application environment followed by threat assessments on what threat motives could include neighboring data or application access from the subject application that is being threat modeling. The following is a simple representation of the order of the threat analysis.

As shown in Figure 7.24, the selected team members will provide quick ideas and evidence as to what data, components, human/physical assets, and/or third-party infrastructures are most likely to be prime targets. Collecting the thoughts and feedback of team members will yield a summary of threat possibilities that reflect possible motives and targets at different levels. Looking at these variables in a cross section of different applications for different industries is presented as follows.

Table 7.12 provides a quick way to list threat scenarios for any type of application. From such a simple breakdown, we can further build upon what we have built in terms of a threat model for our application. In this activity, we can begin to focus on the data, human, physical, and third-party targets within our application, along with their associated threat motives.

| Threats to application data • IP, Customer/Client PII, Confidential Data, etc. | ➡ | Threat to application components • Components enumerated in Stage II | ➡ | Threats to human and physical resources • Employees, buildings, customers | ➡ | Threats to affiliated infrastructures/ applications • Connected global infrastructures |

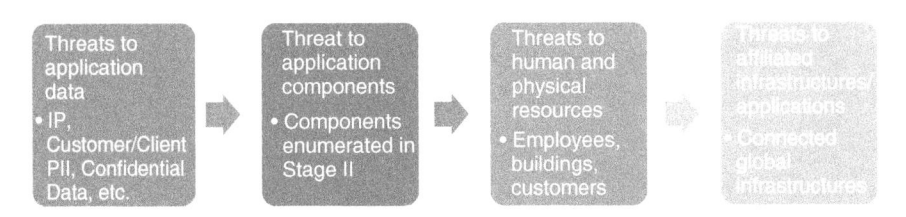

Figure 7.24   Areas to Consider around Threat Evaluation

TABLE 7.12 Sample Threat Considerations for Various Applications

Threat Considerations	Online Banking App	Transcription Software (Health care)	Multitenant Cloud Service Offering (CRM)
Data component target	Customer PII, Credentials, Bank account info, Source code, admin credentials, certificates	Patient Health Info	PII of online records, Business Intelligence/ Recon, Credential data,
App component target	Published web service APIs, mobile client computing apps, Source code repositories, domain controllers, DNS servers, CA server, token server	Backend data server, fileserver components, Stored library components, source code repository	Virtual Host Controllers, Virtual Network Management Interfaces, Management Interfaces, Published web service interfaces, FTP services, Administrative interfaces to virtual infrastructure
Human component target	Not likely	Not likely	Not likely
Physical component target	Not likely	Patient	Main Data Center Facility
Affiliate target	Trusted third-party development or IT shop	Outsourced development shop	Redundant site operations
Possible threat agent	Hacker syndicate groups, individual hackers/hackers for hire	Hacker Syndicate Groups, Individual hackers/hackers for hire	Hacker Syndicate Groups, Individual hackers/hackers for hire
Possible threat motive	Identity theft, financial fraud	PII theft, Affect data integrity of PHI (misdiagnosis)	Mass compromise of multitenant PII information and/or systems & infrastructure

EXPLORING THE SEVEN STAGES AND EMBEDDED THREAT MODELING ACTIVITIES   423

Without making any correlative analysis to global trends, it is possible to make simple associations to threats per industry. Certain threats are obvious, such as the threat of financial fraud through credit card data compromises. Others are less obvious, such as the compromise of an obscure third-party parts manufacturer. From information leakages to network breaches, knowing what the threats may be pursuing for the application that is being threat modeled is a question that most product/software team members should be able to answer. Companies that can go through similar exercises, as shown earlier, will quickly discover that they can narrow the focus to a few threats that can be factored into the threat model. Simple inherent threat targets that companies of various industries can factor into their threat analysis are listed in Figure 7.25.

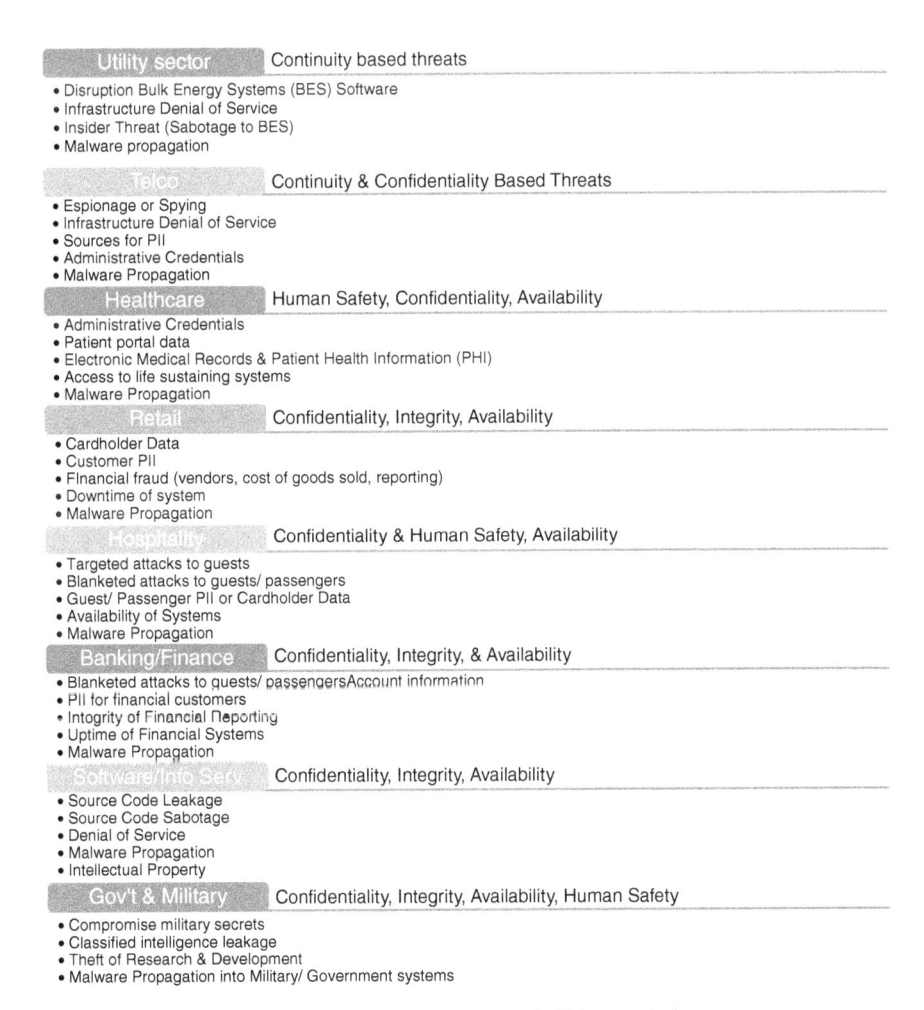

Utility sector — Continuity based threats
- Disruption Bulk Energy Systems (BES) Software
- Infrastructure Denial of Service
- Insider Threat (Sabotage to BES)
- Malware propagation

Telco — Continuity & Confidentiality Based Threats
- Espionage or Spying
- Infrastructure Denial of Service
- Sources for PII
- Administrative Credentials
- Malware Propagation

Healthcare — Human Safety, Confidentiality, Availability
- Administrative Credentials
- Patient portal data
- Electronic Medical Records & Patient Health Information (PHI)
- Access to life sustaining systems
- Malware Propagation

Retail — Confidentiality, Integrity, Availability
- Cardholder Data
- Customer PII
- Financial fraud (vendors, cost of goods sold, reporting)
- Downtime of system
- Malware Propagation

Hospitality — Confidentiality & Human Safety, Availability
- Targeted attacks to guests
- Blanketed attacks to guests/ passengers
- Guest/ Passenger PII or Cardholder Data
- Availability of Systems
- Malware Propagation

Banking/Finance — Confidentiality, Integrity, & Availability
- Blanketed attacks to guests/ passengersAccount information
- PII for financial customers
- Integrity of Financial Reporting
- Uptime of Financial Systems
- Malware Propagation

Software/Info Serv — Confidentiality, Integrity, Availability
- Source Code Leakage
- Source Code Sabotage
- Denial of Service
- Malware Propagation
- Intellectual Property

Gov't & Military — Confidentiality, Integrity, Availability, Human Safety
- Compromise military secrets
- Classified intelligence leakage
- Theft of Research & Development
- Malware Propagation into Military/ Government systems

Figure 7.25   Sample Threat Possibilities per Industry

The last figure was simply meant to be a quick representation of top threats that affect various industries. During the threat analysis, this information is useful in order to determine if the application being threat modeled is subject to the threat possibilities depicted at a macro level. From there, it will be important to narrow down a generic threat against the components identified in stage II of the PASTA methodology. Some questions to pose members of the threat modeling technical group would be the following:

- What current threats exist that are specific to the application model and employed infrastructure model?
  - Sought-after responses will help determine what specific threats are taking place against foundational elements of the product application. Example: Threats to Ruby on Rails framework, exploited in 2012–2013.
- What current threats exist related to key vendors/business associates that may undermine the security posture of the product application?
  - Sought-after response should look to identify process-based risks from operations or third-party components that are to be leveraged by the application.
- What current threats are affecting the industry or underlying target users of the developing product application?
  - Sought-after answers should address threats that have been more prevalent over time, especially in recent history.
- Has the "attractiveness" of the data changed recently? Does it contain more PII than before or information that can be leveraged by the criminally inclined?
  - Sought-after responses would be the ones that identify whether the application data has changed to possibly further entice malicious actors to have an increased appetite to target the application data. Example: LinkedIn's "Intro Service" introduced in 2013–2014.

Threat Classification Some threat modeling methodologies will suggest classification of threats in order to better organize threats into compartmentalized components. If this is beneficial to you and your team, you may consider placing your depicted threats into threat classification models such as STRIDE or DREAD – both from Microsoft. For PASTA, this is not needed; however, it could be easily incorporated into this activity within stage IV if desired. Simply after defining possible threats from the last activity, assign to a category from one of the predefined threat categories in STRIDE (Spoofing, Tampering of Data, Repudiation, Information Disclosure, Denial of Service, and Elevation of Privileges). Some find it easier to see if threats fall into one of these categories, especially if STRIDE and/or DREAD have been introduced along with their respective taxonomies of terms. The only problem is that attack patterns and vulnerabilities do not also leverage the same classification model, thereby making the use of STRIDE or DREAD to be useful within a threat analysis phase of a threat modeling methodology. PASTA does not need these categories to be used in this activity, but instead a conscientious list on viable threat patterns from which attack trees will be later built from.

As stated several times thus far, the activities and stages in PASTA build off of one another. This makes it linear and easy to collaborate on. As we look at the following activities that support stage IV of the PASTA process, it is important to consider what unique attributes and conditions of the application may also influence the types of threats that could materialize. Everything related to deployment location, personnel operating and managing the application, and especially architectural considerations should be always considered when considering what types of threats are most likely to be aimed at the organization and specifically the application being threat modeled.

In this activity, we focused internally on what key members of the organization considered as the most likely threats to the application or product being developed. In the following activity, we will look inwardly again to the organization, but this time not to its people, but rather its process and technological controls for possible guidance on what threats to ultimately consider as part of the overall threat model.

Stage IV: Activity II (S4:A2) – Gather Threat Intelligence from Internal Sources
This activity can be summarized in one sentence:

- *Leverage historical incident reports and security alert data.*

This may be easier than it appears since legal may have different thoughts about people outside of Forensic or Incident Response groups knowing about breaches that have taken place within an organization. This has and will continue to be a roadblock for the industry as a whole since disclosing for the sake of researching and even building a threat model but not disclosing to affected customers is a bit underhanded, although the reasons for each are vastly different. On paper, however, the perception would require some talented finessing. Until then, companies engaged in threat modeling will have to make do with what they have in terms of internal threat data.

Focusing on two key data points, *Reported Incidents* and *Central Log Data* will provide a good basis of internal threat data to later develop into threat intelligence. This threat intelligence, spawn from internal data sources, will then help to substantiate the viability of threats taking place against the application. Externally harvested threat intelligence will be gathered and correlated from outside sources as well, but for this activity, internal log data sources should be the key focus. Some of the best threat intelligence can be formulated by the internal threat data that is collected by an organization. Such data can originate from internal log information, such as central log repositories or an Incident Response database. Products such as Security Incident & Event Monitoring (SIEM) solutions facilitate this greatly. The possibility to channel all internal alerts, incidents, and log data into one vehicle streamlines the process for this activity. Diverse threat data sources, such as platform/system logs, as well as any network-related logs, will provide the type of threat data from which internally harvested threat intelligence can be developed.

In this activity, some degree of Security Operations and/or IT Operations process maturity must preexist. For example, if you do not have a Security Operations Center (SOC) or do not enable logging on your systems or centralize logs to a log aggregation point, then this may be a point in the chapter that you bookmark or simply contemplate its theoretical capabilities in your own company's environment. Additionally, if your company does not keep track of security incidents of varying types, or worse, even know what a security is, it may be time to bookmark this activity for later use. This activity aims to build off of the first activity by refining what types of passive and active recon or attack efforts have taken place over the last twelve (12) months. Much of that effort will depend on good threat data managed by groups such as Security Operations, Incident Response, Network Operations, and other IT areas. Twelve months is usually a good test bed of threat intelligence to look at since it would account for "seasonal" traffic and provides an ample scope of coverage for analysis. It will be a matter of preferences and largely capability and resources if that time span is increased. It should be pointed out that threat modeling members would not be asking for twelve months of logs to be compressed and zipped up for review. That would negate the ability for PASTA to be a streamlined process to accompany an SDLC workflow. Instead, the assumption is that an SIEM or Log Management solution could provide a huge catalyst to review the level of data needed for a lengthy period of time.

The key to any threat data harvesting is centralization. Unfortunately, most organizations, even large enterprises, have trouble fulfilling the control of centralized logging or incident data management. For most companies in the SMB market (and a large bit of mid-cap companies), the maximum scope of their centralization revolves around only network logs. From there, little to no monitoring is typically done. Larger companies have evolved beyond localized logging and have been leveraging the power of centralized logging solutions (Splunk, Sumo Logic, Nagios, etc.) over the past 10 years, thereby making the ability to harvest threat data a reality. More mature processes have sought SIEM solutions from places such as IBM, HP, and beyond in order to aggregate and normalize the terabytes worth of log data from various sources (network, system, and on rare instances, application servers). Although many places are still slow to make the time and financial investment in SIEMs, this has changed greatly in the past five years or so. Slower adoption has been experienced around storing and centralizing application logs; however, regulatory pressures may affect this adoption over the next few years.

SOCs and Network Operation Centers (NOCs) typically collect security/network-related alert data across multiple enterprise assets. Leveraging the data that pertains to assets within the product application technology scope should be made as part of this activity. Alerts against similar product applications within the enterprise or overall IT environment would also be useful to the threat modeling team. Information being sought as part of this activity includes things such as failed login attempts, failed application calls, authentication errors, arbitrary input received, invalid object references, and so on. Moreover, log records that revolve around identity violations, particularly around identity management solutions or services such as Active Directory or LDAP where authentication integration may leverage are worthwhile to review. In general, patterns that reflect anomalies in application usage are good pieces to review as threat intelligence.

Ideally, SIEMs would be the best route for harvesting threat intelligence from internal sources given SIEM's ability to correlate various types of logs beyond just network logs. The SIEM's ability to ingest, normalize, and search for key terms, at a relatively quick rate can allow for a threat modeling team to perform targeted searches around threats that are perceived to be viable against the application. Again, if the application being threat modeled is new, alerts and events of comparable applications could be used as well. This exercise will strengthen initial threat perceptions around the application, thereby substantiating possible threats previously considered for the application.

If logs are not currently centralized and manifested via a central logging solution or SIEM, a basic step for gathering threat intelligence is to review access violations across platform, database, application, and network logs. This should be done for the scope of assets across the application architecture. Typically this may include logs from infrastructure assets, DNS servers, web servers (if applicable), data servers (file systems or relational databases), as well as application server log. If workstation logs are relevant to the application solution, they should also be included in the scope of the review.

Whether audit reports are being collected or not, it is important to identify the following characteristics that should be collected as part of audit logs. Any audit logs that are material to application components (stage II) in the threat model are the key focus. Key activities to identify across log, audit, and/or incident reports are the following:

- Access Control Logs (Identity Management solution (IdM), Network Access Control (NAC), LDAP/ AD Servers, Application Access Logs, System/ Service Logs (RDP, SSH, Platform (*nix, Windows, RADIUS, TACACS+, RACF, TopSecret (Mainframe), etc.)
  - Look for violations in access. This may translate Authorized access during odd hours may also indicate compromised internal actors. Their credentials may have been used to access or conduct unauthorized actions against some facet of the application environment.
    - Abnormal access times by any user
    - Failed login attempts
    - Account lockouts
    - Sudden activity on inactive accounts
    - Sudden activity on active accounts
    - Business logic violations for a given user role (using a report that does not correspond to role)
- Host-based Firewall alert logs
  - Illicit file/ system access requests
  - Access to blocked sites (Ex: known blacklists, etc.)
  - Abnormal disk/ CPU usage levels.
  - Alerts from application whitelisting end point solutions.
- Application Logs
  - Business logic exploitation attempts

- Injection-based attempts (CSRF, XSS, SQLi, etc.)
- Fuzzing attempts
- HTTP Error Codes
- Database level error messages
- Any level of application logs relate to the product application's use cases.
- Privilege escalation attempt
- Infrastructure Logs
  - Firewalls, router logs (egress traffic),
  - Web proxy/ Load balancer logs (if applicable)
  - Netflow traffic for interfaces associated with application environment. Intrusion Detection Systems/ Software (agent based)
  - Observed ARP spoofing attempts
  - IP conflicts
  - Spike in use of a particular network protocol
  - Firewall alerts that show spoofed IP sources or loop-back address
  - IPS/IDS alerts that show MEDIUM to HIGH or even very frequent LOW tripped alerts
  - Unified Threat Management (UTM) or Network Threat Management (NTM) logs.
- Server side logs
  - File system file access violations, SSH logs, Windows Event Logs, sudo logs, and so on.
  - Agent-based logs (Ex: from host-based security on end points – Firewalls, Host Intrusion Prevention)
- Host-based A/V or HIPS agent logs or Application Whitelisting Agent Logs
  - Administrator machine terminals with elevated access to product application features requested or tripped
- Proxy server logs
  - Logs from both network and application proxies.
  - Illicit URI requests or manipulated web requests
  - Excess or spike in HTTP 404, 302, 500 alerts
- Database logs
  - Ex: Business logic logs show anomalies in batch job requests (outside expected timeframes)
- Web server transaction logs
  - Ex: Directory enumeration attempts for folders/ file objects that do not exist.
- Human Resource Reports
  - Personnel write-ups provide non-traditional intelligence on troubled personnel that may pose as threat agents in the event of an insider threat.

- Facilities Management Reports
  o Violations to access from physical areas within a company provide additional threat intelligence as to what internal threats may be present by internal employees or rogue human actors who may have obtained illicit credentials to protected areas. Reviewing timestamps and reconciling user roles to access times may paint a picture of a developing threat. Logs from proxy cards, biometric readers, and other physical access control points that enable logging can be centralized to logging aggregators for easier access and analysis.

The aforementioned list provides easy ways to narrow down viable threat data criteria. This would help to narrow the focus on what to search for in these massive incident event log repositories. For example, related to access control logs, if an application has expected or predictable usage times for certain roles, then reviewing alerts outside of these time windows may represent anomalies and possible indications of illicit access to application data. Outliers or anomalies in normal application use cases are good indicators of possible threat indicators. This is simply one for which there are many per each type of log that can be consumed.

One of the benefits from harvesting log data is that it builds for good threat context. Such information aids in determining if presumed threats have any validity. Threat intelligence may even suggest that active or recent attack patterns are actively present and even have some level of persistence. If the subject application is a new application, but leveraging preexisting infrastructure or assets, then log data around those other application components should be leveraged as part of the threat analysis. Additionally, log data from comparable applications components, having similar technology, use cases, and deployment models, may also be of use.

In terms of roles, working with enterprise system and network administrators will prove to be key allies in fulfilling internal threat intelligence gathering. Being able to gain the help of administrators in network and system operations will determine the success of this activity. In most large enterprises, as long as approved access is granted, many of these SIEM products have a reporting web interface that they can simply log in and run their queries or even set up their batched report requests. Filters are provided in many of the SIEM products today in order to filter queries to down to header level information, IP, action type, TCP protocol, timestamp, and more. For non-web-related applications, establishing criteria for protocol use, authentication types, IP-based header values will be important versus those HTTP headers used in web-related applications.

The next activity in stage IV now builds on our initial threat analysis and review of internal threat data to collaborate with external threat sources. The continued objective is to conclude with a substantiated list of threats for which attack trees will be built in the stages that follow.

Stage IV: Activity III (S4:A3) – Gather Threat Intelligence from External Sources

This stage is about threat intelligence gathering versus amassing threat data. The former is driven by identifying who attackers are, what they are planning and what they are after. The latter is about data used to evaluate whether or not something could be a threat (e.g. – elevated counts to protocol use on a switch or inside network device). We have focused on threat data earlier in this Stage and now we look outwardly for guidance on current threats that could affect our application environment being threat modeled. This activity aims to refine the list of possible threats against the subject application that is being threat modeled.

External threat intelligence gathering has a wider breadth of data to consume and is generally done so by third-party managed security service providers (MSSP). Very few companies have internal resources that harvest external threat data. Even fewer companies have internal resources able to correlate threat data to their own industry trends, company technology footprint, let alone application components. As a result, much of the external threat intelligence data is consumed by SMBs and enterprises alike in the form of subscribed threat feeds. Various types of services offer slightly modified version of this service. Some MSSPs offer a hybrid service where internal alert data from client networks would be mashed with external threat data consisting of reported security incidents, security bulletins, and other security advisories. Other MSSPs simply offer external threat feeds. Many additional service options are also present as well as much of these types of services imply some degree of customization. The relevancy to overall threat analysis is that a broader range of threat data can be analyzed and factored into the threat model.

Regardless if an MSSP is used or if an internal SOC is correlating breach data, reported security incidents, and security advisories, the following criteria can serve as valuable points of guidance for qualifying good threat intelligence to bake-in.

1. Correlate threat intelligence to the perceived threats identified in Activity S4:S1. This external threat intelligence will legitimize the threat perceptions that were internally identified under the first stage.
2. Focus on threats that will adversely affect the use of defined use cases from stage I.
3. Look for threats that are ideally related to your industry segment. Secondly would be that they are related to the employed technology or service model that the application is following (Cloud-SaaS, client server, etc.).
4. Identify threats that, if realized, would present the biggest impact to the application's use, adoption, promotion, or even the company's reputation.
5. Focus on threats that pass a basic supposition of viability. If it sounds too farfetched, you can rest assured that adversaries or hacker groups are also trying to fathom an easier way to conduct their layers of attack.
6. Don't lose site of the big threat picture: data loss, infrastructure compromise, IP Theft, and so on. Keeping site of this will provide the right context to evaluate the threats that are researched in this phase.
7. Do not forget about the threat agent or malicious actor. The threats may seem viable, but it is important to consider who or what would perform the layers of attack that represent a given threat.
8. Make sure that the threat is still relevant. Threat information does have a shelf life since as attackers launch attacks and defenders understand these attacks,

EXPLORING THE SEVEN STAGES AND EMBEDDED THREAT MODELING ACTIVITIES 431

attackers will have to find new ways to attack or different places to attack who may not be informed of latest attack methods.

9. Understand the attack vector relative to the threat identified by the threat intelligence. Examples of attack vectors can be (LAN based, NFC Protocol, "sneaker net," browser based are some examples. Considering the channel of attack will further substantiate the possibility of a threat that is supported by a mature attack vector.
10. Abuse/Misuse Case – Although this is an activity that is really fledged out in Stage VI of the PASTA methodology, it is worth considering what possible abuse cases can be derived from threat patterns. If there are very little to none, then it would be best to focus efforts on more credible threat patterns.

Now that we have come guiding criteria on selecting possible threat sources, here are some actual threat intelligence sources to consider.

- [PLATFORM] Microsoft Security Intelligence Report (http://www.microsoft.com/security/sir/default.aspx)
- [HEALTHCARE] HITRUST Cyber Threat Intelligence and Incident Coordination Center (http://www.hitrustalliance.net/ctas/) – Health care-focused threat intelligence reporting.
  o Health-care Threat Briefing – summary of top threats in the health-care industry.
  o Health-care Industry Threat Report – overall synopsis on threats to healthcare industry.
  o Health-care Incident and Malware Reports – summary of malware reports affecting today's health-care entities; provides indication of targeted malware attacks aimed at either affecting patient lives or compromising patient information.
- [GENERAL] NTT Group has unveiled a new threat intelligence report in 2013 that looks at global threats, cross industries. Regional threat outlooks can be obtained here: http://www.nttgroupsecurity.com/.
- [GENERAL] SANS Internet Storm Center (ISC) – Useful information on regarding spikes in threat data around the world, mostly network focused. (https://isc.sans.edu/reports.html)
- [GENERAL] US-CERT (http://www.us-cert.gov/security-publications) – Summary of threat intelligence data that is industry/platform agnostic.
- [GENERAL] Security Partner Threat Data (McAfee, Symantec, DellSecureWorks, Cyveillance, etc.) – Ongoing briefings of mostly malware or Internet-based threats that have been recorded/logged by some of the world's leading security software firms and their network of security software agents/appliances.

Threat intelligence, generally provided by security and technology firms with a research department, is able to provide either a free or pay for service on active threats.

MSSPs with a research department may be able to provide companies with a periodic feed of active threats as observed across client environments or studied honeypots where some of their vendor technology may be deployed. These security points of presence often have the ability to integrate threat data to a central repository where macro-level analytics can be performed. The dominant focus of threat intelligence today revolves around web infrastructures and network-based appliances/equipment, however, given the rise of use and popularity of mobile platforms in both personal and corporate settings, threat feeds around mobile and other platforms will undoubtedly increase, therefore, those types of feeds should be aggregated whenever possible and if applicable to a company's application development roadmap for products.

Apart from the previously mentioned security companies, the Verizon Business group has recently created the Verizon Enterprise Risk Incident Sharing (VERIS) Framework as well as an accompanying web application that allows for anonymous sharing of security incidents. The result is an online warehouse for identifying incidents that relate to those experienced by a given company or set of companies. The VERIS framework embellishes four key measurable areas that encompass multiple characteristics related to an incident. They are shown as follows in Table 7.13, under the column titled "Metric Area."

Over time, more and more organizations will look to share incident-related information. This sharing has already begun to become aggregated by places like the Verizon VERIS network and the HITRUST Cyber Threat Intelligence and Incident Coordination efforts. Today, MITRE has established TAXII[5] (Trusted Automated eXchange of Indicator Information), which defines a suite of services aimed at exchanging cyber threat information across organizations, industries, and product groups. The service is built around the STIX[6] (Structured Threat Information eXpression) language, which aims to standardize the protocol used when sharing incident or threat information. This structure language is similar to the CCE and CVE languages, which aim to standardize common configuration and common vulnerability lists. Over time, it is expected that the amount of threat intelligence from across multiple industries and organizations will lend to a highly useful list of threats to consider when threat modeling.

Threat intelligence is best leveraged when the information from the threat feed is properly correlated to the application environment that is being studied by the application threat model, in addition to the threats defined to be most relevant from S4:A1. Threat intelligence that conforms to the TAXII structure will also assist in the consumption and sharing of threat intelligence to other sources when needed. Using information from threat feeds would normalize attack, vulnerability, weakness, and other application component data that may be relevant to the threat. These threat feeds serve as counter-intelligence to attacks in cyberspace and provide an opportunity for multiple parallels to be drawn during the threat analysis phase (stage IV) of the proposed threat modeling methodology.

---

[5] http://taxii.mitre.org/.
[6] http://stix.mitre.org/.

TABLE 7.13 VERIS Framework of IR Metrics

Metric Area	Characteristics	Purpose/Additional Metrics
Demographics	Date of incident	Facilitates trending over time
	Primary industry	Facilitates industry-specific analysis and comparisons
	Region of operation	Facilitates regional analysis and comparisons
	Number of employees	Facilitates analysis and comparisons based on organizational size
	Number of dedicated IT security staff	Provides an indicator of the size and budget of the information security program
Incident classification	Agent	Defines internal attack agent, internal, or partner
	Action	Defines whether action is malware, hacking, social, misuse, physical, error, and environmental
	Asset	Asset type, # of assets affected, additional asset details, business function, mgt/administration decisions over time on asset, location/hosting details of asset
	Attribute	Confidentiality, Integrity, Availability, Authenticity, Utility, Possession of Control of Data
Discovery and mitigation	Incident timeline	Initial action to Incident, Incident to Discovery, Discovery to Containment/Restoration
	Incident Discovery	Evidence Sources, Discovery Method, Other Discovery metrics
	Capabilities and remediation	Program Maturity, Control Assessment, 20/20 Hindsight Solution, Cost of 20/20 Hindsight Solution, Corrective action and recommendations
Impact classification	Impact categorization	Direct Impact Categories, Indirect Impact Categories
	Impact estimation	To obtain an estimation of impact in currency (dollars)
	Impact qualification	To understand the severity of the impact relative to the organization's tolerance for loss

Leveraging information from prior incidents is invaluable to many companies wishing to build further context around attacks that they may have witnessed. It also provides a frame of reference to understanding attacks against varying types of application environments. The challenge in analyzing incidents for the benefit of improved threat modeling is the diversity of incident types reported, which makes it prone to have a lot of fractured groups. If reported differences contain more unique properties than similar ones, it will affect the integrity of the threat intelligence that would be formed from such reported incidents.

This forces some degree of synchronization among threat intelligence reports and incident reports. Although the intent by the industry is to have reported incidents provide threat intelligence, the secretive nature of breaches and companies reluctance to anonymously disclose has made the process slow. Threat intelligence service providers are therefore having to introduce other forms of "intelligence" into the threat equation, which is risky and somewhat deceitful practice by many standards. In the future, it is hoped that an increased collaboration of anonymous incident reporting can provide for improved threat intelligence. This would greatly elevate the quality of threat intelligence from which this activity in PASTA would directly benefit from.

Nonetheless, the threat intelligence provided by companies such as Symantec, Intel Security (formerly McAfee), Dell-SecureWorks, or Juniper Networks have their benefits and use during stage IV of the application threat modeling methodology. Wherever the source, it should be mentioned that sources for threat feeds become less reliable over time and in general should be qualified every year to two years in order to make sure that the data sourcing is up to date and comprehensive.

Stage IV:Activity IV (S4:A4) – Update the Threat Libraries   One of the most comprehensive attack libraries is managed by the MITRE organization. The CAPEC (Common Attack Pattern Enumeration & Classification) is an attack library based on prior attack patterns. Attack libraries are helpful to apply to applications and determine if any of the attack patterns are viable given various characteristics (known vulnerabilities, weaknesses, and threats). Pen testing tools have recently begun to incorporate attack libraries into their tool base. Knowing that attack models and attack probes will be presented in Stage VI of the PASTA methodology, it is important to achieve two important tasks for this present activity. These two actions are as follows:

1. Update the threat library from source. Beyond MITRE Corporation's (www.mitre.org) CAPEC library, you may check other sources of application threats/attacks that could provide for the inception of an attack tree. Both OWASP and WASC (Web Application Security Consortium) have top threat listings to web applications, as well as for mobile applications (mobile). These listings can all help to provide a database of threats that can be applied to the threat model. Most pen testing tools and DAST (Dynamic Application Security Testing) already have regularly scheduled updates that incorporate these libraries into the product itself. Some tools that currently update using the CAPEC libraries include the following: MetaSploit Pro (Rapid7), Cenzic Hailstorm (Trustwave), and HP WebInspect. Managing updates to attack libraries is possible outside of these tools; however, it is nice to have them automatically updating during this activity.
2. Consider Threat to Attack Relationship. Building off of the attack library updates and review, an attack tree at this stage will begin to form and capture the threat to attack relationship. Threats cannot be realized without a successful

attack; therefore, a preliminary analysis into the types of attacks that could achieve the identified threats from this stage should be performed.

Stage IV:Activity V (S4:A5) – Threat Agents to Asset Mapping A threat agent is a single individual or group intending to launch a threat into action. Today, nearly all threat agents will be human, but in the future, threats will be orchestrated autonomously by actors in applications. Encompassing the threat agent into the threat model is important because mitigation may apply to preventing or limiting the threat agent's actions via a range of countermeasures. Upon mapping the threat agents to possible targets, preventative, detective, or reactive countermeasures can be considered.

In this activity, we map threat agents to the beginnings of an attack tree. As shown in the following attack tree model, a threat to an embedded medical device, with a subset of use cases is depicted. Threats to each use case are depicted along with a possible threat agent. In this example, there are three possible threats and associated threat agents. Left to right, we have an internal threat agent who may have legitimate or illicit access to affect the monitoring use cases for the application. This may be an insider who may have colluded with an external threat agent in order to affect the target application, and ultimately, the target patient.

The next threat agent is intended to represent a criminal agent who has technical expertise in the software and can introduce an attack payload against the software product. This may have life or death consequences for the patient. For prime global figures or key government officials, this may be a viable threat scenario. The criminal agent represents a hacker for hire who has researched exploit scenarios that succeed against the use case of regulating heartbeats from a Bluetooth-enabled pacemaker.

The last threat agent depicts one that works within a trusted vendor organization. The vendor may produce the target asset and/or software related to the Bluetooth enabled. In this case, the threat agent may have been contracted to alter the data reporting functionality of the use case in order to allow for an unauthorized data request to be sent to the application components executing "Report Medical Data" use cases.

A mapping of all three threat agents is represented in the following partial tree (see Figure 7.26).

Stage IV:Activity VI (S4:A6) – Assign Probabilistic Values around Identified Threats This activity helps to assign a weighted percentage to each identified threat in S4:A1. The probabilistic analysis is based on considerations for access, window of opportunity, ability to repudiate, risk reward (for threat agent), and threat simplicity. Although extremely simplistic, these five pieces of information truly represent whether or not some threats become actionable against a target application or application component. The rationale behind some of these characteristics is also logical since these five threat characteristics would need to be present for a threat to be formed. Evaluating these five attributes around threat should be based on the activities fulfilled up until this point in stage IV, which included industry statistics, threat reports, or security incident reports.

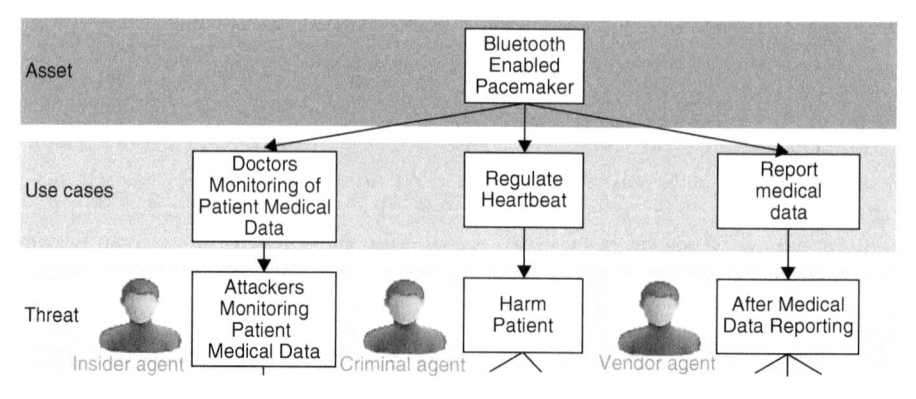

Figure 7.26 Mapping of Threat Agents to Asset Targets

Each of the five criterion is divided into three possible percentage outcomes. They are as follows:

90% – Reflects nearly all aspects of the threat criteria are possible.
50% – Reflects a moderate to large aspect of the threat criteria is possible.
10% – Reflects a limited amount of the threat criteria is possible.

- *Accessibility:* Threat landscape related to target(s) is easily accessible.
  - *90%:* Completely open to all human and/or logical application, network traffic
  - *50%:* Restrictions are in place for access against logical or human interaction.
  - *10%:* Assumed to be impermeable. Recognizing that noting
- *Window of Opportunity:* Nothing impedes threat agents from exercising threat plans and underlying attack patterns.
  - *90%:* Opportunity is always there.
  - *50%:* Opportunity is only present during certain points of time.
  - *10%:* Limited time window for threat to be exercised.
- *Ability to Repudiate:* Is there an opportunity to repudiate threat actions against a target or threat landscape that includes aspects of the application environment.
  - *90%:* Repudiation is nearly guaranteed.
  - *50%:* Opportunity repudiate is only partially present or threat components are only partially able to be repudiated.
  - *10%:* Ability to repudiate is extremely difficult.
- *Risk Reward:* Value of target over risk level to threat agent.
  - *90%:* Value received from successful execution of threat is nearly double level of risk.
  - *50%:* Reward potential is at least 50% of the value of the risk.
  - *10%:* Very little reward percentage in relation to risk level.

- *Threat Simplicity:* Simplicity level of threat. Easiest threats will have reduced layers of attack patterns as well as number of threat agents.
  ○ *90%:* Nearly all of threat plan is simple to execute.
  ○ *50%:* Large part of threat plan is simple to execute.
  ○ *10%:* Very little of the plan is simple to execute.

The numeric probability assigned to identified threats (from S4:A1) and threat-related criteria (mentioned earlier) is not intended to be an advanced form of probabilistic analysis. The noncomplexity is actually a good trait to maintain since much of what people find discouraging about threat modeling is that it is large and complex. Adding complexity to threat modeling is not the best of ideas, especially when trying to foster adoption. Nonetheless this probabilistic activity is intended to create a value percentage around Threat. As a result, thus far, we have a slightly altered *Risk* formulate that resembles the following:

$$(R)\text{isk} = \frac{(T)\text{hreat}_{(P)\text{robability}} \times (V)\text{ulnerability}_{(P)\text{robability}} \times (I)\text{mpact}}{(C)\text{ountermeaures}}$$

Probability in the aforementioned formula is obtained by taking the average percentages of all threat criteria values. In doing so, it provides a probabilistic percentage average that can be used to estimate the likely of a threat to take place, in the absence of knowing what vulnerabilities exist or what countermeasures to mitigate the risks could be developed. Later, we will also begin to explore the other probability coefficient around vulnerabilities.

Exemplifying the use of this form of quantifying threat probability, we look to a quick example in the higher education industry in Table 7.14.

Reverting back to the health-care threat scenario from the prior activity, we can revisit the attack tree to consider probabilities around one of the threat agents. Taking the second threat agent scenario where a hired hacker may be contracted to develop a custom payload for unleashing against a head of nation, we review the following threat criterion for probability (Table 7.15).

The predefined percentage benchmarks may be altered if desired as well. A 58% probability that a targeted threat to a national leader with a pacemaker may be a bit high. Both of the areas around accessibility and the simplicity of the threat could in fact be much lower than 10% considering that state leaders may have considered this risk before and thereby implemented some NFC emission containment safeguards. Additionally, gaining physical access to a national leader may prove difficulty, given their security along with unpublished itineraries. Nonetheless, this exercise provides a good basis for which to consider key characteristics of how probabilistic analysis can be assigned to threats.

Key Roles in Stage IV

Another key member or group to consider from Figure 7.26 is the incident responder or security analyst charged with event or incident monitoring. If incidents are

TABLE 7.14 Threat Analysis of a Mobile Based Loan Application Serving Higher Ed

Application Name:	iLoan4Learning v1.1
Short Description:	Mobile and web-based student loan application for undergraduate students at a major college/university.
Data:	Student PII, approximately 1.3M records.

<table>
<tr><td colspan="3" align="center">Threat Criterion</td></tr>
<tr><td>Threat Criteria</td><td>Probability (%)</td><td>Reason</td></tr>
<tr><td>Accessibility:</td><td>90</td><td>Threat agent's access to app.</td></tr>
<tr><td>Window of opportunity:</td><td>50</td><td>Opportunity is present often.</td></tr>
<tr><td>Repudiation:</td><td>50</td><td>Repudiation can be controlled to some degree by the network and application logs.</td></tr>
<tr><td>Risk reward:</td><td>50</td><td>PII volume equates to large potential payout in black market.</td></tr>
<tr><td>Simplicity:</td><td>10</td><td>There are many needed layers needing to overcome in order to successfully execute this threat.</td></tr>
<tr><td>Average:</td><td>50</td><td>Probability of threat to take place.</td></tr>
</table>

TABLE 7.15 Threat Analysis for Bluetooth Enabled Medical Device

Application Name:	HelloHeart 1.3
Short Description:	Bluetooth-enabled device monitors and controls heartbeat regularity.
Data:	Patient Health Information (PHI), patient safety – loss of life

<table>
<tr><td colspan="3" align="center">Threat Criterion</td></tr>
<tr><td>Threat Criteria</td><td>Probability (%)</td><td>Reason</td></tr>
<tr><td>Accessibility:</td><td>90</td><td>Open NFC protocol; similar device can be purchased for testing.</td></tr>
<tr><td>Window of opportunity:</td><td>10</td><td>Physical proximity needed to release payload.</td></tr>
<tr><td>Repudiation:</td><td>90</td><td>Repudiation is almost guaranteed since application logging is known to not take place.</td></tr>
<tr><td>Risk Reward:</td><td>90</td><td>Bounty compensation is extremely high.</td></tr>
<tr><td>Simplicity:</td><td>10</td><td>Exploit payload would require some R&D time. Physical countermeasures may have already taken place.</td></tr>
<tr><td>Average:</td><td>58</td><td>Probability of threat to take place.</td></tr>
</table>

tracked and managed over time and centralized, threat analysis can leverage historical passive or active attack patterns to support the threat analysis. Incident response analysts, network operation engineers, or security operation center analysts are ideal to work with in Stages 4 of the proposed threat modeling methodology. Depending upon how events, incidents are tracked and managed (by source, by type, by frequency, etc.), some degree of trending analysis can be done and relayed to the threat modeler in order to consider how historical reconnaissance, injection attempts, brute force attacks, phishing campaigns can indicate historical attack trends from which some degree of regression analysis can be performed. If such data is not available for the target application environment, it may be possible to leverage statistics or metrics around similar incidents or events on comparable application environments within the company. Such information provides some degree of contextual basis for understanding motives, target assets, and attack vectors for the subject application environment addressed by the threat model. This provides the improved ability to profile attack patterns based on *actual* events that have taken place against similar environments. It is important to note that this effort is not aimed to *conclusively* profile attackers and their targets based on these events alone, but it obviously lends a great amount of credible and relevant information to the threat model for an application as the motives for historical attacks will be similar if not the same to those of prior attacks, assuming no major change in functionality and/or data use.

Stage IV – Summary on Threat Intelligence and Analysis

Overall, threat intelligence will be a stage filled with research aimed at sustaining a threat model. The threat model will ultimately reflect a tree-like structure that has branches of assets, use cases, abuse cases, vulnerabilities, and attack patterns. These attack trees take full form in Stage VI. The key to this stage, however, is analyzing and collecting good intelligence data from both internal and external sources. The following is an excerpt that reflects the type of content that should be reviewed.

A summary of the activities for this stage is revealed in Figure 7.27.

Stage V – Weakness & Vulnerability Analysis (WVA)

Stage V of PASTA is about identifying vulnerable or weak areas across the application. Our knowledge of inherent risks associated with the application, a refined technology scope, set of use cases, relevant threats will now be the background to discover what vulnerabilities or weaknesses may be present across the application.

The key objective is mapping this information back to the attack tree that was introduced in the threat analysis phase under stage IV. As most IT and Security professionals know, outputs from vulnerability assessment programs are riddled with false positives. Additionally, for the purposes of a threat model, the scope of vulnerabilities may extend outside the scope of the application on which an application threat model is focusing. For this reason, vulnerability trimming will be applied in order to port over relevant and confirmed vulnerabilities to the attack tree. This is the primary

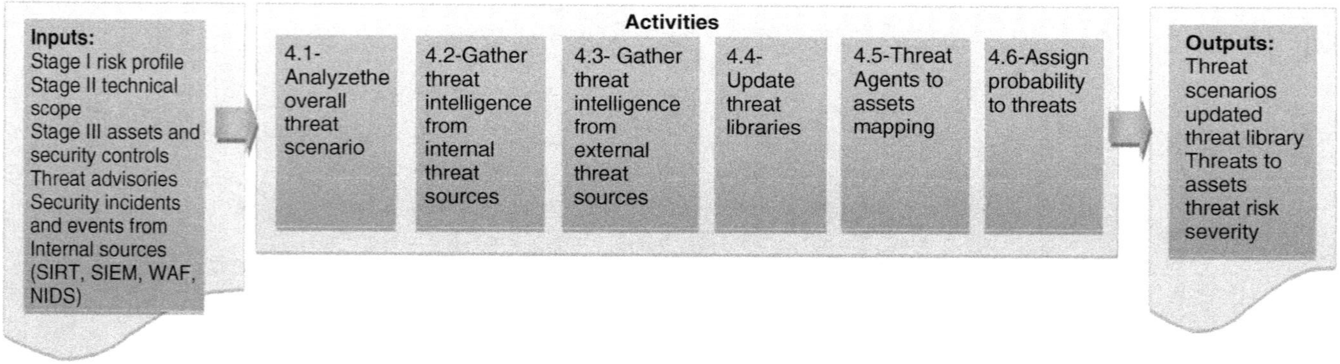

Figure 7.27 PASTA Risk-Centric Threat Modeling – Stage – IV (TA) Threat Analysis

objective. In support of this stage's primary objective, the following tasks are also important to fulfill.

1. Review/correlate existing vulnerability data.
2. Identify Weak Design Patterns in the Architecture.
3. Map threats to vulnerabilities.
4. Provide Contextual Risk Analysis based on Threat-Vulnerability.
5. Conduct Targeted Vulnerability Testing.

Stage V:Activity I (S5:A1) Review/Correlate Existing Vulnerability Data Establishing a historical context for what has been vulnerable or weak across application components is a key place to start Stage V. Doing so provides a glimpse of what areas have historically been more susceptible to exploitation. Using this information, we can align existing vulnerabilities or flaws in network/application design to the threat intelligence and data that has been collected thus far. Additionally, application use cases and objectives can be considered in light of the known vulnerabilities and weak design attributes. Overall, the collective knowledge of prior vulnerabilities and weak or nonexistent control implementations translates to a different level of concern given the background knowledge obtained from the PASTA stages thus far. Knowledge of business objectives, technical scope, and interoperability of application components, threat intelligence, and now, confirmed vulnerabilities and/or weaknesses, provides for a developing picture around contextual risk.

In terms of the age or *freshness* of vulnerability information leveraged as part of this activity, it is important not to consume information that is not too old. This would otherwise minimize the effectiveness of the threat model. The time stamp of old vulnerability data should not exceed a twelve month period, unless the application being threat modeled is a legacy application or one where upgrades or applied patches are scarce due to software incompatibilities. Aside from those exceptions, reviewing vulnerabilities beyond twelve months may be futile since patches, updates, or upgrades may have negated the initial findings.

Key elements that should be extracted from prior vulnerability data should include the following:

- Assets employed by the application (DNS, Proxies, Bastion hosts, etc.)
- Actors (Human, System, or Application-based actors)
- Client software (Browser, Mobile, Traditional Fat Client)
- Server software (IIS, Active Directory, ISA, Exchange)
- Running services (privileged, ephemeral ports)
- Third-party software (Citrix, MS Hypervisor, Oracle IdM)
- Application frameworks (Struts, .NET MVC, Spring MVC)
- Architecture
- Data sinks/sources (e.g. file servers, databases, etc.).

Using the aforementioned as criteria for containers for vulnerability data, scan results, audits, and architectural reviews can be mapped to each of these containers that may be present within the application. Since we know the footprint of application components (thanks to stage II), associating these components can be easily achieved by hostname, IP, namespace, named pipe, DNS name, method call, and so on. An example of this association is provided in the following section (Table 7.16).

The aforementioned artifact shown is simply a representation of how historical vulnerability information can be aggregated into a consolidated artifact. Consolidation of this information can take place in any format; from a spreadsheet to an internal wiki or ticketing/but tracking system. If more enterprise tracking systems are used, these application defects should be labeled appropriately in order to designate them as being part of a threat modeling effort. In doing so, they can be easily retrieved and re-classified once additional design and software flaws are found within Stage V of PASTA. Inherent vulnerabilities across all application components of the target application is simple the starting ground for this stage. The next activity will build on top of these recent preexisting vulnerabilities and look at the current architecture in order to see what design flaws may be present. This is covered in the next activity for this stage.

Stage V: Activity II (S5:A2) Identify Weak Design Patterns in the Architecture An often neglected component to application security is its architecture. In this activity, we will revisit the DFDs produced under stage III (Application Decomposition). As part of this activity, a review of key architectural concerns around data security will be examined in order to ensure that security is applied for data at rest, in transit, and while being processed. These considerations use cases depicted under stage III and identify if the request/responses among application components are not part of a well-designed security architecture.

Secure software design activities center a number of different security themes. These themes need to be addressed on the trust boundaries that have been identified in stage III. A simple list of insecure architecture gaps to identify in this activity is presented as follows:

- Unencrypted authentication channels.
- Noncentralized logging activities.
- Noncentralized or distributed authentication models.
- Unprotected or exposed administrative interfaces.
- Nonsegregated network segments among trust boundaries.
- Liberal application/network ACLs (extended permit ip any, extended permit ip 10.10.10.0 255.255.255.0 any, X Domain Policy wildcard use "*").
- Placement of sensitive network services, such as credential stores, in public/semipublic network areas.
- Use of application services that do not require authentication.
- Nonfederated user models where a single elevated credential serves as the actor to many worker processes across an application environment.

TABLE 7.16 Threat Analysis Artifact against a Single Asset/ Use Case

Targeted Asset	Affected Service	Identified Vulnerability	Description	Affected Actor	Affected Use Case	Impact	Countermeasure
10.51.25.35	SSHD (port 22)/Secure Shell Server	Default SSH password: root with blank password (ssh-default-account-root-no-password)	The root account uses a blank password. This would allow anyone to log into the machine via SSH and take complete control.	SSH User (imager01)	Secure remote copies to physical imaging servers over network.	High	Use the "passwd" command to set a more secure login password. A good password should consist of a mix of lower- and upper-case characters, numbers, and punctuation and should be at least 8 characters long.

(*continued*)

TABLE 7.16 (Continued)

Targeted Asset	Affected Service	Identified Vulnerability	Description	Affected Actor	Affected Use Case	Impact	Countermeasure
imaging1.hc.org	NTPD (port 123)/Network Time Daemon	NTP 'ntpd' Autokey Stack Buffer Overflow Vulnerability (ntpd-crypto-recv-buffer-overflow)	There exists a stack-based buffer overflow in the crypto_recv function found in ntpd before 4.2.4p7 and 4.2.5 before 4.2.5p74. When OpenSSL and autokey are enabled, the flaw allows remote attackers to execute arbitrary code via a specially crafted packet containing an extension field. Additionally, the NTPD was found to be running as the "root" user.	root	Accurate time stamping of medical report data.	High	Update ntpd 4.2.4x to ntpd 4.2.4p7 Download and apply the upgrade from: http://www.eecis.udel.edu/~ntp/ntp_spool/ntp4/ntp-4.2/ntp-4.2.4p7.tar.gz Also associate another actor to run daemon.

Ddc1. careentity.org	DNS Service (port 53)/Domain Name Service server	DNS server allows cache snooping (dns-allows-cache-snooping)	This DNS server is susceptible to DNS cache snooping, whereby an attacker can make nonrecursive queries to a DNS server, looking for records potentially already resolved by this DNS server for other clients. Depending on the response, an attacker can use this info to potentially launch other attacks.	dns-svc	Ensuring the security of PHI and PHI-related systems at Health-care organization.	High	1. Leave recursion enabled if the DNS Server resides on a corporate network that cannot be reached by untrusted clients OR 2. Do not allow public access to DNS Servers performing recursion OR 3. Disable recursion

(*continued*)

TABLE 7.16 (Continued)

Targeted Asset	Affected Service	Identified Vulnerability	Description	Affected Actor	Affected Use Case	Impact	Countermeasure
Db1.health-careentity.com	Multiple Ports: TCP Port 1099 TCP Port 8080 TCP Port 1521	Arbitrary Code Injection (CVE-2013-0422)	Multiple vulnerabilities in Oracle Java 7 before Update 11 allow remote attackers to execute arbitrary code by (1) using the public getMBeanInstantiator method in the JmxMBeanServer class to obtain a reference to a private MBeanInstantiator object, then retrieving arbitrary Class references using the findClass method, and (2) using the Reflection API with recursion in a way that bypasses a security check by the java.lang.invoke.MethodHandles.Lookup.checkSecurityManager method due to the inability of the sun.reflect.Reflection.getCallerClass method to skip frames related to the new reflection API, as exploited in the wild in January 2013, as demonstrated by Blackhole and Nuclear Pack, and a different vulnerability than CVE-2012-4681 and CVE-2012-3174.	oracle	Ensuring the security of PHI and PHI-related systems at Healthcare organization.	High	Update Java Oracle Security Alert CVE-2013-0422 states that Java 7 Update 11 (7u11) addresses this (CVE-2013-0422) and a different but equally severe vulnerability (CVE-2012-3174). Java 7 Update 11 sets the default Java security settings to "High" so that users will be prompted before running unsigned or self-signed Java applets.

Room	MySQL (port 3306)/MySQL Server	Database Open Access (database-open-access)	The database allows any remote system the ability to connect to it. It is recommended to limit direct access to trusted systems because databases may contain sensitive data, and new vulnerabilities and exploits are discovered routinely for them. For this reason, it is a violation of PCI DSS section 1.3.7 to have databases listening on ports accessible from the Internet, even when protected with secure authentication mechanisms.	Root	Ensuring the security of PHI and PHI related systems at Healthcare organization.	Medium	Configure the database server to only allow access to trusted systems. In general, segregation based on internal trust boundaries along with network or application-based access control filters will work adequately. Also associate another actor to run MySQL PID.
IMG501							

- Poor proxy implementation.
- Insecure transport of logging data.
- Excess privileges across system platforms.
- Anonymous actor calls to application service.
- Unencrypted communication channels.
- Unencrypted data storage (online).
- Unencrypted data storage (offline).
- No digital certificates used for Internet facing services.
- No digital certificates used for high-impact processing servers.
- Insecure key management storage.
- No identity validation on actor calls.
- Insecure/unreliable IP protocol used.
- Authentication data send in clear text.
- PII or sensitive client information sent in clear text.
- Weak encryption ciphers used.
- Proximity of high target asset to network perimeter.
- Superfluous use of network services among application components.
- Poor segregation of multitenant data sources.
- Poor network segregation among environments.
- Poor segregation of administrative interfaces.
- Insecure transport layer (TCP).
- No input validation across data interfaces.
- No segmented logging channel.
- No considerations for High Availability (HA) in design.
- Only 1 security zone defined.
- Insecure messaging (Layer 7) protocol used.
- Outdated or insecure service version (WEP, SNMPv2, SSHv1, etc.).
- Insufficient network defenses/lack of stateful packet inspection.
- Little to no business logic validation.
- No standard security API used for authentication, encryption.
- No integrated security domain model.
- Insecure challenge response model.
- No integrated authentication model used.
- Superfluous use of two-way trust exchanges.
- Poor implementation of multifactor authentication.
- Not currently leveraging a security framework.
- Storage of connection strings or application credentials.
- Client-side storage of sensitive data (credentials, etc.).
- Insufficient security in relational/flat file databases.

EXPLORING THE SEVEN STAGES AND EMBEDDED THREAT MODELING ACTIVITIES **449**

- Insecure password storage and retrieval.
- Lack of security attributes/assertions across programmatic interfaces.
- No integrity checks for data processing/transmittal.

Architects should review their network, application, and data designs to ensure that the aforementioned mentioned flaws are not included across various layers of the application. Design flaws or weaknesses need to address application design and not just network design. DFDs will prove instrumental at this point as they will legitimize the need for greater security control to be implemented at those points, along with the previously developed DFDs, in order to ensure that the aforementioned architectural gaps have not been left unmitigated. The key goal from this activity is that security considerations become applied where trust boundaries have been formed (stage III). Trust boundaries mean that two distinct areas of application components should have some level of restricted access control in order to ensure the security, integrity, and authenticity of a communication exchange.

Revisiting one of the DFDs from before, we see some trust boundaries defined in the following figure. Notice some simple inclusions of requirements that were presumed nonexistent in the DFD. By simply analyzing the interaction between a login procedure and a backend college database server, we may note that insufficient controls exist across this trust boundary. As a result, we can denote what additional architectural gaps are present. In this case, countermeasures listed in green for the data flow among the login process and the authentication engine (of the college database) are architectural gaps that can be added as vulnerabilities for this stage (Figure 7.28).

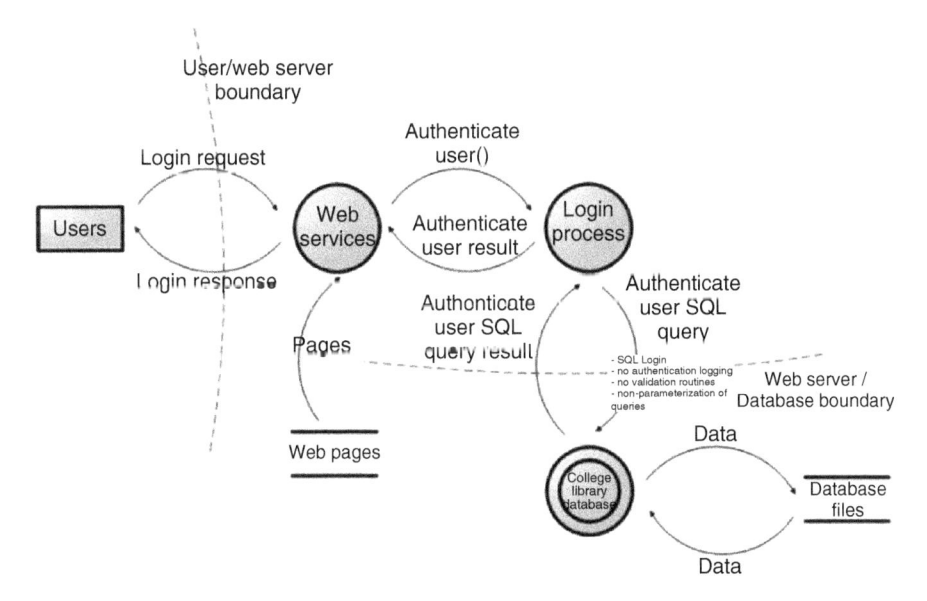

Figure 7.28 Missing Architectural Countermeasures among Application Components

The importance of conducting architectural reviews in this stage is that the other forms of automated assessment tools will not consider design flaws or simply poor architecture. As shown in the aforementioned figure, absent controls (such as those in green) are easily missed by vulnerability scanners or dynamic application scanners. Analyzing the security architecture, we can potentially augment the prior list of known vulnerabilities with more holistic design weaknesses identified from this activity.

Stage V: Activity III (S5:A3) – Map Threats to Vulnerabilities Building off of the attack tree (introduced in stage IV), we can now begin to look at the aggregate of design flaws and software vulnerabilities and map them to branches on the attack tree. This "tree" is maintained as a visual representation of the relationship between vulnerabilities/design flaws and threats. The mapping also provides a relationship node to the use cases affected by the threat. After each stage thus far, a clearer depiction of how the threat affects the application component(s), associated use cases, vulnerabilities and design flaws becomes clearer. One important node in this developing attack tree is the abuse case. The abuse case maps to the use case and plans out a strategy for exploitation, without necessarily knowing an attack vector. The vulnerability node in the attack tree provides a plausible point of entry or kink in the application armor and therefore supports the abuse branch of the tree. We see both the *abuse case* and *vulnerability* layer depicted in Figure 7.29.

In order to keep the figure simple, certain threats have only one defined abuse case; however, one-to-many relationships may exist between threats and underlying

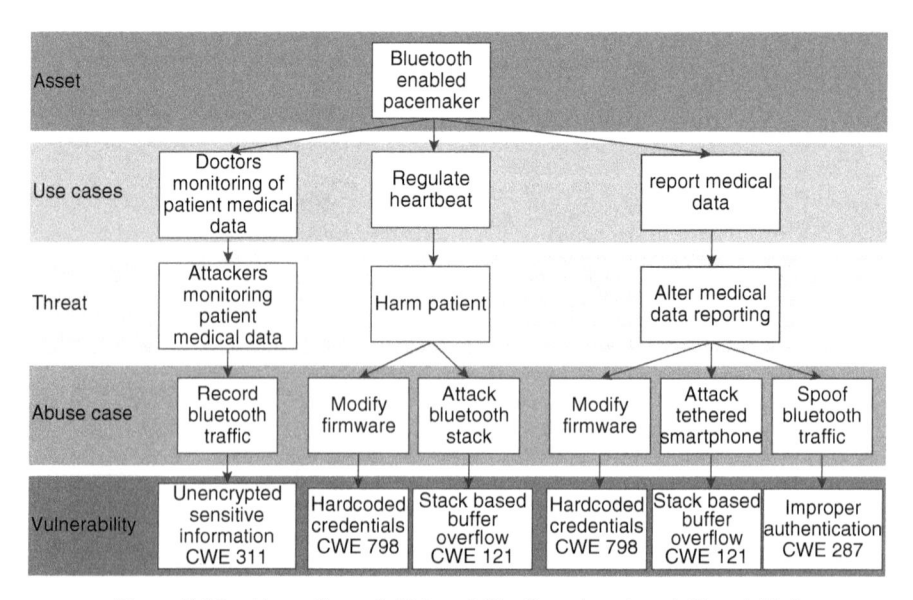

Figure 7.29 Abuse Cases & Vulnerability Branch to Attack Tree Added

branches. You may find more one-to-many relationships as you work through your own application.

This activity can be completed best in Visio and by referencing two distinct libraries: CVE lists and CWE lists. In most cases, vulnerability data from scanning reports will denote either and can be associated to the branch in the tree that corresponds to the analyzed abuse case that could exploit a vulnerability. The abuse case is aimed at being the plan of attack for a threat agent and used for the purpose of realizing one or more facets of their defined threat(s). As shown in the aforementioned figure, these threats affect the security of various associated use cases for the asset or application. The trunk of the tree is the targeted asset which may represent a physical server, a virtual host, a software application, a third-party product, or a database.

Paying attention to the vulnerability branches of the tree, we see that, for example, an abuse case of recording Bluetooth traffic may allow sensitive data to be compromised in transit. This may be something to consider architecturally as part of the product application design in Stage VII (Residual Risk Analysis).

Abuse Cases Abuse cases are supportive steps to achieving a threat's intent. They are a beneficial, yet not mandatory part of the overall attack tree. They help to depict high-level attack plans in manners that are understandable by everyone involved in the threat modeling effort. From architects to business analysts – all participants would appreciate the simplistic terminology associated with abuse cases. This simple terminology makes creating abuse cases quite easy. Simplistically, they can be a distortion of the actual use case name. For example, a use case of "Authenticate User" could have an abuse case named "Steal User Authentication." Another example is the use case of "Provide Secure Checkout Function." The distortion of this use case would lead to the abuse case of "Bypass Checkout Function." Another form of building out abuse cases is to focus on the target of the threat. If the threat's target is data, then abuse cases should be construed based on their relevance to both the application component that they are *abusing* and the threat objective. For example, a threat objective may be to bring down a Bulk Energy System (BES). The abuse cases may include (1) gaining illicit network access, (2) bypassing authentication in FTP infrastructures or (3) phishing the utility company's IT administrators. There are plenty of examples and they can be developed based on simply building the attack trees collaboratively. A brainstorming session among threat modeling participants will quickly build the necessary abuse case layer for the attack tree. Another important point to remember is that multiple abuse cases per use case, therefore it is not necessary to simply think of just one.

In Figure 7.29 (from bottom to top) the vulnerabilities or design flaws facilitate a possible abuse case. The abuse case represents the threat intent from the prior layer of the tree. The threat serves as the pinnacle of the overall threat model against the application as a whole and/or its targeted software components.

Insufficient Vulnerability Data In the case of a new application, historical vulnerability data may not be present. If this is the case, a vulnerability database can be queried for relevancy based on application component name/version. Common Vulnerability Enumeration (CVE) and/or Common Weakness Enumeration (CWE) lists are provided in multiple formats by the MITRE (www.mitre.org) organization as well as included in various vulnerability scanners. Those scanners may or may not have the vulnerability data in a searchable format, but if they do, vulnerabilities may be pulled from the tool and mapped based on the abuse cases. Security advisories/bulletins on employed frameworks or software components are also a good source for vulnerability data to pull from. A special focus open frameworks and client-side plug-ins, if part of the technology scope (stage II), should be regarded. Specific vulnerability briefings on any employed application components are also helpful. Additional sources for vulnerability data that could be used in the absence of prior vulnerability assessment reports are as follows:

- Open Source Vulnerability Database – http://www.osvdb.org.
- Oracle (http://www.oracle.com/technetwork/topics/security/alerts-086861.html).
- Microsoft (http://technet.microsoft.com/en-us/security/dn481339).
- US-CERT (http://www.us-cert.gov/ncas/alerts/).
- Secunia (Security Advisories by Vendor http://secunia.com/community/advisories/vendor/).
- Carnegie Mellon University Vulnerability Notes Database – (http://www.kb.cert.org/vuls/).
- Exploit-DB (http://www.exploit-db.com/) – Contains information on various types of exploits against various types of vulnerable software.
- Security Focus (http://www.securityfocus.com/) – Mixed back of security vulnerabilities across different technology products.
- Cisco Security Advisories (http://tools.cisco.com/security/center/mpublicationListingDetails.x?docType=CiscoSecurityAdvisory).

There is a lot of vulnerability data and without a proper tool or mechanism to consume, query, and organize relevant vulnerability data, a significant amount of time would be require to conscientiously review. For this reason, it may be better to simply address design flaws in the application/network architecture during this iteration of the application threat modeling effort. Alternatively, a targeted vulnerability research effort can be done to identify vulnerabilities for the top and most impacting threats/asset components. If the company has an internal vulnerability database, it may leverage this as a way to correlate relevant vulnerabilities based on the scope of asset components being utilized that may be vulnerable.

Stage V: Activity IV (S5:A4) – Provide Contextual Risk Analysis Based on Threat Vulnerability In this activity, we leverage previously identified and validated vulnerabilities and weaknesses and apply them to the attack tree for better context (in terms of relevance to a targeted asset or component). In doing so, this slowly builds a prioritization model for remediation, based on relevance to use cases, asset components, and threat probabilities. The criterion around threat probabilities (introduced in stage IV), combined with confirmed vulnerabilities can begin to demonstrate the viability of successful abuse cases. Identified threats against asset components that are easy to interface with, having known vulnerabilities or design weaknesses should thus far receive the greatest attention, particularly if the use case pertaining to the asset component supports a key business objective.

Identified vulnerabilities sustain the possibilities for a threat to take place. Not all vulnerabilities are created equal however. Some vulnerabilities or design flaws greatly facilitate certain abuse cases than others. In this activity, developers, architects, certain QA professionals, and strategic third-party security testing partners will help to identify both weaknesses and vulnerabilities that affect the use cases, actors, services, and overall asset function within an application environment.

This activity helps to (1) associate vulnerabilities to assets in the threat model and (2) sustain the viability on how weaknesses and vulnerable components could facilitate the threat depicted. This stage's intrinsic value is in depicting the possibility of attack and also beginning to make an association for how certain attacks could exploit the identified vulnerability or application weakness. The following figure illustrates how the logical flow of contextual analysis should take place across both threats and vulnerabilities. This logical representation presented subsequently provides a way to consider vulnerabilities in the context of the threat, the target asset (or component) and ultimately how it ultimately affects risk levels for the application.

Figure 7.30 provides that logical analysis needed to determine (at various binary decision intervals) how a given vulnerability affects the viability of a threat. This later will translate into a higher probability for a vulnerability to become exploited as well as a greater relevancy to the threat becoming successful. As a result, it provides the opportunity for a premature risk analysis using the contextual variables of threat(s) and application component (or asset). The vulnerabilities relevance to a threat becoming successful is one risk-based consideration while the other explores the viability of the vulnerability to undermine an asset's intended use case(s) (impact). Using this knowledge, we can now factor in this analysis to how targeted vulnerability testing should take place.

Stage V: Activity V (S5:A5) Conduct Targeted Vulnerability Testing This stage is simply not about performing vulnerability testing or having one performed by a third-party group. As most IT and Security professionals know, vulnerability reports can be riddled with false positives and extend beyond a manageable response for remediation. Additionally, scope creep is a common problem for vulnerability tests conducted across many large enterprises and even small businesses. Since much of the scope targets are focused on ranges and network blocks, many of those conducting vulnerability tests have no clue on what they are truly testing in terms of asset use. For this reason, *vulnerability trimming*, or selecting vulnerabilities for tailored testing, based on threat relevance and application component, should be applied. This allows for targeted vulnerability testing to evaluate components that are within the application scope and in support of the overall threat model. The overall threat model

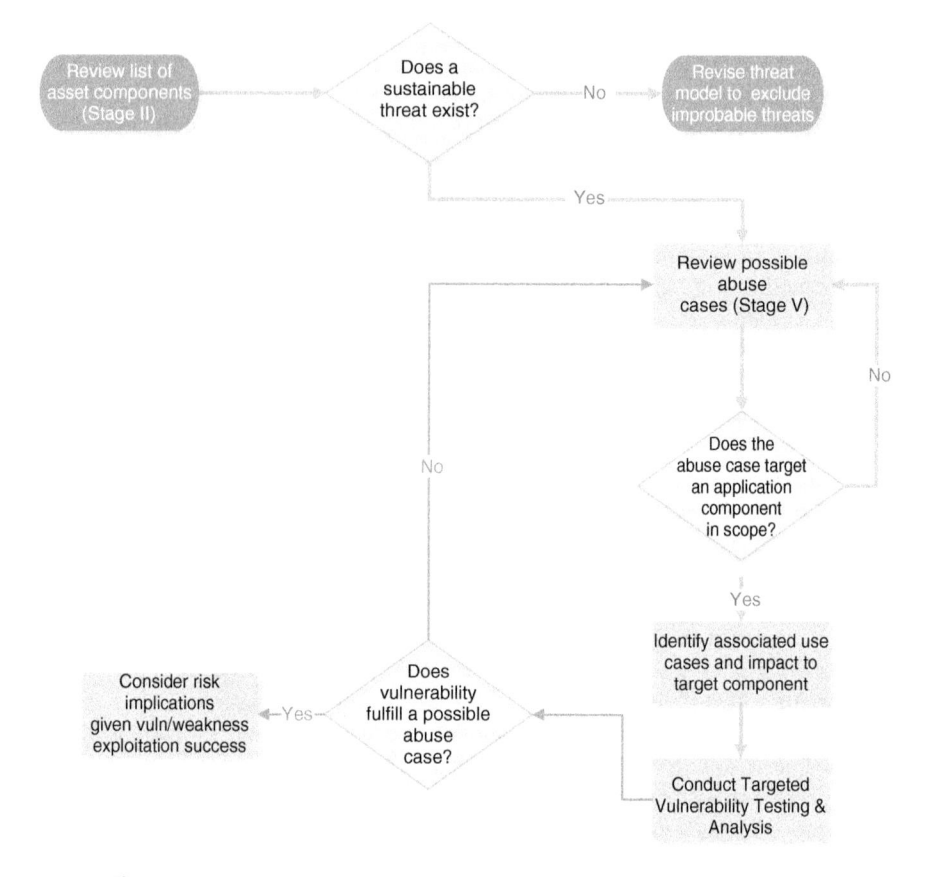

Figure 7.30 Logical Flow Considering Threats to Assets to Vulnerabilities

will have a threat and series of abuse cases that will look to exploit vulnerabilities or design flaws. The tester will have the ability to use CVE and CWE names and description tags in order to appropriately launch vulnerability/weakness checks that support the viability of a threat model. For this activity, we will look to identifying how vulnerability trimming can take place in order that targeted vulnerability scans can be achieved.

Conducting vulnerability scans is largely fulfilled by various active and passive network/application scanners. There may already be a number of tools within your enterprise or security operations team that may be poised to complete such types of vulnerability scanning. In order for targeted vulnerability scans to be properly leveraged, the following scanning techniques or review exercises should be applied.

1. For existing vulnerability reports or scans, if possible, narrow down the scope of components with prior vulnerabilities in order to use as a criteria for scoping out a targeted scan.

EXPLORING THE SEVEN STAGES AND EMBEDDED THREAT MODELING ACTIVITIES 455

2. If those assets or application components have not been scanned, then they should be now. The enumeration and scoping exercises that took place in stage II (Technical Scope) greatly assist in incorporating assets or application components that require greater vulnerability analysis and that are most relevant to the application environment.

   a. From a platform or asset level, use nmap to scan the hosts within the application environment (no CIDR notations or ranges).

   b. Fingerprint services, ports, and OS versions for assets in scope using nmap. Those services, ports, and underlying operating system are all components that are in scope for testing.

   c. Use network-based vulnerability scanners to select the specific component or set of components that are in scope, based on the threat model.

   d. For example, we may want to focus a specific vulnerability test on the components that support the "Forgot Password" feature on a website. The multitiered components would be a client-side technology such as a JAR file or a compiled Flash objective. It also includes the IIS web server and any backend application components at the application or data tiers. See following screenshot and highlighted area for how targeted use cases tied to application components can be tested (Figure 7.31).

   In the aforementioned example, we see that the *forgotpw* page is called in order to retrieve a password for a given user. This use case may be part of

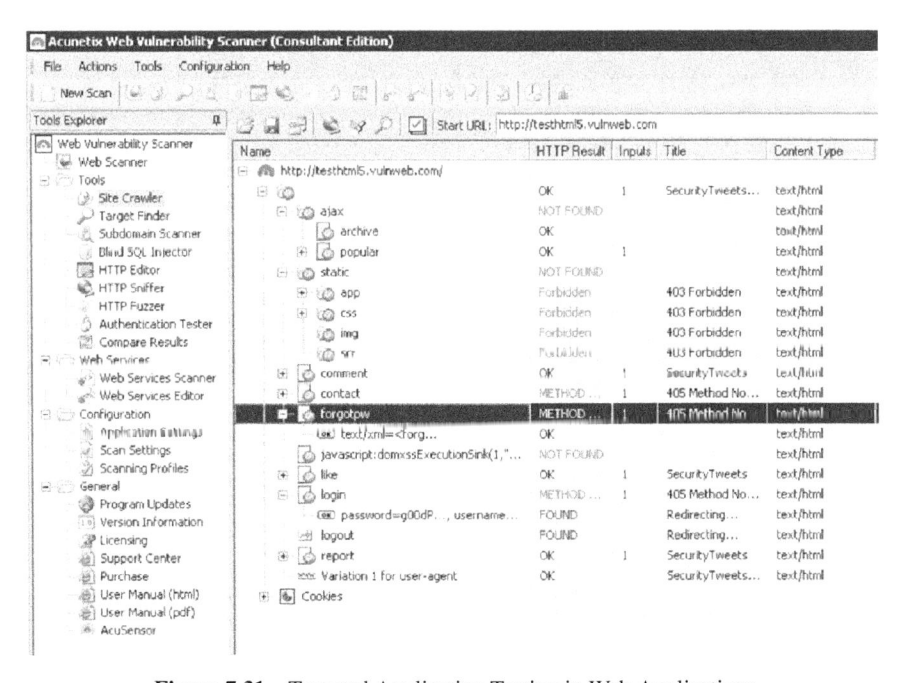

Figure 7.31 Targeted Application Testing in Web Applications

TABLE 7.17 Labeling Relevant Threat Modeling Variables during Targeted Assessment Efforts

Threat Modeling Label	Application Component
Target (asset)	Web portal
Use case	Password reset
Threat	Steal credentials
Abuse case	SQL injection (Time based)
Vulnerability 1	No input validation
Vulnerability 2	No parameterization of queries
Weakness 1	No restrictions to password reset attempts
Weakness 2	Insecure transport layer for sensitive data

a targeted threat in a given threat model. This being the case, we use the context of *component relevancy* and *threat relevancy* to determine that this page and underlying use case should be scanned. Broken up into clear labels, vulnerability testing against this use case should be considered as follows (Table 7.17).

e. Various types of vulnerability scanners will allow for customer scan types or scan modules to be selected. This provides a more targeted approach to not simply select an entire node or range of nodes to scan.

f. If application-based scans are being conducted, one can spider or traverse the branches of a site or individual application component as part of the scan. Application components in the client or presentation tier will relate to technologies that may require static or dynamic application scanners. For example, static source code analyzer may be used to review client-side code such as JavaScript. Application de-compilers will assist to reverse engineer Flash, PowerBuilder, Silverlight, or Ajax files into decipherable code. Once such client-based technologies have been decompiled, they may in turn reveal Application tier components such as exposed web service namespaces, from which now we can leverage web-based proxies to test these exposed tiers for web, mobile, or cloud-based applications. Some of these APIs may in turn leverage messaging frameworks that require testing. Beyond the testing, this activity also helps to reconcile against the activities performed to enumerate the technical components for the application in stage II.

Note: For testing in this activity, it is suggested to use authenticated scans rather than unauthenticated scans. This will ensure that false positives are not tainting the results of this targeting scanning effort.

3. A list of all in-scope assets (from a system level) should be scanned and vulnerabilities correlated to the threats, use cases, and abuse cases denoted in the "living" attack tree. The attack tree is referred to as "living" since it should be continuously updated upon revealing more branches of vulnerabilities. Ensuring that the following relevant platforms are scanned (either manually or via automated tools) is important in order to ensure that *vulnerability trimming* does not exclude relevant components identified by these scans.

a. Distributed servers
b. Midrange servers
c. Personal computing devices
d. Mobile devices
e. Network infrastructure equipment
f. Network appliances
g. Application proxies

Multiple scenarios for targeted testing can be depicted under this section; however, it would really all repeat the same basis formula of simply identifying what vulnerabilities are relevant to two key items: (1) threat attempted to be realized and (2) the target asset or application component. These two variables determine whether or not a given vulnerability is essential for inclusion. The end goal realized by this activity is a tremendous amount of time savings in both the actual vulnerability scanning as well as the review of vulnerability scan results. Last, it makes the results much more topical to the threat model and evolving attack tree that is being built across the PASTA process.

A summary of all the activities for this stage, as well as inputs and outputs, is depicted in Figure 7.32.

Stage VI – Attack Modeling & Simulation (AMS)

This stage's key objective is to complete the attack tree. The attack tree is a centerpiece for application threat modeling because it organizes all of the information around threats, target assets, abuse cases, vulnerabilities, weaknesses, and the exploits that profit from all of the above. In PASTA, this stage will continue to build from its prior stages in the manner just mentioned. Being a risk-centric threat modeling approach, we will determine the probability for a vulnerability to be exploited. As a result, the prior version of the risk equation introduced in stage IV (Threat Analysis) will now encompass another probability coefficient that is tied to the vulnerability variable. The formula will now look as follows:

$$(R)\text{isk} = \frac{(T)\text{hreat}_{(P)\text{robability}} \times (V)\text{ulnerability}_{(P)\text{robability}} \times (I)\text{mpact}}{(C)\text{ountermeasures}}$$

In the last stage, we identified relevant vulnerabilities that relate to both the desired threat as well as the targeted asset. In this stage, we want to model the different types of attacks that would exploit the relevant vulnerabilities for the application, all aimed at realizing the various threat objectives. From a well-defined attack tree, we are able to see the scope of assets, actors, services, and other entities defined in the other stages that came before stage IV (Threat Analysis). The attack tree completion will ultimately reveal different layers of attacks; all mapped to preexisting vulnerabilities that facilitate the exploitation of data, credentials, or simply online reliability of the application or system. The attack tree then becomes a key threat modeling artifact to exemplify which viability of a threat and the affected application components that would succumb to the attacks that achieve said threat.

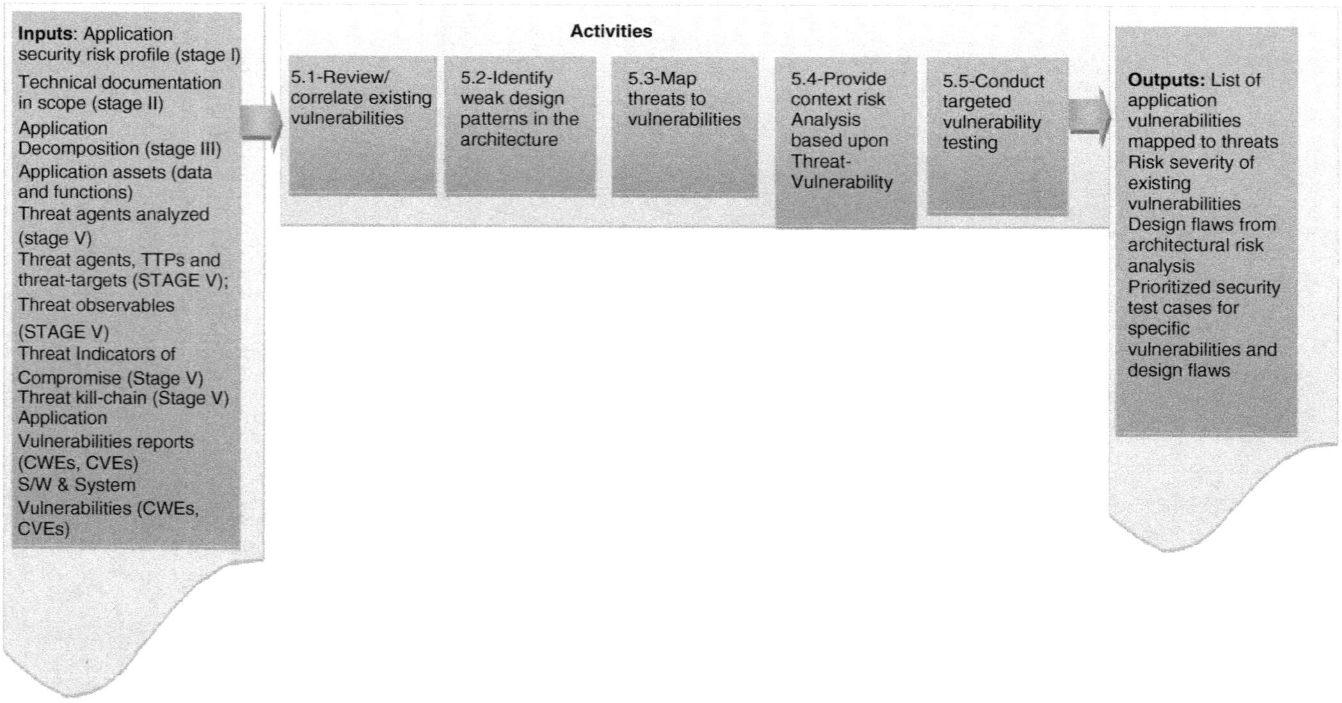

Inputs: Application security risk profile (stage I)
Technical documentation in scope (stage II)
Application Decomposition (stage III)
Application assets (data and functions)
Threat agents analyzed (stage V)
Threat agents, TTPs and threat-targets (STAGE V);
Threat observables (STAGE V)
Threat Indicators of Compromise (Stage V)
Threat kill-chain (Stage V)
Application Vulnerabilities reports (CWEs, CVEs)
S/W & System Vulnerabilities (CWEs, CVEs)

Activities

| 5.1-Review/ correlate existing vulnerabilities | 5.2-Identify weak design patterns in the architecture | 5.3-Map threats to vulnerabilities | 5.4-Provide context risk Analysis based upon Threat-Vulnerability | 5.5-Conduct targeted vulnerability testing |

Outputs: List of application vulnerabilities mapped to threats
Risk severity of existing vulnerabilities
Design flaws from architectural risk analysis
Prioritzed security test cases for specific vulnerabilities and design flaws

Figure 7.32 PASTA Risk-Centric Threat Modeling – Stage V – (WVA) Weakness and Vulnerability Analysis

Activities in this stage are focused on discovering the viability of exploiting identified vulnerabilities and weaknesses around the application. Thus far, the application threat model has depicted what technology footprint the application is to use as well as what is potentially flawed with its innate software, network, or design specifications. This stage aims to determine how viable successful attacks are in exploiting identified and confirmed vulnerabilities in the application. Typically, penetration testing would need to be exercised against the product system to validate previously found weaknesses. For this reason, all of these activities are aimed at running in parallel to the development phase of a generic SDLC life cycle and are to be performed in various degrees. As such, the key activities for this stage are summarized as follows:

- S6:A1 – Analyze possible attack scenarios.
- S6:A2 – Update the attack library/vectors and the control framework.
- S6:A3 – Identify the attack surface and enumerate the attack vectors.
- S6:A4 – Assess the probability and impact of each attack scenario.
- S6:A5 – Derive a set of cases to test existing countermeasures.
- S6:A6 – Conduct attack driven security tests and simulations.

Key artifacts generated from this stage include a fully matured and layered attack tree that visualizes how asset components are affected by identified threats. The following sections illustrate procedures and supporting artifacts that pertain to this stage of PASTA.

Stage VI: Activity I (S6:A1) Analyze the Attack Scenarios The goal for this activity revolves around enumerating and analyzing possible attack scenarios. In doing so, we have to consider the target asset(s) and related threat components. Additionally, we want to build off of the selected threats that have been substantiated by our work under stage IV of the PASTA methodology. Doing so, we can brainstorm what type of attack scenarios could be achieved given the threat intelligence we have of current threats affecting similar application or system environments, as well as the context of what the target asset performs or provides in terms of value to an adversarial group or figure.

Within this in mind, building attack scenarios begins with a re-examination of the threat hierarchy. The progression in an asset-centric threat modeling methodology begins with the asset under this hierarchy. The threat modeling team needs to identify attack branches that stem from the target asset using the following rationale (Figure 7.33).

As shown in attack trees, the threat is prefaced by the use case and followed by an abuse case which provides a counter to the use case's objective. The more of these layers depicted, the clearer the threat model becomes in terms of how attacks become viable and realistic to defend against.

In the following brief example, we take a threat scenario for a restaurant chain whose Point of Sale (POS) system is the subject of threat to capture credit card data.

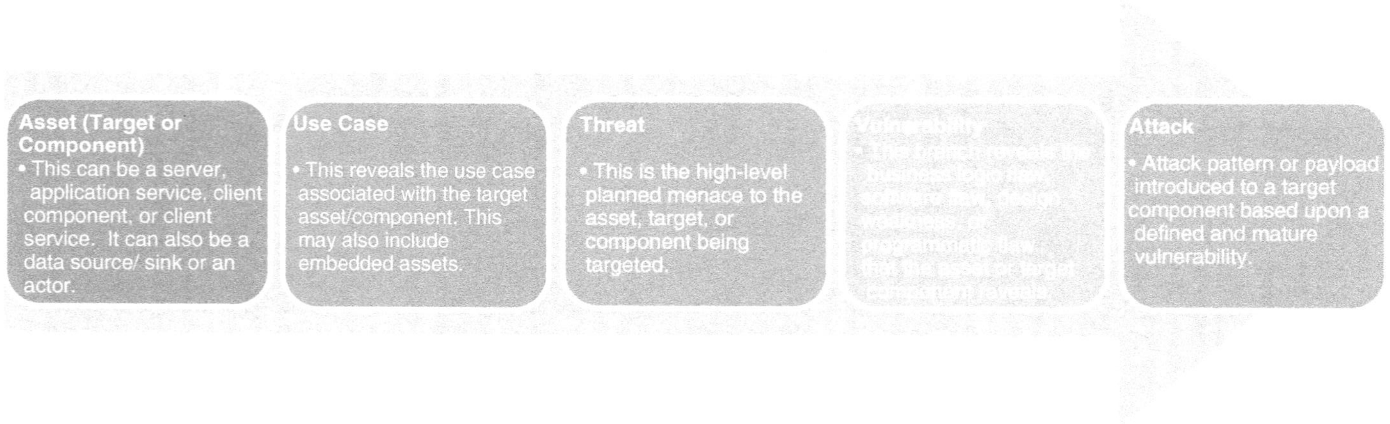
Asset (Target or Component)
• This can be a server, application service, client component, or client service. It can also be a data source/ sink or an actor.
Use Case
• This reveals the use case associated with the target asset/component. This may also include embedded assets.
Threat
• This is the high-level planned menace to the asset, target, or component being targeted.
Vulnerability
Attack
• Attack pattern or payload introduced to a target component based upon a defined and mature vulnerability.

Figure 7.33 Linearly Thinking about Attack Patterns

TABLE 7.18 Attack Considerations for POS at Restaurants

Target Asset	Point of Sale (POS) Device
Asset use case	Process card payments at restaurants
Threat scenario	Install malware to capture card data
Abuse case	Use authorized credentials to install malware
Vulnerability	Users have elevated accounts on POS systems
Attack scenario 1	Deliberate install of malware onto POS by employee
Attack vector 1	Sneaker-net; physical access to POS; Download malware over Internet
Attack scenario 2	Unintentional install of malware onto POS by employee
Attack vector 2	Physical access to POS; Drive by download on allowed Internet site
Attack scenario 3	Compromised update/configuration path to include rogue malware as part of update from system administrator
Attack scenario 3	Update server compromised and unchecked installer introduced malware to target POS.

Using the following given variables, we will proceed to analyze high-level attack scenarios.

In Table 7.18, we see a simple example of how this activity should be carried out. We begin with the logical root of the asset or target subject. This may also be a component of the overall asset used within the application model. The simple example depicted was intended to provide a generic creation of possible attack scenarios that can be considered given other threat characteristics as shown by the aforementioned table. The end goal is to arrive at a list of possible attack scenarios that are operationally possible as well as technically feasible given the known vulnerabilities in the environment.

Stage VI: Activity II (S6:A2) Update Attack Library/Vectors and Control Framework For this activity, we focus on ensuring that our list of attacks as well as possible control measures is vast enough in order to properly build a threat model – a key objective for this stage. The goal of this activity is simply to search for a comprehensive library of attack patterns that traverse a diverse range of attack vectors, or channels of attack. Similarly, we would need to properly develop or maintain a list of possible controls, as part of a broader control framework. This list of controls should equally be vast enough to encompass a diverse set of attack surfaces and attack vectors.

It may be difficult to enumerate different types of attacks if you are not familiar with attack patterns. Attack patterns represent a sequence or nonsequential collection of abusive actions against a target. Each pattern represents a collective of abuse cases for an attack. It is important to ensure that a wide variety of attack patterns are available from which to query and assign to the attack tree. In light of this, it is critical to have a comprehensive and up-to-date attack library. One of the best and comprehensive attack libraries is the CAPEC attack library from MITRE.[7] The CAPEC library boasts approximately 400 attack patterns or CAPECs in their latest (2014) iteration of their library. The library itself has been made searchable by various other sites, namely Security Database,[8] on online PHP application that has made the entire CAPEC v.1.5 version searchable by CAPEC ID. This is truly the most comprehensive threat library out there today; however, if you would like to create your own, that is suitable as well, as long as a unique identifier can be associated with each pattern and that associated control responses are also aligned with the specific control pattern. Homemade attack libraries can be made by amalgamating various sources of information in order to build a custom attack library. Sources may be derived from OWASP,[9] WASC,[10] PTES,[11] or even various resources from the SANS Reading Room.[12] The tool, ThreatModeler™,[13] is a free threat modeling tool that incorporates the CAPEC attack library and allows the threat modeling team to assign attack patterns to threats defined in stage IV. Other tools previously mentioned, such as TAM, do not incorporate all of the CAPEC libraries so mapping attacks to parent node threats will not be as effective using TAM.

If your product team would like to get the CAPEC library directory and parse the entire library, both the data schema and the XML data are available for download at the MITRE site (http://capec.mitre.org/about/documents.html).

It is not suggested that attack libraries become aggregated and correlated separately as this will be very time-consuming. If an internal library is being developed, attack patterns should be added, normalized, and assigned unique category identifiers for ease of cross reference and lookup. Separately, several different pen testing frameworks and tools have the CAPEC library built into the product. Depending on the solution, it may be possible to query this attack library. Ultimately, developing or obtaining an attack library from external sources is simply the initial means for having a diversified pool of possible attack patterns to consider in the context of the threat and the overall threat model.

The benefit about the CAPEC library is that it also comes with an associated "Solutions & Mitigations" & "Controls" section, which essentially translates to the possible countermeasure to resist the attack pattern. A snapshot of what this looks like is as follows and taken from www.security-database.com (Figure 7.34).

CAPEC greatly facilitates the matching of attack patent to possible control measures. For this reason, many manufacturers of pen testing products have adopted the CAPEC library into their own tool solution. These tools are thereby able to ingest the XML CAPEC content and related elements that depict attack characteristics as well as related countermeasures. This eliminates the need of having a distinct attack

---

[7] http://capec.mitre.org/about/index.html.
[8] http://www.security-database.com/capec.php.
[9] https://www.owasp.org/index.php/Category:Attack.
[10] http://projects.webappsec.org/w/page/13246978/Threat%20Classification.
[11] http://www.pentest-standard.org/index.php/Main_Page.
[12] http://www.sans.org/reading-room.
[13] http://myappsecurity.com/threatmodeler/download.

Security Controls

ID	type	Security Control Description
1	Preventative	Avoid providing any indication regarding the validity of user IDs upon failed login attempts. Provide a simple error message such as "Login failed. Try again or contact your administrator" regardless of why a login attempt fails.

Figure 7.34 Snapshot of Related Control from CAPEC ID in Library

library from a library of possible countermeasures, particularly when building both an organic attack library and control framework.

Stage VI: Activity III (S6:A3) Identify the Attack Surface and Enumerate the Attack Vectors In this chapter, we use the approach to identify the full attack surface for the scope of the threat model using the visualization of attack trees. The attack surface will encompass each of the possible attacks that can exploit the vulnerabilities identified from the prior stage. Attack trees provide a visual representation of the relationships among attacks and their vulnerability counterparts, along with the preceding contributing factors that sustain the attack (abuse case, threat, etc.).

A key goal in this activity is to ensure that the attack tree is finalized. We have begun with the target asset and listed underlying functional components (actors, use cases, services, processes, etc.), as well as dysfunctional components (threats, abuse cases, weaknesses, vulnerabilities, attacks, attack patterns, etc.). The final tree can be represented in multiple ways. Traditionally, they are represented via Visio schematic-like drawings, such as the ones previously referenced.

A diagram showing a simplified attack tree is included subsequently. For this exercise, we imagine modeling threats and attacks around a wearable or implantable medical device – a pacemaker. This product is listed in the top row of the attack tree. Please note that for simplicity's sake we have limited this threat model to a single asset and a narrow range of vulnerabilities with which attack mappings will take place.

Prior to introducing the attack tree for the pacemaker, the following are some simple considerations to keep vigilant when developing your own attack tree.

1. (Asset) The application we are using to build the attack tree is a pacemaker.
2. (Use Cases) The base functionality of the pacemaker is to monitor the patient's heart rate, regulate their heart rate, and then connect via Bluetooth to a smart phone in order to send heart rate information to the patient's primary care physician.
3. (Threat) Next, we consider how this functionality could be misused. In this row, we see threats that could occur if this device deviated from the intended use case. For example, if the heart rate regulation abilities functioned in a fashion other than intended, it could cause harm to the patient.
4. (Abuse Case) In the next row, we see what abuse cases could lead to this. Let us focus on attacking the embedded Bluetooth stack.

5. (Vulnerability) In the next row, we will enumerate specific technical vulnerabilities that could foster the aforementioned use case; in this case, it is a buffer overflow within the Bluetooth module's firmware.
6. (Attack Patterns) Next, we list out attack patterns or methodologies that an attacker would utilize with this specific type of technical vulnerability. Here we see that if they opted to create a buffer overflow for the Bluetooth module, their attack pattern would target hardware components. If this were not meant to be a simple and streamlined example, we could add other attack patterns such as a memory corruption attack pattern.
7. (Impact) Finally, we must consider what the ultimate impact of a successful attack would be. In this case, the attacker would have gained full control over the pacemaker's heartbeat regulation capabilities, ultimately allowing them to harm the patient as suggested by the threat row.

The following attack tree builds from the prior tree (Figure 7.29) in the vulnerability stage by adding the CAPEC attack patterns that are relevant for exploiting the identified vulnerabilities/weaknesses in the application model. The various layers can be color-coded for ease of use. This use of color coordination may be used to organize the layers of the attack tree by a criteria determine to be useful and beneficial by the threat modeling team (Figure 7.35).

In reviewing the completed attack tree, we see that the revealed attack surface is inclusive of a PAN (Personal Area Network), given the Bluetooth sniffing attack. We also see that the attack surface encompasses embedded system or software components (CAPEC 440, 401, and 440) that may be vulnerable for alteration. Last, we have a mobile device platform that can serve as an extension to the attack surface given its interoperability with the target asset – the pacemaker. The attack surface encompasses at least three different vectors of attack that could realize the vulnerabilities identified by the threat model. One vector is over near field communications enabled by the Bluetooth technology on both the phone and the pacemaker itself. Another vector is in the development of the pacemaker itself, therefore related to the manufacturing process by the manufacturer. The last is over a mobile device that interfaces with the pacemaker software. Understanding the attack surface, as well as channels of attack, provides a great visualization to share among those engaged in the PASTA process. The completed attack tree provides a great artifact for depicting how attack scenarios profit from the underlying components that facilitate the goals of a defined threat. In the next section, we will address the probabilities associated with each of the identified attack patterns that are part of this threat model.

Stage VI:Activity IV (S6:A4) Assess the Probability and Impact of Each Attack Scenario One key goal in this activity is to review the attack scenarios provided thus far and determine probability for success around exploitation. This pseudo-probabilistic analysis is useful in identifying where the most urgent part of threat mitigation should take place. Using the CAPEC library, some of the elements for each CAPEC provide information on the severity and the difficulty associated with exploiting a target weakness and/or vulnerability. Revisiting the attack tree

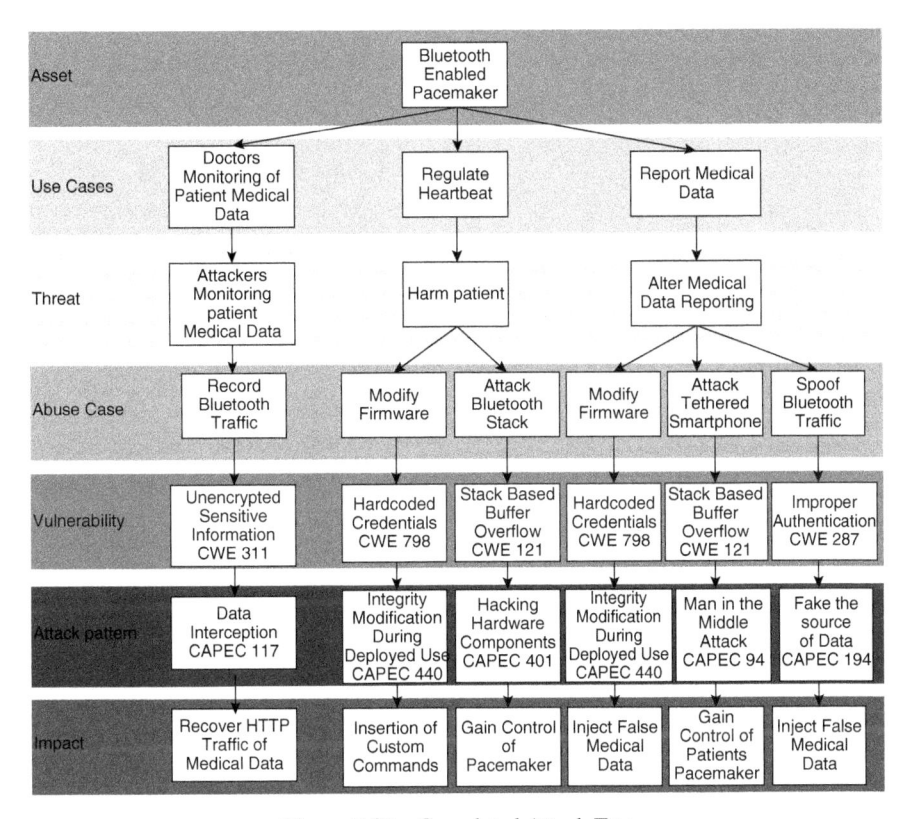

EXPLORING THE SEVEN STAGES AND EMBEDDED THREAT MODELING ACTIVITIES   465

Figure 7.35   Completed Attack Tree

from the prior activity, we take a look at CAPEC-117 (Data Interception). That CAPEC has associated prerequisites and other CAPECs that go with it. See, in the following figure, the other CAPEC associations as well as the weakness (CWE) IDs that are associated with this CAPEC ID of 117[14] (Figure 7.36).

Determining the probability will hinge upon the following criteria for each attack pattern listed on the attack tree. These conditions are as follows:

1. *Attack prerequisites:* Are these prerequisites surmountable for most attackers, based on time allotments, complexity of attack, cost of attack (resources, tools, etc.)?
2. *Weakness/Vulnerability Maturity:* Is the maturity of this weakness or vulnerability widely disclosed, exploited in the wild or is it a new, isolated vulnerability with very little information around PoC?
3. *Hackability:* Can you or your team exploit the vulnerability/weakness? Partially? Fully? This is one of the better indicators and one that will be exercised

---

[14] https://capec.mitre.org/data/definitions/117.html.

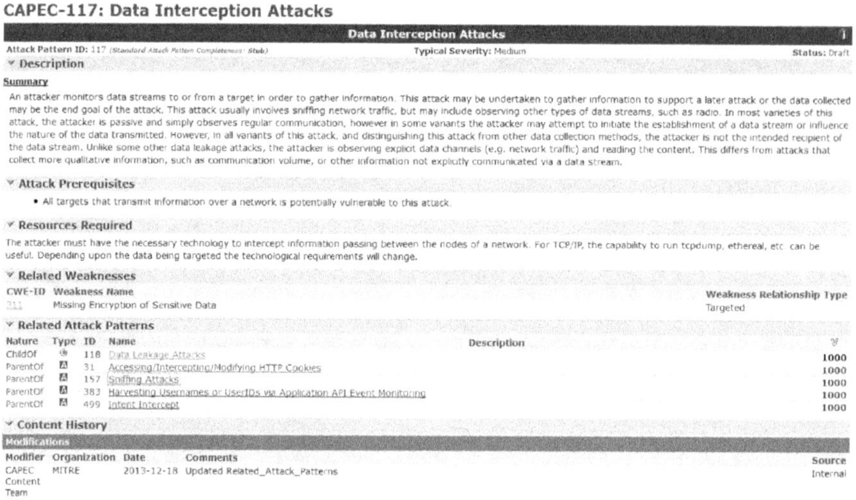

CAPEC-117: Data Interception Attacks

Data Interception Attacks

Attack Pattern ID: 117 (Standard Attack Pattern Completeness: Stub) Typical Severity: Medium Status: Draft

Description

Summary

An attacker monitors data streams to or from a target in order to gather information. This attack may be undertaken to gather information to support a later attack or the data collected may be the end goal of the attack. This attack usually involves sniffing network traffic, but may include observing other types of data streams, such as radio. In most varieties of this attack, the attacker is passive and simply observes regular communication, however in some variants the attacker may attempt to initiate the establishment of a data stream or influence the nature of the data transmitted. However, in all variants of this attack, and distinguishing this attack from other data collection methods, the attacker is not the intended recipient of the data stream. Unlike some other data leakage attacks, the attacker is observing explicit data channels (e.g. network traffic) and reading the content. This differs from attacks that collect more qualitative information, such as communication volume, or other information not explicitly communicated via a data stream.

Attack Prerequisites

- All targets that transmit information over a network is potentially vulnerable to this attack.

Resources Required

The attacker must have the necessary technology to intercept information passing between the nodes of a network. For TCP/IP, the capability to run tcpdump, ethereal, etc. can be useful. Depending upon the data being targeted the technological requirements will change.

Related Weaknesses

CWE-ID	Weakness Name	Weakness Relationship Type
311	Missing Encryption of Sensitive Data	Targeted

Related Attack Patterns

Nature	Type	ID	Name	Description	
ChildOf		118	Data Leakage Attacks		1000
ParentOf		31	Accessing/Intercepting/Modifying HTTP Cookies		1000
ParentOf		157	Sniffing Attacks		1000
ParentOf		383	Harvesting Usernames or UserIDs via Application API Event Monitoring		1000
ParentOf		499	Intent Intercept		1000

Content History

Modifications

Modifier	Organization	Date	Comments	Source
CAPEC Content Team	MITRE	2013-12-18	Updated Related_Attack_Patterns	Internal

Figure 7.36 MITRE CAPEC Library Snapshot – CAPEC 117

in the next activity. If the attack pattern can be successfully executed by your testing team, then it is a good chance that a determined hacker or hacker syndicate will be able to do so with far greater ease, due to greater amount of time and resources that they have to conduct such exploitive measures.

Another simpler approach would be to apply estimates to probabilities based on contextual information on what we know about threat model components. In consideration of this approach, the following areas can be evaluated.

1. *Probability of threat agents, motives, and abuse cases against target assets*
   a. *Probability Coefficient:* The team should assign a probability for the threat to be conducted successfully based on analysis from stage IV (Threat Analysis) and the success of Stage VI (Attack Enumeration). Moreover, the probability could factor in the maturity of the threats and/or attacks within the industry and operational areas where the product application will be implemented.
      i. The probability coefficient should between 10% and 90% as a standard deviation of 10% is assumed on both ends automatically in the formula used in Stage VII. This probability should factor in a subjective analysis on the motives for launching the threat.
      ii. *Example:* Bluetooth Traffic Interception Probability = 25%.
2. *Maturity of vulnerability discovered*
   a. *Probability Coefficient:* The team should assign a probability for the vulnerability that is associated with threat identified in stage IV (Threat Analysis) and base it on the maturity of the vulnerability.

i. The probability coefficient should between 10% and 90% as a standard deviation of 10% is assumed on both ends automatically in the formula used in Stage VII. The percentage reflects the probability that this vulnerability is mature and widely known.
      ii. *Example:* Unencrypted Data Prior to Transport (Design Flaw) = 90%.
   3. *Severity Rating (Threat | Vulnerability | Impact)*
      a. *Threat:* Using a scale of 1-4, denote the severity rating (1 = Low | 2 = Moderate | 3 = High | 4 = Critical) if the threat were realized.
      b. *Vulnerability:* Using a scale of 1-4, denote the severity rating (1 = Low | 2 = Moderate | 3 = High | 4 = Critical) of the identified vulnerability (excluding all other considerations such as accessibility, prerequisites, etc.).
      c. *Impact Level:* Using a scale of 1-4, denote the severity rating (1 = Low | 2 = Moderate | 3 = High | 4 = Critical) of the impact to the business or product objectives if the threat were realized.

Another key objective under this activity is to determine impact. Reverting back to the attack tree figure from the prior page, we see an impact row. The impact is tied to the assumption that the attack pattern will be successful and now we must calculate what the adverse effects are to the business objectives for the application as well as the specific use case affected by the attack pattern. Revisiting CAPEC 117, we see the affected use case of "Doctors Monitoring of Patient Medical Data." The immediate impact of this may not be financial, but may ultimately affect patient safety and privacy. As such, the successful exploitation of this use case needs to be regarded by the threat modeling team in the following manner:

1. Is the successful exploit one that introduces immediate financial loss (one can use the Single Loss Expectancy (SLE) calculation for this, which equals Asset Value (AV) x Exposure Factor (EF). Under this formula, we make EF 100% if the exploit is feasible and proven. The AV in this case is really the patient data. How much is that worth by itself? If needed, this SLE value can then be annualized to an ALE (Annual Loss Expectancy) value, which is simply the SLE value multiplied times the expected frequency of occurrence.
   This is generally an easy criterion to measure. The data by itself may be worth nothing financially; however, knowledge that this attack has taken place must yield speculation that at larger more drastic affect to patient safety is almost certain to follow as most threat agents would not be able to profit by the vital information obtained from the pacemaker device, by itself.
2. Is the successful exploit one that introduces a drawn out financial impact? (e.g. – bad press coverage, class action lawsuits, etc.) How much is it worth in the context of what may follow as a subsequent form of attack that supports a larger threat? This is difficult to perform an accurate valuation on and can largely be based on industry precedence of similar post-exploitation events.

The following chapter will provide more examples via use cases to further exemplify how impact and probabilities can be derived from the attack model.

Stage VI:Activity V (S6:A5) Derive a Set of Attack Cases to Test Existing Countermeasures Now that an attack tree has been formed, it is an opportune time to see if the control framework that is in place can provide some level of inherent threat mitigation. In Stages I and II, we were introduced to controls that could be aligned with the application design. These controls would reflect the control framework for the application. In this activity, we want to select any possible controls that could limit or eliminate any aspect of the threat. This includes the opportunity for an abuse case, the existence of a vulnerability or design weakness or the attack itself. Reverting back to the CAPEC 117 example, if there are features of the pacemaker device that provide for enhanced security, but may not be enabled, then this may be a consideration. Such an inherent security control may already be present in the manufactured medical device but may not have actually been enabled. This is a frequent issue across various frameworks and even third-party services. It is therefore important during Stage II to have a review of all possible inherent control options are determine and enumerated from the technology components identified to be in scope for the application solution.

Once a list of possible inherent countermeasures is identified, the countermeasures should be tested for their effectiveness in limiting the effects of the exploit. Such exploit testing is conducted in the next activity for this stage. It's important to note that the controls selected as part of this activity are already present and don't constitute new countermeasures that need to be developed by the application or system development team.

Stage VI:Activity VI (S6:A6) Conduct Attack Driven Security Tests & Simulations
The key objective for this activity is to demonstrate attack viability by denoting the probability and severity level of the attacks defined in the attack tree. While this has been a challenge among security and IT professionals, this activity will help illustrate which attack patterns may be successful. These values will later be used as part of the overall residual risk formula that is introduced and calculated in Stage VII.

The threat modeler will define the scope for a targeted pen test. No pen test will simply be one with a broad scope. In this stage, the activity should focus only on the vulnerabilities identified from the prior stage. Since the vulnerabilities found in the prior stage were topical to the threats enumerated in stage IV, the workflow of leveraging outputs from the prior stages becomes quite apparent.

When pen testing, the penetration testing team can either look up attack patterns in their respective tools that would exploit the associated vulnerabilities from Stage V. This matching can be done by using the CAPEC number or by using a keyword search, such as "Data Interception," or finding synonyms that reflect the intended attack goal. Testing tools are slowly adopting the CAPEC IDs (which are comparable to the CVE and CWE IDs). These references can be used to identify what attack patterns can be tested. Alternatively, penetration testing team members can look up the vulnerability that corresponds to the attack, by referencing that information again in the vulnerability branch layer of the attack tree. CWEs and CVEs can also be searched in tools such as Metasploit, Armitage, Web Inspect, Hailstorm, and AppScan. In lieu

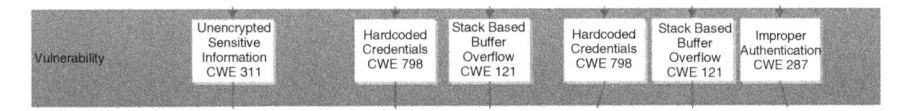

EXPLORING THE SEVEN STAGES AND EMBEDDED THREAT MODELING ACTIVITIES 469

Figure 7.37 Vulnerability Portion of Attack Tree

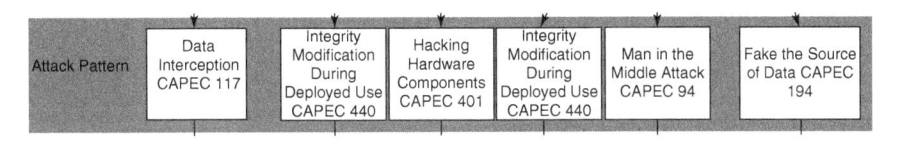

Figure 7.38 Attack Pattern Portion of Attack Tree

of doing batched scanning, these targeted scans along with manual pen tests can be conducted (Figure 7.37).

As an example, some attack module searches can be conducted on the following sites using some of the methods depicted earlier. A list of a few of these sites that can be referenced by the penetration testing team is as follows.

- http://www.exploit-db.com/
- http://www.metasploit.com/modules/framework/search
- http://www.commonexploits.com/

More sophisticated attacks can be achieved by allowing the penetration testing team to develop customized attacks that fulfill the goals of those listed under the attack pattern branch of the attack tree (Figure 7.38).

It is important to note that attacks do not necessarily have to succeed in order for an attack pattern on the attack tree to have some merit. Since results can vary depending on the rules of engagement for the penetration test, the allotted time, and the sophistication of the attack, an unsuccessful attack should simply indicate that the probability level should be throttled down when performing the overall risk analysis on each threat and determining what countermeasures to use and develop.

Most penetration testing software allows you to select attack modules to deliver to a target host. These modules or individual attack scripts, within a penetration testing framework (such as Metasploit Pro, Armitage, or Kali Linux), allow responsible testing members to conduct the testing in accordance with the attack patterns that match those listed under the attack tree. Reverting back to the recently completed attack tree, we can begin to find how these attack patterns can be developed as targeted attacks or using a penetration testing framework.

In Chapter 8, we will go over more specific use cases that provide a wider range of diversity for conducting the Attack Modeling phase. We will also introduce the notion of kill chains as a substitute for attack trees in order that greater options for modeling attacks can be considered.

A visual summary to stage VI is depicted in Figure 7.39.

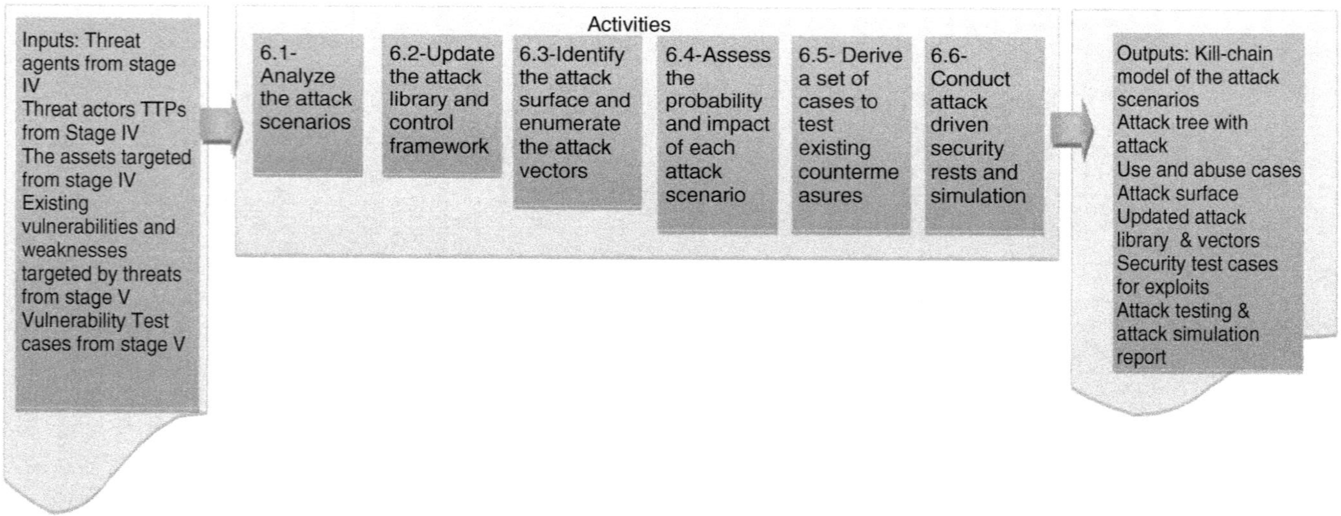

Figure 7.39 PASTA Risk-Centric Threat Modeling – Stage VI – (AMS) Attack Modeling and Simulation

Stage VII – Residual Risk Analysis & Management (RAM)

Stage VII of the PASTA methodology is focused on mitigating threats that matter to the application, product team, and overall business. This is achieved by applying all types of countermeasures that are both effective and topical to the threats and attacks depicted under the PASTA threat model. This approach saves time, is based on evidence or substantiated signs of threat patterns, and fosters a greater understanding of how security impacts application use cases and, to a greater extent, business objectives. The following are the key activities to be performed under this stage.

Stage VII:Activity I (S7:A1) Calculate the Risk of each Threat. This is an activity that borrows from prior efforts around threat analysis and risk evaluation, namely, the portion of the risk formula that deals with probability. As part of this activity, the risk professionals will have the ability to review the threat model and supportive attack trees in order to see how viable identified threat patterns are. Stage IV of the PASTA methodology provides insight to risk professionals as to the prevalence of the threat and the viability of the threat taking place against the target application or system. For each threat in the attack tree or trees that are depicted, a percentage weight of probability should be assigned based on the following conditions:

1. Internal Threat Data
   a. Do logs show that this threat has taken place before?
   b. Is there evidence that shows signs of this threat taking place?
   c. Where in the architecture have key threat data sources been pulled from? High-impact business areas? Confidential areas?
2. External Threat Intelligence
   a. What similar threat events have affected other companies in your industry?
   b. Where have similar threats been seen (across industries)?
   c. Have the threats been focused on architectures that are currently used by the organization and specifically the application undergoing the threat model?
3. Viability of Attacks
   a. Are testing efforts able to successfully exploit weaknesses/vulnerabilities that support this threat?
   b. Is the architecture containing the threat target in a readily accessible area (physically or logically?)
   c. Is the sophistication level low for exploitation of weaknesses/vulnerabilities, related to this attack(s)?

Using these three areas, attack patterns or the associated CAPECS can be assigned a probability percentage of success. This would provide a coefficient that could be used and averaged as a threat probability. Other coefficients of probability are also possible to be placed on the weakness or vulnerability (CWE & CVE respectively) nodes on the attack tree. Bruce Schneier actually has a pretty simplistic, yet effective way to associate branches of a tree with either a probability percentage of occurrence as well as a financial value of impact.[15] Related to the probability percentages, this can be helpful, especially after having tested the application and determine the viability of the attack given test results against known weaknesses or vulnerabilities.

The attack tree, threat analysis from stage IV, and the security testing results should provide a good basis for which to determine the probability of attack layers, supporting a threat, to become viable patterns that yield an overall successful attack.

Stage VII: Activity II (S7:A2) Identify the Countermeasures The objective for this activity to determine the right amount of risk mitigation through the use of agreed upon countermeasures to be developed or designed by the appropriate roles. Software engineers and architects must work together to determine how unacceptable risk levels will be addressed by the implementation of newly proposed countermeasures.

This activity will revisit the threat model and the associated attack tree in order to see what countermeasures can be implemented via architectural design or via software updates to either the codebase or product application. A visual depiction of how countermeasures can be identified for a specific use case using use-abuse case analysis is depicted in Figure 7.40.

As part of this exercise, the threat modeling team can begin to enumerate a vast list of countermeasures that have associated costs and benefits so that product

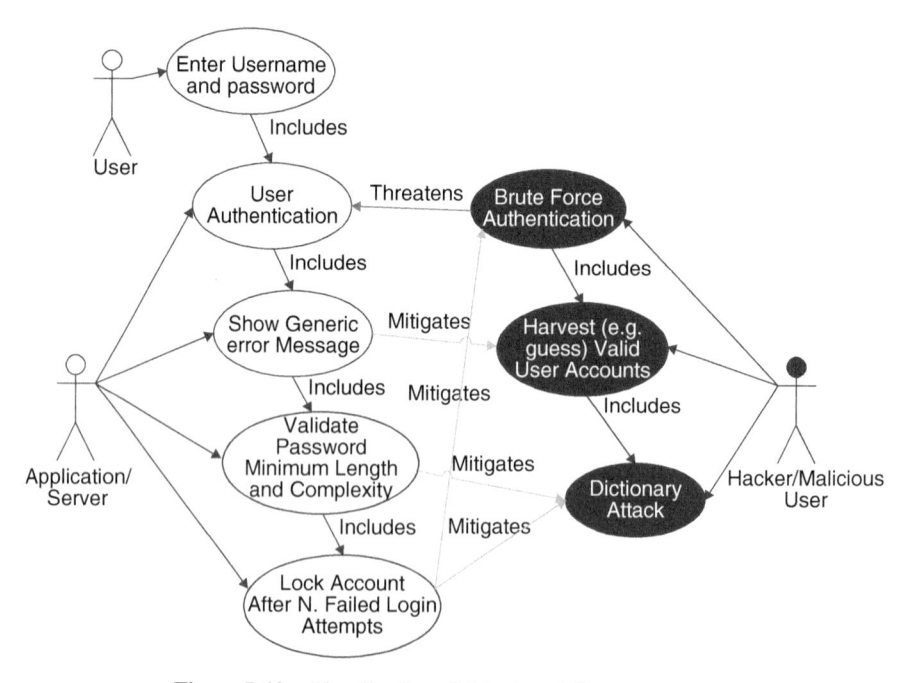

Figure 7.40 Visualization of Attack and Countermeasures

---

[15] https://www.schneier.com/paper-attacktrees-ddj-ft.html#rf1.

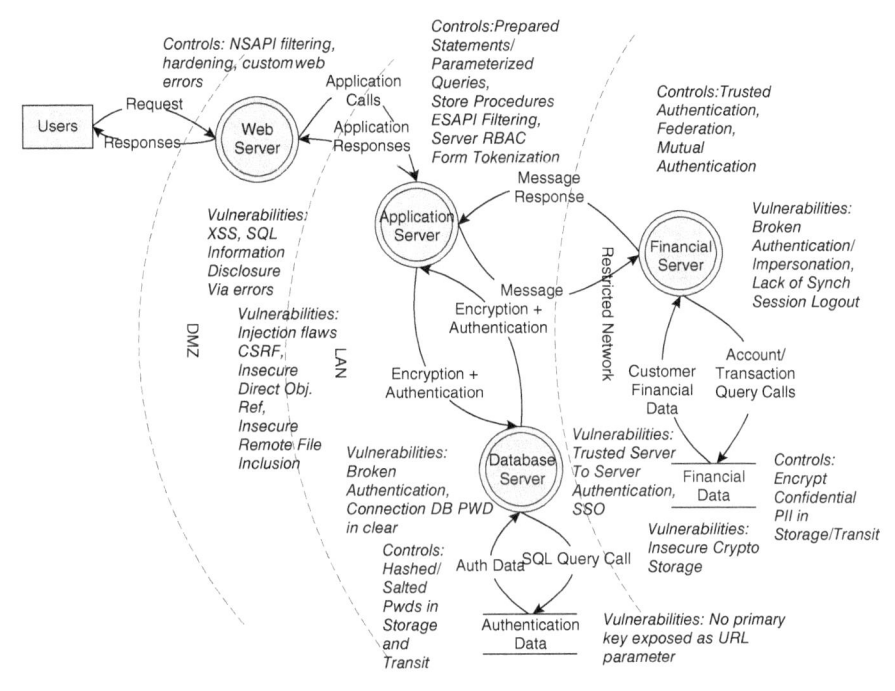

EXPLORING THE SEVEN STAGES AND EMBEDDED THREAT MODELING ACTIVITIES 473

Figure 7.41 Data Flow Diagram With Architectural Risk Analysis of Vulnerabilities and Controls

management groups can be informed on how to make the best decision regarding what countermeasures to develop.

The assignment of architectural countermeasures can be done using a DFD. Many of the threats and vulnerabilities that affect data endpoints could be mitigated architecturally. As a result, exercises based on the following figure can provide a visual indication to the product team on where countermeasures could be placed. (Figure 7.41).

Beyond DFDs, the attack trees can also provide an alternative for depicting the right countermeasures that relate to attack mitigation and ultimately, threat mitigation. The bottom row of the figure that follows details appropriate countermeasures for the threats that have been discussed in the prior activities. Going back to our branch of the tree that shows the attack on the Bluetooth module with a stack-based buffer overflow, we can see that the proper way to deal with this type of threat is to perform security testing that will lead to the identification and elimination of the vulnerability. Even though it is not specifically applicable in this situation, it may make sense to deploy multiple countermeasures. For instance, if we were trying to deploy countermeasures around a cross-site scripting vulnerability in a web application, we could perform security testing around the application environment to identify and eliminate the vulnerability. Additionally, we could also deploy a web application firewall to help prevent the exploitation of the vulnerability. Depending on the

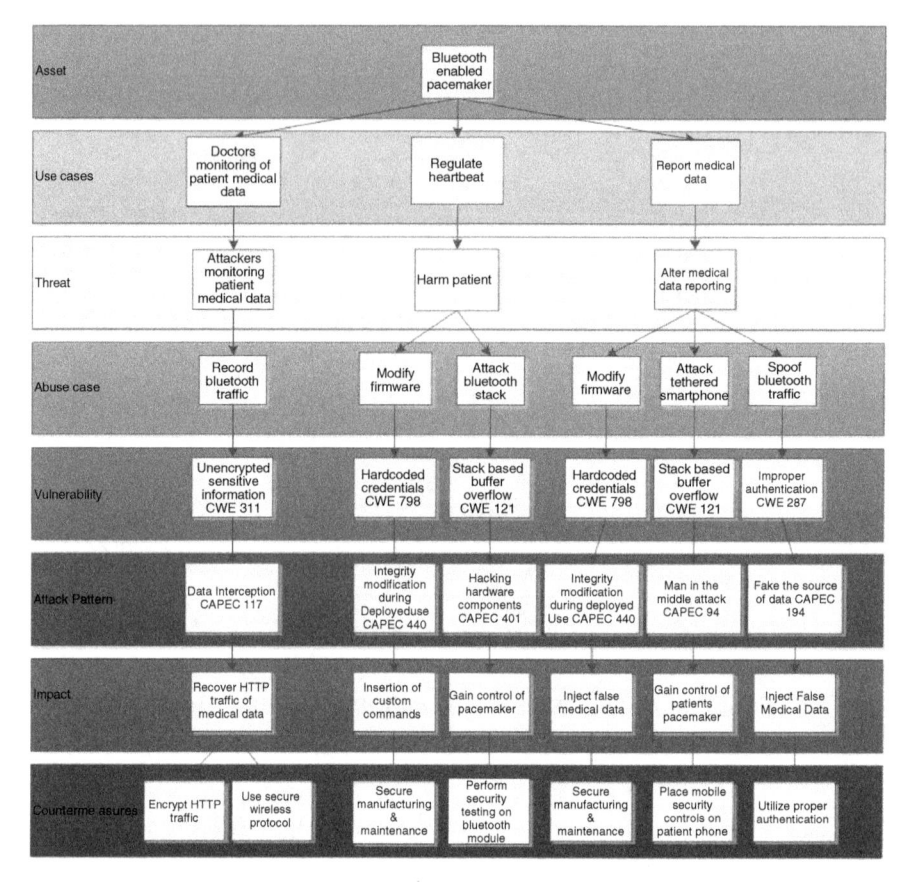

Figure 7.42 Completed Attack Tree w/Countermeasures

severity of the cross-site scripting issue and the criticality of the application, we could even recommend removing affected sections of the code base, or taking the entire application out of the production environment.

A representation of the attack tree, inclusive of the countermeasures that will be developed and mapped to the attack tree, is exemplified in Figure 7.42.

Stage VII: Activity III (S7:A3) Calculate the Residual Risks The objective for this activity revolves around risk analysis. The asset-centric approach in this guide addresses risk a bit differently by considering other variables that are not traditionally covered in risk analysis. These other variables are as follows.

- *Probabilities:* Probability coefficients can be assigned to threats and vulnerabilities in order to determine the likelihood that the vulnerability could be exploited under the observed conditions and based on its publicity. Additionally, the probability associated with the threat should be considered. Is it easy to execute the threat within the application's environment?

- *Countermeasures:* The countermeasures that currently provide some degree of protection against the threat and vulnerability also need to be factored into the risk analysis. Was the penetration testing team given information or certain advantages that allowed them to successfully exploit the application environment?

In consideration of these variables, this risk-centric threat modeling step defines a residual risk. This residual risk is what risk is left upon factoring existing countermeasures into the overall risk analysis. The new residual risk formula would be depicted:

$$\text{Residual Risk} = [(tp * vp)/c] * i$$

Step 1 – Severity Rating
Threat Level (1–4): Determine a threat level for each identified threat.

$$(1 = \text{Low} \mid 2 = \text{Moderate} \mid 3 = \text{High} \mid 4 = \text{Critical})$$

This level of analysis is ported over from stage IV of PASTA. We can translate the qualitative assessment given here or use the probabilistic analysis provided in stage IV of this chapter.
Vulnerability Level (1–4): Determine how critical the vulnerability is in the context of the application or the affected use case.

$$(1 = \text{Low} \mid 2 = \text{Moderate} \mid 3 = \text{High} \mid 4 = \text{Critical})$$

This will use the probabilistic analysis associated with the exploitability of the weakness or attack. This was discussed under stage VI of the PASTA methodology. Alternatively, a quantitative percentage can be assigned based on the qualitative values listed earlier.
Impact Level (1–4): Determine what the business impact would be if the threat was successful.

$$(1 = \text{Low} \mid 2 = \text{Moderate} \mid 3 = \text{High} \mid 4 = \text{Critical})$$

It is best to unitize the impact as discussed under stage I of the PASTA methodology and Stage VI as well where impact level were calculated based on successfully completed attacks. The information provided by the business analyst will ultimately help to further support information from business impact analyses (BIAs) completed around the application environment. This is important to the overall threat modeling process as it helps to identify where countermeasures should be developed by and between actor(s) making an application call to a data source. The threat modeler or facilitator of threat modeling activities should facilitate the activities that take place in stage II in order to ensure that the activities revealed in the RACI diagram per role are completed. Within this stage, the business analyst will help to define the properties of the application data and confirm the supportive technology as well as new technology center to the application environment.

Step 2 – Probability Coefficient   Using a scale from 10% to 90%, assign a percentage for the probability that:

1. The threat will take place.
2. The vulnerability is widely known and can be exploited.
3. The probability that if the threat is imminent, the impact level would be as severe as previously rated.

☞ Note: A scale of 10–90% is used to incorporate a standard deviation percentage since the probability value for an occurrence can never be guaranteed at 100% or 0%.

Step 3 – Number of Countermeasures and the Effectiveness of the Countermeasures   Considering what countermeasures exist in the environment that may not have been tested as part of the exploitation phase of the penetration testing OR considering some proposed countermeasures that could be put into place, list the number of countermeasures that would deter each of the following (a countermeasure can deter or resist more than one of the following choices (examples are also included) (Table 7.19).

The effectiveness of the countermeasures listed can range from 10% to 90%, as nothing would prove to be 100% effective. Since these are subjective values, it is best to use percentages that are rounded to 5 or 10 percentage points.

Additional examples and use cases of risk calculation are provided in Chapter 8.

Stage VII:Activity IV (S7:A4) – Recommend Strategy to Manage Risks   The objective for this activity is to update risk profiles associated with the system or application, in order to have a current account of both risk and risk strategy.

Compliance and risk management teams should work together with threat modeling efforts, as part of a joint working session, in order to update the risk profile of the application and capture the risk values. These risk values can be factored into any formal enterprise risk management suite (e.g. Modulo, Archer Technologies, LockPath GRC) for tracking and reporting.

TABLE 7.19   Residual Risk Analysis

Risk Component	Number of Countermeasures	Effectiveness of Countermeasures	Description of Countermeasures
Threat	2	30% (reduces threat by 30%)	Improved authentication and application whitelisting
Vulnerability	3	90% (addresses vulnerability by this amount)	Patch to software framework
Impact	0	0% (reduces impact that could be realized by this amount)	None

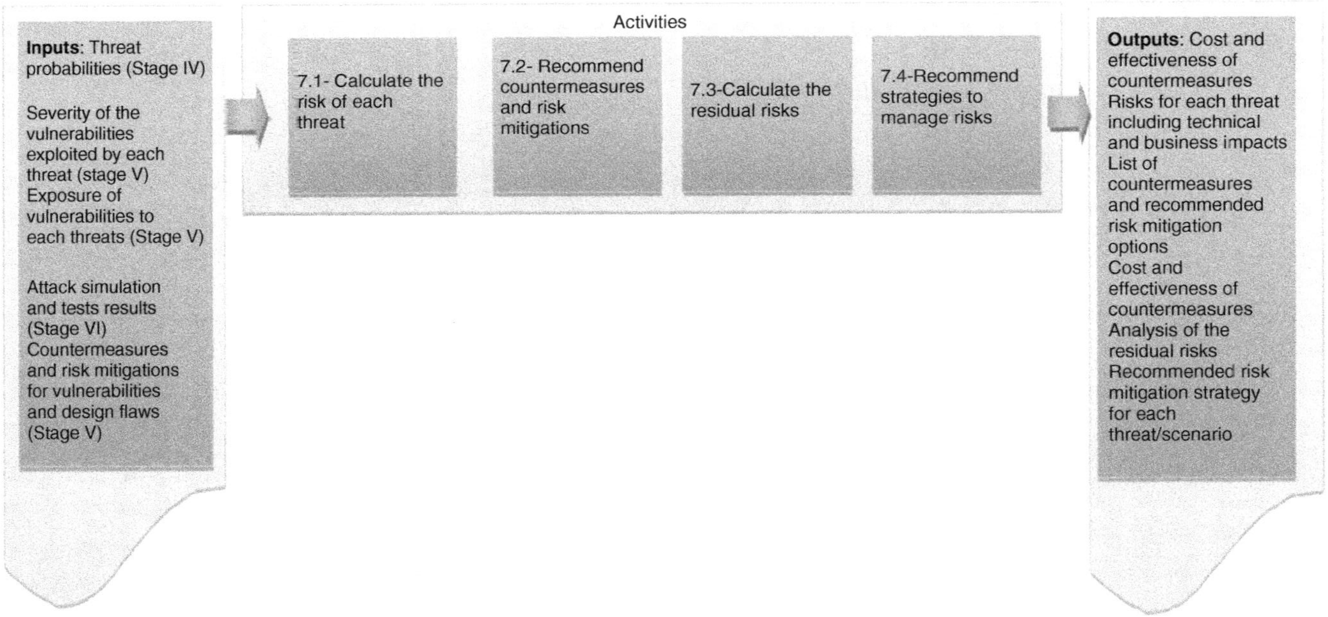

Inputs: Threat probabilities (Stage IV) Severity of the vulnerabilities exploited by each threat (stage V) Exposure of vulnerabilities to each threats (Stage V) Attack simulation and tests results (Stage VI) Countermeasures and risk mitigations for vulnerabilities and design flaws (Stage V)

Activities

7.1- Calculate the risk of each threat

7.2- Recommend countermeasures and risk mitigations

7.3-Calculate the residual risks

7.4-Recommend strategies to manage risks

Outputs: Cost and effectiveness of countermeasures Risks for each threat including technical and business impacts List of countermeasures and recommended risk mitigation options Cost and effectiveness of countermeasures Analysis of the residual risks Recommended risk mitigation strategy for each threat/scenario

Figure 7.43 PASTA Risk-Centric Threat Modeling – Stage VII – (RAM) Risk Analysis and Management

Strategic direction around residual risks needs to come from application owners or product owners. Risk mitigation takes time and money. The risk appetite of the product group and/or overall organization is the one to ultimately decide on what countermeasures to develop. All of this strategy is based on the risk levels identified via the seven stages of PASTA as well the depicted impact revealed by the overall threat model.

As part of succinct, yet highly effective strategy to manage the residual risks identified, the following should be performed:

1. Share residual risk information and overall threat model (attack tree, DFDs, residual risk analysis) with information/application owner.
2. Risk management and compliance professionals should assist in the conveyance of all risk-related items found. They should also extract the relevant security and compliance gaps that the threat model exposes the product, to as well as the risks now linked to the organization.
3. Determine whether the risks depicted by the threat model supersede the costs of neglecting the observed threats. Threats that do not pose a risk level that is above a baseline acceptance of risk should be logged as accepted in an enterprise risk management platform.
4. Threats found to present material risk to the product or overall business should be mitigated using the proposed countermeasures revealed by the threat model. These countermeasures should be formally tracked and measured to completion.
5. The artifacts produced during the threat modeling process should be used to support a new risk profile for the application. The threat model, namely the DFDs and attack trees, should be preserved and revisited when the application environment undergoes a drastic code change and/or component change (e.g. framework, COTS, hosting/deployment model, etc.) Conditions for reevaluating the threat model should be imposed at the conclusion of Stage VII.

CHAPTER SUMMARY

Regardless of the organizational size, application threat modeling allows for a clear roadmap of risk mitigation – a message appreciated and understood by business. Even in a team of one, a well-developed threat model will save time over ad hoc security testing or control gap analysis and control audits. In the chapter that follows, we will build from the notion that security CAN be built in via a risk-centric approach to threat modeling and look at each one of these PASTA stages in greater detail. Chapter 8 also provides a broad range of use cases for how to successfully apply the PASTA methodology.

A diagram summarizing the activities, inputs, outputs for this stage is presented in Figure 7.43.

8

PASTA USE CASE

PASTA USE CASE EXAMPLE WALK-THROUGH

"Tell me and I forget. Teach me and I remember. Involve me and I learn."
Benjamin Franklin

In this chapter, we show how to use the PASTA risk-centric threat modeling process to analyze the risks of specific threat agents targeting a web applications and specifically the web application assets that include customer's confidential data and business critical functionality that the web application provides. Among the web application assets in scope for the protection of threats, we will also consider information technology assets such as the application software components, applications, systems, and services where this software is installed and run. The goal of this risk-centric threat modeling exercise is to determine the technical and business impact of opportunistic and targeted threat actors against the web application assets and to recommend protective and detective security controls that can be designed, implemented, and deployed to protect the web application assets from these threats and reduce the risk to the organization/business, that is, responsibility to either own or manage the web application assets.

Throughout this chapter, we will use NIST National Institute for Standards and Technology terminology and standard definitions for threats, vulnerabilities, attacks, and risks as well as NIST standard definitions for risk management activities such

---

Risk Centric Threat Modeling: Process for Attack Simulation and Threat Analysis, First Edition.
Tony UcedaVélez and Marco M. Morana.
© 2015 John Wiley & Sons, Inc. Published 2015 by John Wiley & Sons, Inc.

as threat analysis and risk management. *Note:* Refer to the book glossary for specific risk management terminology used throughout this book including this chapter. Within this use of terminology and in the context of managing web application risks, the Process for Attack Simulation and Threat Analysis is defined as "*a risk-centric threat modeling process aimed at considering possible threats scenarios, attacks and vulnerabilities within a proposed or existing web application environment for the purpose of assessing the risks and managing technical and business impacts.*"

We already defined the PASTA risk-centric threat modeling process in Chapter 6. What follows after this introduction to PASTA is an example/use case for conducting a risk-based threat modeling of a web application by walking through the various stages and activities of the PASTA Process for Attack Simulation and Threat Analysis. For this walk-through, we choose a web application that can be considered at high risk of attacks from value-driven threat actors seeking to steal confidential data such as bank accounts and credit card data as well compromise business critical functionality that such web application could provide such as accessing and checking bank accounts online, making payments such as paying bills and transfer money. Today such a type of web application, because it stores and processes valued data as well as money, is highly sought target by money-driven threat agents such as fraudster and cyber-criminals. Since such web application can also be reached over the Internet and is highly visible website with globally recognized company, it is also highly sought target by politically motivated threat actors seeking to impact the company reputation with defacing the company website and by attacking it with denial-of-service attacks.

A good example of a web application that fit this profile is a financial type of web application such as online banking. With PASTA, we would like to analyze the threat and risk profile of such web application from both compliance and cyber-threat risk perspective. We would like to determine the technical scope of the web application and identify the assets at risk to determine how well these are protected from targeted and opportunistic attacks. To know how attacks from various threat agents affect the web application before gets attacked we would like to simulate these attacks and identify any security control weaknesses and vulnerabilities that these attacks can possibly exploit. After we have simulated the attacks, we would like to identify countermeasures that can be designed, implemented, and deployed to effectively detect and protect from these attacks and reduce the risk for the organization of possible confidential data compromise and online fraud. These general risk management objectives just stated can be achieved by following the seven stages of PASTA process depicted in Figure 8.1.

A brief summary of what each of these seven stages of PASTA consists of and specifically what will be the goal of each stage as related to the web application context and online banking use case is provided herein. Stage I of PASTA consists of the "Definition the Objectives (DO) for the Analysis of Risks" in stage I, we will demonstrate how to derive the security and compliance requirements, determine the business impacts and derive the risk profile that is the basis of a set of high-level objectives for securing the web application for security/compliance but also for the risks due to emerging cyber-threats affecting the business and technical environment in which the application is planned to operate.

PASTA USE CASE EXAMPLE WALK-THROUGH

STAGE I - Definition of the Objectives (DO)
- DO 1.1 - Document the business requirements
- DO 1.2 – Define the security/compliance requirements
- DO 1.3 – Define the business impact
- DO 1.4 – Determine the risk profile

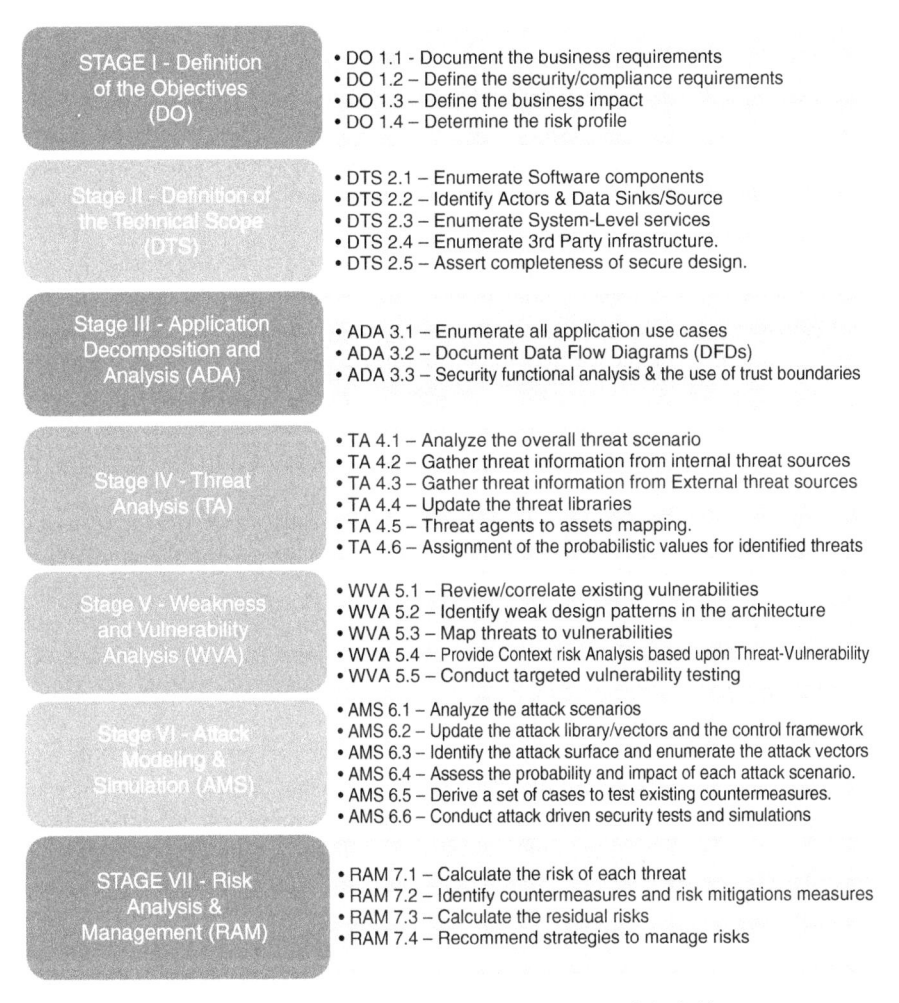

Stage II - Definition of the Technical Scope (DTS)
- DTS 2.1 – Enumerate Software components
- DTS 2.2 – Identify Actors & Data Sinks/Source
- DTS 2.3 – Enumerate System-Level services
- DTS 2.4 – Enumerate 3rd Party infrastructure.
- DTS 2.5 – Assert completeness of secure design.

Stage III - Application Decomposition and Analysis (ADA)
- ADA 3.1 – Enumerate all application use cases
- ADA 3.2 – Document Data Flow Diagrams (DFDs)
- ADA 3.3 – Security functional analysis & the use of trust boundaries

Stage IV - Threat Analysis (TA)
- TA 4.1 – Analyze the overall threat scenario
- TA 4.2 – Gather threat information from internal threat sources
- TA 4.3 – Gather threat information from External threat sources
- TA 4.4 – Update the threat libraries
- TA 4.5 – Threat agents to assets mapping.
- TA 4.6 – Assignment of the probabilistic values for identified threats

Stage V - Weakness and Vulnerability Analysis (WVA)
- WVA 5.1 – Review/correlate existing vulnerabilities
- WVA 5.2 – Identify weak design patterns in the architecture
- WVA 5.3 – Map threats to vulnerabilities
- WVA 5.4 – Provide Context risk Analysis based upon Threat-Vulnerability
- WVA 5.5 – Conduct targeted vulnerability testing

Stage VI - Attack Modeling & Simulation (AMS)
- AMS 6.1 – Analyze the attack scenarios
- AMS 6.2 – Update the attack library/vectors and the control framework
- AMS 6.3 – Identify the attack surface and enumerate the attack vectors
- AMS 6.4 – Assess the probability and impact of each attack scenario.
- AMS 6.5 – Derive a set of cases to test existing countermeasures.
- AMS 6.6 – Conduct attack driven security tests and simulations

STAGE VII - Risk Analysis & Management (RAM)
- RAM 7.1 – Calculate the risk of each threat
- RAM 7.2 – Identify countermeasures and risk mitigations measures
- RAM 7.3 – Calculate the residual risks
- RAM 7.4 – Recommend strategies to manage risks

Figure 8.1 PASTA Threat Modeling: Stages and Activities

Stage II of PASTA consists of the "Definition of the Technical Scope (DTS)" of the process. This stage is where we capture and enumerate the various technical details of users and functional accounts, software and architecture components including system-level services and third-party infrastructure components. After these various components of the application architecture and technology stack that support them are captured through enumeration in checklists and worksheets, they also need to be asserted in the current implementation and included in the technical documentation of the application in scope. This technical documentation that includes the architecture design documentation and technical functional documentation will also include the security requirements previously identified and asserted for completeness.

During stage III, that is during the "Application Decomposition and Analysis (ADA)" of the threat modeling process, we will decompose the application in basic elements of application functionality that includes the various type of users, and their roles, the various type of data that is accessed as data in storage (e.g. databases) or in transit (e.g. data flows), the boundaries of trust that are crossed by the data to access functionality and resources and the security controls that protect data and functions from external and internal threat agents.

Once we have decomposed the application and analyzed how the application components interact with the data in transit and storage and we have identified the data and functional assets inherent risk due to the sensitivity and exposure of these assets, we can start analyzing the various threats against these components and assets to determine if these are potentially at risk of attacks. This can be done during stage IV, "Threat Analysis (TA)." Specifically, we will show how we can conduct the analysis of specific threats targeting the application whose technical scope was defined in stage II and whose functional and data assets were identified in stage III.

Initially we will look at the threat landscape and analyze the threat scenario/environment for the application in scope. Specifically during the threat analysis, we look at analyzing the threat scenarios and we seek to gather threat intelligence from internal as well as external sources to understand the type of threats agents and threat targets sought by these threat agents including the type of weaknesses and vulnerabilities that these threat agents seek to exploit using different Tools, Techniques, and Processes (TTPs).

We will show how the categorization of the threat agents can be done according to their motives (e.g. political, ego-driven, and money-driven), the threat agent's capabilities (e.g. financial resources, attacking tools, and knowledge of attack techniques), and the threat agent caused security incidents (e.g. publicly reported data breaches). In this stage, we will use a model for threat agents that is instrumental to the creation of a threat library/knowledge base that associates threats with the who (i.e. the threat agents or actors) the how (i.e. the attack tools and techniques used and the vulnerabilities that are exploited) and the what (i.e. the targets in terms of data and functional assets sought).

After the threat intelligence information is collected from sources of internal and external threat agents, we will update the threat libraries and map the threats to the assets targeted so that we can model the threats against these assets later on during the attack modeling stage. In this stage, we will show how this threat library/knowledge base can be updated with threat sources from threat intelligence and internal logged events.

We will also show how to assign a probability to these threats so that these can be prioritized later on for risk assessments including vulnerability assessments specifically for the vulnerabilities and weaknesses that these threats seek to exploit and have high probability to be realized in attacks against the application assets (e.g. data and functions).

During stage V, that is, during the "Weakness and Vulnerability Analysis (WVA)," we will show how each threat of the threat library can be associated with a previously assessed vulnerability or gaps in the security controls of the application (e.g. authentication, authorization, encryption, session management, data validation, audit, and logging). During this stage, we also look in depth on how the application is designed, which technical security controls are in place both at the architectural level and functional level to identify any weaknesses that might expose the application assets to the previously identified threats. These are weaknesses in security controls that might expose the assets (e.g. data or functions) to threat agents hence increasing the threat probability of such threat agents to be realized in attacks.

At the end of this stage, we will identify weaknesses and vulnerabilities that need to be prioritized for and validated by security tests in order to reduce the probability risk of each threat. These security assessments will also include security test cases to test the security requirements that were previously documented and included in the technical design in stage II. At the end of stage V, we will have a clearer picture of weaknesses and vulnerabilities affecting the various components of the application architecture and of the type of threat agents that might exploit them in the case of specific attack scenarios.

This will trigger threat-driven security assessments of these vulnerabilities and bring value added for previously executed security assessments that were done blind to threat and by considering weaknesses and vulnerabilities independently from the risk of specific threat actor exploiting them. The mapping of threats to vulnerabilities allows us to move from a vulnerability-centric assessment to a threat/risk-centric assessment. A vulnerability-centric assessment focuses on the identification and remediation of vulnerabilities such as web application vulnerabilities that are either introduced during design (e.g. design flaws) or source code (e.g. coding errors). The identification of the design flaws and coding errors should be the focus of specific assessment such as architectural risk analysis and source code analysis as well as manual assessment such as secure code review, manual security tests such as ethical hacking pen test (referred as black-box testing) and automatic security tests scanning for vulnerabilities such as dynamic and static source code analysis.

When we use the PASTA methodology to conduct a risk-centric threat modeling exercise, the focus of vulnerability assessments is threat/risk centric and PASTA allows us reassess these vulnerabilities with the lenses of threat agents trying to exploit them. By applying the PASTA to the application, we will leverage any vulnerability data of weaknesses and vulnerabilities that was identified in previous vulnerability assessment conducted on the web application in scope for the analysis. The focus of at this stage is to gather data such as vulnerability reports on any vulnerabilities and weaknesses such as design flaws and implementation type of vulnerabilities that are introduced in software and libraries as well as misconfigurations of systems and network infrastructure components and that the threats previously analyzed could target in their exploits and use for attacks against the web application.

Among the weaknesses in security controls any design flaws in the design of the online banking application such as weaknesses in authentication, managing of authenticated sessions, errors in the design of user authorization, missing input validation of data as well as encryption of highly sensitive data such as authentication data, encryption keys and confidential data of customers take a specific focus in the analysis of the risks of the application architecture. At this stage, we should have a good picture of vulnerabilities and weaknesses that have been introduced because of errors in design, source code and implementation of security controls to protect data and functional assets. We can therefore prioritize specific vulnerability assessments such as ethical hacking pen tests and source code analysis and code reviews using both automated and manual techniques to validate and assert the severity of these weaknesses and vulnerabilities in the threat environment that we previously analyzed.

The other core of the PASTA assessment besides the modeling and the analysis of threats are the attack modeling and simulation. During stage VI "Attack Modeling and Simulation (AMS)," we will analyze the attack scenario for each specific threat to determine the likelihood of the threat occurring and the technical impacts in case of exploits of a condition such as either a control gap or vulnerabilities previously identified. The attack scenario will be analyzed by looking at the course of actions and the events that are triggered by the attacks so that these can be detected and alerted for actions (e.g. through a security incident response). Attack trees to learn about the attacker goals and methods can be used as methodology to determine the path of attacks sought by the attackers as path of least resistance and minimum cost hence bearing the highest probability to be executed to cause damage to the application.

Attack modeling seeks to model and simulate the attacks used against the web application to analyze how these attacks operate from the step of initial deployment of the agent of the attack (e.g. malware or bot) to the installation in the compromised systems to the conduction of the exploit of vulnerabilities and weaknesses in the web application's security controls to bypass them and to the final execution of the attack to cause the desired impact including the exfiltration of the data, outage of the online services provided and, last but not least, the steal of monetary assets from the victims (e.g. money from the bank accounts). The modeling of the attacks and the simulation of the attack scenario are critical for the derivation of attack-driven security tests whose goal is to validate how weaknesses and vulnerabilities are exploited as well as the effectiveness of exiting countermeasures in mitigating the impacts. Based on the attack simulations and tests, it is possible to determine which weaknesses and vulnerabilities should be prioritized for fixing including which countermeasures should be designed and deployed to detect and protect from the attacks. The identification of the countermeasures depends on different factors besides the effectiveness and the reduction of the initial risk of each threat to a residual that can be accepted also the costs for implementing them.

At the end of this stage, we will derive a list of attack simulation test cases that include the most probable attacks leading to exploits of control gaps and vulnerabilities and conduct simulated test cases of these attacks to determine whether the security measures that include both detective and preventive controls that are currently deployed are sufficient to mitigate the risk of a threat to be realized. The goal of the simulated tests is to consider additional security measures and controls to determine the security control effectiveness in the prevention and detection of possible attacks.

Finally in stage VII, "Risk Analysis and Management (RAM)" we will analyze the information in hand such as the threats and the simulated tests of attack scenarios to identify the technical impacts and to determine the business impacts on the assets and the type of security measures (e.g. preventive and detective controls) that can be implemented in order to mitigate the risks of the various threats considered including DDoS and malware banking hacking threats. The types of security measures that are recommended are the ones that are proved most effective in the mitigation of the risks of threats. During this stage, we will assess the technical and business impacts with the security measures in place and the reduction of these assuming that additional countermeasures will be deployed. The costs and effectiveness of these security measures will be evaluated and commiserated with the impacts to the business in the case these measures either will not be implemented. In some cases, the risk mitigation strategy consists of transferring the risks to a third-party. Another risk mitigation strategy might consist of eliminating the potential sources for risk such as by taking the critical business functionality off the Internet and made available only to internal users.

Stage I: Definition of The Objectives (DO)

Goals of This Stage The goal of the first stage of the application threat modeling methodology is the definition of the objectives for the analysis and management of the various types of cybersecurity risks affecting the application in scope. In order to derive these objectives, it is important to collect and analyze business requirements, information security policies and standards, privacy laws of organization/business and the application/product that are in scope for the assessment.

Guidance for the Execution of This Stage To define the objectives for the treatment of risk it is necessary to define information security requirements, compliance requirements, data privacy requirements and risk management requirements in the scope of the web application. Prerequisite for the execution of this stage is the reference to information security policies and standards, regulatory compliance, privacy laws, and business requirements.

Since information security policies and regulatory compliance apply also to web application assets that are owned and managed by the organization, it is important to review also application domain specific security standards if these are available. The outcomes of this stage are

1. The initial security and risk profile of the web application in scope for the analysis;
2. A set of documented high-level objectives for managing application risks including noncompliance with information security, unlawful regulatory noncompliance, business continuity risks, financial risks, and security incident risks of the web application.

Specific information security, compliance, and risk mitigation requirements can be documented during the different design phases of the SDLC for both new applications and for application changes. Business risks are derived from a preliminary risk analysis of potential business impacts based on the initial classification of the confidentiality of the data and the value given to the application as an asset for the organization.

In order to be ready to execute this stage, it is mandatory that an organization has adopted information security standards and policies for the protection of the organizational data assets that are processed by software and applications. From the compliance perspective, this includes applicable requirements derived from information security standards (e.g. ISO 27001) and industry specific requirements (e.g. PCI-DSS). For the security risk management perspective, the definition of risk mitigation objectives includes the definition of the inherent risks based upon the initial business functional requirements and exposure of the application assets and the inherent value of the asset.

At high level, a risk statement objective can be "the web application might expose high financial risk assets and functionality such as payment and money transfers to external threat agents and these risks are considered HIGH and need to be prioritized for a focused assessment of the application such as application threat modeling.

At high level, the main objectives include both information security, compliance, and risk management objectives and these constitute the initial set of high levels security and risk mitigation requirements for the application in scope. These are security requirements that can be followed both during design of the web application and to assess the various risks. At this stage, the severity level of cyber threats targeting the application that are received from threat advisories should also be taken into consideration (e.g. in the case of the financial sector, this will be FS ISAC).

Since threats will be later analyzed in stage IV of the PASTA™ threat modeling methodology the initial risk management objectives for these threats are mostly derived from what is known initially about the existing application/product such as the confidentiality of the data stored and processed, the exposure of the application to the Internet or intranet, the functionality at risk such as payments and money transfers as well as any new features and technologies that will be introduced in the application/product and will increase the overall risk profile of the application.

In regard to the risk profile of the application that is derived during this stage, the objective of this initial risk profile is mainly to identify at high level the inherent technical and business risks where the technical risks depend upon the risk of losing confidentiality, integrity and availability of the data assets while the business risks depend on the value given by the business to these assets whose exposure for the business in the case these assets are lost/compromised include a business impact.

Inputs for Conducting This Stage To conduct this stage, it is important to gather and assess information regarding the applicable information security policies and standard, applicable compliance regulations, and data privacy laws as well as to capture high-level business requirements for the application. This information could be already documented and if not documented it needs to be captured by conducting interviews with the application stakeholders including application development units, application business owners, information security teams and continuity of business managers, risk managers and compliance officers.

A nonmandatory list of technical documentation that can be captured for conducting this stage includes the following:

1. High-level business objectives
2. IS policies and standards
3. Data classification policies
4. Compliance regulations and data privacy laws
5. Risk assessment processes and standards
6. Security incident response procedures
7. Asset IT inventory
8. Asset values

Artifacts Produced at the End of This Stage At the end of this stage, we will produce the following artifacts:

1. Functional business requirements
2. Functional security requirements
3. Analysis of business impacts
4. Risk profile of the application/IT asset in scope

Tools The execution of this stage can be facilitated by the availability of IT asset repository that allow the threat modeler user to update the IT asset with the risk profile information, the classification of the data and the security and risk analysis and management requirements that are specific for this asset. A repository of documentation such as web portal to access information security and application security standards and documentation as it applies to the application in scope is also useful. Ideally the threat analyst, application security architect, security software developer, or technical risk manager conducting the application threat modeling assessment should have access to all these resources from share repositories such as MS SharePoint. For conducting this stage, we rely on the use of the tool ThreatModeler™ developed by MyAppSecurity Inc.

Activities to Be Conducted In this Stage This stage consists of the following activities:

 DO 1.1 – Document the business requirements for the new product/IT asset or application in scope for the threat modeling exercise. Application business requirements describe the application functionality from the business objectives perspective that is the service that is provided to customers/users of the application. These business requirements should already be documented otherwise a set of high-level business objectives can be used to derive security functional requirements describing the business functionality of the application in scope.

DO 1.2 – *Define the security requirements:* at high level, these are security requirements for the protection of the data assets and the security parameters such as the confidentiality, integrity, availability, and accountability of the data accessed, processed, and stored by the application. The data protection requirements can be derived in compliance with data privacy laws with scope on the type of data that is considered private and need to be protected (e.g. personal identifiable information (PII)). The compliance driven security requirements depend on different factors such as the type of data that the application is meant to protect and the applicable technical security standards based upon the type of data that is processed: example, if the application handles credit card payment data, the application will be in scope for PCI-DSS technical standards that will drive security requirements for the protection of credit card data that can be documented for the design of the application that process credit card data such as encryption of credit card data during transmission and storage and for masking of the credit card data when is displayed by the application user interfaces.

DO 1.3 – *Define the business impacts* such as the potential impact to the organization/business in the case of the valued asset data such as confidential data and business critical functions are either lost or compromised such as in the case of a security incident. Examples of security incident whose business impacts need to be identified and estimated are the business impacts caused by the loss of confidential data, loss/degradation of services and system/application functionality as well as losses due to fraudulent transactions. Business impacts can be estimated as economic loss based upon the value of the data/functional asset for the organization that is lost in a security incident. Business impacts caused by the loss of the assets can be used to estimate the level of business risk by factoring the estimated frequency of the security incident with a data loss event and the expected monetary value that is lost in that event.

DO 1.4 – *Determine the risk profile* for the application/product in scope. The purpose of the risk profile is to capture the technical and business risks for the application/asset in scope based upon a set of high-level risk analysis and management objectives. From cyber-threat risk perspective, these are risk analysis objectives such as capabilities, motives, and attack vectors used and the determination of how these threats might be realized in attacks to cause a negative impact to the application assets. Technical risk management objectives are aimed at analyzing and reducing the impact of attacks against the application security controls. High-level objectives can be derived from applicable information security policies and standards and the analysis of the impact risk levels estimated in the risk profile assuming the type of threats and the inherent information security risks. Business risk management objectives aim to the management of the estimated impacts caused by cyber-threats when these cause an impact to the business. The estimated business impact need to consider different factors such as legal and regulatory risks for noncompliance, loss of data privacy and the business impacts due to loss of data availability and service, and compromise of critical functionality at risk of security incidents caused by cyber-threats.

- A risk profile can be defined after risk management objectives are identified. In the case of a security incident, risk management objectives ought to consider the risk of cyber-threats besides regulatory compliance and information security risks. The general notion of risks on which the risk-centric methodology is based is that cyber-threat risks is associated with a probability of a cyber-threat to be realized in a cyber-attack that can cause a tangible loss and negative impact due to the compromise of the assets. From quantitative risk management perspective, cyber-threats cause business impacts such as revenue-monetary loss, fraud loss, operational losses, fines and penalties from regulators, data privacy loss fines, license liabilities, and legal costs lawsuits.

The application risk profile is dependent on known information about the application operational environment and the inherent risks such as information security risks factors such as the data exposure, confidentiality and integrity. The non-compliance risks might include a possible loss of privacy and business impacts caused by potential security incidents with breaches of data. Besides the inherent risks that are driven by the asset values, the documented risk profile need to factor the exposure to threats such as the severity level of the cyber-threat as probability of the application product to be attacked. Estimate and assign risk impact levels for threat severity-probability of attacks, technical impacts and business impacts (High, Medium, and Low). The analysis of these risk factors includes also the analysis of the impact to the business based on previous estimates.

Web Application Use Case Example The first activity of this stage consists of the activity "*DO 1.1 – Document the business requirements.*" It is not the objective of stage I to document business requirements but to gather the business requirement for the application in scope. Typically any given product or service including a web application should have the business requirement documented. These are requirements that describe what the new product/IT system, software, and process in scope need to satisfy in order to provide value for the business/organization when satisfied.

Typically business requirements lead to description of WHAT should be implemented by the application and these requirements are documented in Business Requirement Documents (BRD). The definition of how to achieve these business requirements with the application software or product in scope is typically the scope of both functional and nonfunctional requirements that are captured in System Requirement Specifications (SRS) or System Requirement Documents (SRD). For the online banking web application in scope, we would like to capture the specific functional business requirements that describe the functionality of the online banking application as these are describing the various features that the application is meant to provide. The reason we focus on "business features" is because these are "business assets" and therefore need to be protected from risk of threat agents seeking to compromise them for fraudulent transactions as well as for unauthorized access to confidential data. At high level, the business requirements for the online banking application in scope can be described from the perspective of the user bank customer being "the asset" for the organization as well as the confidential data that is stored and processed (e.g. bank accounts, credit card data) and the various business functions that are made available for the user/customer. From this perspective, the business requirements more closely resemble "business use cases" describing business functionality provided to the user of the application. For example, a nonexhaustive list of user business requirements for the online banking application includes the following Business Requirements (BR):

- *BR-1:* A bank customer can register to the online banking site using his debit card information and personal documentation.
- *BR-2:* A registered user can login into the online banking site.
- *BR-3:* A bank user can check his bank account statement, balance, and account transactions.
- *BR-4:* An authenticated user can apply for a new bank account.
- *BR-5:* An authenticated user can apply for a new loan.
- *BR-6:* An authenticated user can apply for a new credit card.
- *BR-7:* An authenticated user can pay bills online.
- BR-8: An authenticated user can transfer funds between accounts.
- *BR-9:* An authenticated user with multifactor authentication can transfer funds to a recipient of an external bank account through ACH.
- *BR-10:* An authenticated user can manage his or her account such as change his or her password, change the contact information (e.g. e-mail, postal address, and phone number).

In the description of these business requirements, we need to include a description of each of the type of users of the application (e.g. bank customer visitor a registered user and an authenticated user), the business function that is provided to each user and the type of data that is handled by the application (e.g. general public information or confidential information of the customer). This emphasis allows later to identify the type of user as well as the type of business functions that need to be provided and the sensitivity of the data that is processed.

As we start a new application threat modeling project, these business requirements can be captured using a threat modeling tool such as ThreatModeler™. In Figure 8.2, we show how the ThreatModeler™ tool wizard allows us to capture the business requirements associated with the online banking application in scope.

Once these business requirements are gathered and associated with the threat modeling project, the next step of the activity consists of conducting the activity *"DO 1.2 – Define the security/compliance requirements."*

PASTA USE CASE EXAMPLE WALK-THROUGH

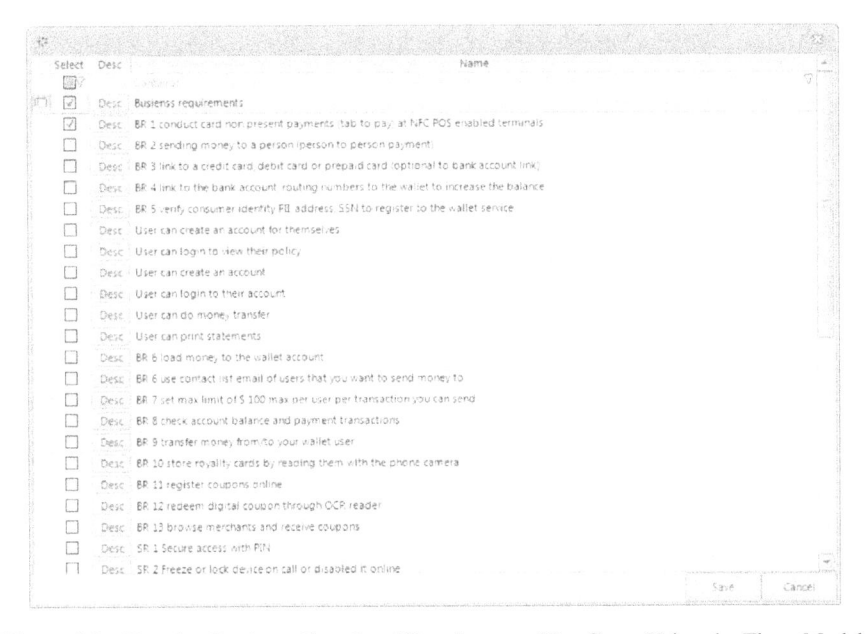

Figure 8.2 Entering Business Functional Requirements/Use Cases Using the ThreatModeler™ Threat Modeling Tool

Since the scope of security requirements is the protection of the confidentiality, integrity, and availability of the data and specifically the security requirements for protecting information that is considered confidential, it is important to identify the type of data that is processed and stored by the application. One possible way to identify which data is processed and stored is to look at each of the business requirements previously defined and identify the data that is stored or processed. The sensitivity of the data, that is, the data classification, depends on the organization's information security policy and the data classification policy. In order to classify the sensitivity of the data, it is necessary that the organization has adopted information security standards and policies (e.g. ISO 27001). These standards and policies need to be aligned with industry specific security requirements as it is mandated by the type of business vertical in which the organization operates and the type of data that is processed. For example, if the organization is developing a website that has in scope payment by processing credit card data, it will be in scope for PCI-DSS. PCI-DSS as well as other regulatory security standards might apply to the online banking application in scope as well. Since confidential data should be considered one of the organization assets that need to be protected, it is important to analyze the business requirements to determine if any confidential data is either processed or stored by the application. An example of this analysis is shown in Table 8.1.

After the type of data and the sensitivity has been identified using the organization data classification policy, it is possible to derive the security requirements for protecting these data based up the classification of the sensitivity of such data.

TABLE 8.1 Sensitive Data Analysis and Business Requirements of Online Banking Application

Business Functional Requirement	Data Classification of Data Processed by Each Business Function in Scope for the Business Functional Requirement
BR-1	Confidential Data (Bank Account, Card Number), Personal Identifiable Information (PII) (SSN, DOB)
BR-2	Username and authentication data (password)
BR-3	Confidential Data (Bank Account, Name, Surname, Address, Account Number)
BR-4	Confidential Data (Bank Account), Personal Identifiable Information (PII) (SSN, DOB)
BR-5	Confidential Data (Bank Account), Personal Identifiable Information (PII) (SSN, DOB)
BR-6	Confidential Data (Bank Account), Personal Identifiable Information (PII) (SSN, DOB)
BR-7	Confidential Data (Bank Account)
BR-8	Confidential Data (Bank Account)
BR-9	Authentication data (Secure Token/PIN), Confidential Data (Bank Account, Routing Number), Personal Identifiable Information (PII)
BR-10	Authentication data (password), Confidential data, Personal Identifiable Information (PII)

At high level, security requirements for the protection of the data that is processed and stored by the application in scope can be derived from the information security policies and standards that adopted by the organization/business. These information security policies and standards apply to all information data assets including the ones that are processed by the online banking application that include PII of customers and authentication data.

Typically information security policies include information security requirements for the security of digital assets (e.g. confidential data and business critical functions) that are owned and managed by the organization. At high level, information security requirements are not associated with the usage and function of the web application but rather are nonfunctional requirements that describe at high level the security constraints such as necessary security requirements that apply to protect the confidentiality integrity and availability of the confidential data and the business functions that handle such information.

From the perspective of the threat modeling exercise, we would like to focus on functional security requirements. These are requirements that need to be satisfied by the security controls such as authentication, authorization, data protection/encryption, data validation/filtering, session management, audit and logging and error management and exception handling.

An example of functional security requirements that can be derived for the online banking application based upon applicable standards and regulations are included herein. *Note: these requirements are not comprehensive of all types of security requirements for an online banking application but provided as an example of high level requirements:*

- *SR-1:* Passwords should be encrypted using irreversible encryption (e.g. hashes) using standard algorithms and minimum key lengths.
- *SR-2:* Passwords should comply with the password management policy (e.g. minimum 8 characters, alphanumeric, masked on display and expired every 90 days).
- *SR-3:* A password can be changed after authentication by providing old and new password. The new password should be typed twice.
- *SR-4:* A password can be reset by validating the username and a set of challenge questions. Upon validation, the user will be redirected to a login page where he would log in using a one-time use only password. The one-time only use password will be sent to the e-mail address on file for that user.
- *SR-5:* An account profile change such as change of mailing address and contact information such as e-mail, phone number requires additional verification of the customer identity (e.g. customer is called by customer support representative to validate his or her identity, customer needs to call the bank to confirm the change request).
- *SR-6:* Access to PII stored by the application requires the use of multifactor authentication such as security token and PIN.
- *SR-7:* Access to high-risk transactions such as transfer of funds to an external account requires use of multifactor authentication such as security token and PIN.
- *SR-8:* Authentication data should always kept encrypted in all systems and environments.
- *SR-9:* Confidential data need to be encrypted in storage and in transit.

These functional security requirements can be documented in the technical design documentation for the online banking application. These security functional requirements are used to assert if are supported with the necessary technical details that should be in scope for the threat modeling exercise during the stage II of PASTA "Definition of the technical scope."

Besides functional security requirements driven by information security policies and standards, it is also important to include security requirements that satisfy regulatory and compliance obligations. Also, these regulatory and compliance obligations need to be in scope for the security functional requirements of the online banking application in scope. For example, in the case of online banking applications, there are several US and international standards and regulatory compliance that might be applicable for the security of online banking application, some of these include:

1. Information Security Policies and Standards (e.g. ISO 27011)
2. Federal Financial Institutions Examination Council's (OCC-FFIEC)

3. Gramm-Leach-Bliley Act of 1999 (GLBA)
4. Sarbanes–Oxley Act of 2002 (SOX)
5. Payment Card Industry Data Security Standard (PCI DSS)
6. Security Breach Notification Laws (SB 1386)

Some of these regulatory bodies and standards also rule specific security requirements that should be in scope for the application and can be added to the list of security requirements previously identified such as

SR-10: Access to high-risk transactions such as transfer of funds to an external account requires use of multifactor authentication such as security token and PIN (mandated by OCC-FFIEC).

SR-11: Credit and debit card holder data such as credit/debit card number should be protected by masked (e.g. show only last four digits) on display and protected with either encryption (e.g. hash) or tokenized while in transit and in storage. The card PINs and the authentication card codes such as CAV2/CVC2/CVV2/CID should never be stored by the application after authorization not even if encrypted (mandated by PCI-DSS).

Additional functional security requirements that should be defined for the application are security functional requirements that satisfy data privacy requirements. These security requirements depend on the various privacy laws in scope that are different by country and jurisdiction and concern the protection of the citizen's data that is considered private by the different data privacy laws in scope for that country and jurisdiction. For example, for what concerns US online banking customers, these are requirements for the protection of PII. An example of the requirements for applications that process and store PII consists of restricting the access to these data only to authenticated and authorized users and to provide disclosure to the customers affected when their PII data is either lost or compromised. In the case of the online banking web application in scope, these privacy security requirements apply to customers' private data such as customer's PII data that is processed and stored by the web application. This also applies to confidential PII data used to identify a customer when applying for a new bank account, when applying for new credit card, when getting a credit report from a credit bureau as well as for identifying a customer to recover or reset passwords and online user accounts.

Depending on the country and state where the private information of the customers is stored, there are different types of privacy laws that should be considered in effect. Specifically what is considered private data varies among countries, for example, under EU directive 95/46/article 2a: *"personal data is any information relating to an identified or identifiable person, an identification number or one or more factors specific to the physical, physiological, mental, economical cultural or social identity."* In the United States of America, what is defined as PII is defined in personal data breach notification laws such as SB 1386 that include the combination of a name and a tax ID such as Social Security Number (SSN), a Driver License Number, and an Account/Credit/Debit card number and a PIN.

Depending on the applicable privacy and data breach notification laws, it is important to derive a security requirement for the protection of personal identifiable data of the customers as well as to provide necessary disclosures, notifications, and options when private information of the customer can be collected and shared with other parties. Another important reason for protecting PII is to protect it from the identity thefts and fraud such as when a fraudster will use stolen identities to impersonate a legitimate user and commit fraudulent transactions. An example of security requirement that can be derived for the application to satisfy the requirement of protection of PII is the following:

SR-12: PII such as Name and Last Name and a Tax ID such as Social Security Number should be encrypted when stored and transmitted and masked when displayed.

The list of security functional requirements SR1 to SR12 shows an example on security functional requirements that can be derived for the online banking application to be compliant with information security policies enforced by the organization to protect the confidential data of the customers as well as by the various regulatory compliance and privacy laws in scope for the protection of the customer's private information.

After the functional security requirements have been defined the next step consists of performing the activity "*DO 1.3 Define the business impact.*" This activity consists of defining what the business impact will be in the case of the application data assets such as confidential data and functionality is being either lost or compromised in security incidents.

Examples of security incidents that impact data assets include loss of availability of data and service such as in the case of accidental outrage or denial-of-service attack and loss of confidentiality and integrity of the data caused by data breach incident.

These examples as relate to the possible loss of confidentiality and integrity and availability of the data consist of either information security impact such as the loss of Confidentiality Integrity and Availability of the data or the associated technical impact caused by loss or degradation of the security control (e.g. encryption, authentication/authorization, digital signing, quality of service) that satisfies protection against that impact. From the business impact perspective, these information security and technical impact translate to business impact when these are associated with the consequences to the business in the case these data and functions are either loss or compromise. At high level, these impacts to the business are associated with the monetary/economical loss associated with the security incident as this security incident might be caused by a threat agent exploiting weaknesses and vulnerabilities in the online banking application to produce a business impact. The definition of the business impacts is often done based upon estimates of the value of the data assets and functions and the assessment of the quantitative risks of security incident events. These business impacts are specific for each type of threat, vulnerability exploits and attacks and the impact on the assets. In stage VII risk analysis and management will provide example on how this business impacts can be calculated.

At this preliminary stage of the risk-based threat modeling exercise, we will focus on high-level estimates of business impacts that can be captured in the risk profile of the online bank application to determine the level of financial business risk for the online bank application.

Business impacts include both tangible and nontangible losses. Tangible losses can be estimated based upon the possible loss of the monetary value of the assets.

Nontangible losses are difficult to estimate since they have an impact on the company brand and reputation and customer perception of the company value. Examples of the possible tangible and nontangible business impacts include the following:

1. *Tangible loss* such as the costs incurred by the organization because of data breach security incident. For each of the banking customers, this cost is estimated to be $355/record (a financial organization Ponemon Institute 2010 data).
2. *Tangible impacts to the business* because of loss and degradation of service caused by a DDoS (Distributed Denial-of-Service attack. The average annual cost of DDoS attacks for a business is estimated to be $187,506/year (based on 2011 Second Annual Cost of Cyber Crime Study Benchmark Study By Ponemon Institute).
3. *Tangible impact caused by online fraud* for example online fraud due to malware banking Trojan compromising a customer PC and successfully conducting a fraudulent transfer up to the max value amount (e.g. $100,000) allow for the personal or business account of the customer/client.
4. *Tangible impacts due to violation of EU data privacy laws* (e.g. up to 1 million EUROs or 2% of worldwide annual turnover whichever is greater under new rules June 2013 proposed by the European Commission).
5. *Tangible impacts due to regulatory fines* imposed by the payment credit card industry (VISA, MasterCard, AMEX, Discover) due to loss of credit card data from their customers (PCI DSS with fines up to $500,000 when credit cardholder data is either lost or stolen).
6. *Nontangible reputational damage* caused by inability of customer to access the remote functions that the online banking application provides such as open bank accounts, pay bills, apply for loans, book resources and services, transfer funds, trade stocks, view account information, download bank statements and others.
7. *Nontangible reputation* loss such as, in the case of publicly traded company, a drop in stock price as consequence of announced security breach.

These estimates of the business impacts are business specific and financial related and are based upon vendor surveys and statistical data of the impact of security incident affecting financial organizations. It is important to notice that this list of business impacts is not all included list of business impact since it might include also lawsuits, legal fees, and additional measures and controls imposed after the security incidents by regulatory bodies and other factors. More accurate estimates can be derived based upon internal sources including cost incurred to recover and technical repairs after

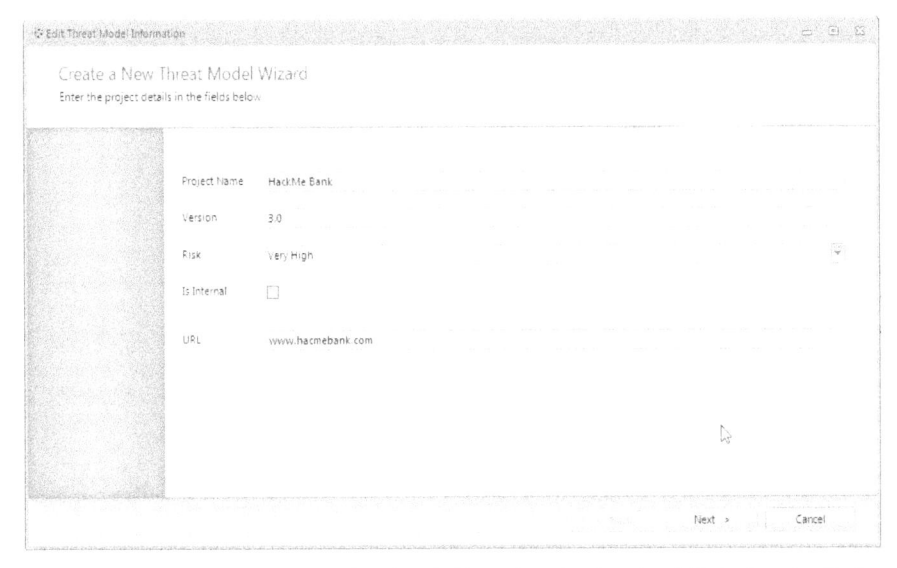

Figure 8.3 ThreatModeler™ Tool Wizard Capturing the Level of Risk for the Project HackMe Bank

incurring in data breach-related security incidents including incidents whose impact for the financial organization has been losses because of online fraud.

Because of the various business impacts calculated herein, the risk of the online banking application project "is considered very high and can be assigned to the new HackMe Bank" project using the ThreatModeler™ wizard screen shown in Figure 8.3.

After the business impacts have been defined, the next step of this stage consists of performing the activity "*DO 1.4 – Determine the risk profile for the application/product.*"

Before defining the risk profile for the online banking application, it is important to identify a set of high-level risk management objectives at organizational level. These are also risk management objectives that apply to the management of risks of the online application in scope and can be followed throughout the application threat modeling assessment process.

These are objectives for the identification and the analysis of threats against the online banking application and the determination of their severity, the analysis of how each of these threats might be realized to cause a negative impact on the application data and functional assets and the determination of the security measures that can be designed and deployed to reduce these risks to manageable levels.

From the perspective of technical risks and specifically for the risks caused by possible design flaws and vulnerabilities in the application, it is also important to articulate the possible impacts of security incidents whose risks need to be managed. This is the risk of security incidents targeting the online bank application and that might expose sensitive data and functionality to different types of impacts such as impact of compromise of confidential data (e.g. information security risks), impact caused by noncompliance such as failing compliance audit with regulation (e.g. unlawful noncompliance, legal and regulatory risks) and business impact such as in the case of a security incident due to the realization of a threat in an attack that will cause a monetary loss of asset values (e.g. confidential data and business functionality).

The types of risk that an online banking application might be subjected to and is worth analyzing further might include the following:

1. *Information security/technical risks*
2. *Unlawful noncompliance* liabilities, legal and regulatory fines
3. *Violation of privacy* laws risks
4. *Business impacts* (e.g. business continuity risks)
5. *Security incident impacts* caused by specific threats

The management of these risks requires the organization to adopt information security policies and standards and have risk management processes in place. At high level, these are standards and processes that impact the organization/business as whole all web applications including the online banking application that is developed and managed by the organization.

This goal of the risk profile of the application is to provide a snapshot of the inherent risks that need to be managed in compliance with the organization risk management process. These risks depend on the inherent characteristics of the application/product in scope for the risk analysis. In the case of an online banking web application, for example, the risk profile can be derived from an IT asset repository that includes information to manage information security requirements, compliance, and risks of the online banking application. From information security perspective, the IT asset repository might include information about the application environment (e.g. Internet or intranet) the inherent risks based upon the classification of the data (e.g. confidential and private PII) and the volumes of such data (e.g. volume of records stored based upon number of users registered). An initial risk level for information security risks can be assigned based on an estimate of the possible levels of impacts due to the loss of confidentiality, integrity, availability of the data stored/processed by the online banking application. The level of impact can be estimated based upon the consideration of the classification of the data and the volumes of this data that can be possibly disclosed, tampered with, or made unavailable in the case of a security incident.

In the case of compliance risks, it is also possible to estimate the possible levels of impact in the case of a possible violation of security standards and regulations such as PCI-DSS in scope for the application whose impact can be estimated as additional costs to the business for fines and legal costs. In the case of privacy risks, the impact can be estimated as direct function of the number of registered users whose compromise of PII might have different levels of impacts and costs for the business.

From risk perspective of the business impacts, a possible estimate can be done as function of the economic levels of the impact of a security incident and the impact of a loss or compromise of a business function such as data compromise due to malware/hacking and impact on the availability of the site when it is attacked by denial of service. Such level of impacts might be determined based upon the monetized amount of estimates of loss of data and service occurred because of the likelihood and impact of security incidents. Methodologies such as business impact analysis and quantitative risk analysis might help to quantify these estimates. These business impacts were previously estimated in the business impact analysis activity and included in the risk profile as estimate of the level of "Business Impact Risks."

Finally the initial risk profile of the application might also include the risks of cyber-threats as level of severity as probability of these cyber-threats to be realized in attacks such as malware/hacking and distributed denial-of-service attacks against the online banking application. The level of severity of these threats might be derived by the estimates provided by security vendors and cyber intelligence providers (Table 8.2).

Stage II Definition of the Technical Scope (DTS)

Goals of this Stage The goal of this stage is to enumerate the details of technical components including architectural and software components that scope for conducting the threat modeling exercise. The technical details should be included in the design and asserted against the security requirements that were previously identified. The technical details that are captured at this stage support the detailed analysis of the application architecture and components in stage III-Application Decomposition and provide the technical scope for assessing the exposure of the application assets (data and functionality) to threats in stage IV-Threat Analysis. The enumeration in the technical scope also seeks to identity all the components of the technical stack that includes the layers of software, processes, servers/systems, and network components that support the application functionality. The objective of this stage is to create a comprehensive list of technology assets that support the application in scope and made the various components of the application architecture.

Guidance for the Execution of This Stage The activities of stage II provide a list of the underlying technology stack of the application in scope such as the platform/system, relevant databases, application servers, network servers, infrastructure equipment, biometric hardware, and any other IT asset that will be used to fulfill the objectives defined under stage I. Essentially, the activities across this stage defines the various components (assets or sub-assets) that will be later dissected by the application threat model.

Any of these technologies could serve as either the immediate attack surface or target component within the threat model. The technology scope therefore helps form the environment in which future attacks will be taking place whose formal methodologies used for attack modeling such as attack kill-chain and attack trees will be representing, along with associated vulnerabilities, attacks, actors, and so on.

Stage II of PASTA (Technical Scope) attempts to answer the common problem or question "I didn't know that we were running/using that technology in our app."

TABLE 8.2 Online Banking Application Risk Profile

IT Asset Risk Profile: Online Banking Application	
General description of the application functionality	The online banking application allows customers to perform banking activities such as financial transactions over the internet. The type of transactions supported by the application includes bill payments, wires, funds transfers between customer's own accounts and other bank institutions, account balance-inquires, transaction inquires, bank statements, new bank accounts loan, and credit card applications. New online customers can register an online account using existing debit card, PIN, and account information. Customers authenticate to the application using username and password and different types of MultiFactor Authentication (MFA) and Risk-Based Authentication (RBA)
Operating environment	Internet (accessible over the Internet by banking customers an intranet only by administrators)
Compliance laws and regulations in scope	ISO 27001, ISO 22301, FFIEC, PCI-DSS, GLBA, SOX, SB 1386, EU Privacy-FTC Safe harbor rules
Sensitive data types	Confidential, Confidential PII, and Authentication Data
High risk transactions	Payments, wire transfers, online access to confidential information and PII
User roles	Visitor, registered user, administrator, customer support representative
Number of users	3 million registered customers
Information security risks	HIGH (High risk for potential loss of data confidentiality, integrity and availability)
Noncompliance risks	HIGH (High-risk impact in the case of violation of compliance regulations in scope)
Business impact risks	VERY HIGH (High risk of loss of revenue and online fraud in the case of denial of service and security incidents)
Privacy violations risks	HIGH (high risk of privacy violation for the volume of users registered)
Threat severity risk	ELEVATED (High risk of cyber-attacks as indicated by FS ISAC for the financial sector) (* this is dynamic value from monthly threat intelligence reports)

Stage II is essentially a large enumeration project. It focuses on itemizing software and hardware assets in order to later define a lean and relevant attack surface whose components could be exploited by various possible threats. Activities in this stage should produce a roster of technological components that are inventoried. This in itself is incredibly useful and can be leveraged over time as the technology scope of the application changes. The roster of application components needs to extend beyond traditional realms (i.e. – server, infrastructure appliance, endpoint, etc.).

The list should span to include layered pieces of technologies that may be embedded. The simple rule is to identify anything that has a direct exposure to a caller or actor, whether it is from a human or a compiled library that only calls another component based upon an event or interpreted result. Essentially, the asset breakdown should extend beyond hardware and include software based technologies such as proxies, middleware, authentication servers, compiled libraries, open source libraries, third-party APIs, browser-based plug-ins, and so on. Today's feature-rich UIs, for example, need to be dissected properly in order to ensure that all of the client and presentation layer technologies are properly enumerated.

Later on, these assets will serve as the main "trunk" to the attack trees focusing on the various assets that can be attacked to be developed in PASTA's stage VI. The tree will ultimately show underlying use cases, data components, and actors interact with each other. From each one of these nodes, further branches can be split out to show unique threats for each underlying node stemming from the initial asset component.

Scoping is important for this exercise as too broad of a scope may confuse the subsequent steps. Too broad of a scope inhibits good analysis. For this reason, a tighter scope of assets is suggested in order that a simpler and more efficient threat model can be created. This stage objective is to capture the technical details of the application/product so it possible to later identify the risks and the technical impacts. The technical details need to be captured and documented including the data assets and architectural components. For the definition of the technical scope, it is important to be able to collect these technical details in design documentation and captured in standard technical design documentation.

A comprehensive documentation should include the architecture design documents inclusive of the architecture components, servers and network infrastructure dependencies, the details of security controls such as authentication, authorizations, data protection in storage and in transit, data filtering, session management as well as details of the design patterns used and the architecture components, data interfaces and the trust boundaries of the application with other application software and software with server components, third-party software libraries and frameworks, servers O.S. and the supporting data center, network infrastructure in support of the application and product in scope.

Since threat modeling focuses on identifying how threats are realized in attacks against the various technical components of the application/product as well as the various components of the technology stack, it is important that this technical information is completed and documented with all the necessary details. These are the details necessary for conducting the threat modeling exercise.

At the project level, it is important to capture the technical details of the design and of the new features/changes introduced in the application/ products so that it is possible to assert the technical impact of these changes. These design changes are ideally documented in the technical documentation that is used for the design and implementation of the application. As the technical details are captured through interviews, questionnaires, and other methods (e.g. analysis of network topology, reverse engineering of code to determine libraries used etc.), they also need to be documented. The final activity consists of validating that the technical documentation is complete by asserting the security requirements and by validating if any technical details are missing and need to be documented in the technical design of the product/application.

Inputs for Conducting This Stage To conduct this stage, it is important to gather information about the technology stack used by the application at the various technology layers including software libraries, API used by the application software, software framework that support the execution environment (e.g. J2EE, dot NET), type of client technologies (e.g. Web 2.0 components, browsers, thick clients) servers (e.g. web servers, application servers, databases) and O.S. (Linux, MS Windows, UNIX) including the various network infrastructure components. The information of the technology stack should be made available based upon available technical documentation and assessable when stored in IT asset repository. In case this information is not readily available, it can be gathered by conducting a series of interviews with the application stakeholders such as application managers and technical SMEs. Some of the information of the technology stack can also be gathered using network scanning and process profiling tools to identify processes and systems running on the application in scope.

Example of documentation that can be reviewed to enumerate the various components of the application architecture and the technology stack includes the following:

(a) Security requirements from stage I
(b) Documentation of the technology stack used by the application components at the different tiers of the architecture
(c) Architecture design documents
(d) Architectural diagrams of the application
(e) Functional and technical specifications
(f) Network diagrams

Artifacts Produced at the End of This Stage At the end of this stage, we will produce details of the technical stack that compromises layers of components and services that are used by the application including the network infrastructure layer and the third-party infrastructure layers/components. The technology stack is also organized by the various architectural tiers of the web application in scope that includes the presentation tier, the business logic tier, and the data tier. The details of the technology stack need to be documented in the technical design documentation and specifications along to the functional security requirements defined in stage I.

Tools The execution of this stage can be facilitated by the use of IT asset repository with up-to-date information on technology stack used by the application as well as architecture design and project level design documentation such as technical specifications and functional level design. A project management workflow tool also helps in enforcing toll gates when this step is performed during the SDLC to ensure that technical documentation is complete with information and security requirements that can be asserted for architectural risks introduced in the design changes during stage III.

PASTA USE CASE EXAMPLE WALK-THROUGH 503

Activities This stage consists of the following activities:

- *DT2 2.1 – Enumerate software components:* The goal of this activity is to enumerate software components used by the application. This information can be collected from the application stakeholders conducting targeted interviews and by using ad-hoc questionnaires. Example of the technical information that is relevant for the analysis and should be collected includes the various software components of the technology stack used in the application architecture such as the programming languages, custom libraries, and third-party software and services. Some organizations that have adopted a repository for manage technical assets including web applications might have this information already stored in the IT asset repository/catalog that include all software components, servers, and network components used by the application and in scope for design changes as well as operation/maintenance;
- *DT2 2.2 – Identify actors and data sinks/source:* The goal of this activity is to identify the various actors (human or application based) that include users and user roles as well as process running under specific functional accounts. These actors can access resources such as files and data based upon permissions set for these resources and mapped to each user/agent or component/agent. The goal of this activity is to determine who the application actors are and the roles and the type of permissions of these actors to access resources including the various components of the application architecture at various tiers as well as layers of the technology stack. The identification of the actors such as users and roles can also be assessed by reviewing access control lists assigned to existing resources such as data and files and by using tools that allow retrieve information on roles and permissions for users to access data and files accessed by software components.
- Configuration files can also be reviewed to identify users and roles. Other techniques to identify users/actors include the audit of databases that store user credentials and architectural components whose function is to manage users and roles such as LDAP-based directory services (e.g. Active Directory, SiteMinder Single Sign On LDAP Servers). The validation might go as far as collecting data from traffic to/from the authentication components and by analyzing how credentials are used by clients and hosts to identify any preshared keys, digital certificates used for authentication engine and by running authentication calls through a proxy to identify authentication calls have been missed in enumeration efforts. Similar to the other activities around enumerating software, systems, and third-party software, this activity is focused on identifying smaller components that actually run or operate within the previously listed exercises. Within these two exercises, we will identify all database, system, and application actors that are making/receiving requests on each asset or across the application environment.
- Besides user actors, processes that run at the application level to perform various tasks such as connecting to databases opening files also need to be enumerated

when these are associated with system accounts and processes running on a system. These are processes that can be enumerated by process IDs (PIDs) and can be mapped to user accounts. This enumeration helps to identify some of the inherent actors on a given system or third-party product. Tools such as SysInternals by Microsoft can be used to conduct this assessment at system/platform level for either a physical or virtual MS Windows host. Beyond using tool-based techniques to extrapolate the actors and services of the product application environment, application architects and members of the development team should be able to create an initial list of actors and required services that sustain the application use contained within the environment. Developers, for example, can perform CRUD exercises to determine what actors will be used to Create, Read, Update, or Delete data from the data repository, whether it is a backend database or a flat file system.

DTS 2.3 – Enumerate system-level services: At system level, processes can run as services. The goal of this activity is to discover what system types or operating systems are being used at the various tiers of the application architecture such as presentation tier, business logical tier, and database tier. Examples of the system services that run in the presentation tier include various processes in support of the interaction of the user with the application and include processes for entering user data such as commands for the application, upload files as well as for visualize and use the data such as running data queries, search and download files, videos and other type of data. At the business logic layer, system-process might run on the application server and use middleware to communicate with other server processes that run the servers (e.g. backend servers) where the data is stored. System-level service enumeration is aimed at identifying what services are running on the various system assets on which much of the application software will be running. Both of these exercises will require the use of some system commands and/or simple tools that facilitate identifying both services and actors in association with various use cases of the product application. A port scanner, for example, would be able to do both the platform identification and the service enumeration for a given scope. If, for example, my test product application runs on a 192.168.52.0/28 network, I can scan that and see what the scope of platforms and services are. Note that system platforms encompass application servers and/or databases within each architectural tier. They also reveal possible third-party products or autonomous application environments (e.g. cloud services, SaaS services) that may support the overall application solution. Third-party products in general are difficult to include in the threat model since they are largely black boxes for which an underlying understanding of technology is absent. Third-party cloud environments are even more complex since the ability to scan or interface with any facet of the cloud infrastructure is not commonly permitted by the cloud or hosted operator. Vendor products and tools, although proprietary in nature, at least present the opportunity for security practitioners to scan and interface with the host in order to ascertain some level of security assurance. Both third-party services

PASTA USE CASE EXAMPLE WALK-THROUGH   505

and appliances should be listed under the correct container for activities under this step.

Enumeration of system-level services can be done by using different tools that are O.S. specific and therefore limited in their capabilities. If there is any diversity of operating systems on the network, then systems administrators will end up with a diversity of report types. Some security scanners (e.g. Tenable's Nessus or Rapid7's NeXpose) today have the system-level scanning capabilities and avoid unnecessary use of time and resources to conduct this assessment.

At the end of this activity, we will produce formalized descriptions of installed packages in a heterogeneous network with much less time and effort than using the aforementioned options. We will also provide functionality well beyond the scope of package management including the ability to identify services open on a given platform as well as the ability to fingerprint the platform OS and any embedded OS that may be present. All of this information helps the threat modeling process by identifying a blueprint of assets with possible inherent vulnerabilities. Such data will be further leveraged in stages IV allowing the mapping of threats to the system-level services enumerated and the various system assets that operate within the different tiers if the architecture such as presentation tier, business-layer tier, and data tier as well as the various trust boundaries of the network architecture such as client, DMZ layer, and internal network layers of traditional three tier web-based application architectures.

Typically architectural tiers represent an abstraction for the network tier, for example, for web applications, the presentation tier is mostly allocated on the client host and the services running on that host to support user interface functionality (e.g. thin-client browsers and thick clients) and the web server providing the web interface as a service (e.g. web service). The identification of client-side technologies that are developed by the product/software development team is also to the enumeration of the various host-level processes that run on the client as well as the web server and this includes also the system level services for presentation layer functionality that includes JavaScript, AJAX, and Silverlight development. At the presentation layer, some degree of input validation is done at the client/browser as well as at the web server (e.g. by filtering request and response using NSAPI filters as example).

A secure architecture typically involves the running of services that can enforce security functions such as authentication, authorization, data validation at the application layer. This includes input validations of requests and responses for data exchanges that are both downstream and upstream. Business logic is also provided by at the application servers that aggregate functionality from data sources. Lastly, a data layer represents where the greatest level of protection should be applied to the assets, given the presumed data centralization of key business and/or client data.

DTS 2.4 – Enumerate third-party infrastructure components: Many application environments use various external networks. Some may be in the form of cloud-based services such as Process as a Service (PaaS), Software as a

Service (SaaS), or Infrastructure as a Service (IaaS), while others will be along the lines of a more traditional third-party ASP or colocation model. Whatever the service, it is important to bring third-party infrastructures into the technical scope. Depending on the relationship and the legal terms around "right to audit," certain automated solutions could be used similar to the activities for a captive or self-hosted model. However, many third-party vendors do not like their environments to be scanned without proper permission, so it is important to ensure that any discovery scanning efforts against a multitenant or shared hosting environment is cleared beforehand. For this reason, realistic actions to perform under this activity include interviews with third-party technology SMEs in order to identify what software, data, platforms, and system services are to support the application, reviews with any existing network design documentation from the third- party and evidence in support of the reviews collected using tools that allow to enumerate software used, data repositories (flat files, relational DB), fingerprint platforms, and ports/services used (may depend on legal agreements with the third party). Generally speaking, it is important to rely on vendor-technical points of contacts to get the necessary information. Today, most account management teams themselves will have the information or know of the internal SME who can provide requested asset/component information pertaining to your hosted solution.

DTS 2.5 – Assert completeness of secure technical design: Once we have identified the various application actors, enumerated all components used at the different layers of the application architecture and the technology stack including software, we would like to review the technical documentation to validate that this information is documented in the technical design is complete and accurate and includes all the necessary details to conduct the application threat modeling exercise.

To make sure that document details are documented including all enumerated components of the technology stack, development teams can be given technical documentation templates for designing the application architecture that include all the design details necessary for the secure design of the application (e.g. security requirements) as well as the details for the application threat modeling exercise. The key items to document are security requirements for the design of security controls for the application/asset in scope. To determine which security controls should be documented and how as well as the security requirements that need to be followed, it is important to rely upon application security standards and guidelines and document templates that include the mandatory sections of the document that need to be documented for the initial technical scope assessment from the information security team. These document templates can also include pointed guidance of which architecture diagrams should be documented and how and include an information security section with mandatory documentation of security controls (e.g. authentication, authorization, data validation, encryption, session management, audit and logging). It should be responsibility of the application design architects to document all the mandatory sections of the architecture design and functional design document. Each design document should include a set of Information Security (IS) requirements as mandated in the template document. The type of classification of the data and the risk levels assigned to this data in the risk profile should be used to define IS requirements for protecting these assets (e.g. confidential data should be encrypted). The technical documentation should provide enough details for identifying and analyzing the presence of gaps in security controls and architectural design flaws. The assertion of the completeness of design needs to include all software components, actors (human and not human), system-level services, third-party infrastructures that were enumerated and captured in the previous activities of this stage of the threat modeling process. The definition of what details should be in scope for technical design also depends on the business and security requirements previously defined and the type of assets such as data and functions that need to be protected for compliance and risk management perspectives. The technical scope assessment of a web application, for example, requires the documentation of logical and network architecture as well as of the application functionality that is exposed through the various channels, proprietary or third-party channels. The enumeration of the human actors drives the enforcement of the user's roles and permissions and the security requirement for the design of authorization controls such as role-based access controls.

Web Application Use Case Example The first activity of this stage consists of the activity *DTS 2.1 – "Enumerate software components."* Software components used by the application can be classified based upon different types of information such as the type of languages used by the application software such as J2EE, .NET, C/C++, PHP, JavaScript, Visual Basic, Python, Shell, Ruby, Objective-C, and C#, the customized and proprietary libraries developed for the various components of the application architecture tiers such as presentation layer (e.g. graphical APIs/libraries), business tier (e.g. business components API/libraries), and data tier (e.g. data access components libraries). These libraries can be developed using standard technologies and APIs such as Web HTTP messaging protocols, XML, and Web 2.0 APIs software components that use AJAX, JSON, and Web 2.0 service protocols such as SOAP and REST used in SOA Service Oriented Architectures. Since most of applications today are developed using third-party libraries and components that are deployed at the different layers and tiers of the application architecture. It is critical to enumerate them as well; these include libraries such as Web APIs that include Apache Struts, Spring, Log4j/NET.

An example of the software (S/W) technology stack of the online banking application in scope is included in Table 8.3.

The information of the application components s/w technology stack can be collected from the application stakeholders conducting targeted interviews and by using ad-hoc questionnaires. Some organizations that have adopted a (IT) Information Technology asset repository for managing technical assets such as IT systems deployed and maintained by the organization including the ones used by the web applications might have this data already stored in the IT asset repository/catalog

TABLE 8.3 Online Banking Application Components S/W Technology Stack

Online Banking Application Technology Stack: Software Components and Libraries	
Programming languages and software development environments	Java/J2EE, JavaScript
Standard software protocols	HTML / HTML5, SOAP, REST, XML, CSS / CSS3, WS Security, SAML
Third-party software frameworks	Java/JDK, JSP Struts, JavaEE (Servlets), JavaScript, Framework, RIA, AJAX, JSON Spring Sprint, Log4J
Custom software libraries and APIs*	Java Banking Platform (JBP)Secure Filtering APIs (SFA)Financial Web Services (FWS)
Third-party software libraries and APIs	MS Active X, Java Applet, Adobe FLASH, JDBC Oracle, TIBCO EMS APIs, SiteMinder SDK

*Note the custom S/W libraries developed for the online bank application are fictional and not used in any specific type of commercial banking application and provided as an example of proprietary custom developed libraries/software.

that include all software components, servers, and network components used by the application and in scope for design changes as well as operation/maintenance.

The next stage activity to follow is *DTS 2.2 – "Identity Actors and Data Interfaces."* The goal of this activity is to determine who the application actors are and the roles and the type of permissions of these actors to access resources including the various components of the application architecture at various tiers as well as layers of the technology stack. The identification of the actors such as users and roles can also be assessed by reviewing access control lists assigned to resources such as data and files and by reviewing how these data and files are accessed by software components.

The definition of the users and roles of each application is typically defined in the RBAC Role base Access Control matrix that defines who the users of the application are, their roles and their permissions to access the various resources (e.g. URLs, functions, data, files) that are stored and protected by the security control of the application. Often these user roles and permissions are defined in application configuration files, these files can also review to validate whether the user role-permission configuration implemented for the application 9e.g. stored in XML configuration policy file) corresponds to the roles and permissions for the users that are documented in technical design.

The definition of the user roles is critical for the application threat modeling exercise since from these roles depend the enforcement of authentication and authorization security controls.

An example of various users of the online banking application that can be defined using ThreatModeler™ and later one used to assign use cases is shown in Figure 8.4.

Besides user actors, processes that run at the application level to perform various tasks such as connecting to databases opening files and so on also need to be enumerated when these are associated with system accounts and processes running on

PASTA USE CASE EXAMPLE WALK-THROUGH

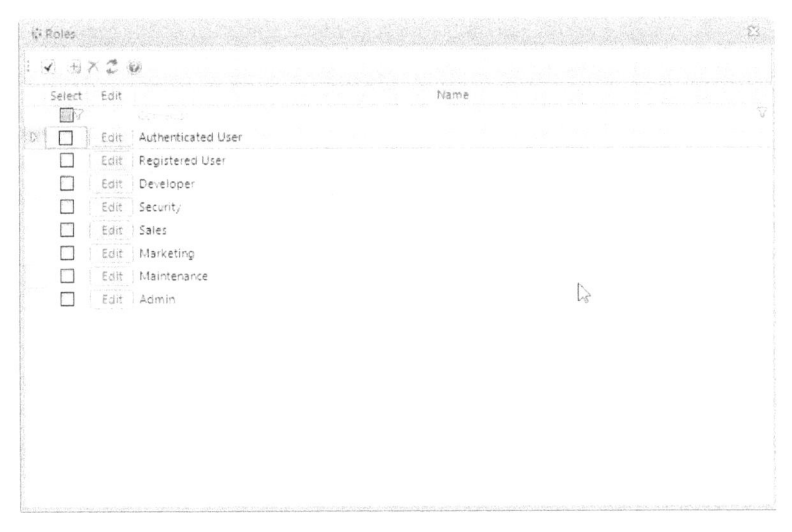

Figure 8.4 HackMe Bank Users

a system. These are processes that can be enumerated by PIDs and can be mapped either to user accounts or to functional/system accounts.

Once the various users have been enumerated defined the next step consists of capture the various data interfaces components that provide connections between the various components of the application architecture. At this stage of the enumeration exercise, it is also important to capture the type of authentication used to authenticate users as well as each connection and the protocol used. An example of this data interface enumeration is provided in Table 8.4.

TABLE 8.4 Online Banking Web Application: Data Interfaces

Data Interface ID	Data Interface Components	User and Server To Server Authentication	Protocol
1	Browser To/From Web Server	UID, Pwd, 2FA	HTTP/SSL
2	Web Server To/From Application Server	Mutual SSL Authentication	HTTP?SSL
3	Application Server To/From Database Server	AppID Pwd	JDBC/SSL
4	Application Sever To/From Messaging Bus Server	AppID Pwd	XML/JMS
5	Application Sever To/From Fraud Detection Web Service	Mutual SSL Authentication	XML/HTTP/SSL
6	Application Server To/From Authentication Storage-Database	AppID Pwd	JDBC/SSL
7	Messaging Bus To/From Mainframe	AppID Pwd	XML/JMS

After we have captured the data interfaces, the next step consists of performing the activity "*DTS 2.3 – Enumerate system-level service*." The goal of this activity is to discover what system types of servers, services, and operating systems are being used in the various tiers of the application architecture such as presentation tier, business logical tier, and database tier. These are tiers that have specific functions. An example of how the various application architectural tiers operate in an online banking application to run a query for bank account activity and present back the process data of account balance that is stored in the database is shown in Figure 8.5.

System-level service enumeration is aimed at identifying what services are running on the various system assets on which much of the application software will be running. Each tier of the application architecture is supported by different types of servers and services specifically:

1. *The presentation tier* is supported by PC clients such as different types of web browsers (Google Chrome, Mozilla Firefox, Microsoft Internet Explorer Safari) and stand-alone user clients-consoles and O.S., (such as Windows,

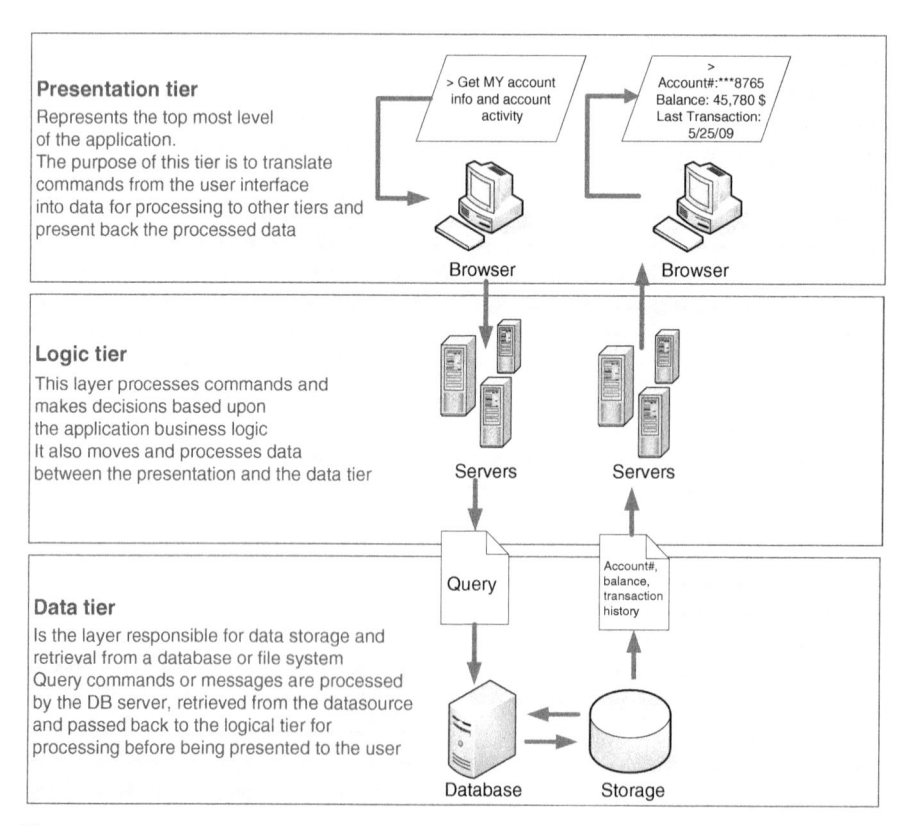

Figure 8.5 Representation of a Bank Account Query Transaction Through the Different Tiers of an Online Banking Application

UNIX, Apple O.S) running on desktops and laptops as well as O.S running on mobile devices (e.g. iPhone IOS, Android).

2. *The business logic tier* is supported by servers such as web servers (e.g. IIS, Apache tomcat) that can deliver web content that can be accessed online and the type of web application servers (e.g. Windows Server, Oracle Java Application Server, IBM WebSphere) that can execute the application business logic and access the various business services and APIs that provide these business services.

3. *The data tier* that is supported by various database and database servers (e.g. SQL Server, Oracle).

Web application architectures include both internal services (e.g. secure file transfers between servers via SFTP Secure File transfer Protocol and managed secure file transfers between mainframes and external services such as web services provided by another business partner that are not hosted in the internal network. The data collected and stored in the application services technology repository including the various types of services deployed with the application architectural components is shown in Figure 8.6.

It is important that each service component is associated with application components as containers of user functionality. An example of associating client site service components with user client presentation tier type of functionality or "widgets" is shown in Figure 8.7.

The next activity is *"DTS 2.4-Enurate Third-Party Infrastructure."* Many application environments use various external networks. Some may be in the form of Cloud-based services such as PaaS, SaaS, or IaaS while others will be along the lines of a more traditional third-party ASP or colocation model. Whatever the service, it is important to bring third-party infrastructures into the technical scope. Generally speaking, it is important to rely on vendor-technical points of contacts to get the necessary information to enumerate the various architectural components. Often times, this information might be considered company proprietary and is not shared with the business partner or client. In this case, it is important to ask the third party to be in scope for a third-party security assessment that will assess the third-party infrastructure components including the security of type of services used by the application. In the case of integration with third-party cloud services, the enumeration of these cloud services can be done using cloud control matrix spreadsheets such as the one documented by the Cloud Security Alliance (CSA) as well as to provide evidence of compliance of industry standards such as SAS 70, SOC, FISMA, PCI DSS, ISO, FIPS-140, ISO/IEC 27001-2005, and others.

After the technology stack of all the application components that are in scope for the application have been enumerated and collected, the next step consists of documenting them in technical documentation. The goal of the activity *"DTS 2.5 – Assert completeness of secure technical design"* is to review the technical design of the application to validate that the details of the application technology stack previously captured/enumerated as well as the security requirements defined in STAGE I are documented in the technical design of the application. The documentation of these

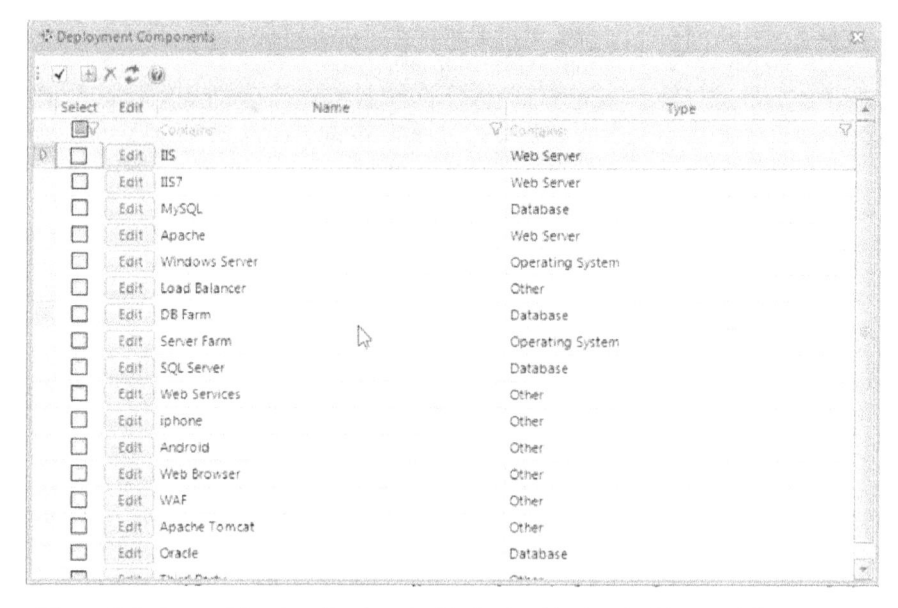

Figure 8.6 Internal Services Deployed with the Application Architectural Components

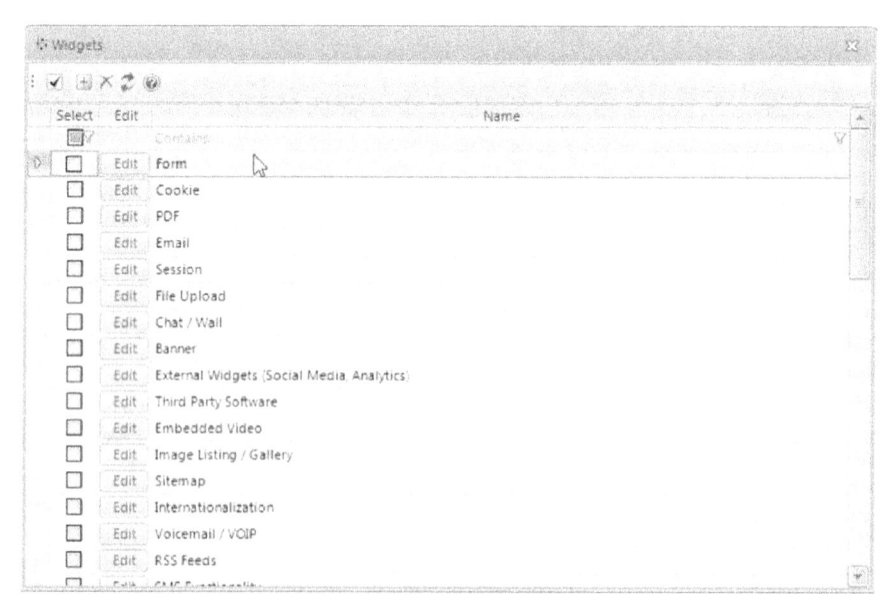

Figure 8.7 ThreatModeler™ Association of Widgets with Client Components

technical details is not only required to make sure that the application in scope will be implemented by following specific functional security requirements but also to make sure that all the technical details that need to be in scope for the application threat modeling exercise are documented and complete.

In the case of the online banking application, for example, the technical details of the application design can be documented in architecture design documents. These architecture design documents should conform to standard document templates and include all the details of the technical stack previously enumerated as well as technical details of the application architecture that can be later reviewed in the weaknesses and vulnerability stage to identify any design flaws in the design of security controls of the application (e.g. authentication, authorization, data protection in storage and transit, session management, data input and output filtering/sanitization, audit and logging, error and exception handling etc).

At high level, the technical design documentation should at a minimum include the following type of technical information:

1. Description of the users of the application and their roles and permissions as it can be documented in a role access control matrix.
2. Description of the application functionality from user perspective (e.g. use cases).
3. The functional security requirement section with description of the design of security controls.
4. Diagram of the logical architecture of the application showing the main architectural components, data interfaces, and communication protocols.
5. The technology stack (type of servers, O.S., software frameworks) from the IT asset repository.
6. The network topology of the application showing the physical location of the various network components including third-party components.

From the perspective of assessing the risk of targeted attacks, at the architectural design level, the documentation should provide enough details of the architecture to determine the level of exposure to external and internal threat agents. For example, all internal and external user and data interfaces to and from the web application in scope need to be properly documented, including the type of data flows (inbound, outbound), the type of authentication of these interfaces (e.g. server to server connections), and the type of protection of the data in transit to/from these interfaces.

For the online banking application, for example, this should include technical design information that shows the type of user interfaces (e.g. web and mobile), the type of servers and protocols and the different trust boundaries of the application architecture. This information can captured and depicted in an architecture design diagram of the online banking application as shown in Figure 8.8. The design documents of the application should include details about the user's roles-permissions, databases where confidential data is stored and the type of

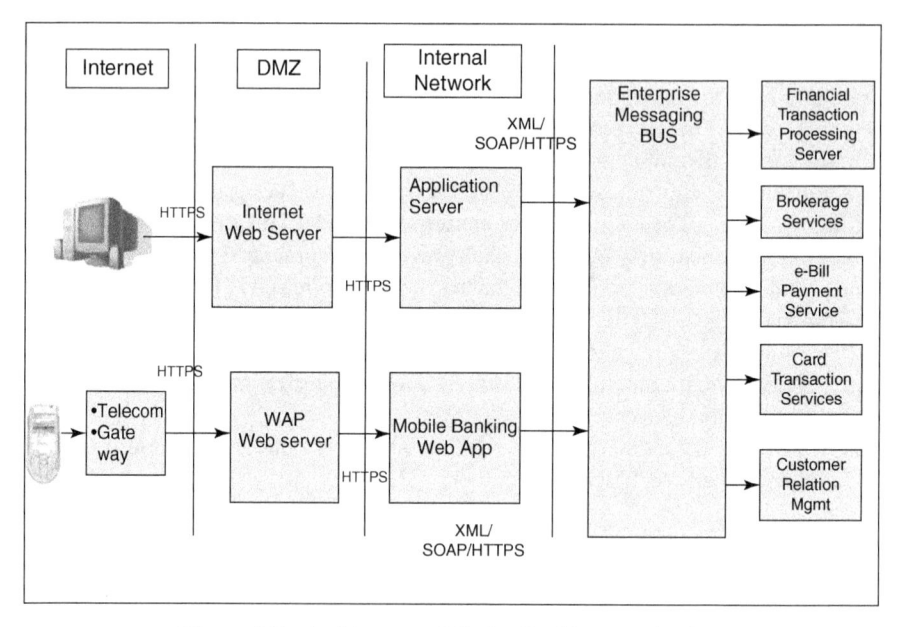

Figure 8.8 Architecture of Online Banking Application

protocols used for transmitting data as well information of the security controls such as user authentication, enforcement of authorizations to access data and functions, type of encryption used in storage and in transit, the type of session management used how is implemented, the type of data filtering APIs used, and the type of audit and logging controls that are implemented to monitor and detect suspicious activities.

At high level, the technical details of what should be documented need to validate that all the data assets at risk are documented including the confidential data and PII data in storage and transit and the security controls to secure access and ensure the confidentiality of such data such as simple and dual authentication factors used. The various types of user functions and user interactions with architectural components can be documented in use cases and sequence diagrams. The technical documentation should provide detail information that described how the various security controls of the application are designed and the security requirements and technology standards used.

After the technical design documentation has been reviewed to assert that the design documentation is complete, a preliminary security review can be conducted to validate compliance of the design with the security requirements that were previously documented in stage I.

A complete architecture design document for the application should include technical details describing how the various security controls should be designed in compliance with technical standards in the case of user authentication, for example, the design should conform to the standard approved design for user authentication and multifactor authentication for online banking applications. The requirement to design multifactor authentication for the online banking application for access of confidential data and for access to high-risk transactions such as payments and transfer of funds is mandated by the previously defined security requirements, *"SR-6: Access to personal identifiable information stored by the application requires the use of multifactor authentication such as security token and PIN"* and *"SR-7: Access to high risk transactions such transfer of funds to an external account requires use of multifactor authentication such as security token and PIN (mandated by OCC-FFIEC)."*

The validation that the design includes a set of design requirements for implementation of multifactor authentication for specific functions can be done by asserting that these requirements are included in the design both at the architectural level and the functional level. The high-level architecture design documentation, for example, should include the technical details of which type of MFA is implemented (e.g. challenge questions, one time passwords/tokens, out of band authentication, certificate-based authentication).

The assertion that the design of the online banking application enforces encryption for data in storage and transit as defined in the security requirements can be done based upon the type of data that is processed and stored by the online banking application. For example, for authentication data, the design of encryption can be reviewed in the design to satisfy the security requirement *SR-1: Passwords should be encrypted using irreversible encryption (e.g. hashes) and using standard algorithms and minimum key lengths* and *SR-8: Authentication data should always be kept encrypted in all systems and environments.*

In the case of credit card data, the design should include specific design requirements for protection of credit card data in storage, transit, and when displayed such as *SR-10: Credit and debit card holder data such as credit/debit card number should be protected by masked (e.g. show only last four digits) on display and protected with either encryption (e.g. hash) or tokenized while in transit and in storage.*

The technical details of the type of controls used for protecting credit card (e.g. masking the card data, rendering the card data unreadable using either encryption or by replacing it with tokens) need to be in scope for the specific functional-technical design. Besides asserting that encryption is implemented by design to protect the confidentiality and integrity of the data, the type of encryption algorithms, key lengths, and their implementation including the protection for encryption keys can also be assessed by the review of the design to make sure that standard encryption algorithms, minimum key lengths, and standard secure key storages are also mandated in the security requirements section of the design documents.

Once the technical scope has been defined and the application security requirements have been asserted to be accurate and complete in the technical documentation of the application architecture and technical specifications, we are ready to conduct the architectural risk analysis and the next stages of the application threat modeling exercise.

Stage III – Application Decomposition and Analysis (ADA)

Goals of This Stage Decomposition of the application in basic components whose security controls and interaction with other components can be analyzed. Examples of components that can be used to describe the security of the application architecture include users, roles, data storages, data flows, functions, security controls, and trust boundaries.

Guidance for Performing This Stage The purpose of the application decomposition is to decompose the application in simple components so that each one can be analyzed for his exposure to threat agents/actors and for specific design flaws and vulnerabilities that these threat agent/actors might seek to exploit. These basic application components consists of the users of the application, their roles, the data assets in storage and transit, the application use cases and the type of functionality that can be assessed by these users, the security controls to protect sensitive data and functions, the analysis of the data flows including entry and the exit points for the data, the trust boundaries to access data and to process the data. Once the application is dissected in the various application components using architecture analysis techniques such as Data Flow Diagrams (DFDs), architectural design reviews, and whiteboard exercises, it will be possible to identify design flaws at component level and later analyze the impact caused by threats exploiting them.

By decomposing the application in architectural components, it is also possible to assert that security requirements for protecting the confidentiality, integrity, and availability of data are enforced by design for each application component. This analysis can be conducted by analyzing the functional design of each component of the application such as the user interfaces and user's functions, the web servers, the application servers, the databases and the backend services as well as the data interfaces, the data flows and the security controls in place to protect the data in transit and in storage in and between components.

Activities This stage consists of the execution of the following activities:

ADA 3.1 – Enumerate all application use cases (e.g. login, account update, delete users, etc) that describe an application business function and how the user interacts with the application to accomplish a specific functionality that the application provides. The use cases can be derived based upon the capture of the business requirements defined in stage I and users and roles of the application defined in stage II. The description/enumeration of the use cases need to include a description of the criticality of the business function being performed that includes the possible impact to the business caused by the impact of possible loss of accountability, availability, confidentiality, integrity of the data and the resulting impact such as economic loss resulting from loss of data including unlawful noncompliance, data privacy violations, and reputational damage.

ADA 3.2 – Document Data Flow Diagrams (DFDs) of the identified architectural components. By creating a high-level DFD of the application, it will be possible to visualize the information flow end to end (ingress/ egress traffic at all layers of the application) and to describe how the data interacts end to end, from the external entities (client, user) to the data store through the processing elements of the application (components, servers). Depending on the detail used (e.g. DFD level 1 or DFD level 2), DFD can be used to describe data flow interactions among architectural components and among different functions of the application functionality. The goal of using high level 1 or 2 DFDs that allow to analyzing architectural level data flows by visually describing how actors (e.g. either users or processes) previously identified interact with the various architectural components enumerated in stage II at different tiers of the application architecture (e.g. presentation tier, business tier and data tier). These components and tiers can be represented within different trust boundaries (e.g. client trust, DMZ trust and internal trust zone), and the various server components that have been enumerated in stage II can be located within these trust boundaries. Example includes locating the external users and client in the external nontrusted zone, web server in the DMZ and application servers, middleware servers and backend servers/databases in the internal trust boundary zone.

ADA 3.3 – Security functional analysis and the use of trust boundaries. The goal of this activity is to analyze the security of the use cases previously identified and how the various data assets identified as components in the DFD are protected by the security controls from functional perspective. The goal is to decompose functionality of the application/system in users, data processed, and security controls that protect that data. Functionality is per se an asset as data that can be protected based upon the risk of the functionality/transaction. This activity is also referred as secure transactional analysis and consists of the analysis of application functions to assert the presence of security controls that protect the confidentiality, integrity, availability, and accountability of these functions. Examples of controls that protect functionality are authentication and authorization, encryption, input and output validation, session management, and audit and logging. At functional level, each one of the application asset and new functionality exposed by the application to a user need to be analyzed from the security perspective to determine whether protective and detective security controls are included in the design of the application. If a gap in a security control is identified, this will constitute a security finding and should be reported and considered for potential exposure. The remediation of this finding needs to consider the effectiveness of the control to mitigate threats and the additional countermeasures that should be put in place to reduce the risk-impact of such threat.

It is important to note that threat agents can exploit different type of vulnerabilities and weaknesses in the application. Examples of vulnerabilities include what constitute either a design flaw or vulnerability in the implementation and/or configuration of the application. Some of the threat agents might also abuse the business logic of which the application is built upon to cause a negative impact. From a threat analysis and modeling perspective, a possible way to identify business logic flaws is to analyze all uses and abused of the application functionality using use and abuse cases.

Input for Conducting This Stage This includes different types of documentation such as

1. Business and security requirements (stage I)
2. Technical scope (stage II)
3. Technology stack (stage II)
4. Secure technical design details (stage III)
5. Architectural design documents and diagrams
6. Functional and technical specifications
7. Data interfaces
8. Users and user interfaces
9. Internal and external infrastructure components

Artifacts Produced at the End of This Stage At the end of this stage, we will produce the following artifacts: decomposition of application architecture and analysis of the data flows processed by each architectural component and of the security controls that protect each component. Specifically, the following information should be analyzed as part of the decomposition analysis of the application.

(a) *Use cases* (login, account updates, delete users, etc.) *interfaces* including the use cases, users roles-permissions (documented use cases and access control matrix)
(b) *Data interfaces and services* system level/process application to application and server to server including hosted by third parties in the cloud (e.g. SaaS, PaaS, and IaaS)
(c) *Decomposition and analysis of the application architecture* including architectural components (documented end-to-end data flows in DFDs, sequence diagrams, and top-down architecture level)
(d) *Functional security control transaction analysis* includes the identification of use cases, functions/transactions, and security controls to protect data and functions

Tools The execution of this stage can be facilitated by the use of visualization tools such as MS Visio that are also incorporated in threat modeling tool from Microsoft SDL Threat Modeling Tool™. Functional asset decomposition is a feature of MyAppSecurity Inc ThreatModeler™ Tool and is used herein as well as the ThreatModeler™ Architectural Analysis features.

Web Application Use Case Example The first activity of this stage consists of the activity *ADA 3.1 – Enumerate all application use cases*. The main goal of this activity is to enumerate the use cases. From the perspective of software and system engineering, use case describes a list of steps and specifically interactions between a user of the application that is defined also as actor and the application to achieve a desired goal. From the perspective of the application threat modeling exercise, a use case describes a business process flow that shows from the architectural stand point how a user interact with the application to perform a business function. These business functions were previously documented at high level as business requirements and should be either documented or captured at more detail level for the review during this stage. If these use cases are part of the design documentation such as UML, use cases can be easily enumerated and analyzed at this stage also by comparing with the business requirements defined in stage I and users and roles of the application defined in stage II.

The use cases that are enumerated in this stage need to describe an application business function and how the user interacts with the application function to accomplish a specific functionality that the application provides. These business functions might have different type of risk depending on how business critical is the process that this use case action allows to perform since might be targeted by a threat agent and cause a possible negative impact to the business such as loss of accountability, availability, confidentiality, integrity, of the function and the data.

In threat modeling, use cases can be represented as user interaction with the various architectural and functional processes provided by application. In the case of the online banking application, the use cases represent actions that are performed by the user to conduct business transactions with the online bank application in scope such as log-on into the online banking site to view the bank account statement and the transactions conduct money transfers and make payments. The visualization of use cases that can be entered using a palette of a tool such as ThreatModeler™ it is shown in Figure 8.9.

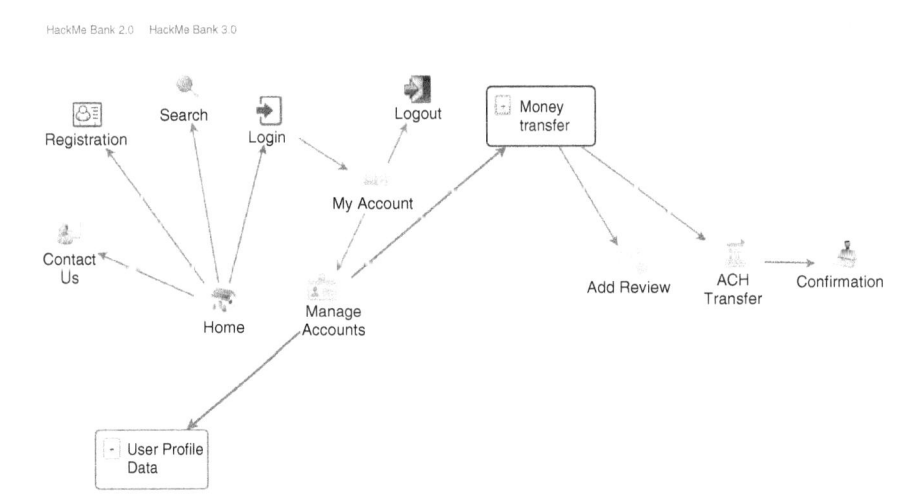

Figure 8.9 Component-Based Functional Use Cases of Online Web Application

Using the ThreatModeler™ tool palette, it is possible to enter each use case using the tool graphical palette to associate users with each component of the application with a functional component. Each functional component is associated with data that is processed by the component as well as with data that is either stored or processed by other functional components.

Similar to architectural level components where the data interactions with components can be expressed in terms of either the user or the data interface and the type of protocol in between as documented in the data interfaces at stage II, the functional interactions among components can also be expressed as interactions of data through communication protocols that are highlighted as arrows between components. In ThreatModeler™ functional components are also associated with the sensitivity of the data that these functional component process either for storage or for transit and this help to assert functional security requirements and security testing requirements for each of these functional components.

Each functional component can also be associated with the data elements such as user and roles with permissions to access or use the component and elements of functionality called widgets that represent how the component interacts with other components to support that functionality (e.g. login interact with the authentication data repository to validate passwords). In ThreatModeler™, each functional component can also be associated with the technology stack and the specific network components such as server components where the functionality of the functional component is installed and deployed.

The decomposition of functional components associated with data processed to and from the component and the associated functionality as defined in the business requirements lays down the foundation of the analysis of threats against data assets and functionality for each component and the evaluation of the exposure to the threat by considering the security measures implemented to protect the data and functionality associated with each component.

After we have captured the use cases, the next step consists of performing the activity *ADA 3.2 – Document Data Flow Diagrams (DFDs)*. The goal of this activity is to visualize the information flow end to end (ingress/egress traffic at all layers of the application) and to describe how the data interacts end to end, from the external entities (client, user) to the data store through the processing elements of the application (components, servers). DFD seek to visualize the following elements of the web application architecture:

1. External entities (users, web browser, e-mail-client, external site/system)
2. Processes (Servers: Web, Application, DB server, functions: input validation, authentication, authorization, session management, encryption)
3. Data flows (inbound/outbound function calls, call types, type of data and protocol)
4. Data stores (file, database, any data at rest)
5. Trust levels and trust boundaries

PASTA USE CASE EXAMPLE WALK-THROUGH 521

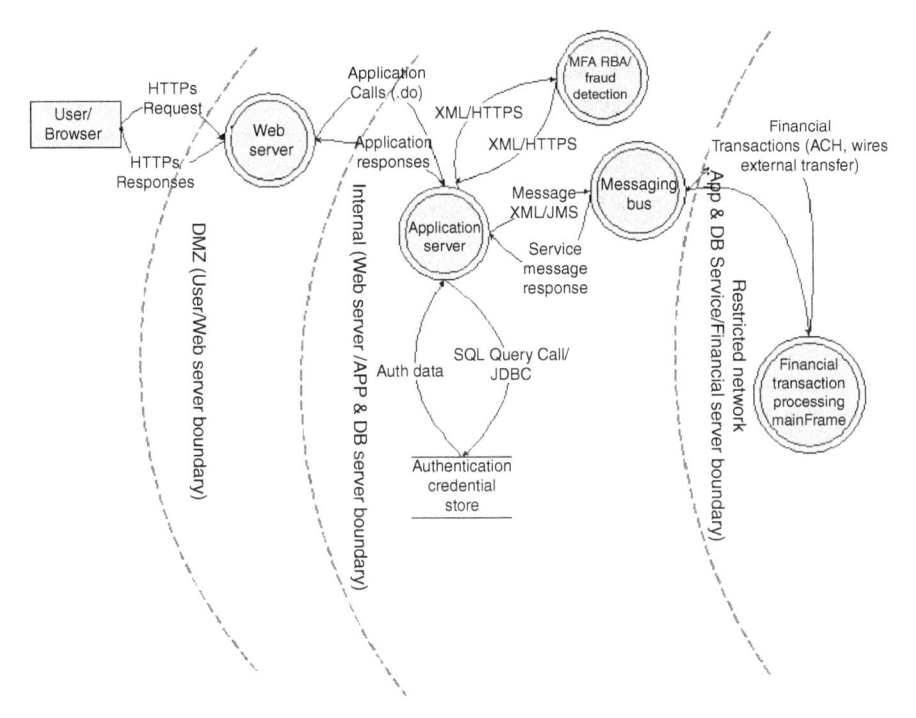

Figure 8.10 Data Flow Diagram for Online Banking Application

The analysis of the application data flows using DFD helps in the identification of the entry and the exit data points at the various trust boundaries and the access levels (anonymous, user authenticated, administrator, super-user) required to access the different architectural components (data, services) within these trust boundaries.

An example of high-level DFD for the online banking application is shown in Figure 8.10.

The DFD in Figure 8.10 can be created using a graphical tool such as MS Visio. The diagram shows the basic data processing components of the architecture of the online banking application that includes the client (e.g. user browser), the web server, the application server, the messaging bus to access the back end services for financial processing as well as web service components providing specific functionality for Risk Based Authentication/MultiFactor Authentication and Fraud Detection. The data storages and the data flows depicting the type of data stored (user authentication data) as well as the data in transit through the various communication channels and protocols between components are also shown. The DFD also shows the various trust boundaries that are crossed by the data to access each of the components: the De-Militarized Zone, the Internal Only Accessed Network, Trust Zone, and the Restricted Only Accessed Network/Trust Zone.

Once the data components have been decomposed in a DFD diagram, it is possible to assert the presence of security controls for protecting the data such as encryption in storage and in transit for confidential and authentication data accessed through these components as well as the presence of other controls such as authentication and authorization, input and output data validation, auditing and logging, and session management. By analyzing the flow of data, it is also possible to identify data entry and exit points to assert input validation and when the data crosses the trust boundaries to assert that access controls are enforced for data to cross that trust boundary.

The next activity to be performed at this stage is *ADA 3.3 – Security functional analysis and the use of trust boundaries*. The goal of this activity is to analyze the security of the use cases from the functional perspective by looking at the enforcement of the security controls such as authentication, authorization, input validation, and data protection in storage and transit for each user action and each type of data crossing the trust boundaries at the entry and exit points of the DFDs.

The visualization of the data flows with DFD allows a threat analysis to look at the data being processed for specific users and use cases from both defensive and offensive perspective to identify if the data coming from a specific user role with specific permissions can be trusted before being processed by processes that reside within trust boundary. A use case of authentication for defensive perspective, for example, needs to enforce protection of the confidentiality, availability, integrity of the authentication data in transit from the user client to the credential storage where the data is stored. From the defensive perspective, for example, each user data input needs to be validated before it can be processed by the application server and the authentication data need to be encrypted in storage at the database credential storage. From the attacker perspective, a threat agent can try different types of attacks against the authentication data flow by trying to spoof and tamper the authentication data in transit as well as by repudiate the authentication source by trying to authenticate from untrusted client. This analysis drives the consideration of security controls such as encrypting the authentication token in transit and in storage with digital hash signing the authentication tokens with digital signatures to provide nonrepudiation. At the entry point before the authentication token is issued after positive authentication, the user provided credentials such as userID and password are validated for malicious input such as SQL injection commands and XSS attack vectors. These validations are enforced within the web server trust boundary and within the applications server internal trust boundary. In essence, the visualization of the data flows with DFD helps to identify how likely attack vectors can impact the data from the entry points by exploiting weaknesses (vulnerabilities) of security controls such as authorization, authentication, and secure communication channels across the different layers of the architecture. These are security controls that need to be identified and included in the application decomposition along with their interaction with the various data and functional assets to assert that they can protect the data assets that are considered sensitive such as authentication and sensitive data as well as the business functionality at risk.

Trust boundaries can also be identified at the level of a process running on the specific component. For example, assuming that a user registers to create an online account to authenticate through Single Sign On (SSO) to the online banking

PASTA USE CASE EXAMPLE WALK-THROUGH 523

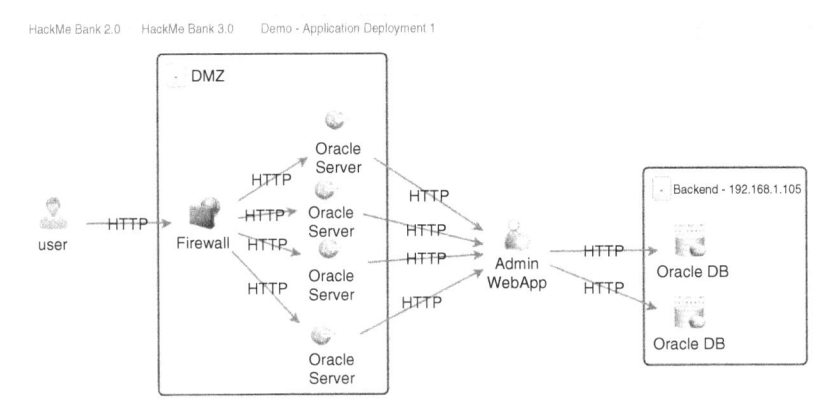

Figure 8.11 Functional Component Trust Boundaries Using ThreatModeler™

application, the user will be under the trust boundary of the registration process. When the user logs into and authenticate to the online banking application, he/she will be in the trust boundary of the web application and the external processes such as browser processes running on his/her desktop/PC. When the authenticated user selects a high-risk business critical transaction such as an ACH (Automated Clearing House) payment, the payment will execute in the trust boundary of that process.

Such visualization of trust boundaries for the user case of user registration, login to manage accounts and make a payment and logout from the online bank application is provided in Figure 8.11. When a user registers to create an account to authenticate through SSO to the web application is under the trust boundary of the registration process. When the user logs into and authenticate, he/she will be in the trust boundary of the web application and the external processes such as browser processes running on his desktop/PC. When the user selects a high-risk business critical transaction such as an ACH (Automated Clearing House) payment, the payment will execute in the trust boundary of that process.

By visualizing the trust boundaries at process/functional level, it is possible to assert the presence of security controls at that level of functionality such as for security controls that protect the confidentiality, integrity, availability, and accountability of the processes that support these functions and specifically high-risk functions such as money payments. Examples of controls that protect functionality are authentication and authorization, encryption, input and output validation, session management, and audit and logging.

The analysis of the application business functions and specifically business critical functions that can be targeted by fraudsters such as transfer of money to external entities, bill payments as well as the process for registration of new accounts, login authentication, and recovery of lost passwords and accounts can also be in scope for specific security functional analysis at the level of each business critical transaction. This activity consists of analyzing each of the business application functions at transactional level to identify the security controls that are in place for validating the data before it is processed by the application, the enforcement of access controls such as authentication and authorization to access the function as well as session management controls, data encryption, error handling, and logging and auditing.

An example of transaction analysis for online banking application is provided in Table 8.5.

In the first row of the matrix herein included, we have listed a number of user functions that are implemented in the online banking application such as password reset, user ID recovery, account registration, log-on, fund transfers (e.g. wires), and payment functions (e.g. bill pay). For each transaction, we have assigned an inherent risk of the transaction that considers both technical and business impact, the classification of the data that is processed by each function/transaction, the type of data that need to be validated before processing and the various types of security controls that are implemented.

This type of analysis allows to assert the security requirements for the implementation of security controls in each transaction of the application, for example, a password recovery has a high inherent risk because of the possible impact on the confidentiality, integrity, and availability of the application in case passwords are compromised. The password recovery function is available to known registered users and requires a validation of the user debit card number, the debit card PIN, and the bank account number in order to be reset. A wire transfer is considered a critical risk transaction since it allows moving money to another bank account in another financial institution and therefore might have a high business impact if this transaction gets compromised. Because of the critical inherent risk of this transaction, strong authentication such as multifactor authentication is required and the function is only available to authenticated users.

Once the user is authenticated the session is managed by the server Role Base Access Controls (RBAC) and the user need to authorize the transaction by acknowledging the amount and the transaction through an Out Of Band (OOB) channel such as SMS message over the mobile phone. The confidential data in transit such as the bank account data to send the money to and the transfer amount can only be sent over encrypted channel. As detection security controls besides the standard audit and logging of security events, money transfers also require the logging of suspicious events that can be correlated with fraudulent transactions.

At functional level, each one of these critical business functions that can potentially be exposed to external threat agents will be later analyzed in stage V Weaknesses and Vulnerability analysis to identify possible design flaws and will be considered a vulnerability-security finding and reported as such and considered for the potential impact. During this stage, the goal is to architectural and functional level decomposition of the application in security controls and assets that include data, data flows, and application functions.

Stage IV – Threat Analysis (TA).

Goals of This Stage The goals of this stage are the analysis of the threat scenarios based on the various sources of internal and external threat intelligence and the

TABLE 8.5 Security Function Transactional Analysis

Application Function	Inherent Risk	Data Classification	User Role	Input Validation and Data validated	User Authentication	User Authorization	Data Encryption	Audit and Logging
Registration	LOW	Confidential and Confidential-PII	Site visitor	ESAPI, card data, PII, demographics	None	None	HTTPS	Server and App. Logs
Login	HIGH	Authentication data	Authenticated user	ESAPI, userID, password, MFA	Simple and multi factor	Server-side RBAC	HTTPS (transit) SHA1-256 (storage)	Server and App. Logs. Security Event Logs
Password recovery	HIGH	Authentication and Confidential-PII	Known registered user	ESAPI, debit card No, PIN, Bank account	Debit card PIN and card No.	Server-side RBAC	HTTPS (transit) SHA1-256 (storage)	Server and App. Logs, Security Event Logs
Access account balance	MEDIUM	Confidential	Authenticated user	ESAPI, Bank account	Simple	Server-side RBAC	HTTPS	Server and App. Logs
Bill payments	HIGH	Confidential	Authenticated user	Payee account, payment amount	Simple and multi factor	Server-side RBAC	HTTPS	Server and App. Logs, Security Event Logs
Fund transfer/wires	CRITICAL	Authentication and Confidential	Authenticated user	ESAPI, bank account data, transfer amount	Multi Factor Only	Server-side RBAC, Out Of Band Auth.	HTTPS	Server and App. Logs. Fraud Event Logs

analysis of the threat agents that within this threat scenario are known to target application security controls weaknesses, flaws in design, and vulnerabilities. Based on the analysis of the threat agents and of the specific characteristics of the threat agents and threat targets, it will be possible to update the threat library and use the information of the threat library for the architectural design reviews and for estimating the risk of the potential impact of these threats based upon the knowledge of known weaknesses and vulnerabilities that these threat agents seek to target. Based on the information of threat intelligence and the analysis of the threat events, it will be also possible to provide an estimate of the probability of these threats to target the application data assets and application functionality in scope.

Guidance for Performing This Stage The objective of the Threat Analysis (TA) stage of PASTA(TM) is to conduct the threat analysis in the context of the application/product in scope. The goal of this threat analysis is to analyze the type of cyber-threat agents such as these being human (e.g. script kiddies, hacktivists, cyber-criminals, fraudsters, cyber-spies) and nonhuman (e.g. malware). These threat agents might intentionally or opportunistically target the application in scope. Initially it is important to capture the threat environment that depends on the business and technical environment in which the application operates. This initial analysis is necessary to characterize the threat landscape.

Every threat environment can be characterized by specific threat agent factors and events. The categorization of the threat agents might include threats that are either human or automated, their capabilities such as the type of skills, the attack techniques and tools at their disposal, their motivations (political, monetary, espionage), their opportunities such as the type of targets that can be explored and attacked and the application vulnerabilities that can be discovered and exploited.

The characterization of the threat landscape largely depends on the information at the disposal of the threat analyst such as threat reports and threat information gathered from different sources of threat intelligence such as the Information Sharing and Analysis Centers (ISACs) and sources of security incidents caused by cyber-attacks such as Web Hacking Incident Database (WHID). The purpose of the analysis of threat intelligence is to determine the level of severity of the threats targeting the application assets (data and functionality) in scope and the threat environment and decide the course of action such as issuing alerts and advisories for customers and clients, monitor specific events for detect incoming attacks and be prepared to respond (e.g. reduce the attack surface, monitor critical functions and set limits on functionality, including blocking access as last resort) in case the application will be attacked.

From the security incident response perspective, the monitoring of specific cyber threats events might rely on the logging of specific suspicious events such as abnormal access control violations and triggers (e.g. velocity checks on application functions, web page errors, etc.). For the correlation of these events, the threat analyst might utilize kill-chain techniques (e.g. chain of events) to determine if these events might indicate the potential course of action of a possible attack.

From the application threat modeling perspective, the analysis of threats and threat events is instrumental to the implementation of a threat analysis engine that correlates threat events with targets and security incidents as well as repository of threat information such as threat knowledge base of threat information and attack libraries that can be used to determine the probability of threat events, extraction of threat parameters and correlation of attack vectors with security controls and vulnerabilities that are affected by these attack vectors. The assignment of a probability value to each threat of the threat library can be based on the analysis and assignment of factors of threat probability such as threat agent capabilities (e.g. level of skills required to perform the attack), motive (e.g. level of possible gain/reward) and opportunity (e.g. the level of sophistication of the resources required to conduct the attack) and of threat events associated with the threat agent (e.g. refer to Structured Threat Information Expression (STIX) for threat actor correlation with threat techniques and procedures and correlation with threat observables and threat indicators and security incidents, course of actions and exploit targets.

Standards methods for scoring the severity of threats might be inherent of the threat agent risk factors to determine probability of threats such as the ones used in the OWASP Risk Rating Methodology and (MOSP) Motive, Opportunity, Skill Required, Population Size, and the risk of threat agents to be capable of exploiting vulnerabilities and produce an impact such as in the case of threat (DREAD) risk rating that stands for Damage Potential, Reproducibility, Exploitability, Affected Users, Discoverability. These factors can be assigned score levels and averaged to determine the overall threat agent likelihood factor (OWASP-MOSP) and threat risk severity (MS-DREAD) (Note in the case of MS-DREAD threats are classified as technical threats using STRIDE Spoofing, Tampering, Repudiation, Information Disclosure, Denial of Service, and Elevation of Privileges).

Once the threat library is updated with new threats, the level of risk as probability and impact for each threat should be estimated. One possible estimation of the relevance of each threat is to enumerate each of these threats to the application security controls to determine whether these controls are present to either reduce or increase the level of risk of the threat. The level of risk of the threat can be calculated as factor of probability of the threat to be realized in an attack as well as the technical and business impact of that threat.

Inputs for conducting this stage include the following:

1. Stage I risk profile
2. Stage II technical scope
3. Stage III assets and security controls
4. Threat intelligence reports and advisories
5. Security incidents and events from internal sources (SIRT, SIEM, WAF, NIDS)

Prerequisites for This Stage To conduct this stage, the following inputs are required.

Artifacts Produced at the End of This Stage At the end of this stage, we will produce the following artifacts:

1. *Threat scenarios for the application/systems in scope* based on the analysis of external cyber-threat advisories (e.g. threat severity level from threat advisory to know how close these threats are to be realized in attacks) as well as internal events such as security incidents that can be correlated with these threats.
2. *Updated threat library* that includes information of each of the threats that are part of the threat scenarios each characterized by threat agent factors (use normalized threat characterization) based upon the information learned from threat intelligence.
3. *Enumeration of threats to application data assets and components:* These are the components in scope for the risk analysis (use DTS for data assets and function asset in scope) that have been decomposed in stage III.
4. *Assignment of the initial risk severity of the threat* as this is the probability and impact for these specific threats targeting application security controls and application components (using threat agent probability factors of skill level, motivation, opportunity). (NOTE Possible threat probability assignment methods are OWASP and DREAD (but considered too subjective) to assign risk to each threat).

Tools The execution of this stage can be facilitated by the use of and standardized by relying on formal methods for the threat analysis such as:

(a) Sources of Open Source Threat intelligence (OSINT) such as threat alerts from various security vendors.
(b) Threat classification methods for categorizing threats (e.g. STRIDE, OWASP, MITRE-STIX, Events-Incidents, Agents, Motives, Damage Potentials, Tools, Exploits, Impacts (application-users).
(c) Risk control frameworks that map threats to assets and controls such as Microsoft STRIDE and Web Application Security Frame.
(d) Threat risk severity calculation formulas from OWASP, FFIEC, and Microsoft (i.e. DREAD) to calculate severity for each threat agent-source by considering the probability of the event.
(e) Threat libraries such as WASC WHID attack library and threat management dashboard integrated in threat modeling tools such as myAppSecurity Inc ThreatModeler™ tool.

Activities This stage consists of the following activities:

T4 4.1 – Analyze the overall threat scenario: Based on correlation of threat agents, events, campaigns, observables, indicators of compromises, techniques, tactics and strategies, and the targets. A visualization of the threat landscape with the correlated threat information with graphics and diagrams allows the threat analyst to analyze the various sources of threat agents with indication of these threats being realized in attacks and correlated with possible security incidents occurring to the web application.

TA 4.2 – *Gather threat information from internal threat sources*: Examples of sources of threat intelligence might be collected as event triggers from different systems at network, system, and application layer. A security event might be considered a suspicious activity that can be monitored and detected. Examples of suspicious activities include repetitive failure of logging into an account as indication of brute force attacks against passwords, logging of traffic from suspicious domain or IP, detecting SQL injection attack vectors using a WAF as indication of a vulnerability scanning and so on. The association of internally logged information with a threat requires aggregation of events from different internal sources (e.g. firewalls, IDS/IPS, servers, network management routers and switches, and vulnerability scan engines), permanent events storage in a database and analysis using threat management systems and log aggregators and security management consoles with analytics and filtering of these events as possible threat event alerts that can be actioned for security incident response as well as for issuing internal threat alerts.

TA 4.3 – *Gather threat information from external threat sources:* Examples of sources of external threat intelligence are external vendors, law enforcement, secret services, (CERT) Computer Emergency Response Teams, and ISACs Information Security Assurance Centers. The type of cyber-threat intelligence information might include OSINT Open Source Intelligence such as publicly released advisories from response centers such as CERT as well as confidential and proprietary sources of threat intelligence. Prior to gather the threat intelligence is important to have established a protocol for threat information sharing and dissemination among parties and a standard to categorize the threat information. Examples of categorization of the threats including the identification of the threat agents (e.g. human, automated), their skills, the group capabilities, motivations, opportunities, the type of targets such as the vulnerabilities exploited and the threat severity as a factor of information of the threat targeting specific industry sectors or even specific assets within that industry sector/vertical using specific type of tools, techniques, and processes (e.g. account takeover with malware, DDoS). This activity includes the threat source/report data collection from source of threat intelligence and aggregation and categorization of threats. Standard threat dissemination protocols such as TAXII and standard threat representation such as STIX can be used for sharing information about threat events that are observable and the type of indication of compromise events of these observables.

TA 4.4 – *Update the threat libraries:* Update the threat libraries for emerging threats whose characteristics are aggregated from the sources of threat. These threat libraries should include information that is actionable for threat-risk mitigation such as the type of threat agents/actors, the threat campaigns, the threat capabilities and tools used by the threat targets such as the company assets (e.g. data and functions), the course of actions, the incidents, and the security incidents observed including the security controls and measures impacted and the vulnerabilities/gaps that are exploited in attacks/incidents known to be attributed to these threat agents

TA 4.5 – Threat agents to assets mapping: Once threats have been visualized, they can be correlated with the application assets such as data and functionality as well as potential vulnerabilities of security controls that protect these assets and might expose these assets to the threats. The correlations of threats to assets support an initial analysis of the risks as factor of likelihood and impact of attacks being realized for these threats.

TA 4.6 – Assignment of the probabilistic values for identified threats: As this is the probability and impact for specific threats previously analyzed to target valued assets of the organization such as confidential and sensitive data stored and processed by an application system as well as business critical operations/functions of that organization/system. Threat probability can be associated with a threat agent probability as a factor of the threat agent skill level, motivation, and opportunity such as availability of cyber-crime tools, knowledge of attacks tools and techniques, use of known processes and procedures for successfully conducting attacks, attack strategies and organization in cyber threat groups (e.g. cyber-criminal groups, hacktivist group etc). At higher level, the probabilistic severity of a threat can be rated as how close is the threat to attack an asset and produce an impact. Attack kill-chain can be used to determine the threat probability such as how far the threat agent is in the execution of the attacks against a target starting from intention and survey initial discovery of the target, research of the target, reconnaissance, exploit of vulnerabilities to conduct the attacks and operation execution and control of the attack against the target. Note: the impact of the threats analyzed during this stage can be considered as unmitigated till a further validation of the presence of design flaws and vulnerabilities (stage V) in these controls as well as possible exploits of these controls by specific attack vectors identified during the attack modeling and simulation stage (stage VI).

Web Application Use Case Example The first activity of the threat analysis stage consists of "*TA 4.1 – Analyze the overall threat scenario.*" In the case of the online banking application in scope, there are several types of threat scenario.

A threat scenario for an online banking application includes the various types of threats such as malware and hacking threats seeking to compromise confidential customer information and to commit fraudulent financial transactions, Distributed Denial-of-Service DDoS threats seeking to flood the website with requests rendering it unserviceable for customers, threats of compromise of confidential data such as PII, bank account data, and credit card data of customers.

Prior to conducting a specific analysis of the various cyber-threat scenarios that are relevant to the online bank application, threats need to be prioritized for the threat analysis. This prioritization might depend on different factors such as publicly available data of data breaches attributed and internal events such as security incidents that can attributed to specific threat actors and threat vectors used by these threat actors.

For example, if we consider the survey of data breach incidents from the 2013 Verizon data breach report, the top threat actions of malware include attack vectors that seek to capture data from user activity using key loggers, form-grabbers, and spyware involving sending data to external site and the installation of a backdoor to allow remote access control. The top hacking threat vectors include exploitation of guessable credentials, backdoors and command and control channels, brute force attacks, and use of stolen login credentials. Within the hacking threat, the most used attack vector used against large organizations are web applications, followed by the installation of backdoors or control channel and remote access by compromise of desktops. Based on the data of this survey, among the various sources of threat agents, external threat agents motivated by financial gain represent the largest threat accounting for 87% of attacks followed by only 5% of internal threat agents, 3% of partners, and another 5% as unknown.

Based on this information, external threat agents motivated by financial gain using malware and hacking techniques to target web applications represent a top priority threat scenario to be considered in the threat analysis. This is based on security incident data breach driven survey approach. In reality, internal threat agents cannot be neglected in the analysis as this might impact the financial organization with the largest impacts. Examples of internal threats against online banking applications include internal threat sources such as disgruntled employees and malware uploaded on internal servers for exfiltration of data from the inside network such as backdoors and sniffers.

Another driver to prioritize the type of threat scenarios is information from threat intelligence of specific threats targeting specific targets such as online banking applications for reputational damage and for cause disruptions of service to customers such as in the case of Distributed Denial-of-Service (DDoS) attacks. Since these types of attacks are politically motivated, they seek to gain attention from public. One method used is to announce the plan to conduct the attacks on social media sites.

An example of gathering of threat intelligence from public sources such as searches of attacks from threat agents is shown in Figure 8.12.

The diagram in Figure 8.12, for example, shows all the recorded events in the public media of the announced campaign of Distributed Denial-of-Service attacks by the Izz ad-Din al-Qassam Cyber Fighters AQCF threat agent group. For most of the financial organizations today, being either large or medium, the threat of DDoS attacks targeting the online banking sites cannot be neglected and need to be prioritized in the analysis of the threat scenarios.

The information of announced attacks of specific threats such as DDoS but also account takeover malware and other threats can be the driver for a more in-depth analysis of these threat scenarios to understand the various steps of the attacks, the types of tools, techniques, and processes used by the threat agents and the type of weaknesses and vulnerabilities that are exploited. This analysis allows to identify

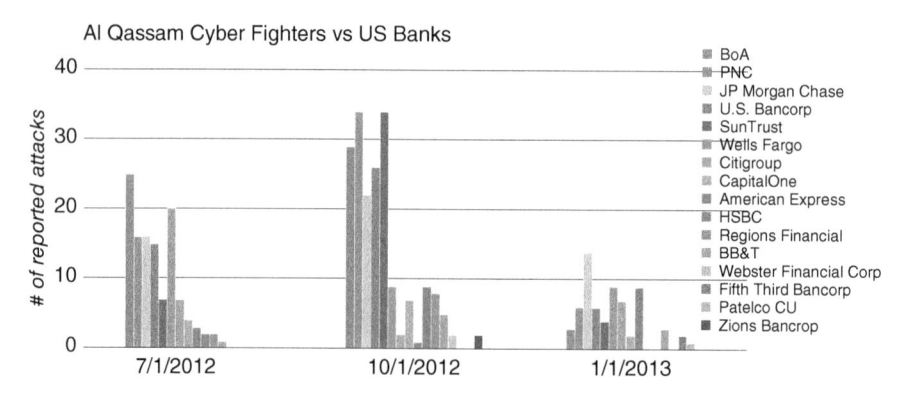

Figure 8.12 Campaign of DDoS Attacks Against Banking Sites Announced by AQCF Threat Agent Group

the effectiveness of current security measures and security controls and to propose improvements to better respond and reduce the impact of these attacks.

In order to analyze the overall threat scenario for the online bank application in scope, it is important to adopt a standard characterization of each type of threats. External threat agents, for example, can be classified as human and nonhuman attacking applications from outside the network perimeter. Depending on the type of external threat agents and the tools at their disposal, different type of malware and hacking techniques could be used. These techniques might not be very sophisticated such as in the case of exploit of server misconfigurations and exploit of vulnerabilities that can be easily identified with the use of free vulnerability scanning tools. These types of threats are also defined as opportunistic. Examples of opportunistic threats consist of threat agents seeking to exploit application vulnerabilities such as weak input validation, weak authentication and authorization, weak session management, gap and weaknesses in the protection of data in storage and transit such as encryption and gaps in auditing and logging of specific events to detect attacks as well as weaknesses in protection of the logs so that attackers can clean up their tracks.

Different from targeted threats, targeted threats might not exploit weaknesses in web applications but seek to compromise the client of the application by installing malware that is designed to attack the application and is designed to specifically bypass applications controls that are typically considered strong such as multifactor authentication and compromise servers by bypassing network layer defenses such as firewalls and intrusion detection systems. Examples of targeted threats against online banking applications include account takeover that consists of compromising the customer banking account by staging an attack that starts by compromising the customer's host computer by social engineering the victim to select malicious links that point to malware. This malware is often banking malware that when executes on the compromised host will hijack the authenticated session and take over the online banking transactions and later respond to a command and control center instructions under the control of the threat agent.

PASTA USE CASE EXAMPLE WALK-THROUGH 533

The analysis of the course of action of these threats is critical to determine which countermeasures might be deployed to proactively detect and protect from these threats. This is the value that threat analysis provides in terms of proactive risk management of these threats before the application will become a target by these threat agents.

From the perspective of proactively mitigating the risk of threats exploiting known vulnerabilities in web applications, today the focus is mainly around vulnerability assessments that identify and fix any vulnerability that can be exploited by the threat agents hence reducing the opportunity for the attacks to exploit them to conduct his attacks. This approach might be sufficient to mitigate the risk of threats opportunistically exploiting known vulnerabilities and weaknesses but might not be enough in the case of advanced and targeted threats including malware hacking and DDoS. For these types of threats, a focused threat analysis and attack modeling is required to identify additional security measures that can be designed and implemented in the web application as well as outside the web application. Such comprehensive analysis of malware banking and DDoS threats need to focus on the understanding of the characteristics of the threat agents and the attack techniques, tools, and strategies used.

To accurately capture the overall threat scenarios, it is important that we adopt a standard categorization for the types of threat agents (e.g. human, automated) and we define them according to their capabilities, motivations, opportunities, the type of vulnerabilities exploited, targets, and cyber-threat severity of incidents being reported. Threat categorization is also useful to create a schema for aggregate threat information that can be later analyzed to determine the threat targets and the type of weaknesses and vulnerabilities that these threats seek to exploit.

In order for the threat intelligence information to be useful for the threat analysis, it is important to categorize the threat sources with specific parameters so that these can be correlated to conduct specific analysis. The more detailed the categorization of the threats the more comprehensive and focused the threat analysis can be.

At high level, threats can be characterized based on the type of threat agents, the threat agent capabilities and motivations, the threat events such as security incidents associated with these threat agents, the threat agent capabilities, the various types of techniques and tools used and the threat targets specifically any type of value assets such as customer sensitive data and money-valued functionality that might also put the online banking application under possible threat of attacks from these threat agents. An example of categorization of threat agents and the type of overall threat scenarios and how they might affect web applications and IT systems of financial institutions is included in Table 8.6.

At high level, the analysis of the overall threat scenario consists of looking at the overall picture of the various types of threats. Based on this high-level view of threats and the correlation of the various parameters that characterize the threats, it is possible to decide which threats are more relevant and to conduct a more focused analysis such as by focusing on the threats that higher probability to attack the online banking application or the ones that might cause the larger impact (e.g. internal threats).

TABLE 8.6 Overall Cyber-Threat Scenarios Affecting Financial IT Systems and Applications

Cyber Threat	Cyber-Crime	Hacktivism
Threat actors	Cyber-gangs, fraudsters	Anonymous Groups, State Sponsored Groups, Script Kiddies
Motivation	Financial gain from stolen money from bank accounts, fraudulent transactions, purchase of good with stolen	Political agendas, cause disruptions, get noticed and damage the company reputation
Goals	Monetize stolen credit card data, online fraud, account takeover, movement of money to fraudulent accounts, counterfeit of credit and to purchase goods and debit card data to withdraw money from ATMs with counterfeit debit and prepaid cards.	Expose confidential data of adversaries to public for political reasons including company and government secrets. Defacing of websites to damage brand and reputation. Denial of service to web sites to gain attention and cause economical damage to organizations.
Events	Security incident reported on 5/9/2013: $ 45 million stolen at ATMs worldwide by breaking into computer systems of card payment processors in the United States and India.	Cyber-threat campaign announced on 5/1/2013: ACQF announced the start of the week nine of the third phase of operation Ababil, the distributed denial-of-service (DDOS) attack against major financial institutions in USA
Capabilities	Global cyber-crime and fraud operations, knowledge of configuration and use of cyber crime-tools such as banking malware and to conduct phishing campaigns to distribute malware and to run exploits of vulnerabilities in applications to install backdoors in systems for stealing sensitive data.	Recruiting of hacktivists threat actors by running campaigns on social media such as twitter, Facebook and YouTube. Capability of conduct coordinated attacks by renting and acquiring cyber-crime tools and botnets. Knowledge of DDoS attack tools as well as of exploit web application vulnerabilities.

(continued)

TABLE 8.6 (*Continued*)

Cyber Threat	Cyber-Crime	Hacktivism
Techniques	Social engineering users to select malicious links Drop malware with key logger/spyware/form grabbing capability to steal confidential data Use of man-in-the-middle attack techniques to bypass MFA and to hijack authenticated session and take over accounts and money movement transactions Use of man-in-the-browser attacks to inject HTML to social engineer users to provide additional ATM PINs and credit card data such as CVV Send stolen credentials to external site/entity Transfer money to money mule accounts Install backdoors on compromised servers allowing remote access to credit card and payment data Install network sniffers to capture payment data in transit from POS and credit card processing	Public recruiting of threat actors through social media outlets and public forums Use of free and off-the-shelf DDoS attacking tools for coordinated attacks against targets Renting of botnets to coordinate DDoS attacks from compromised hosts Exploit of layer 4 (network layer) and layer 7 (application layer) weaknesses and vulnerabilities Exploit of general web-application vulnerabilities, such as XSS, SQL injection, and Directory Traversal for stealing confidential data Used anonymity services to disguise sources of the attacks Post documents obtained from hacking attacks in anonymous web sites (e.g. pastebin)
Targets	Banks and bank customers, merchants, credit card processors, host computers such as desktops and server such as web and application servers and databases, web and mobile applications and POS software and hardware.	Online banking sites, high visibility government sites, sites or services hosted on high-profile web servers, credit card payment gateways, root name servers and services used at Internet service providers

A tool that aggregates threat information such as threat dashboard can be useful for a threat analyst to conduct a more focused analysis of the threats based on specific parameters and narrow down the threats that matter, for example, at the application and project level. Specifically, such threat dashboard could be embedded in an application threat modeling tool and allows the threat analyst/modeler to extract the threat information about the top type of threats and threat targets, the type of data and functional assets being targeted, the vulnerabilities and weaknesses exploited, and the assessed presence of countermeasures and controls to mitigate these threats.

Based upon the data provided in a threat dashboard, a threat analyst can prioritize the enumeration of threats by starting from the ones whose risk is higher. This is the approach of "analysis in-depth first" opposite of the approach of "breadth first" that in essence consists of enumerating all cyber-threats of the threat library that data and functional components are affected to. This type of threat analysis is also referred to as "threat enumeration" and "threat analysis per asset and component" and will be conducted later on during this stage by conducting the activity TA 4.5 threat agents to asset mappings.

After the overall threat scenarios have been analyzed, the next activity consists of *TA 4.1 analyzing threats by gathering threat information from internal sources.* The gathering of threat intelligence is essential activity for proactive cyber-risk management and cyber-threat prevention specifically for the analysis of the specific types of security events that can be monitored to detect the occurrence of attacks as well as for the type of vulnerabilities that can be targeted during these attacks.

Examples of sources of internal threat intelligence include threat events gathered by internal honeypots, threat events correlated by the analysis of application and system logs, information collected from Web Application Firewalls (WAF) set to monitor specific cyber-threat events such as exploit of common vulnerabilities targeting the organization website. SIEM (Security Internet Event Monitoring) can also log threat events when these are logged by different systems and can be correlated with suspicious activities of user actions indicating possible attacks based on specific rules such as velocity checks, authentication failure events, attempts to scan for common vulnerabilities for the sake of later exploit them in an attack. Other internal sources of threat events include events detected by fraud detection systems shared through internal fraud management teams and threat events that might have triggered a security incident by the Security Incident Response Teams SIRTs

Gathering threat intelligence from internal sources provides a lot value for threat prevention when this information is correlated with threat information coming from external sources. This is the focus of the activity *TA 4.1 – Analyzing threats by gathering threat information from internal sources.* Before we gather threat intelligence information from external sources, it is important to cover some basic standard threat categorizations for threat information that is shared across different external threat sources. This standardization of threat information is also important to represent threat information in structured manner that can be shared, understood, and analyzed by different threat analysts. An example of this standardized language for the sharing and analysis of cyber-threats is the STIXthat stands for Structured Threat Information expression.

STIX has been developed by the MITRE Corporation as an open standard for describing cyber threat information in a standardized and structured manner. According to MITRE "*STIX characterizes an extensive set of cyber threat information, to include indicators of adversary activity (e.g., IP addresses and file hashes) as well as additional contextual information regarding threats (e.g., adversary Tactics, Techniques and Procedures [TTPs]; exploitation targets; Campaigns; and Courses of Action [COA]) that together more completely characterize the cyber adversary's motivations, capabilities, and activities, and thus, how to best defend against them.*"

PASTA USE CASE EXAMPLE WALK-THROUGH

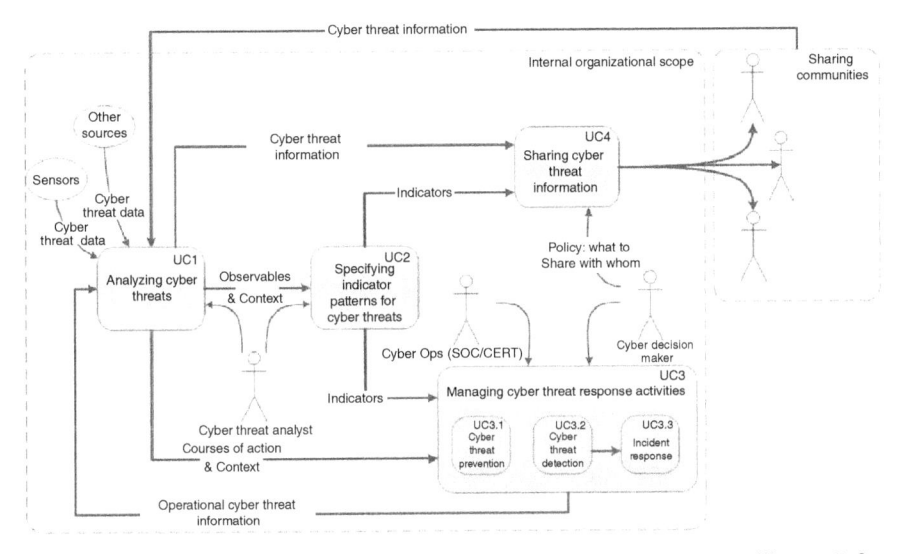

Figure 8.13 Ontology of (STIX) Structured Language for Cyber Threat Intelligence Information (Courtesy of MITRE Corp)[1]

The core use cases of sharing and analyzing cyber threat intelligence are shown in Figure 8.13 as well as specifying indicators patterns for cyber-threats.

From the cyber-threat risk management perspective, the most important aspect of STIX is to use the collected cyber-threat information for preventing or detecting cyber threat activities that includes mitigate vulnerabilities, weaknesses, or misconfigurations that may be targets of exploit. From the threat modeling perspective, STIX cyber-threat syntax includes the notion of threat TTP that stands for Tactics, Techniques, and Procedures that is a representation of the behavior or modus operandi of a cyber-threat agent including the use of particular attack patterns and exploits.

In the STIX cyber threat schema, the tagging of cyber-threat target consists of the "ExploitTarget" and represents a potential victim that may make them susceptible to a particular adversary TTP (e.g. a system vulnerability, application weakness, or configuration issue).

The STIX cyber-threat schema provides a very comprehensive set of attributes that can be used for the analysis of cyber-threats as shown in Table 8.7.

Each of the STIX threat intelligence information sharing attributes has a special meaning. The main cyber-threat attributes of STIX include the following:

1. *Observable* is an event that can be observed in the cyber crime domain. Examples include IP addresses, registry keys, HTTP methods as well as recorded events such as the deletion of a file.

[1] https://stix.mitre.org/images/STIX_Core_Use_Cases_large.jpg.

TABLE 8.7 Structured Threat Information eXpression (STIX) Architecture vs 3.0

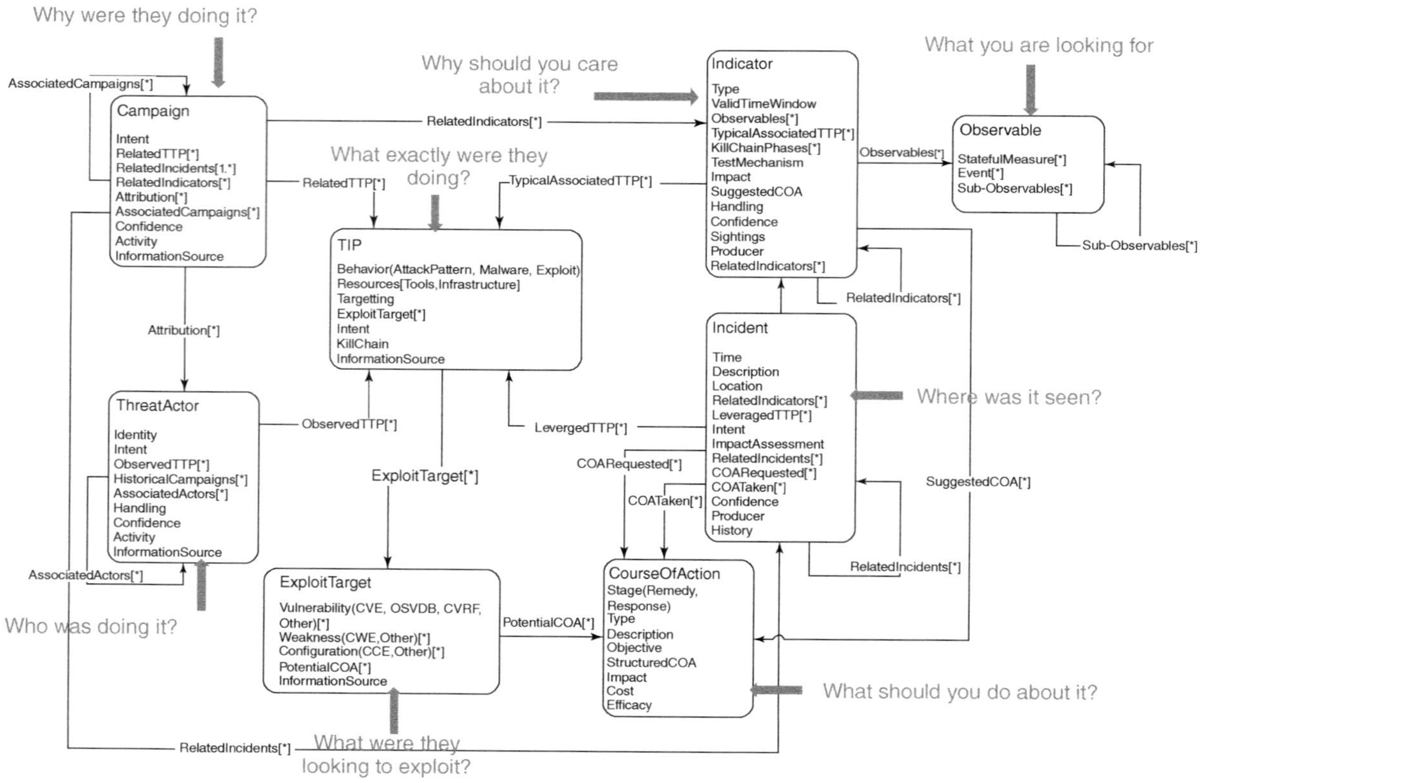

PASTA USE CASE EXAMPLE WALK-THROUGH

2. *Indicator* is a parameter that provides the indication of the cyber-attack context for the observable; for example, if the observable is dropping of a file, the indicator is a malicious file including a zero-day vulnerability or a Trojan.
3. *Incident* describes the activity associated with the attack that includes information of the "who" is involved, the "when," that is, when the incident occurred, the impact, and the Course of Action (CoA) taken in response to the incident.
4. *TTPs* are the Tactics, Techniques, and Procedures that describe how the threat agent operates to conduct attacks.
5. *Exploit Target* is the threat agent target for the exploit. The target can be associated with a vulnerability and a weakness in the system, application, or network being targeted.
6. *Course of Action* is the action that can be taken to prevent, mitigate, and remediate the effects of a given cyber-threat.
7. *Campaign* is a set of adversary activities such as the tactics, techniques and procedures, indicators, exploit targets, and incidents.
8. *ThreatActor* is the cyber-adversary that is the entity perpetrating the attack.

According to STIX definition, an observable is defined as "An Observable is an event or stateful property that is observed or may be observed in the operational cyber domain, such as a registry key value, an IP address, deletion of a file, or the receipt of an http GET. STIX uses Cyber Observable eXpression (CybOX™) to represent Observables."

An example of using STIX language for sharing threat intelligence of an observable is shown in Table 8.8.

The cyber-threat observable has an "observableID," a cybox "ObjectID" and represents a URL (CybOX URI object), the "kill-chain" phase relevant for this observable and a phase ID of the kill-chain. The handling of the threat intelligence information is done according to a marking. The information marking allows a threat analyst to specify how the content within this observable should be handled based upon the color given to the information that maps to different levels of sensitivity of the information. In the example herein, the marking of this information is considered AMBER marking and the sensitivity if "For Official Use Only (FOUO)" a term that under DoD rules usually designates unclassified information.

This threat intelligence information is actionable toward the monitoring of the specific domain as possible source of delivery of malware through drive by download that has Silverlight browser plug-in enabled.

From the application threat modeling perspective, an interesting element of STIX is the "ExploitTarget" construct. This construct allows a threat analyst to map cyber-threats to the exploit targets such as, for example, vulnerabilities that can be exploited to compromise the target and conduct an attack. The "ExploitTarget" construct actually allows a specification of vulnerability that can be exploited such as a Common Vulnerability and Exposure (CVE) type of vulnerability.

TABLE 8.8 Example of Description of Browser Exploit Threat Using STIX

id	Repository-00ff06f0-996d0-44bb-a1263-449cf4a53444
Title	Browser Plug-in Exploits
Type	Domain Watchlist
Alternative_ID	CISCP:indicator-5889988f2381-5887-451d-9b9b-685a15aea480
Description	Browsers were redirected to download files from hacked.acme.com. No further information such as port number or protocol is available.
Observable id	repository-9f6c1099-a630-4d64-bf6c-55997efd5ccf""

	cybox:Object id:	repository-f999ebca-88c2-41f0-87f1-82e641432733
	cybox:Properties:	URIObj:URIObjectType
	URIObj:URIObjectType	Domain Name
	URIObj:Value	Equals hacked.acme.com
	Kill_Chain_Phases	stixCommon
	Kill_Chain_Phase	
	Ordinality	3
	Name	Delivery
	phase_id	stix:KillChainPhase-79a0e041-9d5f-49bb-ada4-832299b162d
	Handling	
	Marking	
	Controlled_Structure	//node()
	Marking_Structure	AMBER
	simpleMarking:Statement	FOUO

An example of a sample of threat intelligence sharing of an observable using STIX is shown in Table 8.8. This is the observable of an exploit of a browser plug-in to redirect the browser to download malicious files from a specific domain and whose kill-chain phase is "delivery."

The STIX cyber-threat schema also incorporates the notion of the "kill-chain." The kill-chain is a representation of the sequence of events that cyber-threat will undertake to realize a threat into an attack that is from the initial reconnaissance events to the execution and maintenance of the attack. A graphical example of the steps pre- and postexploit of vulnerabilities from a cyber-threat is shown in Figure 8.14.

The modeling of attacks with kill-chain is particularly useful to decide which cyber-threat events need to be detected and monitored to respond to cyber-attacks. In the case of cyber-threat against online banking sites, for example, the kill-chain information can be used to decide which threat events can be monitored and correlated as indication of preparation of an exploit (e.g. installing malware on a target machine) and after the exploit take place as indication of execution of the exploit (e.g. stealing of sensitive data).

PASTA USE CASE EXAMPLE WALK-THROUGH

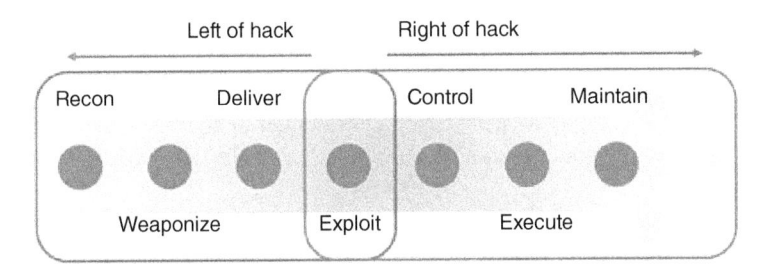

Figure 8.14 Example of Kill-Chain (Courtesy of MITRE corp)[2]

A kill-chain of a malware attack against an online banking site for example might include the following sequence of events:

1. *Reconnaissance* event triggered by the threat agent to learn about the online banking sites that can be targeted such as by crime exploit of common vulnerabilities using scanning tools.
2. *Weaponize* the attack tool trojan/malware by collaborating with other threat actors in the underground cyber-crime forums.
3. *Deliver* of the banking malware to the target (e.g. client machine) such as through e-mail phishing campaigns directly targeting the online banking customers and by injecting malware on servers (e.g. inject malicious links in vulnerable web server/websites) so that it can be later dropped to the victim visiting the site with a cyber-threat technique referred as "drive by download."
4. *Exploit* that is compromise of the client machine with banking malware or the server with backdoors for the sake of stealing sensitive data such as payment data, transactions, and credit card data.
5. *Control* that is the control of configuration of the online banking malware tool by the bot command and control server granting the cyber-threat agent the control to initiate the attack (e.g. when the online banking customer log in to conduct a transfer of money to external account or a payment).
6. *Execution* that is the execution of Man in the Browser (MiTB) to collect sensitive data from the victim and Man-in-the-Middle (MiTM) to conduct the authenticated web session hijacking for bank account takeover and movement of money from the victim account.
7. *Maintenance* that is to maintain persistence on the compromised server at the financial institution to exfiltrate bank account and credit card data from the backdoor installed on compromised server in the internal network.

[2]https://stix.mitre.org/about/.

From the perspective of aggregating the cyber-threat information from sources of threat intelligence such as the FS ISAC (Financial Sharing, Information Security Assurance Center), the classification and structuration of cyber-threat information according to STIX allow performing cyber-threat analysis on various types of cyber-threats attributes and to decide the course of action for responding to these cyber-threats.

Another source of cyber-threat intelligence includes the Web Hacking Incident Database (WHID) that is a project run by the Web Application Security Consortium (WASC) and is dedicated to maintain a list of web application-related security incidents. The data of WHID, for example, includes information about attack methods such as reported incidents caused by cyber-attacks against web applications that are reported in the public domain. These events can be correlated with the attacks observed in the public honeypot and then mapped to the most common vulnerabilities that these attacks seek to exploit.

The information about the attacks against web applications that is collected by the WHID can be later used to prioritize the remediation of vulnerabilities that are observed to be exploited by the attacks observed. WHID attack libraries can be incorporated into threat modeling tools such as ThreatModeler™, which is shown in Figure 8.15.

After the cyber-threat intelligence information has been aggregated and stored in the organization threat intelligence knowledge base, the next step consist of updating the threat libraries that can used to conduct a threat analysis.

Figure 8.15 Web Incident Hacking Database Attack Library

PASTA USE CASE EXAMPLE WALK-THROUGH

Select	Edit	Name	Risk
	Edit	Overflow Buffers	Very High
	Edit	Session Sidejacking	High
	Edit	Clickjacking	High
	Edit	Cross Zone Scripting	High
	Edit	HTTP Request Splitting	High
	Edit	Cross Site Scripting through Log Files	High
	Edit	Cross Site Tracing	Very High
	Edit	Command Line Execution through SQL Injection	Very High
	Edit	Object Relational Mapping Injection	High
	Edit	Cause Web Server Misclassification	High
	Edit	SQL Injection through SOAP Parameter Tampering	Very High
	Edit	JSON Hijacking (aka JavaScript Hijacking)	High
	Edit	Brute Force	High
	Edit	API Abuse/Misuse	Medium
	Edit	Authentication Abuse	Medium
	Edit	Authentication Bypass	Medium
	Edit	Data Excavation Attacks	Medium
	Edit	Data Interception Attacks	Medium
	Edit	Choosing a Message/Channel Identifier on a Public/Multicast Channel	High
	Edit	Double Encoding	Medium

Figure 8.16 ThreatModeler™ Tool Threat Library

This leads to the next activity that *TA 4.4 – Update the threat libraries* with the new aggregated threat information from the different sources of threat intelligence. Threat libraries can be incorporated in threat modeling tools and enumerated against the various security controls of the application to drive security requirements, conduct tests, and identify vulnerabilities. An example of generic threat library that is incorporated in the ThreatModeler™ tool is shown in Figure 8.16.

Threat libraries can be updated with the inclusion of new cyber threats as these are shared from different sources of threat intelligence. As new threats emerge, it is important to reevaluate the application exposure to these threats and specifically derive a new set of security requirements for the secure design of the application architecture whose cyber-threats need to be mitigated and to revisit the architecture design reviews to identify potential design flaws and vulnerabilities that these new threat might seek to exploit and security test the application against new attack vectors that seek to exploit these vulnerabilities and specifically by following the same tactics, techniques, and procedures used by the threat agents.

Since security requirements, security issues, and security tests are associated with architectural components such as web servers, application servers, and databases, the best use of these updated threat libraries is by associating new emerging threats with the data and the components that might be exposed by these threats. Besides the update of the threat library to map to the existing components such as the company assets (e.g. data and functions), it is also important to update the different parameters that characterize each cyber-threat such as the types of threat agents/actors, the threat campaigns announced by the threat agents, the threat agent capabilities and the threat agent tools, techniques and strategies, the security incidents observed including the security controls and the security measures impacted (e.g. authentication, authorization, encryption, input validation, session management), and the control gaps such as design flaws and vulnerabilities that are known to be exploited by these threats.

The mitigation of the risk of new threats might require new countermeasures; hence, when these countermeasures are identified, they need to be incorporated in an updated risk control framework to evaluate new application as well as changes to these applications.

As an example, the update of the threat library to include banking Trojan type of threats drives the update of the risk control framework to include the following new and updated security controls:

- Updated fraud detection and monitoring controls with updated rules
- Updated anomaly user behavior transaction detection rules controls
- New suspicious user activity detection rules to be monitored
- Dual controls for initiate and approved/authorize high-risk transactions such money movements/transfers and payments
- Strong multifactor authentication controls such as OOB One-Time Passwords to authenticate users and authorize money movement transactions and payments
- Use of additional layers for authentication that relies on different factors that can be validated on the device where the transaction originates such as biometrics.
- OOB verification and authorization for money movement transactions (e.g. banking customer receives notification of authorize a transfer over the phone and ought to positively confirm the transaction before execution)
- Use of external device such as USB/token to establish a two-way SSL channel with the online banking site
- Maximum transaction limits on money transfers such as max money value amount per transaction, allowable payment window
- Blacklists and white list of money transfer recipients
- Reputation-based controls to identify "true IP addresses" and block transactions from known bad IPs
- Complex fingerprinting of the device to determine the trustworthiness of the device based upon flash one-time cookie, browser settings, O.S settings, IP address, and geolocation of the device
- Malware detection and protection for client browsers/PCs
- Customer subscription alerts via e-mail or SMS for money movements

Once the threat library has been updated including the new controls that can be assessed and designed for the mitigation of the risks of new cyber threats, the next activity of the threat analysis stage consist of "*TA 4.4 – Correlate threat agents to assets/targets.*" Correlation of the threats with the assets such as the various components of the application architecture is also referred to as threat enumeration in threat modeling.

Threat enumeration focuses on correlating threats to security controls to determine if these threats are either mitigated by the presence of countermeasures or are not mitigated because countermeasures are either missing or have design flaws or vulnerabilities that expose the application assets. From the perspective of application threat modeling, the specific mapping of threats to architectural components of the application architecture including data in storage and in transit is important to be able to visualize how these threats map to the application logical and physical architecture. Specifically it is important to correlate these threats with the assets that in the case of online banking applications include the sensitive data of customers such as bank and credit card data, PII, and application's business critical functionality that can be abused for financial gain. The focus of the threat analysis and correlation with the application assets is called out in the application threat modeling process as specific activity.

For what concerns the data, since data is both in storage and transit, it is important to map these threats not just to the data storages such as databases but also to the data in transit across the different components of the application that includes the different servers allocated in the different tiers of the application architecture shown in Figure 8.8. In the threat modeling example, there are shown the threats enumerated from a small list using STRIDE (e.g. spoofing, tampering, repudiation, information disclosure, denial of service and elevation of privileges) affecting some specific components such as user/browsers and authentication credential store that is considered an high-valued target by the attackers (Figure 8.17).

A STRIDE- based security control risk framework can also be used to assert if the application is designed to include security controls that specifically reduce and control the risks of these threats as shown in Table 8.9.

Another view that can be used for the threat to asset modeling assessment is a defensive view that consist of looking at each of the application security controls from the lenses of an Application Security Framework (ASF) and then determine if any weaknesses and vulnerabilities in the design and implementation of these application security controls expose the application to specific threats as shown in Table 8.10.

Both the STRIDE attacker view and the ASF defensive view for the enumeration of threats are essential for an in-depth analysis of the threats affecting the application data and functional assets.

Threat modeling tools can incorporate these threat and control framework and facilitate the analysis of the threats against the assets such as both the data and the functional components of each basic element of the application. An example of functional level decomposition in support to the analysis of threats against data and "widget" of functionality associated to each component.

The correlations of threats to assets such as data and functional assets lead to the final step of the threat analysis that is *TA 4.6 – Assignment of the probabilistic values for identified threats* that is the estimate of the level of risk for each of the threat being analyzed and modeled. The level of risk for each threat used in the analysis

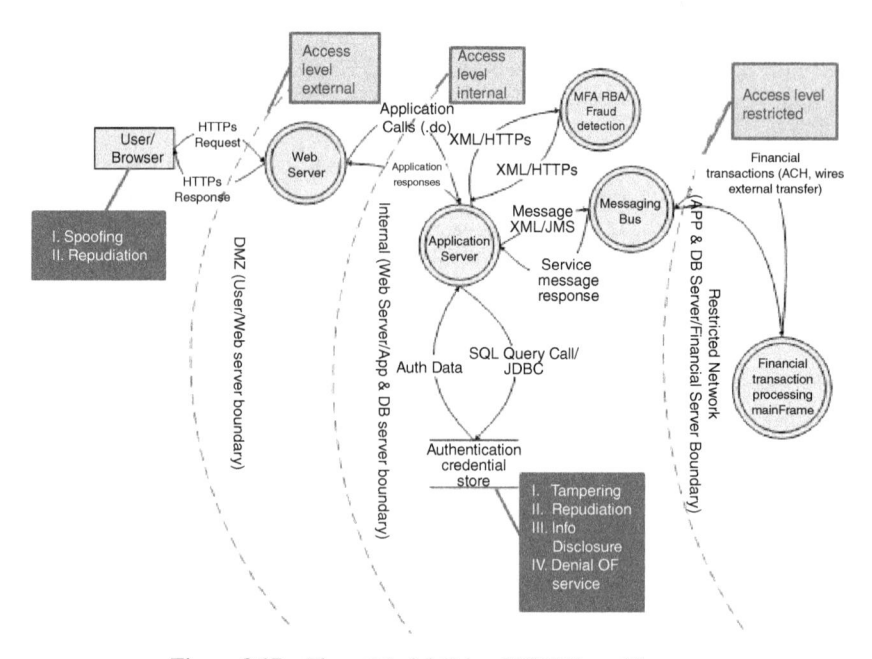

Figure 8.17 Threat Model Using STRIDE per Element

TABLE 8.9 STRIDE Threat List

	STRIDE Threat List	
Type	Examples	Security Control
Spoofing	Threat action aimed to illegally access and use another user's credentials, such as username and password	Authentication
Tampering	Threat action aimed to maliciously change/modify persistent data, such as persistent data in a database, and the alteration of data in transit between two computers over an open network, such as the interest	Integrity
Repudiation	Threat action aimed to perform illegal operation in a system that lacks the ability to trace the prohibited operations.	Non-Repudiation
Information disclosure	Threat action to read a file that they were not granted success to, or to read data in transit.	Confidentiality
Denial of service	Threat action to deny access to valid users such as by making a web server temporarily unavailable or unusable.	Availability
Elevation of privilege	Threat aimed to gain privileged access to resources for gaining unauthorized success to information or to compromise a system.	Authorization

TABLE 8.10 Application Security Frame

Type	Description	Attack Examples
Auditing and logging	Threats caused by failure to maintain detailed and accurate application logs that can allow for traceability and nonrepudiation and provide enough information for administrators to identify security issues and for incident response specialists to trace an attack. An attacker can use logs to obtain critical information about the system as well as tamper them to clear his traces after an attack.	1. Non repudiation 2. Cleaning the logs to remove evidence 3. Inserting of faked logging entries
Authentication	Threats caused by lack of strong protocols to validate the identity of a user to access a system or component outside the trust boundary. An attacker can obtain illegitimate access to the system or its individual components.	1. Impersonation 2. Spoofing attacks 3. Brute force attacks 4. Dictionary attacks 5. Token/Cookie Reply attacks 6. Man in The Middle attacks(MiTM)
Authorization	Threats caused by a lack of mechanisms to enforce access control on protected resources within the system. An attacker can get access to resources that should not have privileges to access to.	1. Escalation of privileges 2. Luring attacks 3. Forceful browsing
Configuration management	Threats caused by insecure deployment and administration. An attacker can get access to system/user data and gain unauthorized access to system functionality	1. Elevation of privileges 2. Unauthorized access to configuration data 3. Unauthorized access to administration interfaces
Data protection in storage and transit	Threats caused by the implementation of encryption and lack of adequate protection for secrets and other data in storage or transit. An attacker can compromise user/system confidentiality and data integrity by bypassing the cryptographic mechanisms used by the system	1. Access to sensitive data in storage 2. Access to secrets (e.g. encryption keys) 3. Eavesdropping of data during transmission 4. Data tampering 5. Brute force attacks to crack encryption

can be evaluated based upon risk factors for the threats such as the probability for the threat to be realized in an attack and conduct an exploit and cause an incident such as compromise of sensitive data and fraud.

This estimate of the risk for each threat at this stage is critical for deciding the course of action to mitigate the risk of the threat. For example, if the threat analysis is conducted to review the impact of new application functionality as well as changes to data that might increase the risk, the analysis of threats at this stage can drive risk management decision at design level such as designing a threat resilient security control that protects the data assets and functionality or otherwise the design of the application must change to remove the threat entirely (e.g. do not store credit card numbers to remove the threat of disclosure). Once a risk severity is assigned to each threat, it can be prioritized to discuss with the business and risk management how the risk of threats should be managed (Figure 8.18).

For the calculation of the risk of threats, a threat analyst can calculate the risk of each threat by using risk calculation formulas. These formulas are based on the assignment of the level of risk, HIGH, MEDIUM, and LOW, to the different factors of risks such as likelihood and impact. The factors of probability of a threat occurring depend on the degree of mitigation of the threat (e.g. the presence or not of a vulnerability) and associated factors for the determination of the likelihood for an attacker to exploit the vulnerability in an attack.

For a given attack, the possible exploit of a vulnerability depends on several factors such as being able to discover the vulnerability, conduct the exploit, and reproduce the exploit in other attacks. From technical impact perspective, the impact can also be further analyzed by assigning values to the damage potential of the threat and the number of affected components.

This analysis of the risk of a threat initially ought to make assumption on the exploitability of a vulnerability that is the realization of a threat in an attack and the presence of vulnerabilities that at this stage can only be roughly estimated since vulnerabilities and attacks are evaluated only during STAGE V Weaknesses and Vulnerability Analysis and STAGE VI Attack Modeling that are essential for the final quantification of risk is STAGE VII Risk Analysis and Management.

At the end of the threat analysis stage, the threat analyst will assign a level of risk to the threat and later revise it higher based upon the analysis of vulnerabilities that map to that threat and the model of an attack that could exploit that vulnerability as shown in Figure 8.19.

Stage V – Weaknesses and Vulnerability Analysis (WVA)

Goals of This Stage The analysis of weaknesses and vulnerabilities and correlation of these with the threats previously analyzed. Any weaknesses and vulnerabilities in the application architecture are also identified during this stage and prioritized for validations/tests along with any weaknesses and vulnerabilities of the application/IT system in scope that were previously analyzed with other assessments.

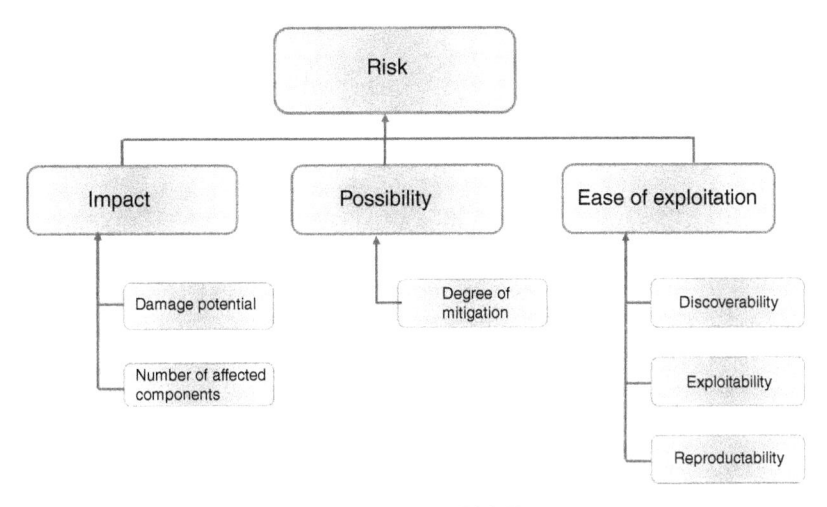

PASTA USE CASE EXAMPLE WALK-THROUGH 549

Figure 8.18 Threat Risk Factors

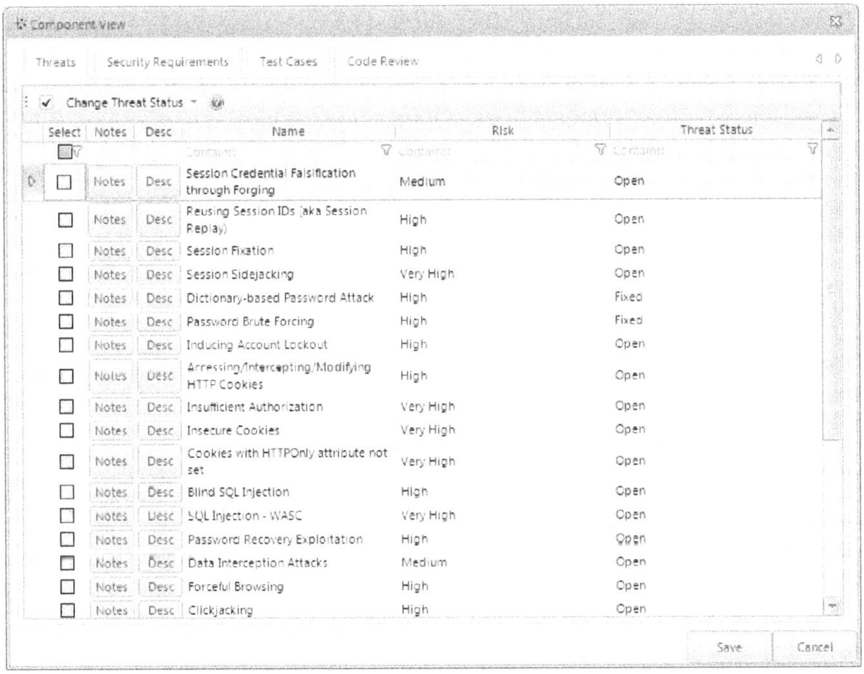

Figure 8.19 Threat Dashboard with Threat Risk and Status

Guidance for Conducting This Stage During this stage, we will reassess any existing vulnerabilities and weaknesses of the several components of the technology stack including software components, servers, and services supporting the application in scope along with any design flaws identified by conducting an architectural risk analysis of the application components. These weaknesses and vulnerabilities will be correlated with information of the threats targeting them as threat target and prioritized for security testing based upon the information of "ThreatTargets," "Observables," and "Indication of Compromise" analyzed from threat reports received from internal and external threat sources. The information about the stage of the attack such as the attack kill-chain stage included in the observable can also be used to prioritize the security tests along with the severity of the vulnerability that was previously tested. The information about the threat agent's TTPs Tools, techniques, and processes that has been observed can also be used for creating specific test cases for these vulnerabilities that are more realistically representative of the threat scenarios.

During this stage, vulnerability reports from different security assessments that were previously executed on the web application such as application dynamic security tests and static application security tests are considered for the analysis. The information about weaknesses and vulnerabilities found in the application constitute the knowledge base of vulnerabilities that is considered for this assessment as well as any design flaws that could be identified during the security review of the application and software architecture.

Previously identified application vulnerabilities can be stored in a vulnerability management repository/knowledge base so can be categorized by application assets. Such vulnerability management repository/knowledge base should be made available for querying based upon the specific assets in scope for the risk analysis identified during stage II and decomposed during stage III. These application and system vulnerability assessments are typically performed in compliance with standards and processes such as security architecture reviews, secure code reviews, manual application security tests, and automatic dynamic and static code analysis scans. The assumption of this stage is that application vulnerabilities can be mapped to impact to each of the web application assets that include source code, architectural components, and data potentially targeted by the threats previously analyzed.

Any gaps in the security controls and weaknesses in the design of these security controls (e.g. design flaws) identified during the application architectural analysis in this stage are also correlated to threats during this stage. At the end of this stage, we would have a mapping of threats to vulnerabilities and control weaknesses (design flaws) of the application, software, and systems in scope to ascertain whether security control weaknesses and application and system vulnerabilities exist and might expose the application assets (data and functions) to attack from threat agents and what their probability is to be targeted by threat agents.

Based upon the mapping of threats to vulnerabilities, it is possible to conduct a more accurate scoring of vulnerability severity. Among the factors that can be used for scoring of risk for vulnerabilities, a threat analyst can use the ease of discovery of the vulnerability, the exposure of the vulnerability to specific threats and the fact that events to exploit the vulnerability are logged and audited. The factors that can be assessed at this stage also include technical impact factors such as impact on data confidentiality, integrity, and availability in case these vulnerabilities are exploited by a specific threat. The calculation of the risk severity of vulnerabilities in presence of threats can use standard vulnerability severity risk scoring methods such as CVSS. Finally the vulnerabilities and threat that have the highest probability and technical impact that can be assessed during this stage can be put in scope for additional security tests to validate the likelihood of exploit and determine the technical impact.

Activities This stage consists of the following activities:

WVA 5.1 – Review/correlate existing vulnerabilities: This activity consists of the review of existing application vulnerabilities affecting security controls that protect assets such as data and functions that are targeted by the threat agents that were previously analyzed. Typically, each organization should have a vulnerability management repository that is a repository that stores vulnerability data from different security tests previously executed on the application/system such as architectural risk analysis, source code analysis, and penetration testing. During this activity, the threat analysis will be querying vulnerabilities previously identified for each web application and select vulnerabilities in security controls that expose specific data and the functional assets such as authentication data, confidential data, and various type of functionality such as user authentication, change of authentication credentials, read access to confidential data, change of confidential data, and others.

WVA 5.2 – Identify weak design patterns in the architecture: After the design of the application has been decomposed in basic architecture elements including the type of data that these components process as data in transit through other components and as data stored, it is possible to analyze the scope for the security control and to assert that security requirements are followed for the secure design of security controls, application architecture, and functionality. Security control gaps to protect the data assets can be identified by following an architectural review process that enumerates the security control to review and provide guidelines to review how these controls should be designed by following security architecture principles and documented security requirements, guidelines, and standards. Security control frameworks can also be used to assess the security strength of the control and commensurate it against the inherent risk of the data and functional asset that the control is required to protect by providing either a detective or protective function. If a design flaw is identified, this should be reported as finding and an initial risk level should be assigned at this point. This risk of such design flaws also depends on the probability of a specific threat agent to exploit that design flaw. Such risk can be initially assigned as this stage by grouping the design flaws using standard weaknesses enumeration methods (CWE) and by using standard risk scoring methods for calculating the risk of the vulnerabilities such as First CVSSvs2. In calculating the risk for design flaws with these methods, it is important to consider the threat agents that might potentially exploit these weaknesses and vulnerabilities and look whether threat intelligence provides information of these threat agents seeking to target these vulnerabilities as a factor of probability of a threat. This activity builds on the previous stages of stage III application decomposition and specifically enumeration of the assets, creation of DFDs, and stage IV threat analysis activities such as mapping of threats to the assets and the probabilistic value assigned to these threats during stage IV.

Note that the risk that is assigned to the design flaw at this stage needs to be revised later on during the attack modeling stage after attack simulation and tests are performed to determine the likelihood and impact of threat agents and attack vectors used by these threat agents in the exploitation of these design flaws.

WVA 5.3 – Map threats to vulnerabilities: This activity will consider each threat of the threat library that is already mapped to a security control identified in stage IV to determine if these controls have vulnerabilities or design flaws that might increase the exposure to each threat. This activity consists of mapping threats to vulnerabilities and architectural design flaws (e.g. control gaps/ weak design of security controls). Design flaws that are previously identified during the application decomposition analysis and assertion should also be mapped to threats.

WVA 5.4 – Provide Context risk Analysis based upon Threat-Vulnerability: With this activity, we will review weaknesses and vulnerabilities in the context of threats. The goal of this activity is to determine the risk severity of weaknesses and vulnerabilities by considering the risk posed by exposure to threats in the context of the overall threat scenarios. Standard factor for calculation of risks includes probability and impact; furthermore, probability factors can be calculated based upon the assignment of values for ease of discovery, ease to conduct the exploit, awareness of the exploit, detection and prevention of exploit of the vulnerability by detective controls. Impact factors are technical impacts on the assets when the vulnerability is exploited such as impact of confidentiality, integrity, and availability of the asset. The risk calculation will use standard grouping for vulnerabilities such as CWE and standard risk scoring methods such as CVSS.

WVA 5.4 – Conduct targeted vulnerability testing: The goal of this activity is to create a suite of security tests for specific weaknesses and vulnerabilities targeted by threat agents. These security tests can be executed using different types of security tests including manual security tests of vulnerabilities, black-box and white-box tests, static and dynamic source code scanning, and manual code reviews. These security tests are no longer blind of threat agents but consider the type of threat agents and attack tools used by these threat agents as these were to exploit the vulnerability in a real attack against the application. The purpose of these tests is to assert the exposure and the risk as technical impact on the assets. For example, this can be a case of testing a known SQL injection vulnerability with specific attack vectors used by the threat agents.

Note: The goal of these tests is not to identify if these vulnerabilities can be exploited (e.g. exploitability tests) but to determine a more accurate value of risk severity of the vulnerability based upon known exposure to threat agents. Seldom by using the same attack vectors used by the threat agents that can be discovered by the analysis of threat targets, additional weaknesses, and vulnerabilities can be identified. This is the case for example when design flaws are identified during the review of the architecture design and the validation of these design flaws by testing also identifies additional instances of similar type of vulnerabilities caused by implementation/coding as well as insecure configuration.

Inputs Used for Conducting This Stage

1. Documented application security risk profile for the assignment of risk to vulnerabilities from stage I.
2. Technical documentation in scope from stage II.
3. Application architecture documents detailing users, components, functions, data assets analyzed in stage III.
4. Application assets (data and functions) targeted by threat agents analyzed in stage IV.
5. Vulnerability reports from previous vulnerability assessments (ethical hacking, source code analysis, secure code review).
6. Documentation from the previous analysis of threats in stage IV including:
   a. Application security controls weaknesses (CWEs) and application, software, and system vulnerabilities (CVEs) targeted by threat agents/actors as Threat-Targets that are part of the threat scenario previously analyzed.
   b. Information from threat intelligence (e.g. threat reports) about the threat TTPs that can be used to prioritize the security tests of the vulnerabilities targeted.
   c. Information from threat intelligence (e.g. threat reports) about the stage of the kill-chain of the attack in which these threats have been observed as threat event as well as IOC indication of compromise.

Artifacts Produced at the End of This Stage At the end of this stage, we will produce the following artifacts:

(a) List of application vulnerabilities and weaknesses affecting the architectural components of the application mapped to threats
(b) Risk severity of the vulnerabilities calculated using standard risk scoring methods (using CVSS) based upon the information of the "threat illumination" of the vulnerability by a threat as (exposure to threats as opportunity and target)
(c) List of identified design flaws from architecture risk analysis
(d) Prioritized security test cases for retesting the presence of vulnerabilities that are targeted by various threats actors

Tools The execution of this stage can be facilitated by the use of vulnerability management repositories such as SVGI Vulnerability Repository, Source: Sourceforge.net Standard vulnerability risk scoring methods (CVSSvs2) to score risks of vulnerabilities. Formal methods to map threats to vulnerabilities and countermeasures such as OWASP threat trees are used for this stage. Vulnerability reports from OWASP (e.g. OWASP Top 10) and WASC as well as MITER CWEs as well as vendors sources of OSINT for threats and vulnerabilities exploited by these threats are used herein. Security test libraries for specific functional components embedded in threat modeling tools such as myAppSecurity ThreatModeler™ are also shown herein to create risk-based test cases for web application vulnerabilities.

Web Application Use Case Example The goals of this stage of application threat modeling exercise are to query existing weaknesses and vulnerabilities, identify any design flaws in the architecture design, and determine the risk, map threats to vulnerabilities and design flaws identified, and prioritize security tests for validation of design flaws and weaknesses and vulnerabilities that were previously identified and now can be reassessed and retested based upon the information of threats targeting them and tools, techniques, and procedures used.

During this stage, we will focus on both weaknesses and vulnerabilities previously tested, as well as the vulnerabilities that are identified during the review of the architecture and need to be validated and tested with security tests. We will first query any known weaknesses and vulnerabilities for the online banking application that was in scope and identify the type application security component that was affected and the assets impacted (data and functionality). We will then proceed to map known threats to these vulnerabilities and the security controls affected including new design flaws identified in this stage and calculate the risk severity of these vulnerabilities based upon exposure to the threat agents. Finally we will prioritize the security tests to test these design flaws and vulnerabilities.

The first activity of this stage consists of the *WVA 5.1 – Review/correlate existing vulnerabilities*. The scope of this activity is the analysis of existing weaknesses and vulnerabilities that were previously identified in performed security assessments on the online banking application such as secure architecture design reviews, source code analysis, and ethical hacking penetration tests of the application. After these weaknesses and vulnerabilities are reported to the business and discussed with application development teams for remediation, they are typically stored in the vulnerability risk management repository so can be queried for each application to track their resolution within the compliance remediation time frames. These vulnerabilities can also be queried for later analysis during this stage of the threat modeling exercise, specifically to correlate them to specific threats and assign a risk score for the severity by considering the probability of threat agents seeking to exploit them. The severity of the vulnerabilities can be calculated using standard risk scoring methods such as CVSS that use factors of probability and impact to determine the impact of threat agents on the assets such as their confidentiality, integrity, and availability.

The previously conducted threat analysis and specifically the information gathered from threat intelligence provide data for the calculation of the factors of probability

PASTA USE CASE EXAMPLE WALK-THROUGH   555

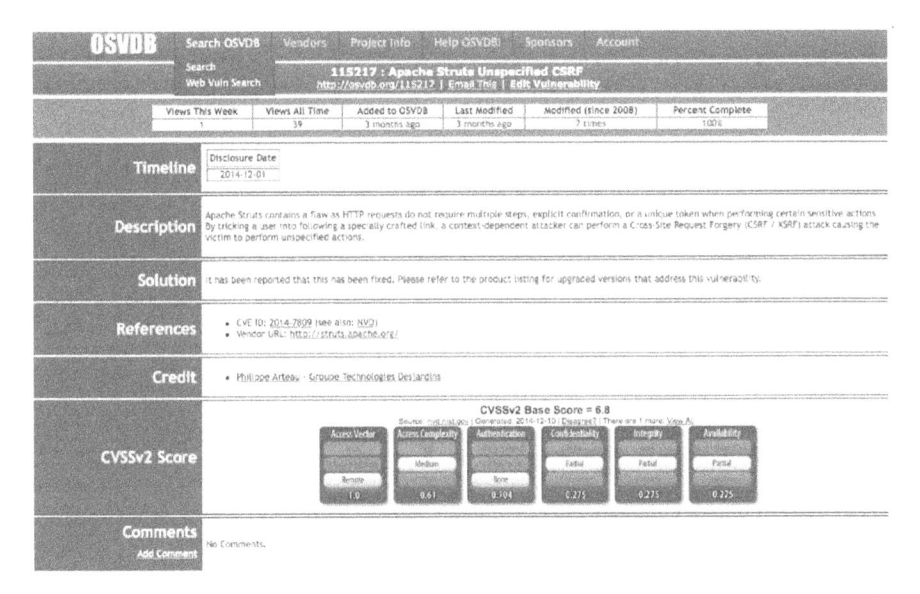

Figure 8.20 OSVDB Open Source Vulnerability Database source http://www.osvdb.org[3]

and impact. For example, the information that application vulnerabilities are currently being exploited by specific types of attacking tools or malware that is used to target online banking sites (e.g. banking malware Trojans) increases the probability of a potential exploit and the risk for the target. The exposure of the vulnerability to specific threat agents and the fact that the exploitation of these trigger events that are monitored and logged for potential Indication Of Compromise (IOCs) decreases the probability of a potential impact.

The analysis of vulnerabilities based upon the information of threat agents and the countermeasures in place is also critical for the derivation of security tests to validate the effectiveness of the existing countermeasures in the mitigation of the risk of threat agents seeking to exploit these known vulnerabilities.

Let us start with the first activity, that is, query existing vulnerabilities in the application. The goal of this activity is to query existing application vulnerabilities by the inventory ID of the inventory of the web application and IT system owned by the organization. Typically, each organization that has rolled out vulnerability assessment processes in compliance with information security standards should have a vulnerability management repository that stores vulnerability data from different security tests previously executed on the application such as architectural risk analysis, source code analysis, and penetration testing.

An example of query for vulnerable application software using the NVD (National Vulnerability Database) as a source using the Open-Source application SVGI's vulnerability repository is shown in Figure 8.20. Through this tool, it is possible to

---
[3] Sourceforge.net.

search for software vulnerabilities based upon the application software used by the application and determine the type of vulnerability grouped according to MITRE CWE and the risk scoring based upon CVSS.

Similar types of repositories can also be used to aggregate vulnerabilities from internal application vulnerability assessment and organized by a repository of IT assets that also includes applications besides IT systems. After we have queried existing vulnerabilities and weaknesses, the next step of this stage is to perform the activity *"WVA 5.2 – Identify weak design patterns in the application architecture."* The goal of this activity is to analyze the architectural components of the application architecture in scope and identify design flaws that might expose application assets (data and functional) at risk and need to be included in prioritized security tests for validations. Architectural design flaws consist of either gaps or weaknesses in security controls that might expose the data and functional assets to potential impacts such as the loss of confidentiality, integrity, and availability of confidential data and business critical functionality.

This activity can be executed at this stage since we have defined the security functional requirements for the application during stage I and defined the application technical scope in stage II including the technology stack of the various components, servers, and services and network components that support the application functionality residing in the hosts and servers located at different tiers of the application architecture (e.g. presentation tier, business tier, and database tier). In stage III, we also have decomposed the application in data and functional assets and we have analyzed trust boundaries and security controls deployed within these trust boundaries to protect sensitive data assets and business critical functions. In stage IV, we have conducted a threat analysis and we have updated the threat library with the information about threats learned from threat intelligence and mapped these threats to the assets. In stage V, we are not ready to identify any design flaws in the architecture that might be exploited by these threats with knowledge of their targeting specific weaknesses and vulnerabilities.

Since the objective of this activity is to analyze the architecture of the application to identify design flaws in security controls, we can start by reviewing any security control that is required to protect highly sensitive data (e.g. security keys, passwords) in storage and in transit. The previously documented DFDs DFDs may be useful to conduct this analysis and any potential design flaw that might expose DFD components (e.g. user client, data assets, processes located in servers in the different trust boundaries) and exposed to a threat agent and threat vector used by the threat agent represents a potential exposure and a security impact for the data assets that these security controls are designed to protect.

The assertion of the design of security controls for protecting the data in storage and in transit as well as the access to the various components of the application architecture can be done by following the flow of data as depicted in the DFD as well as by asserting the security requirement for each functional component. In the case of the online banking application, it can also be done by looking at the data assets in transit and in storage as shown in DFDs and by walking-through each architectural component of the DFD that is traversed by the data in transit. By starting the data flow from the external user interaction with the online banking application, for example, we can look at the data end to end from the user browser to the validation in the authentication credential store. The requirements for security controls such as authentication, session management, input validation, audit and logging, and encryption can be asserted at the level of the component that either process authentication data while in transit or in storage can be asserted by walking through the data flow.

Examples of design flaws that might be identified during this stage include design gaps in security controls that use weak architectural design patterns to protect sensitive data and critical business functionality.

The secure design of these security controls can be reviewed by asserting the security requirements for the design of each security component. If the design misses a requirement for the design of a security control such as access controls for accessing the confidential data, this will potentially expose data and functionality to potential threats. By following the data flow for other type of data such as, for example, data used in financial transactions, it is also possible to identify if there are design flaws in enforcing mutual authentication between the application server and web service calls exposed by the messaging bus as well as enforcement of secondary authentication and session management before allowing the data to cross the trust boundary with the financial processing mainframe.

When this activity is conducted during the SDLC such as in the case of development of a new online banking application or to assess the impact of design changes introduced in an existing online banking application, the assessment of the protection of data that is either stored or processed by each component can be done by asserting the inclusion of specific security requirements for the design of security controls to protect the data in storage, in process, in transit, and on display to users. The lack of design of a security control to meet these requirements is a finding that can be fixed during the design phase of the SDLC by requiring the development teams to include it in the architecture design documents. If these design flaws are identified during the SDLC these can be remediated based upon the analysis of the potential technical impact and likelihood of exploit. The assessment of the risk of the design flaw in the implementation of a security control will be done by analyzing the likelihood of threats and the technical impact in case such threats will exploit these design flaws to impact either the application data or the functional assets.

The architectural analysis of the security components can be done following the decomposition of the architecture of the application by analyzing the design of the security controls and by enumerating a set of requirements to assert that the confidentiality, integrity, and availability of each data component are protected by a secure design of a security control. In the case when security control is either missing in design or cannot be asserted by the documentation, available specific tests should be documented to validate that no security control gaps or vulnerabilities are present.

Architecture analysis reviews can have either positive or negative assertions. A positive assertion consists of identifying the security control as documented and designed by following the security requirement. A negative or failed assertion represents the instance where a security control cannot be asserted in the design because is missing or it is designed without following security requirements and security standards and therefore introduces a design flaw. An example could be, for example, encrypting the authentication data using a nonstandard encryption algorithm or not using standard secure protected storage for keys.

An example of security architecture design guidelines that can be used to review the design of application security controls is shown in Table 8.11.

The assessment of security controls in the application architecture can be done by embedding the security requirements previously documented and security control frameworks such as STRIDE and ASF in threat modeling tools. By using the Threat-Modeler™ tool, for example, it is possible to conduct an architectural risk analysis by reviewing the various security controls of the application and conduct an in-depth design review of each security control. An example of this approach using the ThreatModeler™ tool is included in Figure 8.21.

Once the security control to review is selected (e.g. authorization), a more in-depth security risk control review can be performed by asserting the requirement of the control as this requirement has been reviewed and asserted against the application security design guidelines previously shown. The tracking of the review of application security controls at architectural and functional level can be done by enumerating each security design requirement for this control using a threat modeling tool as shown in Figure 8.22.

The functional decomposition of the application can also be used to assert security requirements for protecting both the data and the functionality associated to each functional component. For example, a login component that allows a user to authenticate and access the wires fund transfer functional component would need to assert the implementation of multifactor authentication during login. The functional decomposition can provide a better assertion of security requirements for protecting data for specific business process implemented by the online banking application such as requests for bank statements, opening bank accounts, money transfers, and payments.

These design flaws can be identified by using the secure functional analysis for business critical functions of the online banking application that was conducted in stage III. Using the results of this analysis, it is possible to assert that security controls implemented protect each of the application business critical functions, as these are functional assets and as data assets have a requirement for the protection of confidentiality, integrity, and availability risks. At high level, this type of analysis allows to analyze the risks of each functional asset based upon the information of the threat targeting it and identify weaknesses in security controls (e.g. MFA that might be bypassed by MiTM attacks) and should be remediated by introducing changes in the design of the application.

After we have identified design flaws and tracked for validation with security testing including the other types of security controls, weaknesses and vulnerabilities that were identified in previous security tests the next step of this stage consist of correlating each of these design flaws, security control weaknesses and vulnerabilities with the threats that were previously analyzed. This is the activity *WVA 5.3- Mapping threat to vulnerabilities*. This activity leverage the results of the threat analysis performed during stage IV and the type of vulnerabilities such as CWE and CVE that are known to be exploited by threat agents of the threat scenarios being analyzed.

TABLE 8.11 Secure Architecture Design Guidelines

Security Control	Secure Architecture Design Requirements
Authentication	Authentication strength should be commiserated to the risk of the data/functionality being accessed; Internal and external connections (user and entity) should be authenticated; Non-repudiation of a connection should be enforced through IP filtering or mutual authentication; Credentials and authentication tokens should be protected with encryption in storage and transit; Protocols used for authentication should be resistant to brute force, dictionary, and session replay attacks; Strong password policies should be enforced; Logging errors should not reveal password hints and valid usernamesAccount lockouts should not result in a denial of service for users
Authorization	Authorization mechanisms should work properly, fail securely, and cannot be circumvented Authorization should be checked on every request and cannot be bypassedServer side; Role-Based Access Controls (RBAC) should be used to restrict access to specific operations The principle of least privilege is used for users and service accounts.Privilege separation is correctly configured within the presentation; business and data access layers Permissions such as Access Control Lists (ACLs) are used for enforcing authorized access to resources
Encryption	No credentials and sensitive data are sent in clear text over the wireSensitive data is encrypted in storage and in transitStandard encryption algorithms and minimum key sizes are being usedDigital signatures are used to protect data integrityPrivate keys are cryptographically protected by either secure file storage or hardware encryption modules
Session	Authentication tokens are sent encrypted over SSLUser is forced to reauthenticate when performing critical functionsAll open sessions are expired at logout and at timeoutSession tokens cannot be replayedSession tokens are changed after authenticationHTTP cookies are set with the secure flag
Input validation	All data types, format, length, and range checks are enforcedAll data sent from the client is validated by the server before processingNo security decision is based upon parameters (e.g. URL parameters) that can be manipulatedInput filtering via white list validation is used to filter malicious dataOutput encoding is used
Error Handling/ Information leakage	All exceptions are properly handled in a structured mannerPrivileges are restored to the appropriate level in case of errors and exceptionsNo system error messages (e.g. memory stack) are returned to the userError messages are scrubbed so that no sensitive information is revealed to the attackerThe application fails in a secure mannerResources are released if an error occurs
Logging/ Auditing	No sensitive information is loggedSecurity events (e.g. authentication, password changes) are loggedAccess controls are enforced on log files to prevent unauthorized accessIntegrity controls are enforced on log files to provide nonrepudiationLog files provide for audit trail for sensitive operations and logging of key eventsAuditing and logging is enabled across the tiers on multiple servers

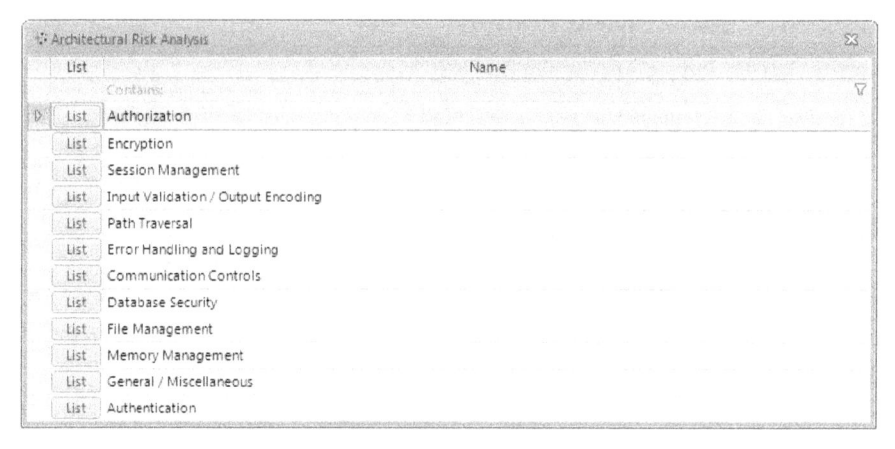

Architectural Risk Analysis

List	Name
	Contains
List	Authorization
List	Encryption
List	Session Management
List	Input Validation / Output Encoding
List	Path Traversal
List	Error Handling and Logging
List	Communication Controls
List	Database Security
List	File Management
List	Memory Management
List	General / Miscellaneous
List	Authentication

Figure 8.21 Architectural Risk Analysis Component of ThreatModeler™

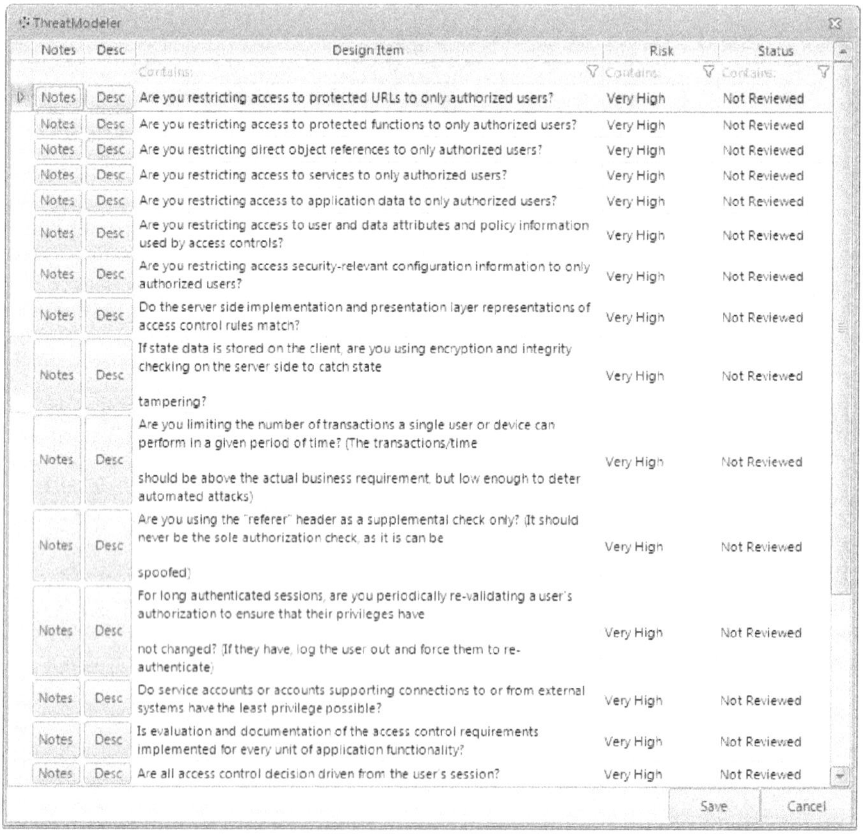

ThreatModeler

Notes	Desc	Design Item	Risk	Status
		Contains	Contains	Contains
Notes	Desc	Are you restricting access to protected URLs to only authorized users?	Very High	Not Reviewed
Notes	Desc	Are you restricting access to protected functions to only authorized users?	Very High	Not Reviewed
Notes	Desc	Are you restricting direct object references to only authorized users?	Very High	Not Reviewed
Notes	Desc	Are you restricting access to services to only authorized users?	Very High	Not Reviewed
Notes	Desc	Are you restricting access to application data to only authorized users?	Very High	Not Reviewed
Notes	Desc	Are you restricting access to user and data attributes and policy information used by access controls?	Very High	Not Reviewed
Notes	Desc	Are you restricting access security-relevant configuration information to only authorized users?	Very High	Not Reviewed
Notes	Desc	Do the server side implementation and presentation layer representations of access control rules match?	Very High	Not Reviewed
Notes	Desc	If state data is stored on the client, are you using encryption and integrity checking on the server side to catch state tampering?	Very High	Not Reviewed
Notes	Desc	Are you limiting the number of transactions a single user or device can perform in a given period of time? (The transactions/time should be above the actual business requirement but low enough to deter automated attacks)	Very High	Not Reviewed
Notes	Desc	Are you using the "referer" header as a supplemental check only? (It should never be the sole authorization check, as it is can be spoofed)	Very High	Not Reviewed
Notes	Desc	For long authenticated sessions, are you periodically re-validating a user's authorization to ensure that their privileges have not changed? (If they have, log the user out and force them to re-authenticate)	Very High	Not Reviewed
Notes	Desc	Do service accounts or accounts supporting connections to or from external systems have the least privilege possible?	Very High	Not Reviewed
Notes	Desc	Is evaluation and documentation of the access control requirements implemented for every unit of application functionality?	Very High	Not Reviewed
Notes	Desc	Are all access control decision driven from the user's session?	Very High	Not Reviewed

Save   Cancel

Figure 8.22 Architectural Risk Analysis of Authorization Controls

Specifically the map of threats to vulnerabilities when is done using the STIX threat language consists of mapping the "Threattarget" attribute with CWEs and CVEs that are known from threat intelligence to be exploited by this threat agent.

Without a mapping of threat to vulnerability that comes from a threat intelligence feed using STIX in which the "threattarget" attribute is populated with the types of CWEs that are known to be exploited by the threat, the threat analyst need to recur to formal methods and conduct this mapping to the best of the knowledge of known application vulnerabilities as these are reported in vulnerability assessments and known threat agents and attacks that seek to exploit them.

One of the formal methods that analysts can use for the mapping of threats to vulnerabilities is the threat tree, an example of, which it is shown in Figure 8.23. In the example shown, a threat agent, the attacker whose goal is to read other user's messages will try to exploit different type of vulnerabilities to reach his goal. Examples of vulnerabilities that the threat agent might seek to exploit includes an SQL injection vulnerability, a design flaw in authorization, a cached page, or file stored on the desktop that can be retrieved by accessing the unattended desktop or even a nonvulnerability such as careless employee who would leave his desktop unattended without logging out hence accessing the logged authenticated session of that user to get his data. The walking of a threat tree from the attacker goals to the vulnerabilities that can be exploited to reach such goals is also useful to determine the course of action (the end of the the branch of the threat tree) to mitigate the risk of these vulnerabilities.

The deliverable of this activity consists of a list of vulnerabilities at the application and system level and their level of exposure to the threats. Since these vulnerabilities affect the different IT assets of the application such as the several architectural components of the web application such as web and application servers and databases as well as the servers and application software on which these applications run and the network where these servers are hosted, it is also important to correlate these vulnerabilities for each IT application assets.

Since this stage builds on top of the previous stages and specifically the assessment of the technical scope for the IT assets in stage II, the decomposition of the application in these IT assets at architectural and technology stack level in stage III including any design flaws identified during the architectural analysis in that stage as well as the threat analysis profile with threat list for web application assets (data and functions) from stage IV, it is possible at this stage also to visually correlate these vulnerabilities with the different components of the application architecture as well as the threats that seek to exploit these vulnerabilities as shown in Figure 8.24.

In the DFD of Figure 8.24, the different components of the online banking application are shown including the flow of the data, the different process/components of the application architecture and the different trust zones/boundaries for accessing the data in and out from these components. Threats such as data compromise, data theft, online fraud, abuse of functionality, abuse of privileges, and denial of services are shown as external threat agent threats.

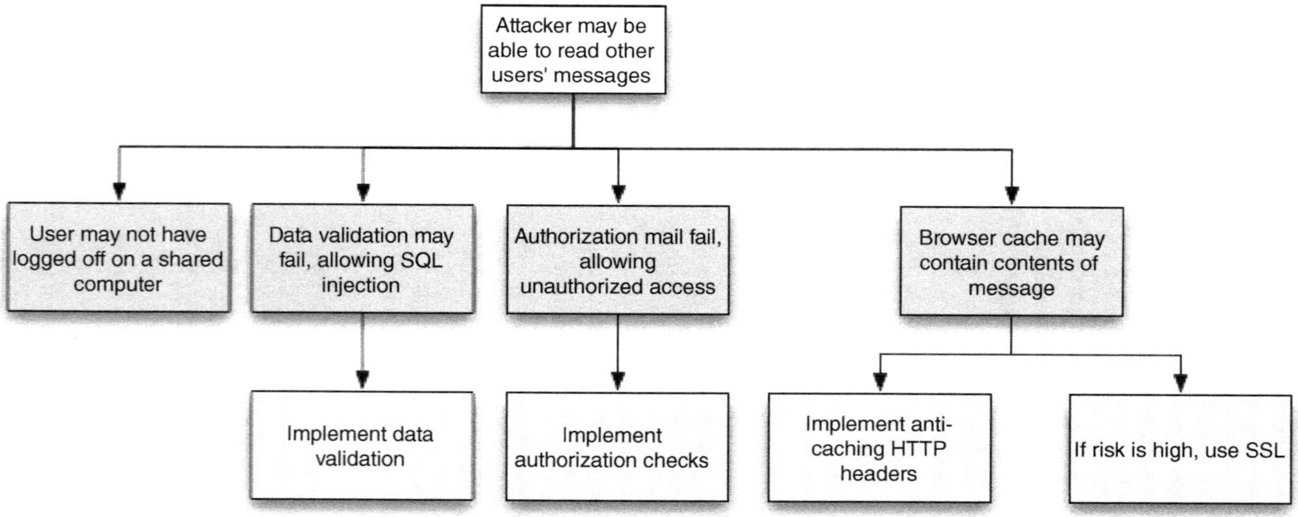

Figure 8.23 Threat Tree (Source OWASP)

PASTA USE CASE EXAMPLE WALK-THROUGH 563

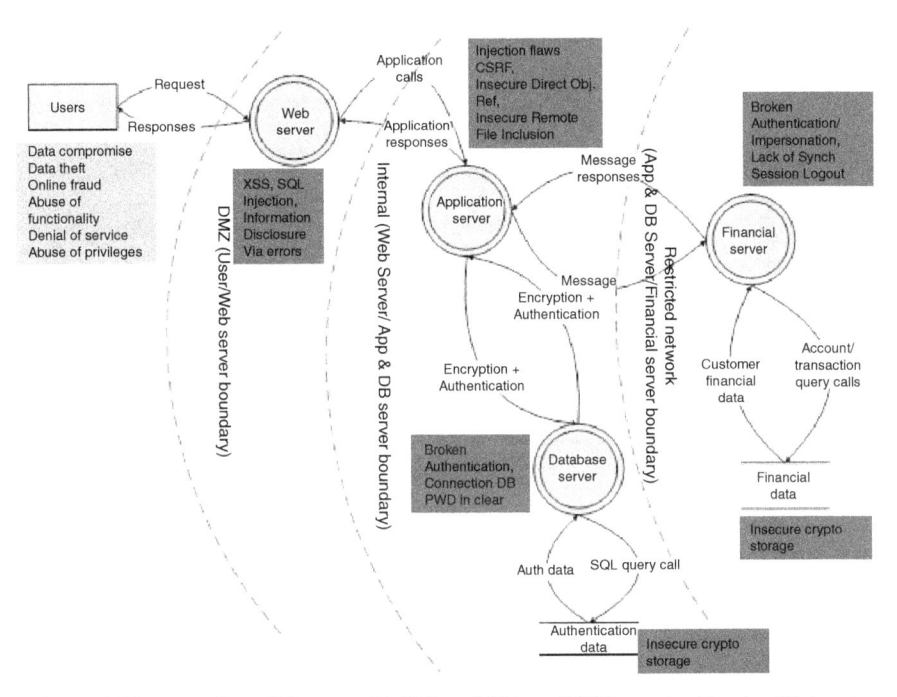

Figure 8.24 Mapping of Threats with Vulnerabilities of Different Application IT Assets

The vulnerabilities that these external threat agents seek to exploit to realize these threats are marked for each component. A threat agent can exploit one of more vulnerability at different layers of the application architecture for the threat agent to be capable of reaching his goal. For example, data compromise and theft might occur because of an exploit of SQL injection vulnerability at the web server and insecure direct object reference at the application server to retrieve financial records for another user or either weak authentication (e.g. passwords in clear or guessable) or insecure session management (e.g. authentication session for accessing the financial server is not in synch and not timing out) at the financial server allowing the external threat agent to login to the database where financial data are stored.

This correlation of threat agents with vulnerability exploits that can be pursued at the different layers of the application architecture is important to determine which vulnerabilities should be prioritized for remediation based upon the risk posed by a threat agent exploiting them. This mapping also allows application security teams to look at the protection of the application from the perspective of trust boundary layers that can breach and decide where and how to apply defense in depth for protecting from these threats. Once the application weaknesses and vulnerabilities are correlated with the application assets and the threat agents, the threat analysis has finally gathered the overall picture of the application threats and vulnerabilities and is ready for the next step, that is, to calculate and assign a risk severity to these vulnerabilities.

This is the objective of the activity *WVA 5.4 "Provide Context risk Analysis based upon Threat-Vulnerability."*

The scoring of the vulnerabilities need to consider both the risk severity of the vulnerabilities that was previously estimated as blinded to threats, that is, without factoring the instance of a threat seeking to exploit the vulnerability in the risk calculation and the risk posed by exposure to known threats.

To assign the risk severity to vulnerabilities, standard accepted risk scoring methods can be used such as CVSS. These methods allow a threat analyst to calculate the score of a vulnerability based upon the assign to different factors such as probability and impact. For calculate probability, the factors that can be considered are the ease of discovery, ease to conduct the exploit, awareness of the exploit, and security controls that might either prevent or detect the exploit of the vulnerability. For the calculation of technical impact caused by an exploit of vulnerabilities, the factors that can be used for the risk calculation are the impact on the confidentiality, integrity, and availability of the data.

The calculation of the severity of vulnerabilities is essential for prioritize these vulnerabilities for threat remediation: vulnerabilities whose severity is ranked HIGH can be prioritized before MEDIUM risk vulnerabilities. The remediation of vulnerabilities can also be prioritized based upon other criteria such as the types or group of vulnerabilities that are found most prevalent and commonly found in web applications and included in the OWASP (Open Web Application Security Consortium) Top Ten 2013, the WASC (Web Application Security Consortium) vs.2, the SANS CWE/SANS Top 25, and MITRE CWE (Common Weaknesses Exposures). These categorizations of vulnerabilities follow different taxonomies but at high level can all be mapped and prioritized accordingly as it is shown in the Table 8.12.

It is important to notice that while OWASP Top Ten is prioritized with OWASP A01 as the most critical weakness and OWASP A10 as the least critical weakness and the same for SANS Top 25, which is a yearly list of the most severe weaknesses, other classifications such as WASC and CWE are not prioritized based upon the same criteria based upon progressive IDs. WASC Threat Classification is a weakness and attack classification maintained by the Web Application 2Security Consortium where IDs are assigned chronologically upon definition of the weakness or attack: WASC TCs lower IDs are not necessarily more severe than WASC TCs with a higher ID, they were just defined earlier. CWE (Common Weakness Enumeration) are also assigned on a sequential basis as they are defined.

It is important to notice that there is a difference between a prioritization by severity based upon the risk score assigned to the vulnerability (e.g. CVSS score), based upon the most prevalent type or group of vulnerabilities (e.g. OWASP) and based upon the most common vulnerabilities found in exploits such as security incidents and instances of compromise.

In essence, the fact that a vulnerability group that is most common (e.g. OWASP A01 Injection) does not mean is the one most exploited in attacks observed from threat intelligence and security incident reports. For example, Imperva's 2013 Web Application Attack Report (WAAR) identifies how many attacks a typical application

PASTA USE CASE EXAMPLE WALK-THROUGH

TABLE 8.12 Mapping of OWASP-WASC and CWE Source CriticalWatch: OWASP to WASC to CWE Mapping, Correlating Different Industry Taxonomy

OWASP Top 10, 2013	WASC v2	CWE/SANS Top 25 2011	CWE-ID	Reference	Dangerous Type		CWE-ID
A01 - Injection	External Control of Assumed-Immutable Web Parameter		CWE-472		WASC-01 Insufficient Authentication		CWE-287
					WASC-02 Insufficient Authorization	6	CWE-862
						15	CWE-863
	File Injection		CWE-98		WASC-33 Path Traversal	13	CWE-22
			CWE-73		Inclusion of Functionality from Untrusted Control Sphere	16	CWE-829
	PHP Injection		CWE-94		Improper Access Control		CWE-284
	WASC-05 Remote File Inclusion		CWE-98		Authentication Bypass Through User-controlled Key		CWE-639
			CWE-426	A05 - Security Misconfiguration	Information Exposure Through an Error Message	39	CWE-209
			CWE-73		Sensitive data under web root		CWE-219
	WASC-19 SQL Injection	1	CWE-89		WASC-13 Information Leakage		CWE-200
			CWE-564			28	CWE-754
	WASC-20 Improper Input Handling	27	CWE-20		WASC-14 Server Misconfiguration		CWE-16
	WASC-23 XML Injection		CWE-91		WASC-15 Application Misconfiguration		CWE-16
	WASC-25 HTTP Response splitting		CWE-113		WASC-16 Directory Indexing		CWE-548
	WASC-28 Null byte injection		CWE-158		WASC-17 Improper Filesystem Permissions	11	CWE-250
	WASC-29 Ldap Injection		CWE-90			17	CWE-732
	WASC-30 Mail command injection		CWE-88				CWE-280
	WASC-31 OS Command Injection	2	CWE-78				CWE-538
	WASC-36 SSI Injection		CWE-97				CWE-552
	WASC-39 Xpath Injection		CWE-643	A06 - Sensitive Data Exposure	WASC-50 Insufficient Data Protection	8	CWE-311
	WASC-46 XQuery Injection		CWE-652			19	CWE-327
A02 - Broken Authentication and Session Management	WASC-01 Insufficient Authentication	5	CWE-306			25	CWE-759
			CWE-287				CWE-326
	WASC-11 Brute Force	21	CWE-307		WASC-04 Insufficient Transport Layer Protection		CWE-311
	WASC-12 Contents Spoofing		CWE-345	A07 - Missing Function Level Access Control	WASC-02 Insufficient Authorization		CWE-285
	WASC-18 Credential/Session Prediction	7	CWE-798		WASC-21 Insufficient Anti-automation		CWE-799
		31	CWE-330				CWE-084
	WASC-37 Session Fixation		CWE-384		WASC-34 Predictable Resource Location		CWE-425
	WASC-47 Insufficient Session Expiration		CWE-613	A08 - Cross Site Request Forgery (CSRF)	WASC-09 Cross-site Request Forgery	12	CWE-352
	Reliance on Untrusted Inputs in a Security Decision	10	CWE-807	A09 - Using components With Known Vulnerabilities	[NO WASC]	16	CWE-829
	Download of Code Without Integrity Check	14	CWE-494	A10 - Unvalidated Redirects and Forwards	WASC-38 URI Redirector Abuse	22	CWE-601
A03 - Cross Site Scripting (XSS)	WASC-08 Cross-site scripting	4	CWE-79				
	WASC-24 HTTP Request Splitting		CWE-93				
A04 - Insecure Direct Object	Unrestricted Upload of File with	9	CWE-434				

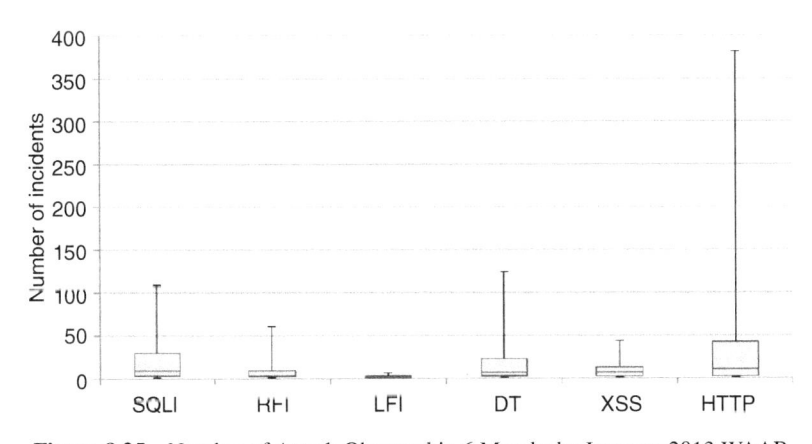

Figure 8.25 Number of Attack Observed in 6 Months by Imperva 2013 WAAR

can expect to suffer annually. This is based on observing and analyzing Internet traffic to 70 web applications during a period of six months. The number of attack incidents observed is shown in Figure 8.25.

According to this report, *"the most prevalent types of attacks are SQL injection, and directory traversal HTTP protocol violations, which often indicate automated threats, evasion techniques, and denial of service attacks."* By comparing with the most prevalent vulnerabilities found in application, we can drive the following conclusions:

1. The top 1 attack HTTP protocol violations (automation attacks) only maps to the top seven vulnerability missing function level access controls and WASC 21 missing antiautomation.
2. The top 2 SQL injection attack maps to the top 1 vulnerability OWASP A01-Injection and WASC-19 SQL Injection.
3. The top 3 directory transversal attack maps to the top 4 common vulnerability OWASP Top 4 Insecure Direct Object Reference, WASC-33 Path Transversal.
4. The top 4 Cross-site scripting attack (XSS) maps to OWASP top 3 (XSS).
5. The top 5 Local File Inclusion attack maps to the top 1 common vulnerability OWASP top 1 injection WASC vs2 File Injection.

If an organization ought to prioritize vulnerabilities based upon attacks observed using this metrics, the focus would be on fixing instances of lack of antiautomation countermeasures, input validation vulnerabilities, insecure direct object reference, and cross-site scripting.

According to the same WAAR report, different business verticals are also differently affected in terms of attacks sought, for example, online retain web applications experience about twice as many of SQL injection attack than other verticals including financial and fewer remote file inclusion attacks than the general application population. It is therefore important to prioritize vulnerabilities based upon observed security incidents and indication of compromises as well as common vulnerabilities observed for applications that belong to the same industry sector.

For the application in scope of the analysis, that is, online banking application, the vertical sector of reference is the financial sector. It is critical that the risk severity of the vulnerabilities identified as being most common in the sector of relevance is also compared with the threat intelligence shared by organizations in the same sector of relevant (e.g. for the financial sector the FS-ISAC) on which attacks are more prevalent and how to detect and block these attacks.

Known vulnerabilities analyzed at this stage and design flaws identified during stage V known to be exploited by the top attacks (e.g. input validation flaws, missing detection and countermeasures against automation attacks/bots) are the ones that should be prioritized. The effort for vulnerability remediation needs to be driven from the perspective of fixing them but also detecting the vulnerabilities by considering also the most effective measures that can detect and block attacks (e.g. black lists of attack sources) that seek to exploit them with countermeasures. In order to prioritize the monitoring effort on attacks, it is important to be able to acquire threat intelligence on malicious sources and apply this intelligence in real time. Since this threat intelligence can only be seen by analyzing data gathered from a large set of potential victims, it has to be gathered from information assurance centers such as FS ISAC.

At the end of this activity, it is important to produce a report of vulnerabilities for the online banking application that is correlated to the threats affecting each security component of the application. The risk severity of these vulnerabilities will be updated by taking into consideration the likelihood of threat agent seeking to exploit them. This report also includes updated risk for control gaps/design flaws exposing data assets/functions to threats previously analyzed in stage IV (Architectural risk analysis activity)

Once the risk severity of the vulnerabilities has been analyzed based upon threat analysis information and the severity risk information has been updated in the knowledge base of exploitable weaknesses for the online banking application to prioritize the vulnerability remediation effort, the next activity of this stage consists of *"WVA 5.4 – Conduct targeted vulnerability testing."* The goal of this activity is to conduct targeted vulnerability tests. These tests will also include a set of new test cases that include the knowledge of threats targeting these vulnerabilities from the threat to vulnerability mapping analysis done previously. The scope of these targeted vulnerability tests is to revalidate known vulnerabilities previously identified as these were identified by previous application security assessments such as security design reviews, source code reviews, and application static and dynamic tests. These security tests will also validate any design flaws and vulnerabilities that are part of the knowledge based and are considered at high risk of being exploited by threat agents.

The value added by conducing these targeted vulnerability tests comes from testing known and new vulnerabilities as a real threat agent will try to identify them for later exploit them in an attack and using the same tools and attack techniques known from the threat intelligence and threat analysis. The purpose of these tests is also to determine the exposure and the risk as technical impact on the application assets including confidential and sensitive data as well as business critical functions that can be targeted by specific threats. For example, this can be a case of testing a known SQL injection vulnerability that was previously assessed and remediated but can know be retested with the knowledge of specific threat vectors (e.g. encoded threat vectors seek to bypass known filtering in place) and by using the same attack tools (e.g. Havij SQL injection tool) used by known threat agents.

When creating these test cases, it is important to be able to correlate the security test cases that apply to each functional component of the application and correlate these with the threat being analyzed in stage V and the security requirements documented during stage I as well as vulnerabilities identified in previous assessments that belong to that component under review. An example of deriving security test cases for each functional component for the login functional component of the online banking application (refer to the Hacme Bank ThreatModeler™ template and project) is shown in Figure 8.26.

These security test cases can be executed during this stage of the assessment as well as during the validation phase of the SDLC to reassess the risk posed by these vulnerabilities in the presence of security measures such as protective application security controls (e.g. authentication, authorization, encryption, data input validation, session management) as well as countermeasures that can detect specific threat triggered events (e.g. application and system logs).

By looking at each functional component of the application and by analyzing security functional requirements, threats targeting weaknesses and vulnerabilities including the ones identified as design flaws during the architectural risk analysis

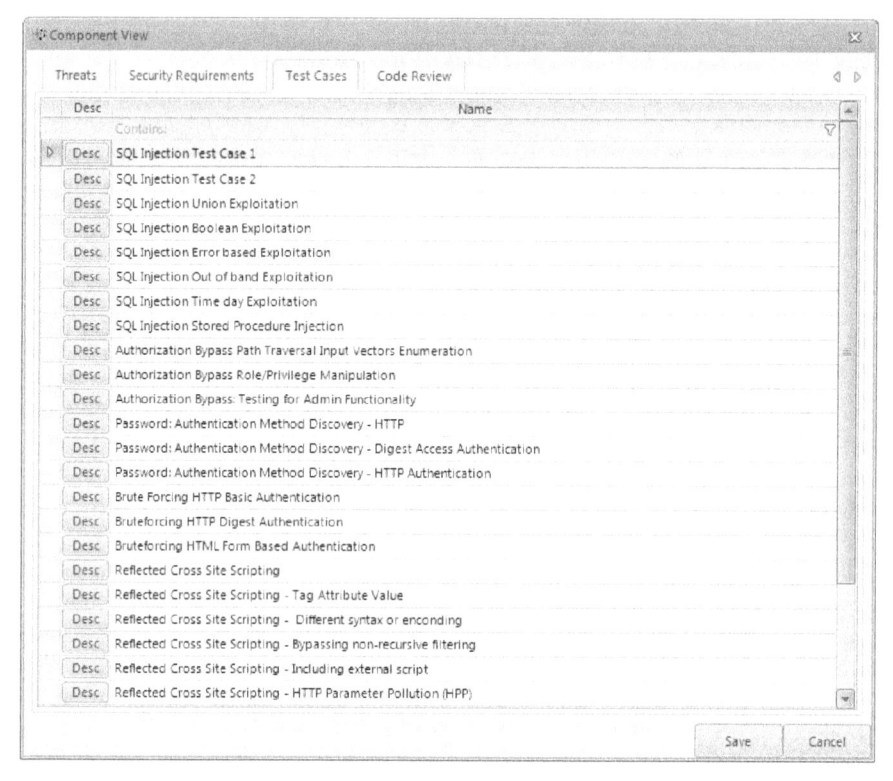

Figure 8.26 Test Cases to Validate Vulnerabilities at Component Functional Level ThreatModeler™

that affecting these security controls associated with functional components and the security tests that can validate these security controls weaknesses and vulnerabilities, we have an actionable view to assess the risk of each functional component, and we can track each threat to mitigate the impact by applying fixes of these weaknesses and vulnerabilities as well as by applying additional countermeasures when the remediation of these vulnerabilities is not enough to mitigate the impact. Since, to determine the extent of the impact, it is important to look at the specific of the attacks and how these vulnerabilities are exploited prior to conducting these attacks, we would need to conduct an attack modeling exercise. This attack modeling will be performed in the next stage of PASTA, stage VI Attack Modeling and Simulation.

Stage VI – Attack Modeling and Simulation (AMS)

Goal of This Stage The goal of this stage is to analyze and model the attacks against the application. The analysis of the attacks relies on the analysis of the chain of events such as kill-chain reported by threat intelligence or as root cause analysis of a security incident that was analyzed "post mortem." Based on the analysis of the attacks and the previous identification of the threat agent (TTPs) Tools, Techniques, and Processes, it is possible to analyze the course of actions of the various attack scenarios and associate with the TTPs used by the threat agents/actors of these attack scenarios. Once the attack scenarios have been analyzed and the various attack vectors are identified and updated in the attack libraries, the next step consists of deriving a set of cases to test existing countermeasures and conduct attack-driven security tests and simulations. The objective of these test cases is to simulate realistic attack scenarios and determine if exploits from the threat agents are possible and identify countermeasures to prevent and detect the attack vectors used.

Guidance for Conducting This Stage The scope of the Attack Modeling and Simulation (AMS) stage is to create an attack model to simulate attacks against the application and to determine whether these attacks could result in possible impacts on the application assets such as sensitive data and business critical functions. By analyzing the various attack scenarios in the attack model, it would be possible to determine the effectiveness of application security controls in mitigating the impact of these attacks. The modeling of these attacks starts by considering the threat scenario that was previously analyzed in stage IV including the various types of threat agents/actors identified in that threat scenarios. These threat agents are also known to use specific tools, techniques, and procedures (TTPs) to conduct their attacks. In this stage, we focus on these TTPs as well as on the various attack vectors used by these threat agents. Some of the TTPs and attack vectors can be attributed to specific threat agents, their capabilities and motivations as well as the tools used such as cyber-crime tools to conduct these attacks.

Attack modeling considers both opportunistic exploit of weaknesses and vulnerabilities in web applications and targeted attacks against products/applications. This attack modeling relies on the knowledge of the threat agent kill-chain and on the analysis of the overall threat scenarios. The attack vectors that are identified by the analysis of the attack scenarios will enumerate all types of possible attacks and the specific types of security controls (e.g. authentication) that are attacked and will document how these can be attacked by using an attack library.

Some of these attacks can also opportunistically target known vulnerabilities that are accessible through user and data interfaces including vulnerabilities that should be considered inherent of the technology stack such as software framework and service vulnerability used by the application. For example, mobile applications have inherent vulnerabilities that might be exploited by specific threat agents using different attack vectors. These attacks might follow a specific chain of events such as will seek to compromise the mobile device first and then bypass authentication controls such as multifactor authentication with (MiTMo) Man-in-the-Mobile Attacks.

One of the techniques that can be used for modeling attacks includes attack trees. Attack trees help to create a model of how the attacker's main goals can be realized by following a specific branch of the attack tree. The model of attacks with attack trees help to identify the most probable path that can be followed by an attacker to reach his goals. Another method that can be used to model attacks is to analyze the business use cases and identify the possible abuse cases that can be followed by the attacker to bypass security controls.

After the various attack scenarios have been analyzed, the next step consists of analyzing how threat agents can conduct attacks to cause an impact on the application.

Since an attack describes how a threat can be realized, the probability of a threat to be realized in an attack depends on several factors and among them the costs for an attacker to conduct the attack based upon the attacking tools at his disposal and the opportunities to exploit known vulnerabilities. To assess the probability of a threat to be realized in an attack to cause an impact, it is important to assign the values to the costs of the attacks and the benefit for the attacker as gain and choose to simulate the attacks that maximize the gain and minimize the costs for the attackers.

An attack scenario might occur because of the exploit of specific vulnerabilities that increase the probability of a threat to conduct successful attacks against the application assets. The analysis of the probability of possible attacks among the various options of attack available to an attacker can be done by analyzing attacks using attack trees. By analyzing the various possible paths for conducting attacks with an attack tree, it is possible to determine the attacker's course of actions and attack events that have higher probability to succeed in achieving the attacker's goal. By modeling attacks using attack tree, we can model each step of the attack as the opportunity that an attacker has to move to the next step of the attack till it reaches the desired goal for the attacker. The realization of an attack can be analyzed by assigning conditions to each node of the attack tree. At each node of the attack tree, an attacker has the options of "OR" (one attack or another can be chosen) or "AND" (both attack paths can be chosen). For example, a threat agent seeking to compromise the data in a database for the attack scenario of a banking Trojan needs to own the client "AND" attack the application "OR" attack the application directly. Given that the probability of attacking the client is lower than attacking the application directly, it will choose that attack path. The probability of success is given by the consideration of all single probabilities of each node whose conditions need to be fulfilled in order for the attacker to reach his goal. Once the most probable attack paths have been analyzed including the application components, processes, and security controls that a threat agent need to transverse on its way to the target, it is possible to create specific test cases for simulating the attacks.

Attack trees can have different scope such as network layer scope, architectural level scope, and functional level scope. The analysis of attacks using attack trees at the network later can be useful to analyze (CNE) Computer Network exploits as well as (CAN) Computer network attacks. At the application layer that is the focus of risk-centric application threat modeling, attack trees can be used to analyze exploits of vulnerabilities affecting architectural components including the various services, API and libraries, and system-level processes that support the application functionality.

The analysis of sequence of events that attackers follow when conducting attacks against the application assets, the analysis of the attack surface to identity the application data entry points that are sought to conduct the attacks as well as the analysis of the most probable attack scenario based upon the analysis of the attack trees helps in the derivation of test cases to simulate the attack scenarios. Once each of the attacks is simulated with tests, it is possible to determine for each threat agent the probability to achieve his desired impact such as exfiltration of data, stealing money, and fraud. The analysis of impacts include both technical impacts such as loss of data confidentiality, integrity, accountability, and availability as well as business impact as monetized loss associated with a data asset. The determination of the probability of threats to be realized in attacks and the likelihood of the attack to produce either a technical or business impact allows determining the risk of each attack. The identification of the various events of an attack leading to an exploit of vulnerabilities to cause an impact is critical to determine the detective controls that can be deployed to detect these events as indication of an attack and to decide the appropriate response to mitigate the impact.

Once the attack has been analyzed and simulated, it is possible to update the attack library with the mapping of threats, controls, and vulnerabilities that these attacks seek to exploit. This attack library can be inclusive of all known attack vectors. These attack vectors can be later used for the creation of specific tests for testing the resilience of security controls and countermeasures to these types of attack vectors.

Inputs for Conducting This Stage Since attacks describe that threat agents might exploit security controls and weaknesses to cause an impact, the type of information that is required for modeling of attacks is the knowledge of the threats and of the vulnerabilities. The type of documentation that can be useful for modeling attacks includes:

1. Threat scenarios analyzed in stage IV.
2. Threat agents analyzed in stage IV.
3. Threat actors TTPs analyzed in stage IV.
4. The assets targeted by threats analyzed in stage IV.
5. Existing vulnerabilities and weaknesses targeted by threats analyzed and mapped in stage V.
6. Results of testing of vulnerabilities and design flaws executed during stage V.

Artifacts Produced at the End of This Stage At the end of this stage, we will produce the following artifacts:

(a) *The model of the attack scenarios* including the course of action of the attacks using kill-chain model that is followed by the different threat agents/actors.
(b) *Attack trees* with the determination of the most probable attack paths leading to exploits and identification of various vulnerabilities and security controls that might be bypassed.
(c) *Use and abuse cases* covering bypass of security controls and abuse of functionality for fraud and data compromise.
(d) *The attack surface* that is targeted by threat agents previously identified in the attack modeling scenarios (analyzed for threats and data entry points previously identified stage IV Threat Analysis).

(e) *Updated attack library* with new attacks that can be enumerated for simulating/ testing the various attack scenarios.

(f) *Documented test cases* that can be used to test the resilience of the application in the presence of specific conditions of exposure of vulnerabilities as well as by considering the real attack scenarios, automated and not, single or group based, capabilities, motivations, cyber-attack tools and techniques used in real attack case scenarios.

(g) *Attack testing/simulation report* that includes the results of the test cases for testing the various attack scenarios for vulnerabilities and design flaws. The report includes the assessment of risks of each security issue (design flaws, vulnerabilities) that is identified such as probability and technical impact can be determined based upon the results of the test/simulation.

Tools The execution of this stage can be facilitated by the use of WASC WHID attack libraries and threat-driven test cases to simulate attacks included in myAppSecurity ThreatModeler™. MS STRIDE methodology is used here to derive and prioritize threat-driven test cases. Formal methods for capturing attack scenario used here is Lockheed™ kill-chain and use of kill-chain in MITRE STIX for threat-vulnerability-attack correlation. Analysis of attacks and probability includes the use of formal methods such as Amoroso attack trees. Standard use and abuse cases and MITRE CAPEC attack patterns are also used for this stage. Attack analysis and intelligence are also provided by sources of OSINT threat intelligence and vendor reports.

Activities This stage consists of the following activities:

AMS 6.1 – Analyze the attack scenarios: An attack scenario can be created for each threat agent based upon the information captured from various sources such as threat intelligence, logged security events incidents and the analysis post mortem of security incidents. Threat agents can be classified based upon their motives and capabilities. Examples include hacktivists, script kiddies, cyber-criminals, fraudsters, and government/state and corporate-sponsored spies. A threat agent might rely on different type of manual attack techniques and automated attacking tools. The attacks against the targets can follow a chain of events such as the attack course of action. The analysis of the sequence of events of a cyber-attack helps to model the attack scenario. The model of the attack scenario also includes the attacking vectors used and the specific vulnerabilities that are exploited by the threat agents to realize their goals such as data compromise, data theft, online fraud, abuse of functionality, denial of service, and abuse of privileges as example. The outcome of this activity is to create attack stories that describe how the various threat agents might attack the application.

AMS 6.2 – Update the attack library/vectors and the control framework: After the attack scenario has been analyzed and modeled, it would be possible that some of the attack vectors attributed to the threat agent's attack techniques and tools used are not part of the threat library and therefore need to be updated including the type of countermeasures that have been found effective in either detecting or preventing the attacks. The new countermeasures that should be considered in the threat library might include new emerging threat attack vectors analyzed in the attack modeling exercise as well as updated vulnerabilities and weaknesses and gaps in preventive and detective security controls. (*Note:* It is important to revisit the control assessment risk framework to add new preventive and detective controls as options to mitigate the attacks.)

AMS 6.3 – Identify the attack surface and enumerate the attack vectors: Against the data entry points of the application. Use the up-to-date threat library to identify the type of attack vectors that can be used, the type of vulnerabilities of the architecture components that can be exploited and the security controls that should be in place to detect and prevent the attacks.

AMS 6.4 – Assess the probability and impact of each attack scenario: Determine the probability of each attack of the threat scenario using attack trees (probability of exploit producing the desired technical and business impact that maximize gain for the attacker). Identify the various security controls that can be bypassed and functionality that can be abused leading to the exploit and impact. Each attack scenario can be associated with the probability of the attack and the impact so can be prioritized for the analysis and mitigation.

AMS 6.5 – Derive a set of cases to test existing countermeasures: These test cases are both threat driven using threat classification (e.g. STRIDE) and threats, vulnerabilities identified in each architectural components. Attack driven test cases can be documented based upon the previous analysis of the attack chain of events and the attack vectors used by the attackers. Additional tests can be created using use and abuse cases. Each test case can be prioritized based upon the risk that was previously calculated for each of the attack scenarios using attack trees.

AMS 6.6 – Conduct attack driven security tests and simulations: The scope of these tests is to identify vulnerabilities and design flaws that are exploited by the attack and determine the risks as factor of probability and the impact. The risk ought to factor the technical impact (loss of confidentiality, integrity, accountability, and availability) of these exploits using the results of the simulated attack exercise. After each test case is executed, the risk values that were previously assigned to each threat should be revised higher or lower depending on the results of the tests.

Web Application Use Case Example Before we start modeling the attacks targeting application in scope, it is important to highlight the difference between threats and attacks. There is a difference between threats and attacks and it is important not to confuse the two: threats describe negative events or conditions with potential for damage, whereas attacks describe how threats are realized to produce exploits and instances of compromise of data and functionality.

Examples of threats affecting online banking applications include breaches of confidential data of customers such as bank accounts and credit card data, fraudulent transactions such as unauthorized money transfers and denial of service to online accounts and transactions. Examples of attacks describing how these threats can be realized include exploit of SQL injection vulnerability to gain unauthorized access to confidential data, exploit of social engineering to install key logger malware on the bank customer's PC, compromises of user's login credentials including multifactor authentication credentials with MitM attacks and session hijacking and account takeover for transferring money to fraudulent accounts.

The description of how a threat is realized that is the definition of an attack also includes the notion of vulnerability since vulnerabilities describe opportunities for a threat agent to conduct an attack, for example, by exploiting a vulnerability to install malware on the client or to break into the web application (e.g. exploit of SQL injection vulnerabilities in the web application). Since attacks are best used to describe how threats can be realized through vulnerability exploits, we need first to analyze the threats and the vulnerabilities. This is the reason why in PASTA stage VI (AMS) Attack Modeling and Simulation comes after Vulnerability and Weakness Analysis (WVA) (stage VI) and Threat Analysis (TA) (stage V).

For the objectives of this stage, that is, the modeling of attacks to simulate the attack scenario with security test cases, we need first to analyze the attack scenario. This is accomplished by executing the stage activity *"AMS 6.1 – Analyzing the attack scenarios."* To perform this activity, the threat analyst/modeler needs to consider the type of threat agents of the threat scenarios previously analyzed and describe how an attack takes place as sequence of steps that the threat agent/actor might follow. The description of how threats of specific threat scenario can be realized to produce the desired impact such as compromise of confidential data and fraudulent transactions is the objective of the attack modeling. As minimum requirement, the description of the attack scenario needs to be comprehensive and detailed and to include the description of the attacking tools (e.g. cyber-crime toolkits), attacking techniques, and attack vectors used by the attackers against the target in this case the online banking application. The analysis of threat targets done in stage IV is also very critical for the modeling of attacks since it provides mapping of threat targets to application vulnerabilities that could be exploited during the attack. Another important element for modeling attacks is the indication of compromise and the security events that can be monitored as indication of security incidents. These security events might be triggered and detected as indication of compromise of confidential data and fraudulent transactions.

The analysis of attacks starts first and foremost with the analysis of the threat agent's characteristics specifically the type of threat agents that might target the online banking application. This analysis was done during stage IV. At high level, the threat agents attacking the online banking application might include internal threat agents such as malicious users and disgruntled employees as well as external threat agents that can be classified based upon their motivations and capabilities as hacktivists, script kiddies, cyber-criminals, fraudsters, and government/state and corporate-sponsored spies.

Each of these threat agents that were previously analyzed to target the online banking application might have different motives and capabilities and uses different types of attack techniques and tools. Some of these attacks might require the usage of sophisticated attacking tools also known as crimeware that is specifically designed by cyber-crime organizations to attack specific targets (e.g. malware banking Trojans used to attack online banking applications and botnet-based DDoS tools). The attacks used by threat agents to attack online banking sites are not all sophisticated necessarily rather might rely on exploit of common vulnerabilities and the attack vectors be included in freely available tools such as application security vulnerability scanners.

The various agents targeting the online bank application for an exploit might rely on an arsenal of different type of attack techniques, tools, and attack strategies in order to achieve their goals. For the sake of the use case shown herein, we focus on the known attack scenarios of fraudsters targeting an online banking application for online fraud, identity theft, stealing of confidential data of customers, and hacktivists targeting online banking applications with distributed denial of service.

When tasked to conduct the modeling of attacks against the online banking application, a threat analyst could rely on previous knowledge gathered on the attacks that take place after a security incident. Typically what follows after a security incident has been contained is the analysis of the incident to identify the type of vulnerabilities that were exploited as well as the preventive and detective controls that were bypassed during the course of the attack. An analysis of a security incident postmortem might also identify the sequence of events that is followed by an attacker firstly for conducting the exploit to own the target and secondly to use the compromised target to steal confidential data.

The information of the sequence of events that is followed by a threat agent to conduct and exploit of a weaknesses or vulnerability as well as to compromise the target to either steal confidential data or alter the integrity of financial transactions to commit fraud is a critical piece of information that can used for the attack analysis and simulation. This critical type of information is known with the term of "kill-chain" and is usually associated with a threat agent and can be included in the threat intelligence reports that threat intelligence sources might shared with interested parties (e.g. as threat intelligence information shared among financial institutions that are part of information assurance sharing information centers).

In the case of the online banking application, for example, and for the attack scenarios in scope that includes client compromise with banking malware and distributed denial-of-service attacks, several attack vectors can be analyzed based upon the information gathered by threat intelligence. Specifically this threat intelligence might include information about the specific attack vectors used to conduct the exploits such as to compromise the client's PC/browser through drive by downloads and MitB and compromise of the "secure" online channel established between the client PC/browser and the online banking application using MitM and compromise of the authenticated session to perform unauthorized financial transactions using session hijacking.

For the analysis of the attack scenario, it is necessary to capture the sequence of events that lead to exploits and compromises of data and functionality. By analyzing

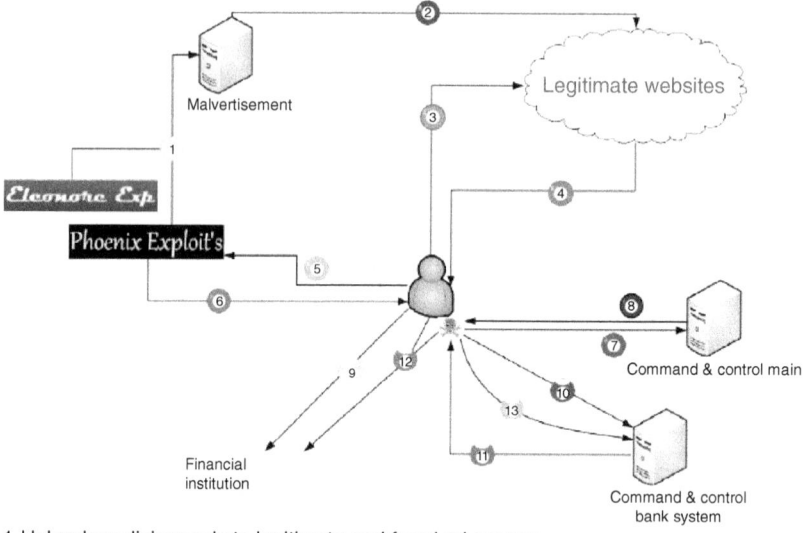

Figure 8.27 Sequence of Events Followed in Banking Trojan Attacks

1. Uploads malicious ads to legitimate and fraud ad servers
2. Malicious Ads published on legitimate websites
3. User accesses infected website
4. Website content contains redirection to exploit kit
5. User is redirected to exploit kit
6. User's PC exploited and payload downloaded successfully
7. Trojan reports in to C&C server
8. C&C server sends instructions to trojan
9. User accesses FI web site
10. Trojan reports on user activity to C&C server
11. C&C server sends commands to manipulate transaction
12. Bank transaction is altered to unauthorized payee
13. Trojan reports back success/fail to C&C server

the sequence of events of the attack, it is also possible to identify the type of security controls that are either compromised or bypassed and the vulnerabilities and weaknesses that are exploited by the attacker. An example of this sequence of events used in a banking malware attack against the user's online banking financial transactions is shown in Figure 8.27.

This figure shows the sequence of events that is followed by a fraudster to steal money from a victim's bank account starting with a compromise of the victim's PC with banking malware/Trojan.

PASTA USE CASE EXAMPLE WALK-THROUGH 577

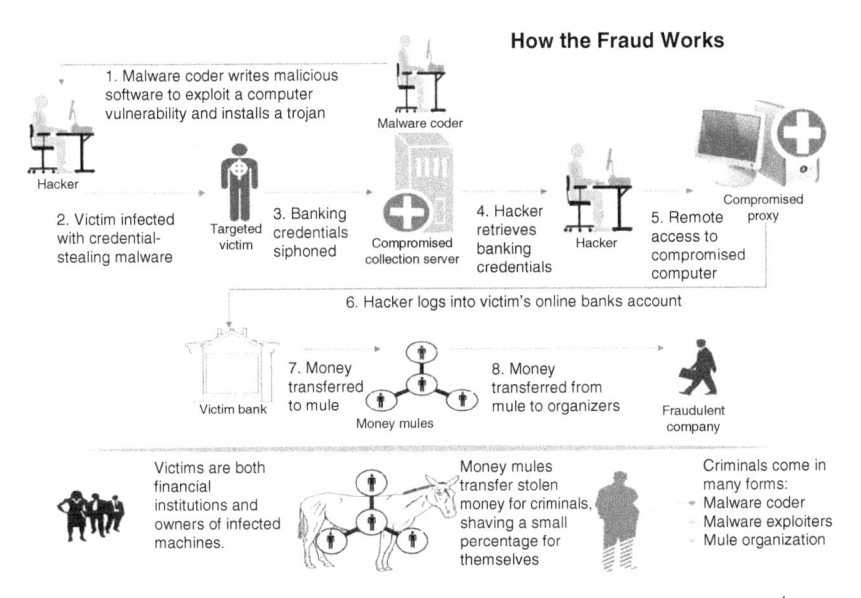

How the Fraud Works

Figure 8.28 Anatomy of Account Takeover and Fraudulent Wire Transfer[4]

Figure 8.28 shows the type of threat actors that are involved in the malware banking attack and the various techniques and strategies that use for conducting fraud such as stealing money from the bank account of the victim.

To model the attacks, we need to start from the analysis of the attack. Once we have modeled the attack scenario, we can analyze more in detail the attacking vectors used and the specific vulnerabilities that are exploited in the attack. At the beginning of the attack modeling exercise, attack scenarios can be modeled at high level by creating attack stories that describe how the various steps taken by the threat agents to achieve their goals.

Once the attack scenario is captured and we have identified the type of threat agents/actors and the attacking tools, techniques, and processes used, we can start to analyze more in detail the attack tools to extract the information about the attack vectors. An example of attacking tools that should be analyzed includes the various types of toolkits used by the attacker to create Trojan/banking malware and analyze the various types of vulnerability exploits and the various types of attack vectors used. An example of this type of analysis is shown in Figure 8.29.

By the analysis of the attack vectors used in banking malware/Trojans, it can be concluded that different types of infection techniques can be used by attackers in order to compromise the target client PC: this include social/engineering phishing, drive by download, malicious and exploit of common vulnerabilities in web applications as well as the browser. Once the malware is installed in the client/browser, an

---
[4]http://krebsonsecurity.com/tag/operation-trident-breach/.

Trojan MB - MitB MM - MitM B - Both O - Other	Infection Method					Attack Capabilities									Timing		Type	
	Phishing	Drive-by Download	Malicious Web Link	Malicious Ad	Virus Infection	HTTP Injection	Browser Redirect	From Grabbing	Credential Theft	Keystroke Logging	By Pass MFA	Screen Capture/Video	Certificate Theft	Install Backdoor	Instant Message	Real-Time	Out of Band	Automated	Manual
						MB	MM	B	B	B	B	O	O	O	O				
ZeuS	*	*	*	*	*	*	*	*	*	*	*	*	*	*	*	*	*	*	*
Spy Eye	*	*	*	*	*	*	*	*	*	*	*	*		*		*	*	*	*
InfoStealer	*	*	*	*	*	*		*	*	*	*	*	*			*			*
SilentBanker	*	*	*	*	*	*	*	*		*	*	*	*	*		*	*		*
URLZone	*	*	*	*	*	*		*		*	*	*		*		*	*	*	*
Clampi/Bugat/Gozi	*	*	*	*	*	*			*							*			*
Haxdoor	*	*	*	*	*	*		*		*				*		*			*
Limbo	*	*	*	*	*	*		*		*	*			*		*			*

Figure 8.29 Attack Vectors Used in Banking Trojan Malware, Source OWASP Anti-Malware Knowledge Base

attack agent can be activated under control of the command and control server to initiate several types of attacks against the online banking application using attack vectors such as MitM and MitB attacks. These attack vectors use redirects to redirect the victim to malicious sites, allow the fraudster to steal user's authentication credentials including multifactor authentication, take over the victim's bank account and compromise the integrity of the transaction including changing the recipient of the money transfer, changing the amount of money to be transferred, and install backdoors on compromised servers with the ability to take commands and steal confidential data.

The reverse engineering of the attacking tools and techniques used by the attackers helps to capture the attack vectors and use them for security testing. The analysis of the attack scenario is very critical and needs an in depth analysis, specifically in the cases of banking malware and DDoS attacks, it is critical to understand the sequence of the attack from the initial step of the reconnaissance of the target to the final step of realize the threat that is to achieve the attacker goals such as stealing sensitive data of customers, stealing money from bank accounts, and denial of service to access the online banking site including ability to authenticated and conduct business transactions such as checking account balance, paying bills, and other financial transactions that are available online.

In order to capture the attack scenario and specifically to dissect an attack by qualifying the events and the various activities conducted during each event, it is important to follow a model for quantifying and qualifying the various cyber-threat activities. One possible method to capture the qualifying events of an attack so that the defender can act a proper response is the "kill-chain" method. The kill-chain method was originally developed by the military as US (DoD) Department of Defense technique to locate, track, target, engage, and eliminate threat agents.

From the perspective of cyber-attack detection and eradication of the threat agents, a kill-chain model can be adopted to cyber-attacks for analyzing the actions taken by cyber-threat agents so that these can be used to capture the attacker's logical progression into steps that lead to the attacker goals such as data compromise and financial gain. The phases of the attack kill-chain consist of (1) Reconnaissance (2) Weaponization, (3) Delivery, (4) Exploitation, (5) Installation, (6) Command and Control, and (7) Action and Objectives. This technique has been adopted to cyber security and in particular intrusion security and incident response. This section will adopt kill-chain to analyze the various steps of the attack workflow that motivated threat actors to attack an online banking application.

The model and simulation of the attacks can also follow the sequence of events that were previously analyzed and shared by the threat intelligence sources. An example of information that is critical for the modeling of an attack is the sequence of events before and after an exploit that is the kill-chain phase of the attack. A threat observable event can be correlated to a kill-chain to determine if this observable is correlated to a kill-chain event such as a pre- or a postevent of an exploit of vulnerability. These events can help the threat analyst in the simulation of the attack by simulating the sequence of events in a security test. The security test can be conducted as a simulation exercise of the attack that is as much as possible realistic of the attack vectors, attacking tools and application vulnerabilities that are exploited.

Kill-Chain Attack Analysis of Banking Malware Attack Scenarios An example of capturing the attack scenario for the various phases of the kill-chain of malware banking/Trojan attacks is included herein:

1. *Kill-chain step 1 of the malware attack: Reconnaissance:* This step of the attack consists of the research, identification, and selection of targets for malware based attacks. During this phase, the attackers scan and identify sites that embed advertisements and are vulnerable to malicious advertisement uploads (e.g. iFRAME vulnerabilities, SQL Injection). Research of client vulnerabilities (e.g. browser plug-ins, flash vulnerabilities) that can be exploited for dropping malware (e.g. XSS, XFS-click-jacking, spear-phishing social engineering and drive-by-download attacks) as well as vulnerabilities of web applications that can be exploited to attack online banking sites. Derive a set of requirements for

the development of the malware as attacking tool crimeware that can exploit vulnerabilities for both droppings and exploitation/installation;

2. *Kill-chain step II of the malware attack: Weaponization:* During this step, the threat agents engineer the malware to satisfy the attack requirements. This includes also acquiring crimeware tool kit by cybercriminals that can be customized to conduct the attack. The attackers engineer online banking malware to include both disclosed (e.g. CVEs) learned from reconnaissance and undisclosed (e.g. "zero-day") vulnerabilities. Vulnerabilities are aggregated into crimeware kits using custom exploit code intended for a specific online banking URLs. Custom exploit code might include attack vectors after learning about the internal network of the bank as well as after reverse engineering the source code of the web application and understanding of the online banking site functionality. Final assembly/packaging of the malware might use open source, toolkits, and use of architected botnets of java toolkits, php scripts, or command line batches. Less skilled attackers can acquire these banking Trojan kits from cybercriminals and configure them to attack online banking sites of specific FIs (Financial Institutions); this phase of the attack includes the transmission and delivery of the malware to the target environment.

3. *Kill-chain step III of the malware attack:* Delivery of the malware (e.g. dropping of malware on target PC/server) might occur via different infection methods such as

    a. drive-by-download browsing a malware infected site to install malware on the client host;

    b. remote command execution exploiting SQL injection or other vulnerabilities to upload malware on the targeted internal server host;

    c. phishing e-mail impersonating the bank/FI with malicious link pop-ups and with malicious attachments (e.g. adobe pdf);

    d. search a site that point search to malicious URL pointed by infected Search Optimization Engine (SOE);

    e. malware installed by disgruntled employee allowing outbound web traffic to C&C from that server;

    f. unauthorized access to internal network of the bank by third-party contractor;

    g. malware installed on BYOD allowing access to internal network resources;

    h. source code with embedded backdoors by rogue S/W developer/contractor;

    i. third-party provisioned software/hardware with backdoor capabilities;

    j. malicious link delivering malware posted by threat actor on social media (e.g. Facebook) and shared with a social media group.

4. *Kill-chain step IV of the malware attack: Exploitation:* This phase of the attack consists of the triggering and activating the malware to exploit vulnerabilities on the client and the server. Once the malware is delivered to the target using one of the delivery methods (e.g. drive by download, opening attachment in e-mail), it will start to execute and scan for vulnerabilities that can be used for the installation and later for the execution of the attack under the control of

the fraudster/cybercriminal. Client vulnerabilities that are exploited for installation via drive by download includes several O.S and browser vulnerabilities listed with known CVEs and zero-days. These vulnerabilities might or might not require admin access to the target PC. Web application vulnerabilities that can be exploited to attack online banking website include common vulnerabilities that facilitate the installation of the malware on the client (e.g. XSS) as well as vulnerabilities that can used to install malware on web server (e.g. iFrames) and to gain access to databases (e.g. SQL injection) and later operation of the malware under command and control of the fraudster that facilitate bank account takeover (e.g. session hijacking)

5. *Kill-chain step V of the malware attack: Installation:* The goals of this phase of the attack are the installation of the malware on the client including possible remote backdoor on online banking application server for persistent access to the application. Once the CVE vulnerability is identified by the dropped malware, the online banking Trojan will install various malware packages (e.g. key loggers) on the client PC. In the cases when the exploitation/compromise also includes access to the internal servers, for example, through the exploit of a server vulnerability (e.g. command injection, SQL injection, remote file inclusion) by direct access to server through the internal network, the malware will install on the server. Example of malware installed on the server includes backdoors by exploiting vulnerabilities on the server and exfiltration data from these servers through remote access to that system as well as packet sniffers to capture data from the network.

6. *Kill-chain step VI of the malware attack: Command and Control:* During this phase of the attack, the attacker will establish a channel to enable remote control of the malware installed on client and server hosts. The banking Trojan will send messages out to the Internet to establish a communication channel to the attacker. Once the channel is open, the threat agent will have access to their target environment and receive command from the bot Command and Control (C&C) so that it can fully operate to control online banking sessions initiated by the client as well as to remote access both client and server hosts for exfiltration data and manipulate financial transactions (e.g. money transfers/wires).

7. *Kill-chain step VII of the malware attack: Action and Objectives:* This step of the attack includes the execution of the malicious/fraudulent actions such as exfiltration of online banking credentials and movement of money from the customer account to the fraudsters. This step of the kill-chain is when the attacker will attempt to accomplish their intended goal by operating the malware by following a sequence of events:

    a. Once the customer log-on the online banking site, the banking malware will report on the customer activity to the C&C server.
    b. The C&C server will send commands to the banking Trojan to steal authentication data, multifactor authentication credentials (e.g. challenge questions), and PII from the victim. The attack vectors include the following:
        i. Logging keystrokes
        ii. Form grabbing for transaction authentication numbers (TAN)

iii. Taking screenshots
iv. Exporting private key certificates
v. Exporting protected storage passwords
vi. Monitoring for file transfer and e-mail passwords (FTP and POP3)
vii. Routing connections through the infected machine
c. The banking credentials will be sent to malware operators in near real time (using Jabber).
d. The fraudster manipulates the online transaction by exploiting full control of the user's session and the web channel through different attacks (e.g. session hijacking/automatic transaction hijacking (ATH), MiTM).
e. The bank transaction is manipulated and is altered to send money to unauthorized payee (e.g. money mule).
f. The banking malware Trojan reports back the success/fail to C&C server.
g. The money stolen from the customer bank account is transferred from mule to fraudsters.

Similarly to the analysis of the online banking malware attacks, we can use the kill-chain for modeling of distributed denial-of-service attacks scenarios:

Kill-chain analysis of DDoS attack scenarios: An example of capturing the attack scenario for the various phases of the kill-chain of DDoS includes the following:

1. Kill-chain step I of the DDoS attack: Reconnaissance. This step of the attack consists of the research, identification, and selection of targets for DDoS attacks. The most likely threat agents targeting online banking sites for DDoS are politically motivated hacktivists for damaging the reputation of the financial institution, money-driven fraudsters seeking to distract the financial institution during account takeover attempts and country-state sponsored attackers seeking to disrupt the financial operations of a state owned or country's government operated online banking site. In general, the likely targets of DDoS attacks are public and private organizations with high visibility. Once the threat agents have decided which private or government operated Financial Institution will be targeted by a DDoS campaign, they will start to search for the most visible websites (Note: one potential method to assess the web site visibility is to use web analytics such as Alexia rankings for company websites). After a list of target websites has been identified, the threat agents will conduct a survey of the security of the target websites. The goal of this survey is to identify website vulnerabilities and weaknesses that can be exploited with specific attack vectors. Since DDoS seek to attack websites directly, the focus is on exploit of application layer and network layer type of vulnerabilities that lead to DDoS exploits. According to threat intelligence reports gathered during stage IV, for example, a DDoS reconnaissance phase of DDoS campaigns previously conducted by hactivist threat actors consists of the following activities:

i. Scanning for web application vulnerabilities (e.g. directory traversal, SQL injection, XSS)
ii. Scanning for pre-authenticated web pages of the web application which are time-consuming and resource consuming and might lead to exhaustion of the server resources (e.g. download of large PDF files, use of search engines that are not cached involving high consumption of CPU resources)

After these application vulnerabilities and weaknesses have been identified similarly to how penetration testers find web application vulnerabilities using commercially available pen testing tools (e.g. Havij automated SQL injection tools, Acunetix web vulnerability scanner, Nikto web scanner), the threat actors will conduct a preliminary preattack test to validate their findings using different attack vectors. Some of these application attack vectors such as HTTP GET Flood to attack a vulnerable web page are already part of freely available DDoS attack tools (e.g. High Orbit Ion Cannon (HIOC), BroBot DDoS, DirtJumper, Pandora). The attackers will also inspect the HTTP layer for exploit of vulnerabilities leading to DDoS such as testing with web methods the HTTP web server supports (e.g. POST or GET methods), checking if the web server timeout connections and checking if session creation can be abused to exhaust resources on the web server. After the attacker has conducted a set of preattack tests, it will have identified vulnerabilities and weaknesses in the online banking web application that can be targeted and the specific attack vectors that can be used for exploit them.

2. *Kill-chain step II of the DDoS attack: Weaponization.* After the DDoS attackers have scanned the target web sites for weaknesses and vulnerabilities to exploit and tested the attack vectors against the target, the next step consists of preparing the DDoS attack by configuring and engineering tools and various techniques to attack the web site target. Specifically in this phase, the threat agents will prepare the attack by weaponizing DDoS attack tools with attack vectors that seek to exploit network layer and application layer vulnerabilities for DDoS. Most of DDoS attack tools are botnet-based attack tools and consist of a network of enabled bots that can be coordinated by a command and control center host to flood the targeted online banking web site with malicious traffic. The attack vectors used for weaponize DDoS attack tools seek to exploit both traditional network layer (level 3 and 4 of OSI stack) and application layer (level 7 of OSI stack) vulnerabilities. DDoS attack tools are engineered and customizable to attack specific targets and to conduct a mix of application layer attack on HTTP, HTTPS, and DNS and network layer volumetric attacks on a variety of network protocols (e.g. TCP, UDP, ICMP). Since DDoS attack tools are freely available for download and are written as toolkits in programmable languages (e.g. PHP), they can be easily adapted and customized to include specific attack vectors for DDoS such as UDP, TCP floods, HTTP GET/POST floods, and configured to use proxies to hide the IP-source of the attacks. The weaponization of the DDoS tools can be as simple as configuring them to attack a specific target UR: or IP address and select the various attack parameters

(e.g. port number, protocol) that are part of the exploit. The URLs that are attacked are specifically resource-intensive URLs such as pre-authenticated downloads of large files such as PDF documents, images, and video from the web server. When resource-intensive URLs also include search pages that are not cached and can be abused to exhaust the search engine URLs, these are also weaponized at this stage by injecting iFrames in another compromised website, which pointed to the target online banking site search URL.

3. *Kill-chain step III of the DDos attack: Delivery.* Once the malicious code of the DDoS agent is weaponized and packaged in a Trojan virus or a computer worm, the next step is to deliver it to the target. In this step, the target is the host that the bot master seeks to compromise to become a "zombie." This web server "zombie" will be later controlled by the command and control server and used in a coordinated DDoS attack against the online banking site. The possible ways to deliver DDoS agents on the targets include spam campaigns with malicious code for download and execution as well as use of worms that exploit a particular vulnerability in a system of software and spread through other machines so these will become botnet "zombies" as well.

4. *Kill-chain step IV of the DDoS attack: Exploitation.* In this step of the attack, the vulnerabilities of the hosts where the DDoS Trojan is dropped are exploited to compromise the host and later install the DDoS agent. The malware that is dropped on the host can exploit known CVEs and weaknesses in the secure configuration of the hosts as well as web server vulnerabilities (e.g. iFrame injection, remote file inclusion) that can be used to upload malware with the DDoS agent on the compromised host. The DDoS bot agents can also exploit vulnerabilities in software that is used for managing content on the web server such as Content Management Systems (CMS) software from Joomla and WordPress.

5. *Kill-chain step V of the DDoS attack: Installation.* After the DDoS master has uploaded the malware on the vulnerable hosts, the next step consists of the installation of the DDoS agents and Command and Control Servers so these become part of the DDoS botnet. Once the DDoS agents are installed on the hosts, these are turned into "zombies," which are controlled by the bot master through the Command and Control (C2) servers. The C2 Servers themselves can also be installed on compromised hosts. The installation of DDoS agents includes download of updated malware from the C2 server and installation of backdoors that can be programmed to later receive remote commands and direct the flood of HTTP and UDP traffic to the online banking site targeted. This backdoors of the DDoS agents are written using script programming languages such as PHP and JavaScript and can be controlled remotely by the bot master using APIs. These APIs allow the bot master to configure the DDoS agent and upload updated attack scripts.

6. *Kill-chain step VI of the DDoS attack: Command and Control.* Once the DDoS bot agent is installed on the hosts, they become controlled by the DDoS bot master. To complete the installation of the DDoS bot agent on the host target, the DDoS bot agent will also call home the C2 server to receive the updated attack scripts for the malware to conduct the attacks against the target. In order

to execute DDoS attacks, the DDoS agent need to establish a communication channel with the DDoS Command and Control (C2) servers so that it can receive and execute commands. Depending on the type of C2 architecture being used for the DDoS botnet, the DDoS agent will communicate with the DDoS C2 server through different channels and protocols such as IM, IRC, HTTPs, P2P, and even social media such as Twitter and Facebook. This communication with the C2 server allows the bot master to coordinate and launch the DDoS attack of several DDoS agents against the online banking site target.

7. *Kill-chain step VII of the DDoS attack: Action and Objectives.* This is the step of the attack where the activities originated by the threat agent in control of the DDoS botnet including DDoS agents and DDoS C2 are directed against the online banking site target. Once the DDoS botnet is established, it can be used directly by the bot master that developed it to direct DDoS attacks against the target or it can rented for use by other threat actors. This step of the kill-chain is when the threat agent will attempt to accomplish their intended goal by directing specific attack vectors against the online banking site. These attack vectors are directed to exploit web site vulnerabilities such as SQL injection, Directory Transversal, and XSS as precursor phase to DDoS attacks whose objective is the exfiltration of sensitive customer data (e.g. bank account data credit card data) from the online banking site that is attacked. Following the findings of reconnaissance such as pre-authenticated web pages hosting large files (e.g. a BMP image or a PDF document of 5 MB of size or later), the attackers will send automated simultaneous requests by configuring the HTTP GET Flood attack vector of automated tools to download these files as well as exploit of search engine backend by running repetitive queries.

The DDoS attacks are typically automated and depending on the DDoS attacking tool used and how the DDoS attack bot agent is designed or weaponized, several DDoS attack vectors can be used against the online banking site. Examples of the sequence of attacks using an automated DDoS tool such as BroBot include the following commands and attack vectors:

1. The DDoS bot agents receive commands with the attack instructions in the form of HTTP GET and POST request parameters from DDoS bot C2 server.
2. The DDoS bot agents are instructed to attack the target web server URL with the following attack vectors:
    a. TCP flood at a specific port;
    b. UDP flood;
    c. HTTP GET flood of specific URL/web page (e.g. large file download);
    d. HTTP POST flood of specific URL (e.g. large file upload);
    e. HTTP GET flood with randomized HTTP "User-agents" against a specific URL;
    f. HTTPS GET flood of specific URL.

Other tools used for DDoS attacks include Dirt Jumper that allows the bot master to conduct the following attacks:

1. HTTP GET Flood: causes web server by repeating conventional HTTP requests and as soon as the bot receives the response from the server breaking the underlying TCP connection and sends a new HTTP request
2. HTTP File Downloading Flood: download/request larger (more bandwidth consuming) files (e.g. large pdf files)
3. POST HTTP Flood: send random usernames and passwords (embedded in HTTP-POST packets) to the online banking site
4. TCP SYN attack: sends a TCP SYN request and immediately closes the connection without waiting for the response from the server
5. HTTP Download: In this type of attack, the bot leaves the server in the state of "waiting" after establishing a full TCP connection
6. Socket attack: concentrate on a particular socket on the victim server.
7. HTTP POST of large request (larger than 1 GB) bytes in length with the purpose of congesting the server's upload channel

Once we have captured the attack scenarios for malware account takeover and DDoS attacks, we can map the various phases of the attack kill-chain to various security measures that can be taken prior to the phase of the attack when the attack take place that is the phase of actions and objectives.

Since application threat modeling is first and for most a security engineering activity, it is important to use the information extracted from the attacks such as the attack vectors and the vulnerabilities that are exploited by these attacks to design countermeasures that can detect and protect from these attack vectors. Since these attack vectors change with the emerging threats as well as the type of vulnerabilities that are exploited, the next step consists of documenting the attack vectors and security controls that protect and detect these attack vectors using the analysis of the attack scenario as a reference.

This is the goal of the *AMS activity 6.2 – Update the attack library/vectors and the security controls of the threat-risk specific control/measure framework."* The goal of this activity is to extract the information about the attack events and attack vectors used to conduct the attack scenario.

Once the new attack vectors have been identified, these can be included in an updated attack library/knowledge base. This attack library can be later used for derive security requirements for security controls that need to be designed and implemented as well as to derive security test cases.

Prior to documenting the attack vectors, it is important to analyze from the attack scenario that was previously captured and documented using the kill-chain the various security measures such as detective, protective, proactive, and reactive controls that can be documented in a risk control framework. After these security measures have been documented, the next step consists of extracting information of the various attack vectors that can be used for testing the application resilience to these attack vectors including exploits of known vulnerabilities and weaknesses associated with these vectors.

As an example of security measures that can be documented using the kill-chain scenarios previously captured for malware attacks is shown in Table 8.13.

By analyzing the attack scenario captured with through the kill-chain of banking malware attacks against the online banking application and the various steps of the malware attack have been captured, it is possible to map to the various steps of the attacks analyzed through the kill-chain to security measures such as detective and preventive controls that can be deployed to monitor, detect, and protect from the attacks.

The standardized method to capture and analyze the attack vectors using the kill-chain are STIX threat schema attributes from threat intelligence such as the "KillChainType" that is attack specific and the "KillChainPhaseType" that is kill -chain attack specific and any "KillChainPhaseReferenceType."

To determine which phase of the kill-chain specific, the malware banking threat observable is and focus on the security measures that can detect, deny/prevent and disrupt the attack before reaches the last phase of the kill-chain, action and objectives that is when the attack is executed against the target. For example, if an observable provided by the threat intelligence is the receipt of HTTP GET of exploit of specific vulnerability and indication of compromise that provide the context that that observable is associated with banking malware Trojan and the kill-chain is phase three that is "Exploitation" the financial institution can undertake actions for the detection of the attack such as:

1. Detect scanning of web application vulnerabilities (CWEs) exploited by that observable (Note is STIX is used the "ExploitTarget" parameter can be used to determine which system or web application vulnerability, weakness, or configuration issue are exploited).
2. Monitor suspicious activities in application log that can be attributed at that event (e.g. as indication of automatic scan of web application vulnerabilities against the target web application).
3. Monitor application layer exploits with Web Application Firewall (e.g. by looking at the specific HTTP GET URL and attack vector used).
4. Look at alerts from host and Network Intrusion Detection Systems (NIDS) (e.g. by looking at the IP of the source of the attack).
5. Error logging and exception handling (e.g. application logs such as web server errors of page not found that can be correlated to the HTTP GET attack).

As preventive measures such as to deny the opportunity for the attacker/threat agent to install the banking malware on the client browser the focus should be on measures such as prioritize the remediation of the vulnerabilities that the attack vector seek to exploit during the malware installation phase such as common vulnerabilities that facilitate the installation of the malware on the client (e.g. XSS) as well as vulnerabilities that can be used to install malware on web server (e.g. iFrames) and

TABLE 8.13 Malware Banking Trojan Kill-Chain and Security Measures

Phase Kill Chain	Detect	Deny	Disrupt	Degrade	Deceive	Destroy
Reconnaissance	Web Analytics Open Source Threat intelligence (OSINT)					
Weaponization	Specific threat Intelligence on this activity (from sting operation, monitoring of threat-agent communications)	Control developer access to online banking business critical source code	Obfuscate source code that might be potentially targeted			
Delivery	Inform bank customers on cyberthreats Enforce visual trust indicators on browser (e.g. EV SSL) Digital sign e-mails from Banks/FIs	Lock access to removable media Control access for third party vendors Filter employee access to social media Filter access to malicious URL/links Filter malicious attachments in e-mails	Coordinated law enforcement-vendor malware/botnet takedowns			

Exploitation	Detect scanning of web application vulnerabilities (CWEs) Monitor suspicious activities in application logs Monitor application layer exploits with WAF Host and Network Intrusion Detection Systems Error logging and exception handling	Fix and patch host, system and web application vulnerabilities (CWEs) at different layers (network, system, technology stack, application)	Data Execution Prevention Enforce minimum privileges (e.g. no admin access)
Installation	Anti-Malware S/W on client Fingerprint known good S/W installations Logging suspicious installation activity	Deny system access to non admin privileges Sandboxing browser and applications Desktop virtualization and containment	Limit access to users systems and applications from known/ suspicious software installations on clients/ servers

(*continued*)

TABLE 8.13 (Continued)

Phase Kill Chain	Detect	Deny	Disrupt	Degrade	Deceive	Destroy
Command and control	Adopt APT C2 detection services from third parties Monitor and detect unusual communication channels and patterns (e.g. IRC, P2P, HTTP, IM, Social Media)	Deny access to IM, IRC, Social Media Filter malicious inbound C2 communications Block known HTTP C2 command with WAF	Coordinated law enforcement-vendor C2 server network takedown	Degrade C&C communication to malware agent	DNS redirect	
Actions and objectives	Detect attack malware banking Trojan attack events and banking malware based attack vectors used for exfiltration of online banking credentials and movement of money (refer to kill chain action and objectives analysis) Logging of suspicious activities related to banking malware Fraud detection rules for malware initiated fraud	2-Way Out Of Band (OOB) Authentication OOB Transaction Validation Authorization Maker/Checker Dual Controls for High Risk Transactions (Payments and Money Transfers) Deny user access to business critical functions based on fraud detection rules	Coordinated law enforcement seize of compromised bank accounts, suspend compromise accounts and credit cards, block fraudulent accounts	Degrade Web Response Slow down the attacker with antiautomation	Honeypots Web page decoys	

to gain access to databases (e.g. SQL injection) and later operation of the malware under command and control of the fraudster that facilitate bank account takeover (e.g. session hijacking).

From a proactive risk management approach perspective, that is, to take measures to detect and prevent malware banking attacks before the banking malware is dropped on the client machine, that is, the malware delivery phase, several actions can be taken to improve awareness of online banking customers of specific attacks before taking any action that facilitates malware compromise through browsing of infected web sites (e.g. drive by downloads) and through phishing (e.g. by clicking on attachments and links that are apparently trustworthy but in reality are malicious). For internal employees, banks can take the following measures to protect from malware compromise:

1. Lock access to removable media (e.g. USB devices)
2. Control access for third-party vendors to the internal network
3. Filter employee access to social media (e.g. Facebook, Twitter)
4. Filter access to malicious URL/links
5. Filter malicious attachments in e-mails

These measures should be in place prior to the detection of malware such as banking Trojans trying to compromise bank employees for internal attacks such as specifically to compromise data processes by business critical systems as well as hosts of internal employees who have access to customer and client data such as bank accounts, tax forms with confidential-PII that can be targeted by malware banking attacks.

If the source of infected websites used to deliver malware is known by threat intelligence sources, another action that can be taken by the organization prior to becoming the target of malware banking attacks is to try to take legal action to disrupt the delivery of the malware with drive by download and phishing. This type of activities consists of try to preempt the attacks before these take place by trying to coordinate with law enforcement and security vendor actions against cyber-criminals. Actions that can be taken with security vendors are trying to eradicate malware from compromised web servers that are known to deliver malware as well as to take down services that serve as command and control centers of banking malware and botnets.

Prior to delivery phase, other actions that can be taken are to learn from threat intelligence source if the online banking site is mentioned in underground forums as possible target for the attacks by monitoring threat actor activity in this forums. This might include discussions on how to configure a cybercrime tool kit to attack a specific URL of an online banking site and any discussions in the underground forums on how to weaponize the banking malware and the botnet to attack specific online banking sites.

In the cases when the scripts used by the banking malware are written with attack vectors that attack the online banking application of a specific bank and the specific functionality and web pages, the knowledge of the script is critical to take actions to test these attack vectors in a testing laboratory and engineer countermeasures to protect the various URLs targeted by these attack vectors. Often the malware attacking tools are engineered to exploit the specific design flaws in the online banking site that could have been very difficult without the knowledge of the source code. One possibility to make more difficult for threat actors to reverse engineer the source code is to obfuscate the source code, that is, to require the source code to be obfuscated.

After the analysis of the attack scenario by using the kill-chain is completed, there are two groups of attack vectors that can be extracted for engineering and testing web applications:

1. Preattack vectors used by the threat actors for the delivery of malware and for the exploitation of vulnerabilities to upload and install the malware on the target system/host/application
2. Attack vectors used to pursue the actions and objectives of the attacker such as for exfiltration of sensitive data from the web application and for execute fraudulent transactions

Examples of preattack vectors are the ones exploiting vulnerabilities that allow the installation scripts on the client browser such as XSS and remote command execution via SQL injection into web URLs, auto-executed infections, for example, when a user unintentionally browse a website that is infected advertisement/flash video and user executed infections, that is, when user is lured via social engineering to open malicious attachments, deceptive pop-ups, and selecting URLs pointing to malicious URL. According to the 2013 Verizon DBIR (Data Breach Investigation Report) among all the preattack vectors, the majority are direct installed and injected by an attacker. From the perspective of protecting web applications for delivering malware that can attack the application directly to install malware on serves or indirectly by installing scripts on the client, identifying and fixing of vulnerabilities such as SQL Injection, XSS, and XFS need to be prioritized.

These types of web vulnerabilities that can be exploited for installation of malware need be categorized in relation to the specific threat agent and the threat target for the specific phases of the kill-chain that map to kill-chain delivery such as delivery of the payload, exploitation of vulnerability and installation of malware. This mapping of vulnerabilities to threat agents and threat targets was the goal of stage V of PASTA, WVA (Weakness and Vulnerability Analysis) that was intended to be performed prior to this phase.

In the case of malware banking Trojan attacks, since the attack vectors seek to compromise the browser by exploiting vulnerabilities of the browser prior to attack the web application, the mitigation of such weaknesses and vulnerabilities also reduces the opportunity for an attacker to compromise the client prior to attack the web application. The figure herein, for example, shows CVEs that can be exploited by drive-by-download attacks to compromise the client with banking malware (Figure 8.30).

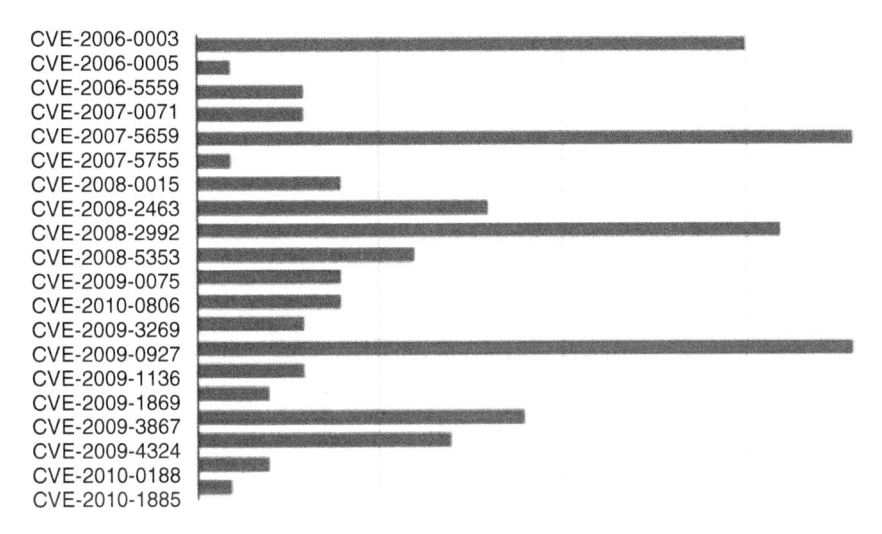

```
CVE-2006-0003
CVE-2006-0005
CVE-2006-5559
CVE-2007-0071
CVE-2007-5659
CVE-2007-5755
CVE-2008-0015
CVE-2008-2463
CVE-2008-2992
CVE-2008-5353
CVE-2009-0075
CVE-2010-0806
CVE-2009-3269
CVE-2009-0927
CVE-2009-1136
CVE-2009-1869
CVE-2009-3867
CVE-2009-4324
CVE-2010-0188
CVE-2010-1885
```

Figure 8.30 CVEs Exploited by Drive-By-Download Attacks

TABLE 8.14 Attack Vectors Used By Banking Malware

	Online Banking Malware Attack Vector(s)
AV1	Capture authentication data from user activity using key logger
AV2	Take screenshots of the user's browser session to defeat virtual keyboard
AV3	Exfiltration confidential data and send to external server
AV4	Redirect to another site URL or IP address
AV5	Update modules/scripts for the malware installed
AV6	Initiate client attacks (XSS, MiTB)
AV7	Initiate web-based attacks (MiTM, Session Hijacking)
AV8	Spoof SMS OTPs sent to fraudster's mobile (MoITM)
AV9	Capture data from volatile memory (e.g. RAM)
AV10	Capture secrets (private keys, certificates) stored on the client device (mobile or desktop)
AV11	Capture sensitive data stored on cashed data/temporary files
AV12	Install backdoor to allow remote access/control
AV13	Listen and execute commands to update malware agent and exfiltration data
AV14	Manipulate money transfer transactions to send money-to-money mule accounts

For the sake of engineering attack resilient web applications, the most realistic assumption is to assume that client PC and browsers are compromised and determine how to detect and prevent malware-based attack vectors to break into the online web application to compromise sensitive data and to conduct fraudulent transactions. A nonexhaustive example of a list of attack vectors used by banking malware is shown in Table 8.14

TABLE 8.15 DDoS Attack Vectors Extracted from the Analysis of DDoS Attacks Against Web Applications

	DDoS Bot Agent(s) Attack Vector(s)
AV1	HTTP GET file downloading flood: causes web server by repeating conventional HTTP requests
AV2	HTTP POST flood: send random usernames and passwords (embedded in HTTP-POST packets)
AV3	HTTP file downloading flood: download/request larger (more bandwidth consuming) files
AV4	Malformed HTTP requests: slowloris attack---
AV5	HTTP download: leaves the server in the state of "waiting" after a full TCP connection
AV6	HTTP POST of large request (larger than 1 GB) bytes
AV7	Slow HTTP POST attack
AV8	TCP SYN flood attack: sends a TCP SYN request and immediately closes the connection
AV9	UDP flood
AV10	ICMP flooding
AV12	Smurf attacks
AV13	DNS attacks (IP spoofing, open recursion, and amplification)

Ideally, each type of cyber threat should have a list of attack vectors that can be queried for and used to derive security requirements and security tests to determine the resilience of the web application to these attacks. As for malware-based attack vectors shown herein, a list of DDoS attack vectors can also be extracted by the analysis of the kill-chain of DDoS and specifically for the Kill-chain step VII of the DDoS attack: Action and Objectives.

In the case of DDoS, these types of attack vectors include both layer 7 and layers 3 and 4 attack vectors that we had previously analyzed and captured during the analysis of DDoS attack scenario using the kill-chain methodology. A nonexhaustive list example of DDOS attack vectors is included in Table 8.15.

One important goal that needs to be achieved during this phase of PASTA is to document attack vectors in attack pattern/libraries that can be actionable for the derivation of security requirements for engineering the online banking application for opportunistic and targeted attacks. This goal can be pursued by adopting a standardized attack library.

An open source standardized attack library that is available today to describe attacks, attack vectors and associated weaknesses (e.g. CWE-IDs) these attack vectors seek to exploit is the MITRE's Common Attack Pattern Enumeration (CAPEC). According to MITRE, "*CAPEC is collection of attack patterns available in the Common Attack Pattern Enumeration and Classification (CAPEC™) initiative, we can help identify opportunities for improving the resilience, integrity, and reliability of our software-based mission capabilities, as well as make our software less susceptible to attack.*"

PASTA USE CASE EXAMPLE WALK-THROUGH   595

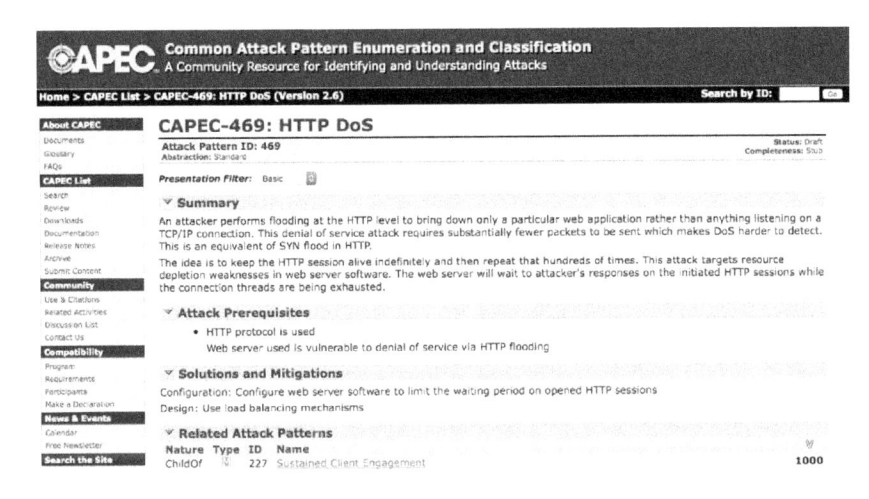

Figure 8.31   CAPEC Attack Pattern for HTTP DoS[5]

The sources of CAPEC are both exploits from proof of concept exploits of vulnerabilities and the research from malware analysis and analysis of attacks observed in security incidents.

In the context of attacks against web applications, CAPEC attack libraries can be used to identify the high-risk weaknesses (e.g. CWEs) that can be exploited by a specific attack and determine a set of security requirements and test cases and tools that can be used to test the resilience of the application against DoS attack vectors.

An example of using standard attack patterns to categorize attacks for HHTP DoS is shown in Figure 8.31.

CAPEC attack patterns also document how to conduct an exploit to test the weaknesses that the attack pattern seeks to exploit. For example, in the case of CAPEC-66:SQL injection, the attack execution flow provides the tester with the attack step techniques to survey the application to determine use controllable input that is susceptible to SQL injection and to exploit the SQL injection vulnerability.

Table 8.16, for example, shows the SQL injection attack steps and the environment that can be replicated in a test to determine whether user-controllable input susceptible to injection.

A positive test of this sequence of event consists of receiving an error message from server indicating that there was a problem with the SQL query. A negative test consists of receiving a normal response from the server. The outcome of this test can be considered positive if at least one user-controllable input susceptible to injection found.

A second series of tests using the CAPEC SQL injection attack sequence consists of a try to conduct the exploit as the attackers do that is to "*add logic to the query to extract information from the database, or to modify or delete information in the database.*" This is shown in Table 8.17.

---
[5] http://capec.mitre.org/data/definitions/469.html.

TABLE 8.16 CAPEC SQL Injection Attack Sequence 1. Determine User-Controllable Input Susceptible to Injection

ID	Attack Step Technique Description	Environments
1	Use web browser to inject input through text fields or through HTTP GET parameters.	env-Web
2	Use a web application debugging tool such as Tamper Data, TamperIE, WebScarab, and so on to modify HTTP POST parameters, hidden fields, nonfreeform fields, and so on.	env-Web
3	Use network-level packet injection tools such as netcat to inject input	env-Web env-ClientServer env-Peer2Peer env-CommProtocol
4	Use modified client (modified by reverse engineering) to inject input.	env-ClientServer env-Peer2Peer env-CommProtocol

TABLE 8.17 CAPEC SQL Injection Attack Sequence 1. 2. Experiment and try to exploit SQL Injection Vulnerability

ID	Attack Step Technique Description	Environments
1	Use public resources such as "SQL Injection Cheat Sheet" at http://ferruh.mavituna.com/makale/sql-injection-cheatsheet/, and try different approaches for adding logic to SQL queries.	env-Web env-ClientServer env-Peer2Peer env-CommProtocol
2	Add logic to query, and use detailed error messages from the server to debug the query. For example, if adding a single quote to a query causes an error message, try : "' OR 1=1; --," or something else that would syntactically complete a hypothesized query. Iteratively refine the query.	env-Web env-ClientServer env-Peer2Peer env-CommProtocol
3	Use "Blind SQL Injection" techniques to extract information about the database schema.	env-Web env-ClientServer env-Peer2Peer env-CommProtocol
4	If a denial-of-service attack is the goal, try stacking queries. This does not work on all platforms (most notably, it does not work on Oracle or MySQL). Examples of inputs to try include: "'; DROP TABLE SYSOBJECTS; --" and "'); DROP TABLE SYSOBJECTS; --." These particular queries will likely not work because the SYSOBJECTS table is generally protected.	env-Web env-ClientServer env-Peer2Peer env-CommProtocol

TABLE 8.18 CWEs Exploited in SQL Injection Attacks (CAPEC SQL Injection)

CWE-ID	Weakness Name	Weakness Relationship Type
89	Improper neutralization of special elements used in an SQL command ("SQL Injection")	Targeted
74	Improper neutralization of special elements in output used by a downstream component ("Injection")	Secondary
20	Improper input validation	Secondary
390	Detection of error condition without action	Secondary
697	Insufficient comparison	Secondary
713	OWASP Top Ten 2007 category A2 – injection flaws	Secondary
707	Improper enforcement of message or data structure	

TABLE 8.19 CAPEC-66 Security Requirements For Mitigation of Risk of SQL Injection Attacks

ID	Security Requirement
SR1	Special characters in user-controllable input must be escaped before use by the application
SR2	Only use parameterized stored procedures to query the database
SR3	Input data must be revalidated in the parameterized stored procedures
SR4	Custom error pages must be used to handle exceptions such that they do not reveal any information about the architecture of the application or the database

The outcomes for conducting the exploit test are also described in the CAPEC attack pattern such as success in the case the attacker/tester achieves goal of unauthorized system access, denial of service, and so on or failure in the case the attacker is unable to exploit the SQL injection vulnerability.

The CAPEC attack patterns also describe the application weaknesses that are in scope for the security tests since these are sought to be exploited by the attacker using this attack pattern and attack vectors. This is shown in Table 8.18.

The relevant security requirements and security principles are also documented in CAPEC and these can be used for engineering the web application and make it less susceptible to these attacks. An example is shown in Table 8.19.

CAPEC attack libraries can be integrated in threat modeling tools and assist the threat modeler in creation of security test cases that can be used to identify weaknesses and vulnerabilities that might be part of the legacy online web application that might have been introduced by the architectural and design changes of the application.

The other important requirement is to keep the attack library associated with the assets impacted/targeted and weaknesses and vulnerabilities exposed by the security controls in front of these assets. The association of threat actors, vulnerabilities,

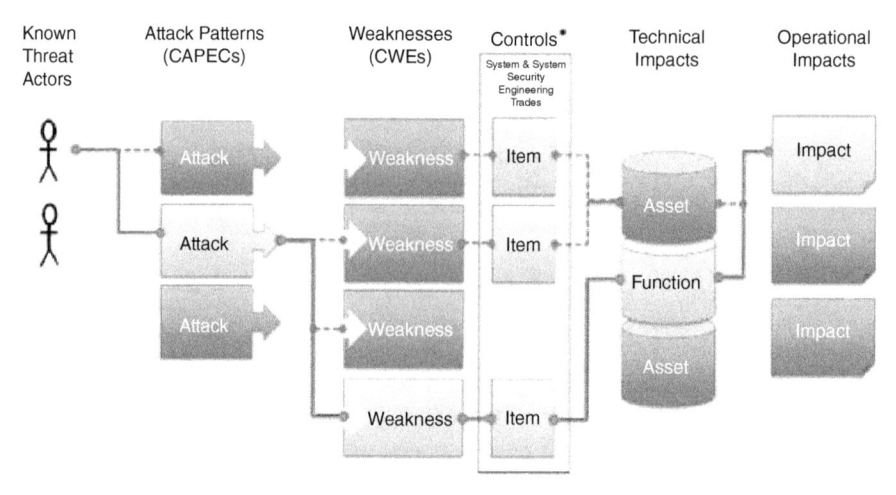

Figure 8.32 Engineering for Attacks Source MITRE[6]

weaknesses, and holistic security controls (e.g. security by design, deployment, and test controls) to cause technical impacts to assets is shown in Figure 8.32.

The standardization of attack patterns is critical for the threat and attack modeling exercise and for the engineering of secure web applications. The use of standard attack library like CAPEC helps security testers to identify vulnerabilities and test the resilience of security controls to specific attacks. These attack libraries should include the attack vectors derived from the analysis of the various type of threats and incidents using external sources such as Information Sharing Assurance Center (ISACs), the Web Hacking incident Data Bases (WHID and well as internal sources such as security logged events from logs/SIEMs, WAFs and honeypots.

Ideally each organization should have a repository of attack libraries that is kept up to date based upon the various sources of threat intelligence, security incidents and research on attack vectors used in attacking tools against the specific target in scope, that is, the online banking application.

Attack libraries can be actionable for the attack-driven engineering of secure web applications when are integrated in a threat modeling platform. An example of WHID attack library that is integrated in a threat modeling tool ThreatModeler™ is shown in Figure 8.33.

In the example shown, the attack vectors map to web hacking security incidents that have been observed against online banking sites and aggregated in the (WHID) Web Hacking Incident Database that is maintained by the (WASC) Web Application Security Consortium organization. These attack vectors are associated with the functional components of the online banking application that were previously analyzed. By enumerating the various attack vectors that target the functional component, the threat modeler can assert that security requirements are documented in architecture

[6]http://cwe.mitre.org/community/swa/attacks.html.

PASTA USE CASE EXAMPLE WALK-THROUGH 599

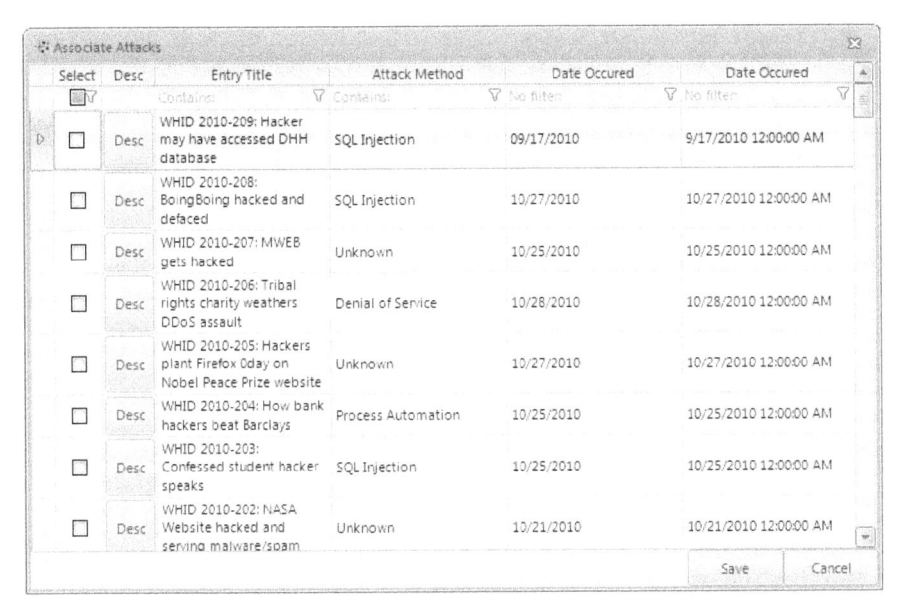

Select	Desc	Entry Title	Attack Method	Date Occured	Date Occured
☐	Desc	WHID 2010-209: Hacker may have accessed DHH database	SQL Injection	09/17/2010	9/17/2010 12:00:00 AM
☐	Desc	WHID 2010-208: BoingBoing hacked and defaced	SQL Injection	10/27/2010	10/27/2010 12:00:00 AM
☐	Desc	WHID 2010-207: MWEB gets hacked	Unknown	10/25/2010	10/25/2010 12:00:00 AM
☐	Desc	WHID 2010-206: Tribal rights charity weathers DDoS assault	Denial of Service	10/28/2010	10/28/2010 12:00:00 AM
☐	Desc	WHID 2010-205: Hackers plant Firefox 0day on Nobel Peace Prize website	Unknown	10/27/2010	10/27/2010 12:00:00 AM
☐	Desc	WHID 2010-204: How bank hackers beat Barclays	Process Automation	10/25/2010	10/25/2010 12:00:00 AM
☐	Desc	WHID 2010-203: Confessed student hacker speaks	SQL Injection	10/25/2010	10/25/2010 12:00:00 AM
☐	Desc	WHID 2010-202: NASA Website hacked and serving malware/spam	Unknown	10/21/2010	10/21/2010 12:00:00 AM

Figure 8.33 WHID Attack Library in ThreatModeler™

design for mitigating the risk of these attack vectors and that security test cases have been created to "close the threats," that is, the various functional components have been tested against these attack vectors.

Once the attack libraries have been updated, the next step to follow consists of *AMS 6.3 – Identify the attack surface and enumerate the attack vectors against the data entry points of the application.*

The main objective of attack surface analysis is to characterize the exposure to the various attack vectors to attack the data that is processed by the online banking application through the various entry and exit points, trust boundaries, vulnerabilities and weaknesses of security controls, and the assets that could be impacted such as data and functions.

To conduct this attack surface analysis, it is important to visualize the previously analyzed architecture diagrams and DFDs including the entry and exit points, the trust boundaries, the assets, and the weaknesses and vulnerabilities and to identify the various security measures and countermeasures in place that act as barriers and challenges to the various attack vectors to conduct exploits. The analysis of the attack surface leverages the information of threat agents (e.g. internal and external) and attack vectors previously analyzed as used by these threat agents for the pursuit of these attacks and exploits.

Ideally a threat modeler should be able to conduct a walk-through of the data from the entry points representing the "attack surface" of the possible attacks and the initial "source" of the attack vector to the final destination or "sink" of the attack vector that produces the desired impact (e.g. compromise of the data asset).

For the sake of this use case, we define attack surface the collection of entry point into the web application that includes both internal and external user interfaces, as well as data interfaces such as the connections among the various tiers of the application architecture. Once the various data entry points are listed, we can associate them with the various security controls in place and enforced at the various trust boundaries such as user authentication and authorization required for access, input data validation, mutual authentication, and data encryption enforced to protect the data and the sensitivity of the data asset that is exposed to the interface including the type of transactions available.

Once the various architectural elements of the attack surface have been captured through the analysis of the architecture diagrams and the DFDs, it is possible to use as measurement of attack risk such as potential exposure and impact of attacks. The attack surface measurement is relative to the various factors that characterize the inherent risk and exposure of the online banking application to potential attacks such as the fact that the application is Internet, intranet, or extranet facing application, has value assets (e.g. confidential data) and functions (e.g. payments, wire transfers) being exposed to the Internet users, integrates with other applications such as through SSO/federation, support different type of devices (e.g. web and mobile), and integrates with business critical backend services (e.g. SaaS, web services)

Once the organization has decided what architectural component best characterizes the attack surface of the web application, it is possible to use as a relative measure of risk being introduced in the design such as addition of new user and data interfaces that might increase the risk of attacks such as new avenues and potential impact from attacks.

An example of capture of attack surface for online banking application based on the same architectural diagrams and DFDs used for previous stages of PASTA (Figures 6.1 and 6.2) is shown herein in Table 8.20.

In the example shown, we have defined the attack surface for the online banking application as baseline and compared with application changes that were introduced to determine the increased risk such as additions of new URLs, web services, and devices. In the example shown, the attack surface has increased as well as the attack risks due to the addition of pre-authenticated URLs to download files and videos (e.g. large PDFs and flash video streaming) and to conduct web searches. These changes represent an increased risk of attacks from threat agent-actors to cause denial of service by running automation scripts that direct a flood of HTTP GET request to download these files and videos for upstream pipe saturation DDoS and for exploitation of search engine vulnerabilities.

The other increased risk due to the increased attack surface is caused by the support of mobile banking through thick (smartphone applications) and thin (web based) mobile clients. This increased risk can be measured as increased exposure to malware attacks specifically targeting mobile devices if bank customers with mobile banking applications installed.

Additional changes that increase the attack surface for the online banking application and the risk of attacks are the deployment of new Web 2.0 features such as widgets components using AJAX since these new components might introduce new

TABLE 8.20 Attack Surface of Online Banking Application

	Online Banking Application Attack Surface Changes		
Component	Trust Zone	Application Baseline	Application Features/ Changes (New Release)
User interfaces	Internet	Pre-authenticated URLs-Visitors Post-authenticated URLs-Auth-Users	Pre-authenticated URL-Visitors-File Download Pre-authenticated URL-Visitors-Search API Queries
User devices	Internet	Web Client Browsers	Mobile Thick Client Mobile Thin Client
Data interfaces	DMZ	Web Client-Web Server-HTTPS	Web2.0 Client (Flash, Ajax)-Mobile Web Gateway-HTTPS
	Internal	Web Server-App Server-HTTPS AppServer-DB Credential Store-JDBC-SSL AppServer-Risk Base Authentication-HTTPS-XML AppServer-Enterprise Messaging Bus-SOAP-HTTPS Enterprise Messaging-Financial Processing Mainframe-MQ-SSL AppServer-Fraud Detection Service–HTTPS-XML Appserver-Secure File Transfer Server-SFTP	Mobile-Web Gateway-Mobile Banking Application HTTPS Mobile Banking Application-SOAP-HTTPS Web Server-Search APIs-SOAP-HTTPS Web Server-Secure Token Service-HTTPS-XML
Admin interfaces	Internal	Post-authenticated URL-Admin-Users-Intranet	Post-authenticated URL-Admin-Users-Intranet

and existing vulnerabilities both in the client and on the server and additional avenues for attacking the online banking application from the Internet.

The aggregation of other financial services websites through Single Sign on/Federation also increases the attack surface because the increased number of users can now single sign on and can be potentially the target of malware banking attacks and the increased number of financial transactions are available for attackers that were not available prior to the SSO to these financial sites. For example, when before the services that could be targeted only included services provided by the bank, the aggregation of other financial services through sign on (e.g. electronic bill payment services, credit card payment services etc) increases the risk of these services of being attacked by one entry point, that is, the user interface to SSO to the online banking site.

In addition, the new data interfaces that are accessible only through the internal network such as web services that expose the backend financial services through the mobile client through the common enterprise messaging bus also represent an internal threat agent attack risk; hence, these need to be secured by ensuring that requests of internal connectivity to these interfaces are repudiated for internal host that cannot be mutually authenticated to these interfaces by enforcing mutual certificate authentication for all web service calls as an example.

Once the attack surface is measured and compared with the baseline, it is possible to make informed decisions such as reducing the attack surface and the risk that is to minimize the risk exposure of the assets to the various threat agents and attack vectors and vulnerabilities that these threat agents could exploit in a targeted or opportunistic attacks against the online banking application. Examples include moving CPU resource-intensive URLs with static content such as videos and files that can be targeted by DDoS attacks to third-party CDN (Content Delivery Networks as well as by caching pre-authenticated web searches that use the Search APIs so these cannot be exploited.

To reduce the risk of additional vulnerabilities that might be introduced by Web 2.0 client components, the organization can introduce additional software assurance services such as application threat modeling, source code reviews/scans and pen tests specifically for threats targeting these components. Attack vectors specifically exploiting Web 2.0 vulnerabilities such as the ones categorized by WASC as Web 2.0 threats need to be incorporated and augment the current application vulnerability assessment/tests.

For the increased exposure caused by the use of mobile devices and online banking applications that are installed on mobile devices to transact with the bank, additional security engineering processes need to be enforced for reviewing and certifying the secure development and provisioning of these online banking applications. Specifically since mobile devices and applications are primary target for malware attacks including for attacking online banking applications as well as online banking credentials, specific security measures and controls need to be engineered and deployed to reduce the exposure of attack vectors targeting both mobile devices, desktops, and online banking applications such as MoITM Mobile-In-the-Middle attacks (e.g. attacks that seek to compromise the mobile device when used for out-of-band one-time password verification and authorization). Specifically mobile-based online banking applications need to be in scope for testing with attack vectors that are specific for attacks targeting weaknesses and vulnerabilities that are inherent of the mobile O.S (e.g. Android, IoS) where the mobile application is installed and the provisioning process of the application on the device (e.g. AppleStore and Android marketplace).

The example of attack surface measurement for the online banking application in scope that is provided herein is meant to capture the risk exposure to the various attacks and attack vectors at high architectural design level. The approach considered is from the perspective of the attacker's opportunity as this being an external threat agent seeking to attack the online banking application remotely for stealing confidential data such as online banking credentials, credit card data, and bank account data, committing fraudulent transactions such as by stealing money from the victim's bank account through banking malware and distributed denial of service both as diversion attack and for reputational damage.

At lower level, that is, detail functional design including source code, the attack surface might consider specific attacks against application software, processes, and permissions to execute these processes including open ports, named pipes, PRC endpoints, null sessions, installed services, services running defaults and as System, and files and permissions set for these files. Once these parameters are measured as is done in Microsoft's (RASQ) Relative Attack Surface Quotient, they represent an opportunity to measure improvements in security of products. At the source code level, that is, the analysis of attack vectors that can be used to exploit coding issues, the attack surface can also be used to determine the increased risk represented by the introduction of changes in source code and make defensive coding decisions on exposing API calls to internal service calls and access to input data and data files that might represent an avenue for specific attack vectors.

In the case of Microsoft products, at Operative System Level, the attack surface can be analyzed using the attack surface analyzer to determine if system misconfigurations such as weak ACLs, installing services, changing firewall rules and so on that might expose a Window's System installation to specific threat agents and attack vectors.

From the attacker perspective, the online banking application attack surface is represented by all possible attack vectors and avenues at disposal of the attacker that include exploit of weaknesses and vulnerabilities at the various layers of the technology stack including the internal and external networks, the various systems and hosts that the web application is designed to be installed and run. By keeping this in mind, it is important that whenever a new change is introduced to the application being this just a new configuration change, system upgrade changes, connectivity changes, and last but not least new services and features added, it is reviewed for the additional risks that are introduced as exposure of new attack vectors specifically targeting vulnerabilities and weaknesses introduced by changes in design, coding, and configurations.

Once we have documented the attack surface of the online banking application and captured at high level, the exposure to potential attacks for the design, implementation, and configuration changes that are introduced, the next step consists of estimating the probability of these attack vectors to cause an exploit and determine the desired impact. This is the goal of the activity *AMS 6.4 – Assess the probability and impact of the exploit of each attack scenario.* At high level, attack probability, that is, the possibility of an attack to cause an impact can be estimated using attack trees.

Attack trees are formal attack models that threat analysts can use to analyze the probability of the attacker's goals to be realized by considering the various tools, techniques, and opportunity for exploit at disposal to the attacker. For an attacker, a user interface, data interface application weakness or vulnerability including server or application mis-configuration represent an opportunity and an avenue for an attack. Now the question for an attacker is, given various opportunities for attacking the web application as well as TTPs Tools, Techniques and Processes required to achieve the goal, what is the attack path that is most likely to succeed and cheaper in terms of costs to bear to acquire tools, techniques, and familiarize with attack processes? For example, in the case of a threat agent such as a cyber-criminal whose business is to create malware such as banking malware that can be sold or rented to other cyber-criminals to steal money from their bank account, the main question is which vectors of attack lead to the ultimate goal that is to create a cyber-crime tool that can exploit various types of weaknesses and vulnerabilities to achieve the attacker's goal, that is, stealing money from bank accounts. Attack tree analysis of attacks is what malware writers use to walk through the various possible exploits including social engineering exploits, use of phishing scam tools, exploit of vulnerabilities in client browsers, web application vulnerabilities, and security control weaknesses such as weak user authentication and multifactor authentication that is currently used by banks.

The main objective of the malware writer is to engineer a cyber-crime tool kit that is both sophisticated and flexible enough to bypass common security controls deployed by most banks and adapted for dissemination using different delivery methods and to conduct different type of attacks such as MitM and MitB attacks. By writing such cyber-crime tool, cyber-criminal will also write procedural instructions to both operate the tools and to commit the fraud. For example, to escape most of money laundry controls in place at banks to prevent moving money to bank accounts black-listed as fraudulent by (AML) Anti Money Laundry controls fraudsters figure out that the proceeds of fraudulent wire transfer can be sent first to "money mules" in essence person that can transfer money acquired illegally through a courier service or electronically on behalf of the fraudster for a fee. As part of the cyber-crime scheme that involves using banking malware money mules are hired through work at home schemes.

From the defender perspective, conducting the same type of analysis of the attacker using an attack tree to analyze how the attacker goal can be realized and the various possible avenues to conduct the attacks, this possible avenues can be analyzed by assigning conditions to each node of the attack tree as either "OR" or "AND" conditions. For example, a threat agent seeking to compromise the online banking application using a banking Trojan can attack the client "AND" attack the application "OR" attack the application directly. Given that the probability of attacking the client is lower than attacking the application directly, it will choose that attack client path.

The probability of success is given by the consideration of all single probabilities of each node whose conditions need to be fulfilled in order for the attacker to reach his goal. The attack tree model of banking malware attacks is shown in Figure 8.34.

The attack path of banking malware attack threat agent and the coordinate action of the fraudster agent are shown herein. The path of the malware attack that is followed by the banking malware is shown in the left of the attack tree while the manual steps of the attack that are followed by the fraudster are shown on the right of the attack tree.

PASTA USE CASE EXAMPLE WALK-THROUGH

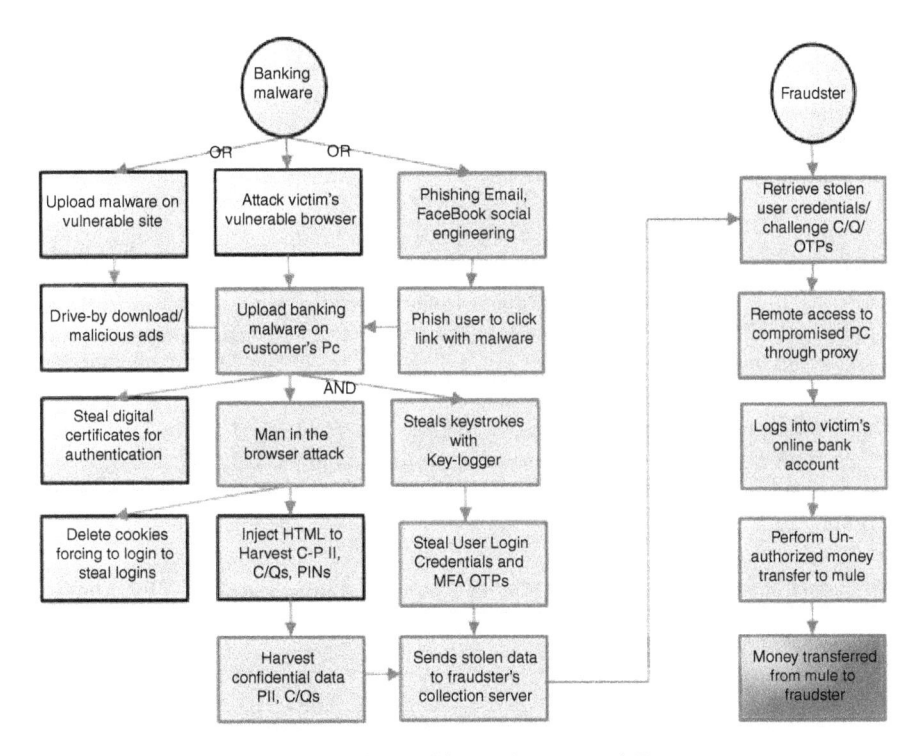

Figure 8.34 Banking Malware Attack Tree

At root of the attack tree the malware attack can use any of the attack delivery methods considered in the branches of the first node such as (1) upload banking malware on vulnerable website with direct attack (e.g. IFrame injection), (2) attack the client directly by remote exploit of browser vulnerabilities, or (3) perform the social engineering attack to phish the use to click on links with malware.

The assumption is that the social engineering attack is the attack vector of choice for uploading malware on customer's PC. From threat intelligence, it is known that banking malware spreads mostly either by drive by download or by phishing. The assumption that attackers seek to compromise the targeted host by luring customers with phishing e-mails is the assumption that the weakest link in every attack is always the human element and therefore social engineering and phishing represent a low cost, high-gain opportunity for attacker to spread malware. The attack tree shown in Figure 8.34 shows in each leaf the various possible steps that a fraudster could follow in the pursuit of his final goals that are harvest confidential data and credentials from the victim and commit account take wire fraud. Once the malware is installed and the client host machine is uploaded, installed, and configured on targeted client host, it will execute the various attacks such that it is designed to harvest confidential data from the bank customers using MiTM, stealing credentials by logging keystrokes. After the malware has sent the stolen online banking site credentials and customer sensitive data to the fraudster, it will wait to execute commands from the fraudster's controlled command and control server. The path that is followed by the fraudster includes a series of steps such as remote connecting to the compromised host through a proxy to anonymize his actions, taking over the customer account by hijacking the session, manipulate the transaction to move money to a money mule account and least but not last have the money mule sending the stolen money to the fraudster's account (typically in another country).Once the path of the most probable attack for the banking malware threat in scope has been analyzed, the next logical step of the threat analysis is to derive test cases for simulating the attacks and understand how the exploit occurs and specifically to identify which vulnerabilities and weaknesses are exploited and security controls are bypassed to realize the threat.

This leads to the next activity of the attack modeling that is *AMS 6.5 – Derive a set of cases to test existing measures.* These test cases can be derived with the knowledge derived from the analysis of the attack scenarios including the kill-chain sequence of event that lead to the attack operation and execution, the update of the attack library with the attack vectors learned from the attack scenarios, the analysis of the attack surface to determine the possible avenues of attack vectors from the perspective of the attackable data entry points, and the analysis of the attack trees to determine the most probable attack paths that are pursued by the attacker to reach his goals.

For the derivation of the security test cases to simulate the attacks, two criteria can be used:

1. Test cases for testing the several weaknesses (CWE) and vulnerabilities (CVEs) that attack vectors seek to exploit during the various phases of the attack kill-chain (e.g. using ThreatTarget STIX mapping to CVEs and CWEs) and to conduct the attack (e.g. using CAPEC-CWE mapping).
2. Test cases for testing the possible abuses of security controls including the bypassing of multifactor authentication and traditional client-based security measures (e.g. browser security, antiviruses, and antispyware).

For the first group of test cases that are attack driven, the derivation of the security test cases builds upon the analysis of the kill-chain derived security requirements. These security requirements are different from the security requirements that were written in stage I in response to information security policies and compliance as well as for secure the online banking application functionality including online banking transactions and for protection of the confidentiality, integrity, and availability of sensitive customer information. These security requirements are validated with functional driven test to validate that security controls function as is "accepted" by design, implementation, and configuration.

The security test cases that are documented in this stage of the attack modeling and simulation consist of attack-driven security test cases whose goal is to verify the resilience of the application when attacked with the same attacking tools, techniques, and procedures used by the threat agents being this both automated and human threat agents.

Through the analysis of the attack scenarios of malware banking and DDoS threats by using the kill-chain method, security measures can be identified to detect, deny, disrupt, deceive, and destroy the malware-based and DDoS-based attacks. Specifically, the effectiveness of these security measures in mitigating the attacks need to be validated in simulated attack exercises. The attack vectors that are extracted from the analysis of the attack scenarios and specifically also from sources of threat intelligence, root cause analysis of security incidents and malware analysis/reverse engineering are instrumental to update information on the security measures that need to be validated in order to detect and protect from these attack vectors. Security measures and controls that are known to be effective in mitigating the risk of these attacks can be uploaded for each attack pattern as shown by using standard attack patterns such as CAPEC or by using threat modeling tools such as ThreatModeler™ where attacks, security requirements for controls and measures, and test cases are mapped to each functional component of the online banking application.

After these security controls and measures are documented in design and implemented in the online banking application, they might still be affected by weaknesses and vulnerabilities that these specific attacks seek to exploit; therefore, a list of specific test cases to test these vulnerabilities and weaknesses should be created. The various weaknesses and vulnerabilities that threat agents seek to exploit were also identified by threat intelligence as threat target-vulnerability mapping and analyzed in stage IV weaknesses and vulnerability analysis to prioritize security tests. These tests seek to identify the presence of vulnerability but not necessarily for security assurance perspective and are compliance driven. The security tests that are derived at this stage are realistic attack driven and are aimed at conducting an exploit of the vulnerability with the realistic attack vectors used by the attackers to produce the same impact. For this reason, it is important to scope vulnerability and weaknesses test for exploit using the same attack scenario and the same attack vectors used by the attackers.

Attack libraries and patterns are key for attack-driven security tests and assist in defining the behavior of the online banking application when is attacked and to prevent or to react to a specific type of likely attack.

From the development perspective, attack libraries help to identify the positive security requirements for designing security controls such as authentication, authorization, input validation, and application functionality, and validate that are resistant and resilient to the specified attacks such as malware banking and DDoS.

Attack libraries also help to identify appropriate negative security requirements (misuse/abuse cases) to specify the behavior of the online banking application when faced with the specified attacks. Negative security requirements can be contained in each attack pattern by fleshing out the details of the various steps for misuse or abuse of functionality that are undertook by the attacker and help to identify weaknesses in security controls and missing security functionality that could enable such an attack. The methodology that can be used to derive negative security requirements following an understanding of the attack scenarios, attack libraries/patterns, and attack tree analysis includes misuse and abuse cases.

Figure 8.35 shows an example of use and abuse cases to derive negative security requirements to strengthen the design of MFA Multifactor Authentication for the online banking application. On the left-hand side of the abuse case diagram are

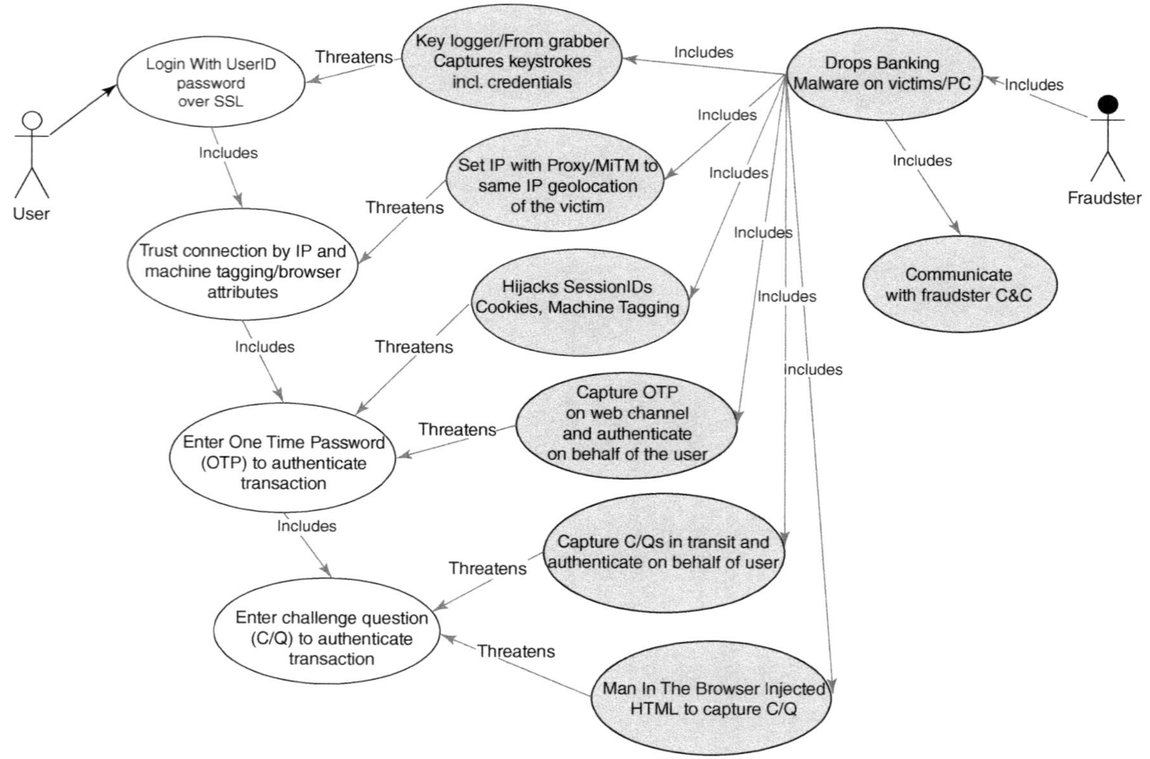

Figure 8.35 Use and Abuse Cases for MFA Controls

depicted the various steps/use cases followed by a bank user when logging to an online web application using standard MFA controls deployed by a bank. On the right-hand side of the diagrams are the steps followed by a fraudster that "threaten" to compromise the MFA functionality for bypassing the log-on authentication steps.

In the example shown in Figure 8.35, the fraudster controls the banking malware dropped on the client host and initiates a set of abuses of MFA that are learned from the malware banking attack scenario previously analyzed. From the abuse case analysis, it is analyzed how the attacker can abuse both single authentication credentials and MFA controls including, risk-based authentication factors such as IP geo-location, machine tagging, and MFA used to authenticate money movement transactions such as One-Time Passwords (OTPs) and Challenge/Question (C/Q) factors, one time passwords.

Based upon this analysis, it is possible to derive missing security requirements and test cases to protect user logging as well as test the threat resilience of multifactor authentication controls to these types of attacks.

Based upon the analysis of the attack tree as an example, the following Security Test (ST) cases can be derived for malware banking-based attacks:

1. *ST1-Malware-delivery-web-based attack test:* Test the security controls of the online banking application using attack vectors that seek to exploit vulnerabilities and exploits used for dropping banking malware on the client such as, XSS, XFS, and iFrame injection exploits.

2. *ST2-Malware-delivery-client-based attack test:* Test the client hosts for exploit of browser vulnerabilities in the executable environment of the client host/PC that are used for drive by download and phishing such as browser plug-ins, adobe and macromedia flash and active X controls.

3. *ST3-Malware-action on objectives attack test:* Test the impact of malware banking attack actions targeting online banking application for vulnerabilities and weaknesses assuming compromise of malware on the client to attack. Attacks vectors to be used for testing the online web application include MitM, MiTB, and session hijacking attacks. These exploit of weaknesses by these attack vectors such as lack of mutual authentication, expired or insecure certificates and cryptographic storage, lack of (OOBA) 2-way Out Of Band Authentication, session fixation and hijacking, and authentication weaknesses (Note the complete list of CVEs and CWEs is extracted from the mapping of threats to vulnerabilities and attacks that are documented in the attack libraries and patterns).

At more detailed level, attack-driven security tests can be derived from the previously defined attack vectors used in malware-based attacks as shown in Table 8.21.

Similarly for DDoS attacks, the following attack-driven test cases can be derived based upon the analysis of the attack vectors used by DDoS agent attack tools. An example is shown in Table 8.22.

Attack-driven tests validate the realization of the attack to accomplish their intended goal of the attack such as stealing confidential information and online banking credentials of a customer, manipulate money transfers, and steal money

TABLE 8.21 Malware-Based-Attack-Driven Security Test Cases

Attack Vector	Attack Description	Security Test Case	Test Case Description
\multicolumn{4}{c}{Online Banking Malware Attack Vector(s) and Security Test Cases}

Attack Vector	Attack Description	Security Test Case	Test Case Description
AV1	Capture authentication data from user activity using key logger	ST1	Test effectiveness of antimalware software and sandboxing/virtualization to detect and prevent malware installation on host PC/workstations
AV2	Take screenshots of the user's browser session to defeat virtual keyboard	ST2	Test capability of frame grabbing malware to capture virtual keyboard keystrokes if effective test alternative methods for trusted UI and OOBV
AV3	Exfiltration confidential data and send to external server	ST3	Test detection of unauthorized HTTP traffic from/to internal host to outside the company network
AV4	Redirect to another site URL or IP address	ST4	Test for invalidated redirect and forwards and filtering of known URLS used for malware delivery at corporate gateways
AV5	Update modules/scripts for the malware installed	ST5	Test detection and filtering of command and control traffic to malware compromised clients
AV6	Initiate Client Attacks (XSS, MiTB)	ST6	Test for client attacks vulnerabilities (CVEs) and weaknesses (CWEs). Test effectiveness of MiTB defenses such as antimalware, client sandboxing virtualization and OOBA
AV7	Initiate Web-based Attack (MiTM, Session Hijacking)	ST7	Test for CVEs and CWEs that facilitate MiTM and Session Hijacking
AV8	Spoof SMS OTPs sent to fraudster's mobile (MoITM)	ST8	Test resilience of SMS OTPs to MoTIM attacks
AV9	Capture data from volatile memory (e.g. RAM)	ST9	Test device memory protection controls and crypto routines
AV10	Capture secrets (private keys, certificates) stored on the client device (mobile or desktop)	ST10	Test secure storage of secrets (keys, authentication data) and validated against weaknesses and vulnerabilities of key management and encryption
AV11	Capture sensitive data stored on cashed data/temporary files	ST11	Test for caching of confidential and authentication data
AV12	Install backdoor to allow remote access/control	ST12	Test for user access restrictions (authN and authZ), unauthorized communication ports and audit and logging enabled for suspicious

(continued)

PASTA USE CASE EXAMPLE WALK-THROUGH   611

TABLE 8.21 (*Continued*)

Online Banking Malware Attack Vector(s) and Security Test Cases				
Attack Vector	Attack Description	Security Test Case	Test Case Description
AV13	Listen and execute commands to update malware agent and exfiltr$$$	ST13	Test filtering of C2 commands to download malware package updates to internal servers using various communications controls (IM, IRC, HTTPs, P2P)
AV14	Manipulate money transfer transactions to send money to money mule accounts	ST14	Test for impersonation/account take over through session hijacking to tamper money transfer parameters. Test effectiveness of MFA controls deployed (e.g. H/W OTPs, OOB SMS OTPs, C/Qs, RBAs)

from bank accounts and take off the online banking site with denial-of-service attacks.

These specific attack-driven test cases can be added to threat-driven security test cases. The difference between attack-driven and threat-driven test cases is that threat-driven test the realization of a threat into an attack whose successful validation of the test is to ascertain that the threat can be realized.

For example, the following security test cases are generic threat driven using the STRIDE (Spoofing Tampering Repudiation Information Disclosure, Denial of Service and Elevation of Privilege) classification:

1. *ST1-Spoofing Identity:* Test attempts to impersonate a user by sniffing user credentials on the wire or in persistent storage.
2. *ST2-Spoofing Identity:* Test that security tokens (e.g. cookie) issued before authentication cannot be replayed to bypass authentication.
3. *ST1-Tampering data:* Test with a web proxy that is not possible to tamper and replay authentication and sensitive data.
4. *ST2-Tampering data:* Test strength of password hashes against replay attacks (e.g. use of salted hashes).
5. *ST1-Repudiation:* Test mutual authentication and/or digital signatures to enforce trusted connection between client and server and between server to server/point to point connections.
6. *ST2-Repudiation:* Test that all security events are audited and logged.
7. *ST1-Information:* Disclosure: Test that the access of nonpublic data requires authentication.
8. *ST2-Information:* Disclosure: Test that error messages and exceptions do not disclose useful information to an attacker.

TABLE 8.22 DDoS Attack Driven Security Test Cases

	DDoS Bot Agent Attack Vector(s) and Security Test Cases		
Attack Vector ID	Attack Description	Security Test ID	Test Description
AV1	HTTP GET File Downloading Flood: causes web server by repeating conventional HTTP requests	ST1	Test Resilience of Web Server to HTTP GET Flooding Attacks Pre-Authentication and determine degradation/denial of service/CPU
AV2	HTTP POST Flood: send random usernames and passwords (embedded in HTTP-POST packets)	ST2	Test Resilience of Online Banking Application Against HTTP POST flooding targeting login web pages determine degradation/denial of service
AV3	HTTP File Downloading Flood: download/request larger (more bandwidth consuming) files	ST3	Scan online banking application for pre-authentication URLS that allow to download videos and large PDF files. Use HTTP GET flood testing tools to flood request to download videos and large PDF files and determine degradation and denial of service
AV4	Malformed HTTP Requests: Slowloris attacks	ST4	Test Web Server for HTTP GET requests with malformed HTTP headers to determine degradation/denial of service
AV5	HTTP Download: leaves the server in the state of 'waiting' after a full TCP connection	ST5	Test HTTP download attacks used by DDoS attack tools such as Pandora and DireJumper against web server to determine degradation/denial of service
AV6	HTTP POST of large request (larger than 1GB) bytes	ST6	Test effectiveness of filtering of large HTTP request (e.g. limitation of max size of HTTP requests at web server NSAPI filters as well as at Application Server servlet filters)
AV7	Slow HTTP POST Attack	ST7	Test resilience of web servers against sloe HTTP Post attacks
AV8	TCP SYN, UDP, ICMP flooding attacks	ST8	Test data center network devices resilience against traditional L3 and L4 DDoS attacks (e.g. TCP Syn flood, PING flood, UDP Floods etc.)
AV9	DNS Attacks (IP spoofing, open recursion and amplification)	ST9	Test for attacks against DNS server including DNS amplification attacks exploits

PASTA USE CASE EXAMPLE WALK-THROUGH   613

9. *ST3-Information*: Disclosure: Test that processes do not cache or log passwords, session information, or PII.
10. *ST1-Denial of Service:* Test that you cannot flood either a process (e.g. HTTP GET and POST requests to the web server) or a service (e.g. web service calls) with so much data so that it stops responding to valid requests.
11. *ST2-Denial of Service:* Test that malformed data (e.g. malformed HTTP headers, XML files etc) cannot crash the process.
12. *ST1-Elevation of Privilege:* Test that user cannot tamper client parameters or forceful browsing to elevate his privileges.
13. *ST2-Elevation of Privilege:* Test that a process cannot be forced to load a command shell, which in turn will execute with elevated privileges.

Threat-driven security tests can be associated with component of the application architecture and security control that is changed/modified to determine the exposure to generic threats.

Threat-driven test cases can also embedded in a threat modeling and tool and retrieve to validate threat mitigation at each component, that is, to assert that the risk of the threat is mitigated by security requirements asserted by review of design and security test cases executed to validate these requirements.

In Figure 8.36, we show an example of security test cases that can be extracted for each functional component of the online banking application and mapped to threats, security requirements, and code snippets that serve as reference to conduct a source code review to assert the implementation of these security requirements in the source code.

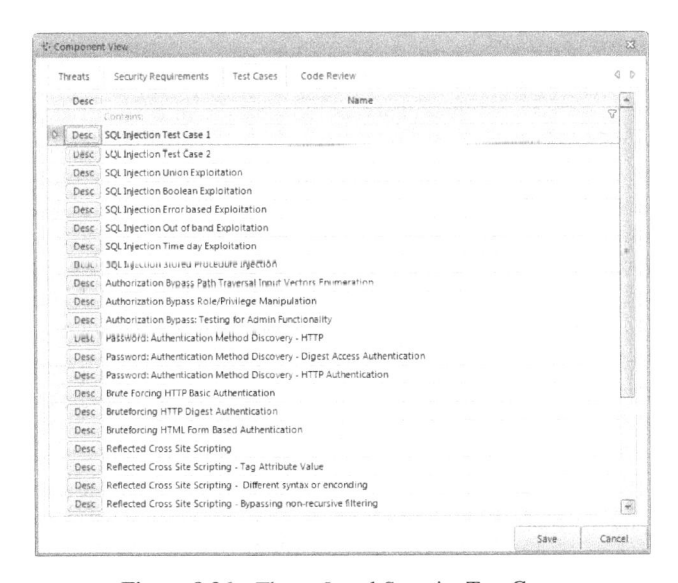

Figure 8.36 Threat-Level Security Test Cases

Once various test cases have been documented, the next and last stage of attack modeling and simulation stage is to conduct an attack simulation exercise for the threats considered that includes, in this case, malware banking and DDoS attacks. This is the goal of the activity *AMS 6.6 – Conduct attack driven security tests and simulations*. The scope of these simulation attack exercises is to identify vulnerabilities and design flaws that are exploited by the attack and determine the risks as factor of probability of attack and the impact of these attacks but also to identify any weaknesses and vulnerabilities that these attack exploit and to learn how to respond in the case of security incidents caused by these attacks.

Prior to execute these simulation attack exercises, it is important to document an attack-driven testing strategy that can be followed by the organization with specific goals that need to be met. An example of goals for an attack-driven security testing strategy include the following:

- Identify the most likely attack course of action against your web application and your customers (difficulty of attack is the least and the impact is the highest);
- Identify the attack surface and the attack vector entry points;
- Identify the access levels required to conduct the attack;
- Test for vulnerabilities and design flaws that these attacks could exploit as used in real case scenarios;
- Test for abuse of functionality/business logic by deriving test cases using use and abuse cases;
- Test the same attack vectors used by the attack tools to try to evade security controls;
- Test defenses at the different layers of the architecture to validate the defense in depth against threats identified in the application threat model.

At the end of the execution of the attack simulation and test exercise, it is important to produce an attack simulation test report for the threat scenarios considered that includes the results of the security test cases and the identification of the exposure of vulnerabilities to these attacks as well as bypass of security controls to cause an impact. The attack simulation report includes the results of the security tests and the security issues identified and the risk of each security issue (design flaws, web application and system vulnerabilities, weaknesses in security controls).The risk severity of each security issue can be estimated based upon the probability of the attack to cause an impact and can be determined based upon the review of the results of the test/simulation.

The results of the security tests cases can be mapped to the various threat agents to determine if the risk of threats is mitigated. Some of these threats might be considered unmitigated and open because of the presence of weaknesses and vulnerabilities in security controls and therefore considered of a certain risk. This risk of these threats can be calculated based upon risk calculation formulas to determine the probability, and the risk severity of the vulnerabilities can also be calculated based upon different scoring methods such as CVSS. These final calculations of the level of risks for each threat based upon the various factors that can be considered in the analysis such as quantitative and qualitative risk analysis are the objective of stage VII.

Stage VII – Risk Analysis and Management (RAM)

Goal of This Stage   The goal of this last stage is to analyze the risk of each threat and attack scenario that was previously simulated, recommend countermeasures that can minimize this risk, and recommend strategies for managing these risks. The initial risk of each threat is calculated based upon qualitative and quantitative risk calculation methods, and the risk after countermeasures and risk mitigations are applied (e.g. residual risk) of each threat is also calculated by considering the effectiveness of each countermeasure and risk mitigation. Finally different risk strategies to manage the technical and business impact of the threat analyzed are also recommended in this stage.

Guidance for Conducting This Stage   The objective of the risk analysis and management (RAM) stage is to analyze the various risks of the threats, the attacks that are used to realize these threats, and the vulnerabilities that can be exploited and produce an impact on the application assets that include both data and functionality. The analysis of risk includes the calculation of the risk levels of the analysis of the probability and factors of technical impact such as loss of confidentiality, integrity, availability, accountability as well as business impact such as the various monetary legal impacts to the business that include business continuity loss, fraud monetary loss, noncompliance violations, and data privacy law violation impacts.

For the assessment of technical impact factors and business factors, it is possible to use technical risk and business risk calculation formulas used by each business. Examples of generic risk assessments for technical risks include the standard scoring methods for vulnerabilities such as First CVSS and the categorization of vulnerabilities such as Mitre's CVE. The analysis of technical and business impacts can consider the specific factors for assigning the probability and impact of threats. Once the risks are assigned to each one of the attack scenarios and vulnerabilities identified in the attack simulation analysis, the next step is to recommend the adoption of new countermeasures to reduce the impacts of threats and recommendations for fixing any design flaws and vulnerabilities that were previously identified during the attack simulation tests.

Recommendations for the adoption of countermeasures need to follow a risk mitigation strategy and a risk management process. The risk management process might dictate whether a risk should be mitigated by implementing countermeasures of the risk that can be either transferred to a third party with cyber-insurance or accepted when compensating controls could be identified. Any recommendations of new countermeasure need to consider both the costs and the benefits such as the effectiveness of these countermeasures in reducing the various impacts of threats targeting the application. The cost of countermeasures can be calculated based on their total cost of ownership that includes the cost of acquiring, deploying, and maintaining such countermeasure. The costs of countermeasures need to commensurate with the potential impacts. The selection of countermeasures should also factor the residual risks after these countermeasures are deployed to determine their effectiveness as a whole. After the countermeasures are identified, the decision of whether to implement these countermeasures need to align with the organization risk mitigation strategies and the objectives for the treatment of risk defined in STAGE I.

Activities This stage consists of the following activities:

RAM 7.1 – Calculate the risk of each threat: The goal of this activity is to analyze the technical impact caused by the attacks that were previously analyzed and factor the probability to determine the risk of each threat to be realized in an attack. Examples of technical impacts include the loss of confidentiality, integrity, availability, and accountability of data and functionality. By associating the probability of each threat occurring based upon the capabilities and motivation of each threat agent, it is possible to assign the risk to each threat attack. Once the technical impacts have been calculated, it is also possible to associate the value of the asset impacted and such as the monetary value of the asset that is at risk to be compromised and quantify the business impact caused the various types of threats and exploits;

RAM 7.2 – Recommend countermeasures and risk mitigations: The goal of this activity is to recommend security measures to detect and protect from the various attack scenarios. Examples of countermeasures are detective and protective security measures and controls that mitigate the impact of attacks against the application assets (data and functionality). Besides identifying countermeasures, the focus of this activity is also to select risk mitigations for the various types of weaknesses and vulnerabilities that attacks might exploit in an attack. Among risk mitigations, design and code changes are also recommended during this stage: these are corrective action plans and design and coding changes whose goal is mitigate the root causes of weaknesses and vulnerabilities such as design flaws or implementation type of vulnerabilities; the types of countermeasures include preventive and detective security controls that are found effective in mitigating the impact of the attacks that were previously simulated. These countermeasures can be deployed in addition to fixing of any design flaws, coding errors, and mis-configuration issues vulnerabilities that were identified to be exploitable with attack simulations and tests previously executed.

RAM 7.3 – Calculate the residual risks: The goal of this activity is to calculate the levels of residual risk both qualitatively and quantitatively after the different countermeasures and risk mitigation options such as design changes for fixing design flaws and code changes to fix coding issues have been deployed in production. The residual risk calculation is the basis to decide if the deployment of countermeasures reduces the risk to a level of LOW risk that is acceptable by the organization. The calculation of the residual risk for a countermeasure depends on the estimate on how much effective is the countermeasure when it is deployed. For example, after the attack analysis and simulation, it is found that new countermeasures need to be deployed such as two-factor out-of-band authentication solutions that are effective to mitigate MiTM and MiTB type of attacks seeking to compromise single factor and multifactor authentication using traditional hardware and software OTPs. The effectiveness of various OOBA authentication options to mitigate the risk varies depending upon the type of OOBA solution that is selected such as OOBA with biometrics that includes a voice authentication, fingerprints, SMS OTPs, and 2-way 2FA Second Factor Authentication using a completely independent secure authentication channel. The effectiveness of this countermeasure when considered as a whole by applying defense in depth is also enhanced when is used in conjunction with other countermeasures such as antimalware on the client and detective controls on the server to detect anomalies in transactions as indication of compromise. The deployment of these countermeasures in support of the principle of defense in depth is critical to reduce the overall amount of risk for MiTm and MiTB to a residual level of LOW that might be deemed acceptable by the organization based upon the accepted risk mitigation strategy.

- By analogy, the deployment of design changes and implementation changes to remediate weaknesses and vulnerabilities can also be considered as countermeasures to mitigate the risk of threat agents and the impact of attack vectors used by these threat agents. Specifically once different type of design options might be implemented to remediate a weaknesses in a security control such as a weakness in a security control that provides data filtering/input validation of malicious commands, the effectiveness of the risk mitigation option can be calculated as a factor to select the remediation that is most effective to mitigate the risk. For example, input filtering for malicious input might include the implementation of an API that filters attack vectors and their encoded versions in different characters to prevent attackers to bypass the filtering. As for new countermeasures, the effectiveness of changes introduced in the application such as deployment of APIs to filter malicious commands from attack vectors increases when these APIs are deployed at different layers of the application architecture such as by deploying NSAPI filters at the web server in the DMZ and servlet filters at the application server located with the internal trusted network.

RAM 7.4 – Recommend strategies to manage risks: the goal of this activity is to recommend the actions that should be taken to treat the risks of each threat and reduce the technical and business impacts to the organization. At this stage of the risk analysis and management, the risk manager has all the information on the table such as the results of the attack simulation exercise, information about the weaknesses, and vulnerabilities that are exploited by these attacks and the selection of different types of countermeasures with different effectiveness and level of residual when deployed as well different options to remediate weaknesses and vulnerabilities previously identified. Each of these countermeasures includes associated costs for design and implementation and effectiveness in reducing the initial risk to a residual level that might be deemed acceptable by the organization.

Based upon this information, it is possible to decide how to treat the risk by recommending different risk mitigation options that align with the organization risk mitigation strategy. This risk mitigation strategy might consist of the following options:

1. Accepting the risk when it is deemed acceptable by the organization based upon the risk level and the presence of compensating controls/measures.
2. Applying the countermeasures/risk mitigations to reduce the risk to acceptable levels.
3. Transferring the risk to a third party such as by signing cyber-insurance.
4. Avoiding the risk such as in the case of deciding not to implement the application feature or storing valued assets that might put the application at risk.

If the risk mitigation strategy followed includes accepting the risk such as by filing a risk exception, it is important that this risk exception is documented and signed off by the business that is ultimately responsible to accept the risk. This risk acceptance certification is also important to provide as visibility to auditors and forensics investigators in the case the organization suffered a security incident whose application impacted was in scope for the application threat modeling exercise to assert whether the root causes of the security incident were also identified as security issues in the application threat modeling exercise whose impact to the business was analyzed and accepted by the business owners including the possible liability of data losses and compromises in the case of security incident exploiting the issues being identified.

If the risk mitigation strategy followed consists of applying countermeasures and risk mitigations, it is important to validate them with security tests after these are deployed and implemented. The results of these tests serve the purpose of certification and assurance that the risks of the threats considered are now mitigated. This assurance also provide visibility to the business owners, risk managers, and auditors who have responsibility in making assertions on whether risks are managed in alignment with business objectives, risk management objectives, and compliance with information security policies and technical standards. At this last stage of the threat modeling exercise, the various security requirements that were identified in stage I can be asserted based upon the results of the threat modeling assessment and the attack-driven security tests cases that were executed in stage IV to validate that these security requirements are validated and tested and the risk of the various threats being considered are now mitigated and closed.

If the risk mitigation strategy consists of transferring the risk to a third party such as in the case of not implementing the countermeasure risk mitigation option but relying on a third party that will assume the costs and the liabilities for implementing it based upon a contract with the business, it is important that the business that accepts to transfer the risk to the third party/vendor also legally bind the liabilities in a legal contract with the vendor. An example of this transfer of risk through transfer of liability is the signing of a contract agreement such as a Service Level Agreement (SLA) with a third-party vendor that takes responsibility in either implementing the countermeasures or taking the risks and the liability in the case of a security incident.

The option of avoiding the risk might be taken by risk management together with the business and the development organization and might include the option of not implementing changes in the application that might increase the attack surface and the risk such as exposing functionality that is considered too risk to be exposed online, not storing secrets such as passwords even if encrypted on mobile devices, not moving business critical services, and customer confidential information on the cloud and other changes that might be considered to bear too much risk for the organization. When making these decisions, it is important to articulate to the decision from business perspective. For example, if a decision ought to be made not to implement a certain application feature/functionality, it is important to commiserate that decision with the potential monetary loss that might be incurred by the business is such application feature/functionality will get compromised by attacks targeting that feature/functionality. If this decision was not made in stage I at the beginning of the assessment based upon the analysis of business requirements and business impacts can be made at this stage after all technical and business risks have been considered.

Input for This Stage This includes one or more of the following:

1. Threat probabilities (stage IV)
2. Severity of the vulnerabilities exploited by each threat (stage V)
3. Exposure of vulnerabilities to each threats (stage V)
4. Attack simulation and tests results (stage VI)
5. Countermeasures and risk mitigations for vulnerabilities and design flaws (stage V)

Artifacts Produced at the End of This Stage At the end of this stage, we will produce the following artifacts:

(a) Analysis of risks each threat including technical and business impacts
(b) List of countermeasures and recommended risk mitigation options for reducing the various impacts of the attacks
(c) Calculation of the residual risks after countermeasures and various options for remediated vulnerabilities are applied
(d) Cost of the countermeasures and risk mitigation options
(e) Recommended risk mitigation strategies for each threat/scenario

Tools The execution of this stage can be facilitated by the use of risk calculators from FIRST such as CVSSvs2, OWASP risk calculation methods, MS™ DREAD for threat-risk severity and industry accepted risk calculation methods for quantitative and qualitative risk calculations. Control risk frameworks that map threats to security controls can be used for identification of countermeasures. Vendor-supplied reports on cost of countermeasures and vendor-unbiased threat intelligence reports on countermeasure effectiveness can also be used. The ThreatModeler™ tool threat management dashboard is also used herein for tracking the risk management of various threats against the online banking application.

Web Application Use Case Example At this stage of the threat modeling exercise, the focus is on the factors that can help to quantify and qualify the risk of each threat so that informed risk decisions for the management of risks can be made. From the information security risk perspective, the main concern is the protection of the confidentiality, integrity, and availability of the data hence the factors that are assessed to quantify and qualify risk are factors of technical impact caused by weaknesses and vulnerabilities in a security control or measures on the confidentiality, integrity, availability, accountability of the data.

A qualitative level of risk can be assigned to the degree of degradation of the security control caused by weaknesses and vulnerabilities that correlate to increased exposure and partial or complete loss of the security attributes of the asset that need to be protected such as Confidentiality, Integrity, and Availability. A step further when this loss is associated to the value of the asset can also be quantified as business impacts that can be either directly or indirectly associated with the business value of the asset lost as well as with the consequences of loss such as additional economic penalties such as fines for noncompliance violations and for data privacy law violations.

Standard methodologies and risk formulas can be used for assigning the various levels for the probability and impact including the standard scoring methods to determine the risk severity of vulnerabilities such as First CVSS and for the categorization of vulnerabilities such as Mitre's CVE. The determination of the business impact caused by the loss of the assets needs to factor the probability of a security incident occurring that might compromise the asset and multiply that probability with the impact that is determined as monetary value expected caused by the security incident. Once technical and business impact are quantified, the next step in the risk management stage is to identify security measures that can reduce the risk including corrective action plans for fixing any design flaws and vulnerabilities that are found exploitable during the attack simulation exercise and validated with attack-driven tests.

The threat risks can be mitigated by reducing the opportunity of attacks to exploit known weaknesses and vulnerabilities in security controls as well as by adopting new countermeasures against these threats. A risk management decision is generally required when the level of risk is higher than that the organization is willing to accept. In this case, the risk manager who ought to make that call whether the risk should be mitigated, transferred, or accepted need to consider both the costs and the benefits of countermeasures. Typically the cost of countermeasures includes the cost of acquisition, deployment, and maintenance and need to commensurate with the potential impacts that the organization might occur if the countermeasure is not implemented. The selection of countermeasures should also factor the effectiveness of the countermeasures and the residual risks after each of these countermeasures are deployed to determine their effectiveness as a whole. After the countermeasures are identified and recommended to executive management and business sponsors, it is important to provide information to support whether the decision of mitigating risks aligns with the organization risk mitigation strategies and the objectives for the treatment of risk that were defined in STAGE I at the beginning of the threat modeling exercise.

PASTA USE CASE EXAMPLE WALK-THROUGH

The first activity of this stage consists of the activity *RAM 7.1 – Calculate the risk of each threat*. The goal of this activity is to analyze the risk of the threat as technical impact caused on the asset. The risk of a threat can be calculated based upon different factors and methodologies. The risk of threat from probability perspective represents a possibility of that threat to be realized in an attack and cause a compromise. Formulas that can be used to assess the risk of a threat include assigning levels of probability and impact for the threat and multiply with the severity of weaknesses and vulnerabilities using CVSS scoring that the threat seek to exploit and the impact on the assets (data and functions) resulting from the security incident such as data breach where the data is known to be compromised due to the successful attack on the target.

The first step consists of assigning the severity of the vulnerabilities for each security control is affected by the threat based upon the updated information that comes from the analysis of threats, vulnerabilities, and attacks.

The CVSS scoring method can be used for assigning the risk severity using a standard and consistent method that is based on the following factors:

- Base Metrics
  - Access Vector (AV)
  - Access Complexity (AC)
  - Authentication (Au)
  - Confidentiality Impact(C)
  - Integrity Impact (I)
  - Availability Impact (A)
- Temporal Metrics
  - Exploitability (E)
  - Remediation Level (RL)
  - Report Confidence(RC)
- Environmental Metrics
  - Collateral Damage Potential (CDP)
  - Target Distribution (TD)
  - Security Requirements (CR, IR, AR)

To calculate the severity of each vulnerability, the Online Calculator – http://nvd.nist.gov/cvss.cfm?calculator&adv&version=2 can be used and the CVSS vs2 guide can be found herein: CVSSv2 guide – http://www.first.org/cvss/cvss-guide.html.

Once the various risk scores are assigned to the vulnerabilities and weaknesses that map to the threat previously analyzed, the next step consists of assigning the risk likelihood to a threat that is the probability of a threat to occur. For assigning that probability, several methods can be used, but unfortunately none of them is accepted standard. For example, in OWASP risk methodology, threat likelihood factors that are considered are the threat agent factors such as the skills required by the threat agent to conduct the exploit (e.g. high-level skills correlated to low probability), the motivation/reward (e.g. high reward associated with high probability), opportunity (e.g. full access to resources such as tools to conduct the attack associated with high probability), and size (e.g. the larger the group/population of attacker the higher the probability). The OWASP risk methodology can also be used to calculate vulnerability factors and technical and business impact factors and is documented herein: https://www.owasp.org/index.php/OWASP_Risk_Rating_Methodology and a risk calculator is provided herein: http://paradoslabs.nl/owaspcalc/.

Note: OWASP risk rating methodology is currently under review because it does not provide consistent risk calculations but is reported herein as reference for calculating the threat probability only as one of the methods that can be used. The authors of this book recommend using standard formulas and methods that provide consistent risk ratings for both vulnerability risks and threat probability.

Other nonstandard risk rating methodologies that can be sued to rank the severity of threats include the Microsoft DREAD methodology that is based upon the following factors to calculate the risk of a threat:

- *D*amage potential as the damage if the vulnerability is exploited.
- *R*eproducibility as how easy is it to reproduce the attacks.
- *E*xploitability as how easy is it to launch an attack.
- *A*ffected users as a rough percentage as how many users are affected.
- *D*iscoverability as how easy is it to find the vulnerability.

The risk ranking of a threat can be assigned by using the DREAD Threat Risk Ranking Table http://msdn.microsoft.com/en-us/library/ff648644.aspx#c03618429_011 and by averaging the value with the formula:

$$Risk = (D + R + E + A + D)/5$$

A more generic formulation for calculating risk is based on the definition of risk as *"The likelihood that threat will exploit a vulnerability to cause an impact to the system"*:

$$Risk = Threat \times Vulnerability \times Impact$$

By putting the emphasis on assets as relate to impact, another empirical calculation for risk can be based on the following definition: *"Risk is the probability of an attack on an asset exposed by vulnerability"*:

$$Risk = Vulnerability \times Asset \times Attack$$

Once the technical impacts have been calculated, it is also possible to associate the monetary value of the asset that is at risk to be compromised and quantify the business impact caused the various types of threats and exploit. If the risk that is calculated is a technical risk, the risk factors considered are the loss of confidentiality,

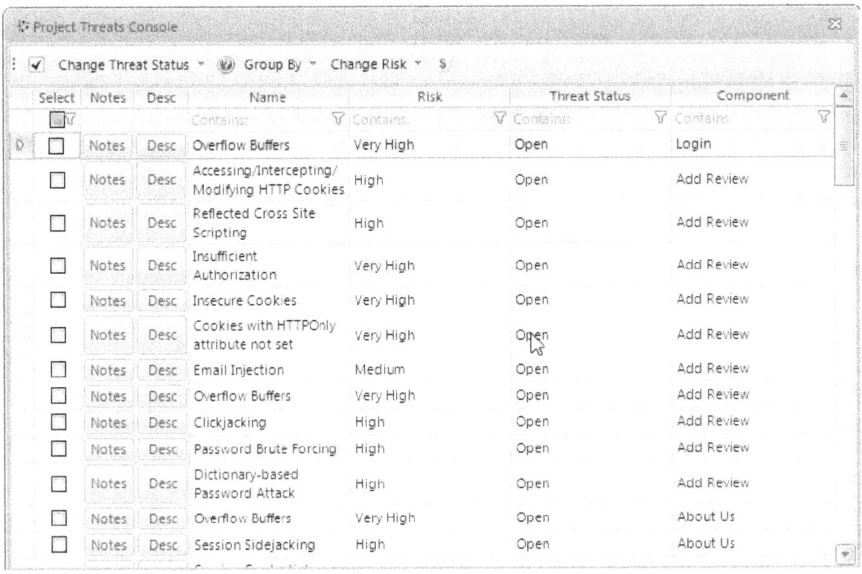

PASTA USE CASE EXAMPLE WALK-THROUGH 623

Select	Notes	Desc	Name	Risk	Threat Status	Component
	Notes	Desc	Overflow Buffers	Very High	Open	Login
	Notes	Desc	Accessing/Intercepting/Modifying HTTP Cookies	High	Open	Add Review
	Notes	Desc	Reflected Cross Site Scripting	High	Open	Add Review
	Notes	Desc	Insufficient Authorization	Very High	Open	Add Review
	Notes	Desc	Insecure Cookies	Very High	Open	Add Review
	Notes	Desc	Cookies with HTTPOnly attribute not set	Very High	Open	Add Review
	Notes	Desc	Email Injection	Medium	Open	Add Review
	Notes	Desc	Overflow Buffers	Very High	Open	Add Review
	Notes	Desc	Clickjacking	High	Open	Add Review
	Notes	Desc	Password Brute Forcing	High	Open	Add Review
	Notes	Desc	Dictionary-based Password Attack	High	Open	Add Review
	Notes	Desc	Overflow Buffers	Very High	Open	About Us
	Notes	Desc	Session Sidejacking	High	Open	About Us

Figure 8.37 Threat and Risk Dashboard

integrity, availability, and accountability of data and functionality. By associating the probability of each threat occurring based upon the capabilities and motivation of each threat agent, it is possible to assign the risk to each threat. The risk for each threat can be calculated, assigned to each threat and tracked for risk mitigation using a threat-risk management dashboard as shown in Figure 8.37.

In the cases when the impact can be associated to the value of an asset, it can be used to determine the business impact. For example, if the maximum value of a functional asset such as money transfer is $ 1 MM per transaction from one account in a single transaction, it is possible to estimate the business impact in the calculation of risk as this transaction can be potentially compromised causing a maximum impact of that amount.

The standard formula that can be used for the quantitative assessment of risk is ALE = ARO × SLO, where (ARO) is the Rate of Occurrence (ARO) or the annual frequency of the security incident causes by that threat and Single Loss Expectancy (SLE) or probability of a loss as a result of a security incident caused by that threat. The SLE can be factored further as by considering the SLE = AV × EF where AV is the Asset Value (AV) and EF is the Exposure Factor (EF).

Factors of probability and impact can also be displayed in the so-called heat map to calculate qualitative level of risk for both technical and business risks. For example, for each specific threat agent, the threat event such as the occurrence of a security incident caused by a malware-based attack or a DDoS can be rated as Very LOW or rare event, LOW or unlikely event, MEDIUM or possible event, HIGH as likely event and Very HIGH as very likely. The level of impacts can be calculated as associated with monetary losses if such security incident ought to occur such as Very LOW for

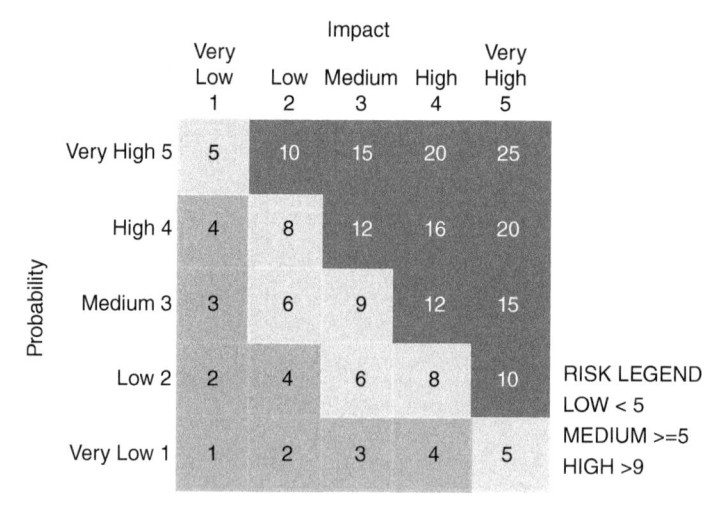

	Impact Very Low 1	Low 2	Medium 3	High 4	Very High 5
Very High 5	5	10	15	20	25
High 4	4	8	12	16	20
Medium 3	3	6	9	12	15
Low 2	2	4	6	8	10
Very Low 1	1	2	3	4	5

RISK LEGEND
LOW < 5
MEDIUM >=5
HIGH >9

Figure 8.38   Risk Calculation Heat Map

losses up to $100, LOW up to $1 MM, MEDIUM up to $5 MM, HIGH up to $10 MM, and Very HIGH for monetary losses more than $10 MM.

By entering these values in the heat map, it is possible to calculate the overall risk from the business impact perspective. By using the heat map, for example, the monetary impact due to the max amount of $1 MM is considered LOW and the probability of the malware event is considered HIGH, and the overall risk of malware banking attacks is considered MEDIUM. The risk calculation of heat map is shown in Figure 8.38.

In the heat map, the lower band represents the LOW risk, which is the risk that is acceptable based upon the organization risk management policy and appetite for risk. The middle band represents medium level risk and the higher band represents high risk. Both medium and high risks need to be addressed and high-risk remediation has priority over medium risks.

By following one of these risk assessment methodologies, at the end of this activity, the risk manager would have calculated the risk for each threat including technical and business impacts and entered in the risk management dashboard. An example of the risk dashboard showing the status of the threats (open, closed, mitigated, etc.) and the risk associated to the technical risks, which is the risk of the vulnerabilities associated to each threat is shown in Figure 8.39. In risk dashboard, 23 issues are reported to be of very high risk, 38 issues are of high risk, 8 are of medium risk and 5 are of low risk. The risk dashboard help risk managers to prioritize the fixing of issues whose unmitigated threats are considered very high and high risks.

Once each of the threats being assessed has assigned a risk, the next step of the risk assessment and management consists of performing the activity *RAM 7.2 – Identify the countermeasures and risk mitigations*. The goal of this activity is to recommend security measures to detect and protect from the various attack vectors as well as promote changes to the online banking application to remediate vulnerabilities and

PASTA USE CASE EXAMPLE WALK-THROUGH 625

Figure 8.39 ThreatModeler™ Threat-Risk Management Dashboard

weaknesses such as design flaws and web application type of vulnerabilities that were previously assessed and validated as exploitable with attack-driven security tests; the term *countermeasures* is referred herein as a broad term that includes preventive and detective security controls as well as fixing of any design flaws and vulnerabilities identified in the threat-driven and attack-driven security tests. In this broad definition of countermeasures for threats, a control gap such as missing authentication for example is also considered a countermeasure.

Ideally at this point of the threat modeling exercise, countermeasures are already documented and mapped to each instance of a threat and attack vector and can be queried through the threat modeling tools for each architectural and functional component of the online banking application. When using a tool such as ThreatModeler™, for example, each functional component has associated security controls that can be implemented to mitigate specific threat targeting the functional component. An example of countermeasures associated with threats to the log-in component is shown in Figure 8.40.

The goal of this activity is to query each of the functional component that the online banking application has been decomposed to the assert if the countermeasures associated with threats have been asserted in design and validated with threat-based and attack-based security tests. For the countermeasures that are not being implemented yet for which the threats are still open and unmitigated hence representing a

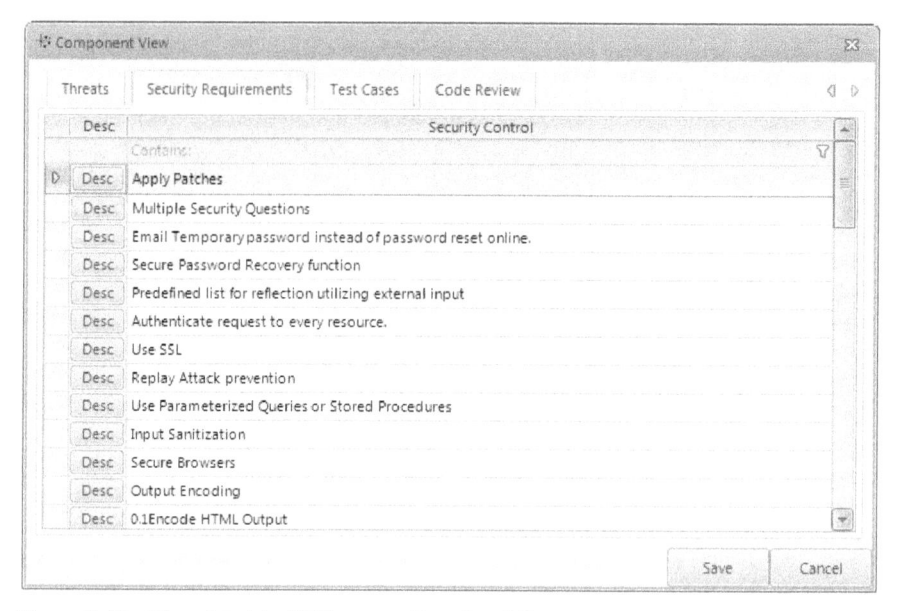

Figure 8.40 ThreatModeler™ Threats to Functional Components and Security Controls That Mitigate These Threats

risk, the goal of this activity is to determine whether these countermeasures should be implemented based upon the risk posed by each threat.

To make this determination, it is important to have an high-level architectural and data flow view of the threats, the attack vectors, the vulnerabilities and vulnerabilities that these threats and attack vectors seek to exploit and the countermeasures that can be deployed within each trust boundary and each data entry and exit point of the architecture to reduce the level of risk. This holistic architectural and data flow view of threats, attacks, vulnerabilities, and countermeasures allows a threat analyst-risk manager to assess the overall risk and the effectiveness of the countermeasures at the different architectural tiers of the online banking application and determine if these can work together to provide risk mitigation as following the various security requirements and security architecture design principles.

An example of this high-level threat and countermeasures holistic view superimposing on DFDs of the online banking application in scope for threat modeling with countermeasures to mitigate the exploit of vulnerabilities by attack vectors that are initiated by various types of threats is shown in Figure 8.41.

This high-level view of threats and countermeasures in place to protect and detect from attacks of various threats is very critical for threat and risk management. Using the military battlefield metaphor, an architectural view of the data flows and view of threats, attacks, vulnerabilities, and countermeasures is as critical for a risk manager to manage the risk of cyber-threats as it is for a military general the view of the battlefield to manage his defensive positions against the enemy. This view of

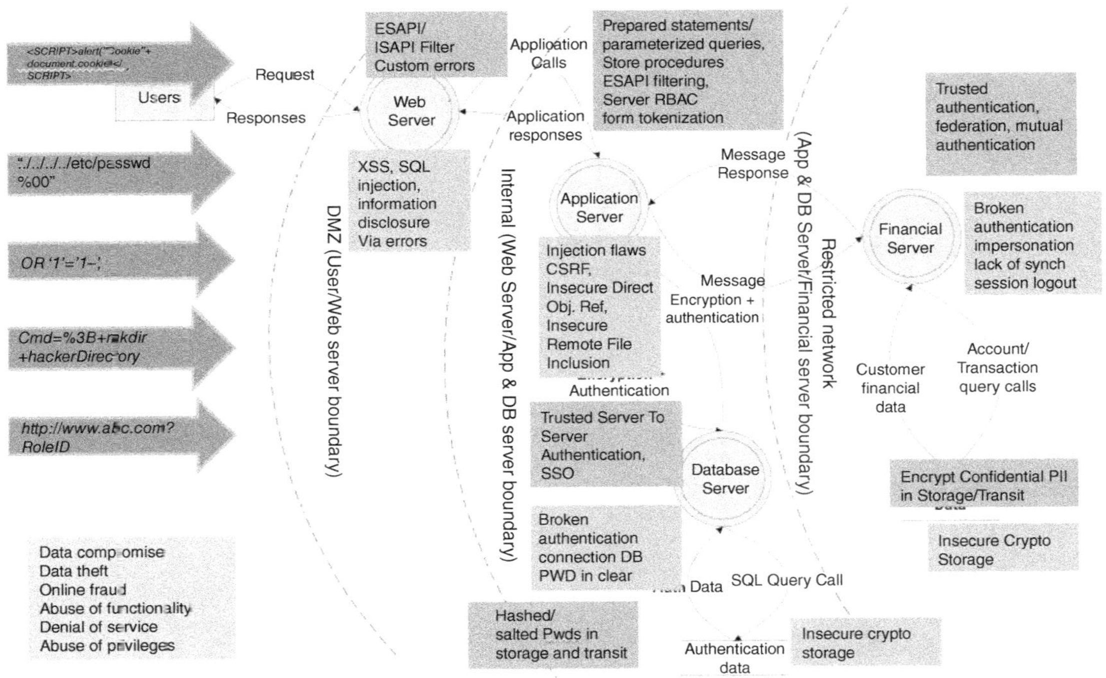

Figure 8.41 High Level View of Threats-Attacks-Vulnerabilities-Countermeasures of Online Banking Application

TABLE 8.23 Security Measures Proposed for Mitigate the Risks of Malware Banking and DDoS Threats

Attack-Vulnerability-Countermeasure Analysis

Attacks	Phishing, Drive by Download, MiTM, MiTB, MiTM, banking Trojans (Zeus) and C&C botnet control, host and application vulnerability exploits	DDoS reconnaissance, coordinated and targeted DDoS attacks against application and network layer, exploit of web application vulnerabilities
Attack targets	Financial Institutions, card merchants and credit card processors, web and mobile banking sites	Financial institutions, online banking sites, stock exchange web sites, visible credit card web sites
Attack impacts	HIGH: Monetary loss, online fraud, identity theft, wire fraud	HIGH: Reputational Damage via Defacement, Business Disruption, Online Revenue Loss
Attack probability	HIGH: Low cost and risk and high reward for threat agents, low cost of acquisition of cyber crime tools, basic knowledge of hacking tools/techniques	HIGH: Easy recruitment of attackers through social media, availability of free DDoS tools, low cost for renting DDoS botnets, basic knowledge of hacking tools/techniques
Vulnerability exploited	Social engineering, browser/PC vulnerability exploits XSS, SQL Injection, weaknesses in traditional MFA, weakness in virus signature detection, nonrepudiation for connections, indirect	Web Application Vulnerabilities, XSS, SQL Injection, Weaknesses in anti-DDOS defenses at network and application layer, Limited Web Traffic Capability/Architectures
Effective preventive controls	Consumer's education, client antimalware, 2-way Out of Band (OOB) authentication, OOB wire transaction confirmation, maker/checker for transaction initiation/approvals	Anti-DDOS defenses at edge of internet, internet and network (LAN) anti-DDOS layers such as IP filtering, malicious traffic scrubbing and URL blocking at the application layer (e.g. WAF)
Effective detective controls	Fraud detection, suspicious web application activity detection, out of band (e.g. SMS) transactional activity alerts	Network anomaly traffic/bandwidth detection, Real time DDOS Alerts, WAF application layer DDOS attack monitoring

countermeasures represents a defensive baseline that is used as reference to evaluate the security posture of the online banking application to general threats and attacks.

In the case of specific threats such as banking malware and DDoS that are in scope for this threat modeling example, the goal is also to recommend various security measures such as preventive and detective controls that can reduce the attack probability and impact of these threats as shown in Table 8.23.

After the various options of countermeasures have been recommended, the next step in the risk analysis and management stage is to conduct the activity *RAM 7.3 – Calculate the residual risks*. There is a residual risk associated with each threat." We can consider residual risk the risk left after we have applied security controls that reduce the likelihood and impact of the risk posed by a specific threat agent.

The level of reduction of risk provided by the adoption of a countermeasure can be calculated as a factor the risk control mitigation effectiveness such as the reduction of the overall risk factored as likelihood and impact of each threat.

The more effective the countermeasure in mitigating the risk of a threat, the less residual risk caused by the threat. We previously defined in Chapter 5 the amount of "Risk Mitigation (RM)" of the initial risk as a function of the "Control Effectiveness (CE) with the following empirical the formula:

$$RM = IR \times CE$$

The control effectiveness factors both the effectiveness of the control to reduce the likelihood and the impact on the asset value. For example, assuming a countermeasure is 40% effective (it works 40% of the time) and reduces the potential impact by 80%, the overall control effectiveness is 32% (40% × 80%). The amount of Risk Mitigation gained by applying this countermeasure is therefore 32%.

Since there is no one countermeasure alone that mitigates the risk of one threat, it is important to consider the cumulative effectiveness of countermeasures when these are deployed together. This is also very useful for a risk manager to determine if the recommended countermeasures provide an overall reduction of initial risk to an acceptable level.

For example, let us consider that both preventive and detective DDoS countermeasures are applied for mitigating the threat of DDoS and among them some are more or less effective in mitigating the risk. In the case of a DDoS threats, for example, countermeasures might be deployed at different layers of the OSI stack such as OSI layer 7 (application layer) measures such as web application firewall and layer 3 (network layer) countermeasures such as IP whitelists and blacklists, and rate controls. These countermeasures when deployed together can be considered 64% effective that is work 80% of the time and mitigates 80% of the impact. Detective DDoS countermeasures such as monitoring malicious DDoS traffic and issue alerts on suspicious spikes of the network traffic is not considered effective as preventive countermeasures but as effective "defense in-depth" measures since buy the organization that is attacked by DDoS some time to react with DDoS protection countermeasures such as blocking rules for source IPs and scrubbing of malicious traffic.

The Residual Risk (RR) is the amount of Initial Risk (IR) subtracted from the Risk Mitigation (RM) provided by preventive and detective countermeasures when both are deployed to mitigate the risk of DDoS threats. In simple terms, RR can be expressed by the following formula:

$$RR = IR \times (1-CE)$$

Assuming that the initial risk is HIGH (10 risk score) and that an acceptable risk is LOW (less than 5 risk score), the countermeasures deployed for preventing and detecting DDoS attacks need to reduce the level of risk at a level that is acceptable that is LOW risk. Assuming the effectiveness of the countermeasures that are deployed is 64% that will reduce the risk to a level of 3.6 that is considered LOW.

The final activity of the risk analysis and management consist of the activity *RAM 7.4 – Recommend strategy to manage risks*. The goal of this activity is to recommend a risk mitigation strategy to reduce the impact that the exploitation of malware and DDOS threat against the online banking application. In general, a risk mitigation strategy includes four options to mitigate threats:

1. Risk Mitigation – decrease the risk by applying countermeasures, fixing vulnerabilities
2. Risk Acceptance – doing nothing because the risk is either low or is compensated by existing security measures/controls
3. Risk Avoidance – removing the feature that causes the risk
4. Risk Transference – pass risk to an externality/third party using cyber-insurance

A possible risk mitigation strategy could be to fix only MEDIUM- and HIGH-risk vulnerabilities whose cost to design and implement fix is less than the potential business impact derived by the exploitation of the vulnerability. A similar risk mitigation strategy for malware banking attacks, for example, would be to deploy additional countermeasures such as ant-malware software, 2-way out of band authentication for wire transfers, and detective measures such secure event management and log aggregation and behavioral-based fraud detection systems. Another strategy could be to accept the risk when the technical impact such as the loss Confidentiality, Integrity, and Availability implies a small degradation of the service and not a loss of a critical business function. This can be, for example, a viable threat mitigation option for DDoS attacks. In some cases, transfer of the risk to another service provider might also be an option when the cost to implement the countermeasure can be too high and not as effective as being deployed on the premise of the organization's data center such as in the case of adopting cloud services for protection of DDoS attacks.

The decision which strategy is most appropriate depends on different factors that need to be assessed such as the business impact an exploitation of a threat can have, the likelihood of its occurrence, and the costs for transferring (i.e. costs for insurance) or avoiding (i.e. costs or losses due to redesign) it. That is, such decision is based on the risk a threat poses to the online banking application as this is a company asset. Ultimately the overall risk has to take into account the business impact of each threat since this is a critical factor for deciding the risk management strategy.

The risk mitigation strategy is also chosen based upon the effectiveness of the countermeasure considered in reducing the risk to a LOW residual as well as the cost of implementing the proposed countermeasures. In the case of DDoS, for example, assuming the potential economic impact caused by a DDoS attack against a website is $187,506 (year average impact according to 2011 Second Annual Cost of Cyber

Crime Study Benchmark by Ponemon Institute), and a benchmark of control effectiveness in reducing the risk is 64% the max cost that should be allocated annually for rolling our countermeasures for the protection of DDoS is $187,506. Within this boundaries of cost and minimum control effectiveness countermeasures that exceed the effectiveness in mitigating the risk and cheaper to acquire, deploy, and maintain are the one that can be recommended for adoption in the risk mitigation strategy.

GLOSSARY

INFORMATION SECURITY AND RISK MANAGEMENT TERMINOLOGY

"Half of the communication battle in information security today is caused by not agreeing on a common terminology for information security and risk management"
                                                        Dr. Gary McGraw, CTO Cigital

Introduction

When using the PASTA risk-centric threat modeling process for threat model and conducting the various stages and activities, it is important to use a risk management language and terminology that is industry standard terminology for works such as threats, vulnerabilities, attacks, and risk and of other terminology used to describe activities in the information security and risk management domains. Throughout this book and specifically for the execution of PASTA as risk-centric threat modeling process, we use standard definitions for threats, attacks, and vulnerabilities such as the ones documented in the various National Institute of Standards and Technologies (NIST) standards and guidelines and SPs (Special Publications). At high level, the definition of the information security and risk management terminology is included in this glossary while more specific terminology definitions provided in the glossary section.

Risk Centric Threat Modeling: Process for Attack Simulation and Threat Analysis, First Edition.
Tony UcedaVélez and Marco M. Morana.
© 2015 John Wiley & Sons, Inc. Published 2015 by John Wiley & Sons, Inc.

For what concern the definition of threats, we refer to the NIST SP 800-37 "*Guide for Applying the Risk Management Framework to Federal Information Systems.*" This guide defines a threat as "*Any circumstance or event with the potential to adversely impact agency operations (including mission, functions, image, or reputation), agency assets, or individuals through an information system via unauthorized access, destruction, disclosure, modification of information, and/or denial of service.*" A threat is often associated to a threat source where "*a threat source is either: (i) intent and method targeted at the intentional exploitation of vulnerabilities; or (ii) a situation and method that may accidentally trigger vulnerabilities.*"

For the definition of the activity of "threat analysis" in the context of risk assessments and threat modeling that is referred in several chapters of this book, we refer to the definition of NIST SP 800-30 "Guide for Conducting Risk Assessments." "*A threat analysis consists on the examination of threat-sources against system vulnerabilities to determine the threats for a particular system in a particular operational environment.*" In the NIST guidelines definition of threats, there is a notion of vulnerabilities as these vulnerabilities can be exploited by threat agents to cause an impact. A vulnerability is defined in several of NIST special publications, the one that is closer to the concept of vulnerability in risk-based threat modeling is found in NIST SP 800-30: as "*a flaw or weakness in system security procedures, design, implementation, or internal controls that could be exercised (accidentally triggered or intentionally exploited) and results in a security breach or a violation of the system's security policy.*"

When dealing with threats and vulnerabilities, it is important not to confuse the two definitions: threats represent a potential for damage while vulnerabilities represent a condition and an opportunity for a threat agent to realize that damage. For example, threats represent a potential for a bad event, intentionally or not intentionally initiated by a threat agent in the presence of vulnerabilities.

A condition for vulnerability might consist of an opportunity for a threat to cause a negative impact to the organization such as by breaking into the application database to steal confidential and sensitive data. This opportunity might depend also on the exposure of the application/system to the threat agent. A group of threat agents might be correlated with a threat actor campaign against the organization and the application as well as other factors that can characterize the threat environment and exposure to threats in which the application operates to.

For a web application that process credit card data for payments, for example, the online environment represents an opportunity for external threat agents to attack the application. For analyzing a threat, it is important to characterize the threats using different factors such as the threat capabilities, the tool, attack methods, techniques, and tactics used by the threat agents and the threat targets. Threat actors and groups of threat actors might have different motivations such as fraud motives associated to cyber-criminals and fraudsters, government, and commercial espionage associated with cyber-spies and political motives associated with hacktivist groups. In order to analyze threats and threat agents/actors, it is important to dissect threats and characterize them accordingly to their specific characteristics.

Vulnerabilities as well can be characterized by different factors such as their root causes, the type of security controls that the vulnerability impact to and their security factors such as the confidentiality, integrity, and availability of the data that is exposed by the presence of that vulnerability. Since vulnerabilities represent conditions and opportunities for threat agents to cause an impact, the risk factors are also associated with the probability and impact of possible exploit of the vulnerability by threat agents.

Threats and vulnerabilities have a different meaning depending on if these are seen from the perspective of an attacker or from the perspective of a defender. For an attacker perspective, vulnerabilities are opportunities to attack an application to achieve specific goals such as stealing confidential information. A vulnerability such as weak encryption used to protect the data or weak authentication to access that data might facilitate a threat agent to access such as confidential data by brute forcing authentication and as well as by performing an attack against the weak encryption used by the application. From a defender perspective, vulnerabilities represent security issues. These vulnerabilities need to be fixed before applications are put into production hence preventing of them being opportunistically exploited by a threat agent/actor.

Threats are associated to vulnerabilities and to attacks but attacks should not be confused with threats: attacks describe how threats can be realized to cause an impact to an asset such as a loss of confidentiality, integrity, and availability of that asset. A threat represents a potential of a threat agent attacking a target and therefore are a possibility for an attack. A standard definition of attacks is covered in NISP 800-28v2, Guidelines on Active Content and Mobile Code: *"Attacks are the realization of some specific threat impacting the confidentiality, integrity, accountability, or availability of a computational resource."* For example an information disclosure threats can be realized by a threat agent through exploit of SQL injection type of vulnerabilities. To discover the SQL injection vulnerability, an attacker will first probe the application web pages with a vulnerability scanner and then manually inject SQL commands in the application web pages in the attempt to alter the SQL query statement. The attacker goal is to gain unauthorized access to confidential information such as credit and debit card data stored in the database.

From the defender perspective, the analysis of an attack includes the analysis of the course of action of the various events that lead to an exploit of a vulnerability. The analysis of the course of action of an attack helps to identify the events and the type of security measures that can be deployed to detect the various attack events that can be triggered during an attack and the countermeasures to protect the assets from the attacks.

Threats, vulnerabilities, and attacks are the basic elements whose analysis allows the assessment of risk. Information security risks are often associated with the factors of probability (or occurrence) and of impacts (e.g. technical and business). The NIST publication, NIST 800-33 Underlying Technical Models for Information Technology Security provides a standard definition of information security risk *"The probability of a particular threat-source will exercise (accidentally trigger or intentionally exploit) a particular information system vulnerability and the resulting impact if this should occur."* In this NIST standard definition of risk, there is emphasis on the probability of a threat source to exercise a vulnerability to cause an impact.

The analysis of threats also includes the analysis of the probability of the occurrence of a threat event and of the likelihood of threat agent to successfully conduct attacks seeking to exploit vulnerabilities. For example, a threat probability can be associated with the occurrence of threat events (based upon past events) such as previously observed security incidents and vulnerability exploits. Threat probabilities can also be associated with the inherent characteristics of the threat agent such as his motivations in attacking certain targets and the capabilities and opportunities to conduct these attacks.

The attack probability can be associated with the probability of a threat to be realized in attack and to succeed to produce an impact such as compromise of data. The modeling of the most probable paths of attacks with an attack tree: some attack paths are subject to possible choices of attacks that can be pursued by an attacker when these have higher probability of success of the attacker objectives by minimizing the costs of the tools and computer resources that are required to conduct them.

When the course of action of an attack is known from a previous attack or security incident occurring, it is possible to associate the probability of the threat to be realized in an attack and an exploit or compromise by the detection of the specific events that lead to that exploit. A formal method that can be used for this analysis is the "kill chain" method. By analyzing attacks through the "kill chain," it is possible to define a sequence of events that can be correlated with a course of action of attacks and exploits. The closer the event is to an indication of compromise the higher the probability of the threat to be realized.

The likelihood and impact are used as factors for quantifying or qualifying risks during a risk assessment exercise. A standard definition for risk assessment can be found in NIST SP 800-30, Guide for Conducting Risk Assessments: "*a risk assessment is the process of identifying the risks to system security and determining the probability of occurrence, the resulting impact, and additional safeguards that would mitigate this impact.*" The assessment of the impacts depends on the different factors given to the impact such as technical and business. A technical impact can be calculated as the impact of an exploit of the application vulnerability that exposes the assets (e.g. data, functionality) to either a partial or a total loss of the confidentiality, integrity, and availability characteristics of these assets. A business impact instead can be factored as function of the value of the asset that is being impacted as monetary loss. One possible methodology to determine the business impact of a threat event is the quantitative risk methodology. Typically qualitative risk methodologies factor both the occurrence of a security incident event and the monetary loss caused by that event to calculate the business impact.

Once technical risks and business risks are assessed using the various risk calculation formulas that are part of the organization risk assessment process, the next step is to identify the best strategy to manage risk. The standard definition of risk management for information systems is documented in NIST 800-30, risk management is *"The total process of identifying, controlling, and mitigating information system–related risks. It includes risk assessment; cost-benefit analysis;*

INFORMATION SECURITY AND RISK MANAGEMENT TERMINOLOGY 637

and the selection, implementation, test, and security evaluation of safeguards. This overall system security review considers both effectiveness and efficiency, including impact on the mission and constraints due to policy, regulations, and laws."

A more compressive standard definition of risk management includes the documentation of a risk mitigation strategy as defined in NIST SP 800-53r2, Recommended Security Controls for Federal Information Systems and Organizations: *"The process of managing risks to organizational operations (including mission, functions, image, or reputation), organizational assets, or individuals resulting from the operation of an information system, and includes: (i) the conduct of a risk assessment; (ii) the implementation of a risk mitigation strategy; and (iii) employment of techniques and procedures for the continuous monitoring of the security state of the information system. (FIPS 200)"*

The purpose of this glossary is to provide a reference to standard (e.g., – NIST) terminology for information security and risk management. This glossary is also searchable through FISMAPEDIA http://fismapedia.org.

Each term in the glossary is provided with the NIST (SP) Special Publication document reference and the "definition" within quotes. The NIST SP documents are published by NIST on http://csrc.nist.gov/publications/PubsSPs.html.

National Institute of Standard & Technology (NIST) Information Security and Risk Management Glossary

Acceptable Risk (NIST SP 800-16): The level of Residual Risk that has been determined to be a reasonable level of potential loss/disruption for a specific IT system.

Access Control (NIST SP 800-47): The process of granting access to information technology (IT) system resources only to authorized users, programs, processes, or other systems.

Adequate Security (NIST SP 800-16): Security commensurate with the risk and magnitude of the harm resulting from the loss, misuse, or unauthorized access to or modification of information. This includes assuring that systems and applications operate effectively and provide appropriate confidentiality, integrity, and availability, through the use of cost-effective management, acquisition, development, installation, operational, and technical controls.

Agent (NIST SP 800-51r1): A program used in distributed denial of service (DDoS) attacks that sends malicious traffic to hosts based on the instructions of a handler. Also known as a bot.

Assessment Procedure (NIST SP 800-37): A set of activities or actions employed by an assessor to determine the extent to which a security control is implemented correctly, operating as intended, and producing the desired outcome with respect to meeting the security requirements for the system.

Asset (NIST SP 800-26): A major application, general support system, high impact program, physical plant, mission critical system, or a logically related group of systems.

Assurance (NIST SP 800-30): Grounds for confidence that the other four security goals (integrity, availability, confidentiality, and accountability) have been adequately met by a specific implementation. "Adequately met" includes (1) functionality that performs correctly, (2) sufficient protection against unintentional errors (by users or software), and (3) sufficient resistance to intentional penetration or bypass.

Attack (NIST SP 800-28v2): The realization of some specific threat that impacts the confidentiality, integrity, accountability, or availability of a computational resource.

Audit (NIST SP 800-32): Independent review and examination of records and activities to assess the adequacy of system controls, to ensure compliance with established policies and operational procedures, and to recommend necessary changes in controls, policies, or procedures. (NS4009)

Audit Trail (NIST SP 800-47): A record showing who has accessed an IT system and what operations the user has performed during a given period.

Authentication (NIST SP 800-32): Security measure designed to establish the validity of a transmission, message, or originator, or a means of verifying an individual's authorization to receive specific categories of information. (NS4009)

Authenticity (NIST SP 800-37): The property of being genuine and being able to be verified and trusted; confidence in the validity of a transmission, a message, or message originator. See authentication.

Authorization (NIST SP 800-33): The granting or denying of access rights to a user, program, or process.

Availability (NIST SP 800-30): The security goal that generates the requirement for protection against Intentional or accidental attempts to (1) perform unauthorized deletion of data or (2) otherwise cause a denial of service or data, unauthorized use of system resources.

Availability (NIST SP 800-33): The security objective that generates the requirement for protection against intentional or accidental attempts to (1) perform unauthorized deletion of data or (2) otherwise cause a denial of service or data.

Baseline Security (NIST SP 800-16): The minimum security controls required for safeguarding an IT system based on its identified needs for confidentiality, integrity and/or availability protection.

Blacklist (NIST SP 800-90): A list of discrete entities, such as hosts or applications, that have been previously determined to be associated with malicious activity.

Blended Attack (NIST SP 800-33): Instance of malware that uses multiple infection or transmission methods.

Boundary Protection (NIST SP 800-53r2): Monitoring and control of communications at the external boundary of an information system to prevent and detect malicious and other unauthorized communications, through the use of boundary protection devices (e.g., proxies, gateways, routers, firewalls, guards, and encrypted tunnels).

INFORMATION SECURITY AND RISK MANAGEMENT TERMINOLOGY 639

Brute Force Attack (NIST SP 800-72): A method of accessing an obstructed device through attempting multiple combinations of numeric/alphanumeric passwords.

Buffer Overflow (NIST SP 800-28v2): A condition at an interface under which more input can be placed into a buffer or data holding area than the capacity allocated, overwriting other information. Attackers exploit such a condition to crash a system or to insert specially crafted code that allows them to gain control of the system.

Business Continuity Plan (NIST SP 800-34): The documentation of a predetermined set of instructions or procedures that describe how an organization's business functions will be sustained during and after a significant disruption.

Business Impact Analysis/BIA (NIST SP 800-34): An analysis of an information technology (IT) system's requirements, processes, and interdependencies used to characterize system contingency requirements and priorities in the event of a significant disruption.

Business Recovery Plan (NIST SP 800-34): The documentation of a predetermined set of instructions or procedures that describe how business processes will be restored after a significant disruption has occurred.

Certificate (NIST SP 800-32): A digital representation of information, which at least (1) identifies the certification authority issuing it, (2) names or identifies its Subscriber, (3) contains the Subscriber's public key, (4) identifies its operational period, and (5) is digitally signed by the certification authority issuing it.

Chain of Custody (NIST SP 800-72): A process that tracks the movement of evidence through its collection, safeguarding, and analysis lifecycle by documenting each person who handled the evidence, the date/time it was collected or transferred, and the purpose for the transfer.

Compensating Security Controls (NIST SP 800-18r1): The management, operational, and technical controls (e.g. – safeguards or countermeasures) employed by an organization in lieu of the recommended controls in the low, moderate, or high baselines described in NIST SP 800-53, that provide equivalent or comparable protection for an information system.

Compromise (NIST SP 800-32): Disclosure of information to unauthorized persons, or a violation of the security policy of a system in which unauthorized intentional or unintentional disclosure, modification, destruction, or loss of an object may have occurred.

Computer Security Incident Response Team/CSIRT (NIST SP 800-61): A capability set up for the purpose of assisting in responding to computer security-related incidents; also called a Computer Incident Response Team (CIRT) or a CIRC (Computer Incident Response Center, Computer Incident Response Capability).

Confidentiality (NIST SP 800-30): The security goal that generates the requirement for protection from intentional or accidental attempts to perform unauthorized data reads. Confidentiality covers data in storage, during processing, and in transit.

Configuration Control (NIST SP 800-18r1): Process for controlling modifications to hardware, firmware, software, and documentation to protect the information system against improper modifications before, during, and after system implementation.

Contingency Plan (NIST SP 800-57P1): A plan that is maintained for disaster response, backup operations, and post-disaster recovery to ensure the availability of critical resources and to facilitate the continuity of operations in an emergency situation.

Countermeasures (NIST SP 800-53r1): Actions, devices, procedures, techniques, or other measures that reduce the vulnerability of an information system. Synonymous with security controls and safeguards.

Cryptanalysis (NIST SP 800-57P1): (1) Operations performed in defeating cryptographic protection without an initial knowledge of the key employed in providing the protection. (2) The study of mathematical techniques for attempting to defeat cryptographic techniques and information system security. This includes the process of looking for errors or weaknesses in the implementation of an algorithm or of the algorithm itself.

Data Integrity (NIST SP 800-57P1): A property whereby data has not been altered in an unauthorized manner since it was created, transmitted, or stored. In this recommendation, the statement that a cryptographic algorithm "provides data integrity" means that the algorithm is used to detect unauthorized alterations.

Denial of Service/DoS (NIST SP 800-61): An attack that prevents or impairs the authorized use of networks, systems, or applications by exhausting resources.

Digital Signature (NIST SP 800-32): The result of a transformation of a message by means of a cryptographic system using keys such that a Relying Party can determine (1) whether the transformation was created using the private key that corresponds to the public key in the signer's digital certificate; and (2) whether the message has been altered since the transformation was made.

Distributed Denial of Service/DDoS (NIST SP 800-61): A DoS technique that uses numerous hosts to perform the attack.

Event (NIST SP 800-61): Any observable occurrence in a network or system.

False Positive (NIST SP 800-86): Incorrectly classifying benign activity as malicious.

Honeypot (NIST SP 800-61): A host that is designed to collect data on suspicious activity and has no authorized users other than its administrators.

Identification (NIST SP 800-47): The process of verifying the identity of a user, process, or device, usually as a prerequisite for granting access to resources in an IT system.

Identity (NIST SP 800-33): Information that is unique within a security domain and which is recognized as denoting a particular entity within that domain.

Incident Handling (NIST 800-61r1): The mitigation of violations of security policies and recommended practices.

Information Owner (NIST SP 800-53r1): Official with statutory or operational authority for specified information and responsibility for establishing the controls for its generation, collection, processing, dissemination, and disposal.

Information Resources (NIST SP 800-18r1): Information and related resources, such as personnel, equipment, funds, and information technology.

Information Security (NIST SP 800-37): The protection of information and information systems from unauthorized access, use, disclosure, disruption, modification, or destruction in order to provide confidentiality, integrity, and availability.

Information Security (NIST SP 800-66): Protecting information and information systems from unauthorized access, use, disclosure, disruption, modification, or destruction in order to provide:

a. availability, which means ensuring timely and reliable access to and use of information. (44 U.S.C., Sec. 3542)
b. confidentiality, which means preserving authorized restrictions on access and disclosure, including means for protecting personal privacy and proprietary information; and
c. integrity, which means guarding against improper information modification or destruction, and includes ensuring information.

Information Security Policy (NIST 800-53r1): Aggregate of directives, regulations, rules, and practices that prescribes how an organization manages, protects, and distributes information.

Information System Owner (or Program Manager) (NIST SP 800-53r1): Official responsible for the overall procurement, development, integration, modification, or operation and maintenance of an information system.

Information System Security Officer (NIST SP 800-53r1): Individual assigned responsibility by the senior agency information security officer, authorizing official, management official, or information system owner for maintaining the appropriate operational security posture for an information system or program.

Inside Threat (NIST SP 800-32): An entity with authorized access that has the potential to harm an information system through destruction, disclosure, modification of data, and/or denial of service.

Integrity (NIST SP 800-37): Guarding against improper information modification or destruction, and includes ensuring information nonrepudiation and authenticity. (44 U.S.C., Sec. 3542)

Intrusion Detection System/IDS (NIST SP 800-47): A software application that can be implemented on host operating systems or as network devices to monitor activity that is associated with intrusions or insider misuse, or both.

IT Security (NIST SP 800-47): Technological discipline concerned with ensuring that IT systems perform as expected and do nothing more; that information is provided adequate protection for confidentiality; that system, data, and software integrity is maintained; and that information and system resources are protected against unplanned disruptions of processing that could seriously impact mission accomplishment. Synonymous with Automated Information System Security, Computer Security, and Information Systems Security.

IT Security Architecture (NIST SP 800-33): A description of security principles and an overall approach for complying with the principles that drive the system design; e.g., guidelines on the placement and implementation of specific security services within various distributed computing environments.

IT Security Goal (NIST SP 800-33): To enable an organization to meet all mission/business objectives by implementing systems with due care consideration of IT-related risks to the organization, its partners, and its customers.

Least Privilege (NIST SP 800-57P2): A security principle that restricts the access privileges of authorized personnel (e.g., program execution privileges, file modification privileges) to the minimum necessary to perform their jobs.

Major Application (NIST SP 800-34): An application that requires special attention to security because of the risk and magnitude of the harm resulting from the loss, misuse, or unauthorized access to, or modification of, the information in the application. A breach in a major application might comprise many individual application programs and hardware, software, and telecommunications components. Major applications can be either a major software application or a combination of hardware and software in which the only purpose of the system is to support a specific mission-related function.

Malicious Code (NIST 800-53r1): Software or firmware intended to perform an unauthorized process that will have adverse impact on the confidentiality, integrity, or availability of an information system. A virus, worm, Trojan horse, or other code-based entity that infects a host. Spyware and some forms of adware are also examples of malicious code.

Malware (NIST SP 800-114): A computer program that is covertly placed onto a computer with the intent to compromise the privacy, accuracy, or reliability of the computer's data, applications, or OS. Common types of malware threats include viruses, worms, malicious mobile code, Trojan horses, rootkits, and spyware.

Management Controls (NIST SP 800-16): Management controls are actions taken to manage the development, maintenance, and use of the system, including system-specific policies, procedures, and rules of behavior, individual roles and responsibilities, individual accountability and personnel security decisions.

Minimum Level of Protection (NIST SP 800-16): The reduction in the Total Risk that results from the impact of in-place safeguards.

Minor Application (NIST SP 800-18r1): An application, other than a major application, that requires attention to security due to the risk and magnitude of harm resulting from the loss, misuse, or unauthorized access to or modification of the information in the application. Minor applications are typically included as part of a general support system.

Misconfiguration (NIST SP 800-40): A configuration error that may result in a security weakness in a system.

Mitigate (NIST SP 800-66): To select and implement security controls to reduce risk to a level acceptable to management, within applicable constraints.

Mobile Code (NIST SP 800-53r1): Software programs or parts of programs obtained from remote information systems, transmitted across a network, and executed on a local information system without explicit installation or execution by the recipient.

Mutual Authentication (NIST SP 800-32): Occurs when parties at both ends of a communication activity authenticate each other.

Nonrepudiation (NIST SP 800-53r1): Assurance that the sender of information is provided with proof of delivery and the recipient is provided with proof of the sender's identity, so neither can later deny having processed the information.

Operational Controls (NIST SP 800-53r1): The security controls (e.g. – safeguards or countermeasures) for an information system that are primarily implemented and executed by people (as opposed to systems).

Out-of-Band (NIST SP 800-32): Communication between parties utilizing a means or method that differs from the current method of communication (e.g. – one party uses U.S. Postal Service mail to communicate with another party where current communication is occurring online).

Outside Threat (NIST SP 800-32): An unauthorized entity from outside the domain perimeter that has the potential to harm an Information System through destruction, disclosure, modification of data, and/or denial of service.

Packet Sniffer (NIST SP 800-86): Software that monitors network traffic on wired or wireless networks and captures packets.

Patch (NIST SP 800-45): A "repair job" for a piece of programming; also known as a "fix." A **patch** is the immediate solution to an identified problem that is provided to users; it can sometimes be downloaded from the software maker's Web site. The **patch** is not necessarily the best solution for the problem, and the product developers often find a better solution to provide when they package the product for its next release. A **patch** is usually developed and distributed as a replacement for or an insertion in compiled code (that is, in a binary file or object module). In many operating systems, a special program is provided to manage and track the installation of patches.

Patch Management (NIST SP 800-61): The process of acquiring, testing, and distributing patches to the appropriate administrators and users throughout the organization.

Plan of Action and Milestones (PoAM) (NIST SP 800-53r1): A document that identifies tasks needing to be accomplished. It details resources required to accomplish the elements of the plan, any milestones in meeting the tasks, and scheduled completion dates for the milestones.

Penetration (Pen) Testing (NIST SP 800-53AdF): A test methodology in which assessors, using all available documentation (e.g., system design, source code, manuals) and working under specific constraints, attempt to circumvent the security features of an information system.

Policy (NIST SP 800-26): A document that delineates the security management structure and clearly assigns security responsibilities and lays the foundation necessary to reliably measure progress and compliance.

Potential Impact (NIST SP 800-53r2): The loss of confidentiality, integrity, or availability could be expected to have (i) a limited adverse effect (FIPS 199 low); (ii) a serious adverse effect (FIPS 199 moderate); or (iii) a severe or catastrophic adverse effect (FIPS 199 high) on organizational operations, organizational assets, or individuals (FIPS 199).

Port Scanning (NIST SP 800-61): Using a program to remotely determine which ports on a system are open (e.g. – whether systems allow connections through those ports).

Potential Impact (NIST SP 800-53r1): The loss of confidentiality, integrity, or availability could be expected to have (i) a limited adverse effect (FIPS 199 low); (ii) a serious adverse effect (FIPS 199 moderate); or (iii) a severe or catastrophic adverse effect (FIPS 199 high) on organizational operations, organizational assets, or individuals.

Privacy (NIST SP 800-32): Restricting access to subscriber or Relying Party information in accordance with Federal law and Agency policy.

Privacy Impact Assessment (NIST SP 800-53r1): An analysis of how information is handled (i) to ensure handling conforms to applicable legal, regulatory, and policy requirements regarding privacy; (ii) to determine the risks and effects of collecting, maintaining, and disseminating information in identifiable form in an electronic information system; and (iii) to examine and evaluate protections and alternative processes for handling information to mitigate potential privacy risks.

Private Key (NIST SP 800-57P1): A cryptographic key, used with a public key cryptographic algorithm, that is uniquely associated with an entity and is not made public. In an asymmetric (public) cryptosystem, the private key is associated with a public key. Depending on the algorithm, the private key may be used to:

1. compute the corresponding public key,
2. compute a digital signature that may be verified by the corresponding public key,
3. decrypt data that was encrypted by the corresponding public key, or
4. compute a piece of common shared data, together with other information.

Privileged Function (NIST SP 800-53r1): A function executed on an information system involving the control, monitoring, or administration of the system.

Privileged User (NIST SP 800-53r1): Individual who has access to system control, monitoring, or administration functions (e.g., system administrator, information system security officer, maintainer, system programmer).

Procedures (NIST SP800-26): Contained in a document that focuses on the security control areas and management's position.

Profiling (NIST SP 800-61): Measuring the characteristics of expected activity so that changes to it can be more easily identified.

Protective Distribution System (NIST SP 800-18r1): Wire line or fiber optic system that includes adequate safeguards and/or countermeasures (e.g., acoustic, electric, electromagnetic, and physical) to permit its use for the transmission of unencrypted information.

Public Key (NIST SP 800-57P1): A cryptographic key used with a public key cryptographic algorithm that is uniquely associated with an entity and that may be made public. In an asymmetric (public) cryptosystem, the public key is associated with a private key. The public key may be known by anyone and, depending on the algorithm, may be used to:

1. verify a digital signature that is signed by the corresponding private key,
2. encrypt data that can be decrypted by the corresponding private key, or
3. compute a piece of shared data.

Public Key Infrastructure/PKI (NIST SP 800-32): A set of policies, processes, server platforms, software, and workstations used for the purpose of administering certificates and public-private key pairs, including the ability to issue, maintain, and revoke public key certificates.

Relying Party (NIST SP 800-32): A person or agency who has received information that includes a certificate and a digital signature verifiable with reference to a public key listed in the certificate, and is in a position to rely on them.

Remediation (NIST SP 800-40): The act of correcting a vulnerability or eliminating a threat. Three possible types of remediation are installing a patch, adjusting configuration settings, and uninstalling a software application.

Remediation Plan (NIST SP 800-40): A plan to perform the remediation of one or more threats or vulnerabilities facing an organization's systems. The plan typically includes options to remove threats and vulnerabilities and priorities for performing the remediation.

Residual Risk (NIST SP 800-33): The remaining, potential risk after all IT security measures are applied. There is a residual risk associated with each threat.

Risk (NIST SP 800-18r1): The level of impact on agency operations (including mission, functions, image, or reputation), agency assets, or individuals resulting from the operation of an information system given the potential impact of a threat and the likelihood of that threat occurring (NIST SP 800-30).

Risk Assessment (NIST SP 800-30): The process of identifying the risks to system security and determining the probability of occurrence, the resulting impact, and additional safeguards that would mitigate this impact. Part of Risk Management and synonymous with Risk Analysis.

Risk Management (NIST SP 800-30): The total process of identifying, controlling, and mitigating information system-related risks. It includes risk assessment; cost-benefit analysis; and the selection, implementation, test, and security evaluation of safeguards. This overall system security review considers both effectiveness and efficiency, including impact on the mission and constraints due to policy, regulations, and laws.

Role-Based (NIST SP 800-16): Mapped to job function, assumes that a person will take on different roles, over time, within an organization and different responsibilities in relation to IT systems.

Roles and Responsibilities (NIST SP 800-16): Functions performed by someone in a specific situation and obligations to tasks or duties for which that person is accountable.

Rootkit (NIST SP 800-61r1): A set of tools used by an attacker after gaining root-level access to a host to conceal the attacker's activities on the host and permit the attacker to maintain root-level access to the host through covert means.

Safeguards (NIST SP 800-53r1): Protective measures prescribed to meet the security requirements (i.e., confidentiality, integrity, and availability) specified for an information system. Safeguards may include security features, management constraints, personnel security, and security of physical structures, areas, and devices. Synonymous with security controls and countermeasures.

Safeguards (NIST SP 800-53r1): Protective measures prescribed to meet the security requirements (i.e., confidentiality, integrity, and availability) specified for an information system. Safeguards may include security features, management constraints, personnel security, and security of physical structures, areas, and devices. Synonymous with security controls and countermeasures.

Sanitization (NIST SP 800-18r1): Process to remove information from media such that information recovery is not possible. It includes removing all labels, markings, and activity logs. (CNSS Inst. 4009, Adapted)

Scanning (NIST SP 800-61): Sending packets or requests to another system to gain information to be used in a subsequent attack.

Secret Key (NIST SP 800-57P1): A cryptographic key that is used with a secret key (symmetric) cryptographic algorithm that is uniquely associated with one or more entities and is not made public. The use of the term "secret" in this context does not imply a classification level, but rather implies the need to protect the key from disclosure.

Security (NIST SP 800-66): Protecting information and information systems from unauthorized access, use, disclosure, disruption, modification, or destruction in order to provide-A. integrity, which means guarding against improper information modification or destruction, and includes ensuring information nonrepudiation and authenticity;B. confidentiality, which means preserving authorized restrictions on access and disclosure, including means for protecting personal privacy and proprietary information; andC. availability, which means ensuring timely and reliable access to and use of information. See Information Security. (44 U.S.C., Sec. 3542).

Security Category (NIST SP 800-53r1): The characterization of information or an information system based on an assessment of the potential impact that a loss of confidentiality, integrity, or availability of such information or information system would have on organizational operations, organizational assets, or individuals.

Security Control Assessment (NIST SP 800-53AdF): The testing and/or evaluation of the management, operational, and technical security controls in an

INFORMATION SECURITY AND RISK MANAGEMENT TERMINOLOGY   647

information system to determine the extent to which the controls are implemented correctly, operating as intended, and producing the desired outcome with respect to meeting the security requirements for the system.

Security Control Baseline (NIST SP 800-53r1): The set of minimum security controls defined for a low-impact, moderate-impact, or high-impact information system.

Security Control Enhancements (NIST SP 800-18r1): Statements of security capability to (i) build in additional, but related, functionality to a basic control; and/or (ii) increase the strength of a basic control.

Security Controls (NIST SP 800-69): A protective measure against threats.

Security Domain (NIST SP 800-33): A set of subjects, their information objects, and a common security policy.

Security Functions (NIST SP 800-53r1): The hardware, software, and firmware of the information system responsible for supporting and enforcing the system security policy and supporting the isolation of code and data on which the protection is based.

Security Goals (NIST SP 800-30): The five security goals are integrity, availability, confidentiality, accountability, and assurance.

Security Impact Analysis (NIST SP 800-37): The analysis conducted by an agency official, often during the continuous monitoring phase of the security certification and accreditation process, to determine the extent to which changes to the information system have affected the security posture of the system.

Security Incident (NIST SP 800-53r1): An occurrence that actually or potentially jeopardizes the confidentiality, integrity, or availability of an information system or the information the system processes, stores, or transmits or that constitutes a violation or imminent threat of violation of security policies, security procedures, or acceptable use policies.

Security Label (NIST SP 800-18r1): Explicit or implicit marking of a data structure or output media associated with an information system representing the FIPS 199 security category, or distribution limitations or handling caveats of the information contained therein.

Security Objective (NIST SP 800-18r1): Confidentiality, integrity, or availability.

Security Perimeter (NIST SP 800-53r1): All components of an information system to be accredited by an authorizing official and excludes separately accredited systems, to which the information system is connected. Synonymous with the term security perimeter defined in CNSS Instruction 4009 and DCID 6/3.

Security Plan (NIST SP 800-53r1): Formal document that provides an overview of the security requirements for the information system and describes the security controls in place or planned for meeting those requirements.

Security Policy (NIST SP 800-33): The statement of required protection of the information objects.

Security Requirements (NIST SP 800-18r1): Requirements levied on an information system that are derived from laws, executive orders, directives, policies, instructions, regulations, or organizational (mission) needs to ensure the confidentiality, integrity, and availability of the information being processed, stored, or transmitted.

Senior Agency Information Security Officer (NIST SP 800-37): Official responsible for carrying out the Chief Information Officer responsibilities under FISMA and serving as the Chief Information Officer's primary liaison to the agency's authorizing officials, information system owners, and information system security officers.

Sensitive Information (NIST SP 800-26): Information whose loss, misuse, or unauthorized access to or modification of could adversely affect the national interest or the conduct of Federal programs or the privacy to which individuals are entitled

Sensitivity (NIST SP 800-16): The degree to which an IT system or application requires protection (to ensure confidentiality, integrity, and availability), which is determined by an evaluation of the nature and criticality of the data processed, the relation of the system to the organization missions and the economic value of the system components.

Signature (NIST SP 800-61): A recognizable, distinguishing pattern associated with an attack, such as a binary string in a virus or a particular set of keystrokes used to gain unauthorized access to a system.

Social Engineering (NIST SP 800-114): A general term for attackers trying to trick people into revealing sensitive information or performing certain actions, such as downloading and executing files that appear to be benign but are actually malicious.

Specification (NIST SP 800-53AdF): An assessment object that includes document-based artifacts (e.g., policies, procedures, plans, system security requirements, functional specifications, and architectural designs) associated with an information system.

Spyware (NIST SP 800-28v2): A program embedded within an application that collects information and periodically communicates back to its home site, unbeknownst to the user.

Standard (NIST SP 800-66): A rule, condition, or requirement (1) Describing the following information for products, systems, services or practices (i) Classification of components. (ii) Specification of materials, performance, or operations; or (iii) Delineation of procedures; or (2) With respect to the privacy of individually identifiable health information. (45 C.F.R., Sec. 160.103)

Subsystem (NIST SP 800-18r1): A major subdivision or component of an information system consisting of information, information technology, and personnel that perform one or more specific functions.

Supplementation (Assessment Procedures) (NIST SP 800-53AdF): The process of adding assessment procedures or assessment details to assessment procedures in order to adequately meet the organization's risk management needs.

Supplementation (Security Controls) (NIST SP 800-53AdF): The process of adding security controls or control enhancements to the low, moderate, or high security control baselines in NIST Special Publication 800–53 in order to adequately meet the organization's risk management needs.

System (NIST SP 800-40): A set of IT assets, processes, applications, and related resources that are under the same direct management and budgetary control; have the same function or mission objective; have essentially the same security needs; and reside in the same general operating environment. When not used in this formal sense, the term is synonymous with the term "host". The context surrounding this word should make the definition clear or else should specify which definition is being used.

System Security Plan (NIST SP 800-53r1): Formal document that provides an overview of the security requirements for the information system and describes the security controls in place or planned for meeting those requirements.

System-Specific Security Control (NIST SP 800-37): A security control for an information system that has not been designated as a common security control.

Tailored Security Control Baseline (NIST SP 800-53r1): Set of security controls resulting from the application of the tailoring guidance to the security control baseline.

Tailoring (Assessment Procedures) (NIST SP 800-53AdF): The process by which assessment procedures defined in Special Publication 800-53A are adjusted, or scoped, to match the characteristics of the information system under assessment, providing organizations with the flexibility needed to meet specific organizational requirements and to avoid overly-constrained assessment approaches.

Tailoring (Security Controls) (NIST SP 800-53AdF): The process by which a security control baseline selected in accordance with the FIPS 199 security categorization of the information system is modified based on (i) the application of scoping guidance; (ii) the specification of compensating security controls, if needed; and (iii) the specification of organization-defined parameters in the security controls, where allowed.

Technical Controls (NIST SP 800-16): Hardware and software controls used to provide automated protection to the IT system or applications. Technical controls operate within the technical system and applications.

Test (NIST SP 800-53AdF): A type of assessment method that is characterized by the process of exercising one or more assessment objects under specified conditions to compare actual with expected behavior, the results of which are used to support the determination of security control effectiveness over time.

Threat (NIST SP 800-37): Any circumstance or event with the potential to adversely impact agency operations (including mission, functions, image, or reputation), agency assets, or individuals through an information system via unauthorized access, destruction, disclosure, modification of information, and/or denial of service. (CNSS Inst. 4009, Adapted)

Threat (NIST SP 800-53r1): Any circumstance or event with the potential to adversely impact agency operations (including mission, functions, image, or reputation), agency assets, or individuals through an information system via unauthorized access, destruction, disclosure, modification of information, and/or denial of service.

Threat Assessment (NIST SP 800-53r1): Formal description and evaluation of threat to an information system.

Threat Source/Agent (NIST SP 800-33): Either (i) intent and method targeted at the intentional exploitation of a vulnerability or (ii) the situation and method that may accidentally trigger a vulnerability.

Total Risk (NIST SP 800-16): The potential for the occurrence of an adverse event if no mitigating action is taken (i.e., the potential for any applicable threat to exploit a system vulnerability).

Trojan Horse (NIST SP 800-47): A computer program containing an apparent or actual useful function that also contains additional functions that permit the unauthorized collection, falsification, or destruction of data.

Trusted Path (NIST SP 800-18r1): A mechanism by which a user (through an input device) can communicate directly with the security functions of the information system with the necessary confidence to support the system security policy. This mechanism can only be activated by the user or the security functions of the information system and cannot be imitated by untrusted software.

Trustworthy System (NIST SP 800-32): Computer hardware, software and procedures that (i) are reasonably secure from intrusion and misuse; (ii) provide a reasonable level of availability, reliability, and correct operation; (iii) are reasonably suited to perform their intended functions; and (iv) adhere to generally accepted security procedures.

Unauthorized Access (NIST SP 800-61r1): A person gains logical or physical access without permission to a network, system, application, data, or other IT resource.

Unauthorized Disclosure (NIST SP 800-57P1): An event involving the exposure of information to entities not authorized access to the information.

User (NIST SP 800-53r1): Individual or (system) process authorized to access an information system.

Victim (NIST SP 800-61): A machine that is exploited.

Virus (NIST SP 800-40): A program designed with malicious intent that has the ability to spread to multiple computers or programs. Most viruses have a trigger mechanism that defines the conditions under which it will spread and deliver a malicious payload of some type.

Vulnerability (NIST SP 800-44): A security exposure in an operating system or other system software or application software component. A variety of organizations maintain publicly accessible databases of vulnerabilities based on the version number of the software. Each vulnerability can potentially compromise the system or network if exploited.

Vulnerability Assessment (NIST SP 800-53r1): Formal description and evaluation of the vulnerabilities in an information system.

Web Bug (NIST 800-46): Tiny images, invisible to a user, placed on web sites in such a way that they allow third parties to track use of web servers and collect information about the user, including IP address, Host name, browser type and version, operating system name and version, and web browser cookie.

Workaround (NIST 800-40): A configuration change to a software package or other information technology resource that mitigates the threat posed by a particular vulnerability. The workaround usually does not fix the underlying problem (unlike a patch) and often limits functionality within the IT resource.

Worm (NIST 800-40): A type of malicious code particular to networked computers. It is a self-replicating program that works its way through a computer network exploiting vulnerable hosts, replicating and causing whatever damage it was programmed to do.

REFERENCES

1. Davis T.E. Autopsy of a Mega-Casualty Event: What Are the Principles? Seminar Series, Centers for Disease Control, Atlanta, 2004.
2. Hall Ken, Tyree Barry N. Army Unit Status Reports move online. Available at http://www4.army.mil/news/article.php?story=8656.
3. Peretti Kimberly Kiefer. Data breaches: what the underground world of "carding" reveals. Santa Clara Computer and High Technology Journal, 25, (2), Article 4, 2008.
4. Arlene M. Stillwell, Roy F. Baumeister, Regan E. Del Priore, We're all victims here: toward a psychology of revenge . Journal Basic and Applied Social Psychology, 30, (3) 2008, 253–263.
5. Schneier Bruce. Beyond fear: thinking sensibly about security in an uncertain world, May 4, 2003.
6. Fowler S, Stanwick V. *Web Application Design Handbook*. Morgan Kaufman Publishing, July 7, 2004.
7. Trust, Reputation, and Security: Theories and Practice. *AAMAS 2002 International Workshop, Bologna, Italy, July 15, 2002. Selected and Invited Papers.* Lecture Notes in Computer Science. Lecture Notes in Artificial Intelligence, Vol. 2631. Falcone, R.; Barber, S.; Korba, L.; Singh, M. 2003, 235 Softcover. ISBN: 978-3-540-00988-7.
8. The Business Case for the Microsoft Security Development Lifecycle (SDL). Available at http://msdn.microsoft.com/en-us/security/cc420637.aspx.
9. Shirley C. Payne. (2006). A Guide to Security Metrics, SANS Reading Room. Available at http://www.sans.org/reading_room/whitepapers/auditing/a_guide_to_security_metrics_55?show=55.php&cat=auditing.

Risk Centric Threat Modeling: Process for Attack Simulation and Threat Analysis, First Edition.
Tony UcedaVélez and Marco M. Morana.
© 2015 John Wiley & Sons, Inc. Published 2015 by John Wiley & Sons, Inc.

10. Visual Studio Developer Center. Designing for Scalability. Available at http://msdn.microsoft.com/en-us/library/aa291873%28VS.71%29.aspx.
11. Ambler SW. The object primer. In: *Business Process Modeling*. Cambridge University Press; 2004. Chapter 9.
12. PBS Frontline: Hackers:Interviews, Interview with James Adams. Available at http://www.pbs.org/wgbh/pages/frontline/shows/hackers/interviews/adams.html.
13. CERT Advisory CA-1997-28 IP Denial-of-Service Attacks. CERT. 1998. Retrieved May 2, 2008.
14. Shostack Adam. Experiences Threat Modeling at Microsoft.
15. Genome Threat Modeling & Design Review. Available at http://msdn.microsoft.com/en-us/library/dd831971.aspx#CRT.
16. Bocan Valer, Cretu Vladimir. Mitigating Denial of Service Threats in GSM Networks. Available at http://www.dataman.ro/wp-content/uploads/2007/06/ares-2006-mitigating-denial-of-service-threats-in-gsm-networks.pdf.
17. Methods of Attack View. Available at http://capec.mitre.org/data/graphs/1000.html.
18. The security of applications: not all are created equal. Available at http://www.netsourceasia.net/resources/atstake_app_unequal.pdf.
19. Risk based testing. Available at http://www.owasp.org/images/4/41/IMI_2009_Security_Summit.ppt.
20. RUP. Available at http://en.wikipedia.org/wiki/IBM_Rational_Unified_Process.
21. Security in Agile. Available at http://www.webadminblog.com/index.php/2008/09/25/security-in-agile-development-owasp-appsec-nyc-2008/.
22. Agile-SDL streamline security practices for Agile development. Available at http://msdn.microsoft.com/en-us/magazine/dd153756.aspx.
23. Modeling Tool (TAM). Available at http://msdn.microsoft.com/en-us/security/aa570413.aspx.
24. The SDL threat modeling tool: the SDL threat modeling tool secure code reviews. Available at http://www.slideshare.net/marco_morana/secure-code-reviews-presentation.
25. Gonzales Albert. Wikipedia Profile. Available at http://en.wikipedia.org/wiki/Albert_Gonzalez.
26. DataLoss DB open Security Foundation. Available at http://datalossdb.org/.
27. PCI DSS. Available at http://usa.visa.com/download/merchants/cisp-list-of-pcidss-compliant-service-providers.pdf.
28. One year later Five takeaways from the TJX breach. Available at http://www.highbeam.com/doc/1G1-170405594.html.
29. Heartland Settles With VISA. Available at http://www.scmagazineus.com/heartland-settles-with-visa-funds-to-go-to-issuing-banks/article/160943/.
30. 126-million spent so far to respond to heartland breach. Available at http://www.scmagazineus.com/126-million-spent-so-far-to-respond-to-heartland-breach/article/136491/.
31. $ 19.4 million to settle claims related to the hacker intrusion. Available at http://www.scmagazineus.com/heartland-posts-q2-loss/article/141291/.
32. Court gives preliminary ok to 4m consumer settlement in heartland case. Available at http://www.businessweek.com/idg/2010-05-07/court-gives-preliminary-ok-to-4m-consumer-settlement-in-heartland-case.html.

REFERENCES

33. The HeartLand Breach. Available at http://www.bankinfosecurity.com/heartland_breach.php.
34. Heartland breach expenses pegged at 140M so far. Available at http://www.computerworld.com/s/article/9176507/Heartland_breach_expenses_pegged_at_140M_so_far?taxonomyId=17.
35. Lessons learned from the TJ Maxx Data Breach. Available at http://www.nealofarrell.com/index.php/bio/74.html.
36. Survey: Half of businesses don't secure personal data. Available at http://news.cnet.com/8301-1009_3-10360639-83.html.
37. Julia S. Cheney, (2010). Heartland payment systems: lessons learned from a data breach, Available at http://www.philadelphiafed.org/payment-cards-center/publications/discussion-papers/2010/D-2010-January-Heartland-Payment-Systems.pdf.
38. Financial services – information sharing and analysis center. Available at http://www.fsisac.com/.
39. FDIC warns banks to watch for 'money mules' duped by Hackers. Available at http://www.wired.com/threatlevel/2009/10/money_mules/.
40. Danmec/Asprox SQL injection attack tool analysis. Available at http://www.secureworks.com/research/threats/danmecasprox/?threat=danmecasprox.
41. DDoS Tools. Available at http://ddanchev.blogspot.com/2008/02/blackenergy-ddos-bot-web-based-c.html.
42. Zeus botnet analysis: Past, present and future threats. Available at http://searchsecurity.techtarget.com/tip/0,289483,sid14_gci1514783,00.html.
43. The security of applications not all are created equal. Available at http://www.securitymanagement.com/archive/library/atstake_tech0502.pdf.
44. Advanced persistent threats. Available at http://www.damballa.com/knowledge/advanced-persistent-threats.php.
45. An introduction to factor analysis of information risk (FAIR). Available at http://www.riskmanagementinsight.com/media/docs/FAIR_introduction.pdf.
46. Microsoft threat modeling. Available at http://www.microsoft.com/security/sdl/getstarted/threatmodeling.aspx
47. NIST risk management framework. Available at http://csrc.nist.gov/groups/SMA/fisma/framework.html.
48. Practical threat analysis. Available at http://www.ptatechnologies.com/.
49. OCTAVE (Operationally Critical Threat, Asset, and Vulnerability Evaluation[SM]). Available at http://www.cert.org/octave/.
50. TARA Threat Agent Risk Assessment. Available at http://download.intel.com/it/pdf/Prioritizing_Info_Security_Risks_with_TARA.pdf.
51. Trike. Available at http://trike.sourceforge.net/.
52. IT risk assessment frameworks: real-world experience. Available at http://www.csoonline.com/article/592525/it-risk-assessment-frameworks-real-world-experience?page=1.
53. NIST SP 800–30 risk management guide for information technology systems. Available at http://csrc.nist.gov/publications/nistpubs/800-30/sp800-30.pdf
54. Common vulnerability scoring system (CVSS-SIG). Available at http://www.first.org/cvss/.

55. Architectural risk analysis. Available at https://buildsecurityin.us-cert.gov/bsi/articles/best-practices/architecture.html.
56. Duncan Gardham. (2009). Cold war enemies Russia and China launch a cyber attack every day. Available at http://www.telegraph.co.uk/technology/news/6727100/Cold-war-enemies-Russia-and-China-launch-a-cyber-attack-every-day.html.
57. John Leyden. (2010). Security experts dissect Google China attack. Available at http://www.theregister.co.uk/2010/01/14/google_china_attack_analysis/.
58. Charles Hawley. (2010) What are google's real motives in China?. Available at http://www.spiegel.de/international/business/0,1518,671926,00.html.
59. Hernan Shawn, Lambert Scott, Ostwald Tomasz, Shostack Adam. DFD Symbols, "Uncover Security Design Flaws Using The STRIDE Approach". Available at http://msdn.microsoft.com/en-us/magazine/cc163519.aspx#S2.
60. Shostack Adam. STRIDE chart. Available at http://blogs.msdn.com/b/sdl/archive/2007/09/11/stride-chart.aspx.
61. Meier JD, Mackman Alex, Dunner Michael, Vasireddy Srinath, Escamilla Ray, Murukan Anandha. Chapter 3 – Threat Modeling, Microsoft's Pattern & Practices. Available at http://msdn.microsoft.com/en-us/library/ff648644.aspx.

INDEX

A
Abuse Cases, 452–453
Access Control, 152
Access Levels, 232
Adherence with Information Security, 96–100
Adherence with Software Engineering, 100–101
Advanced Persistent Threats (APTs), 252–253
Agile SDLC, 219
Analyse Attack Scenarios, 461–463, 532, 576–588
Analysis of Attacks, 71–74
Analysis of Attack scenarios, 461–463
Analysing Vulnerabilities and Impacts, 73–76
Anatomy of Account Takeover Fraud, 579
API example, 415
Application Assets, 126–127
Application Containers, 379–381
Application Decomposition & Analysis, 178–182, 393–419, 518–526
Application Design & Development, 24

Application Security Frame, 550
Application Security Goals, 257
Application Service Levels, 226
Application Risk Assessments, 91–92
Application Risk Management, 275–282
Application Walkthrough, 14–15
Architecture Components, 562
Architecture Diagrams, 210
Architecture Risk Analysis, 254
Architectural Analysis with DFDs, 408–415, 524–526
Assess Probability and Impact of Attack Scenarios, 466–469
Assert Completeness of Secure Technical Design, 513–517
Asset, 259
Asset Management, 296
Asset Variables, 182
Assignment of Probabilistic Values for Identified Threats, 547–548
Assurance, 238
Attacks, 45–48, 293
Attack Analysis in Threat Modeling, 130, 571–572

Risk Centric Threat Modeling: Process for Attack Simulation and Threat Analysis, First Edition.
Tony UcedaVélez and Marco M. Morana.
© 2015 John Wiley & Sons, Inc. Published 2015 by John Wiley & Sons, Inc.

Attack & Countermeasure Analysis, 630
Attack Surface Analysis, 226, 369, 465–466, 601–603
Attack Tree 48, 607
Attack Vector Analysis, 580
Attack Vectors Used by Banking Malware, 595
Attack Vectors Used Against Web Applications, 596
Attack Modeling and Simulation, 187–189, 459–473, 570–617
Attack Modeling, 305
Audit and Compliance, 236
Audit and Risk Management, 236–239
Audit Logs, 429–431
Awareness, 323–324

B

Banking Trojan Attacks, 578–580
Benefits of Threat Modeling, 289
Blind Threat Modeling, 382
Build in Security Maturity Model (BSIMM), 95
Building Security in the SDLC, 195–198
Building Security in Agile Sprints, 222
Business Functionality, 347
Business Impact Estimates, 274
Business Impact, 355–360
Business Impact of Vulnerabilities, 135–136
Business Liabilities, 347
Business Logic Attacks, 257
Business Objectives Mapping to Security Requirements, 348
Business Requirements, 351

C

Capability Maturity Model (CMM), 320
Campaign Against Online Banking Sites, 534
CAPEC Attack Libraries, 464–465
Catching Up With Emerging Threats, 257
CERT, 310
Change Control, 152
Challenges of Securing Software Using Agile SDLC, 220
CISO, 140–142, 246, 282, 310, 331
  oversight in threat modeling, 140–142, 331
  role in incident response, 310
  responsibility, 246

risk managment, 282
Conduct Attack Driven Security Tests and Simulations, 470–472
Considerations For Factoring Business Impact, 359
Configuration Management, 153
Common Attack Pattern Enumeration and Classification (CAPEC), 165, 595–600
Compliance as Factor for Information Security Assurance, 257
Compliance as Factor in Risk Reduction, 236–241
Compliance in Risk-Centric Threat Modeling, 331
Compliance Requirements, 350–353
Compliance and Information Risk Management, 290–291
Components in Scope for Threat Modeling (example), 364
Computer Security Incident Handling Guide, 308–309
Contextual Risk Analysis, 454–455
Control Analysis, 298
Control Gap Analysis, 247
Control Requirements, 298
Correlation of Threat Agents to Asset Targets, 546–547
Correlate Vulnerability Data, 443–444
Countermeasures, 627
Cybercrime Gangs, 235
Cyberthreat, 259, 260, 291, 303, 311
  alert levels, 311
  analysis, 259–260
  dissecting, 303
  risks, 291
CRUD Entitlements, 37
CVEs Vulnerability Types Exploited by Drive by Download, 595
CVSS Vulnerability Risk Scoring, 623

D

Derive Attack Driven Test Cases to Test Countermeasures, 470
Data Flow Analysis, 398–408
Data Flow Diagrams (DFDs), 110, 212, 232, 403, 405, 407, 408
  security centric DFDs for distributed attacks, 159

INDEX 659

revisiting DFDs in architectural analysis, 451
symbols, 156
syntax, 402
Data Breach Incidents, 235, 242–243, 235–259
  economic impact, 242
  cost estimates, 242–243
  lesson for risk management, 235–259
  notification laws (SB 1386), 255
Data Sinks & Sources, 369–376
Defence in Depth, 295
Define Activities, 349–369
Define Objectives of Threat Modeling, 172–174, 346–348, 487–501
Define Participants, 364–366
Define Roles 366–367
Define Business Requirements, 349–350, 492
Define Business Impact (example), 497–498
Define Security Requirements (example), 490, 495–497
Defining The Technical Scope of Threat Modeling, 174–178, 369–393, 501–526
Defining the "who", "what", "when", "where", 176
Defining Participants, 386–390
Denial of Service Attacks, 163, 257
Derivation of Test Cases for Testing Countermeasures, 608–617
Design For Resilience, 200
Design Flaws, 104–118
  examples, 107–108
  identification, 104–118
  remediation, 113–118
  root cause analysis, 114–115
Detection and Analysis, 311
Determine the Risk Profile (example), 499–501
Difference Between Top Vulnerabilities and Top Exploits, 567–568
Distributed Denial of Service Attacks (DDoS) Risk Analysis Examples, 265–269, 313, 532–535
Document business requirements (example), 489
Documenting DFDs in a threat model (example), 522–523

Dynamic Application Security Testing Tools (DAST), 105
Dynamic Analysis, 229
DREAD Threat Risk Calculation, 624

E
Effectiveness of Security Controls, 247
Elicitation of Security Requirements, 206–207
Embedding Threat Modeling in the SDLC, 197
Emerging Threats, 67, 244–245
Empirical Risk Calculation Formulas, 265, 267, 268, 439, 459, 631–633
End-to-End View of Security Controls, 215
Engineering for Attacks, 600
Enumeration of Use Cases, 395–398
Enumeration of Software Components (example), 509–510
Enumeration of System-Level Services (example), 511–512
Enumeration of Technical Scope, 177
Enumeration of Third Party Infrastructure Components (example), 512–513
Estimates of Business Impacts of Data Breach Incidents, 257
Exposure to Vulnerabilities as Factor for Risk, 263–264
Executive Sponsorship, 139
Exploring Stages and Activates of PASTA Threat Modeling, 345–480
Expected Outputs of Stage I of PASTA Threat Modeling, 339–343

F
Factors Influencing Attack Probability, 128–129
FAIR, 296
False Negatives & Positives, 105
False Sense of Security, 257
Final Security Review, 225
Financial Impact Estimates, 269, 357
Functional Requirements, 399–400
Functional Analysis and Trust Boundaries, 408–416
Fuzz Testing Process, 226

G
Governance Risk Control (GRC), 331

GRC Cross Section of Threat Modeling Team, 331
GRC Artefacts, 353–355

H

Hardening Guidelines For Inherent Risk Mitigation, 383–385
High Level View of Threats-Attacks-Vulnerabilities-Countermeasures, 629
Hybrid Software Security Assessments, 229–232

I

Identify Actors And Data Interfaces (example), 510–511
Identify Weak Design Patterns in The Application Architecture, 557–560
Identify the Attack Surface, 465–466
Identify Weak Design Patterns in Architecture, 444–452
Initial Risk Profile, 301–302
Integrating Threat Modeling in Agile, 219–222
Integrating Threat Modeling in the SDLC, 196–233
Impact Analysis, 297
Impact of Procurement, 390–392
Inputs and Outputs of PASTA Process, 324–325
Information Security Reviews, 88–89
Information Security Risk Defined, 292
Information Security & Risk Management, 289–301
Information Security Assurance, 290
Information Sharing and Analysis Centers (ISACs), 255, 310
Inherent Risk, 362–363
Inherent Risk Profile by Application Type, 363
Inherent Challenges to Threat Modeling, 320
ISAC Alert Levels, 311–312
ISO/IEC 27001, 294–296, 488

J

Judging by Motives, 12
Justification for Investing in Security, 295

K

Kill-chain Attack Modeling, 542–544

Kill-chain Analysis of Banking Malware Attacks, 581–584
Kill-chain Analysis of DDoS Attacks, 584–588

L

Labelling Threats & Application Components, 458
Lesson Learnt from Security Incidents, 249–250–251
List of Insecure Architecture Gaps, 444–451
Logical Flow Considering Threats to Assets, 456
Low Hanging Fruits (LHF), 105

M

Malware Threats, 251–252
Man-in the Middle (MiTM) Attacks 216, 251, 253, 607
Man-in the Browser (MiTB) Attacks, 257, 304
Mapping Threats To Vulnerabilities, 452, 565
Mapping Threat Modeling Activities, 299
Mapping Test Cases to Vulnerabilities, 132–133
Maturity, 323
Microsoft SDL, 222–229
Minimal Threat Modeling Requirements, 225
Misconfigurations, 217
Missing Architectural Countermeasures, 451
MITRE Corp Security Content, 189
Mobile Web Application Example, 180, 414
Modeling and Simulation, 459–473
Multi Factor Authentication (MFA), 252

N

NIST Risk Terminology 635–653
NIST Risk Assessment Methodology, 297–298
Number of Attacks Observed, 567–568

O

OCTAVE, 296
OWASP Guide for Building Secure applications, 116
OWASP Mapping to WASC, 567
OWASP Top Ten, 240, 241, 292
Out of Band Authentication (OOBA), 253

P

PASTA Risk–Centric Threat Modeling in the Details, 345–480
PASTA Risk-Centric Threat Modeling Use Case, 481–633
Patch Management, 153
Performing the DFD exercise, 398–408
PCI-DSS, 216, 236–238, 240
PCI-DSS Audits & Data Breaches, 240
PCI-DSS Fines, 241
PCI-DSS Effectiveness, 247–249
Phishing, 257
Post-Mortem Incident Analysis, 249–250
Proactive Risk Mitigation Strategy, 277
Privacy Testing, 225
Privacy Requirements, 352
Probability of Attacks, 466–469, 605–608
Process IDs, 374–375
Process Areas For Threat Modeling, 139
Process and People, 334–335
Process for Attack Simulation and Threat Analysis (PASTA), 171–194
Provide Context Risk Analysis, 566

Q

Qualified Security Assessors (QSA), 236–239
Quantitative Risk Analysis, 272–275, 625–626

R

Rational Unified Process, 217–218
Reducing the Attack Surface, 604–605
Reasons For Security Failure, 20
Relationship Among Assets, Use Cases and Actors, 181
Regulatory Compliance, 360
    and business impact, 361
Review and correlate vulnerabilities, 556
Remote Access Tools (RATs), 253
Requirement Scope Creeps, 348–349
Resilience to Attacks, 200–201
Residual Risk Analysis and Management, 62, 270–272, 473–480
    calculate residual risk, 62, 270–272, 473, 476–478
    identify countermeasures, 474–475
    recommend strategy to manage risks, 478–480
Risk Analysis, 261–275, 297

Risk Analysis and Management, 305–307, 617–633
Risk Analysis with Threat Models, 60–62
Risk Assessors, 331
Risk Based Threat Modeling, 167–168, 284, 282–289
Risk Based Security Requirements, 207
Risk Calculations, 265–275
    factoring likelihood and impact, 265
    reference scale, 266
Risk Centric Threat Modeling, 319–344
    preparedness, 321
    team selection, 325–326
    supporting personnel, 327–328
    security operations, 329–330
    mapping to security processes, 336–338
Risk Characterization, 259, 262–263
Risk Culture, 281
Risk Determination, 298
Risk DREAD, 116, 168–170
Risk Heat Maps, 266, 268, 294, 626
Risk Management, 275–278, 297
Risk Mitigation, 631–633
Risk Mitigation Strategy, 63–82, 66–67, 253–259, 276–277, 298–299, 480
Risk Profile, 363, 502
Risk Reporting, 298
Risk Terminology, 259 also see Glossary, 635–653
Roles and Benefits of Threat Modeling, 69
Root Cause Analysis, 115
    in application security reviews, 230
    after security incidents, 316–317

S

Security Analysis, 9–17
Secure Architecture Design Reviews, 201–202
Secure Architecture Design Guidelines, 561
Secure By Design, 84–88, 222
Security Centric Threat Modeling, 156–157
Security Content Automation Protocol (SCAP), 188
    bank sys admin case study, 157–158
    for complex attacks, 158
Secure Coding and Threat Modeling, 213
Security Development Lifecycle (SDL), 222–229
    agile SDL, 225–226

Security Development Lifecycle (SDL) (*Continued*)
  line of business SDL, 226
  phases, 227
  security principles incorporated in the SDL, 224
Security Design Reviews, 108, 209–210
  design flaw identificaton, 108–109
Security Enhanced SDLC, 222–229
Security Functional Analysis, 524–526
Security Functional Transactional Analysis, 527
Security In the Software Development Life-Cycle, 92–104
  adopting it, 102–104
Security Incident Response, 283–317
  assessment, 313–315
  escalation procedures,315
  containment and eradication, 315–316
  response, 307–317
  preparadness, 308
  event monitoring, 303
  course of action, 283–284
  handling process, 310
  root cause analysis, 316–317
Security Improvements with Threat Modeling, 82–92
Security Measures For Mitigating Risk, 80–82
  derived using kill-chain attack analysis, 590–592
Security Objectives in Support of Business Objectives, 175
Security Operation Centre (SOC), 426–428
Security Operations, 55–57
Security Requirements, 82–84
Security Requirements, 199–200
  engineering, 206
  for conducting a threat model in SDL, 228
Security Risk Assessment, 223
Security Risk Management, 57
risk components, 58
Security Test Case, 470–472, 611
Security Testing 202–203
Security Testing Tools, 54
  effectiveness of automated tools, 105–108
  coverage, 106
Source Code Analysis & Threat Modeling, 231

Software Components, 369
  enumeration, 371–374
Software Development, 149
  expertise leveraged for threat modeling, 149–151
System and Network Administration, 151–152
Software Assurance Maturity Model (SAMM), 95
Software Enumeration, 377
Sprints (Agile), 219
Stages of PASTA methodology (in summary), 173
Static Application Security Testing (SAST), 105
Static Analysis, 229
STRIDE, 39, 160–165
  categorization table, 164
  classification model, 166
  per element example, 548
  threat list, 549
Structured Threat Information Expression (STIX), 434, 538–542
SQL Injection, 112–113, 235, 255, 274–275, 307
  data breach incidents, 235
  risk mitigation strategy, 255
  impact estimates, 274–275
  remediation options, 307
SQLi-CAPEC, 598–599
System Characterization, 298
System Level Services, 376

T
Targeted Vulnerability Testing, 455–459, 569–570
Taxonomy of Attacks, 46
Technical Scope Definition, 369–371
Technical Design, 379
  assertion of completeness, 379–382
Testing with threat models, 214–217
  test case derivation, 214–215
  prioritization, 215
Test Cases, 470, 612–616
Test Techniques, 261
Threat Modeling in the SDLC, 224
Threat Modeling Activity Integration, 218–219
Third Party Infrastructures, 369

enumeration, 377–379
Threats, 42, 118–123, 131–132, 259, 625
  classification, 42
  analysis of countermeasures, 118–123
  mapping to vulnerabilities, 131–132
  risk, 259
  and risk dashboard, 625
Threat actors, 260
Threat Analysis, 68–71, 182–185, 296, 302–304, 419–441, 526–549
  agents to asset mapping,437
  assignment of probability, 437–439
  frequency, 17
  sources of info gathering, 18
  and risk management, 64–65, 259–282
  effectiveness, 258
  factors influencing attacks, 183
  threat re-examination, 419–420
  key roles, 440–441
  objectives, 421
  threat scenario analysis, 422–427
  threat intelligence gathering, 427–431
  threat possibilities per industry, 425
  threat library updates, 436
Threat Agents, 124–125
Threat Anatomy, 33–48
Threat Attributes, 259–260
Threat Driven Test Cases, 613–615
Threat Factors, 10–16
Threat Intelligence, 65–66
Threat Intelligence Gathering, 427–436
  internal sources, 427–431
  external sources, 431–436
Threat Libraries, 111–113, 545
  using STRIDE, 11
  updates, 436–437
Threat Management Dashboard, 551, 637
Threat Methodologies, 138–194
Threat Modeling, 1, 35–36, 210–211
  approaches, 154–155
  areas of collaboration, 141
  art of espionage, 7
  baseline, 225
  benefits for various roles, 27–29
  business case, 21–24
  classification, 37
  collaboration among stakeholders, 48–53
  criteria for defining scope, 92
  criteria for updating it, 94
  definition, 1–3
  development metrics, 25
  elements of risk, 59–60
  expertise, 146, 148–149
  in military strategy, 3–9
  mapping to security processes, 143–145
  origin and use, 3–7
  preventive risk management, 30–31
  rationale for integration in SDLC, 94–96
  scalability factors, 25–26
  security benefits, 29
  software security assessments and, 202
  software risks management, 204
  time commitments, 153
Threat Modeling Tools, 170–171, 228, 333–334
Threat Risk Rating Table Example, 169
Threat Risk Factors, 551
Threat Scenarios, 125
  analysis, 125–126, 422–427
  affecting financial IT systems and applications, 536–537
Threat Scenario of Financial IT Systems and Applications, 536
Threat Sources to Consider, 433
Threat Targets, 127
Threat Tree, 203, 213
Tools, Techniques and Procedures (TTPs), 571
Total Cost of Ownership (TCO), 295
TJ Maxx Data Breach Incident, 235–238
Training and Awareness, 202
Trusted Automated exchange of Indicator Information (TAXII), 434
Trust Boundaries, 408

U

Unlawful Compliance Risks, 291
Update Attack Libraries 463–465, 545
Update Control Frameworks, 463–465, 546
Update Attack libraries and Control Frameworks, 463–464
Use and Abuse Cases, 207–208, 610
Use Case Diagrams, 85
Use Cases Derived From Business Objectives, 350
Use Cases Derived From Functional Requirements, 401

Use Cases Enumeration, 395–398
Use Cases Visualization Example, 521
Using Containers to Organize DFDs, 404–451

V

Verizon Enterprise Risk Incident Sharing (VERIS), 434–435
Vulnerability, 259
  analysis, 304–305
  characterization with threats and assets, 262
  exposure, 292
  mapping to attacks, 41–42
  risks and impacts, 76–80, 261
Vulnerability Assessments, 296
  and integration with threat modeling, 147
Vulnerability CVSS Risk Severity Calculations, 116, 134, 278
Vulnerability Data Sources, 454
Vulnerability Management, 89–90
Vulnerability Risk Management, 290
Vulnerability Testing, 455–459

W

Walk-Through Use Case of PASTA Risk Centric Threat Modeling, 481–633
Waterfall SDLC, 205
Weakness & Vulnerability Analysis, 185–197, 441–459, 549–570
Weak Design Patterns in Architecture, 444–452
Web Application, 278
  security risks, 278–282
  characterization, 300–302
  use cases, 302
  user roles, 302
  trust boundaries, 302
  targeted vulnerability testing, 457–459
Web Application Firewall, 313
Web Hacking Incident Database (WHID), 544, 601

X

XSS vulnerabilities, 233, 304–305

CPSIA information can be obtained
at www.ICGtesting.com
Printed in the USA
BVHW040031200419
545959BV00008B/27/P